New in This Edition

PROFESSIONAL EDUCATION SERVICES, LP
The Professional's Choice for Quality CPE

8303 Sierra College Blvd., Suite 146
Roseville, CA 95661

Order: 1-800-998-5024
Customer Service: 1-800-990-2731
Fax: (916) 791-4099

Not-for-Profit Organization Audits

2001
ENGAGEMENT REVIEW BOARD

2001

MILLER

Not-for-Profit Organization Audits

**Complete Audit
Program and
Workpaper
Management
System**

Warren Ruppel

Harcourt
Professional Publishing

San Diego New York Chicago London

Copyright ©2000 by Harcourt, Inc.

Printed in the United States of America

ISBN: 0-15-607190-8

00 01 02 MG 3 2 1

Contents

PART I. FINANCIAL STATEMENT AUDITS

PART II. SINGLE AUDITS UNDER OMB CIRCULAR A-133

APPENDIX

Our Commitment to You

Thank you for ordering 2001 *Miller Not-for-Profit Organization Audits: Complete Audit Program and Workpaper Management System*. Each year we bring you the very best engagement guides available with accompanying electronic workpapers and practice aids. To confirm the technical accuracy and quality control of our materials, Harcourt Professional Publishing voluntarily submitted to a peer review of our publishing system and our publications.

We were not surprised when the SEC Practice Section of the AICPA Division for CPA Firms accepted the unqualified peer review report reproduced on the following page. As we go to press, all fieldwork for our next peer review and the peer review report has been completed but is now under consideration by the AICPA. If you need a copy of the new Peer Review Letter to provide to the team captain of your peer review team, please call our Technical Support representative toll-free at (888) 551-7127.

In addition to peer review, our publications undergo strict technical and content reviews by qualified practitioners. This ensures that our books and practice aids meet "real-world" standards and applicability. We also rely on our Editorial Review Board (listed at the front of this book) for product development guidance.

In other words, our publications are reviewed every step of the way—from conception through production—to assure you of the finest products on the market.

Moreover, we now provide the unique Miller Engagement System™ software, that links all Microsoft Word and Excel documents in a dynamic client binder. This system will save you time and money, and it is now included with every single Miller engagement title at no extra charge.

If you do not wish to use the Miller Engagement System™, stand-alone versions of the workpapers are provided in electronic formats for Word 7 and Excel 7 (Office 95). Users with WordPerfect 7 or higher will be able to open any Work 7 format. Users with Lotus 1-2-3 or other Excel-compatible spreadsheet programs will be able to open the Excel 7 Workbook in most cases.

In response to favorable feedback, we continue to publish the most portable product on the market, making it easy for you to have needed information at the audit site.

Updated annually, peer-reviewed, technically accurate, convenient, and practical—2001 *Miller Not-for-Profit Organization Audits* shows our appreciation for the value of your time and our commitment to creating books and practice aids you can trust.

Peer Review Letter

 *Caldwell, Becker, Dervin, Petrick & Co., L.L.P.*
CERTIFIED PUBLIC ACCOUNTANTS

January 14, 1997

The Board of Directors
Harcourt Brace & Company

We have reviewed the system of quality control for the development and maintenance of Not-for-Profit Organization Audits, May 1996 edition ("materials") of Harcourt Brace & Company (the company) in effect for the year ended December 31, 1996 and the resultant materials in effect at December 31, 1996 in order to determine whether the materials are reliable aids to assist users in conforming with those professional standards the materials purport to encompass. Our review was conducted in accordance with the standards for reviews of quality control materials and guidelines for review of continuing professional education programs promulgated by the peer review committee of the SEC practice section of the AICPA Division for CPA Firms.

In performing our review, we have given consideration to the following general characteristics of a system of quality control. A company's system for the development and maintenance of quality control materials and continuing professional education programs encompasses its organizational structure and the policies and procedures established to provide the users of its materials with reasonable assurance that the materials are reliable aids to assist them in conforming with professional standards in conducting their accounting and auditing practices. The extent of a company's quality control policies and procedures for the development and maintenance of the materials and the manner in which they are implemented will depend upon a variety of factors, such as the size and organizational structure of the company and the nature of the materials provided to users. Variance in individual performance and professional interpretation affects the degree of compliance with prescribed quality control policies and procedures. Therefore, adherence to all policies and procedures in every case may not be possible. As is customary in a review of quality control materials and continuing professional education programs, we are issuing a letter under this date that sets forth comments related to certain policies and procedures or compliance with them or to the resultant materials. None of these matters were considered to be of sufficient significance to affect the opinion expressed in this report.

Our review and tests were limited to the system of quality control for the development and maintenance of the aforementioned materials of Harcourt Brace & Company and to the materials themselves and did not extend to the application of these materials by users of the materials nor to the policies and procedures of individual users.

In our opinion, the system of quality control for the development and maintenance of the quality control materials and continuing professional education programs of Harcourt Brace & Company was suitably designed and was being complied with during the year ended December 31, 1996 to provide users of the materials with reasonable assurance that the materials are reliable aids to assist them in conforming with those professional standards the materials purport to encompass. Also, in our opinion, the materials referred to above are reliable aids at December 31, 1996.

Caldwell, Becker, Dervin, Petrick & Co., L.L.

CALDWELL, BECKER, DERVIN, PETRICK & CO., L.L.P.

20750 Ventura Boulevard, Suite 140 · Woodland Hills, CA 91364
(818) 704-1040 · (213) 873-1040 · FAX (818) 704-5536

Preface

The 2001 *Miller Not-for-Profit Organization Audits* combines into one comprehensive, easy-to-use guide everything an auditor needs to perform audits of financial statements, audits in accordance with *Government Auditing Standards*, and single audits in accordance with OMB Circular A-133. Comprehensive coverage of the relevant technical literature is combined with user-friendly advice based on actual experience, resulting in a technically sound and extremely usable audit guide. In addition, 2001 *Not-for-Profit Organization Audits* maximizes the use of electronic practice aids and now includes the ePace! engagement trial balance package and Excel electronic workpapers. Electronic versions of audit programs, workpapers, reports, correspondence, and a comprehensive disclosure checklist enable independent auditors to eliminate many of the time-consuming clerical work too often performed during audits.

Notable additions for this year include coverage of the following:

- FAS-136, "Transfers of Assets to a Not-for-Profit Organization or Charitable Trust That Raises or Holds Contributions for Others." Specific guidance is provided for auditors in examining the FASB's long-awaited standard for determining when a pass-through contribution is accounted for as a revenue or a liability.

- FAS–137, "Accounting for Derivative Instruments and Hedging Activities—Deferral of the Effective Date of FASB Statement No. 133," which gives not-for-profit organizations with derivatives and hedges (and their auditors) a little more time to implement the complex requirements of FAS-133.

- SAS-89, "Audit Adjustments," which affects engagement letters, representation letters, and communications with audit committees, focusing attention on passed or waived audit adjustments and defining management's and the auditor's role in their disposition.

- Two new Amendments to *Government Auditing Standards* regarding (1) documentation requirements when auditors assess control risk at the maximum level for controls that depend significantly on computerized information systems and (2) specific communications with organizations being audited regarding the scope of internal control and compliance work performed under *Government Auditing Standards*.

- Two new Amendments to the OMB Circular A-133 Compliance Supplement; some fine-tuning of requirements accompanies the numerous new programs added to this document.

- Revisions to OMB's Circular A-110, "Uniform Administrative Requirements for Grants and Agreements with Institutions of Higher Education, Hospitals, and Other Not-for-Profit Organizations," including what has changed (and not changed) as to requirements for making public the results of federally sponsored research.

- The President's Council on Integrity & Efficiency's newly revised "Uniform Quality Control Review Guide for A-133 Audits" and "Uniform Guide for Initial Review of A-133 Audit Reports."

"Audit Cost-Savings Tips" have been added throughout the book to assist auditors in applying new audit approaches that can save many hours of audit time. In addition, the continuing audit implications of the Year 2000 Issue are addressed.

Part I covers the requirements for performing an audit of the financial statements of a not-for-profit organization. It incorporates all of the needed guidance for implementation of the numerous recent accounting standards affecting not-for-profit organizations, including FASB Statements 116, 117, 124, and 136; SOP 98-2; and the AICPA Audit and Accounting Guide for not-for-profit organizations. New auditing standards are covered completely. The format follows the natural progression of an audit of a not-for-profit organization's financial statements: Chapter 1 provides background information on the not-for-profit industry and the types of audit circumstances likely to be encountered. Chapters 2 and 3 cover preplanning and planning activities that should occur before and immediately after the start of the audit, including client acceptance considerations. Chapter 4 examines the increasingly important topic of internal control considerations. Chapters 5 and 6 focus specifically on the various types of accounts likely to be encountered in an audit of a not-for-profit organization's statement of financial position and statement of activities, along with a discussion of audit concerns and audit strategy. Chapter 7 describes various sampling methodologies and the extent of audit procedures. Chapter 8 focuses on the tax considerations that must be addressed in auditing a not-for-profit organization. Chapters 9 and 10 provide guidance on concluding the audit and reporting on the financial statements.

Part II of 2001 *Not-for-Profit Organization Audits* covers the additional procedures that must be performed in the conduct of audits of not-for-profit organizations in accordance with *Government Auditing Standards* and OMB Circular A-133. The format of Part II is similar to that of Part I, enabling the auditor to easily build the additional requirements onto the requirements of a financial statement audit. Chapters 11 and 12 introduce the single audit concept and review the relevant technical literature that affects this type of audit. Chapter 13 focuses specifically on the requirements of *Government Audit-*

ing Standards. Chapters 14 and 15 describe the preplanning and planning activities relating to the Circular A-133 requirements, while Chapters 16 and 17 focus on the additional requirements relating to internal controls over federal awards and compliance, including the requirements for auditing subrecipients of federal awards. Chapters 18 and 19 provide guidance for concluding the audit and reporting in accordance with the many reporting requirements in *Government Auditing Standards* and Circular A-133.

All-New Miller Engagement System™

This powerful new software will link all of the Miller Word and Excel practice aids we have supplied you in dynamic client binders, so you only have to add information once and have it populate all related documents. The system integrates seamlessly with the ePace! Engagement trial balance package, and it provides you the means by which to move to a paperless audit environment.

IMPRESS™ Cross-References

IMPRESS stands for the Integrated Miller Professional Reference and Engagement Series System. It is the system by which all Miller publications are thoroughly cross-referenced to one another on a chapter-by-chapter basis. The system is designed to facilitate comprehensive research and to assure that you will always find the complete answers you need. The IMPRESS™ Cross-References at the beginning of each chapter refer you to corresponding chapters in other Miller publications as well as to related chapters in the 2001 *Miller Not-for-Profit Organization Audits*.

Acknowledgments

Stephen Kattell, CPA, of Davis Monk and Co.; James Ulvog, CPA, of Capin Crouse LLP; and George Georgiades, CPA, deserve special thanks for their many useful and practical suggestions, which have incorporated into this book. Richard Bonacci and Cate DaPron of Harcourt Professional Publishing provided thoughtful oversight of this project, which is instrumental in ensuring that the book lives up to the expectations of its readers.

On a personal level, my wife, Marie, and my sons, Christopher and Gregory, are a constant source of support and inspiration, and I dedicate this book to them.

Warren Ruppel
New York, New York

About the Author

Warren Ruppel, CPA, began his career in 1979 with KPMG Peat Marwick after graduating from St. John's University, New York. He served numerous audit clients, including many not-for-profit organizations and governments that received federal financial assistance. In 1989, he joined Deloitte & Touche to specialize in audits of not-for-profit organizations and governments.

Mr. Ruppel has since served as the chief financial officer of a not-for-profit organization subject to the requirements of A-133, as a partner in a small CPA firm, and as an assistant comptroller for accounting for a large municipal government. He has written and conducted numerous training courses and seminars over the course of his career and is widely published in the areas of not-for-profit and governmental accounting and auditing. In addition, he has taught for the New York State Society of CPAs and has been an Adjunct Lecturer of Accountancy at the Bernard M. Baruch College of the City University of New York.

Mr. Ruppel is a member of the American Institute of Certified Public Accountants and the New York State Society of CPAs. He is a former president of the New York chapter of the Institute of Management Accountants. He is also a member of the Special Review Committee of the Government Finance Officers Association.

Accounting Resources on the Web

The following World Wide Web addresses are just a few of the resources on the Internet that are available to practitioners. Because of the evolving nature of the Internet, some addresses may change. In such a case, refer to one of the many Internet search engines, such as Yahoo! (http://www.yahoo.com).

AICPA   http://www.aicpa.org/

American Accounting Association   http://www.rutgers.edu/ accounting/raw/aaa/

ePace! Software   http://www.epacesoftware.com/

FASB   http://www.rutgers.edu:80/Accounting/raw/fasb/

Fedworld   http://www.fedworld.gov

GASB   http://www.rutgers.edu/Accounting/raw/gasb/index. html

General Accounting Office   http://www.gao.gov/

Harcourt Professional Publishing   http://www.hpponline.com

House of Representatives   http://www.house.gov/

IRS Digital Daily   http://www.irs.ustreas.gov/prod/cover.html

Library of Congress   http://www.lcweb.loc.gov/homepage/

Office of Management and Budget   http://www.gpo.gov/ usbudget/fy1996/fy1996.html

Securities and Exchange Commission   http://www.sec.gov/

Miller Engagement System™

The publisher is proud to introduce a revolutionary tool for the busy practitioner. New to this edition, the Miller Engagement System™ will:

- Link all Miller Word and Excel practice aids
- Add and link all of your own existing Word™ and Excel™ documents
- Manage workpapers through dynamic client binders
- Pull data from one location to populate all related workpapers
- Update an entire client binder each year with a few keystrokes
- Help you create master templates for different industries and different types of clients
- Pave the way for a paperless audit environment
- Integrate seamlessly with the ePace! Engagement™ trial balance software

Our goal in offering this software is to provide you with an unexcelled tool for audit efficiency and effectiveness. Miller Engagement System™ lets you enter recurring data (such as customer name and address) just once and have it populate the entire set of workpapers for the client.

No other system provides you with the immediate integration of your favorite Word and Excel documents. No other system puts you in charge of—not at the mercy of—your workpapers. The Miller Engagement System™ is simply the best electronic workpaper management system available today.

To demonstrate the added power of linking the Miller system with the ePace! Engagement trial balance package, we've included a free 30-day trial version with your CD-ROM. (For more information, see "About the CD-ROM and Quick Installation Instructions" in the back of your guide.) When you use the trial balance software with the Miller system, the numbers will populate the appropriate fields in your Word and Excel documents.

Disc Contents

Print versions of the electronic workpapers are located throughout this reference guide. See the chapter tables of contents for exact page numbers. All electronic workpapers included on the CD-ROM are identified in the reference guide by the disc icon that appears at right. This icon is displayed in the upper corner of each workpaper, sample letter, or sample report included on the disc.

SAMPLE CORRESPONDENCE— FINANCIAL STATEMENT AUDIT

SAMPLE REPORTS—FINANCIAL STATEMENT AUDIT

CIRCULAR A-133 WORKPAPERS

CIRCULAR A-133 SAMPLE REPORTS

CIRCULAR A-133 REFERENCE

FEDERAL GOVERNMENT DOCUMENTS

Federal Legislation

---

*These files are in Adobe® Acrobat® PDF format. The Adobe
Acrobat Reader can be downloaded free of charge from http://
www.adobe.com/proindex/acrobat/headstep.html.

EXCEL WORKPAPERS

The following workpapers are accessed through the *Excel* software. Each *Not-for-Profit Organization Audits* workpaper submenu option is listed below, with the individual workpapers contained under that submenu option.

	File Name	*File Type*
Inventory Price Test—Purchased Goods	AG-3	Excel
Receiving Cutoff	AG-4	Excel
Shipping Cutoff	AG-5	Excel
Inventory Analytical Procedures	AG-6	Excel

Property, Plant and Equipment Workpapers

Property, Plant & Equipment Summary Analysis	AJ-1	Excel
Property, Plant & Equipment Analytical Procedures	AJ-2	Excel
Property Additions	AJ-3	Excel
Property Deletions	AJ-4	Excel

Prepaids & Accruals Workpapers

Prepaid Insurance	AH-1	Excel
Prepaid & Accrued Property Taxes	AH-2	Excel
Other Prepaid Expenses	AH-3	Excel
Accrued Liabilities Analytical Procedures	LD-1	Excel

Accounts Payable, Notes Payable and Long-Term Debt Workpapers

Accounts Payable Confirmation Results	LA-1	Excel
Debt Obligations & Interest Analysis	LB-3	Excel
Debt Obligations & Interest Analytical Procedures	LG-1	Excel

Equity, Revenue, Expense & Other Miscellaneous Workpapers

Analysis of Equity Accounts	EA-2	Excel
Revenue & Expenses Analytical Procedures	OC-1	Excel
Analysis of Legal Fees	OE-1	Excel
Analysis of Unrecorded Audit Differences	G-7	Excel

Cross-Reference

ORIGINAL PRONOUNCEMENTS TO
NOT-FOR-PROFIT ORGANIZATION AUDITS

This locator provides instant cross-reference between original pronouncements and the pages in this publication where the pronouncements appear. Original pronouncements are listed numerically or alphabetically, and the chapters in which the pronouncements appear in *2001 Not-for-Profit Organization Audits* are listed underneath.

STATEMENTS ON AUDITING STANDARDS

ORIGINAL PRONOUNCEMENT	*NOT-FOR-PROFIT ORGANIZATION AUDITS* REFERENCE
SAS-1 Codification of Auditing Standards and Procedures	Ch. 10: Reporting Ch. 11: Introduction to Circular A-133 Audits
SAS-7 Communications Between Predecessor and Successor Auditors	Ch. 14: Preplanning for a Circular A-133 Audit
SAS-12 Inquiry of a Client's Lawyer Concerning Litigation, Claims, and Assessments	Ch. 9: Concluding the Audit
SAS-19 Client Representations	Ch. 9: Concluding the Audit
SAS-29 Reporting on Information Accompanying the Basic Financial Statements in Auditor-Submitted Documents	Ch. 18: Reporting Under Circular A-133
SAS-31 Evidential Matter	Ch. 3: Audit Planning Ch. 4: Internal Control Considerations Ch. 6: Statement of Activities Ch. 15: Planning for a Circular A-133 Audit

SAS-35
Special Reports—Applying Agreed-Upon
Procedures to Specified Elements, Accounts,
or Items of a Financial Statement

Ch. 13: Government Auditing Standards

SAS-39
Audit Sampling

Ch. 7: Extent of Auditing Procedures and Sampling
pling
Ch. 17: Compliance and Subrecipient Considerations
erations

SAS-45
Omnibus Statement on Auditing Standards—
1983

Ch. 3: Audit Planning

SAS-47
Audit Risk and Materiality in Conducting an
Audit

Ch. 3: Audit Planning
Ch. 7: Extent of Auditing Procedures and Sampling
pling
Ch. 9: Concluding the Audit
Ch. 15: Planning for a Circular A-133 Audit

SAS-54
Illegal Acts by Clients

Ch. 3: Audit Planning
Ch. 12: Technical Resources for A-133 Audits

SAS-55
Consideration of the Internal Control
Structure in a Financial Statement Audit

Ch. 3: Audit Planning
Ch. 4: Internal Control Considerations
Ch. 16: Internal Controls Over Federal Awards

SAS-56
Analytical Procedures

Ch. 3: Audit Planning
Ch. 4: Internal Control Considerations
Ch. 9: Concluding the Audit
Ch. 15: Planning for a Circular A-133 Audit

SAS-58
Reports on Audited Financial Statements

Ch. 10: Reporting

SAS-59
The Auditor's Consideration of an Entity's
Ability to Continue as a Going Concern

Ch. 9: Concluding the Audit
Ch. 10: Reporting

SAS-60

Communication of Internal Control Structure
Related Matters Noted in an Audit

Ch. 10: Reporting

SAS-61

Communication with Audit Committees

Ch. 10: Reporting

SAS-62

Special Reports

Ch. 10: Reporting
Ch. 13: Government Auditing Standards

SAS-64

Omnibus Statement on Auditing Standards—
1990

Ch. 10: Reporting

SAS-65

The Auditor's Consideration of the Internal
Audit Function in an Audit of Financial
Statements

Ch. 4: Internal Control Considerations

SAS-67

The Confirmation Process

Ch. 6: Statement of Activities

SAS-68

Compliance Auditing Applicable to
Governmental Entities and Other Recipients
of Governmental Financial Assistance

Ch. 13: Government Auditing Standards

SAS-70

Reports on the Processing of Transactions by
Service Organizations

Ch. 3: Audit Planning
Ch. 5: Statement of Financial Position
Ch. 13: Government Auditing Standards

SAS-73

Using the Work of a Specialist

Ch. 3: Audit Planning

SAS-74

Compliance Auditing Considerations in
Audits of Governmental Entities and
Recipients of Governmental Financial
Assistance

Ch. 3: Audit Planning
Ch. 4: Internal Control Considerations
Ch. 12: Technical Resources for A-133 Audits
Ch. 13: Government Auditing Standards

SAS-77

Amendments to SAS No. 22, "Planning and
Supervision," No. 59, "The Auditor's
Consideration of an Entity's Ability to
Continue as a Going Concern," and No. 62,
"Special Reports"

Ch. 9: Concluding the Audit
Ch. 10: Reporting

STATEMENTS OF POSITION
OF THE AUDITING STANDARDS DIVISION

SOP 78-10

Accounting Principles and Reporting
Practices for Certain Nonprofit Organizations

Ch. 1: Introduction and Background

SOP 94-3

Reporting of Related Entities by Not-for-
Profit Organizations

Ch. 1: Introduction and Background
Ch. 2: Preplanning Audit Activities
Ch. 3: Audit Planning
Ch. 5: Statement of Financial Position
Ch 10: Reporting

SOP 98-2

Accounting for Costs of Not-for-Profit
Organizations and State and Local Governmental Entities That Include Fund-Raising

Ch. 1: Introduction and Background
Ch. 2: Preplanning Audit Activities

SOP 98-3

Audits of States, Local Governments, and
Not-for-Profit Organizations Receiving
Federal Awards

Ch. 12: Technical Resources for A-133 Audits
Ch. 14: Preplanning for a Circular A-133 Audit
Ch. 15: Planning for a Circular A-133 Audit
Ch. 16: Internal Controls Over Federal Awards
Ch. 17: Compliance and Subrecipient Consid-
erations

STATEMENTS ON QUALITY CONTROL STANDARDS

ORIGINAL PRONOUNCEMENT	*NOT-FOR-PROFIT ORGANIZATION* *AUDITS* REFERENCE

SQCS-2

System of Quality Control for a CPA Firm's
Accounting and Auditing Practice

Ch. 14: Preplanning for a Circular A-133 Audit

STATEMENTS ON STANDARDS FOR ATTESTATION ENGAGEMENTS

ORIGINAL PRONOUNCEMENT	*NOT-FOR-PROFIT ORGANIZATION* *AUDITS* REFERENCE

SSAE-1

Attestation Standards

Ch. 13: Government Auditing Standards

SSAE-2
Reporting on an Entity's Internal Control over
Financial Reporting

Ch. 13: Government Auditing Standards

SSAE-3
Compliance Attestation

Ch. 13: Government Auditing Standards

AUDIT AND ACCOUNTING GUIDES

ORIGINAL PRONOUNCEMENT	*NOT-FOR-PROFIT ORGANIZATION AUDITS* REFERENCE
Audit Sampling	Ch. 7: Extent of Audit Procedures and Sampling
Audits of Not-for-Profit Organizations	Ch. 1: Introduction and Background

AICPA SEC PRACTICE SECTION

ORIGINAL PRONOUNCEMENT	*NOT-FOR-PROFIT ORGANIZATION AUDITS* REFERENCE
How the Use of a Service Organization Affects Internal Control Considerations	Ch. 3: Audit Planning

FINANCIAL ACCOUNTING STANDARDS BOARD STATEMENTS

ORIGINAL PRONOUNCEMENT	*NOT-FOR-PROFIT ORGANIZATION AUDITS* REFERENCE
FAS-5 Accounting for Contingencies	Ch. 3: Audit Planning Ch. 10: Reporting
FAS-13 Accounting for Leases	Ch. 5: Statement of Financial Position
FAS-57 Related Party Disclosures	Ch. 2: Preplanning Audit Activities Ch. 3: Audit Planning
FAS-93 Recognition of Depreciation by Not-for-Profit Organizations	Ch. 1: Introduction and Background Ch. 5: Statement of Financial Position

FINANCIAL ACCOUNTING STANDARDS BOARD
CONCEPTS STATEMENTS

FASB Concepts Statement No. 6
Elements of Financial Statements

> Ch. 1: Introduction and Background
> Ch. 6: Statement of Activities

GENERAL ACCOUNTING OFFICE PUBLICATIONS

ORIGINAL PRONOUNCEMENT

NOT-FOR-PROFIT ORGANIZATION
AUDITS REFERENCE

Government Auditing Standards[1]

> Ch. 2: Preplanning Audit Activities
> Ch. 11: Introduction to Circular A-133 Audits
> Ch. 12: Technical Resources for A-133 Audits
> Ch. 13: Government Auditing Standards
> Ch. 14: Preplanning for a Circular A-133 Audit
> Ch. 15: Planning for a Circular A-133 Audit
> Ch. 16: Internal Controls Over Federal Awards
> Ch. 17: Compliance and Subrecipient Considerations
> Ch. 18: Reporting Under Circular A-133
> Ch. 19: Concluding the A-133 Audit

Amendments to *Government Auditing Standards*

> Ch. 11: Introduction to Circular A-133 Audits
> Ch. 13: Government Auditing Standards
> Ch. 14: Preplanning for a Circular A-133 Audit

FEDERAL LEGISLATION

ORIGINAL PRONOUNCEMENT

NOT-FOR-PROFIT ORGANIZATION
AUDITS REFERENCE

Single Audit Act Amendments of 1996

> Ch. 11: Introduction to Circular A-133 Audits

Internal Revenue Code Section 501

> Ch. 8: Tax Considerations

OFFICE OF MANAGEMENT AND BUDGET PUBLICATIONS

ORIGINAL PRONOUNCEMENT

NOT-FOR-PROFIT ORGANIZATION
AUDITS REFERENCE

OMB Circular A-21[1]
Cost Principles for Educational Institutions

> Ch. 12: Technical Resources for A-133 Audits

OMB Circular A-110[1]
Uniform Administrative Requirements for Grants and Agreements with Institutions of Higher Education, Hospitals, and Other Nonprofit Organizations

> Ch. 12: Technical Resources for A-133 Audits
> Ch. 16: Internal Controls Over Federal Awards

---

[1] Original text is supplied on the disc accompanying this Guide.

OMB Circular A-122[1]
Cost Principles for Nonprofit Organizations

Ch. 12: Technical Resources for A-133 Audits

OMB Circular A-133[1]
Audits of States, Local Governments, and
Not-for-Profit Organizations

Ch. 1: Introduction and Background
Ch. 2: Preplanning Audit Activities
Ch. 7: Extent of Audit Procedures and Sampling
Ch. 12: Technical Resources for A-133 Audits
Ch. 13: Government Auditing Standards
Ch. 14: Preplanning for a Circular A-133 Audit
Ch. 15: Planning for a Circular A-133 Audit
Ch. 16: Internal Controls over Federal Awards
Ch. 17: Compliance and Subrecipient Considerations
Ch. 18: Reporting Under Circular A-133
Ch. 19: Concluding the A-133 Audit

Compliance Supplement

Ch. 12: Technical Resources for A-133 Audits
Ch. 15: Planning for a Circular A-133 Audit
Ch. 16: Internal Controls over Federal Awards
Ch. 17: Compliance and Subrecipient Considerations
Ch. 18: Reporting under Circular A-133

Amendments to OMB Circular A-133
Compliance Supplement

Ch. 12: Technical Resources for A-133 Audits

PUBLICATIONS OF THE PRESIDENT'S COUNCIL
ON INTEGRITY AND EFFICIENCY

ORIGINAL PRONOUNCEMENT

NOT-FOR-PROFIT ORGANIZATION
AUDITS REFERENCE

Position Statement No. 6: Questions and
Answers on OMB Circular A-133

Ch. 12: Technical Resources for A-133 Audits
Ch. 14: Preplanning for a Circular A-133 Audit
Ch. 15: Planning for a Circular A-133 Audit

Federal Cognizant Agency Audit Organization Guidelines

Ch. 12: Technical Resources for A-133 Audits

Guide for Initial Review of A-133 Audit
Reports[1]

Ch. 12: Technical Resources for A-133 Audits

Guide for Quality Control Review for A-133
Audits[1]

Ch. 12: Technical Resources for A-133 Audits

---

[1] Original text is supplied on the disc accompanying this Guide.

Not-for-Profit Organization Audits

PART I
FINANCIAL STATEMENT AUDITS

CHAPTER 1
INTRODUCTION AND BACKGROUND

CONTENTS

Chapter 1
INTRODUCTION AND BACKGROUND

CROSS-REFERENCES

2001 Miller Not-for-Profit Organization Audits: Chapter 14, "Preplanning for a Circular A-133 Audit"

2001 Miller Audit Procedures: Chapter 1, "Preengagement Activities"

2000 Miller GAAP Guide: Chapter 58, "Not-for-Profit Organizations"

2000 Miller Not-for-Profit Reporting: Chapter 2, "Overview of Current Pronouncements"

DISTINGUISHING CHARACTERISTICS OF NOT-FOR-PROFIT ORGANIZATIONS

Not-for-profit organizations have several unique characteristics, both financial and nonfinancial, that distinguish them from commercial enterprises. These distinguishing features include the following:

- Revenue sources and methodology in collecting and recognizing revenue
- Financial position and performance indicators
- Organizational structure and support
- Operating environment and public scrutiny

These characteristics make the audit of the financial statements of a not-for profit organization different from the audit of a typical commercial enterprise. The following discussion provides an overview of some of the differences (and in some cases similarities) of not-for-profit organizations when compared to commercial enterprises for each of these features.

Revenue Sources and Methodology in Collecting and Recognizing Revenue

As with many specialized industries, many of the differences among organizations in different industries relate to the organization's revenue streams (i.e., how it receives and/or earns its revenue). A hospital's revenues are earned in a much different way than a mutual fund's. A manufacturer's revenues are quite different from an insurance company's. Similarly, a not-for-profit "earns" much of its revenue in ways that are, for the most part, different from the ways that commercial enterprises earn their revenues.

Generally, a not-for-profit's revenues will fall into one or more of the following categories:

- Contributions from the general public, corporate donors, and foundations
- Fund-raising campaigns or annual events
- Grants and contracts with foundations, other not-for-profit organizations, or governmental entities
- Charges for specific services rendered
- Investment earnings

Contributions from the General Public

Not-for-profit organizations solicit general support contributions from a variety of different sources in a variety of different ways. These contributions can range from multimillion dollar contributions from large corporations, individuals, or foundations to the spare change collection canisters found near the cash registers of small stores. In general, the larger the contribution, the more personal interaction there will be between a not-for-profit organization and the donor. For large contributions, the not-for-profit organization may agree to recognize the donor in some way, such as dedicating a room of an office to the donor or naming an award after the donor. Other large donors request that their contributions remain anonymous. Large donations often carry more restrictions in regard to how they may be spent. Temporary or permanent restrictions are important factors in determining the proper accounting treatment of contributions.

Small cash contributions represent a different side of the general support contribution picture. Small contributions may be collected by volunteers or other intermediary organizations and then remitted to the not-for-profit organization. Obviously, the not-for-profit organization should take reasonable precautions over the handling of cash contributions. These types of contributions can be the most difficult to control since the dollar amounts collected most likely will not justify the cost of elaborate internal control structures.

Within these two extremes of general support contributions is a wide variety of methods for soliciting contributions, including direct mail solicitations, telephone solicitations, and radio, television, and print advertising. More recently, many not-for-profit organizations are using web-based solicitations .Each of these methods will result in contributions of various sizes. They also may result in contributions in the form of cash, checks, credit card charges, pledges to pay at a later date, formal bequests, or "in-kind" contributions of some type of goods or services.

Auditors must design their audit procedures to verify the various types of general support revenues that may be pledged or collected. The requirements of FASB Statement (FAS) No. 116 (Accounting for Contributions Received and Contributions Made) also must be considered to determine the proper accounting treatment of contributions received and pledged.

Fund-Raising Campaigns or Annual Events

Many not-for-profit organizations find that organizing their fund-raising appeals into a campaign or special event presents a better opportunity to focus attention on their fund-raising activities, increasing their chances of success.

A fund-raising campaign usually has a specific goal that is to be accomplished over a specified period of time. Often these campaigns are associated with capital projects. For example, a university may announce a capital campaign to raise $50 million by the year 2005 to begin construction of a new library. The campaign may have "chairs," individuals who have made significant contributions to encourage other individuals or companies to make contributions. In fact, many not-for-profit organizations make sure that they have commitments for a significant part of the campaign's goal before they announce the campaign with any publicity. The commitments already obtained will encourage potential donors to contribute and will increase the likelihood that the campaign will be viewed as a success.

A not-for-profit organization may stage a special event to focus attention on its fund-raising efforts. These events can also serve as a forum to familiarize donors with the programs that the organization is providing. The types of special events can vary widely and may include annual awards dinners, exhibitions, concerts, outings, dinners with celebrities or dignitaries, and receptions. Often, not-for-profit organizations recruit "chairs" or "sponsors" to underwrite some or all of the event's expenses. This greatly increases the event's chances for financial success.

Because these special events may be infrequent, not-for-profit organizations may lack control over their financial aspects. The number of unexpected problems or costs associated with special events may be high. Therefore, in addition to auditing the revenue recognition issues, the auditor should review the reasonableness of any campaign start-up expenses. Not-for-profit organizations in the past may have recorded these as a deferred asset if the expenses for the campaign or special event were incurred in an earlier accounting period than the one in which the revenue is recognized. However, as will be discussed later, the AICPA Audit and Accounting Guide (AICPA Guide) requires that those expenses be recorded when incurred. The auditor should review the accounting propriety of any deferral considering this guidance.

Grants and Contracts with Foundations, Other Not-for-Profit Organizations, or Governmental Entities

Not-for-profit organizations often obtain a substantial amount of their funding from grants and contracts. These types of agreements enable the not-for-profit organization to conduct a wide range of activities, from university-level research and development to the provision of food or shelter to the indigent. Both grant and contract agreements are contractual in nature but have differing characteristics.

The deliverables in a grant are generally less specific than would be found in a contract, and a grant generally provides the not-for-profit organization with greater flexibility in providing the goods or services desired by the grantor. For example, a research grant cannot specify that a desired result will be achieved. It can specify that a particular level of effort will be made to pursue the desired outcomes of the grant. It may also specify periodic reporting requirements as well as ownership of rewarding discoveries as a result of the research performed.

A contract generally specifies a level of goods or services that must be provided by the not-for-profit organization. For example, a local government may enter into a contract with a not-for-profit organization requiring the not-for-profit to provide day care services for children referred by the local government. The contract most likely will specify the number of children that must be served, the hours of operation, the compensation per child, the number of staff on duty per child, etc.

A number of audit considerations arise when a not-for-profit organization receives funding through grants or contracts. Classification of revenues and receivables as increases in permanently restricted net assets, temporarily restricted net assets, or unrestricted net assets must be reviewed for propriety. Grants and contracts usually impose various requirements and restrictions on the not-for-profit organization, noncompliance with which may be material to the financial statements. These restrictions usually include grant or contract budgets with which the not-for-profit organization must comply. (There generally are fewer restrictions imposed by grants than by contracts.) If any of the funding for the grants or contracts originates with the federal government, additional audit requirements, established by the Single Audit Amendments Act of 1996 and OMB Circular A-133 (Audits of States, Local Governments and Non-Profit Organizations), may be triggered. The auditor has certain responsibilities if he or she becomes aware of the need for a Circular A-133 audit but has not been engaged to perform this type of audit. These responsibilities are discussed in the chapter titled "Preplanning Audit Activities," and specific guidance on performing an audit in accordance with Circular A-133 is found in Part II of this Guide.

Charges for Specific Services Rendered

An auditor who is familiar with the audits of commercial enterprises should be able to apply these same skills to audit the revenues earned by a not-for-profit organization that charges fees for services rendered. These charges may encompass the basic functions of the not-for-profit organization. For example, a university may charge students tuition and fees for particular classes and credits. These charges also may be ancillary to the basic mission of the not-for-profit organization. For example, a professional organization may charge for a publication it produces. Certain not-for-profit organizations also are considered "membership" organizations, whereby, in return for an annual fee, the members of the organization will be entitled to certain information or other services that can be provided by the not-for-profit organization. Labor unions are another example of organizations that provide services to their members for a fee, in this case fees that are referred to as union dues. Not-for-profit organizations often use fee-for-service activities to augment their program activities. For example, a museum may sell subscriptions to a magazine or newsletter that it publishes.

An auditor's consideration of the not-for-profit's earnings process as it relates to charges for services will be similar to the auditor's consideration of a commercial enterprise. Auditors also need to be aware of the nature of charges for services to determine whether these charges fall within the organizations "exempt function" for Internal Revenue Code purposes or whether any net earnings from these revenues would be subject to unrelated business income tax.

Investment Earnings

Investment earnings are significant to many not-for-profit organizations that rely on the earnings from a corpus of investment capital to provide annual operating support. For example, universities are well-known for their reliance on the earnings of endowment funds to supplement their operating revenues. While audit procedures may be similar to those performed in an audit of a commercial enterprise, the auditor will have several additional matters to consider. Generally accepted accounting principles for the accounting of investments and their earnings are slightly different for not-for-profit organizations than for commercial enterprises, and the auditor must be familiar with these differences. Proper classification of investment earnings, including the reporting of unrealized gains and losses on investments that are restricted, is both new and complex. It will require particular attention from auditors until not-for-profit organizations become familiar with the requirements, resolve some ambiguities in the guidance, and develop routing and systems to simplify the accounting process. New accounting requirements for recording derivatives are also applicable to not-for-profit organizations and will require attention when implemented. In addition, Statement of Position (SOP) 94-3 (Reporting of Related Entities by Not-for-Profit Organizations) may have an impact on the manner in which a not-for-profit organization reports investments in for-profit entities and the manner in which financially interrelated not-for-profit organizations are reported.

In addition, if a not-for-profit organization relies on the earnings from investments for operations, there may be pressure on the investment managers to produce higher earnings, which may result in the acceptance of a higher level of investment risk than might otherwise be appropriate. Auditors should be alert for any investment valuation issues that such a riskier portfolio may present, particularly in light of the unfortunate but well-publicized circumstances in which organizations have incurred significant losses from derivatives and other synthetic securities.

Financial Position and Performance Indicators

The readers of the financial statements of not-for-profit organizations generally read them for different reasons than the readers of commercial enterprise financial statements. Readers of not-for-profit organization financial statements are more likely to be interested in the efficiency of the organization in providing services, rather than in its increases in net assets. Creditors, however, are the exception. They read the statements of both types of organizations with the same objective: to determine the ability of the organization to satisfy its financial obligations.

The statement of financial position presented in accordance with FAS-117 (Financial Statements of Not-for-Profit Organizations) provides information about liquidity as well as classification of net assets. The auditor must ensure that the ordering of assets on the statement as to liquidity, and the classification of net assets into the appropriate categories, has been done appropriately. The FASB issued a special report in December 1994 titled "Results of the Field Test of the Proposed Standards for Financial Statements of Not-for-Profit Organizations and Accounting for Contributions," which found a diversity in practice in the classification of net assets for similar programs and circumstances. Auditors will have to analyze this area carefully to ensure proper classification.

The performance indicators for not-for-profit organizations are different from those of commercial enterprises. Net earnings, earnings per share, and comprehensive income are key indicators for a commercial enterprise, but are not relevant to a not-for-profit organization. Generally, a not-for-profit organization is operating at its optimum level when it is breaking even—when its revenues equal its expenses. A not-for-profit organization cannot operate indefinitely when its expenses exceed its revenues, because eventually the corpus of its net assets will be depleted and it will not be able to meet its financial obligations. Conversely, a not-for-profit whose revenues exceed its expenses on a consistent basis will eventually erode its ability to raise funds, because donors will question why fund raising is necessary when the organization has excess funds.

Another key indicator for not-for-profit organizations is the proportion of the organization's program and supporting services to its total expenses. Donors are extremely interested in knowing how much of each dollar that they donate to the not-for-profit organization will go to the programs of the not-for-profit organization and how much will go to support and administration. Certainly, the higher percentage of program expenses to total expenses, the more favorably the not-for-profit organization will be viewed by potential donors. In addition, the percentage of contributions to fund-raising expenses provides an indication of the efficiency and effectiveness of a not-for-profit organization's fund-raising efforts. As a general rule, donors do not like to see a large percentage of their contribution used for the expenses of raising funds from other donors.

Auditors should perform procedures to ensure that the not-for-profit organization is classifying program and supporting expenses properly, so that these two percentages are properly stated. New requirements for accounting for the cost of activities that have both programmatic and fund-raising aspects ("joint costs") will be an important new area for auditors. The importance of this may be missed by auditors who normally audit commercial enterprises, since classification of expenses ordinarily is not as significant in an audit of a commercial enterprise.

Organizational Structure and Support

The organizational support and structure of not-for-profit organizations generally is weaker than that found in commercial enterprises.

> **OBSERVATION:** Some audit guides designed for not-for-profit organizations refer to this as a weakness in personnel. The author served for a time as the chief financial officer of a not-for-profit organization and found many exceptional employees there. The weakness really relates to the amount of investment that a not-for-profit organization is able or willing to make in improving and updating its systems and processes as well as to the level of investment that it is willing to make in the individuals who perform financial and accounting-related functions.

In most instances, financial personnel in not-for-profit organizations are competing for resources with program personnel. Since its programs are the heart of a not-for-profit organization, there is a natural tendency to commit resources to them. This may lead to some neglect of financial systems and an unwillingness to spend money to update computer systems, etc. Appropriate staff training and development is sometimes neglected as well, particularly when volunteers are being used for some financial functions.

Not-for-profit organizations that compete with other not-for-profit organizations for grants and awards also may try to keep their overhead rate as low as possible. This can directly affect the not-for-profit's willingness to make the necessary investments in financial systems and personnel.

Weaknesses in financial personnel can occur when a not-for-profit organization fails to attract and retain the best possible financial personnel. This can occur for a number of reasons. Working at a not-for-profit organization is sometimes viewed as low-paying, with few perquisites. Since many not-for-profit organizations are small to medium-sized, a clear career path is not always an attraction, and financial personnel are not always sure that their skills are transferable to commercial enterprises. During periods of tightness in the market for skilled labor, not-for-profit organizations often find it difficult to recruit staff with the appropriate skill sets. Nevertheless, working for not-for-profit organizations is attractive to many people for a number of reasons. Many financial personnel have a great deal of enthusiasm for the work of the not-for-profit organization, and the turnover rate of staff at not-for-profit organizations tends to be lower than in many commercial enterprises.

During the last few years, the tremendous demand for information technology (IT) professionals has created a shortage of individuals with these skills. The shortage has resulted in rapidly rising wages for IT professionals, which can impair a not-for-profit organization's ability to attract and retain qualified IT staff. Even with the winding down of Year 2000 software remediation efforts, the shortage of IT professionals will continue to plague not-for-profit organizations.

Auditors should be aware of the potential weaknesses in organizational structure and support described above and should incorporate this awareness into their evaluation of the not-for-profit organization's internal control and their design of an effective audit strategy. Auditors also should consider the assignment of staff with appropriate levels of experience to audits of not-for-profit organizations, so that any potential weaknesses in the organization's systems, processes, or personnel can be adequately addressed. Auditors should also clearly understand how much the not-for-profit organization may need to rely on the auditor to propose audit adjustments for any of the otherwise routine "closing" journal entries.

Operating Environment and Public Scrutiny

Although many auditors regard the audit of not-for-profit organizations as having little or low risk, this is not necessarily the case. It is true that not-for-profit organizations are not publicly traded entities where material misstatement of net earnings and earnings per share is likely to bring a significant amount of legal exposure to the auditor. On the other hand, auditors of not-for-profit organizations have the same legal exposure to creditors of the organization being audited as do auditors of commercial enterprises.

More importantly, not-for-profit organizations operate under a great deal of public scrutiny. These organizations accept public funds and are expected to use these funds in a very efficient manner, with virtually no waste or abuse. If a not-for-profit organization misspends public funds, its reputation and the reputation of its auditor will be severely damaged. In a number of instances in the recent past, very well-known not-for-profit organizations have been severely criticized for acts that probably would go unnoticed at a commercial enterprise. Many of these instances of misappropriation or imprudent spending of funds normally would not be discovered during an audit performed in accordance with generally accepted auditing standards. Recent revisions to auditing standards pertaining to an auditor's consideration of the existence of fraud during an audit of financial statements may also lead to an over-expectation of the responsibly and capability of an auditor to detect fraud.

However, this does not mean auditors should greatly expand the scope of their audits of not-for-profit organizations to detect these instances. Auditors must consider the contributors and grantors to a not-for-profit organization as among the readers of their report (as they would consider other readers) as well as the requirements of generally accepted auditing standards when designing an audit approach and making decisions during the course of an audit on considerations such as materiality.

An audit in accordance with generally accepted auditing standards will not detect all matters that the public might view negatively. In addition, some matters will be viewed negatively even if the related accounting is appropriate and the proper internal controls were used. For example, the public criticized the "golden parachute" of one organization's departing senior executive, even though it consisted entirely of the individual's accrued vacation time.

Developing and maintaining a successful audit practice of not-for-profit organizations is a challenging, yet profitable, endeavor. Not-for-profit organizations have unique characteristics, operating environments, and accounting conventions. An auditor who understands these factors will be able to perform not-for-profit organization audits properly, technically, and professionally, and will be successful in attracting and retaining not-for-profit organization clients.

PURPOSE OF THIS GUIDE

The purposes of this Guide are as follows:

1. To describe and explain the unique characteristics of not-for-profit organizations and the unique accounting conventions they employ.

2. To provide a comprehensive audit approach to performing audits of not-for-profit organizations. The objective of the design of the approach is that it be sufficiently complete so that auditors need not look to numerous other reference sources. At the same time, the approach presented cannot be so detailed or inflexible that it (a) becomes cumbersome for the auditor to work with or (b) cannot be easily modified to be used with the approach normally used by the auditor in his or her audits of commercial organizations.

3. To provide the auditor with detailed information on audits in accordance with Circular A-133. (All of the information and practice aids necessary to perform an audit of a not-for-profit organization in accordance with Circular A-133 are included in this audit practice guide.)

4. To provide the auditor with the tools necessary to implement changes in accounting and auditing standards and requirements.

5. To provide the auditor with practice management information specifically relating to audits of not-for-profit organizations, including suggestions on marketing and proposal development, staff administration and training considerations, risk assessment and client acceptance considerations, and techniques to improve the profitability of these types of audits.

Organization of the Guide

This Guide is divided into two main sections:

1. *Financial Statement Audits*   Provides a walk-through of the various stages of a financial statement audit, with emphasis on considerations important in audits of not-for-profit organizations. These stages include:

   a. Obtaining background information and reviewing applicable professional literature (Chapter 1)

   b. Performing preplanning activities (Chapter 2)

   c. Planning the audit (Chapter 3)

   d. Internal control considerations (Chapter 4)

   e. Performing substantive tests of accounts in the statement of financial position (Chapter 5) and statement of activities (Chapter 6)

   f. Audit sampling (Chapter 7)

   g. Special considerations relating to federal taxation (Chapter 8)

   h. Concluding the audit (Chapter 9)

   i. Reporting (Chapter 10)

2. *Single Audits Under OMB Circular A-133*   Provides specific guidance relating to audits of not-for-profit organizations that receive federal awards. The guidance covered includes information on the following:

   a. Introduction to Circular A-133 audits (Chapter 11)

   b. Technical resources needed to perform Circular A-133 audits (Chapter 12)

   c. *Government Auditing Standards* (Chapter 13)

   d. Performing preplanning activities for an audit in accordance with OMB Circular A-133 (Chapter 14)

   e. Planning the audit in accordance with OMB Circular A-133 (Chapter 15)

   f. Internal controls over federal awards (Chapter 16)

   g. Compliance and subrecipient considerations (Chapter 17)

   h. Reporting according to OMB Circular A-133 (Chapter 18)

   i. Concluding the audit in accordance with OMB Circular A-133 (Chapter 19)

Throughout the Guide, "Observations" provide additional insights into the technical material being covered. In addition, "Audit Cost-Saving Tips" provide practical suggestions for saving audit hours, resulting in lower costs for the not-for-profit organization and higher profit margins for the auditor.

Electronic Workpapers

Not-for-Profit Organization Audits was designed to make your audit engagements as efficient as possible. To that end, the Guide comes with all workpapers, sample reports, sample letters, disclosure checklist, and model audit programs on disc. These electronic versions of the Guide's practice aids can be printed and photocopied, or you can use your word processing program to customize the files for specific engagements and clients.

As you will notice, many of the practice aids in your book contain a disc icon (like the one shown to the right) in the upper right hand corner. This icon indicates that the workpaper, report, etc., also can be found on the accompanying disc, and can be customized and completed on a computer.

Although not reproduced in this Guide, complete audit programs for both financial statement audits and single audits are included on the disc. These programs, and the other workpapers, are designed to be flexible to meet your needs. They may be used as stand-alone materials or as supplements to your existing audit materials.

Instructions for using the electronic workpapers accompanying this Guide are included starting on page 801. These aids are easy-to-use and can speed the audit process, and we hope you will take advantage of them.

PROFESSIONAL LITERATURE ISSUED BY THE FINANCIAL ACCOUNTING STANDARDS BOARD

Historically, the FASB has issued very few Statements of Financial Accounting Standards specifically addressing not-for-profit organizations. However, in the last few years it has issued three significant FASB Statements for not-for-profit organizations. These important Statements which relate to not-for-profit statements are FAS-117 (Financial Statements of Not-for-Profit Organizations), FAS-116 (Accounting for Contributions Received and Contributions Made), and FAS-124 (Accounting for Certain Investments Held by Not-for-Profit Organizations). The proper implementation and continued use of these three Statements is of concern for auditors, particularly in the early years following implementation. The following are brief summaries of (1) two FASB Concepts Statements that address issues for nonbusiness organizations and elements of financial statements, and (2) the FASB Statements that specifically address issues related to not-for-profit organizations.

FASB Concepts Statement No. 4

The FASB discusses the financial reporting and other issues relating to not-for-profit organizations in Concepts Statement No. 4 (Objectives of Financial Reporting by Nonbusiness Organizations). While not providing an exact definition of a not-for-profit organization, Concepts Statement No. 4 does provide the following distinguishing characteristics of "nonbusiness" organizations:

- Receipts of significant amounts of resources from resource providers who do not expect to receive either repayment or economic benefits proportionate to resources provided
- Operating purposes that are other than to provide goods and services at a profit or profit equivalent
- Absence of defined ownership interests that can be sold, transferred, or redeemed, or that convey entitlement to a share of a residual distribution of resources in the event of liquidation of the organization

Concepts Statement No. 4 also describes what it does *not* consider to be nonbusiness organizations. The organizations not considered nonbusiness or not-for-profit organizations include all investor-owned enterprises and entities that provide dividends, lower costs or other economic benefits directly and proportionately to their owners, members, or participants, such as mutual insurance companies, credit unions, farm and rural electric cooperatives, and employee benefit plans. These organizations are outside the scope of this Guide.

In addition to discussing the distinguishing characteristics of nonbusiness organizations, Concepts Statement No. 4 provides a useful discussion of the types of users of nonbusiness organization financial statements as well as their possible interests. The readers and users of financial statements are important to auditors not only because auditors are legally exposed to those readers and users, but also because the anticipated financial statement users can affect the auditor's materiality decisions throughout the audit. Concepts Statement No. 4 states:

> Among present and potential users are members, taxpayers, contributors, grantors, lenders, suppliers, creditors, employees, managers, directors and trustees, service beneficiaries, financial analysts and advisors, brokers, underwriters, lawyers, economists, taxing authorities, regulatory authorities, legislators, the financial press and reporting agencies, labor unions, trade associations, researchers, teachers, and students.

Concepts Statement No. 4 continues by categorizing these potential users into the following groups:

- Resource providers, which include those who are compensated for their services, such as employees and vendors, and those who are not directly and proportionately compensated, such as members and contributors
- Constituents, which are those who use or benefit from the services rendered by the organization
- Governing and oversight bodies, which include those responsible for setting policies and for overseeing and appraising managers of not-for-profit organizations, such as boards of trustees, councils, or other bodies with similar authority
- Managers, which include those individuals responsible for carrying out the policy mandates of the governing bodies as well as managing the day-to-day operations of the not-for-profit organization

> **OBSERVATION:** Resource providers include typical credit providers, such as banks or other financial institutions. The use and reliance of creditors on the financial statements of not-for-profit organizations is an important consideration for auditors because it may be a significant area of legal exposure for the auditor. This is sometimes overlooked by auditors who consider audits of not-for-profit organizations to be relatively risk-free.

Concepts Statement No. 4 also establishes the objectives of financial reporting for nonbusiness organizations. The financial reporting of nonbusiness organizations should include information that is useful in:

- Making resource allocation decisions.
- Assessing services and ability to provide services.
- Assessing management stewardship and performance.
- Providing information about economic resources, obligations, net resources, and changes in them.

Auditors should keep these reporting objectives in mind when planning and performing an audit of a not-for-profit organization.

FASB Concepts Statement No. 6

The FASB issued Concepts Statement No. 6 (Elements of Financial Statements) in December 1985. It addresses a broad range of reporting issues primarily for commercial enterprises, but also presents a substantial discussion of reporting concepts related to not-for-profit organizations. The concepts and terminology discussed in this Concepts Statement are similar to the terminology and requirements adopted by FAS-117, which are discussed more fully below. In other words, these concepts were almost ten years old when they were formally adopted and required to be implemented.

Concepts Statement No. 6 defines the net assets of a not-for-profit organization as a residual, which is the difference between an organization's assets and liabilities. Unlike those of a commercial enterprise, however, the net assets of a not-for-profit organization do not represent an ownership interest, such as shareholders' equity.

Concepts Statement No. 6 identifies three classes of net assets, the same three classes identified in FAS-117: permanently restricted net assets, temporarily restricted net assets, and unrestricted net assets.

Further discussion of these concepts and the resulting reporting requirements is provided in the discussion of FAS-117. These concepts are included in the audit approach and other materials presented throughout this Guide.

FASB Statement No. 117

FAS-117 (Financial Statements of Not-for-Profit Organizations) is a very significant document for accounting and financial reporting for not-for-profit organizations. It standardizes the financial reporting requirements for not-for-profit organizations and modifies and updates the existing requirements to improve the financial reporting of not-for-profit organizations.

FAS-117 was issued in June 1993. It adopts the definition of *not-for-profit organization* originally contained in Concepts Statement No. 4, which is described above. Briefly, FAS-117 specifies that the financial statements of a not-for-profit organization should include the following:

- Statement of financial position
- Statement of activities
- Statement of cash flows

The disclosures previously provided in the statement of functional expenses, concerning the natural classification of expenses (such as salaries, rent, and utilities), are still required for voluntary health and welfare organizations and are encouraged for all other not-for-profit organizations. The information may be presented in a separate schedule or may be included in the footnotes to the financial statements.

> **OBSERVATION:** Voluntary health and welfare organizations are formed to provide voluntary services for various segments of society, usually concentrating on solving health and welfare problems. Although by definition these organization are supported by voluntary contributions from the public, they also may perform fee-for-service activities. A complete definition of voluntary health and welfare organizations is presented in FAS-117.

The statement of financial position reports the *net assets* of the not-for-profit organization, replacing the previously used term *fund balance*. The focus of the statement of financial position is on the assets and liabilities of the organization as a whole, compared with the formerly used *fund break-out* that was commonly reported in the organization's balance sheet. The statement of financial position reports the amounts of net assets of a not-for-profit organization in each of three classes of net assets—permanently restricted net assets, temporarily restricted net assets, and unrestricted net assets.

The statement of activities of a not-for-profit organization classifies revenues, expenses, gains, and losses within the three classes of net assets. The focus of the statement of activities is on the organization as a whole, and it should provide information about expenses reported by their functional classification, such as major classes of program services and supporting activities (if not provided in the notes to the financial statements).

FAS-117 includes the statement of cash flows as one of the basic financial statements of a not-for-profit organization. FAS-117 amends FAS-95 (Statement of Cash Flows) to remove FAS-95's previous exemption of its requirements for not-for-profit organizations. FAS-117 also amends FAS-95 in various sections to incorporate appropriate terminology and provide some specific guidance for not-for-profit organizations.

FASB Statement No. 116

FAS-116 (Accounting for Contributions Received and Contributions Made) was issued concurrently with FAS-117 in June 1993. Its impact on the financial statements of not-for-profit organizations is not as significant or pervasive as FAS-117's, since it addresses only one aspect of an organization's financial statements: contributions. However, since a large proportion of not-for-profit organizations receive contributions in some form, these organizations and their auditors must be familiar with the contents of FAS-116.

The provisions of FAS-116 have been considered in the design of the audit procedures for contributions and contributions receivable included in this Guide. The chapters of this Guide titled "Statement of Financial Position" and "Statement of Activities" provide more detailed information on FAS-116, which supplements the following overview.

FAS-116 applies to all entities that receive or make contributions, not solely to not-for-profit organizations, although these organizations will be the most affected by the requirements.

FAS-116 requires that contributions received, including unconditional promises to give, be recognized as revenues in the period received. These contributions should be recognized at their fair values. Conversely, contributions made, including unconditional promises to give, are recognized as expenses in the period made at their fair values. Conditional promises to give, whether received or made, are recognized when the conditions are substantially met. To be consistent with the requirements of FAS-117, contributions received by not-for-profit organizations would be classified as those that increase permanently restricted net assets, those that increase temporarily restricted net assets, or those that increase unrestricted net assets. Donor-imposed restrictions that expire are recognized in the period that they expire.

Certain of the provisions of FAS-116 were clarified by FASB Interpretation (FIN)-42 (Accounting for Transfers of Assets in Which a Not-for-Profit Organization Is Granted Variance Power). In addition, in July 1998 the FASB issued an Exposure Draft for a proposed Statement titled "Transfers of Assets Involving a Not-for-Profit Organization That Raises or Holds Contributions for Others." Both of these documents address the accounting for situations where a not-for-profit organization raises resources for one or more other not-for-profit organizations and then transfers those resources to the not-for-profit organization(s) that may, or may not, be specified by the original donor. FIN-42 and the recently issued FAS-136, "Transfers of Assets to a Not-for-Profit Organization or Charitable Trust That Raises or Holds Contributions for Others" (which includes the requirements of FIN-42), are discussed as part of the relevant discussion of FAS-116 provided in this Guide and in the chapter titled "Statement of Activities."

FAS-116 allows certain exceptions for contributions of services and contributions of works of art, historical treasures, and similar assets. Briefly, these exceptions are as follows:

- Contributions of services are recognized only if the services received:

  — Create or enhance nonfinancial assets, or

  — Require specialized skills, are provided by individuals possessing those skills, and typically would need to be purchased if not provided by donation.

- Contributions of works of art, historical treasures, and similar assets are not required to be recognized as revenue and capitalized if the donated items are added to collections held for public exhibition, education, or research in furtherance of public service rather than for financial gain.

FAS-116 requires certain disclosures for collection items not capitalized and for receipts of contributed services and promises to give.

FASB Statement No. 124

The FASB issued Statement No. 124 (Accounting for Certain Investments Held by Not-for-Profit Organizations) in November 1995. This Statement requires the use of fair value when measuring investments for financial reporting purposes. It applies to most, but not all, of the types of investments held by not-for-profit organizations.

> **OBSERVATION:** FAS-124 is the not-for-profit version of the guidance that was provided to commercial organizations by FAS-115 (Accounting for Certain Investments in Debt and Equity Securities). Not-for-profit organizations were in need of guidance in this area, because investment valuation practices previously relied on inconsistent guidance in the older AICPA audit and accounting guides that provided different requirements for different types of not-for-profit organizations.

The measurement standards of FAS-124 apply to equity securities that have readily determinable fair values (except where the equity method is being used or for investments in consolidated subsidiaries) and all debt securities. Fair value is considered to be readily determinable if one of the following three conditions is met:

- Sales prices or bid/asked quotations are currently available on a securities exchange registered with the United States Securities and Exchange Commission and in the over-the-counter market, where quotations are publicly reported by either the National Association of Securities Dealers Automated Quotations system or the National Quotation Bureau. Restricted stock would not meet this definition.

- For equity securities that are traded on only foreign exchanges, the foreign market must be of a similar breadth and scope to one of the United States' markets referred to above.

- For mutual fund investments, the fair value per share or unit is determined and published and is the basis for current transactions.

> **OBSERVATION:** FAS-124 reminds not-for-profit organizations that they are also subject to the disclosure requirements of other FASB Statements that relate to the investment area. These include: FAS-105 (Disclosure of Information about Financial Instruments with Off-Balance-Sheet Risk and Financial Instruments with Concentrations of Credit Risk), FAS-107 (Disclo-

sures about Fair Value of Financial Instruments), and FAS-119 (Disclosure about Derivative Financial Instruments and Fair Value of Financial Instruments). In addition, FAS-126 (Exemption from Certain Required Disclosures about Financial Instruments for Certain Nonpublic Entities), which amends FAS-107, must also be considered.

In accounting for unrealized gains or losses on investments, FAS-124 does not make a distinction in accounting between unrealized and realized gains and losses and other investment income. Under FAS-117, investment gains and losses are reported in the statement of activities as increases or decreases in unrestricted net assets unless their use is temporarily or permanently restricted by explicit donor stipulation or by law. Guidance is also provided for when investments held as part of endowment funds that are temporarily restricted or permanently restricted incur losses and fall below donor stipulated amounts. Complete coverage of these situations is provided in the chapter of this Guide titled "Statement of Financial Position."

Additional guidance on reporting investments and changes in the fair values of investment from reporting period to reporting period is provided in the new AICPA Guide. The chapter of this Guide titled "Statement of Financial Position" fully integrates the guidance of the AICPA Guide and FAS-124.

FASB Statements No. 93 and No. 99

The FASB issued FAS-93 (Recognition of Depreciation by Not-for-Profit Organizations) in August 1987. It requires that all not-for-profit organizations recognize the cost of using long-lived tangible assets—depreciation—in externally issued financial statements. Also required are the disclosures required by Accounting Principles Board (APB) Opinion No. 12 (Omnibus Opinion—1967) regarding the disclosure of information about depreciable assets and depreciation.

FAS-99 (Deferral of the Effective Date of Recognition of Depreciation by Not-for-Profit Organizations) extended the effective date of FAS-93, which became effective for financial statements issued for fiscal years beginning on or after January 1, 1990. Clearly, depreciation should now be recorded by all not-for-profit organizations.

AMERICAN INSTITUTE OF CERTIFIED PUBLIC ACCOUNTANTS

The AICPA has taken a significant step to update its accounting and auditing guidance for not-for-profit organizations with the issuance of its Guide for not-for-profit organizations. In addition to the AICPA Guide, two AICPA Statements of Position (94-3 and 98-2) are of particular concern to not-for-profit organizations. Each of these three AICPA documents is discussed in the following pages.

AICPA Audit and Accounting Guide: Not-for-Profit Organizations

The AICPA issued the AICPA Guide titled *Not-for-Profit Organizations* to update its accounting and auditing guidance for not-for-profit organizations and to provide additional guidance relating to FAS-117, FAS-116, and FAS-124. The AICPA Guide has been amended by SOP 98-2, as discussed in the section on SOP 98-2. In addition, SOP 98-3 (discussed in Part II) supersedes Part VII of the AICPA Guide, which covers audits of federal financial assistance.

Applicability

The definition of a *not-for-profit organization* in the AICPA Guide is not the same as the definition in FAS-116. The AICPA Guide states that it:

> ...applies to nongovernmental not-for-profit organizations of the following kinds:
> - Cemetery organizations
> - Civic and community organizations
> - Colleges and universities
> - Elementary and secondary schools
> - Federated fund-raising organizations
> - Fraternal organizations
> - Labor unions
> - Libraries
> - Museums
> - Other cultural organizations
> - Performing arts organizations
> - Political parties
> - Political action committees
> - Private and community foundations
> - Professional associations
> - Public broadcasting stations
> - Religious organizations
> - Research and scientific organizations

- Social and country clubs
- Trade associations
- Voluntary health and welfare organizations
- Zoological and botanical societies

This list does not necessarily include all organizations that meet the definition of a not-for-profit organization in FASB Statement No. 116. This Guide applies to all organizations that meet the definition, regardless of whether they are included in this list.

Care must be exercised in applying the appropriate accounting principles to not-for-profit organizations. An organization would follow the guidance of the AICPA Guide if it meets the definition of a *not-for-profit organization* provided by FAS-116, even if it is not included in the list of organizations provided above. These organizations also should follow generally accepted accounting principles for not-for-profit organizations as prescribed by the FASB.

In addition, the AICPA Guide specifically states that it does not apply to not-for-profit organizations that provide health care services. These organizations should follow the AICPA Audit and Accounting Guide titled *Health Care Organizations*.

Sometimes not-for-profit organizations have strong ties or affiliations with governmental entities. Determining whether these organizations were "governmental" or "nongovernmental" has been less than clear in the past. The AICPA Guide specifically states that it applies to "nongovernmental" not-for-profit organizations and provides a definition of when an organization should be considered to be governmental. It states:

Nongovernmental organizations are all organizations other than governmental organizations. Public corporations and bodies corporate and politic are governmental organizations. Other organizations are governmental organizations if they have one or more of the following characteristics:

(a) Popular election of officers or appointment (or approval) of a controlling majority of the members of the organization's governing body by officials of one or more state or local government;

(b) The potential for unilateral dissolution by a government with the net assets reverting to a government; or

(c) The power to enact and enforce a tax levy.

Furthermore, organizations are presumed to be governmental if they have the ability to issue directly (rather than through a state or municipal authority) debt that pays interest exempt from federal taxation. However, organizations possessing only that ability (to issue tax-exempt debt) and none of the other governmental characteristics may rebut the presumption that they are governmental if their determination is supported by compelling, relevant evidence.

Governmental entities   In August 1995, the GASB issued Statement No. 29 (The Use of Not-for-Profit Accounting and Financial Reporting Principles by Governmental Organizations). According to this Statement, governmental entities should *not* change their accounting and financial reporting to apply the provisions of FAS-116, FAS-117, or other FASB Statements or Interpretations that are limited to not-for-profit organizations or that address issues primarily concerning these organizations. GASB-29 permits governmental entities that have applied the accounting and financial reporting principles applicable to not-for-profit organizations prior to the issuance of those Statements or Interpretations (as modified by all applicable FASB pronouncements issued through November 30, 1989, and by most applicable GASB pronouncements) to continue to do so, pending GASB pronouncements on the accounting and financial reporting model for governmental entities. As an alternative, these governmental entities could change to the current governmental financial reporting model.

Governmental colleges and universities   GASB-15 (Governmental College and University Accounting and Financial Reporting Models) requires that governmental colleges and universities use one of two accounting and financial reporting models. One of these models, referred to as the "AICPA College Guide model," encompasses the accounting and financial reporting guidance in the AICPA document "Audits of Colleges and Universities" (ACU) and SOP 74-8 (Financial Accounting and Financial Reporting by Colleges and Universities), as modified by all applicable FASB pronouncements issued through November 30, 1989, and all applicable GASB pronouncements. The AICPA Guide does not change the applicability of the ACU and SOP 74-8 (Financial Accounting and Financial Reporting by Colleges and Universities) to governmental colleges and universities that use the AICPA College Guide model. Thus, even though the AICPA Guide supersedes ACU and SOP 74-8, some governmental colleges and universities will still be using the guidance in these documents.

The effect of the consideration of governmental entities and governmental colleges and universities using documentation that has otherwise been superseded should not affect auditors performing audits of nongovernmental not-for-profit organizations. However, auditors should be aware of these circumstances in the event that they are engaged to audit a governmental entity or a governmental college or university.

Applicable Professional Literature

One of the more useful features of the AICPA Guide is its analysis of the applicability of professional literature. The status and applicability to not-for-profit organizations of professional standards such as APB Opinion, FASB Statements, and FASB Interpretations is listed in excellent detail.

Statement of Position 94-3

The AICPA issued SOP 94-3 (Reporting of Related Entities by Not-for-Profit Organizations) in September 1994 to standardize the guidance for reporting a not-for-profit organization's related entities. The focus of the guidance of SOP 94-3 is on a not-for-profit organization's investments in for-profit entities and the reporting for financially interrelated not-for-profit organizations.

Investments in For-Profit Entities

The reporting guidance provided by SOP 94-3 is based on the consolidation guidance provided to commercial enterprises. The following specific guidance for investments of not-for-profit organizations in for-profit entities is as follows:

- Not-for-profit organizations should consolidate a for-profit entity in which it has a controlling financial interest through direct or indirect ownership of a majority voting interest if consolidation would be required by the guidance of Accounting Research Bulletin (ARB) No. 51 (Consolidated Financial Statements), as amended by FAS-94 (Consolidation of All Majority-Owned Subsidiaries).

- Not-for-profit organizations reporting the investments in common stock of a for-profit entity should use the equity method of accounting if the guidance of APB Opinion No. 18 (The Equity Method of Accounting for Investments in Common Stock) would require the equity method to be used.

- Not-for-profit organizations that are reporting their investment portfolios at market value may do so instead of reporting those investments by the equity method, which otherwise would be required by the SOP.

Reporting for Financially Interrelated Not-for-Profit Organizations

SOP 94-3 provides the following guidance for reporting by financially interrelated not-for-profit organizations:

- A not-for-profit organization should consolidate another not-for-profit organization in which it has a controlling financial interest through direct or indirect ownership of a majority voting interest, unless control is likely to be temporary or does not rest with the majority owner, in which case consolidation is prohibited.

- A not-for-profit organization should consolidate another not-for-profit organization if the reporting not-for-profit organization has both:

  — Control of the other not-for-profit organization, as evidenced by either a majority ownership or a majority voting interest in the board of the not-for-profit organization, and

  — An economic interest in the other not-for-profit organization.

  If control is likely to be temporary or does not rest with the majority owner, consolidation would be prohibited.

- If a not-for-profit organization exercises control of another not-for-profit organization in which it has an economic interest by means other than majority ownership or majority voting interest in the board of the other not-for-profit organization, the not-for-profit is permitted, but not required, to consolidate the other not-for-profit organization. If control is likely to be temporary or does not rest with the majority owner, consolidation is prohibited.

In circumstances where either (but not both) control or an economic interest exists, the financial statement disclosures required by FAS-57 (Related Party Disclosures) should be made.

In addition, not-for-profit organizations that otherwise would be prohibited from presenting consolidated financial statements under the provisions of SOP 94-3, but that currently present consolidated financial statements in conformity with the guidance of SOP 78-10, may continue to present consolidated financial statements.

Auditors should be careful to identify all potential entities (both for-profit and not-for-profit) for consideration of applying the above rules. These considerations are analyzed in this Guide in the chapter titled "Preplanning Audit Activities."

Statement of Position 98-2

SOP 98-2 (Accounting for Costs of Activities of Not-for-Profit Organizations and State and Local Governmental Entities That Include Fund-Raising) was issued by the AICPA in March 1998. This is long-anticipated guidance for determining when not-for-profit organizations may allocate costs between program activities and fund-raising if the activity has elements of each of these two activities.

Effective Date

SOP 98-2 is effective for financial statements for years beginning on or after December 15, 1998, with earlier application encouraged. If comparative financial statements are presented, retroactive application is permitted, but not required.

Accounting Guidance

Under the guidance of SOP 98-2, costs of a joint activity that are identifiable with a particular function are charged to that function (program, management and general, or fund-raising). Joint costs are allocated between fund-raising and the appropriate program or management and general function if all three criteria established by SOP 98-2 are met. These three criteria are as follows:

- **Purpose** The purpose criterion is met if the purpose of the joint activity includes accomplishing program and management and general functions.

- **Audience** SOP 98-2 establishes a rebuttable presumption that the audience criterion is *not* met if the audience of the joint activity includes prior donors or is otherwise selected on the basis of its ability or likelihood to contribute to the not-for-profit organization.

- **Content** The content criterion is met if the joint activity supports program or management and general functions, as follows:

  — *Program* The joint activity calls for specific action by the recipient that will help accomplish the not-for-profit organization's mission.

  — *Management and general* The joint activity fulfills one or more of the not-for-profit organization's management and general responsibilities through a component of the joint activity.

Allocation Methods

SOP 98-2 requires that when costs of joint activities are allocated, the cost allocation method should be rational and systematic, resulting in a reasonable cost allocation that is applied consistently across similar facts and circumstances.

Disclosure Requirements

When the costs of joint activities are allocated, SOP 98-2 requires the following disclosures:

- The types of activities for which joint costs have been incurred
- A statement that such costs have been allocated
- The total amount allocated during the period covered by the financial statements and the portion allocated to each functional expense category

The chapter of this Guide titled "Statement of Activities" provides more information on applying SOP 98-2, particularly in the document for determining whether the purpose criterion has been met.

> **OBSERVATION:** This SOP is an important pronouncement for not-for-profit organizations and will require attention by the auditor. As mentioned earlier in this chapter, reporting a high percentage of program expenses relative to total expenses is an important objective for not-for-profit organizations, because this information is very important to donors. Donors want to know that a high percentage of their contribution is going toward doing the work of the not-for-profit organization instead of being used for administrative or fund-raising activities. In designing their audit approach to joint cost allocation, auditors must be cognizant of the importance donors place on these reported amounts.

> **OBSERVATION:** During 1998, Statement of Position 98-3 (Audits of States, Local Governments, and Not-for-Profit Organizations Receiving Federal Awards) was issued. This Statement affects the audits of many not-for-profit organizations that receive federal funds. The Statement is discussed in Part II of this Guide.

INTERNAL REVENUE CODE CONSIDERATIONS FOR NOT-FOR-PROFIT ORGANIZATIONS

A discussion of professional literature affecting the accounting and auditing of various types of organizations would rarely include references to the Internal Revenue Code, except perhaps to address income tax expenses and liabilities. Although the Internal Revenue

Code does not establish any accounting, financial reporting, or auditing requirements for not-for-profit organizations, the existence and operations of many of these organizations are closely tied to the Code. Therefore, a brief overview of the Internal Revenue Code definitions of not-for-profit organizations is provided, as is an overview of the section of the Internal Revenue Code that applies to most not-for-profit organizations.

The Internal Revenue Code uses the term *exempt organizations* to focus on not-for-profit organizations' tax-exempt status. Under Section 501 of the Internal Revenue Code, a variety of organizations, generally not-for-profit groups organized for charitable or mutual benefit purposes, may gain exemption from income taxation. Section 501(c) provides for the general exemption from income tax for a variety of organizations. Specifically, Section 501(c)(3) covers a corporation (and any community chest, fund, or foundation) organized and operated exclusively for religious, charitable, scientific, testing of public safety, literary, or educational purposes, or to foster national or international amateur sports competition or for the prevention of cruelty to animals.

Other commonly used sections of the Internal Revenue Code are as follows:

- *Section 501(c)(4)*   Civic league, an organization not organized for profit but operated exclusively for the promotion of social welfare or a local association of employees

- *Section 501(c)(6)*   Business league, chamber of commerce, real estate board, board of trade, or professional football league

- *Section 501(c)(7)*   Club organized for pleasure, recreation, and other not-for-profit purposes (social and recreation clubs)

- *Section 501(c)(8)*   Fraternal beneficiary society, order, or association

- *Section 501(c)(9)*   Voluntary employees' beneficiary organization

- *Section 501(c)(10)* Domestic fraternal society or association

- *Section 501(c)(19)* Post or organization of past or present members of the U.S. Armed Forces

- *Section 501(c)(23)* Political organization

The above list illustrates the breadth of organizations that are considered tax-exempt under the Internal Revenue Code. However, it gives only a brief title to the types of organizations. Consult the Internal Revenue Code and Regulations for a more thorough analysis. The chapter titled "Tax Considerations" discusses the tax-related considerations that an auditor of a tax-exempt not-for-profit organization will need to consider. The chapter also discusses the ramifications when an exempt organization performs activities outside of its tax-exempt function.

NOT-FOR-PROFIT ORGANIZATIONS COVERED BY THIS GUIDE

This Guide is designed primarily for use by auditors engaged to audit organizations that meet the definition of *not-for-profit organizations* in FAS-116. These include nongovernmental colleges and universities. Governmental colleges and universities and other governmental entities are outside the scope of this Guide.

Auditors of organizations that do not meet the definition of a not-for-profit organization in FAS-116, or the AICPA Guide (such as governmental not-for-profit organizations), may find the audit approaches and procedures and practice management materials included herein to be useful. However, these auditors should make sure that the accounting principles used for accounting and financial reporting for these organizations are appropriate.

SUMMARY

Auditors undertaking an audit of a not-for-profit organization must be aware of some significant differences between auditing a not-for-profit organization and auditing a commercial enterprise. In addition, the professional literature providing both audit and accounting guidance for auditors of not-for-profit organizations is different in a number of aspects from that used for commercial enterprises and recently has been significantly changed. Auditors must be prepared to implement the new authoritative professional literature and to understand the unique characteristics of these organizations. The next several chapters will provide specific hands-on guidance to enable the auditor to perform an audit of a not-for-profit organization in a cost-effective manner.

CHAPTER 2
PREPLANNING AUDIT ACTIVITIES

CONTENTS

Chapter 2
PREPLANNING AUDIT ACTIVITIES

CROSS-REFERENCES

2001 Miller Not-for-Profit Organization Audits: Chapter 14, "Preplanning for a Circular A-133 Audit"

2001 Miller Audit Procedures: Chapter 1, "Preengagement Activities"

2000 Miller GAAP Guide: Chapter 14, "Equity Method"

2000 Miller GAAS Guide: Section 220, "Independence"; Section 310, "Appointment of the Independent Auditor"; Section 311, "Planning and Supervision"

The auditor and not-for-profit organization should undertake certain preplanning activities before beginning to plan the audit. These activities will vary depending on whether the audit engagement is new or recurring. In addition, preplanning activities will be more extensive during the not-for-profit organization's first audit.

The auditor and not-for-profit organization should consider the following preplanning activities:

- Performance of procedures for an auditor to determine whether to accept an audit engagement
- Performance of procedures for an auditor to determine whether to continue an existing audit engagement relationship
- Determination of the reporting entity of the not-for-profit organization that is being audited
- Determination of whether the scope of the audit engagement is appropriate
- Documentation of the terms of the audit engagement in an engagement letter

Performance of Procedures for an Auditor to Determine Whether to Accept an Audit Engagement

Before an auditor accepts an engagement to audit a not-for-profit organization, he or she should perform procedures to ensure that it would be appropriate to accept the engagement. The considerations that should be made include the following:

- Independence of the auditor in relation to the not-for-profit organization
- Reputation and integrity of the not-for-profit organization and its management and board of directors
- Information obtained from communications with the not-for-profit organization's predecessor auditor
- Qualifications and abilities of the auditor and/or his or her audit staff to perform the audit in a competent, professional, and timely manner
- Capability of the not-for-profit organization (or the auditor) to prepare financial statements that are fairly presented in accordance with generally accepted accounting principles based on the not-for-profit organization's ability to accurately collect and record its financial transactions in its accounting records
- The auditor's practice issues—which include the ability to use available audit staff effectively to perform the audit in a timely and profitable manner—and the other effects on the audit practice of accepting an engagement to audit a not-for-profit organization
- Preparation of adequate documentation of the above considerations in the auditor's files and working papers

Independence

Auditors must follow the requirements of the Code of Professional Conduct of the AICPA when performing audits of not-for-profit organizations. Rule 101 (Independence) of the Code of Professional Conduct states, "A member in public practice shall be independent in the performance of professional services as required by standards promulgated by bodies designated by Council."

Interpretation 101-1 of Rule 101 provides examples of when an auditor's independence would be considered impaired. These examples include the following:

- Auditors who have or are committed to acquire any direct or material indirect financial interest in the organization being audited

- Auditors who are trustees of a trust (or executors or administrators of any estate) that has or is committed to acquire any direct or material indirect financial interest in the organization being audited

- Auditors who have any joint or closely held business investment with the organization being audited or with any officer, director, or principal stockholders thereof that was material in relation to the auditor's own net worth or the net worth of the auditor's firm

- Auditors who have any loan to or from the organization being audited or with any of its officers, directors, or principal stockholders (exceptions to this rule include home mortgages made under normal lending procedures, terms, and requirements)

- Auditors who are connected with the organization being audited as a promoter, underwriter, or voting trustee, as a director or officer, or in any capacity equivalent to that of a member of management or an employee

- Auditors who are trustees for any pension or profit-sharing trust of the organization being audited

Potential auditors of not-for-profit organizations should keep in mind that these rules require independence not only from the not-for-profit organization being audited, but, in many instances, from the officers and directors of the not-for-profit organization as well. Therefore, auditors should consider any business dealings or loans that they might have with the officers and particularly the directors of the not-for-profit organization before accepting the audit engagement. Not-for-profit organizations frequently have boards of directors or trustees made up of prominent individuals, so the auditor should be particularly careful of these requirements as they relate to not-for-profit organizations.

Interpretation 101-3 discusses the impact on an auditor's independence when the auditor provides accounting services to the entity being audited. This Interpretation is particularly relevant to auditors of not-for-profit organizations. Many small (and some not so small) not-for-profit organizations are not able or willing to expend the resources to hire the appropriate accounting personnel for their operations to permit them to take full responsibility for the preparation of their financial statements. These organizations sometimes rely on bookkeepers or other administrative personnel to perform day-to-day accounting and to handle payroll. In these cases, the auditor may find himself or herself actually preparing financial statements, preparing closing journal entries, choosing among various accounting principles, or implementing new accounting principles.

According to Interpretation 101-3, auditors must meet the following requirements to remain independent of a not-for-profit organization for which they provide accounting services:

- The not-for-profit organization must accept responsibility for the financial statements. The management of the not-for-profit organization must be familiar enough with the financial activities and condition of the organization, as well as applicable accounting principles, to reasonably be able to accept this responsibility. A statement of responsibility by the management of the not-for-profit organization without the basis described above would not be adequate. When such familiarity is lacking, the auditor may discuss the accounting and financial matters with members of management so that they are able to take this responsibility.

- The auditor cannot assume the role of management or employee of the not-for-profit, performing such acts as executing transactions, having custody of assets, or exercising any other authority on behalf of the not-for-profit organization.

- If the auditor is preparing financial statements based on books and records that he or she has maintained, the auditor must comply with all applicable auditing standards when opining on the financial statements. The audit must be performed in accordance with generally accepted auditing standards, including tests of the records that have been maintained by the auditor.

The Interpretations of Rule 101 present a discussion of the general context of independence that the auditor must consider. They are provided to give the auditor a sense of the issues of which he or she must be aware to determine independence. Where there is any indication that independence may be impaired, the auditor should consult the AICPA Code of Professional Conduct for more specific guidance.

In addition to the general guidance provided above, the Code of Professional Conduct addresses other questions regarding specific instances for consideration in determining independence in its Interpretations and Rulings, such as issues concerning former practitioners who have sold their practices or left their audit firms, loans from organizations, litigation with audit clients, effects of the financial interests or positions within the organization of family members, entering into cooperative agreements with clients, the provision of extended audit services to clients, and a number of other even more specific matters.

The following are some of the more specific items addressed in the Interpretations and Rulings directly affect auditors of not-for-profit organizations:

- Interpretation 101-4 (Honorary Directorships and Trustees of Not-for-Profit Organizations)—An auditor may lend his or her name to a not-for-profit organization as an honorary director or trustee of the organization, to lend prestige to the organization. In order for the auditor's independence not to be impaired, certain conditions must be met. The auditor's position must be clearly honorary, and the auditor must not be able to vote or otherwise participate in the management of the organization or the activities of the organization's board of directors or trustees. If the auditor is listed on the organization's letterhead or other externally circulated materials, the auditor's position must be clearly indicated as honorary.
- Ethics Ruling Section 191(2) (Association Membership)—An auditor's independence is not impaired if he or she joins a trade association that is an audit client, provided that the auditor does not serve as an officer, director, or in any capacity equivalent to that of a member of management.
- Ethics Ruling Section 191(14) (Member on Board of Directors of Federated Fund-Raising Organization)—An auditor who serves as an officer or director of a federated fund-raising agency (such as the United Way) would not have his or her independence impaired with respect to the local charities for which the federated fund-raising agency raises funds provided that the federated fund-raising agency does not exercise managerial control over the local charities participating in the fund-raising organization.
- Ethics Ruling Section 191(16) (Member on Board of Directors of Nonprofit Social Club)—An auditor would not be independent of a not-for-profit social club if the auditor serves on the board of directors of the social club, because the board of directors has the ultimate responsibility for the affairs of the social club.
- Ethics Ruling Section 191(17) (Member of Social Club)—This item involves the independence of an auditor who is a member of a social club (for example, a country club or tennis club) in which the membership requirements require the auditor to acquire a pro-rata share of the club's equity or debt securities. As long as the auditor does not serve on the club's governing board or take part in the management of the club, the auditor's independence would not be considered impaired. The equity or debt securities are not considered a direct financial interest within the meaning of Rule 101.
- Ethics Ruling Section 191(48) (Faculty Member as Auditor of a Student Fund)—This item relates to a full- or part-time faculty member of a university who is asked to audit the financial statements of a student fund for which the university:
  — Acts as a collection agent for student fees and remits them to the student fund, and

— Requires that a university administrator approve and sign the student fund checks.

In this case, the independence of the faculty member as an auditor would be considered to be impaired with respect to the student fund, since the faculty member would be auditing several of the management functions performed by the university, which is the faculty member's employer.

- Ethics Ruling Section 191(64) (Member on Board of Organization for Which Client Raises Funds)—An auditor's independence would be considered impaired with respect to an entity that exists solely to raise funds for an organization if the member serves on the board of directors of the organization. However, if the auditor's directorship on the board is clearly honorary, the auditor's independence would not be considered impaired.

- Ethics Ruling Section 191(82) (Campaign Treasurer)—This item involves whether the independence of an auditor who has been asked to serve as the campaign treasurer of a campaign organization for a candidate for mayor would be impaired with respect to the political party with which the candidate is associated, the municipality of which the candidate may become mayor, and the campaign organization. Independence would not be considered to be impaired with respect to the political party or the municipality. However, because of the auditor's role as treasurer, he or she would not be considered independent with respect to the campaign organization itself.

The consideration of independence should be documented in the working papers, and the independence requirements should be maintained throughout the course of the audit and should be reviewed before any subsequent audits of the not-for-profit organization are undertaken.

For small, medium-sized, and large firms, a system to monitor independence requirements and to periodically confirm the independence of the professional staff of the audit firm should be obtained and reviewed by the appropriate administrative personnel or professional staff coordinator. The system established should reflect the size of the audit firm in terms of the number of partners and staff and the number and nature of the clients that are being served.

Reputation and Integrity

Before undertaking an audit of a not-for-profit organization for the first time, an auditor should take certain steps to investigate whether he or she is satisfied with the integrity of the not-for-profit organization and its key management and board of directors. These procedures will enable the auditor to reach a conclusion about whether to accept the audit engagement.

There are no standards in generally accepted auditing standards that set a level of integrity or other criteria for the auditor to judge the prospective client. It is the auditor's decision whether to accept the engagement after obtaining information about the degree of integrity of the not-for-profit organization, its governing board, and its management. An auditor performs these procedures to try to avoid the difficulties that will arise if he or she accepts an audit engagement and later discovers that the not-for-profit organization, through its employees or board of directors, has committed illegal acts or engaged in other questionable activities. If these acts have been committed and the auditor discovers them after beginning the audit, the auditor may be faced with numerous potential reporting requirements and may be affected by any negative publicity or sanctions by regulatory bodies that are directed at the not-for-profit organization.

Auditors should not accept the integrity of management or the board of directors at face value merely because they are connected with a not-for-profit organization that is performing some public good deeds or activities. While a general statement that lack of integrity in management in not-for-profit organizations is less of a concern than in commercial enterprises may have some validity, there is no reason for an auditor to abandon a healthy level of professional skepticism before accepting a not-for-profit organization as an audit client. There are enough instances of improprieties by management and others employed by not-for-profit organizations to justify the effort required by the auditor in addressing this concern before accepting the engagement. In addition, the auditor should be convinced that the purpose of the organization is to carry out its exempt purpose, rather than to provide benefits to its founders, management, or others.

The extent of the procedures performed should be a matter of professional judgment, based on the individual circumstances of the potential audit client. The AICPA has issued a guide titled "Quality Control Policies and Procedures for CPA Firms" that provides some examples of procedures that auditors should consider before accepting an audit assignment. The guide covers the determination of the auditor's independence, communication with the predecessor auditor, and other procedures.

Some suggested procedures that are particularly appropriate for not-for-profit organizations are as follows:

- Obtain and review available financial information regarding the prospective client, such as annual reports, interim financial reports, budgets, or other reports to regulatory agencies, such as reports filed with state charitable agencies. Also review the organization's federal income tax returns.

- Inquire of third parties about any information regarding the prospective client and its management and board of directors that may have a bearing on evaluating the prospective client. Inquiries may be directed toward the prospective client's bankers, legal counsel, investment management firm, and, if applicable, underwriters or investment bankers. Any others in the financial or business community who may have some knowledge of the particular organization also should be considered for inquiry.

- Obtain a listing of the members of management and the board of directors of the not-for-profit organization. Inquire with the parties described above whether they have had dealings with these individuals in the course of the not-for-profit's business dealings and whether they would have any information that would be useful to the auditors.

> **OBSERVATION:** The auditor should be very careful not to overstep the limits of reasonableness in inquiring about individuals, particularly board members, who are associated with the not-for-profit organization only on a part-time basis. Inquiries generally should be limited to information about the individuals in the course of their dealings with the business of the not-for-profit organization. For example, if the organization's banker is also a board member's personal banker, inquiries about personal affairs would not be appropriate.

- Obtain a credit report on the not-for-profit organization. This will provide evidence on how the organization pays its bills and will indicate any potential difficulties the auditor may have collecting audit fees.

- Consider any unusual circumstances in the operating environment of the organization or other unusual circumstances with the organization itself that may have a bearing on the performance of the audit. For example, a not-for-profit organization may obtain most of its revenues from a contract for some particular service that it provides to a state or local government. The auditor should inquire and evaluate the likelihood that this significant contract is either a long-term contract or a short-term contract with a good chance of being renewed.

The procedures discussed above are not mandatory or required by generally accepted auditing standards. They are suggested procedures to help the auditor limit his or her exposure to taking on an audit client without integrity. Even if questions are raised during such inquiries, an auditor is not precluded from undertaking the engagement. Rather, the auditor would consider these findings when planning, designing, and performing the audit.

Communications with Predecessor Auditors

As with any new audit in accordance with generally accepted auditing standards, in the first year that an auditor succeeds another auditor in the audit of the financial statements of a not-for-profit organization the auditor should communicate with the predecessor auditor. Statement on Auditing Standards No. 84 (Communications Between Predecessor and Successor Auditors) (SAS-84) provides guidance to successor auditors on communications with predecessor auditors. SAS-84 is effective for engagements that are accepted after March 31, 1998.

The initial communication with the predecessor auditor should occur and be evaluated before the successor auditor accepts the engagement. The auditor should confirm the prospective client's permission to contact the predecessor auditor in order to comply with the AICPA Code of Professional Conduct, which precludes an auditor from disclosing confidential information obtained during the course of an audit engagement unless the client specifically consents to the disclosure. If the client refuses to grant this permission, the successor auditor should consider the client's reasons for denying permission and determine whether this denial is itself sufficient reason for not accepting the audit engagement.

The auditor's inquiries of the predecessor auditor before accepting the engagement should include, among other things, information that might bear on the integrity of management and on disagreements between the predecessor auditor and management, if any, about accounting principles, auditing procedures, or other similarly significant matters. Inquiry should also be made of any communications to audit committees or others with equivalent authority and responsibility regarding fraud, illegal acts by clients, and internal control related matters. In addition, the auditor should inquire about the predecessor auditor's understanding of the reasons the client decided to change auditors. If the predecessor auditor's responses are limited or insufficient for the successor auditor, then the successor auditor will need to consider the implications of these limitations in information when deciding whether to accept the audit client.

After accepting the engagement and beginning the audit, the successor auditor will need to obtain additional information, as described below, from the predecessor auditor. As a practical matter, the successor auditor would be best served by obtaining all of this information at one time from the predecessor, particularly for smaller audit engagements, where the length of time for performing the additional procedures and inquiries should be limited. This additional information may be invaluable to the successor auditor for audit planning purposes, so the sooner it is obtained, the better.

> **OBSERVATION:** Understandably, the predecessor auditor may be reluctant to make working papers available or discuss accounting or auditing matters with the successor auditor until after the successor auditor actually accepts the audit engagement. This may require the auditor to obtain the additional information from the predecessor auditor after accepting the engagement.

After accepting the audit, the successor auditor will need to obtain information that has continuing accounting significance. When performing an audit for the first time, an auditor will need to satisfy him- or herself that the balances in the balance sheet accounts at the beginning of the year are fairly stated and that accounting principles have been properly applied. Analyses prepared by the predecessor auditor of end-of-the-year account balances would be useful to the successor auditor in this respect. In addition, information about the accounting principles applied (for example, depreciation methods, and estimated lives of classes of assets) will enable the successor auditor to determine if accounting principles have been consistently applied from year to year. While this information may be obtainable through other methods, obtaining it from the predecessor auditor is easier and is likely to be more reliable than information obtained directly from the client or from other sources. The information should be obtained through discussions with the predecessor and through a review of the predecessor auditor's working papers.

The successor auditor's review of the predecessor's audit working papers may affect the nature, timing, and extent of the successor auditor's procedures with respect to opening balances and consistency of accounting principles. However, SAS-84 reiterates that the nature, timing, and extent of audit procedures performed and the conclusions reached by the successor auditor are solely his or her responsibility. In reporting on the audit, the successor auditor should not make reference to the report or work of the predecessor auditor as the basis, in part, for the successor auditor's own opinion.

> **OBSERVATION:** This does not change the reference that is made to the predecessor auditor when prior financial statements that have been audited by the predecessor auditor are presented in the comparative financial statements of the current year.

Information obtained from the predecessor auditor should be appropriately documented, including information on acceptance of the engagement, audit evidence about the opening balances of accounts in the year to be audited, and information on the consistency of accounting principles.

The following two Exhibits are based on sample letters that are provided in SAS-84 to:

- Obtain the not-for-profit organization's consent and acknowledgment to the predecessor auditor to release information to the predecessor auditor (Exhibit 2-1)
- Obtain the successor auditor's acknowledgment as to the use of the predecessor auditor's working papers by the successor auditor (Exhibit 2-2)

These sample letters are presented for illustrative purposes only. They are not required by SAS-84.

EXHIBIT 2-1
NOT-FOR-PROFIT ORGANIZATION'S CONSENT AND ACKNOWLEDGMENT TO THE PREDECESSOR AUDITOR

[Letterhead of predecessor auditor]

[Date]

[Name and address of not-for-profit organization]

You have given your consent to give [*name of successor auditor*], as successor independent auditor for [*name of not-for-profit organization*], access to our working papers for our audit of the [*date of statement of financial position*] financial statements of [*name of not-for-profit organization*]. You have also given your consent to us to respond fully to [*name of successor auditor*]'s inquiries. You understand and agree that the review of our working papers is undertaken solely for the purpose of obtaining an understanding about [*name of not-for-profit organization*] and certain information about our audit to assist [*name of successor auditor*] in planning the audit of the [*date of statement of financial position*] financial statements of [*name of not-for-profit organization*].

Please confirm your agreement with the foregoing by signing and dating a copy of this letter and returning it to us.

Attached is the form of the letter we will furnish to [*name of successor auditor*] regarding the use of the working papers.

Very truly yours,

[*Predecessor auditors*]

Accepted:

[*Name of not-for-profit organization*]

By:_____   Date:_____

EXHIBIT 2-2
SUCCESSOR AUDITOR'S ACKNOWLEDGMENT AS TO THE USE OF THE PREDECESSOR AUDITOR'S WORKING PAPERS

[Letterhead of predecessor auditor]

[Date]

[Name and address of successor auditor]

We have previously audited, in accordance with generally accepted auditing standards, the *[date of statement of financial position]* financial statements of *[name of not-for-profit organization]*. We rendered a report on those financial statements and have not performed any audit procedures subsequent to the audit report date. In connection with your audit of *[name of not-for-profit organization]*'s *[date of financial statements being audited by successor auditor]* financial statements, you have requested access to our working papers prepared in connection with that audit. *[Name of not-for-profit organization]* has authorized our firm to allow you to review those working papers.

Our audit, and the working papers prepared in connection therewith, of *[name of not-for-profit organization]*'s financial statements were not planned or conducted in contemplation of your review. Therefore, items of possible interest to you may not have been specifically addressed. Our use of professional judgment and the assessment of audit risk and materiality for the purpose of our audit mean that matters may have existed that would have been assessed differently by you. We have no representation as to the sufficiency or appropriateness of the information in our working papers for your purposes.

We understand that the purpose of your review is to obtain information about *[name of not-for-profit organization]* and our *[date of financial statements audited by predecessor]* audit results to assist you in planning your *[date of financial statements to be audited by successor auditor]* audit of *[name of not-for-profit organization]*. For that purpose only, we will provide you access to our working papers that relate to that objective.

Upon request, we will provide copies of those working papers that provide factual information about *[name of not-for-profit organization]*. You agree to subject any such copies or information otherwise derived from our working papers to your normal policy for retention of working papers and protection of confidential client information. Furthermore, in the event of a third-party request for access to your working papers prepared in connection with your audits of *[name of not-for-profit organization]*, you agree to obtain our permission before voluntarily allowing any such access to our working papers or information otherwise derived from our working papers, and to obtain on our behalf any releases that you obtain from such third party. You agree to advise us promptly and provide us a copy of any subpoena, summons, or other court order for access to your working papers that include copies of our working papers or information otherwise derived therefrom.

Please confirm your agreement with the foregoing by signing and dating a copy of this letter and returning it to us.

Very truly yours,

[*Predecessor auditor*]

Accepted:

[*Successor auditor*]

By: _____ Date:_____

SAS-84 acknowledges that even with the client's consent, access to the predecessor auditor's working papers may still be limited. Experience has shown that the predecessor auditor may be willing to grant broader access if given additional resources concerning the use of the working papers. Accordingly, the successor auditor might consider agreeing to the following limitations on the review of the predecessor auditor's working papers in order to obtain broader access:

- The successor auditor will not comment, orally or in writing, to anyone as a result of the review as to whether the predecessor auditor's engagement was performed in accordance with generally accepted auditing standards.
- The successor auditor will not provide expert testimony or litigation support services or otherwise accept an engagement to comment on issues relating to the quality of the predecessor auditor's audit.
- The successor auditor will not use the audit procedures or results thereof documented in the predecessor auditor's working papers as evidential matter in rendering an opinion on the financial statements being audited by the successor, except as contemplated by SAS-84.

SAS-84 provides a sample paragraph to reflect these additional agreements, which is modified below, for inclusion in the letter provided in Exhibit 2-2:

> Because your review of our working papers is undertaken solely for the purpose described above and may not entail a review of all of our working papers, you agree that (1) the information obtained from the review will not be used by you for any other purpose; (2) you will not comment, orally or in writing, to anyone as a result of that review as to whether our audit was performed in accordance with generally accepted auditing standards; (3) you will not provide expert testimony or litigation support services or otherwise

accept an engagement to comment on issues relating to the quality of our audits; and (4) you will not use the audit procedures or results thereof documented in our working papers as evidential matter in rendering your opinion on the (date of financial statements being audited by successor) financial statements of (name of not-for-profit organization), except as contemplated in Statement on Auditing Standards No. 84.

SAS-84 also addresses the situation where an auditor is asked to audit and report on financial statements that have been previously audited and reported on (a reaudit of financial statements). In this case the auditor performing the reaudit is considered a successor auditor and the auditor that originally audited the financial statements is considered a predecessor auditor. As such, the guidance provided by this section for predecessor and successor auditors applies.

However, SAS-84 provides that the information obtained from inquiries and review of the predecessor auditor's working papers is not sufficient to provide a basis for expressing an opinion. In addition, the nature, timing, and extent of the audit work performed and the conclusions reached in a reaudit are solely the responsibility of the successor auditor performing the reaudit. Accordingly, if in performing the reaudit the successor auditor is unable to obtain sufficient competent evidential matter to express an opinion on the financial statements, the successor auditor should qualify or disclaim an opinion on the reaudited financial statements.

If, during an audit or reaudit, a successor auditor becomes aware of information that leads him or her to believe that the financial statements reported on by the predecessor auditor may require revision, the not-for-profit organization should be so informed and the matter or matters should be discussed with the predecessor auditor and the client. This would then be considered by the predecessor auditor in accordance with the procedures that are followed when an auditor subsequently discovers facts that may have affected the financial statements previously reported on.

Qualifications and Abilities of the Auditor

Before accepting an engagement to audit a not-for-profit organization, the auditor should review whether he or she (if practicing as a sole proprietor) or the audit firm has the appropriate qualifications and capability to perform the audit in a professional manner. This review is particularly important if the auditor is considering accepting its first not-for-profit organization audit client.

- *Accounting and taxation knowledge* The auditor should consider whether the audit firm and the particular individuals that will be assigned to the audit have sufficient experience to undertake an audit of a not-for-profit organization. If the audit firm or any individual auditor has no experience with not-for-profit organizations, continuing professional education courses on not-for-profit organizations may be appropriate. In addition, the auditor should determine whether he or she has adequate access to the appropriate professional literature.

Another important element the auditor should consider is his or her knowledge of the tax implications of not-for-profit organizations. The auditor must be familiar with the federal income tax rules relating to not-for-profit organizations, not just individual, partnership, and corporate taxation. In addition, the auditor should be familiar with the annual return for exempt organizations on Form 990 and the requirements of the state regulatory authorities in the state(s) in which the not-for-profit organization is located and in which it solicits funds.

- *Compliance with grants and contracts* Auditors of not-for-profit organizations also must be able to address any requirements imposed on the not-for-profit organization by any grant or contract under which the organization obtains funding and performs services. These agreements may have specific reporting requirements (such as supplemental schedules to the financial statements or special reports) and often impose deadlines for when audited financial statements must be submitted to the grantor or contractor agency. The auditor must be able to respond to these specific requirements to ensure the not-for-profit organization's compliance with terms and conditions of the grants or contracts.

- *Single audit and other audit requirements* The auditor should inquire about any requirements to perform the audit in accordance with the U.S. General Accounting Office's *Government Auditing Standards*, which may be included in a grant or contract. If the not-for-profit organization receives federal funds, the requirements of OMB Circular A-133 (Audits of States, Local Governments and Non-Profit Organizations) may apply. OMB Circular A-133 also may apply when the federal funds pass-through a state or local government unit or another not-for-profit organization (a primary recipient) to the not-for-profit organization being audited (a subrecipient). The auditor should try to become aware of these requirements before accepting the engagement by inquiring of management and reviewing the prior year's financial statements. The auditor should consider these additional requirements, if present, when deciding whether to accept the engagement. Circular A-133 and *Government Auditing Standards* contain many additional audit and reporting requirements, specific continuing education requirements for audit staff, and requirements for quality review of the audit firm. These requirements are covered in Part II (Single Audits Under OMB Circular A-133).

- *Staffing capabilities* In addition to the technical skills that are necessary to perform an audit of a not-for-profit organization, the auditor must consider whether he or she or the audit firm has the necessary resources in terms of number of staff to perform the engagement, the availability of these staff members during the time that the audit will be completed, the number of physical locations of the not-for-profit organization, and the feasibility of sending staff to some or all of these locations.

The number of locations at which the auditor will need to perform procedures will also affect the auditor's decision on whether it has the capability to perform the audit. The auditor may not be able to determine which locations will need to be visited before accepting the audit engagement, but he or she will need to assess how many locations will require simultaneous audit test work to be performed and whether the auditor has the audit staff available to meet those needs.

The auditor should determine the optimal level of staffing for the audit of the not-for-profit organization, including, if applicable, the number of hours of time that partners, managers, senior accountants, and staff accountants are likely to spend on the engagement. The audit may range in size from very small, where one person can complete the audit within a week, to very large, where it may take several months for teams of auditors working at several locations to complete the audit. The auditor needs to determine whether this commitment will be possible given the existing client assignments of the audit firm. Not-for-profit organizations generally have fiscal year ends other than December 31. This allows auditors some relief in terms of staffing since the audit work for not-for-profit normally is performed outside of the January through April time period when audit firms are busy with commercial audit clients and tax preparation services.

AUDIT COST-SAVINGS TIP: Flexibility in scheduling audits of not-for-profit organizations is one reason that auditors often accept fees for audits of not-for-profit organizations that are lower than what they ordinarily receive for audits of commercial enterprises. However, auditors must be sure that the audit will actually be performed outside of the auditor's normally busy time. For example, client delays may cause an audit scheduled for the summer to not start until the winter, which is usually not desirable. The auditor may lessen this risk by specifying different hourly rates for peak and off-peak season work.

- *Operations outside of the United States* Frequently, not-for-profit organizations receive funding from federal sources to provide educational and humanitarian aid in locations outside of the United States, most often in developing countries. Before accepting the engagement, the auditor should consider whether procedures must be performed at these locations, whether the auditor will be able to travel to the foreign locations, whether a foreign audit firm can be subcontracted to perform the audit procedures at the foreign locations, or whether original supporting documentation must be sent from the foreign location to the location where the audit is being performed in the United States.

- *Remedying deficiencies* After reviewing whether it has the appropriate qualifications and capabilities to accept an audit engagement for a not-for-profit organization, the auditor may find that he, she, or the firm has deficiencies in certain technical areas or in staffing capabilities. This does not preclude the auditor from accepting the audit engagement, but it may point to areas where the auditor needs to make investments, in technical skills, staffing, or both, in order to be in a position to accept the engagement.

Not-for-Profit Organization's Ability to Prepare Financial Statements

The auditor must make an initial assessment about whether the not-for-profit organization keeps adequate books and records to accurately capture and record its financial transactions and to provide a reliable basis on which to prepare financial statements. This consideration is often referred to as the "auditability" of the organization, and is of particular concern for not-for-profit organizations, particularly smaller ones. A not-for-profit organization's programmatic concerns may outweigh its concerns over financial record keeping and controls, which may lead to inadequate record keeping and controls.

Determination of "auditability" is not the same as the initial assessment of control risk that is performed during the planning phase of an audit. Rather, it is an initial assessment by the auditor that the not-for-profit organization maintains records in sufficient detail and completeness to permit the preparation of financial statements.

> **AUDIT COST-SAVINGS TIP:** Correctly assessment of the condition of a not-for-profit organization's financial records will usually have a significant impact on the audit's ultimate profitablility for an auditor.

Weaknesses in financial record keeping may or may not signal that the records are auditable. For example, a not-for-profit organization may only record its disbursements in a checkbook and may not prepare timely bank reconciliations. If the not-for-profit organization did maintain the supporting documentation for its disbursements and did maintain a record and control over its cash receipts, the organization will most likely still be auditable. Disbursements recorded in a checkbook and cash receipts can be entered into a general ledger system and a bank reconciliation can be prepared as of year end. Admittedly, there are serious control difficulties, but it is likely that the auditor will be able to expand his or her procedures to perform an audit in accordance with generally accepted auditing standards and to issue an opinion on the financial statements.

Conversely, a not-for-profit may collect many of its contributions in cash. The organization may pay certain expenses from its cash collections and deposit the net revenue at the end of each month into its checking account. Additional expenses are paid by check, although some of the supporting documentation has not been retained. Clearly, an auditor will have difficulty determining the gross revenues of the organization and its total expenses. In addition, the extremely weak controls over cash may prohibit the auditor from determining whether all cash collections have been used by the not-for-profit organization for their intended purpose, and from determining whether the disbursements from the checking account were appropriate. Accordingly, an auditor would have difficulty concluding that this hypothetical not-for-profit organization is auditable.

The most effective way for the auditor to obtain information about a not-for-profit organization (in addition to reviewing audited financial statements and management letters from the prior years) is to perform a site visit at the not-for-profit organization. During a site visit, the auditor can meet with members of management as well as accounting and finance personnel to pursue questions about auditability. Information obtained during these visits also may prove valuable in determining the extent of audit effort that will be required and, on a more positive level, help the auditor to better understand the business and needs of his or her prospective audit client. This understanding will enable the auditor to provide the client with a better, more focused, level of service.

The site visit should include discussions with senior executives, both financial and programmatic staff, although the emphasis in the discussions should be with the accounting staff. A walk-through of the accounting department, including perusing documentation, general ledgers, or management reports would be very helpful. Discussions with the prospective client's data processing personnel also will be important to understanding the extent of the not-for-profit's computerization. Information about employee turnover in these positions during the past year also may be important to the auditor.

In general, the smaller the not-for-profit organization, the more likely that the auditor will have concerns about auditability. Larger not-for-profit organizations will be more likely to have been audited in prior years, and the individuals at larger not-for-profit organizations will be familiar with the types of information that must be available in order for an auditor to complete an audit. Smaller organizations requiring first-year audits tend to be those that are just starting to meet an audit threshold established by a state agency regulating charities. Auditors of not-for-profit organizations should be particularly aware of the auditability issues where the pressure of such regulatory requirements are compelling the not-for-profit organization to have an audit of its financial statements.

Performance of Procedures for an Auditor to Determine Whether to Continue an Existing Audit Engagement Relationship

Auditors should have a policy on how frequently or under what circumstances they should reevaluate continuing client relationships to determine whether to continue to provide audit services to a particular not-for-profit client.

The AICPA guide titled "Quality Control Policies and Procedures for CPA Firms" lists certain significant changes that may cause the auditor to want to reevaluate the audit relationship. The changes listed are changes in:

- Management
- Directors
- Ownership
- Legal counsel
- Financial condition
- Litigation status
- Nature of the client's business
- Scope of the engagement

Such changes should not be assumed to be indicators requiring the termination of an audit client relationship. They simply indicate that the auditor may want to reevaluate the relationship.

Before beginning each year's audit for recurring audit clients, the auditor may wish to review informally many of the factors that were considered in deciding whether to accept the client originally. For example, the auditor may consider the following:

- Significant changes in the size of the not-for-profit organization and/or its number of operating locations

- Significant technical developments occurring since the last audit that may require the auditor to obtain technical information or attend continuing professional education courses

  OBSERVATION: Being in a position to help a not-for-profit organization implement SOP 98-2 and report on financial statements prepared in accordance with this requirement is an excellent example of a technical change that may have a significant impact on an auditor of a not-for-profit organization.

- Availability and qualifications of the auditor's staff who would be assigned to the audit engagement

- Changes in the independence of the auditor or other members of the audit firm relative to the specific not-for-profit organization

- Changes in the scope of services that must be provided to the not-for-profit organization

  OBSERVATION: For example, a not-for-profit organization may accept federal funds under a contract or grant for the first time. The auditor will need to consider whether he or she has the capability to meet the requirements of OMB Circular A-133.

The auditor should prepare planning documentation stating whether there are any significant changes that would effect the decision to retain the client, and the auditor's resolution and conclusion on the effect of these changes.

In addition to the more technical matters discussed above, the auditor should evaluate the business aspects of retaining an audit client. Consideration should be given to the relative profitability of the audit in the prior years and the impact on profitability that any changes in the organization or the scope of services to be provided may have in the succeeding year's audit.

  OBSERVATION: When engagements become unprofitable, auditors often increase their fee quote for the succeeding year. If the client accepts the increased fee, then the profitability of the audit becomes more acceptable to the auditor. If the client rejects the increased fee quote and terminates the relationship with the auditor, then the auditor has removed an unprofitable account from his or her business. While this passive approach has its advantages, the auditor may wish to work more proactively with a not-for-profit audit client to find ways to make

> the audit more efficient and more profitable to the auditor. A discussion of additional supporting schedules and analysis that might be prepared by the client instead of by the auditor is an example of how this improved profitability might be accomplished without jeopardizing the relationship with the client.

Whether the reason for terminating an existing audit client relationship is for technical considerations or for business reasons, the auditor should make the concerns known to the not-for-profit organization as soon as possible. These organizations often have more formalized procurement processes and will need more time to hire a new auditor. Termination of the relationship will be easier if the not-for-profit organization has sufficient time to hire a new auditor.

Determination of the Reporting Entity

As part of the preplanning phase of an audit engagement, the auditor should determine exactly what entities will be included in the reporting entity on whose financial statements the auditor will report. The auditor must understand how both for-profit organizations in which the not-for-profit organization has a financial interest and interrelated not-for-profit organizations will be accounted for and reported.

This determination will be fundamental to all of the other considerations that are being made during the preplanning phase. For example, the auditor cannot determine if he or she meets the independence requirements without knowing the composition of the not-for-profit organization's reporting entity.

SOP 94-3 (Reporting of Related Entities by Not-for-Profit Organizations) addresses the reporting entity issue. This SOP does not provide guidance on how to prepare consolidated financial statements, nor does it provide guidance for reporting by commonly controlled not-for-profit organizations for which no parent–subsidiary relationship exists. The FASB's ongoing project on consolidations includes a phase on presentation of consolidated financial statements for not-for-profit organizations. Until this project is complete and the FASB provides specific not-for-profit consolidation information (which may be several years away), the requirements of SOP 94-3 should be implemented using the guidance that is already available in the professional literature for presenting consolidated financial statements.

SOP 94-3 first deals with not-for-profit organizations that have investments in for-profit entities. Guidance is provided for not-for-profits with investments in majority-owned subsidiaries and investments in common stock of for-profit entities with a 50 percent or less voting interest.

Majority-Owned For-Profit Subsidiaries

When a not-for-profit organization has a controlling financial interest in a for-profit entity through either direct or indirect ownership of a majority of the voting interest in that for-profit entity, the not-for-profit should follow the guidance in ARB-51 (Consolidated Financial Statements) (as amended by FAS-94 [Consolidation of All Majority-Owned Subsidiaries]) to determine whether the financial position, results of operations, and cash flows of the majority-owned subsidiary should be included in its financial statements. Thus, the accounting and reporting for majority-owned subsidiaries is the same as that for commercial enterprises.

Common Stock Investments with 50 Percent or Less Voting Interest

When a not-for-profit organization owns 50 percent or less of the voting interests in a common stock investment, the not-for-profit organization should account for the interest using the guidance of APB Opinion No. 18 (The Equity Method of Accounting for Investments in Common Stock). Thus, if APB Opinion No. 18 would require the use of the equity method to account for this investment, then the not-for-profit organization should use the equity method to account for the investment, with one exception (described in the following paragraph). The not-for-profit organization should also make whatever disclosures required by APB Opinion No. 18.

When a not-for-profit organization reports its investment portfolios at market value in conformity with some of the AICPA Audit Guides, the not-for-profit may continue to do so instead of applying the equity method of accounting to the common stock investments.

Figures 2-1 and 2-2 present decision trees for these types of investments that are included as Appendix D of SOP 94-3.

The second major topic covered by SOP 94-3 is the reporting by a not-for-profit organization of financially interrelated not-for-profit organizations. The financial reporting is governed by the relationship between the not-for-profit organizations, which is affected by three factors: ownership, control, and economic interest. SOP 94-3 provides specific definitions of *control* and *economic interest*, as follows:

> *Control*—The direct or indirect ability to determine the direction of management and policies through ownership, contract, or otherwise.
>
> *Economic interest*—An interest in another entity that exists if (a) the other entity holds or utilizes significant resources that must be used for the unrestricted or restricted purposes of the not-for-profit organization, either directly or indirectly by produc-

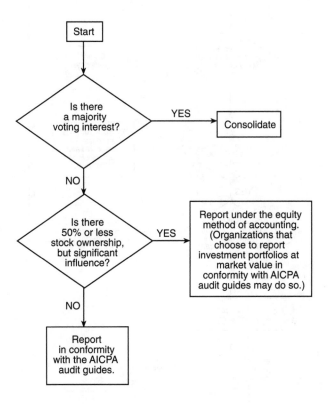

Figure 2-1. *Ownership of a for-profit entity.*

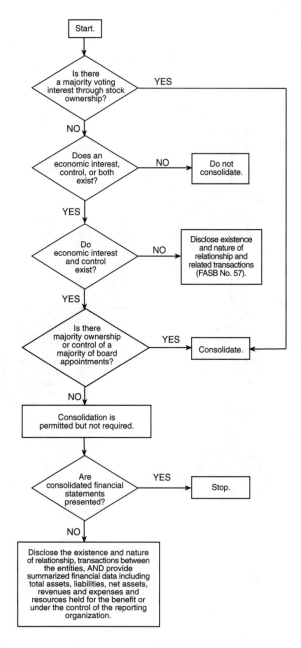

Figure 2-2. *Relationship with another not-for-profit organization.*

ing income or providing services, or (b) the reporting organization is responsible for the liabilities of the other entity.

The following are examples of economic interests:

- Other entities solicit funds in the name of and with the expressed or implied approval of the reporting organization, and substantially all of the funds solicited are intended by the contributor or are otherwise required to be transferred to the reporting organization or used at its discretion or direction.
- A reporting organization transfers significant resources to another entity whose resources are held for the benefit of the reporting organization.
- A reporting organization assigns certain significant functions to another entity.
- A reporting organization provides or is committed to provide funds for another entity or guarantees significant debt of another entity.

Controlling financial interest by majority of voting interest   A not-for-profit organization that has a controlling financial interest in another not-for-profit organization through direct or indirect ownership of a majority voting interest in that other not-for-profit organization should consolidate the other organization. However, if control is likely to be temporary or does not rest with the majority owner, then consolidation is prohibited.

Control through majority ownership interest   Control may not be obtained through ownership of a majority voting interest, but through a majority ownership interest or majority voting interest of the board of the other entity. An "ownership" interest is distinguished from a "voting" interest since the ownership of a not-for-profit organization may take a number of forms. As described in SOP 94-3, not-for-profit organizations may exist in various legal forms, such as corporations issuing stock, corporations issuing ownership certificates, membership corporations issuing membership certificates, joint ventures, and partnerships.

> **Example:** A "majority voting interest in the board of the other entity" is illustrated by SOP 94-3 in the following example. Entity B has a five-member board, and a simple voting majority is required to approve all board actions. Entity A will have a majority voting interest in the board of Entity B if three or more Entity A board members, officers, or employees serve on or may be appointed at Entity A's discretion to the board of Entity B.

However, if three of Entity A's board members serve on the board of Entity B but Entity A does not have the ability to require that those members serve on the Entity B board, Entity A does **not** have a majority voting interest in the board of Entity B.

Where control is obtained through a majority ownership interest (other than by ownership of a majority voting interest) or through a majority voting interest in the board of the other entity (as described in the above example) and the not-for-profit organization has an economic interest in the other not-for-profit organization, then consolidation is required. However, if control is likely to be temporary or does not rest with the majority owner, then consolidation is prohibited.

Control through means other than majority ownership or voting interest   Control of another not-for-profit organization may take forms other than majority ownership or voting interests. For example, control may take the form of a contract or affiliation agreement. In these circumstances, consolidation of the other not-for-profit organization is permitted but not required. However, if control is likely to be temporary, consolidation is prohibited.

If the other not-for-profit elects not to consolidate another not-for-profit organization meeting the above criteria, SOP 94-3 specifies the following disclosures that should be made in the notes to the financial statements of the not-for-profit organization:

- Identification of the other organization and the nature of its relationship with the reporting organization that results in control
- Summarized financial data of the other organization including:
  - Total assets, liabilities, net assets, revenue, and expenses
  - Resources that are held for the benefit of the reporting organization that are under its control
- Disclosures set forth in FAS-57 (Related Party Disclosures)

The disclosures required by FAS-57 that would be in addition to those required above are summarized as follows:

- The nature of the relationships involved
- A description of the transactions between the entities, including transactions to which no amounts or nominal amounts were ascribed for each of the periods for which statements of activities are presented, and such other information as deemed necessary to understand the effects of the transactions on the financial statements

- The dollar amounts of transactions for each of the periods for which statements of activities are presented and the effects of any change in the method of establishing the terms from that used in the preceding period

- Amounts due from or to related parties as of the date of each statement of financial position presented and, if not otherwise apparent, the terms and manner of settlement

Transactions involving related parties cannot be presumed to be carried out on an arm's-length basis, as the requisite conditions of competitive, free-market dealings may not exist. Auditors should consult FAS-57 if they encounter this situation to be sure that all of the required disclosure details are provided.

Existence of either control or an economic interest, but not both In instances where both control and economic interest do not exist, the presentation of consolidated financial statements is precluded (with one exception discussed in the following paragraph), but the disclosures set forth in FAS-57 are required. The existence of an economic interest does not automatically mean that the other organization is a related party requiring the disclosures of FAS-57, so the individual circumstances should be evaluated in light of the requirements of FAS-57.

Entities that otherwise would be prohibited from presenting consolidated financial statements under the provisions of SOP 94-3, but that are currently presenting consolidated financial statements in conformity with the guidance of previous accounting standards, may continue to do so.

The auditor should be familiar with the requirements of SOP 94-3 during the preplanning phase of the audit engagement to ensure that he or she has considered the reporting entity requirements and, to a more limited extent, the disclosure requirements that will need to be applied in the financial reporting by the not-for-profit organization.

Determination of Whether the Scope of the Audit Engagement Is Appropriate

One important step in the preplanning phase of the audit is to make sure that the appropriate scope of the audit engagement has been determined. There may be expanded reporting or audit requirements in contracts or grant agreements under which the not-for-profit organization has received funding. The auditor should be aware of these requirements and should be able to meet the requirements in the time frame required by the contracts or grants. The auditor also should consider that the contractors and grantors will be important readers of the financial statements on which he or she is issuing an audit opinion.

Single Audits

The most common type of scope expansion for not-for-profit organizations involves the requirements triggered when the not-for-profit organization receives certain levels of funding that originates with a federal grantor agency. It is important for the auditor to be familiar with these additional requirements, which arise from *Government Auditing Standards* (commonly called the "Yellow Book") and OMB Circular A-133. These requirements and, more importantly, the dollar thresholds at which they are triggered are summarized below.

> **OBSERVATION:** Part II of this Guide provides complete information on the procedures for performing an audit in accordance with OMB Circular A-133.

Circular A-133 was revised several years ago. The revised Circular changed the threshold for when an audit in accordance with the Circular is required. The new requirement is that not-for-profit organizations that expend $300,000 or more in a year in federal awards are required to have a single audit or (if certain criteria are met and an election is made) a program-specific audit. Not-for-profit organizations that expend less than $300,000 a year in federal awards are exempt from federal audit requirements; however, records must be available for review or audit by appropriate officials of the federal agency, pass-through entity, and the United States General Accounting Office.

While the threshold requirement seems straightforward, applying it to actual organizations and their circumstances is difficult. Some of the terms in the prior Circular A-133 were not clearly defined, and interpretations and modifications to the rules developed.

Not-for-profit organizations (and their auditors) that receive *any* federal funding should carefully refer to Part II for potential applicability of audit requirements under Circular A-133.

Completion of the Client Acceptance Decision

Once the auditor has made the considerations described throughout this chapter, he or she must decide whether to perform audit services for a prospective new audit client or whether to continue audit services for a recurring audit client. The ultimate decision maker in the process depends on the size of the audit firm. Sole practitioners will decide for themselves. In larger firms, the ultimate decision may rest with an office managing partner or partner in charge of an audit practice within an office. In both cases, the decisions are likely to be made based on the preliminary recommendation of an audit engagement partner who has been responsible either for identifying a potential new audit client or for past audit services to a recurring client.

Whatever the decision-making process within individual audit firms, the underlying analysis and procedures performed in support of the decision must be appropriately documented. Exhibit 2-3 presents a model client acceptance/continuation form. The form should be appropriately modified to meet the circumstances of the particular audit firm that is using the form as well as the particular circumstances of the client relationship that is being considered.

Establishing an Understanding of the Terms of the Audit Engagement with the Client

In October 1997, the AICPA issued Statement on Auditing Standards No. 83 (Establishing an Understanding with the Client) (SAS-83). SAS-83 was effective for engagements for periods ending on or after June 15, 1998.

SAS-83 provides that the auditor and the client should establish an understanding of the terms of an engagement. The term *engagement* includes the audit of financial statements as well as other engagements performed by independent auditors. The understanding should include the objectives of the engagement, management's responsibilities, the auditor's responsibilities, and limitations of the engagement.

The auditor should document this understanding in the working papers, preferably through a written communication with the client. Thus, although SAS-83 states that obtaining an engagement letter is preferred, it is still not required. If the auditor believes that an understanding with the client has not been established, the auditor should not accept or perform the engagement.

SAS-83 lists a number of matters that should be included in the understanding with the client. These specific matters are all included in the sample engagement letter provided in Exhibit 2-4 (see page 70). If a written engagement letter is not obtained from the client, documentation should be included in the working papers that the matters included in the sample engagement letter are understood and agreed to by the client.

An engagement letter is a document that specifies the nature and terms of the audit engagement that the not-for-profit is engaging the auditor to perform. The letter is signed jointly by the auditor and the not-for-profit organization, although traditionally it is prepared by

EXHIBIT 2-3
NEW AUDIT CLIENT ACCEPTANCE/CLIENT CONTINUATION
FORM FOR NOT-FOR-PROFIT ORGANIZATIONS

SECTION I: GENERAL/BACKGROUND INFORMATION

Prospective Client: _____

Address: _____

Telephone: _____

Fax: _____

Firm File Number/Client Identification Number: _____

Key Client Personnel

President/Executive Director: _____

Chief Financial Officer: _____

Controller/Accounting Manager: _____

General Counsel: _____

Chair of the Board of Directors: _____

Chair of Audit Committee: _____

Other Key Board of Directors Members (including affiliation):

_____

_____

_____

Type of Legal Form (corporation, membership, etc.):

_____

Internal Revenue Code Section Exemption: _____

Has an IRS tax determination letter been issued? ❑ Yes ❑ No

State charities organization reporting requirements? ❑ Yes ❑ No

States requiring registration/audited financial statements: _____

_____

_____

_____

List any for-profit entities that may be considered for accounting for using the equity method or considered for consolidation with the not-for-profit organization:

_____

_____

_____

List any interrelated not-for-profit organizations that may be related to the prospective audit client by ownership, control, and economic interest:

_____

_____

_____

SECTION 2: COMMUNICATION WITH PREDECESSOR AUDITOR

Document below the communication(s) with the predecessor auditor before accepting the engagement.

Name of predecessor auditor: _____

Name of partner contacted: _____

Telephone number: _____

Did the partner confirm the following representations of the not-for-profit organization?

	Yes	No	N/A
1. The firm is not involved in disputes with the not-for-profit organization over accounting policies, audit procedures, or other significant matters.	_____	_____	_____
2. There are no unpaid fees due the auditor from the not-for-profit organization.	_____	_____	_____

Describe below the predecessor auditor's comments regarding the integrity of the management and board of directors of the not-for-profit organization.

_____

_____

_____

Describe below the predecessor auditor's understanding of the not-for-profit organization's reason for changing auditors.

_____

_____

SECTION 3: OTHER COMMUNICATIONS

Describe briefly below any additional communications that were made with parties outside of the prospective not-for-profit audit client, including the organization's attorneys and bankers. Include the name of the firm; the name, position, and telephone number of contacts; and their comments on the integrity of management and the board of directors and other reasons that may affect acceptance of this engagement, including promptness in payment of invoices:

Contact #1   _____

              _____

              _____

Contact #2   _____

              _____

              _____

Contact #3   _____

              _____

              _____

SECTION 4: INDEPENDENCE

The following section should be completed to determine whether the firm is independent with respect to the prospective client and whether audit services may be performed. Any affirmative responses should be adequately explained if it is determined that they do not impair independence.

	Yes	No	N/A
Are any of the firm's personnel or relatives of the firm's personnel associate with the not-for-profit organization in any of the following capacities:			
1. Members of management or employees.	___	___	___
2. Members of the board of directors, trustees or other governing board.	___	___	___

	Yes	No	N/A

3. Owners, with either a direct or a material indirect financial interest.

Does the firm provide any of the following services to the not-for-profit organization?

1. Performance of responsibilities usually associated with management or other employees of an organization, such as executing transactions or having custody of assets.

2. Processing or controlling of the accounting transactions that will form the basis of the financial statements.

3. Performance of any advocacy work that might bias the firm in favor or opposed to any of the organization's programs or other services.

Is the firm's independence impaired by any other relationship or factor, including:

1. Litigation between the firm and the not-for-profit organization.

2. Unpaid fees that are owed to the firm from the not-for-profit organization.

3. Any other relationship or factor that might impair independence.

SECTION 5: SERVICES TO BE PROVIDED TO THE PROSPECTIVE CLIENT

The following services will be provided to the prospective client upon acceptance of the engagement:

	Yes	No	N/A

1. Audit of organization-wide financial statements in accordance with generally accepted auditing standards.

2. Audit of individual location or fund financial statements.

3. Audit in accordance with *Government Auditing Standards*.

4. Audit in accordance with OMB Circular A-133.

	Yes	No	N/A
5. Special audit procedures required by other than federal funding source.			
6. Special reports or schedules required by other than federal funding sources.			
7. Federal income tax preparation service, such as Form 990.			
8. State charities department registration form preparation.			
9. Consulting services, such as accounting or internal control analyses.			

SECTION 6: MANAGEMENT'S CAPABILITY AND INTEGRITY

	Yes	No	N/A
1. Have any of the communications with parties outside of the not-for-profit organization indicated any reasons for concern about management's integrity?			
2. Does management appear to have a sufficient understanding of the operations of the organization, its financial positions and results of activities, and related accounting principles to take responsibility for the financial statements?			
3. Does management or appropriate financial personnel have an adequate understanding of disclosure requirements, valuation issues, and judgments necessary for a fair presentation of the financial statements?			
4. Has the organization or management been the subject of criticism because of integrity or capability either in the press or from oversight and regulatory agencies, such as state charities regulators or the Internal Revenue Service?			
5. Are there any operational risks to which management has subjected the organization that do not seem justifiable?			
6. Does management have an adequate understanding of the organization's investment policies to minimize the risk of loss from unanticipated events?			

	Yes	No	N/A

7. Has there been excessive turnover in management personnel?

8. Is the board of directors or other governing board sufficiently active to monitor the actions of the president or executive director?

9. Is the not-for-profit organization able to pay its liabilities in a timely manner?

SECTION 7: SUFFICIENT ACCOUNTING RECORDS TO PROVIDE THE BASIS OF FINANCIAL STATEMENTS PREPARED IN ACCORDANCE WITH GENERALLY ACCEPTED ACCOUNTING PRINCIPLES

	Yes	No	N/A

1. Does the prospective client maintain sufficient accounting records that are auditable and will support the information presented in the financial statements?

2. Does it appear that the prospective client maintains adequate documentation to support the transactions recorded in the accounting records?

3. Do accounting staff appear sufficient in number and able to maintain the accounting system and recognize errors in the recording of transactions?

4. Are sufficient reconciliations performed to provide comfort in the recording of transactions (e.g., bank reconciliations, comparing physical inventory to inventory maintained in the accounting records)?

SECTION 8: USERS OF FINANCIAL STATEMENTS

Document below the potential readers and users of the financial statements that will be audited:

	Yes	No	N/A

1. Creditors of the organization, including banks and other lending sources.

		Yes	No	N/A
2.	State charities registration departments.	___	___	___
3.	Other affiliated or controlling not-for-profit organizations.	___	___	___
4.	Members of the not-for-profit organization.	___	___	___
5.	Contributors and potential contributors.	___	___	___
6.	Grantor or contractor entities providing funding sources for the organization.	___	___	___
7.	General public.	___	___	___
8.	News media and other public information depositories.	___	___	___

SECTION 9: AUDITOR'S CAPABILITIES

		Yes	No	N/A
1.	Does the firm have sufficient staff available professionally service this prospective client?	___	___	___
2.	Are staff to be assigned sufficiently familiar with the not-for-profit industry to perform the audit?	___	___	___
3.	Are any specialized skills, such as exempt-organization tax specialists or computer specialists, available if needed for this particular audit engagement?	___	___	___
4.	Does it appear that an adequate audit fee will be obtainable to make this engagement profitable to the firm?	___	___	___

SIGNATURES   ___

Prepared by _____   Date _____

Reviewed by _____   Date _____

Reviewed by _____   Date

Final approval to accept or
to reject this prospective client
for an audit engagement by: _____

Date: _____

the auditor on the auditor's stationery. This does not preclude the not-for-profit organization from requesting that any particular term or circumstance that it would like to include in the letter be included.

The letter should be signed by the auditor and the not-for-profit organization after the auditor has performed his or her client acceptance or retention procedures and has decided to accept or continue the audit engagement, but before the commencement of the audit planning or fieldwork.

While the preparation of an engagement letter was not required by previously generally accepted auditing standards, nor is it required by SAS-83, auditors generally recognize it as a helpful document. The letter serves to notify the not-for-profit organization client formally of the general nature of the audit that is to be performed, including its limitations, and is a formal acknowledgment by the not-for-profit organization of its responsibilities relating to the financial statements and other aspects of the audit. The engagement letter is also a convenient format for documenting understandings reached between the auditor and the not-for-profit organization regarding deadlines, audit fees, and the extent of assistance that the not-for-profit organization will provide to the auditor during the course of the engagement. Any additional services beyond the audit of financial statements that will be performed by the auditor, such as the preparation of tax returns or reports to state charities monitoring departments, also can be included in the engagement letter. Exhibit 2-4 provides a standardized engagement letter; it should be modified to meet the circumstances of the audit engagement for which it is being used.

SUMMARY

The preplanning phase of the audit is an important step in ensuring that an auditor is able to deliver high quality, professional services to an audit client in compliance with all applicable professional standards and qualifications. It gives the auditor an appropriate foundation to move on to the next phase of an audit engagement, which is to perform formal audit planning procedures. These are discussed in the following chapter, "Audit Planning."

EXHIBIT 2-4
ENGAGEMENT LETTER[1]

[*Letterhead of the auditor*]

[*Date*]

[*Not-for-profit organization's name and address*]

This letter sets forth our understanding of the terms and objectives of the services we are to provide to [*name of not-for-profit organization*] for the [*period being audited*] ending [*date of end of period or year being audited*] and the related fee arrangements.

We will audit the statement of financial position as of [*date of period/year end*] and the related statements of activities and cash flows[2] for the [*period/ year*] then ended, the objective of which is the expression of an opinion on the financial statements.[3]

Our audit will be conducted in accordance with generally accepted auditing standards and will include tests of the accounting records of [*name of not-for-profit organization*] and other procedures that we consider necessary in the circumstances to enable us to express an opinion that the financial statements are fairly presented, in all material respects, in conformity with generally accepted accounting principles. If our opinion is other than unqualified, we will discuss the reasons for being unable to issue an unqualified opinion with you in advance. If, for any reason, we are unable to complete the audit, or are unable to form, or have not formed, an opinion, we may decline to express an opinion or decline to issue a report as a result of the audit.

As part of our audit, we will obtain an understanding of the organization's internal control to plan the audit and to determine the nature, timing, and extent of auditing procedures necessary for expressing our opinion concerning the financial statements and not to provide assurance on the internal control or to identify reportable conditions. However, we are responsible for ensuring that the audit committee (or others with equivalent authority or responsibility) are aware of any reportable conditions which come to our attention. The management of [*name of not-for-profit organization*] is responsible for establishing and maintaining effective internal control over financial reporting. To fulfill this responsibility, estimates and judgments by management are required to assess the expected benefits and related costs of internal control policies and procedures. The objectives of internal control are to provide management with reasonable, rather than absolute, assurance that assets are safeguarded against loss from unauthorized use or disposition, and that transactions are executed in accordance with management's authorization and recorded properly to permit the preparation of financial statements in accordance with generally accepted accounting principles. Because of inherent limitations in any internal control, errors may nevertheless occur and not be detected. Also, projection of internal control to future periods is subject to the risk that procedures may become inadequate because of changes in conditions, or that the effectiveness of the design and operation of policies and procedures may deteriorate.

Our audit will include procedures designed to provide reasonable rather than absolute assurance that the financial statements are free of material mis-statements, whether caused by error or fraud. As you are aware, however, there are inherent limitations in the auditing process. For example, audits are based on the concept of selective testing of data being examined and are, therefore, subject to the limitation that such matters, if they exist, may not be detected.

Our responsibility as auditors is limited to the period covered by our audit and does not extend to any later periods for which we are not engaged as auditors.

We understand that you will provide us with the basic information required for our audit and that you are responsible for the accuracy and completeness of that information. We understand that you are also responsible for identifying and ensuring that [*name of not-for-profit organization*] complies with the laws and regulations applicable to its activities. We will advise you about appropriate accounting principles and their application and will assist in the preparation of your financial statements; however, the responsibility for the financial statements remains with you. This responsibility includes the maintenance of adequate records and related internal control structure policies and procedures, the selection and application of accounting principles, and the safeguarding of assets. At the conclusion of the engagement, management will provide to us a representation letter that, among other things, will confirm management's responsibility for the preparation of financial statements in accordance with generally accepted accounting principles; the availability of financial records and related documents; compliance with provisions of laws, regulations, contracts and grants; the completeness and availability of all minutes of board of directors (and committee) meetings; and the absence of fraud involving management or those employees who have significant roles in internal controls.[4]

Our audit is not specifically designed and cannot be relied on to disclose reportable conditions, that is, significant deficiencies in the design or operation of the internal control. However, during the audit, if we become aware of such reportable conditions or ways that we believe management's practices can be improved, we will communicate them to you in a separate letter.[5, 6]

We expect to begin our audit on [*date*] and to issue our opinion on your financial statements no later than [*date*].[7]

Our fees for these services will be based on the actual time spent at our standard hourly rates, plus out-of-pocket costs, which include travel, report production, typing, postage, delivery charges, etc. Our standard hourly billing rates vary according to the responsibility and experience of the staff assigned to your audit engagement.[8] Our invoices for these fees will be presented to you monthly and are payable upon presentation. Based upon our preliminary estimates, our audit fee should approximate $ [*XX,XXX*].[9] This estimate is based on the anticipated cooperation from your staff and the assumption that unexpected circumstances will not be encountered during the audit. If significant additional time is necessary, we will discuss this with you and arrive at a new fee estimate before the occurrence of the additional costs.

We appreciate the opportunity to be of service to [*name of not-for-profit organization*] and believe that this letter accurately summarizes the significant terms of our engagement. If you have any questions or comments, please let us know. If you agree with the terms of our engagement as described in this letter, please sign the enclosed copy and return it to us.

Very truly yours,

[*Auditor's Signature*]

Agreed:

[*Name of Not-for-Profit Organization*]

By:

Name: _____

Title: _____

Date: _____

---

[1] In December 1999, the AICPA issued Statement on Auditing Standards No. 89, "Audit Adjustments," which is effective for audits of financial statements for periods beginning on or after December 15, 1999, with early adoption permitted. In addition to its requirement for communication of audit adjustments to audit committees and for obtaining management's representation as to the effect of unrecorded audit adjustments, SAS-89 adds the following to the list of matters that are generally included in the understanding with the client:

> Management is responsible for adjusting the financial statements to correct material misstatements and for affirming to the auditor in the representation letter that the effects of any uncorrected misstatements aggregated by the auditor during the current engagement and pertaining to the latest period presented are immaterial, both individually and in the aggregate, to the financial statements taken as a whole.

[2] Voluntary health and welfare organizations and, if applicable, other not-for-profit organizations should include a statement of function expenses in the scope of statements to be audited.

[3] Insert a paragraph in this location to describe any other statements or schedules that are to be included in the auditor's audit scope, including those that the auditor will report on "in relation to" the basic financial statements. Also, the engagement letter may confirm the understanding that certain information will not be audited, for example, any tables or schedules that are to be included in an auditor-submitted document, but which the auditor did not include in the scope of his or her audit.

[4] At this point in the letter, the auditor should identify any specific assistance that will be provided by the not-for-profit organization. This can range from the number of hours that internal audit staff will be made available to the independent auditor to assist in the audit of the financial statements, to who will be responsible for physically typing the financial statements. The more specific information that is provided, the better the auditor's position later to adjust the audit fee if the not-for-profit organization does not live up to its commitment to perform certain tasks. Specificity also will be of benefit in that the not-for-profit organization commits in writing to perform certain tasks, which increases the likelihood that they will actually be performed.

[5] The auditor should specify any services in addition to the audit of financial statements that will be provided. This might include such items as preparation of tax returns, preparation of state charities department reports, or filings or other procedures that the auditor agrees to perform, such as counting immaterial petty cash funds that are maintained by the not-for-profit organization's local district offices, which might not otherwise have been performed in an audit in accordance with generally accepted auditing standards. The auditor's reporting on the results of any additional procedures performed at the not-for-profit organization's request also should be specified.

[6] Because of the potential significant impact of the Year 2000 issue on not-for-profit organizations, it is suggested that the following language be added to the engagement letter:

> Furthermore, our audit, including the limited inquiries we will make in connection with Year 2000 issues, is not designed to, and does not, provide any assurance that Year 2000 issues that may exist will be identified, or on the adequacy of [*name of not-for-profit organization*]'s Year 2000 remediation plans with respect to operational or financial systems, or on whether [*name of not-for-profit organization*] is or will become Year 2000 compliant on a timely basis. Year 2000 compliance is the responsibility of management. However, we may communicate matters that come to our attention relating to the Year 2000 issue that, in our judgment, may be of benefit to management.

[7] The timing of services that will be provided in addition to the audit of the financial statements should also be specified, including the deadlines for any deliverables on the part of the auditor.

[8] This paragraph should be modified to reflect the specific fee nature of the engagement to which the letter applies. For example, the fee might be a fixed fee, which includes out-of-pocket expenses, or discounts may be given to the not-for-profit organization from the auditor's standard billing rates.

[9] This section also should address the fees for the performance of any additional procedures beyond the audit of the not-for-profit organization's financial statements.

CHAPTER 3
AUDIT PLANNING

CONTENTS

CHAPTER 3
AUDIT PLANNING

CROSS-REFERENCES

2001 MILLER NOT-FOR-PROFIT ORGANIZATION AUDITS: Chapter 7, "Extent of Audit Procedures and Sampling"

2001 MILLER AUDIT PROCEDURES: Chapter 3, "Audit Planning"; Chapter 4, "Audit Risk and Materiality"; Chapter 7, "Analytical Procedures"

2000 MILLER GAAS GUIDE: Section 311, "Planning and Supervision"; Section 312, "Audit Risk and Materiality in Conducting an Audit"; Section 316, "Consideration of Fraud in an Financial Statement Audit"

The effectiveness of the planning phase of an audit engagement will determine whether the audit is performed in accordance with professional standards, on a timely basis, and in a manner that will be profitable to the auditor. Effective audit planning also will increase the likelihood that the organization being audited will receive efficient, high-quality service.

Although professional auditing literature and professional development seminars emphasize the importance of effective audit planning, this phase of the audit is probably the most neglected. Most auditors would agree that planning is a critical element to a successful audit, yet its benefits cannot always be clearly identified. For example, the results of a senior auditor's efforts to obtain an understanding of the environment in which the client operates are more difficult to identify than the results of an assistant accountant's efforts to trace twenty disbursements to canceled checks. It may take a great deal of discipline on the auditor's part to put the necessary time into audit planning, especially when the benefits are so hard to define.

Perhaps the best way to promote the benefits of proper audit planning is to emphasize its potential effect on the efficiency of the audit. Competition among audit firms generally is intense, with competition for audits of not-for-profit organizations no less intense.

Auditors who develop the most efficient audit strategy will be the leanest competitors in terms of fees, and they may well be the best competitors in terms of the effectiveness of their audits. Since audits of not-for-profit organizations are often performed at discounts from audit firms' standard billing rates, the need for audit efficiency is even greater when performing audits of these types of organizations.

The best, if not the only, time to design an effective audit strategy is during the planning phase of the audit engagement. Planning an audit that meets the professional requirements and is most efficient in reducing audit risk is only the first part of becoming more efficient. The key is to eliminate those procedures that are not required by the professional auditing literature and have little effect on the reduction of audit risk. Auditors undertaking the audit of a not-for-profit organization for the first time may find it a good opportunity to review the audit strategy that they typically use for their other audit engagements before implementing it for the audit of the not-for-profit organization. Such a review may point to efficiencies that the auditor can adopt not only for the audit of the not-for-profit organization, but for his or her commercial enterprise audits as well.

Overview

This chapter provides a guide to the planning considerations necessary for performing an audit of a not-for-profit organization in accordance with generally accepted auditing standards. Some of these considerations are in addition to, or overlap, the planning procedures normally performed for an audit of financial statements of a commercial enterprise in accordance with GAAS. Planning procedures should be tailored to individual client circumstances, and therefore, the auditor should exercise good judgment when determining which procedures are required during the planning phase of an audit engagement.

Planning for an audit of a not-for-profit organization performed in accordance with GAAS should include the following steps:

- Obtaining an understanding of the not-for-profit organization and the environment in which it operates.
- Performing planning analytical procedures.
- Determining planning materiality levels.
- Obtaining an understanding of the not-for-profit organization's internal controls in accordance with SAS-78.
- Completing the initial audit risk assessment and developing an audit strategy.
- Considering the risk of fraud in an audit of financial statements.

- Considering other audit matters, including:
  — Related-party transactions
  — Errors and irregularities
  — Illegal acts
  — Compliance auditing
  — Use of service organizations
  — Use of the work of specialists
- Considering the impact of the Year 2000 Issue on the audit of the not-for-profit organization
- Documenting the planning phase of the engagement in a planning memorandum.

Obtaining an Understanding of the Not-for-Profit Organization and the Environment in Which It Operates

To design an audit approach for an audit of a not-for-profit organization in accordance with GAAS, the auditor must have a reasonably comprehensive understanding of the not-for-profit organization and its operating environment.

Obtaining an understanding of the not-for-profit organization should include understanding how the organization operates its affairs and its administrative structure. Not all not-for-profit organizations operate in the same manner, and the auditor should obtain a familiarity with the particular organization being audited. The auditor should review an organization chart of the entire organization, and the finance department in particular.

The auditor should have a general understanding or assessment of the extent to which the not-for-profit organization is conscious and supportive of internal controls and of the strength of its financial management. Although the auditor will expand this understanding when assessing the organization's control environment, a preliminary assessment of the control environment is useful during the planning phase of the audit and will be necessary in designing a preliminary audit strategy. During the planning phase, the auditor should begin to make preliminary assessments about whether it may be possible to assess control risk at below the maximum level. A complete discussion of the assessment of control risk and the internal controls in the not-for-profit organization environment is provided in the chapter titled "Internal Control Considerations."

The auditor should obtain a general understanding of the following operating characteristics of the not-for-profit organization for use in designing an audit strategy:

- Extent to which accounting and financial systems are computerized, including the type of computers (mainframe, workstations, networks, or stand-alone personal computers) and the extent of technical competence that the personnel of the not-for-profit organization have to maintain any computerized systems. (The not-for-profit organization's consideration and activities in identifying and resolving any Year 2000 problems in its automated systems should also be understood. This will be addressed in more detail later in this chapter.)

- Existence of an internal audit group or department, whether the independent auditor can rely on its work, and whether staff from the internal audit group or department will be available to assist the independent auditor

> **OBSERVATION:** The auditor may want to consider whether internal audit staff are able to perform some audit procedures at remote or off-site locations that the auditor does not plan to visit.

- Extent of the management of various contracts and grant awards and the individuals in the organization responsible for managing those contracts and grant awards

- The not-for-profit organization's ability to accumulate costs into the categories of program activities, general and administrative activities, and fund-raising activities. (The organization's ability to perform joint cost allocation activities should also be considered.)

- The manner in which indirect costs are accumulated and allocated to the various programs and activities of the not-for-profit organization

- The not-for-profit organization's ability to segregate activities and net assets into the appropriate classifications of net assets—permanently restricted, temporarily restricted, and unrestricted.

- The manner in which any subrecipients of contract and grant awards are monitored and the individuals in the not-for-profit organization responsible for the monitoring procedures

- The extent of financial experience and acumen of the program management and other top management individuals who do not have direct responsibility for the financial affairs of the recipient organization

> **OBSERVATION:** Obviously, the considerations listed above are important during the first year an auditor is engaged to perform a not-for-profit organization audit. However, it is just

as important for the auditor to update his or her understanding of these considerations every year. As the auditor's knowledge of the not-for-profit organization builds from year to year, he or she will derive more and more benefit from being able to review these matters.

Not-for-profit organizations operate in a variety of fields and serve numerous constituencies and purposes. The operating environment issues that affect a major college or university are different from those affecting a human service organization providing meals to the indigent. The college or university may have as a significant concern or exposure area the tax status of revenues obtained by its football team in a corporate-sponsored bowl game. The human service organization may be concerned with having its operations judged efficient, thereby putting the five- and ten-dollar contributions it receives to the fullest use and advantage. Similarly, these organizations may receive federal funding for completely different purposes. For example, it may take years before research performed by the university shows results. The human service organization, on the other hand, may provide daily sustenance to people and have an immediate effect.

The auditor must identify the issues affecting the organization under audit and determine what their implications might be to an audit in accordance with GAAS.

The auditor should consider many factors of the operating environment, including:

- The outlook for the continued solicitation of unrestricted revenues, such as through fund-raising activities, annual giving, bequests, special events, and fee-for-service activities.
- The size of any contract and grant awards programs and their importance to the not-for-profit organization, the status of multi-year contracts or grants, and the prospects for obtaining new contracts or grant awards to replace expiring ones; the outlook for increasing or decreasing contract or grant awards programs in the areas in which the not-for-profit organization operates.
- The ability to manage the compliance requirements of any of the not-for-profit organization's contract or grant awards programs.
- The appropriateness of the resources and experience of the administrative staff and capabilities of the not-for-profit organization, given the outlook for its revenue growth or shrinkage.
- The environmental factors that affect the operating expenses of the not-for-profit organization, such as employee health care costs, technology changes, and other factors affecting the delivery of services by the organization.

- The unique revenue streams of typical not-for-profit organizations. A college or university's primary revenue sources are fee-based (i.e., revenues for tuition and room and board). These revenues are readily attributable to individual students and can be tested in a fairly straightforward manner by the auditor. A small human service provider may collect most of its revenues in the form of cash. These revenues may come in the form of checks or coin donations from a collection canister. The audit of these revenues is not as straightforward as the audit of the fee-based revenues for the college or university. The auditor may find it very difficult to satisfy him- or herself that all revenues have been properly collected and recorded.

- Significant changes to the accounting "environment" for not-for-profit organizations in the past few years, such as the recent requirements of FAS-116 (Accounting for Contributions Received and Contributions Made), FAS-117 (Financial Statements of Not-for-Profit Organizations), FAS-136 (Transfers of Assets to a Not-for-Profit Organization or Charitable Trust That Raises or Holds Contributions for Others), the AICPA Guide, SOP 94-3 (Reporting of Related Entities by Not-for-Profit Organizations), SOP 98-2 (Accounting for Costs of Activities of Not-for-Profit Organizations and State and Local Governmental Entities That Include Fund Raising) and, in particular, OMB Circular A-133 (Audits of States, Local Governments, and Non-Profit Organizations).

- The taxation and regulatory environment of not-for-profit organizations, including maintaining the tax-exempt status of the organization's tax-exempt activities, computing and paying the appropriate taxes on any unrelated business income of the not-for-profit, and creating complex tax structures to create for-profit subsidiaries to earn unrelated business income.

OBSERVATION: Environmental factors affecting not-for-profit organizations include many of the same environmental factors facing commercial enterprises (e.g., personnel and payroll matters, purchasing and procurement, cash management, and facilities management). Auditors should not overlook these environmental/institutional factors when planning their audits. In addition to these factors, the not-for-profit organization may envision a unique role for its auditor. Many not-for-profit organizations, particularly smaller ones, rely on their independent certified public accountant to be a financial expert who can provide advice to management through either a management letter or some less formal verbal communication. Clearly, without understanding the organization and its industry, the outside auditor would be able to provide only superficial advice that the not-for-profit probably could obtain from any certified public accountant (including the auditor's competitors).

Boards of directors of not-for-profit organizations also seem to have a high level of expectation regarding the auditor's duty to understand the not-for-profit organization and its industry. In fact, in the typical board of directors meeting to review a not-for-profit organization's audited financial statements, it is the auditor—not the financial management of the not-for-profit organization—who leads the detailed review of the financial statements. While this is certainly more common for smaller not-for-profit organizations than for larger ones, the auditor in either case must be in a position to comment intelligently on the financial statements and respond to questions from the board of directors. Given the relatively new requirements of FAS-116, FAS-117, FAS-124, and FAS-136, the auditor must be ready to explain and respond to questions about the accounting and reporting changes that have resulted from the implementation of these standards and to discuss the various accounting and reporting questions that arose during implementation and how they were addressed.

> **OBSERVATION:** Auditors should encourage the not-for-profit organization's financial managers to lead the analysis of their organization's financial statements, since the financial statements are their responsibility.

Performing Planning Analytical Procedures

Auditors should consider the requirements of SAS-56 (Analytical Procedures) regarding performing analytical review procedures during the planning phase of the audit engagement for a not-for-profit organization. SAS-56 requires that analytical procedures be applied to some extent to help the auditor plan the nature, timing, and extent of other auditing procedures.

SAS-56 states that analytical procedures performed during the planning phase of the audit should focus on (1) enhancing the auditor's understanding of the client's business and the transactions and events that have occurred since the last audit date and (2) identifying areas that may represent specific risks relevant to the audit. The auditor should look for unusual transactions or the unusual recording of transactions and should evaluate the results of operations or financial condition using ratios and trends to identify matters that might have an effect on audit strategy.

The most common type of analytical procedure performed during the planning phase of an audit engagement is a comparison of the prior-year audited balance sheet and operating results with the current-year balance sheet and operating results. The current-year information is sometimes as of the end of the fiscal year being audited, if the entire audit and its planning occur after the end of the fiscal year.

More often, the auditor begins the audit before the not-for-profit organization's fiscal year end, thus precluding the use of full fiscal-year information for analytical procedure purposes. Or the auditor may begin the audit after the fiscal year end, but so soon after that the full fiscal-year information is not yet available.

In these cases, the auditor should attempt to use interim-period financial information, as close to the fiscal year end as possible, to perform analytical procedures. For operating statement information, the auditor should project the full-year information by comparing the partial-year amounts to those of the prior full year. This projection can be a simple mathematical computation (e.g., the average monthly revenues and expenses for a nine-month period multiplied by twelve to project annual information), or it can be refined for seasonality (e.g., most not-for-profits receive a greater number of contributions from individuals in December than in other months) or other factors (e.g., a new federal awards programs that began halfway through the fiscal year).

Unlike publicly traded companies, not-for-profit organizations are not required to prepare quarterly financial statements. Thus, the auditor may experience some difficulty obtaining interim financial information and may have to consider alternative sources of information and methods other than applying analytical procedures at the financial statement level. These alternative sources and methods could include the following:

- Comparing actual revenues and expenses to amounts budgeted through a certain period. Often, not-for-profit organizations have well-developed budgets that have been scrutinized by their boards of directors. Comparing actual amounts to budgeted amounts can give insights into unexpected activities that may be significant from an audit perspective.

- Reviewing any financial presentations and analyses that have been prepared for the board of directors during the year. Reading the minutes of the board of directors meetings relative to financial operations might also be a tool for understanding the not-for-profit organization and its operations.

- Reviewing the quarterly and/or monthly financial status reports for the not-for-profit organization's contract or grant awards programs. These reports often provide expenditure analyses that can be compared to those of prior periods and/or to budgeted amounts.

- Computing and analyzing financial ratios to increase the auditor's understanding of the financial operations of the recipient organization (e.g., comparing recorded revenue and expense amounts for contract or grant awards programs or comparing general support revenues to the pledges receivable at the fiscal year end).

OBSERVATION: Although none of these techniques may give the auditor all the information needed for planning analytical procedures, two or more of these analyses may provide the auditor with useful information and enable him or her to meet the professional requirements of performing analytical procedures related to planning.

Determining Planning Materiality Levels

Auditors of not-for-profit organizations need to satisfy the requirements of SAS-47 (Audit Risk and Materiality in Conducting an Audit). The term *materiality* is not precisely defined in SAS-47 because materiality is a matter of professional judgment and is influenced by the auditor's understanding of the needs of a reasonable reader of the financial statements who is relying on their content. SAS-47 refers to FASB Concepts Statement No. 2 (Qualitative Characteristics of Accounting Information), which defines *materiality* as "the magnitude of an omission or misstatement of accounting information that, in the light of surrounding circumstances, makes it probable that the judgment of a reasonable person relying on the information would have been changed or influenced by the omission or misstatement."

SAS-47 states that financial statements are materially misstated when "they contain misstatements whose effect, individually or in the aggregate, is important enough to cause them not to be presented fairly, in all material respects, in conformity with generally accepted accounting principles."

The auditor should evaluate both the qualitative and quantitative aspects of a misstatement when considering materiality. A misstatement of a relatively small amount that comes to the auditor's attention could have a material effect on the financial statements. SAS-47 uses the example of an illegal payment of an otherwise immaterial amount which could be material if there is a reasonable possibility that it could lead to a material contingent liability or a material loss of revenue.

OBSERVATION: The example of an illegal payment that might prove to be material to the fair presentation of the financial statements may be particularly relevant for not-for-profit organizations. The negative publicity associated with an illegal act that becomes publicly known may have a significant impact on the not-for-profit organization's ability to raise funds, triggering going-concern considerations that are likely to be more severe than for a commercial enterprise. The impact that such illegal activities might have if they are related to endowment funds also should be considered in light of the not-for-profit organization's potential to retain the endowment funds.

SAS-47 acknowledges that planning an audit to obtain reasonable assurance of detecting misstatements that are believed to be material applies principally to quantitative factors of materiality. It ordinarily is not practical to design audit procedures to obtain reasonable assurance of detecting qualitative factors that might be material to the financial statements. To do so would result in a significant amount of additional time spent on the audit, which could result in audits being unreasonably costly and, as importantly, not timely enough to be optimally useful.

Determining planning materiality for the audit of a not-for-profit organization presents different challenges for an auditor than determining planning materiality for a commercial enterprise. In the audit of a commercial enterprise, a percentage of net income is the most likely starting place to begin determining planning materiality. However, a not-for-profit organization's operations normally are designed to break even. The term *net income* is loosely associated with *changes in net assets*, which normally is budgeted to equal zero. The AICPA Guide provides some general guidance to the auditor. The auditor of a not-for-profit organization may consider materiality from the perspective of the not-for-profit organization's total net assets, various net asset classes, changes in those net asset classes, changes in net asset classes, total revenues, revenues of each net asset class, or total expenses. The auditor also might consider other measures, such as total unrestricted contributions, total program expenses, the ratio of program expenses to total expenses, and the ratio of fund-raising expenses to contributions.

> **OBSERVATION:** The use of the other measures of materiality discussed above reflects some of the unique characteristics of not-for-profit organizations. In the audit of a commercial enterprise, classification of expenses might not be considered as important as in a not-for-profit organization, where classification of expenses as program, general and administrative, and fund-raising is important, reflecting a key need of the readers of these organizations' financial statements.

In planning the audit, the auditor uses his or her judgment to determine materiality levels for each financial statement. Since the financial statements are interrelated, the auditor ordinarily considers materiality for planning purposes in terms of the smallest aggregate level of misstatements that could be considered to be material to any one of the financial statements. For example, if the auditor determines a level of planning materiality for changes in net assets for each of the three classes of net assets—permanently restricted, temporarily restricted, and unrestricted—in the statement of activities and for each of these three classes of net assets on the statement of financial position, the smaller level of materiality would be that which influences the determination of audit risk and the design of an audit strategy.

> **OBSERVATION:** In other words, assume that there is a lower level of materiality for changes in unrestricted net assets in the statement of activities than there is for unrestricted net assets in the statement of financial position. If an auditor is testing general support contributions receivable, the auditor should consider the lower level of materiality for changes in unrestricted net assets when determining audit risk and designing an audit strategy for general support contributions receivable.

The auditor generally is basing quantitative materiality decisions on financial information that is not complete. For example, financial statements may not have been prepared during the time that the auditor is planning the audit engagement. Trial balance information that may be available may have to be significantly adjusted before it supports actual financial statement amounts. In these cases, the auditor should look to other sources to determine materiality amounts. Annualized interim financial statements might be used, although this is often difficult in the not-for-profit organization environment, as described in the discussion of the planning analytical procedures. The auditor also may look to the financial statements of prior periods to estimate the financial statement amounts for the period being audited.

When using estimated financial statement amounts to determine planning materiality, the auditor should compare the estimated amounts with the final amounts to ensure that the estimated amounts provide a reasonable basis. Where significant differences exist, the auditor should determine the effect of these differences on planning materiality to ensure that the appropriate level of audit work was performed to result in an appropriately low level of audit risk. Similarly, if significant additional information comes to the auditor's attention during the course of the audit, he or she should consider whether this additional information would have affected his or her decisions about planning materiality. Accordingly, the auditor may need to assess whether he or she obtained sufficient audit evidence during the audit to result in an appropriately low level of audit risk.

When using planning materiality to design an effective audit approach, the auditor should consider using a dollar amount somewhat less than the actual planning materiality amount in designing audit procedures and sample sizes for individual account balances or classes of transactions. This reduced amount is sometimes referred to as *tolerable error* or *tolerable misstatement*. Tolerable misstatement is the maximum monetary misstatement the auditor can accept at the account balance or class of transactions level without causing the financial statements to be materially misstated. Accordingly, when tolerable misstatement for all balances is combined, it should not exceed planning materiality. In fact, tolerable misstatement is generally set so that when combined, it is substantially less than planning materiality. The tolerable misstatement, for example, might be set at 50 or 75 percent of planning materiality. Using an amount lower than planning materiality in designing testwork and in determining sample sizes will result in the auditor obtaining more audit evidence than if the higher planning materiality amount were used. This will provide for the imprecision inherent in audit tests.

While this might be considered inefficient, in cases where errors are discovered that might require additional audit procedures to be performed, it may prove more efficient to perform some additional procedures or test a few more sample items during the period of time when most of the fieldwork is being performed than to perform these additional procedures during the later stages of the audit. Past experience with the individual client circumstances will provide valuable information about whether a tolerable misstatement amount should be used instead of planning materiality and about the percentage to use if tolerable misstatement is chosen.

Exhibit 3-1 provides a simplified worksheet the auditor may use to document the calculation of planning materiality and tolerable misstatement. The base(s) used for the calculation and the percentages used should be adjusted to reflect the judgments of the auditor relating to the particular client being audited.

Obtaining an Understanding of Internal Control

Auditors are required to consider an organization's internal control in planning and performing audits in accordance with GAAS. A detailed discussion of the considerations that an auditor should make of a not-for-profit organization's internal control for a financial statement audit is provided in the chapter titled "Internal Control Considerations." However, internal control considerations are also a necessary part of the planning of an audit strategy. As part of performing other audit planning procedures, the auditor is obtaining information that will be useful in considering the internal controls of the not-for-profit organization being audited.

The AICPA issued SAS-78 (Consideration of Internal Control in a Financial Statement Audit: An Amendment of SAS-55), which provided a revised definition and description of *internal control* from that originally contained in SAS-55 (Consideration of the Internal Control Structure in a Financial Statement Audit)—to incorporate the definition and description contained in "Internal Controls— Integrated Framework," a report issued by the Committee of Sponsoring Organizations of the Treadway Commission. Complete coverage of the requirements of SAS-78 is provided in the chapter titled "Internal Control Considerations."

EXHIBIT 3-1
PLANNING MATERIALITY CALCULATION WORKSHEET

Name of client: _____

Period of audit: _____

Prepared by: _____ Date _____

Reviewed by:_____ Date _____

General Instructions

This worksheet should be used to calculate planning materiality and, if desired, tolerable misstatements for audits of not-for-profit organizations. This worksheet assumes that an opinion will be issued on the financial statements as a whole. This worksheet should be modified if the audit opinion is to apply to individual classes of net assets and changes in net assets or if the worksheet is to be used to compute materiality for a major program according is subject to the requirements of OMB Circular A-133.

The bases and percentages used on this worksheet should be based on the judgment of the auditor, given the individual circumstances of the entity being audited.

If the audit opinion will be on the consolidated financial information of more than one not-for-profit organization, the amounts used in this worksheet should reflect the consolidated amounts. Any intercompany transactions should be eliminated to reflect the amounts that are estimated to appear in the consolidated financial statements.

Step 1. Materiality calculation based on activities

Base	Amount		Percentage[1]		Materiality Estimate
Total support and revenue	$ _____	x	_____	=	$ _____
Total expenses	_____		_____		_____
Increase in net assets	_____	x	_____	=	_____

Step 2. Materiality calculation based on financial position

Base	Amount		Percentage[1]		Materiality Estimate
Total assets	$ _____	x	_____	=	$ _____
Net assets	_____	x	_____	=	_____

Step 3. Conclusion on planning materiality

Based on the calculations in Steps 1 and 2 above, the range for planning materiality is from $_____ to $_____, and planning materiality is set at $_____.

Step 4. Tolerable misstatement

Tolerable misstatement is the maximum monetary misstatement the auditor can accept at the account balance or class of transactions level without causing the financial statements to be materially misstated. Tolerable misstatement is used in computing sample sizes and in making other decisions regarding the extent of testing. Tolerable misstatement can be computed as follows (common rules of thumb used in practice are to estimate tolerable misstatement as a percentage within 50% to 75% of planning materiality):

Planning Materiality   Percentage   Tolerable
(Amount from Step 3) x (50% to 75%) = Misstatement

$_____   X _____   = _____

---

¹ Use the following table to find the corresponding percentage to be used for calculating the materiality estimate based upon the applicable financial statement amounts:

		Activities			Financial Position	
More than	Equal to or less than	Total support and revenue Use	Total expenses Use	Increase in net assets Use	Total assets Use	Total net assets Use
$0	$50,000	3%	3%	6%	3%	6%
50,000	100,000	2.5%	2.5%	5%	2.5%	5%
100,000	500,000	2%	2%	4%	2%	4%
500,000	1,000,000	1%	1%	2%	1%	2%
1,000,000	5,000,000	.5%	.5%	1%	.5%	1%
5,000,000	10,000,000	.25%	.25%	.5%	.25%	.5%
10,000,000	50,000,000	.20%	.20%	.35%	.20%	.35%
	50,000,000	.1%	.1%	.2%	.1%	.2%

While SAS-78 changed the way auditors consider internal control, auditors will continue to use the guidance of SAS-47 in considering internal control risk, along with inherent risk and detection risk, in planning and performing an audit of financial statements.

After obtaining the understanding described above, the auditor makes an assessment of control risk for the various assertions that are embodied in the account balance, transaction class, and disclosure components of the financial statements. The auditor may assess control risk at the maximum level, which represents the greatest probability that a material misstatement that could occur in an assertion will not be prevented or detected on a timely basis by a not-for-profit organization's internal control. In this case, the auditor believes that the policies and procedures are unlikely to apply to an assertion or are unlikely to be effective. The auditor also may believe that evaluating the effectiveness of the related policies and procedures would not be inefficient.

In other cases, the auditor may believe that the not-for-profit's policies and procedures may be effectively designed and operating to support assessing control risk at below the maximum level for a particular assertion. The auditor may then obtain evidential matter to support his or her assessment of control risk for an assertion at below the maximum level. The evidential matter is obtained from tests of controls, which may be performed at the same time the auditor is obtaining an understanding of the not-for-profit organization's policies and procedures for a particular assertion. Alternatively, the auditor may perform tests of controls concurrently with other tests, such as substantive tests, to improve the efficiency of the audit.

The auditor uses the knowledge obtained by understanding the elements of internal control and the assessed level of control risk to determine the nature, timing, and extent of substantive tests for financial statement assertions.

The AICPA Guide lists considerations an auditor should make that relate specifically to not-for-profit organizations. When obtaining an understanding of the not-for-profit organization's control environment, the auditor should consider the following:

- The role of management and the board of directors
- The frequency of board meetings
- The qualifications of management and board members
- The board members' involvement in the organization's operations
- The organizational structure

The AICPA Guide also lists characteristics that may be found in the four other components of the internal control of a not-for-profit organization that ordinarily would not exist in for-profit entities. It states that the auditor should obtain sufficient knowledge of the organization's accounting system and control procedures to understand how:

- Restricted contributions are identified, evaluated, and accepted.
- Promises to give are valued and recorded.
- Contributed goods, services, utilities, facilities, and the use of long-lived assets are valued and recorded.
- Compliance with donor restrictions and board designations is monitored.

- Reporting requirements imposed by donors, contractors, and regulators are met.
- Conformity with accounting presentation and disclosure principles, including those related to functional and natural expense reporting and allocation of joint costs, is achieved.
- New programs are identified and accounted for.

These considerations are included in the discussion of internal control included in the chapter titled "Internal Control Considerations."

Completing the Initial Audit Risk Assessment and Developing an Audit Strategy

SAS-47 provides guidance on an auditor's consideration of audit risk (and materiality) when planning and performing an audit of financial statements in accordance with GAAS. The auditor needs to consider audit risk, together with materiality, when determining the nature, timing, and extent of audit procedures and the evaluation of those procedures.

SAS-47 defines *audit risk* as "the risk that the auditor may unknowingly fail to appropriately modify his opinion on financial statements that are materially misstated. According to SAS-47, financial statements are materially misstated when "they contain misstatements whose effect, individually or in the aggregate, is important enough to cause them not to be presented fairly, in all material respects, in conformity with generally accepted accounting principles."

SAS-47 clarifies some important considerations for an auditor performing an audit in accordance with GAAS. The auditor should recognize that there is an inverse relationship between audit risk and materiality. For example, there is usually a lower risk that an account balance is misstated by a very large amount and a higher risk that an account balance is misstated by a very small amount. The auditor must consider this relationship when evaluating the information gathered during the fieldwork stage of the audit and must compare it to the relationship the auditor thought would exist during the planning phase of the audit.

An auditor should not be willing to accept more audit risk than that established during audit planning for a particular account because he or she discovered an increase in risk as a result of auditing other account balances. The auditor must either accept a higher level of materiality (i.e., be willing to accept a larger misstatement of the account balances) or perform additional or different audit procedures to reduce the audit risk for the account balance to what the auditor originally had planned.

The auditor needs to evaluate audit risk at the account balance (or class of transactions) level to appropriately design and evaluate audit procedures that will lead to an acceptable level of risk for the entire engagement. Beyond that, the auditor must evaluate audit risk for the assertions relative to each account balance or class of transactions.

For example, when assessing audit risk, the auditor may be willing to accept a level of audit risk that pledges receivable are properly valued that is different than the acceptable audit risk that cash is properly valued. A fuller discussion on how to make these assessments is provided below.

SAS-47 provides guidance for evaluating the components of audit risk. Audit risk consists of two components: (1) the risk that the account balance or class of transactions is materially misstated and (2) the risk that the procedures performed by the auditor will not detect the misstatement.

The first component of audit risk is further divided into two risks: (1) inherent risk and (2) control risk. The second component of audit risk (the risk that the auditor will not detect the misstatement) is referred to as detection risk.

The following are definitions of the three individual, independent risks that comprise audit risk:

Inherent risk The susceptibility of an assertion to a material misstatement, assuming that there are no related internal control structure policies and procedures. The risk of such misstatement is greater for some assertions and related balances or classes than for others.

Control risk The risk that a material misstatement that could occur in an assertion will not be prevented or detected on a timely basis by the entity's internal control policies or procedures. That risk is a function of the effectiveness of the design and operation of internal control policies and procedures in achieving the entity's broad internal control objectives relevant to an audit of the entity's financial statements. Some control risk will always exist because of the inherent limitations of any internal control.

Detection risk The risk that the auditor will not detect a material misstatement that exists in an assertion. Detection risk is a function of the effectiveness of an auditing procedure and of its application by the auditor. It arises partly from uncertainties that exist when the auditor does not examine 100 percent of an account balance or class of transactions and partly because of other uncertainties that exist even if the auditor were to examine 100 percent of the balance or class. Such other uncertainties arise because an auditor might select an inappropriate auditing procedure, misapply an appropriate procedure, or misinterpret the audit results.

> **OBSERVATION:** In other words, detection risk would not be completely eliminated even if the auditor tested all of the items in a population. The risk that the auditor will not perform the audit procedures correctly or that the audit procedures are not properly designed to identify an error remains.

The auditor should ensure that the audit strategy he or she employs will result in an appropriately low level of risk for his or her audit of financial statements in accordance with GAAS. This includes an assessment of the risk that the financial statements will be materially misstated because of violations of laws and regulations that have a direct and material effect on the determination of financial statement amounts.

The auditor begins to design an audit strategy by assessing control risk for each of the assertions inherent in the financial statements and the detail accounts. *Assertions* are defined by SAS-31 (Evidential Matter) as:

> Representations by management that are embodied in the financial statement components. They can be either explicit or implicit and can be classified according to the following broad categories:
>
> - Existence or occurrence
> - Completeness
> - Rights and obligations
> - Valuation or allocation
> - Presentation and disclosure

An auditor designs an audit strategy to obtain sufficient competent evidential matter for each of management's assertions about the financial statements of the not-for-profit organization. To obtain evidence relevant to the assertions, the auditor must develop audit objectives for each material account and class of transactions and then design audit procedures to obtain the evidence that will enable him or her to meet those audit objectives. These audit procedures will be compiled into an audit program, which will guide the auditor's performance of procedures throughout the audit and will ensure that the audit objectives for each assertion for all material accounts and classes of transactions are met.

When determining the audit procedures, the auditor must assess audit risk for *each* assertion relative to *each* material account and class of transactions. To do so, the auditor uses the three components of audit risk: inherent risk, control risk, and detection risk.

Inherent Risk

For inherent risk, the auditor assesses the susceptibility of each assertion to material misstatement. To illustrate, the auditor's assessment of the assertion for the existence of cash is quite different from the assessment of the existence of a building. The rights of the holder of a $100 bill are fairly clear—the holder of the bill is likely the owner of the bill and has the right to the bill. On the other hand, the occupant of a building may not be its owner. The building may be leased, or there may be liens against the building that preclude the named owner of the building from having clear title.

To assess audit risk properly, the auditor should determine the inherent risk for each assertion for each material account balance and class of transactions. This can be a difficult and cumbersome task. However, to be in compliance with SAS-47, the auditor should consider the requirements carefully and adequately document the action taken.

SAS-47 does not specify the underlying components of inherent risk, but the auditor should consider the following factors when making assessments of inherent risk for assertions for account balances and classes of transactions:

- *Size and volume of transactions* The size and the number of similar transactions affect inherent risk. Large transactions generally have a higher level of inherent risk than smaller transactions because of the larger financial statement impact that the larger transactions will have. Also, a higher volume of transactions generally indicates a higher inherent risk. If a large number of transactions are not recorded properly, there is a greater risk that the financial statements will be misstated.

- *Complexity of the transactions* Transactions that are complex and require a high degree of sophistication to record will have a higher inherent risk than simpler transactions.

- *Susceptibility to theft or fraud* Accounts that are subject to fraud or theft (such as an asset that is vulnerable to theft or an account payable that can be created for a fictitious vendor) carry a higher inherent risk than accounts that are not subject to the same susceptibility (such as land and buildings owned by the not-for-profit organization).

- *Prior-period misstatements* Accounts or classes of transactions that required significant adjustments in prior years' audits have a higher level of inherent risk than accounts or classes of transactions that required only few or minor adjustments in prior years' audits.

- *Competence of client personnel* The auditor should evaluate the competency of the client personnel responsible for recording the transactions for an account or class of transactions. If prior experience or other observations indicate that individuals recording transactions for an account or class of transactions are doing so accurately, this is an indication of lower inherent risk. If the auditor expects problems with the work of certain client individuals or is suspect of their judgment, then a higher level of inherent risk is indicated.

- *Degree of judgment required*   Some accounts or classes of transactions require more judgment in their recording than others. The more judgment that is required on the part of the client personnel in recording a transaction, the higher the level of inherent risk that is indicated.

Control Risk

The second component of audit risk is control risk—the risk that a material misstatement could occur and not be prevented or detected by the not-for-profit organization's internal control on a timely basis. Again, the auditor must assess control risk for each assertion as it relates to each material account balance and class of transactions.

Based on his or her understanding of the internal control of the not-for-profit organization, the auditor may choose to assess control risk at the maximum level for each assertion as it relates to material account balances and classes of transactions. The auditor may believe that the controls in place are inadequate or are not being performed effectively. The auditor also may believe that it would be more efficient to assess control risk at the maximum and increase the amount of substantive test work that is performed. This has the effect of decreasing the amount of detection risk, enabling the auditor to assess control risk at the maximum level while still maintaining an acceptable level of audit risk.

If the auditor's initial understanding of the internal control indicates that controls are properly designed and are being properly performed, the auditor may choose to assess control risk below the maximum. Assessing control risk below maximum allows the auditor to accept a greater level of detection risk and to perform less substantive test work.

Detection Risk

Finally, detection risk must be determined for each assertion for each material account balance or class of transactions. This determination is made, as described above, by the auditor's consideration of the assessment of inherent risk and control risk for each assertion for each material account balance and class of transactions. Detection risk must be at an appropriate level so that when it is considered together with inherent risk and control risk, an appropriately low level of audit risk is obtained for each assertion, for each account balance or class of transactions. The auditor's determination of planning materiality is also a consideration in determining detection risk.

Audit Strategy

After assessing audit risk and its three components for all assertions, the auditor develops an overall audit strategy. This includes determining audit objectives for the significant account balances and classes of transactions and incorporating the risk-assessment decisions into the design of audit procedures.

The audit procedures developed are clearly affected by the audit strategy. For example, if the auditor chooses to assess control risk at below the maximum level, the audit program will have to reflect the test work the auditor performs on the internal control procedures. Conversely, if the auditor chooses to assess control risk at the maximum level, the audit program will have to include enough substantive test work for the auditor to obtain sufficient evidence about the account balances or classes of transactions and thus reduce detection risk to an acceptable level.

Documentation

Documentation of the audit risk assessments described above can be quite cumbersome. Documentation should include for each significant account balance or class of transactions the following assessments:

- *Inherent risk* Indicate whether inherent risk is high, moderate, or low for each of the assertions:
  - Existence or occurrence
  - Completeness
  - Rights and obligations
  - Valuation or allocation
  - Presentation and disclosure
- *Control risk* Indicate whether control risk is maximum, moderate, or minimum for each of the assertions:
  - Existence or occurrence
  - Completeness
  - Rights and obligations

— Valuation or allocation

— Presentation and disclosure

- *Detection risk*   Indicate whether detection risk is high, moderate, or low for each of the assertions:

— Existence or occurrence

— Completeness

— Rights and obligations

— Valuation or allocation

— Presentation and disclosure

When making these assessments, the auditor must make sure that there is an internal consistency among the three risk assessments. For example, if control risk is assessed at the maximum level for an assertion of an account balance, one ordinarily would expect the detection risk for that assertion to be assessed as high. If it is not, documentation in the working papers should clarify such apparent inconsistencies.

Exhibit 3-2 provides an example of a worksheet for documenting the assessment of inherent risk for the assertions of a particular account balance or class of transactions. Exhibit 3-3 provides an example or a worksheet for summarizing the assessments of risk for the various assertions relating to a particular account balance or class of transactions.

Consideration of Fraud in a Financial Statement Audit

In January 1997, the AICPA issued Statement on Auditing Standards No. 82 (Consideration of Fraud in a Financial Statement Audit). SAS-82 provides important guidance and requirements for auditors in considering the existence of fraud in an audit of financial statements performed in accordance with generally accepted auditing standards.

Auditors have always been responsible for detecting material misstatements of financial statements, even when caused by errors or fraud. This concept was refined somewhat by SAS-54 (Illegal Acts by Clients) for illegal acts which have a direct and material effect on financial statements. SAS-82 expanded the concept of the auditor's responsibility for considering fraud which could result in a material misstatement of financial statements, by providing:

- A description of fraud and its characteristics

- A requirement that auditors assess the risk of material misstatement due to fraud. SAS-82 provides categories of fraud risk factors to be considered in the auditors' assessment.

EXHIBIT 3-2
INHERENT RISK ASSESSMENT WORKSHEET

Name of client: _____

Period of audit: _____

Account balance(s)/Class(es) of transactions: _____

Prepared by: _____ Date _____

Reviewed by:_____ Date _____

This worksheet should be used to document the assessment of inherent risk for the account balance(s) or class(es) indicated above. For each of the factors below (and any other risk factors that are considered relevant in the circumstances) indicate an assessment of inherent risk as High, Moderate, or Low. After completing this process, assess inherent risk for this account balance or class of transactions for each of the financial statement assertions listed below.

		High	*Moderate*	*Low*
1.	Size and volume of transactions			
2.	Consistency of activity through-out the year			
3.	Complexity of transactions			
4.	Types of misstatements that might occur			
5.	Misstatement due to fraud			
6.	Competency of related client personnel			
7.	Degree of judgment required			
8.	Prior-year audit findings			
9.	Other			

Based on the assessments made above, conclude on the assessment of inherent risk for each of the financial statement assertions listed below:

		High	*Moderate*	*Low*
1.	Existence or occurrence			
2.	Completeness			

	High	Moderate	Low
3. Rights and obligations	_____	_____	_____
4. Valuation or allocation	_____	_____	_____
5. Presentation and disclosure	_____	_____	_____

Describe below (if applicable) any additional considerations made in this inherent risk assessment:

_____

_____

_____

EXHIBIT 3-3
AUDIT RISK PLANNING SUMMARY WORKSHEET

Name of client: _____

Period of audit: _____

Account balance(s)/Class(es) of transactions: _____

Prepared by: _____   Date _____

Reviewed by:_____   Date _____

General Instructions

The purpose of this worksheet is to summarize the planned levels of risk of the three components of audit risk—inherent risk, control risk, and detection risk—made during the planning phase of the audit. These planned levels of risk are the basis of the audit strategy designed for the above listed account balance(s) or class(es) of transactions. If during the course of the audit, any of the planned risk levels must be changed, the change also should be documented on this form. The effect the change had on the audit procedures to be performed should be described.

Use the following as a key for indicating the planned levels of risk:

H = High or maximum

M = Moderate

L = Low or minimum

Planning Risk Assessment

Indicate below the planned levels of each of the three components of audit risk made during the planning phase of the audit of the above listed not-for-profit organization

Assertion:	Inherent	Control	Detection
1. Existence or occurrence	_____	_____	_____
2. Completeness	_____	_____	_____
3. Rights and obligations	_____	_____	_____
4. Valuation or allocation	_____	_____	_____
5. Presentation and disclosure	_____	_____	_____

Changes in Risk Assessment

Indicate below *only the changes in the planned levels of each of the three components that changed during the course of the audit* (if applicable).

If there were no changes in the initial planned levels of risk, check "Not Applicable" below to indicate that the assessment made during the planning phase of the audit did not change during the course of the audit as a result of audit evidence obtained.

Assertion:	Inherent	Control	Detection
1. Existence or occurrence	_____	_____	_____
2. Completeness	_____	_____	_____
3. Rights and obligations	_____	_____	_____
4. Valuation or allocation	_____	_____	_____
5. Presentation and disclosure	_____	_____	_____

For any changes indicated, provide a brief explanation below for the reason for the change, indicate the change in any audit procedures performed, and provide a cross-reference to any additional audit procedures performed.

_____

_____

_____

_____

- Guidance on how the auditor should respond to the results of the assessments
- Guidance on the evaluation of audit test results as they related to the risk of material misstatement due to fraud
- Documentation requirements
- Guidance regarding the auditor's communication about fraud to management, the audit committee, and others

The following sections describe SAS-82's guidance on each of these topics. In addition, checklists have been included based on SAS-82's guidance which are provided in the practice aids section of this Guide.

Description and Characteristics of Fraud

There are two types of misstatements that are important to an auditor's consideration of fraud in a financial statement audit:

1. Misstatements arising from fraudulent financial reporting refer to intentional misstatements or omissions from financial statements that may involve the following:

   — Manipulation, falsification, or alteration of accounting records or supporting documents from which financial statements are prepared

   — Misrepresentation in, or intentional omission from, the financial statements of events, transactions, or other significant information

   — Intentional misapplication of accounting principles relating to amounts, classification, manner of presentation, or disclosures

2. Misstatements arising from misappropriation of assets involve the theft of a not-for-profit organization's assets where the effect of the theft causes the financial statements not to be presented in accordance with generally accepted accounting principles

Both of these types of fraud are likely to be accompanied by falsification of documentation or collusion with other individuals to hide the fraud. Given this, auditors cannot obtain absolute assurance that they will detect all fraud that may materially misstate the financial statements. Rather, auditors will obtain reasonable assurance that material misstatements, including misstatements resulting from fraud, are detected.

Assessment of the Risk of Material Misstatement Due to Fraud

The most important aspect of SAS-82 is that it requires auditors to assess the risk of material misstatements of financial statements that may result both from fraudulent financial reporting and from misappropriation of assets. An auditor should assess this risk as he or she would assess the other components of audit risk—inherent, control, and detection risks—as part of the audit planning process. An auditor may choose to assess the risk of material misstatement due to fraud separately from the other components of audit risk. However, SAS-82 acknowledges that the risk of misstatement due to fraud is combined with inherent risk and control risk. Therefore, SAS-82 permits the auditor to elect to assess the risk of misstatement due to fraud as a component of both inherent and control risks. This is the preferred approach, since logically the risk of misstatement due to fraud is part of inherent risk and control risk.

OBSERVATION: The inherent risk and control risk assessment practice aids in this Guide have been updated to include the considerations of the fraud risk factors contained in SAS-82. In addition, a Fraud Risk Assessment Worksheet (Exhibit 3-4) has been included. The model audit programs have also been updated to reflect these required considerations, including inquiries of management as to their assessment of the risk of fraud. Using these updated practice aids will assist the auditor in complying with the requirements of SAS-82.

SAS-82 makes the auditor's consideration of the risk of misstatement due to fraud broad and not specific, requiring considerable judgment on the part of the auditor. For example, one of the fraud risk factors concerns individual employee financial stress. Logically, a financially stressed employee is more likely to misappropriate assets than an employee who is not financially stressed. However, SAS-82 does not require the auditor to evaluate the financial condition of all of a not-for-profit organization's employees. Rather, such information obtained in the course of the regular audit may make this fraud risk factor more important than it would otherwise be. For example, if there was a high expectation that the organization was going to lay employees off in the near future, the auditor might presume financial stress.

The auditor should consider fraud risk factors continuously, not just in the planning phase of the audit. SAS-82 states that identification of fraud risk factors should occur while the auditor is performing client acceptance/retention procedures, during engagement planning, and while obtaining an understanding of internal controls, while conducting field work.

SAS-82 identifies some examples of conditions identified during field work that might support or change a judgment regarding the assessment of the risk of misstatement due to fraud. These examples are:

Discrepancies in the Accounting Records

- Transactions not recorded in a complete or timely manner or improperly recorded as to amount, accounting period, classification, or entity policy.
- Unsupported or unauthorized balances or transactions.
- Last-minute adjustments by the entity that significantly affect financial results.

Conflicting or Missing Evidential Matter

- Missing documents.
- Unavailability of other than photocopied documents when documents in original form are expected to exist.
- Significant unexplained items on reconciliations.

EXHIBIT 3-4
FRAUD RISK ASSESSMENT WORKSHEET

Name of Client: _____

Period of Audit: _____

Prepared by: _____ Date: _____

Reviewed by:_____ Date: _____

General Instructions

This worksheet is designed to assist the auditor in assessing the risk of material misstatement of the financial statements due to fraud in accordance with Statement on Auditing Standards No. 82, "Consideration of Fraud in a Financial Statement Audit" (SAS-82). The auditor should consider the results of this assessment as part of the inherent risk and control risk assessment in planning the audit of the financial statements.

For each fraud risk factor, the auditor should assess whether this risk factor exists for the particular client being audited. The auditor should than determine whether the planned audit procedures are sufficient to address each risk factor identified or whether audit procedures should be expanded to address the risk factors.

In addition, the auditor should determine if there are other fraud risk factors that should be considered and should update the fraud risk assessment throughout the audit to ensure that the results of the audit procedures support the initial assessment of the risk of material misstatement of the financial statements due to fraud.

Indicate below whether there was any change in the fraud risk assessment during the audit and the affect on audit procedures (if any) of the change in the assessment:

Did the fraud risk assessment change during the course of the audit? Yes_____ No_____

If yes, complete page 9 of this worksheet, indicating the change in the risk assessment and the effect on audit procedures.

Risk Factors Relating to Misstatements Arising from Fraudulent Financial Report

Management's Characteristics and Influence Over the Control Environment

	Risk Factor Present	Planned Audit Procedures Adequate	Additional Audit Procedures Required	Cross-Reference to Additional Audit Procedures
1. Motivation for management to engage in fraudulent financial reporting, including:				
a. Significant portion of management's compensation includes bonuses or other incentives, the value of which is contingent upon the organization achieving unduly aggressive targets for operating results, financial position or cash flow.			___	___
b. Excessive interest by management to maintain the organization's operating results or key performance ratios through the use of unusually aggressive accounting practices.			___	___
c. A practice by management of committing to analysts, creditors, and other third parties in what appears to be unduly aggressive or clearly unrealistic forecasts.			___	___
d. An interest by management to pursue inappropriate means to minimize reported results for regulatory or tax purposes (e.g., maintaining tax-exempt status or underreporting un-related business income).			___	___

2. Failure by management to display and communicate an appropriate attitude regarding internal control and the financial reporting process, including:

   a. An ineffective means of communicating and supporting the organization's values or ethics, or communicating inappropriate values or ethics.

   b. Domination of management by a single person or a small group without compensating controls, such as effective oversight by the board of directors or audit committee.

   c. Inadequate monitoring of significant controls.

   d. Management's failure to correct known reportable conditions on a timely basis.

   e. Management setting unduly aggressive financial targets and expectations for operating personnel.

   f. Management displaying a significant disregard for regulatory authority.

   g. Management continuing to employ ineffective accounting, information technology, or internal auditing staff.

3. Nonfinancial management's excessive participation in, or preoccupation with, the selection of accounting principles or the determination of significant estimates.

4. High turnover of senior management, counsel, or board members.

5. Strained relationship between management and the current or predecessor auditor, including:

   a. Frequent disputes with the current or predecessor auditor on accounting, auditing, or reporting matters.

	Risk Factor Present	Planned Audit Procedures Adequate	Additional Audit Procedures Required	Cross-Reference to Additional Audit Procedures
b. Unreasonable demands on the auditor, including unreasonable time constraints for completing the audit or the issuance of the auditor's reports.				
c. Formal or informal restrictions on the auditor that inappropriately limit his or her access to people or information or his or her ability to communicate effectively with the board of directors or the audit committee.				
d. Domineering behavior by management when dealing with the auditor, especially involving attempts to influence the scope of the auditor's work.				
6. Known history of securities or other law violations, or claims against the organization or its senior management alleging fraud or violations of such laws.				

Risk Factors Relating to Industry Conditions

	Risk Factor Present	Planned Audit Procedures Adequate	Additional Audit Procedures Required	Cross-Reference to Additional Audit Procedures
7. New accounting, statutory, or regulatory requirements that could impair the financial stability or operations of the organization.				
8. High degree of competition or market saturation and declining operating margins, including:				
a. Demand for the services of the organization.				

b. Competition for contributions or other sources of funding. |___|___|___|

9. Declining industry or field with increasing organization failures and significant declines in service user demands. |___|___|___|

10. Rapid changes in the field, such as high vulnerability to rapidly changing technology or rapid service obsolescence. |___|___|___|

Risk Factors Relating to Operating Characteristics and Financial Stability

11. Inability to generate cash flows from operations while reporting increases in net assets from operations. |___|___|___|

12. Significant pressure to obtain additional capital considering the financial position of the entity, including need for funds to finance major research and development or capital expenditures. |___|___|___|

13. Assets, liabilities, revenues, or expenses are based on significant estimates that involve unusually subjective judgment or uncertainties, or that are subject to potential significant change in the near term in a manner that may have a financially disruptive effect on the organization, such as ultimate collectibility of receivables, timing of revenue recognition, realizability of financial instruments based on the highly subjective valuation of collateral or difficult-to-assess repayment sources, or significant deferral of costs. |___|___|___|

14. Significant related-party transactions that are not in the ordinary course of business or with related organizations not audited or audited by another firm. |___|___|___|

15. Significant, unusual, or highly complex transactions, especially

	Risk Factor Present	Planned Audit Procedures Adequate	Additional Audit Procedures Required	Cross-Reference to Additional Audit Procedures
those close to year end, that pose difficult "substance over form" questions.				
16. Significant bank accounts or subsidiary or branch operations in jurisdictions for where there appears to be no clear business justification.				
17. Overly complex organizational structure involving numerous or unusual legal entities, managerial lines of authority, or contractual arrangements without apparent business purpose.				
18. Difficulty in determining the organization that or individual(s) who controls the organization.				
19. Unusually rapid growth and positive operating results, especially compared with that of other organizations in the same field.				
20. Especially high vulnerability to changes in interest rates.				
21. Unusually high dependence on debt or marginal ability to meet debt repayment requirements; debt covenants that are difficult to maintain.				
22. Unrealistically aggressive fund-raising or results-oriented in-centive programs.				
23. Threat of imminent bankruptcy or foreclosure.				

24. Adverse consequences on significant pending transactions, such as a contract award or business combination, if poor financial results are reported.

25. Poor or deteriorating financial position when management has personally guaranteed significant debts of the organization.

Risk Factors Relating to Misstatements Arising from Misappropriation of Assets

Risk Factors Relating to Susceptibility of Assets to Misappropriation

26. Large amounts of cash on hand or processed.

27. Inventory characteristics, such as small size, high value, or high demand.

28. Easily convertible assets, such as bearer bonds, works of art or historical treasures, or computer chips.

29. Fixed asset characteristics, such as small size, marketability, or lack of ownership identification.

Risk Factors Relating to Controls

30. Lack of appropriate management oversight (e.g., inadequate supervision or monitoring of remote locations).

31. Lack of job applicant screening procedures for employees with access to assets susceptible to misappropriation.

32. Inadequate record keeping with respect to assets susceptible to misappropriation.

	Risk Factor Present	Planned Audit Procedures Adequate	Additional Audit Procedures Required	Cross-Reference to Additional Audit Procedures
33. Lack of appropriate segregation of duties or independent checks.				
34. Lack of appropriate system of authorization and approval of transactions (e.g., in purchasing).				
35. Poor physical safeguards over cash, investments, inventory, or fixed assets.				
36. Lack of timely and appropriate documentation for transactions.				
37. Lack of mandatory vacations for employees performing key control functions.				

Changes in Fraud Risk Misstatement

During the course of the audit, it may come to the auditor's attention that additional fraud risk factors exist or that the auditor's assessment of fraud risk factors needs adjusting. Other conditions may be identified during field work that change or support a judgment regarding the assessment. Consider the following:

Condition	Change in Risk Factor?
1. Transactions not recorded in a complete or timely manner or improperly recorded as to amount, accounting period, classification, or organization policy.	_____
2. Unsupported or unauthorized balances or transactions.	_____
3. Last-minute adjustments by the organization that significantly affect financial results.	_____
4. Missing documents.	_____
5. Only photocopied documents are available when original documents are expected to exist.	_____
6. Significant unexplained items on reconciliations.	_____
7. Inconsistent, vague, or implausible responses from management or employees to inquiries or analytical procedures.	_____
8. Unusual discrepancies between the organization's records and confirmation replies.	_____
9. Missing inventory or physical assets of significant magnitude.	_____
10. Denied access to records, facilities, certain employees, customers, vendors, or others from whom audit evidence might be sought.	_____
11. Undue time pressures imposed by management to resolve complex or contentious issues.	_____
12. Unusual delays by the organization in providing requested information.	_____
13. Tips or complaints to the auditor about fraud.	_____
14. Other conditions. _____	

Effect of the above, or other conditions, on the assessment of the risk of fraud

Nature of fraud risk factor _____

Describe condition _____

Effect on Audit Procedures _____

Resolution _____

- Inconsistent, vague, or implausible responses from management or employees arising from inquiries or analytical procedures.
- Unusual discrepancies between the entity's records and confirmation replies.
- Missing inventory or physical assets of significant magnitude.

Problematic or Unusual Relationships Between the Auditor and Client

- Denied access to records, certain employees, customers, vendors, or others from whom audit evidence might be sought.
- Undue time pressures imposed by management to resolve complex or contentious issues.
- Unusual delays by the entity in providing requested information.
- Tips or complaints to the auditor about fraud.

The Auditor's Response to the Results of the Assessment

After the auditor considers the risk factors involved in misstatement of financial statements due to fraud (as updated by additional evidence obtained throughout the course of the audit), the auditor must determine whether the audit procedures he or she has performed adequately address the risks of fraud that have been identified. The auditor may find that the risk of fraud is such that the procedures normally performed in an audit of financial statements (i.e., prior to the applicability of SAS-82) are adequate to address the risks of fraud identified using the guidance of SAS-82. On the other hand, the auditor may determine that the risks of fraud he or she has identified require modification of the planned audit approach to adequately address those risks.

SAS-82 describes these modifications in an audit approach as either modifications in overall considerations or modifications in considerations at the account balance, class of transactions, or assertion level.

The effect on overall considerations from judgments about the risk of material misstatements due to fraud are described by SAS-82 as follows:

- *Professional skepticism* Including increased sensitivity in the selection of the nature and extent of documentation to be examined that supports material transactions and an increased need to corroborate management explanations or representations concerning material matters.
- *Assignment of personnel* Including the knowledge and skill levels of the personnel assigned to the audit and the extent of their supervision.
- *Accounting practices and policies* Including further consideration of management's selection and implementation of the organization's accounting policies.
- *Controls* Including consideration that some fraud risk factors that affect controls may affect the auditor's ability to assess control risk below the maximum level. If the auditor is not assessing control risk below the maximum level, the existence of control-related fraud factors may emphasize the importance of the auditor's understanding and considering any controls that the entity has in place to address the identified fraud risk factors. In addition, an increased sensitivity to management's ability to override controls may be appropriate.
- *Nature, timing, and extent of audit procedures* Including some of the following examples:
  — *Nature* More evidential matter may be needed from independent sources.
  — *Timing* More substantive audit procedures may need to be performed at or near year end than would otherwise have been performed.
  — *Extent* Increased sample sizes or more extensive analytical procedures may be needed than would otherwise have been performed.

SAS-82 also addresses the effect of the fraud risk factors on considerations at the account balance, class of transaction, and assertion levels. If fraud risk factors indicate a particular risk applicable to specific account balances or types of transactions, audit procedures should be considered that will limit audit risk to an appropriate level in light of the risk factors identified.

SAS-82 also includes guidance on the evaluation of audit test results, documentation of the auditor's risk assessment and response, and communication about fraud to management, the audit committee, and others. This guidance has been incorporated into the appropriate topics in this Guide.

Considering the Impact of the Year 2000 Issue on the Audit of the Not-for-Profit Organization

Not-for-profit organizations and their auditors must be aware of the potential impact of the Year 2000 Issue on the operations of the organization. Initial concerns about the impact of the Year 2000 Issue focused on mainframe computer systems whose software coded years as two digits (with the year 2000 thus being interpreted as the year "00," resulting in obvious problems with program logic wherever a date is encountered). As the problem has been further studied and analyzed, a high level of concern has developed that the Year 2000 Issue may have much broader impact on all organizations, including not-for-profit organizations. Effects on computerized systems, including individuals' personal computers and computers that are part of a local area network, must be considered along with the effects the problem may have on other systems that utilize some type of computer chip—telephone systems, fax and photocopier machines, medical devices used at healthcare facilities, etc. The impact of the Year 2000 Issue on third parties with which the not-for-profit organization interacts—such as donors (particularly major donors), vendors, banks and other financial institutions, and office space providers—may also have a significant effect.

> **OBSERVATION:** The following discussion of the Year 2000 Issue is carried forward from last year's edition of the Guide. While auditors will be using the current edition of the Guide subsequent to January 1, 2000, the discussion is included because many aspects of the Year 2000 Issue may take several months or more to become apparent. Therefore, auditors should continue to use this guidance, as appropriately modified for audits performed during the year 2000.

The AICPA has issued a report titled *The Year 2000 Issue—Current Accounting and Auditing Guidance* (the "Year 2000 Report") to assist financial statement preparers and auditors in handling the Year 2000 Issue when auditing financial statements. The document was prepared by a task force of practitioners in public practice and staff of the AICPA. Although it is not an authoritative document, it is an excellent resource (with references to relevant authoritative documents) that auditors will find invaluable in their handling of the Year 2000 Issue. It is available for downloading at the AICPA's web site (www.aicpa.org/members/y2000/index.htm). The report covers accounting and auditing issues for both public and nonpublic entities. The following discussion focuses on the guidance the document provides for nonpublic entities.

Accounting Issues

The Year 2000 Report addresses several accounting issues regarding the Year 2000 Issue that financial statement preparers should consider:

- Accounting for the costs of addressing the Year 2000 Issue (External and internal costs specifically associated with modifying internal-use software for the Year 2000 Issue should be expensed as incurred.)
- Revenue and loss recognition for software developers, such as the timing of revenue recognition as well as product warranty, product defect liability, and product return liability
- Impairment issues for inventories of hardware devices that are not Year 2000 ready, as well as the possible impairment of fixed assets containing software or hardware components, and for capitalized costs of software developed or obtained for internal use if that software has not been modified to be Year 2000 ready
- Disclosures under SOP 94-6 (Disclosures of Certain Significant Risks and Uncertainties), such as impairment or amortization of capitalized software costs, inventory valuation, long-term contract accounting, warranty reserves, reserves for sales returns and allowances, or litigation, if it is reasonably possible that the amounts in the financial statements could change by a material amount within one year from the date of the financial statements (based on the facts and circumstances existing at the date of the financial statements)

Auditing Issues

The Year 2000 Report also discusses several auditing Interpretations the AICPA has issued that address the Year 2000 problem. Below is a list of these auditing Interpretations, with some of their more important points noted:

- Interpretation of SAS-22 (Planning and Supervision)

  The auditor's responsibility relates to the detection of material misstatements of the financial statements being audited, whether the misstatements are the result of the Year 2000 Issue or have some other cause.

  — An auditor does not have a responsibility to detect current or future effects of the Year 2000 Issue on operational matters that do not affect the entity's' ability to prepare financial statements in accordance with GAAP or an other comprehensive basis of accounting.

— An audit of financial statements conducted in accordance with GAAS does not contemplate that the auditor would need to assess whether data processing errors caused by the Year 2000 Issue could result in material misstatements of financial statements in periods subsequent to the period being audited.

— If an auditor becomes aware that an entity's computer programs that currently process data correctly will not process data correctly for future financial statements, this weakness should not be considered a reportable condition.

OBSERVATION: The AICPA guidance seeks to make clear that the auditor has limited responsibility for Year 2000 issues. Auditors of not-for-profit organizations are likely to encounter boards of directors who believe that the auditor's role is much greater—namely, that the auditor should provide assurance that the organization is or will be Year 2000 compliant. The auditor would be well served by making sure that both the oversight board of directors and the organization's management understand the auditor's responsibilities.

• Interpretation of SAS-59 (The Auditor's Consideration of an Entity's Ability to Continue as a Going Concern)

The Year 2000 Issue can cause conditions and events that, when considered in the aggregate, indicate there could be substantial doubt about an entity's ability to continue as a going concern. These conditions and events may be in one or more of the following categories:

— *Noncompliant computer systems* System failures or processing errors cause a condition or an event if they currently have a significant adverse financial effect on an entity or are expected to have such an effect within a reasonable period of time.

— *Actions of others affecting the entity* Because of the entity's Year 2000 compliance status, customers, vendors, lenders, insurers, regulators, or other third parties cease to do business with the entity, refuse to extend financing, demand accelerated loan payments, or take significant regulatory actions against the entity.

— *Problems of customers, vendors, and service providers* Significant customers stop purchasing from, vendors stop selling to, or service providers stop providing services to an entity because of these outside parties' own Year 2000 compliance problems.

— *Related costs* Year 2000–related remediation costs, asset impairments, or other loss provisions are of such magnitude that they cause violations of existing loan covenants or otherwise cause severe financial difficulties.

The auditor does not have a responsibility to plan and perform procedures solely to identify conditions and events relating to the Year 2000 Issue. If such conditions and events do come to the auditor's attention, the auditor should consider these in the aggregate regarding the organization's ability to continue as a going concern. If there is substantial doubt about the organization's ability to continue as a going concern for a reasonable period as a result of the Year 2000 Issue, the auditor should consider management's plans for dealing with the adverse effects of these conditions and events. The auditor should plan and perform procedures, including using the work of a specialist, to obtain evidential matter about those elements of the plan that are particularly significant. In these circumstances, if management does not have a plan, the absence of such a plan would ordinarily result in the auditor concluding that such doubt about the organization's ability to continue as a going concern is not alleviated.

The auditing Interpretation indicates that the following elements of management's Year 2000 remediation plan are particularly significant:

— Identification of mission-critical systems (including related hardware and software that are not Year 2000 compliant)

— Identification of products being sold that contain noncompliant components or of services being provided using noncompliant resources

— The dates on which mission-critical systems are expected to fail

— The dates by which mission-critical systems are expected to be Year 2000 compliant

— Plans for replacing or remediating and testing mission-critical systems

— Contingency plans for addressing situations where mission-critical systems are not expected to be Year 2000 compliant before failure resulting from the arrival of the year 2000

— Procedures for identifying hardware and software failures that may occur

— Plans for identifying significant customers, vendors, and service providers that may be unable to purchase from, supply, or provide service to the organization as a result of their own Year 2000 compliance problems, and plans for minimizing the effects on the organization

— Identification of regulatory requirements for reporting Year 2000 compliance efforts

— Procedures for monitoring and evaluating the progress of remediation efforts, including timetables and resource requirements, and for taking any necessary corrective action if established schedules are not met.

Exhibit 3-5 is a checklist that an auditor may use in evaluating management's Year 2000 remediation plans. The checklist incorporates the elements listed above.

The auditing Interpretation makes several other very important points about the auditor's responsibilities regarding the Year 2000 Issue. First, an audit conducted in accordance with GAAS does not provide assurance as to whether an entity will be Year 2000 compliant. Second, procedures performed on management's remediation plans might include making inquiries, reading reports about Year 2000 remediation efforts, and reading documentation of monitoring activities. In considering management's process and progress for remediation, the auditor does not need to independently test whether systems are Year 2000 compliant.

The Year 2000 Report also includes guidance on the auditor's consideration of Year 2000 disclosures in the financial statements. For nonpublic organizations that are considering including voluntary disclosures about Year 2000 issues in the financial statements, the auditor must be very careful in determining whether he or she has sufficient competent evidential matter regarding the information disclosed. The auditor may conclude that the Year 2000 information should be included outside the financial statements or labeled "unaudited," particularly if the disclosures contain subjective or forward-looking information.

> **OBSERVATION:** The auditor (and, in actuality, the not-for-profit organization itself) should avoid making statements in note disclosures or other written documents, such as management letters, that "All actions have been taken (or are being taken) to ensure that all of the not-for-profit organization's systems are fully Year 2000 compliant" or similar affirmative statements. Neither the not-for-profit organization nor its auditor will really know if systems are Year 2000 compliant until the year 2000. Also, not all Year 2000 problems will be readily apparent on January 1, 2000. They may take longer to make themselves known. This is forward-looking information that an auditor cannot obtain sufficient evidence to support and with which he or she should not be associated. In addition, there would be no assurance that all affected systems have been identified, nor is there any assurance that third parties with which the not-for-profit organization does business are Year 2000 compliant.

EXHIBIT 3-5
YEAR 2000 ISSUES QUESTIONNAIRE

Name of Client: _____

Period of Audit: _____

Prepared by: _____ Date: _____

Reviewed by: _____ Date: _____

General Instructions

This questionnaire provides a listing of sample inquiries that are designed to assist in understanding the not-for-profit organization's Year 2000 remediation efforts.

The inquiries are designed to provide auditors with a general understanding of the impact of Year 2000 issues on the not-for-profit organization's electronic processing, the status of activities to remediate such impact, and the level of senior management and board of directors (or audit committee) participation in, or awareness of, those activities. The inquiries relate to the organization's process for remediating Year 2000 issues, not to the effectiveness of that process or its ultimate success.

The information obtained as a result of completing the questionnaire should be used to monitor the organization's progress toward achieving Year 2000 compliance. This information may be useful in several audit areas, including disclosures of commitments and contingencies and going-concern considerations. The information may also be useful in developing management letter comments.

	Yes	No	N/A	Notes
1. Has a formal Year 2000 oversight committee or similar group been established?	____	____	____	_____
2. If so:				
a. Does it have representation from all significant areas of operation of the organization, including information technology and legal counsel?	____	____	____	_____
b. Does it include a member of the organization's senior management who is responsible for Year 2000 remediation efforts?	____	____	____	_____
c. Does it include representation from the organization's internal audit function?	____	____	____	_____

	Yes	No	N/A	Notes

3. Is the status of Year 2000 efforts regularly reported to the board of trustees (or audit committee or others with equal authority and responsibility)?

4. Has an inventory been taken of the organization's computer systems and other technology that may be impacted by the Year 2000 Issue? Consider the following:

   a. Does the organization maintain an inventory of computing platforms, including mainframe systems, mid-range systems, LAN systems, and stand-alone PCs?

   b. Does the organization maintain an inventory of nontraditional computing platforms and devices such as imaging/work flow systems?

   c. Does the organization require a warranty in contracts with software vendors and other vendors about Year 2000 compliance?

   d. Has contact been made with software vendors and outside service providers (including service organizations) whose systems interface electronically with the organization's systems, in order to ascertain the status of their Year 2000 remediation efforts?

5. Has the organization completed an analysis to determine the scope of its Year 2000 issues?

6. After the impact on the organization of not correcting specific Year 2000 issues was determined, were the results used to establish priorities and to develop contingency plans?

7. Does the organization have a budget for its Year 2000 efforts?

8. Does the organization have procedures for monitoring its Year 2000 efforts?

9. Does the organization have contingency plans for mission-critical

	Yes	No	N/A	Notes

systems in the event that those systems do not become Year 2000 compliant when their Year 2000 compliance would be required?

10. Has the organization determined when its mission-critical system will fail because of the Year 2000 problem?

11. Do Year 2000 issues affect the processing of transactions and data for the year under audit?

12. Has senior management considered the legal exposure of not being Year 2000 compliant in time and management's responsibility for financial disclosure related to Year 2000 compliance?

13. Does the organization have plans to disclose Year 2000 matters in connection with issuing its financial statements for the year under audit?

14. If the organization is subject to regulatory oversight, has it been subjected to regulatory inquiries or other requirements regarding Year 2000 issues?

15. If the conversion, testing, and implementation stages of the Year 2000 plan have begun, have problems been encountered that could have a significant impact on the timetable for completing the Year 2000 remediation? If so, have contingency plans been reevaluated?

16. If delays, failures, or other problems have been encountered with vendors, outside service providers, customers, or intermediary efforts, have contingency plans been developed?

17. Do the organization's internal auditors have a role in conversion, testing, and implementation activities, and do they plan to test interfaces with vendors, customers, and intermediaries?

18. When does the organization expect to complete its Year 2000 project?

If the Year 2000 disclosures are included outside the financial statements in a client-submitted document, the auditor should read and consider these disclosures in accordance with SAS-8 (Other Information in Documents Containing Audited Financial Statements).

If the disclosures are included outside the financial statements in an auditor-submitted document, the auditor should refer to SAS-29 (Reporting on Information Accompanying the Basic Financial Statements in Auditor-Submitted Documents). Under SAS-29, if the auditor concludes that the accompanying information is materially misstated in relation to the basic financial statements taken as a whole but the client will not change the information, the auditor either modifies his or her report on the accompanying information and describes the misstatement or refuses to include the information in the document.

Considering Other Audit Matters

As a rule of thumb, the more audit matters that an auditor considers during the planning phase of the audit, the more smoothly and efficiently the audit engagement will be performed. By anticipating potential areas of audit concern or areas where additional audit procedures will need to be performed during the planning phase of the audit engagement, the auditor will be able to incorporate these requirements into the planned procedures at the start of the audit, rather than trying to address these additional matters after the majority of the fieldwork has been completed.

The following sections describe some of the matters that an auditor should address during the planning phase of the audit of a not-for-profit organization to increase the efficiency of the audit.

Related-Party Transactions

The chapter titled "Preplanning Audit Activities" provides information for an auditor to use to determine whether a not-for-profit organization has any related organizations (both for-profit and not-for-profit) whose inclusion or disclosure in the financial statements of the not-for-profit being audited must be considered. In certain instances, SOP 94-3 requires that disclosures of related-party transactions and other matters required by FAS-57 (Related Party Disclosures) be made. The auditor should review the discussion of SOP 94-3 to ensure that sufficient information will be obtained during the course of the audit to enable the required disclosures to be made. In addition, where transactions with related parties are known to exist, the auditor should plan an audit strategy and procedures to obtain some assurance that all significant related-party transactions (or other relationships) have been identified, so that a complete and adequate disclosure can be made.

In addition to disclosures on affiliated organizations, other related-party disclosures may be required in the financial statements of the not-for-profit organization. The auditor should consider the need to identify these transactions when planning the audit. SAS-45 (Omnibus Statement on Auditing Standards—1983) provides guidance to auditors pertaining to related-party transactions. This guidance as it relates specifically to not-for-profit organizations is discussed in the following paragraphs.

SAS-45 acknowledges that an audit performed in accordance with GAAS would not be expected to provide assurance that all related-party transactions will be discovered. However, the auditor should be aware of the possible existence of material related-party transactions that could affect the financial statements and of common ownership or management control relationships for which FAS-57 would require disclosure even though there were no transactions. In addition, the auditor should be sensitive to circumstances where potential conflicts exist between a governing board member's financial interests and his or her duties as a governing board member. SAS-45 describes audit procedures the auditor should consider both to determine whether related parties exist and to identify transactions with parties known to be related parties.

Determining the existence of related parties for a not-for-profit organization may include the following procedures:

- Evaluating the not-for-profit organization's procedures for identifying and properly accounting for related-party transactions.

- Requesting from the management of the not-for-profit organization the names of all related parties and inquiring about whether there were any transactions with these parties during the period being audited.

- Reviewing any filings with regulatory authorities, including state charities regulatory departments or debt offering statements, for the names of related parties and for other businesses in which officers and directors occupy directorship or management positions.

- Determining the names of all pension and other trusts established for the benefit of employees and the names of their officers and trustees.

- Reviewing prior years' working papers for the names of known related parties.

- Inquiring of predecessor, principal, or other auditors of related entities concerning their knowledge of existing relationships and the extent of management involvement in material transactions.

- Reviewing material investment transactions during the period under audit to determine whether the nature and extent of investments during the period create related parties.

SAS-45 lists the following procedures for identifying material transactions with parties known to be related and for identifying material transactions that may be indicative of the existence of previously unknown related-party relationships:

- Providing audit personnel performing segments of the audit or auditing and reporting separately on the accounts of related components of the reporting entity with the names of known related parties so that they may become aware of transactions with such parties during their audits.

- Reviewing the minutes of the board of directors and executive and operating committees for information about material transactions authorized or discussed at their meetings.

- Reviewing information filed with regulatory authorities for information about material transactions with related parties.

- Reviewing any conflict of interest statements obtained by the not-for-profit organization from its management.

- Reviewing the extent and nature of business transacted with major donors, suppliers, borrowers, and lenders for indications of previously undisclosed relationships.

- Considering whether transactions are occurring, but are not being given accounting recognition, such as receiving or providing accounting, management, or other services at no charge or some other individual or organization absorbing corporate expenses.

- Reviewing accounting records for large, unusual, or nonrecurring transactions or balances, paying particular attention to transactions recognized at or near the end of the reporting period.

- Reviewing confirmations for compensating balance arrangements for indications that balances are or were maintained for or by related parties.

- Reviewing invoices from law firms that have performed regular or special services for the not-for-profit organization for indications of the existence of related parties and related-party transactions.

- Reviewing confirmations of loans receivable and payable for indications of guarantees. When guarantees are indicated, determine their nature and the relationships, if any, of the guarantors to the not-for-profit organization.

When related-party transactions are identified, SAS-45 directs the auditor to perform procedures necessary to obtain satisfaction regarding the purpose, nature, and extent of the transactions and their effects on the financial statements. The auditor should obtain and evaluate sufficient competent evidential matter, which should extend beyond making inquiries of management. According to SAS-45, the auditor should consider the following procedures:

- Obtaining an understanding of the business purpose of the transaction.

- Examining invoices, executed copies of agreements, contracts, and other pertinent documents, such as receiving reports.

- Determining whether the transaction has been approved by the not-for-profit organization's board of directors or other appropriate officials.

- Testing for reasonableness the compilation of amounts to be disclosed, or considered for disclosure, in the financial statements.

- Arranging for the audit of interorganization account balances to be performed at concurrent dates, even if the fiscal years differ, and for the examination of specified, important, and representative related-party transactions by the auditors for each of the parties, with appropriate exchange of relevant information.

- Inspecting or confirming collateral to obtain satisfaction concerning its transferability and value.

SAS-45 also lists additional procedures that can be performed when necessary to understand a particular transaction. Auditors confronted with significant related-party transactions that they are having difficulty understanding and interpreting should refer to SAS-45 for these additional procedures.

The procedures above are not required. They should be considered in light of the circumstances of the not-for-profit organization being audited. Auditors must keep in mind, however, that the definition of related parties in FAS-57 includes a not-for-profit organization's management and members of management's immediate family, as well as affiliated entities. Transactions with brother–sister organizations and certain national and local affiliates as well as entities whose officers or directors are members of the not-for-profit organization's governing board may have to be disclosed according to the requirements of FAS-57. Therefore, auditors should be appropriately concerned about identifying and understanding related-party transactions when auditing a not-for-profit organization to ensure that the requirements of FAS-57 are met.

Illegal Acts

The auditor's responsibility to detect and report financial statement misstatements resulting from illegal acts having a direct and material effect on the determination of financial statement amounts is the same as that for errors and irregularities described above. There are other types of illegal acts (referred to in SAS-54 [Illegal Acts by Clients] simply as *illegal acts*) that may have a material indirect effect on the financial statements of the organization being audited.

Not-for-profit organizations are affected by many laws and regulations relating to such matters as equal employment opportunity, occupational health and safety, food and drug administration, etc. These laws and regulations relate more to a not-for-profit organization's operations, rather than its financial and accounting aspects. Their potential indirect effect on the financial statements is generally the result of the need to disclose a contingent liability because of the allegation or determination of an illegality.

SAS-54 describes the auditor's responsibility with respect to detecting, considering the financial statement effects of, and reporting these other illegal acts. The auditor should be aware that such illegal acts may have occurred. If specific information comes to the auditor's attention that provides evidence concerning the existence of possible illegal acts that could have a material indirect effect on the financial statements, the auditor should apply audit procedures specifically directed to ascertaining whether an illegal act has occurred. However, an audit performed in accordance with GAAS provides no assurance that illegal acts will be detected or that any contingent liabilities that may result will be disclosed.

SAS-54 states that the auditor should make inquiries of management concerning the client's compliance with laws and regulations. The auditor also should inquire of management, where applicable, concerning:

- The client's policies regarding the prevention of illegal acts

- The use of directives issued by the client and periodic representations obtained by the client from management at appropriate levels of authority concerning compliance with laws and regulations

The auditor should include written representations from the client regarding illegal acts in the client representation letter obtained from the client at the end of fieldwork. (See the chapter titled "Concluding the Audit" for an example of a client representation letter.)

The auditor does not need to perform any further procedures in this area absent any specific information concerning possible illegal acts. However, when applying audit procedures and evaluating the results of those procedures, the auditor may encounter specific information that raises a question about possible illegal acts. SAS-54 provides the following examples:

- Unauthorized transactions, improperly recorded transactions, or transactions not recorded in a complete or timely manner in order to maintain accountability for assets
- Investigation by a governmental agency, an enforcement proceeding, or payment of unusual fines or penalties
- Violations of laws or regulations cited in reports of examinations by regulatory agencies that have been made available to the auditor
- Large payments for unspecified services to consultants, affiliates, or employees
- Sales commissions or agents' fees that appear excessive in relation to those normally paid by the client or to the services actually received
- Unusually large payments in cash, purchases of bank cashiers' checks in large amounts payable to bearer, transfers to numbered bank accounts, or similar transactions
- Unexplained payments to government officials or employees
- Failure to file tax returns or pay government duties or similar fees that are common to the entity's industry or the nature of its business

Awareness of these factors during audit planning will enable the auditor to be cognizant of the potential specific instances that may indicate illegal acts throughout the course of the audit.

Compliance Auditing

Not-for-profit organizations frequently receive governmental financial assistance. Governmental assistance may be from one or more levels of government—federal, state, or local. In addition, not-for-profit organizations often receive financial assistance from nongovernmental sources. To receive this assistance, the not-for-profit organization may make contractual commitments to comply with the donor or contractor's requirements. Auditors must address these compliance requirements in an audit of a not-for-profit organization performed in accordance with GAAS.

For financial assistance received from nongovernmental sources, the auditor's objective for testing compliance with contractual terms is to determine whether there is a contingent liability on the part of the not-for-profit organization to return all or part of the financial assistance to the donor or contractor because of the not-for-profit organization's failure to comply with any contractual terms of the contract or grant agreement.

The auditor may encounter a wide range of noncompliance instances, with varying degrees of seriousness, which will require careful evaluation using the guidance of FAS-5 (Accounting for Contingencies). For example, assume that a not-for-profit organization receives a grant or contract from a local religious institution to provide temporary shelter to homeless individuals. The grant or contract calls for the not-for-profit organization to provide the services to a minimum of 20 individuals each day for a period of three months. The not-for-profit organization is advanced all of the funds under the grant or contract prior to the delivery of the services. If the not-for-profit organization provides all of the services required by the agreement, and assuming that it is a fixed-price grant or contract, the not-for-profit organization probably would not have to refund any of the advance to the religious institution. The auditor should perform some procedures, such as inquiry and observation or a test check of the attendance logs, to obtain evidence of compliance with the requirements to ensure him- or herself that the grant or contract funds were actually "earned" by the not-for-profit organization and that there is no contingent liability to the religious organization.

However, if the not-for-profit organization provided no services, and there has been no subsequent agreement to provide the services at a later time within the period being audited, there is a strong likelihood that the not-for-profit organization will have to refund the advance to the religious institution. Therefore, the auditor should expect a liability for this refund to be recorded in the not-for-profit organization's financial statements.

Between total compliance and total noncompliance are various levels of noncompliance for which the accounting and financial statement disclosures are not so evident. For example, perhaps only 18 individuals were served on one particular day (two below the daily minimum), or perhaps there was a two-day delay before the services actually were started. The auditor will need to evaluate, using the guidance of FAS-5, whether a contingent liability exists that will have to be recorded or disclosed.

During the planning phase of the engagement, the auditor should determine the extent of compliance requirements that the not-for-profit organization has in its various contract and grant agreements. The not-for-profit organization's controls over compliance with these terms also should be considered. More formal guidance for considering compliance with governmental financial assistance is provided in SAS-74 (Compliance Auditing Considerations in Audits of Governmental Entities and Recipients of Governmental Financial Assistance) and discussed below. The auditor may want to use the concepts for designing audit procedures for nongovernmental entitles that are described below for compliance auditing of governmental financial assistance.

Federal, state, and local governments provide financial assistance to not-for-profit organizations as primary recipients, subrecipients, or beneficiaries. The forms of governmental financial assistance may be cash and other assets, loans, loan guarantees, and interest-rate subsidies. By accepting such assistance, the not-for-profit organization may be subject to laws and regulations that have a direct and material effect on the determination of amounts in the financial statements.

SAS-74 requires that the auditors of these organizations obtain an understanding of the possible effects on financial statements of laws and regulations that are generally recognized to have a direct and material effect on the determination of amounts in the organization's financial statements. The auditor also should assess whether management has identified laws and regulations that have a material and direct effect on the determination of amounts in the organization's financial statements and should obtain an understanding of the possible effects on the financial statements of such laws and regulations. SAS-74 contains the following procedures the auditor may consider when assessing such laws and regulations and when obtaining an understanding of their possible effects on the financial statements:

- Consider knowledge about such laws and regulations obtained in prior years' audits.
- Discuss such laws and regulations with the not-for-profit organization's chief financial officer, legal counsel, or grant administrators.
- Obtain written representation from management regarding the completeness of management's identification.
- Review the relevant portions of any directly related agreements, such as those related to grants and loans.
- Inquire of the office of the federal, state, or local auditor, or other appropriate audit oversight organization, about the laws and regulations applicable to entities within their jurisdictions, including statutes and uniform reporting requirements.
- Review information about compliance requirements, such as the information included in the *Compliance Supplement* issued to OMB Circular A-133; the Government Printing Office's Catalog of Federal Domestic Assistance; and state and local policies and procedures.

When the not-for-profit organization receives federal awards, either as a primary recipient or as a subrecipient, there may be additional audit requirements, including additional compliance auditing requirements. The applicability of these requirements is discussed in the chapter titled "Preplanning Audit Activities." The performance of audits under these two documents is covered in Part II of this Guide.

Use of Service Organizations

Not-for-profit organizations may use the services of service organizations, such as discretionary investment management services or payroll processing services. Also, the not-for-profit may use service organizations to process student financial aid payments and contributions. SAS-70 (Reports on the Processing of Transactions by Service Organizations) provides guidance on the factors the auditor should consider when auditing the financial statements of a not-for-profit organization that uses a service organization to process some of its transactions. Auditors also should consider the not-for-profit organization's compliance with laws, regulations, and contractual agreements that may apply when service organizations are used to process transactions. The not-for-profit organization retains the responsibility for ensuring that transactions are processed in compliance with any applicable laws, regulations, and contractual agreements.

Certain policies, procedures, and records of the service organization may be relevant to the not-for-profit organization and may affect the user not-for-profit organization's ability to record, process, summarize, and report financial data consistent with the assertions in its financial statements. SAS-70 lists the following factors that the auditor of the not-for-profit organization should consider to determine the significance of these policies, procedures, and records to planning the audit:

- The significance of the financial statement assertions that are affected by the policies and procedures of the service organization

- The inherent risk associated with the assertions affected by the policies and procedures of the service organization

- The nature of the services provided by the service organization and whether they are highly standardized and used extensively by many user organizations or are unique only to a few

- The extent to which the not-for-profit organization's internal control policies and procedures interact with the policies and procedures of the service organization

- The not-for-profit organization's internal control policies and procedures that are applied to the transactions affected by the service organization's activities

- The terms of the contract between the not-for-profit organization and the service organization (for example, their respective responsibilities and the extent of the service organization's discretion to initiate transactions)

- The service organization's capabilities, including its:
  — Record of performance
  — Insurance coverage
  — Financial stability
- The auditor's prior experience with the service organization
- The extent of auditable data in the not-for-profit organization's possession
- The existence of specific regulatory requirements that may dictate the application of audit procedures beyond those required to comply with GAAS

The auditor also should consider whether the not-for-profit organization has information about the service organization (such as procedures manuals or technical manuals) and the existence of reports by the service organization's external or internal auditors or by regulatory authorities.

After considering the above factors, the auditor of the not-for-profit organization should decide whether he or she is able to obtain a sufficient understanding of internal control to plan the audit. If the auditor concludes that he or she needs additional information, he or she should arrange through the not-for-profit organization to obtain sufficient additional information from or about the service organization.

In August 1999, the Professional Issues Task Force of the AICPA's SEC Practice Section issued Practice Alert 99-2, "How the Use of a Service Organization Affects Internal Control Considerations" (PA 99-2). This Practice Alert points out examples in professional practice where auditors did not obtain SAS-70 reports when they should have, as well as instances where auditors did obtain SAS-70 reports but those reports were not adequate for the circumstances in which they were used. The increasing popularity of outsourcing activities makes these weaknesses in audit processes even more important.

An auditor of a not-for-profit organization may need to obtain an understanding of the controls at a service organization if the transactions processed or the accounts affected by the service organization are material to the not-for-profit organization's financial statements. In some circumstances, the dollar amounts of the transactions may not be material, but by their nature the transactions would require the auditor to obtain an understanding of the service organization's controls because of the potential for improper processing of the transactions to result in material unrecorded liabilities. Obtaining a SAS-70 report is one way to obtain an understanding of these controls.

An auditor can only assess control risk at below the maximum for these controls if evidential mater is obtained by:

- Testing the user organization's controls over the activities of the service organization
- Obtaining a service auditor's report on controls placed in operation and tests of operating effectiveness, or a report on the application of agreed-upon procedures that describes relevant tests of controls (Note that the service auditor's report in this case must report on operating effectiveness, not just the controls placed in operation.)
- Performing tests of controls at the service organization

If the not-for-profit organization auditor will rely on the report of the service auditor (second bullet above), the auditor should determine that whether the specific tests of controls and results of the service auditor's reports are relevant to the assertions that are significant in the not-for-profit organization's financial statements. One of the deficiencies noted in PA 99-2 is that auditors sometimes simply obtain a SAS-70 report from the service organization's auditor and do not determine whether it is the correct type of report or whether it covers the relevant controls of the service organization. If the service auditor's report on controls is as of a date outside of the not-for-profit organization's financial statements being reported upon, the auditor may need to obtain information to update the SAS-70 report. PA 99-2 specifies the following procedures that may be used to update a service organization's auditor's report:

- Discussions with user organization personnel who would be in a position to know about changes at the service organization
- Review of current documentation and correspondence issued by the service organization
- Discussions with service organization personnel or with the service organization auditor

Significant changes in the service organization's controls would require that the not-for-profit organization's auditor attempt to gain an understanding of the changes and consider the effect of those changes on the audit.

Using the Work of Specialists

Not-for-profit organizations or their auditors may engage a specialist to provide some special skills or knowledge about complex or subjective matters that may be material to the financial statements. A not-for-profit organization, for example, may need to use the work of a specialist to assist in the valuation of contributed assets, particularly such assets as collection items. Auditors should use the guidance of SAS-73 (Using the Work of a Specialist) when they engage a specialist to assist in the performance of the audit.

Documenting the Planning Phase of the Engagement in a Planning Memorandum

The planning procedures described above are an integral part of an audit in accordance with GAAS. The auditor should ensure that his or her working papers properly document the planning process that has been performed.

Certain assessments and conclusions are easily documented in checklists or matrices. For example, in assessing the inherent and control risks and the planned level of detection risk for each assertion for material account balances and classes of transactions, the auditor should use a standardized worksheet. This is the most efficient way to accomplish such a detailed analysis, enabling the auditor to spend more time on the assessment process itself than on the documentation of the process.

In addition, the assessment of the risk components will be referenced to audit objectives and audit procedures contained in the programs the auditor develops. Such correlation in and of itself adequately documents the effect the auditor's risk assessment has on audit objectives and procedures.

Certain considerations, however, do not lend themselves to formatted working papers or standardized audit programs. These considerations, as well as other information that the auditor may wish to document for convenience, should be documented in a planning memorandum.

The planning memorandum is the part of the documentation that indicates that appropriate planning procedures have been performed. Its format can vary greatly and usually depends on the individual style of the auditor or of the firm with which he or she is affiliated. Some auditors, for example, have general guidelines for the contents of planning memoranda and leave the writing to the individual auditor in charge of the audit engagement. Other auditors use a standardized form with a fill-in-the-blank approach that encourages efficiency and completeness, but does not encourage the incorporation of information that is not required but would be useful.

Similarly, the length of planning memoranda can vary widely. While a half-page boilerplate memorandum will in almost all circumstances be inadequate, a 50-page tome for a small to medium-sized not-for-profit organization may signal that too much time is being spent on form over substance. A two- to five-page document generally will provide adequate content and detail.

The planning memorandum for an audit engagement should expand on the planning memorandum typically prepared for audits of financial statements of commercial enterprises in accordance with GAAS. Some general suggestions for content are as follows:

- State clearly that the audit will be performed in accordance with GAAS. Identify any special reporting requirements as well as the auditor's consideration of whether the requirements of *Government Auditing Standards* or OMB Circular A-133 apply.

- Identify the reporting entity of the not-for-profit organization that will be audited (including or excluding affiliated/consolidated organizations and the accounting treatment for significant investments in for-profit subsidiaries) and the period that will be covered by the audit.

- Describe planned reliance on the work of other auditors and the coordination of work and/or reporting requirements with other auditors.

- Outline the time plan needed to complete the audit, including audit hours by critical or significant audit areas and the deadline for submission of the final report to the client.

- Supply names, titles, telephone numbers, etc., of key client personnel and, if applicable, of contacts at any other audit firms.

- Supply specific information about the assistance the not-for-profit organization plans to provide, as well as the auditor's expected role in actual financial statement preparation.

- Briefly describe the not-for-profit organization's operations, including the types of programs it administers, with an expanded discussion of any programs or activities initiated during the period being audited.

- Briefly describe any trends in the environment in which the not-for-profit organization operates.

- Discuss the assessment of the risk of misstatement of the financial statements due to fraud.

- Discuss any specific areas where the auditor expects to assess control risk at below the maximum level for financial statement reporting purposes.

- Indicate the approach the auditor will use to document and test (if applicable) internal controls. Indicate the planned effect of testing these controls on the test work to be performed on account balances.

- Document any significant use of service organizations by the not-for-profit organization and the intended approach to obtain sufficient information regarding internal control structure to plan the audit.

- Analyze planning materiality, including the calculation of planning materiality levels at the financial statement level and the calculation of tolerable misstatement, or refer to the worksheet where these calculations were performed.
- Refer to the planning analytical procedures that were performed and the plan for addressing any unusual findings as a result of those procedures.
- Analyze the effect, if any, of any new pronouncements on accounting and auditing.
- Document the auditor's planned approach for considering the organization's Year 2000 efforts.
- Document that the individual auditors and the audit firm have complied with appropriate independence requirements.
- Discuss any significant follow-up activities that will need to be performed to consider the effect of any significant prior-year audit findings.
- Identify the staff to be assigned to the audit engagement, including any specialists.

> **OBSERVATION:** Since much of the information in the planning memorandum does not change significantly from year to year, but simply needs updating, this is an excellent area in which to begin to incorporate personal computers and word processing into the preparation of audit working papers. Auditors should consider developing a template for planning memoranda specifically for audits of not-for-profit organizations.

Upon completion of the planning memorandum, all of the auditors who will work on the engagement should acknowledge in writing that they have read and understand the planning memorandum.

The above suggestions are a guide that should be tailored to the individual audit. Effective use of planning memoranda helps satisfy the GAAS requirements. It also helps the auditor understand the overall approach to the audit, and it identifies many of the issues that will be encountered during the course of the audit so they can be resolved early.

SUMMARY

Effectively planning the audit of a not-for-profit organization will help the auditor ensure that the audit will meet all professional standards and requirements and will be performed in the most

efficient manner possible. Upon completing the planning procedures described above, the auditor should begin to focus on his or
her consideration of the internal control environment, which is the
subject of the chapter titled "Internal Control Considerations."

CHAPTER 4
INTERNAL CONTROL CONSIDERATIONS

CONTENTS

CHAPTER 4
INTERNAL CONTROL CONSIDERATIONS

CROSS-REFERENCES

2001 MILLER NOT-FOR-PROFIT ORGANIZATION AUDITS: Chapter 16, "Internal Controls over Federal Awards"

2001 MILLER AUDIT PROCEDURES: Chapter 5, "Internal Control

2000 MILLER GAAS GUIDE: Section 319, "Consideration of Internal Control in a Financial Statement Audit"; Section 322, "The Auditor's Consideration of the Internal Audit Function in an Audit of Financial Statements"

Overview

The chapter on audit planning provides an overview of the issues the auditor should consider regarding the not-for-profit organization's internal control when designing an audit strategy for an audit in accordance with GAAS. This chapter focuses specifically on what an auditor needs to consider relating to internal control and the assessment of control risk when performing an audit of the financial statements of a not-for-profit organization in accordance with GAAS.

Consideration of Internal Control in a Financial Statement Audit

SAS-78 (Consideration of Internal Control in a Financial Statement Audit: An Amendment of SAS No. 55) revised the definition and description of *internal control* contained in the AICPA Statements on Auditing Standards to incorporate the definition and description contained in *Internal Controls—Integrated Framework*, a report issued by the Committee of Sponsoring Organizations of the Treadway Commission (COSO).

Definition

SAS-78 revises the definition of *internal control* to conform to the definition in the COSO report, as follows:

> Internal control is a process, effected by an entity's board of directors, management, and other personnel, designed to provide reasonable assurance regarding the achievement of objectives in the following categories:
>
> (a) reliability of financial reporting
>
> (b) compliance with applicable laws and regulations, and
>
> (c) effectiveness and efficiency of operations

Components of Internal Control

The three elements of the internal control structure described by SAS-55 (Consideration of the Internal Control Structure as a Financial Statement Audit) were replaced by SAS-78 with the five components outlined in the COSO report. The five components of internal control are the control environment, risk assessment, control activities, information and communication, and monitoring.

1. *Control environment* The control environment sets the tone of an organization, influencing the control consciousness of its people. It is the foundation for all other components of the internal control structure, providing discipline and structure.

2. *Risk assessment* Risk assessment involves the entity's identification and analysis of relevant risks to the achievement of its objectives and the entity's formation of a basis for determining how the risks should be managed.

3. *Control activities* Control activities are the policies and procedures that help ensure management directives are carried out.

4. *Information and communication* Information and communication involves the identification, capture, and exchange of information in a form and time frame that enables people to carry out their responsibilities.

5. *Monitoring* Monitoring is a process that assesses the quality of the internal control structure's performance over time.

Internal Control Objectives and Components

SAS-78 points out that there is a direct relationship between the objectives of internal control (i.e., what a not-for-profit organization is trying to achieve with internal controls) and the components of internal control themselves. SAS-78 describes the following three broad categories of objectives:

- *Financial Reporting Objectives* Clearly, the auditor will be concerned with internal controls that relate directly to an organization's objective of being able to prepare financial statements that are fairly presented in accordance with generally accepted accounting principles.

- *Operations and Compliance Objectives* Organizations typically have internal control objectives that relate to how the organizations control the way they do business and how they comply with legal and other requirements. If an organization has controls that are used to monitor nonfinancial operating data, the controls may or may not be relevant to the auditor, depending on whether the auditor would use such data for purposes such as performing substantive analytical procedures. An auditor may also find that certain controls over compliance are relevant to his or her audit of financial statements. For example, a not-for-profit organization's controls for maintaining compliance with the requirements to remain a tax-exempt organization would clearly be relevant to an auditor. In addition, when an auditor is using the guidance of SAS-74 (Compliance Auditing Considerations in Audits of Governmental Entities and Recipients of Governmental Financial Assistance) because a not-for-profit organization receives governmental financial assistance, controls over compliance become clearly relevant to an audit of financial statements.

- *Safeguarding Assets* One objective of internal control is to help organizations safeguard assets against unauthorized acquisition, use, or disposition. These controls may be relevant to the preparation of financial statements as well as to operations. Generally, an auditor of financial statements will view as relevant those controls that are used to prepare financial statements.

Consideration of Internal Control in Planning and Performing an Audit of a Financial Statement

The actual audit requirements of SAS-78 relating to internal controls are not very different from those of SAS-55. There are more differences in terminology and framework than in the actual application of the consideration of internal controls to the audit of financial statements. In other words, the auditor considers internal controls differently under SAS-78, but for the most part uses this consideration the same way he or she used the consideration of internal control "structure" under SAS-55.

The following pages describe the process of considering internal controls in an audit of financial statements, define and clarify the five components of internal controls under SAS-78, and outline the types of considerations that the auditor should be making for each of the five internal control components.

Nature of Internal Control

First, the auditor should be aware that the organization being audited is not likely to have placed its internal controls in five neat categories to conform with SAS-78. Thus, the auditor considers the same controls that he or she had considered under SAS-55 and is simply using a different framework to consider/classify the controls.

The auditor should also be aware that there are limitations to internal controls. Internal controls cannot provide absolute assurance to a not-for-profit organization's management that its internal control objectives will be met. Internal controls provide only reasonable assurance. They are subject to human errors and mistakes, faulty judgments in decision making, and circumvention through collusion.

Consideration of Internal Controls in Planning an Audit

To plan an audit of the financial statements of a not-for-profit organization, the auditor should first have a sufficient broad understanding of each of the five components of internal control. That broad understanding will help the auditor to plan and perform procedures by which he or she can (a) understand the design of any specific organization controls that are relevant to the audit of financial statements and (b) assess whether the organization has placed those specific controls in operation. This knowledge is used to:

- Identify types of potential misstatements
- Consider factors that affect the risk of material misstatement
- Design substantive tests

The nature, timing, and extent of procedures that the auditor selects to obtain the understanding of internal control will vary depending on the size and complexity of the organization, the auditor's previous audit experience with the organization, the nature of the specific controls involved, and the nature of the organization's documentation of specific controls.

The auditor obtains information about whether internal controls have been placed in operation, i.e., whether the organization is using them. This does not mean that the auditor is responsible for obtaining knowledge about the operating effectiveness of internal controls (that is, how the control is applied), the consistency with which it is applied, or by whom it was applied. SAS-78 does not require the auditor to obtain knowledge about the operating effectiveness of controls, although an auditor who is assessing control risk at below the maximum level will need to be concerned with some or all of the factors of operating effectiveness.

The auditor also may gain information on internal control from other sources, such as the following:

- *Prior-year audit* Not only does the prior-year audit give the auditor information on the internal control structure itself, it also lets the auditor reevaluate whether he or she had a sufficient understanding of the internal control structure in the prior year to properly plan the audit. The auditor may choose in the current year to expand on the understanding of the internal control structure to plan the audit more effectively.

- *Understanding of the not-for-profit organization's industry* While one might say that all not-for-profit organizations are in the same industry, the range of services that they provide varies widely. An auditor of a college or university will be in a better position to assess the sufficiency of his or her understanding of internal control of that college or university if he or she has audited several similar institutions in the past. The same statement can be made for auditors of trade associations, human services agencies, cultural institutions, etc.

- *Inherent risk assessment* The auditor's assessment of inherent risk should be considered when determining the sufficiency of the understanding of internal control. The greater the auditor believes the inherent risk is for the assertions for all or some of the not-for-profit organization's account balances or classes of transactions, the greater the understanding of internal control the auditor will want to obtain.

- *Complexity of not-for-profit organization's systems and operations* The more complex the systems and operations of the not-for-profit organization being audited, the greater the understanding of internal control the auditor will need to obtain. The size of the not-for-profit organization also tends to be a factor in complexity. Generally, larger organizations have more complex systems in operation. It will be much more difficult for the auditor to design and perform effective substantive tests if the auditor does not obtain a greater understanding of internal control. For a small not-for-profit organization with relatively simple operations, the understanding of internal control needed to plan the audit effectively will be much less.

- *Extent of computerization and computer controls used by the not-for-profit organization*   The greater the extent of computerization, the greater the understanding of internal control the auditor will need. Manual general ledger systems generally require less explanation and understanding than do highly sophisticated computer systems. Also, the auditor should consider the extent of the not-for-profit organization's use of computer controls compared to manual controls. For example, two computer-generated reports are produced on a monthly basis, one that totals cash receipts applied to accounts receivable collections and the other that totals cash collections from receivables that have been posted to the cash account. A computer control may exist that automatically compares these two amounts (which in this simplistic example should be the same) and that produces a report only if there is a difference in the two amounts. In another organization, this computer control may not exist, but a data control clerk may compare the amounts from the two reports manually and document the comparison in some manner. The auditor in the first instance will need to know more about internal control than the auditor in the second to gain an understanding of how the internal control procedures work.

An auditor uses all of the factors mentioned above to determine the extent of his or her understanding of internal controls. An auditor also must consider the fraud risk factors that relate to internal controls that are included in SAS-82 (see the chapter titled "Audit Planning" for a full discussion of the implications of SAS-82). As a general rule, the more complex and sophisticated the operations and systems of a not-for-profit organization are, the more attention the auditor will need to give to internal control.

Overview of Internal Control Components

The following pages describe the five components of internal controls and provide an overview of an auditor's understanding of each of these components relating to a financial statement audit based upon the guidance of SAS-78.

Control Environment

The first component of internal control—the control environment—sets the tone of an organization and influences the control consciousness of the organization's personnel. Control environment factors include the following:

- *Integrity and ethical values* Integrity and ethical behavior are the product of an organization's ethical and behavioral standards, how they are communicated, and how they are reinforced in practice. They include communication of ethical and behavioral standards through policy statements and codes of conduct, and by example. They also include management's actions to remove or reduce incentives and temptations to act illegally or unethically.

- *Commitment to competence* Management's commitment to competence means that it determines the skills and knowledge that are required to perform jobs and functions within the organization and makes sure that these jobs and functions are performed by staff who possess the required knowledge and skills.

- *Board of directors or audit committee participation* The control environment is enhanced by the independence of the oversight's board from management, the experience and stature of its members, the extent of its involvement and scrutiny of activities, the appropriateness of its actions, its ability and commitment to ask difficult questions of management, and its relationship with internal and external auditors.

- *Management's philosophy and operating style* Management's characteristics may include its approach to taking/monitoring business risks, attitudes and actions toward financial reporting (i.e., conservative or aggressive), and attitudes toward information processing and accounting personnel and their functions.

- *Organizational structure* An appropriate organizational structure considers key areas of authority and responsibility and the appropriate lines of reporting for personnel and functions.

- *Assignment of authority and responsibility* Authority and responsibility for activities should be appropriately established, with reporting relationships and hierarchies established.

- *Human resource policies and practices* Human resource policies and procedures related to hiring, orientation, training, evaluating, counseling, promoting, compensating, and taking remedial actions.

The auditor should obtain sufficient knowledge of the control environment to understand management's and its oversight board's attitude, awareness, and actions concerning the control environment, considering both the substance of controls and their collective effect. In understanding the substance of controls, auditors should be aware that controls, such as a written policy, may exist, but may be ignored by senior management and others in the organization. In this example there is no substance to the control that exists. In understanding the collective effect of controls, the auditor needs to make similar considerations to understanding the substance of a control. The existence of a human resource policy for hiring or promoting is of little value if the control is routinely overridden by management.

Risk Assessment

The second component of internal control under SAS-78 is risk assessment. This should not be confused with an auditor's assessment of risk. Rather, it refers to an organization's risk assessment for financial reporting purposes—that is, the organization's identification, analysis, and management of risks relevant to the preparation of financial statements that are fairly presented in conformity with generally accepted accounting principles. These risks are those that affect an organization's ability to record, process, summarize, and report financial data consistent with the assertions of management in the financial statements. SAS-78 lists the following as examples of these types of risks:

- Changes in operating environment
- New personnel
- New or revamped information systems
- Rapid growth
- New technology
- New lines, products, or activities
- Corporate restructurings
- Foreign operations
- Accounting pronouncements

The auditor should gain an understanding of how management considers these risks and decides what actions to take. For example, auditors might want to understand how management identifies these risks, estimates the significance of the risks, assesses the likelihood of the occurrence of the risks, and then relates this information to financial reporting.

Control Activities

The third component of internal control—control activities—is the policies and procedures that ensure that the required actions are taken to address risks to achieving the organization's objectives. SAS-78 categorizes control activities into the following categories:

- *Performance reviews*   These are analytical control procedures wherein actual performance is compared to budgets, forecasts, and prior period performance. Operational information is compared with financial information. An important aspect of this control is not just that someone or some software is preparing the comparisons, but that someone determines whether variances are reasonable or whether expected variances actually occurred.

- *Information processing*   These are the general and application controls over information systems that are performed to check the accuracy, completeness, and authorization of transactions. General controls include control over data center operations, system software acquisition and maintenance, and access security and application system development and maintenance. Application controls apply to the processing of individual applications that help ensure that transactions are valid, properly authorized, and completely and accurately processed.

- *Physical controls*   These controls include the physical security of assets, including safeguards, such as secured facilities, over access to assets and records; authorization for access to computer programs and data files; and periodic counting and comparison with amounts shown on control records.

- *Segregation of duties*   This control encompasses assigning different people the responsibilities of authorizing transactions, recording transactions, and maintaining custody of assets.

The auditor should obtain an understanding of those control activities relevant to planning the audit. This understanding is likely to be obtained during the auditor's efforts to obtain knowledge about the documents, records, and processing steps in the financial reporting system (discussed in the following section, Information and Communication). The auditor may believe that the understanding he or she obtained about control activities from this process is sufficient, or the auditor may believe that he or she needs to obtain additional information about control activities to plan the audit. SAS-78 provides that audit planning ordinarily does not require an understanding of the control activities related to each account balance, transaction class, and disclosure component in the financial statements or to every assertion relevant to them.

Exhibit 4-1 provides a useful tool for documenting their understanding for individual account balances or classes of transactions. Not-for-profit organizations are often subject to laws and regulations on compliance that could have a direct and material impact on its financial statements. Exhibit 4-2 (see page 207) provides a tool to document control activities relating to compliance with these laws and regulations.

EXHIBIT 4-1
UNDERSTANDING OF INTERNAL CONTROL FORM

NAME OF NOT-FOR-PROFIT ORGANIZATION: _____

DATE OF FINANCIAL STATEMENTS: _____

INSTRUCTIONS

This form has been designed to assist auditors in obtaining the information necessary to evaluate a not-for-profit organization's internal control. This form is based on the criteria for an effective internal control as set forth in *Internal Control—Integrated Framework* (the COSO Report) included in SAS-78. Each question should be answered by a check mark in the appropriate column ("YES," "NO," or "N/A"). The questions have been prepared so that a positive answer will indicate a satisfactory degree of internal control. A negative answer should influence the auditor to amplify the answer or to cover the related question with a supplemental statement in order to make the understanding more informative and meaningful.

For subsequent years, the internal control form must be reviewed and updated as follows:

a. The auditor performing each section of the audit should review the previously completed form and determine what changes, if any, the client has made in the organization's internal control.

b. If the form is completed normally there are few changes in a particular audit area, the original answers should be crossed out and the current answers should be indicated and verified by the auditor in red. If the changes for a particular audit area are numerous, the original page should be marked "superseded" and a new page should be completed.

c. If the form is completed electronically, changes should be made each year and the completed, updated form reprinted each year.

d. The auditor updating the audit area should sign and date each section when he or she has completed the updated review of that section.

This form is divided into six major sections: (1) control environment, (2) risk assessment, (3) control activities, (4) information and communication, (5) monitoring, and (6) understanding of account balances and classes of transactions. Before completing this form, the auditor should be familiar with the concepts discussed in the chapter "Internal Control Considerations."

SECTION I—CONTROL ENVIRONMENT

Section I of the form is designed to help the auditor obtain an understanding of the entity's control environment, which sets the tone of an organization

(text continues on page 208)

and influences the control consciousness of its people. According to SAS-78, the control environment encompasses the following factors:

- Integrity and ethical values
- Commitment to competence
- Board of directors or audit committee participation
- Management's philosophy and operating style
- The entity's organizational structure
- Assignment of authority and responsibility
- Human resource policies and practices

		Yes	*No*	*N/A*
1.	Does management adequately convey the message that integrity cannot be compromised?	___	___	___
2.	Does a positive control environment exist, whereby there is an attitude of control consciousness throughout the organization, and a positive "tone at the top?"	___	___	___
3.	Is the competence of the organization's staff (including volunteer staff) commensurate with their responsibilities?	___	___	___
4.	Is management's operating style, the way it assigns authority and responsibility and organizes and develops its people appropriate?	___	___	___
5.	Does management understand the requirements of laws, regulations, contracts, and grant agreements pertinent to its activities?	___	___	___
6.	Does management adequately consider the potential effects of taking unusual risks?	___	___	___
7.	Are financial statements submitted to and reviewed by management, the board of directors, or the audit committee at regular intervals?	___	___	___
8.	Does management demonstrate concern about and willingness to correct important weaknesses in the system of internal control?	___	___	___
9.	Does the organization maintain up-to-date accounting policies and a procedures manual? If yes, obtain copies.	___	___	___
10.	Is a chart of accounts maintained and does it describe the nature of each account? If yes, obtain a copy.	___	___	___
11.	Does management periodically review insurance coverage?	___	___	___

	Yes	No	N/A

12. Does management have a history of establishing reliable accounting estimates? ___ ___ ___

13. Is there a low turnover of management positions, especially financial management? ___ ___ ___

14. Are key operating positions adequately staffed, therefore avoiding constant crisis? ___ ___ ___

15. Is there adequate coordination between accounting and EDP departments, resulting in timely reports and closings? ___ ___ ___

16. Is there an organization chart that reflects the areas of responsibility and the line of reporting? If yes, obtain a copy. ___ ___ ___

17. Are there formal job descriptions that clearly set out duties and responsibilities? ___ ___ ___

18. Are backgrounds and references of applicants for financial and key management positions investigated? ___ ___ ___

19. Are personnel policies and employee benefit plans documented and communicated to employees? ___ ___ ___

20. Is a formal conflict of interest policy or code of conduct in effect? If yes, obtain a copy. ___ ___ ___

21. Are employees who handle cash, securities, and other valuable assets bonded? ___ ___ ___

22. Do related employees, if any, have job assignments that minimize opportunities for collusion? ___ ___ ___

23. Are employees adequately trained to meet their assigned responsibilities? ___ ___ ___

24. Is rotation of duties enforced by mandatory vacations? ___ ___ ___

25. Is job performance periodically evaluated and reviewed with employees? ___ ___ ___

26. Has management established adequate policies and procedures for the development, modification, and use of computer programs and data files? ___ ___ ___

27. Does the entity have a board of directors or an audit committee? If yes: ___ ___ ___

    a. Does the board or committee take an active role in overseeing the organization's policies and practices? ___ ___ ___

    b. Does the board or committee approve the appointment of the organization's independent auditors? ___ ___ ___

	Yes	No	N/A

c. Does the board or committee have sufficient knowledge, experience, and time to serve effectively? _____ _____ _____

d. Does the board or committee constructively challenge management's planned decisions and take appropriate action if necessary (for example, conducting special investigations)? _____ _____ _____

e. Does the board or committee meet in a timely manner with the chief accounting officer and internal and external auditors to discuss the reasonableness of the financial reporting process, the system of internal control, and other significant matters? _____ _____ _____

f. Does the board or committee review the scope of activities of the external and internal auditors at least annually? _____ _____ _____

g. Does the board or committee regularly receive and review key information, such as financial statements, major marketing initiatives, significant contracts, and negotiations? _____ _____ _____

h. Does a process exist for informing the board or committee in a timely manner of sensitive information, investigation, and improper acts (e.g., significant litigation, investigations by regulatory or funding agencies, embezzlement, misuses of corporate assets)? _____ _____ _____

i. Is there appropriate oversight in determining the compensation and benefits of executive officers? _____ _____ _____

j. Is the board or committee sufficiently involved in establishing and evaluating the effectiveness of the "tone at the top" (e.g., approving the organization's code of conduct or policy and procedure manual)? _____ _____ _____

ADDITIONAL COMMENTS—CONTROL ENVIRONMENT

_____

_____

_____

SECTION II—RISK ASSESSMENT

Section II of the form is designed to help the auditor obtain sufficient knowledge and understanding of the organization's risk assessment process, which is an organization's "identification, analysis, and management of risks relevant to the preparation of financial statements that are fairly presented in conformity with generally accepted accounting principles."

According to SAS-78, risks can arise or change due to circumstances such as the following: changes in operating environment; new personnel; new or revamped information systems; rapid growth; new technology; new programs, products, services, or activities; changes in the level and source of funding; foreign operations; expiration of major contracts or grants; and changes in accounting pronouncements.

	Yes	No	N/A
1. Has management established clear organization-wide objectives and are they consistent with its business plans and budgets?	___	___	___
2. Has management established objectives for key activities and are they consistent with and linked to the organization-wide objectives and strategies?	___	___	___
3. Has management identified the resources and critical factors that are important to achieving its objectives (e.g., financing, personnel, facilities, technology, etc.)?	___	___	___
4. Does management consider risks arising from external sources (e.g., funding sources, creditors' demands, competitors' actions, regulation, natural events)?	___	___	___
5. Does management consider risks arising from internal sources (e.g., retention of key personnel or changes in their responsibilities, compensation and benefit programs to keep the organization competitive, the adequacy of backup systems in the event of failure of systems that could significantly affect operations)?	___	___	___
6. Does management identify and monitor significant shifts in the not-for-profit industry in which it operates (e.g., voluntary health and welfare organizations, professional associations, country clubs)?	___	___	___
7. Does management identify and monitor significant shifts in the organization's programmatic activities (e.g., changes in program beneficiaries' demographics, needs, or activity patterns)?	___	___	___
8. Does management consult with its legal counsel regarding the implications of any new legislation or regulation?	___	___	___
9. Are new employees in key positions adequately supervised to ensure that they understand and perform in accordance with the organization's policies and procedures?	___	___	___
10. Are procedures in place to assess the effects of new or redesigned information systems and to monitor new technologies?	___	___	___

	Yes	No	N/A

11. Are procedures in place to handle rapidly increasing volumes of information?

12. When considering development of new programs or product lines, does management give appropriate consideration to major factors such as program service requirements, ability to provide the services, and the impact on the organization's financial operating results?

13. In connection with restructurings, are staff reassignments and reductions appropriately analyzed for their potential effect on operations or on the morale of the remaining employees?

14. Does management keep abreast of the political, regulatory, business, and social culture of areas in which foreign operations exist and are personnel made aware of accepted customs and rules?

15. Is management aware of the existence of new accounting or reporting pronouncements and how they may affect the organization's financial reporting practices?

ADDITIONAL COMMENTS—RISK ASSESSMENT

_____

_____

_____

SECTION III—CONTROL ACTIVITIES

Section III of the form is designed to help the auditor obtain an understanding of the client's control activities. Control activities are the policies and procedures that help ensure that management's directives are effective in processing and preparing financial statements. To successfully address risks and achieve its objectives, management must institute various control activities, such as segregation of duties, physical controls, and a system of approvals.

	Yes	No	N/A

1. Does management have clear objectives in terms of budget, financial, and operating goals? If yes, are such objectives:
   a. Clearly written?
   b. Actively communicated throughout the organization?
   c. Actively monitored?

	Yes	*No*	*N/A*

2. Do the planning and reporting systems in place:

   a. Adequately identify variances from planned performance?   —— —— ——

   b. Adequately communicate variances to the appropriate level of management?   —— —— ——

3. Does the appropriate level of management:

   a. Adequately investigate variances?   —— —— ——

   b. Take appropriate and timely corrective action?   —— —— ——

4. Has management established procedures to prevent unauthorized access to, or destruction of, documents, records, and assets?   —— —— ——

5. Has management established policies for controlling access to computer programs and data files?   —— —— ——

6. Does management adequately monitor such policies?   —— —— ——

7. Are amounts recorded by the accounting system periodically compared with physical assets?   —— —— ——

8. Are control and subsidiary accounts reconciled regularly and discrepancies reported to appropriate personnel?   —— —— ——

9. Are signatures required to evidence the performance of critical control functions, such as reconciling accounts?   —— —— ——

10. Are general journal entries, other than standard entries, required to be approved by a responsible official not involved with their origination?   —— —— ——

11. Are accounting estimates and judgments made only by knowledgeable and responsible personnel?   —— —— ——

12. Does the accounting system provide in a timely manner the necessary information for the preparation of financial statements and related disclosures in accordance with generally accepted accounting principles or another comprehensive basis of accounting and, where applicable, single audit requirements?   —— —— ——

13. Are financial statements and related disclosures prepared and reviewed by competent personnel who are knowledgeable of the factors affecting the company's financial reporting requirements?   —— —— ——

ADDITIONAL COMMENTS—CONTROL ACTIVITIES

SECTION IV—INFORMATION AND COMMUNICATION

Section IV of the form is designed to help the auditor obtain an understanding of the client's information and communication systems. Information is identified, captured, processed, and reported by information systems. Relevant information includes industry, economic, and regulatory information obtained from external sources, as well as internally generated information.

Communication is inherent in information processing. Communication involves providing a clear understanding of individual roles and responsibilities in an effective manner. This may be accomplished through policy manuals, accounting manuals, or other means, and can be made orally.

	Yes	No	N/A

Information

1. Does the organization have mechanisms in place to obtain relevant external information (e.g., on major donors or contractors, programs of similar organizations that compete for funds, legislative or regulatory developments, and economic changes) and internally generated information critical to the achievement of the organization's objectives?

2. Is the information provided to the right people in sufficient detail and on time to enable them to carry out their responsibilities efficiently and effectively?

3. Is the development or revision of information systems over financial reporting based on a strategic plan and interrelated with the organization's overall information systems and is it responsive to achieving the entity-wide and activity-level objectives?

4. Does management commit the appropriate human and financial resources to develop the necessary financial reporting information systems?

Communication

5. Does management communicate employees' duties and control responsibilities in an effective manner?

6. Are communication channels established for people to report suspected improprieties?

	Yes	No	N/A

7. Does communication flow across the organization adequately (e.g., from shipping to accounting) to enable people to discharge their responsibilities effectively?   ____ ____ ____

8. Does management take timely and appropriate follow-up action on communications received from program services recipients, customers (where applicable), contributors, vendors, regulators, or other external parties?   ____ ____ ____

9. Do other parties outside the organization review and follow up on the organization's actions (e.g., an active review of bank loan agreements) or subrecipient monitoring performed by pass-through grantors?   ____ ____ ____

ADDITIONAL COMMENTS—INFORMATION AND COMMUNICATION

_____

_____

_____

SECTION V—MONITORING

Section V of the form is designed to help the auditor obtain an understanding of the organization's monitoring system. Monitoring is a process that assesses the quality of internal control performance over time. It involves (1) timely evaluation by appropriate personnel of the design and operation of controls, (2) identifying areas of improvement and corrective actions, and (3) follow-up procedures to determine that necessary actions are implemented. Monitoring can be accomplished in manners such as the following: ongoing internal activities, internal audit function, and external monitoring activities.

	Yes	No	N/A

1. Is operating information used to manage operations integrated or reconciled with data generated by the financial reporting system?   ____ ____ ____

2. Are customer complaints about billings investigated and any internal control deficiencies corrected?   ____ ____ ____

3. Are communications from vendors and monthly statements of accounts payable used as a control monitoring technique?   ____ ____ ____

4. Are internal control recommendations made by external auditors (and internal auditors, if applicable) implemented?   ____ ____ ____

5. Does management receive feedback from training seminars, planning sessions, and other meetings on whether controls operate effectively?   ____ ____ ____

	Yes	No	N/A

6. Does the organization take a fresh look at the internal control system from time to time and evaluate its effectiveness? If yes: ____ ____ ____

    a Does the evaluation process include checklists, questionnaires, or other tools? ____ ____ ____

    b. Are the evaluations documented? ____ ____ ____

7. Does the entity have an adequate internal audit function? If yes, do the internal auditors: ____ ____ ____

    a. Possess adequate training and experience? ____ ____ ____

    b. Adhere to applicable professional standards? ____ ____ ____

    c. Have an adequate documentation of the organization's internal control? ____ ____ ____

    d. Perform tests of controls and substantive tests? ____ ____ ____

    e. Have adequate documentation of their work? ____ ____ ____

    f. Submit reports on their findings to the board of directors or audit committee in a timely manner? ____ ____ ____

    g. Follow up on corrective actions taken by management? ____ ____ ____

    h. Have direct access to the board of directors or audit committee? ____ ____ ____

    i. Have direct access to records and the scope of their activities is not limited? ____ ____ ____

ADDITIONAL COMMENTS—MONITORING

_____

_____

_____

SECTION VI—UNDERSTANDING OF ACCOUNT BALANCES AND CLASSES OF TRANSACTIONS

Section VI of the form is designed to help the auditor obtain an understanding of the account balances and classes of transactions that are significant to the financial statements. In determining which account balances or classes of transactions are significant to the financial statements, the auditor should consider the following factors:

1. The size and volume of individual items comprising the account balance or class of transactions and the relative materiality of the balance or class to the overall financial statements.

2. Complexity and contentiousness of accounting issues affecting the balance or class.

3. Frequency or significance of difficult-to-audit transactions affecting the balance or class.

4. Nature, cause, and amount of known and likely misstatements detected in the balance or class in the prior audit.

5. Susceptibility of related assets to misappropriation.

6. Competence and experience of personnel assigned to processing data that affect the balance or class.

7. Extent of judgment involved in determining the total balance or class.

8. Complexity of calculations affecting the balance or class.

For each audit area deemed significant, the auditor should obtain sufficient knowledge of the accounting system to understand:

- How and by whom the transactions are initiated

- The accounting processing involved from initiation of a transaction to its inclusion in the financial statements, including how the computer is used to process data

- The supporting documents involved, including accounting records and journals, source documents, and electronic means involved in the processing of the transactions

- The documents and reports generated by the accounting system

The aforementioned understanding of the accounting system is the minimum requirement that the auditor should comply with for each audit area deemed significant. After obtaining such an understanding, the auditor may wish to obtain a further understanding of control activities. A further understanding of control activities would generally not be considered necessary for most small businesses. Nevertheless, the auditor may find it necessary to obtain a further understanding of control activities under the following circumstances:

1. The auditor needs an understanding of control activities to adequately plan the audit.

2. The auditor plans to test controls.

3. The auditor needs such an understanding for purposes of management letter recommendations or other similar purposes.

In summary, for each significant audit area, the auditor should always obtain an understanding of the accounting system and give adequate consideration to whether it is necessary to obtain a further understanding of control activities.

After considering these factors, check in the appropriate column below (1) which audit areas are deemed significant, and obtain an understanding of the accounting system for these areas, and (2) whether a further understanding of control activities will be obtained:

		Check Significant Audit Area (and Obtain Understanding of Accounting System)	Check Only If Further Understanding of Control Activities Will Be Obtained
I.	CASH	_____	_____
II.	INVESTMENTS	_____	_____
III.	CONTRIBUTIONS AND OTHER RECEIVABLES AND REVENUE	_____	_____
IV.	INVENTORIES AND COST OF SALES	_____	_____
V.	PROPERTY, PLANT, AND EQUIPMENT	_____	_____
VI.	PREPAID EXPENSES, DEFERRED CHARGES, INTANGIBLES, AND OTHER ASSETS	_____	_____
VII.	ACCOUNTS PAYABLE AND PURCHASES	_____	_____
VIII.	PAYROLLS AND OTHER LIABILITIES	_____	_____
IX.	DEBT AND LEASE OBLIGATIONS	_____	_____
X.	NET ASSETS	_____	_____
XI.	TAX CONSIDERATIONS	_____	_____
XII.	COMMITMENTS AND CONTINGENCIES	_____	_____
XIII.	COMPUTER CONTROLS	_____	_____

After completing each applicable audit area in this section, the auditor should document his or her assessment of control risk in the space provided after each area. For audit areas not checked, control risk is considered to be assessed at the maximum level. **The auditor should note that control risk cannot be assessed below the maximum level unless tests of controls** are performed; therefore, when considering assessing control risk below the maximum (i.e., moderate or low), the auditor should evaluate whether the effort to be expended on tests of controls would justify a reduction in the effort related to the performance of substantive tests and, therefore, result in audit efficiency.

I. CASH

INTERNAL CONTROL OBJECTIVES

- Access to cash, cash receipts, and cash disbursements records is restricted.
- Cash receipts are recorded correctly as to account, amount, and period and are deposited promptly intact.
- Cash receipts are applied properly to donor/customer balances.
- Cash disbursements are made for goods or services authorized and received.
- Cash disbursements are recorded correctly as to account, amount, and period.
- Cash balance records are reconciled regularly to bank statements and differences are investigated.

POTENTIAL ERRORS AND FRAUD

Cash Receipts

- Cash receipts are recorded incorrectly.
- Items are sold for cash or cash contributions are received, the revenue is not recorded, and the cash is misappropriated.
- Checks received are deposited but not recorded; checks are written to employees for the same amount and also are not recorded.
- Receipts from donors or others are misappropriated, and collectible contributions or other receivables are written off or otherwise credited.
- Lapping occurs (e.g., cash receipts are misappropriated and shortages are concealed by delaying postings of cash receipts).

Cash Disbursements

- Payment is made for goods or services that are not authorized or not received.
- Checks are made out to wrong payees.
- Invoices are paid twice.
- Vendor invoices are altered and photocopied to conceal alteration; payment benefits third parties.
- Check signature or endorsement is forged.
- Disbursements are misclassified or not recorded.

- Disbursements are recorded at the wrong amount or in the wrong period.
- Checks are issued for the benefit of employees or third parties, and payees are changed in the cash disbursements journal.
- Cash disbursements journal is overstated; overstated amount is recorded and the difference is misappropriated.
- Kiting occurs (exploiting the time required for a check to clear the bank ["float" period] to conceal shortage of cash).

UNDERSTANDING OF ACCOUNTING SYSTEM

1. How and by whom are the transactions initiated?

   _____

   _____

   _____

2. Describe the source documents that support the transactions.

   _____

   _____

   _____

3. Describe the computer media that are used in the processing of accounting information.

   _____

   _____

   _____

4. Describe the documents and reports generated by the accounting system.

   _____

   _____

   _____

5. Describe the accounting processing, records, and files (including how frequently they are updated) that are used to process the transactions, including how transactions are reflected in journals of original entry and in the general ledger.

   _____

   _____

   _____

FURTHER UNDERSTANDING OF CONTROL ACTIVITIES

Cash Receipts

	Yes	No	N/A

1. Is mail opened by someone independent of cashier, accounts receivable bookkeeper, or other accounting employees who may initiate or post journal entries?

2. Is the delivery of unopened business mail prohibited to employees having access to the accounting records?

3. Does the employee who opens the mail:

    a. Place restrictive endorsements ("For deposit only") on all checks received?

    b. Prepare a list of the money, checks, and other receipts?

    c. Forward all remittances to the person responsible for preparing and making the daily bank deposit?

    d. Forward the total of all remittances to the person responsible for comparing it to the authenticated deposit ticket and amount recorded?

4. Is a lock box used?

5. Is an independent listing of cash receipts prepared before the receipts are submitted to the cashier or accounts/contributions receivable bookkeeper?

6. Does an independent person verify the listing against the deposit slips?

7. Are employees responsible for fund-raising functions and activities independent of employees responsible for the accounting function?

8. Is a copy of the listing of cash receipts provided to employees responsible for fund-raising activities?

9. Do cash sales or cash contributions occur? If yes:

    a. Are cash receipts prenumbered?

    b. Is an independent check of prenumbered receipts done daily and reconciled to cash collections?

    c. Are cash register tape totals reconciled to amount of cash in drawer?

    d. Do cash refunds require approval?

10. Are authenticated deposit slips retained and reconciled to the corresponding amounts in the cash receipts records?

11. Are cash receipts deposited intact daily?

	Yes	No	N/A

12. Is the bank deposit made by someone other than the cashier or the accounts receivable bookkeeper? ___ ___ ___

13. Are employees who handle receipts bonded?

14. Is the accounts/contributions receivable bookkeeper restricted from:

    a. Preparing the bank deposit? ___ ___ ___

    b. Obtaining access to the cash receipts book? ___ ___ ___

    c. Having access to donor/customer collections? ___ ___ ___

15. Are banks instructed not to cash checks drawn to the order of the organization? ___ ___ ___

16. Is the cashier restricted from gaining access to the accounts/contributions receivable records, bank statements, and donor/customer statements? ___ ___ ___

17. Does a person independent of the cash receipts and receivables functions compare entries to the cash receipts journal with:

    a. Authenticated bank deposit slips? ___ ___ ___

    b. Deposit per the bank statements? ___ ___ ___

    c. Listing of cash receipts prepared when mail is opened? ___ ___ ___

18. Are areas where physical handling of cash takes place reasonably safeguarded? ___ ___ ___

19. Is information adequately captured from remittances for accurate posting of credits to customer/donor accounts, for proper classification regarding its sources (e.g., interest income, sale of property, loan proceeds), or for net asset class? ___ ___ ___

20. Do postings to the general ledger control and subsidiary accounts include the date on which the remittance was received? ___ ___ ___

21. Are postings to the general ledger made by a person independent of the cash receipts and receivables functions? ___ ___ ___

22. Are donor/customer complaints handled by a person independent of the cashier or accounts/contributions receivable functions? ___ ___ ___

Cash Disbursements

	Yes	No	N/A

1. Are all disbursements made by check except those from petty cash? ___ ___ ___

2. Are prenumbered checks used and all numbers accounted for? ___ ___ ___

	Yes	No	N/A

3. Are voided checks properly defaced and retained? ___ ___ ___

4. Are dual signatures required for checks over a predetermined amount? If yes: ___ ___ ___

   a. Are the check signers independent of each other? ___ ___ ___

   b. Is approved supporting documentation presented to each check signer? ___ ___ ___

5. Is signing of checks in advance or in blank prohibited? ___ ___ ___

6. Are checks payable to "cash" or "bearer" prohibited? ___ ___ ___

7. Is access to unused checks limited to authorized persons? ___ ___ ___

8. Is a check-signing machine used? If yes: ___ ___ ___

   a. At all times, are the keys, signature plate, and operation of the signing machine under control of the official whose signature is on the plate? ___ ___ ___

   b. Are the employees who have custody of the keys and plate, and who operate the check-signing machine, independent of check-preparation functions and denied access to blank checks? ___ ___ ___

   c. Are the checks issued to the machine operator counted in advance, and reconciled with the totals indicated on the check-signing machine by someone other than the machine operator? ___ ___ ___

9. Are invoices, vouchers, and other supporting documents presented with the checks submitted for signature? ___ ___ ___

10. Are supporting documents for checks properly canceled (e.g., stamped "paid") to avoid duplicate payment? ___ ___ ___

11. Do proper safeguards exist to prevent checks that have been mailed from returning to the accounts payable bookkeeper or to the employee who drew the checks? ___ ___ ___

12. Is the check-signing function independent of purchasing, cash bookkeeping, and preparation of checks? ___ ___ ___

13. Are bank accounts and check signers authorized by the board of directors? ___ ___ ___

14. Are all checks promptly recorded upon issuance and listed in detail (e.g., in a check register)? ___ ___ ___

	Yes	No	N/A

15. Are payroll checks drawn against a separate bank account? ___ ___ ___

Petty Cash Funds

	Yes	No	N/A

1. Are petty cash funds maintained on an imprest basis? If yes, are they: ___ ___ ___

   a. Reasonably small in amount? ___ ___ ___

   b. Kept in a safe area? ___ ___ ___

   c. Regularly counted by someone other than the custodian? ___ ___ ___

2. Are petty cash disbursements:

   a. Supported by prenumbered vouchers? ___ ___ ___

   b. Restricted to a predetermined maximum dollar amount? ___ ___ ___

3. Are vouchers canceled or marked to prevent duplicate reimbursement? ___ ___ ___

4. Do advances to employees and IOU's require proper approval? ___ ___ ___

5. Are checks for reimbursement of petty cash funds:

   a. Made out to the order of the custodian? ___ ___ ___

   b. Subject to the same review and approval as invoices? ___ ___ ___

6. Are surprise counts made at reasonable intervals by an employee independent of the custodian? ___ ___ ___

Cash Reconciliations

	Yes	No	N/A

1. Are bank statements, related canceled checks, deposit tickets, and related memos received directly from the bank by the employee performing the reconciliations? ___ ___ ___

2. Are bank accounts reconciled monthly by a person independent of cash receipts, general ledger, contributions or other receivables, or accounts payable functions? ___ ___ ___

3. Do bank reconciliation procedures include:

   a. Accounting for the sequence of all check numbers? ___ ___ ___

   b. Examining the paid checks for date, name, endorsement, and cancellation and comparing them to the cash disbursements journal? ___ ___ ___

	Yes	No	N/A
c. Comparing the detail of bank deposits to cash receipts records?	___	___	___
d. Investigating other reconciling items (e.g., checks returned for insufficient funds)?	___	___	___
e. Following up on old outstanding checks?	___	___	___
4. Is independent review performed of monthly bank reconciliations?	___	___	___

ASSESSMENT OF CONTROL RISK

(High/Maximum, Moderate, or Low)

	Financial Statement Assertions				
	Existence or Occurrence	Completeness	Rights and Obligations	Valuation or Allocation	Presentation and Disclosure
Assessment of control risk	___	___	___	___	___

II. INVESTMENTS

INTERNAL CONTROL OBJECTIVES

- Investment transactions are authorized and recorded correctly as to account, amount, and period.
- Income earned on investments is recorded correctly as to account, amount, and period.
- Loss in value of investments is promptly detected and provided for.
- Investment instruments are adequately safeguarded.
- Pledging of investments is authorized.
- Investments are properly valued and classified as long-term or short-term.
- Investments that are subject to donor restrictions are appropriately restricted and classified.
- Donor-restricted and board-designated investment funds are not used for unauthorized purposes.

POTENTIAL ERRORS AND FRAUD

- Investments are made that are not authorized.
- Investments are purchased but not recorded; investments are recorded but not purchased.
- Investments are sold but not recorded; investments are recorded as sold but not sold.
- Investments are valued incorrectly.

- Unwarranted investment losses are incurred or potential investment gains are not realized.

- Unauthorized pledging of investments takes place for the benefit of employees or third parties.

- Restricted investments are sold or otherwise used in violation of a donor restriction.

- Donor-restricted and board-designated investment funds are used for unauthorized purposes.

UNDERSTANDING OF ACCOUNTING SYSTEM

1. How and by whom are the transactions initiated, and how they are authorized?

2. Describe the source documents that support the transactions.

3. Describe the computer media that are used in the processing of accounting information.

4. Describe the documents and reports generated by the accounting system.

5. Describe the accounting processing, records, and files (including how frequently they are updated) that are used to process the transactions, including how transactions are reflected in journals of original entry and in the general ledger.

FURTHER UNDERSTANDING OF CONTROL ACTIVITIES

	Yes	No	N/A
1. Are securities kept in a safe vault? If yes:	___	___	___
a. Is a record kept of all visits to the vault?	___	___	___
b. Is the presence or signature of two or more designated persons required to open the vault?	___	___	___
c. Is a detail record (e.g., certificate number, description) kept of each security?	___	___	___
d. Are the securities periodically inspected and compared with detailed investment records by employees independent of the custodian and with the general ledger?	___	___	___
2. Are all securities held in the name of the entity?	___	___	___
3. Is custody of investment securities held by the entity assigned to bonded employees?	___	___	___
4. Is the custodian of securities independent of the accounting function?	___	___	___
5. Are purchases, exchanges, sales, and pledges of investments initiated and approved by designated officers?	___	___	___
6. Are investment transactions approved in consideration of donor restrictions and board designations of investment funds?	___	___	___
7. Are investments held in custodial accounts with a bank, trustee, or broker? If yes:	___	___	___
a. Are account statements from these parties regularly reconciled with the general ledger control account?	___	___	___
b. Is there a periodic review of the reputation and financial position of the parties that are ensuring completion of investment transactions?	___	___	___
8. Is documented management authorization of transactions compared with evidence of execution of transactions (e.g., brokers' advices) promptly, and are differences investigated?	___	___	___
9. Are procedures adequate to ensure that investment income is recorded in the proper net asset class and collected in a timely manner?	___	___	___
10. Are the carrying values of investments reviewed periodically to determine if adjustments are needed for permanent impairment in value?	___	___	___

Yes   No   N/A

11. Are investments that have been written off or fully reserved against followed up on regarding their possible realization? ___ ___ ___

12. Is a periodic review of the investment portfolio made by designated officers? ___ ___ ___

ASSESSMENT OF CONTROL RISK

(High/Maximum, Moderate, or Low)

Financial Statement Assertions

	Existence or Occurrence	Completeness	Rights and Obligations	Valuation or Allocation	Presentation and Disclosure
Assessment of control risk	___	___	___	___	___

III. CONTRIBUTIONS AND OTHER RECEIVABLES AND REVENUE

Note: The internal control considerations for not-for-profit organizations should consider both the billing and collection of resources from donors and contractors as well as fee-for-service activities and sales of products, which are functions similar to those performed by commercial enterprises.

INTERNAL CONTROL OBJECTIVES

- Where applicable, services provided or products shipped are billed and properly and promptly recorded in the general ledger and subsidiary records.
- Contracts and grants are properly billed and recorded in the general ledger and subsidiary records.
- Billings and revenues are recorded correctly as to account, net asset classification amount, and period.
- Recorded billings are for valid transactions.
- Customer returns and other allowances are approved and recorded correctly as to account, amount, and period.
- Uncollectible accounts are promptly identified and provided for.
- Customer orders require approval of credit and terms in accordance with management's authorization before acceptance.
- Unpaid pledges are billed periodically and are only written off with proper approval.

POTENTIAL ERRORS AND FRAUD

- Goods are shipped or services rendered but not billed; contribution, contract, and other receivables are not recorded.

- Billings are recorded, but goods are not shipped or services are not rendered at all or are not rendered until the following period.
- Contributors, contractors, and others are billed at incorrect amounts.
- Revenues are recorded in the wrong period or net asset class to achieve desired operating results.
- Orders from customers with poor credit are accepted and normal or favorable credit terms are granted.
- Orders are accepted at terms other than those established by management.
- There is an unwarranted granting of credit under a kickback arrangement.
- Receivables are aged incorrectly, and potentially uncollectible amounts are not recognized.
- Receivables are improperly written off to conceal misappropriation of cash receipts.
- Credits issued for returns or allowances are not earned or are not in accordance with company policy.

UNDERSTANDING OF ACCOUNTING SYSTEM

1. How and by whom are the transactions initiated?

_____

_____

_____

2. Describe the source documents that support the transactions.

_____

_____

_____

3. Describe the computer media used in the processing of accounting information.

_____

_____

_____

4. Describe the documents and reports generated by the accounting system.

_____

_____

_____

5. Describe the accounting processing, records, and files (including how frequently they are updated) that are used to process the transactions, including how transactions are reflected in journals of original entry and in the general ledger.

_____

_____

_____

FURTHER UNDERSTANDING OF CONTROL ACTIVITIES

Sales and Shipping

	Yes	No	N/A
1. Are sales orders approved by someone independent of marketing and order entry (e.g., credit manager) before acceptance and before any orders are shipped?	___	___	___
2. Are there adequate procedures for assigning credit limits to new customers? If yes:	___	___	___
a. Is the credit of prospective customers investigated before it is extended to them?	___	___	___
b. Are credit limits approved by designated personnel independent of marketing, billing, collection, and accounting functions?	___	___	___
c. Are credit limits regularly reviewed and compared to balances outstanding?	___	___	___
3. Is there timely communication of credit limits, and changes thereto, to personnel responsible for approving sales orders?	___	___	___
4. Are standard price lists used for basic sales prices and credit terms? If yes:	___	___	___
a. Are they reviewed periodically?	___	___	___
b. Are deviations from the price lists approved by designated employees?	___	___	___
5. Are shipping documents prepared for all goods shipped? If yes:	___	___	___
a. Are the documents prenumbered?	___	___	___
b. Is the numerical sequence of the shipping documents checked and controlled?	___	___	___
c. Does the shipping department double check the quantities shown on the shipping documents?	___	___	___

Yes   No   N/A

d. Do the documents clearly indicate pertinent information such as description of quantities and goods shipped, date of shipment, shipment destination, and means of shipment?   ____ ____ ____

6. Are shipping documents reviewed and compared with billings promptly to ensure that all goods shipped are billed?   ____ ____ ____

7. Are unfilled sales orders reviewed periodically and followed up on?   ____ ____ ____

Customer Returns and Allowances

Yes   No   N/A

1. Are returns, allowances, discounts, and other credits approved before issuance by a person who does not handle cash and receivables functions?   ____ ____ ____

2. Are receiving reports prepared for all sales returns by the department receiving the incoming materials?   ____ ____ ____

3. Are credit memos for returned goods:

   a. Supported by adequate documentation from the receiving department?   ____ ____ ____

   b. Prenumbered and the numerical sequence accounted for?   ____ ____ ____

   c. Recorded in a timely manner?   ____ ____ ____

4. Are customer claims for repairs under guarantees/warranties checked for compliance with terms of sale?   ____ ____ ____

Billings and Valuation

Yes   No   N/A

1. Are sales and contract invoices:

   a. Prenumbered and issued in numerical sequence?   ____ ____ ____

   b. Prepared for all shipments of goods or provision of services?   ____ ____ ____

   c. Compared with shipping documents, customer orders, or contract status reports?   ____ ____ ____

   d. Checked for clerical accuracy?   ____ ____ ____

   e. Verified for prices and rates used?   ____ ____ ____

   f. Checked for credit terms?   ____ ____ ____

Yes　No　N/A

2. Are adequate records maintained of daily sales (e.g., in a sales journal) and compared to postings to the general ledger? ＿＿ ＿＿ ＿＿

3. Are receivables postings reconciled to the sales journal or contract revenue schedules or logs? ＿＿ ＿＿ ＿＿

4. Is the billing function performed by employees who are independent of the programmatic selling, credit, inventory custody, and cash functions? ＿＿ ＿＿ ＿＿

5. Are employees who are responsible for maintaining receivables ledgers independent of the general ledger function? ＿＿ ＿＿ ＿＿

6. Are receivables aged regularly? If yes: ＿＿ ＿＿ ＿＿

　　a. Are they reviewed regularly by designated personnel? ＿＿ ＿＿ ＿＿

　　b. Are past due or delinquent accounts or unusual items investigated in a timely manner? ＿＿ ＿＿ ＿＿

　　c. Are credit balances investigated? ＿＿ ＿＿ ＿＿

7. Are the receivable subsidiary ledgers reconciled regularly to the related general ledger control accounts? ＿＿ ＿＿ ＿＿

8. Are statements of accounts mailed periodically? If yes: ＿＿ ＿＿ ＿＿

　　a. Are they sent by an employee who is independent of the receivables and cash functions? ＿＿ ＿＿ ＿＿

　　b. Are discrepancies and complaints investigated by the same employee? ＿＿ ＿＿ ＿＿

9. Is the receivables detail reviewed periodically to determine the need for a valuation allowance for doubtful accounts? ＿＿ ＿＿ ＿＿

10. Are write-offs of uncollectible receivables approved by an employee other than the credit manager or the accounts receivable bookkeeper? ＿＿ ＿＿ ＿＿

11. Are receivables that have been written off turned over to collection agencies or lawyers? ＿＿ ＿＿ ＿＿

12. Does a responsible official, senior to the receivables bookkeeper, approve journal entries affecting receivables? ＿＿ ＿＿ ＿＿

ASSESSMENT OF CONTROL RISK

(High/Maximum, Moderate, or Low)

Financial Statement Assertions

	Existence or Occurrence	Completeness	Rights and Obligations	Valuation or Allocation	Presentation and Disclosure
Assessment of control risk					

IV. INVENTORIES AND COST OF SALES

Note: While inventory is often not a significant account balance for a not-for-profit organization, many organizations do engage in selling goods from inventory, so an auditor may desire to consider the internal controls over inventory in a manner similar to what would be performed for a commercial enterprise.

INTERNAL CONTROL OBJECTIVES

- Inventories are purchased only with proper authorization.
- Inventories received are recorded correctly as to account, amount, and period.
- Inventories are adequately safeguarded.
- Transfer of finished goods to customers and other dispositions (e.g., scrap sales) are recorded correctly as to account, amount, and period.
- Production costs and costs of sales are properly accumulated and classified in the accounting records.
- Inventory balances recorded in the accounting records are evaluated periodically by comparison with actual quantities on hand (i.e., physical inventory).
- Costs are assigned to inventories in accordance with the stated valuation method.
- Obsolete and slow-moving inventories are promptly detected and provided for.
- Carrying values of inventories are periodically compared to net realizable value and appropriate adjustments are made.

POTENTIAL ERRORS AND FRAUD

- Entries are not properly reflected in general ledger inventory accounts for purchases, production, or sales transactions.
- Inaccuracies in the detailed perpetual inventory records result in unnecessary materials purchased or units produced, inventory overstock, and obsolescence.
- Undetected physical loss or deterioration of inventory occurs.

- Scrap sales are not monitored or reported.
- Nonexistent inventory items are included in periodic physical count.
- Transfers from raw materials or work-in-process are recorded improperly or in the wrong period.
- Unauthorized adjustment of inventory records is made to conceal misappropriation of assets.
- Inventory records are manipulated to change the reporting of operating results.

UNDERSTANDING OF ACCOUNTING SYSTEM

1. How and by whom are the transactions initiated?

   _____

   _____

   _____

2. Describe the source documents that support the transactions.

   _____

   _____

   _____

3. Describe the computer media that is used in the processing of accounting information.

   _____

   _____

   _____

4. Describe the documents and reports generated by the accounting system.

   _____

   _____

   _____

5. Describe the accounting processing, records, and files (including how frequently they are updated) that are used to process the transactions, including how transactions are reflected in journals of original entry and in the general ledger.

   _____

   _____

   _____

FURTHER UNDERSTANDING OF CONTROL ACTIVITIES

Physical Control, Reconciliations, and Valuation

		Yes	No	N/A
1.	Are all types of inventory (e.g., raw materials, work-in-process, finished goods) adequately safeguarded (e.g., guards, alarms) and insured?	___	___	___
2.	Are employees with access to inventory bonded?	___	___	___
3.	Are offsite inventories stored in bonded warehouses?	___	___	___
4.	Are employees who are responsible for custody of inventory independent of inventory recording and accounting functions?	___	___	___
5.	Are receiving reports for all incoming materials prepared for the accounting department to be matched with purchase orders and invoices?	___	___	___
6.	Are production reports for all materials produced prepared for the accounting department?	___	___	___
7.	Are issuances and shipments made only on signed requisitions?	___	___	___
8.	Are shipping documents prepared for all shipments?	___	___	___
9.	Are physical inventories taken:			
	a. At the end of the fiscal year?	___	___	___
	b. Periodically during the year?	___	___	___
10.	Are written instructions and procedures followed for inventory counts and is compliance with them checked?	___	___	___
11.	Are inventory counts supervised by qualified persons following adequate written instructions and procedures?	___	___	___
12.	Are inventory custodians independent of billing, shipping, and recordkeeping?	___	___	___
13.	Are documents issued in prenumbered order and controlled for:			
	a. Receiving?	___	___	___
	b. Shipping?	___	___	___
	c. Materials requisitions?	___	___	___
	d. Production orders?	___	___	___

	Yes	No	N/A

14. Are priced inventory sheets numerically controlled and verified as to:

    a. Quantities?

    b. Unit cost?

    c. Extensions and footings?

15. Are costs, extensions, and footings of the inventory listings verified by a second person?

16. Is a periodic review made as to potential overstock, slow-moving, and obsolete items by comparing quantities on hand with historical usage?

17. Are adequate controls in place for sale or reuse of scrap or salvaged materials?

18. Is the carrying value of inventory periodically compared to net realizable value, and are adjustments recorded if necessary?

19. Are records maintained for inventory on consignment or in outside warehouses and periodically reconciled to reports received from these parties?

20. Are all inventory adjustments documented, and do they require management approval?

Perpetual Records

	Yes	No	N/A

1. Are perpetual inventory records maintained for:

    a. Raw materials?

    b. Work-in-process?

    c. Finished goods?

    d. Supplies and repair parts?

2. Do the perpetual records show:

    a. Quantities?

    b. Unit costs?

    c. Aggregate dollar values?

3. Are the perpetual records kept by employees who have no access to the inventory?

4. Are significant differences between physical counts and perpetual records investigated promptly?

5. Are perpetual records reconciled periodically to the controlling accounts in the general ledger?

Yes   No   N/A

6. Are the perpetual records adjusted to the physical inventory counts at least once a year, and are such adjustments approved by a responsible employee?   ___   ___   ___

7. Are perpetual inventory records checked regularly by cycle counts? If yes: ___   ___   ___

   a. Are all classes of inventory subjected to cycle counts?   ___   ___   ___

   b. Are significant differences between cycle counts and perpetual records investigated and reconciled?   ___   ___   ___

   c. Are inventory adjustments documented and do they require management approval?   ___   ___   ___

Cost Accounting Processes

Yes   No   N/A

1. Are raw materials issued recorded from production orders or stores requisitions?   ___   ___   ___

2. Are material costs charged to job orders or material usage accounts?   ___   ___   ___

3. Are production labor costs charged to job orders or departmental expense accounts based on payroll records, job tickets, or production reports?   ___   ___   ___

4. Is overhead charged to job orders, departments, or work-in-process based on measure of activity (e.g., direct labor hours or dollars)?   ___   ___   ___

5. Is work-in-process increased for raw materials placed in production?   ___   ___   ___

6. Is work-in-process relieved and finished goods charged based on completed production orders, inspection reports, or finished goods receiving tickets?   ___   ___   ___

7. Are finished goods relieved based on filled sales orders or storekeepers' issue slips?   ___   ___   ___

8. Is the application of materials, labor, and overhead to work-in-process and finished goods inventories reviewed regularly for reasonableness and consistency?   ___   ___   ___

9. Are standard cost variances regularly analyzed and allocated to inventory?   ___   ___   ___

ASSESSMENT OF CONTROL RISK

(High/Maximum, Moderate, or Low)

Financial Statement Assertions

	Existence or Occurrence	Completeness	Rights and Obligations	Valuation or Allocation	Presentation and Disclosure
Assessment of control risk	_____	_____	_____	_____	_____

V. PROPERTY, PLANT, AND EQUIPMENT

INTERNAL CONTROL OBJECTIVES

- Property, plant, and equipment are purchased only with proper authorization.

- Property, plant, and equipment purchases are recorded correctly as to account, net asset classification amount, and period.

- Disposals, retirements, and trade-ins are identified promptly and recorded correctly as to account, amount, and period.

- Property, plant, and equipment are adequately safeguarded and insured.

- Depreciation is calculated correctly using proper lives and methods and is recorded in a timely manner.

POTENTIAL ERRORS AND FRAUD

- Purchases of property are recorded in the wrong account or not recorded.

- Unnecessary property is acquired, resulting in unused or idle capacity.

- Employees are able to conceal unauthorized purchases for their own benefit.

- Property remains in the accounting records after disposal.

- Sales of property are not recorded, and proceeds are misappropriated.

- Wrong lives are assigned to property, resulting in miscalculation of depreciation.

UNDERSTANDING OF ACCOUNTING SYSTEM

1. How and by whom are the transactions initiated?

   _____

   _____

   _____

2. Describe the source documents that support the transactions.

_____

_____

_____

3. Describe the computer media that is used in the processing of accounting information.

_____

_____

_____

4. Describe the documents and reports generated by the accounting system.

_____

_____

_____

5. Describe the accounting processing, records, and files (including how frequently they are updated) that are used to process the transactions, including how transactions are reflected in journals of original entry and in the general ledger.

_____

_____

_____

FURTHER UNDERSTANDING OF CONTROL ACTIVITIES

	Yes	No	N/A
1. Are detailed records maintained and do they include:			
a. Description of asset?	___	___	___
b. Cost?	___	___	___
c. Acquisition date?	___	___	___
d. Depreciation method?	___	___	___
e. Related depreciation?	___	___	___
f. Useful life?	___	___	___
2. Are the detailed records reconciled to the general ledger control accounts at least once a year?	___	___	___

	Yes	No	N/A

3. Are depreciable lives reviewed periodically by management and compared to actual experience for adequacy?   _____ _____ _____

4. Is all property adequately insured and is insurance coverage reviewed periodically?   _____ _____ _____

5. Are assets physically inspected periodically and compared to detailed records?   _____ _____ _____

6. Are acquisitions of property authorized by designated personnel for:

   a. All capital expenditures?   _____ _____ _____

   b. Major renovations?   _____ _____ _____

   c. Major repair jobs?   _____ _____ _____

   d. Research and development projects?   _____ _____ _____

7. Does the organization have a well-defined policy for distinguishing between capital expenditures and repairs and maintenance?   _____ _____ _____

8. Does the retirement or sale of property require the approval of designated personnel?   _____ _____ _____

9. Are procedures adequate to ensure that property physically retired is properly removed from the accounting records and that the proceeds from sale, if any, are properly accounted for?   _____ _____ _____

10. Are the methods of selecting useful lives and depreciation policy clearly defined and approved by designated personnel?   _____ _____ _____

11. Are physical safeguards (e.g., alarms, guards, restricted access) over property adequate?   _____ _____ _____

12. Are the personnel who are responsible for maintaining custody of the property independent of the personnel in charge of maintaining the accounting records?   _____ _____ _____

13. Does in-house construction require authorized work orders?   _____ _____ _____

14. Is construction-in-progress regularly reviewed for adherence to budgeted amounts?   _____ _____ _____

15. Are receiving documentation, purchase order or contract, and invoice matched before transactions are recorded?   _____ _____ _____

ASSESSMENT OF CONTROL RISK

(High/Maximum, Moderate, or Low)

Financial Statement Assertions

	Existence or Occurrence	Completeness	Rights and Obligations	Valuation or Allocation	Presentation and Disclosure
Assessment of control risk	_____	_____	_____	_____	_____

VI. PREPAID EXPENSES, DEFERRED CHARGES, INTANGIBLES, AND OTHER ASSETS

INTERNAL CONTROL OBJECTIVES

- Expenditures resulting in prepaid expenses, deferred charges, intangibles, and other assets are incurred only with proper authorization.

- Prepaid expenses, deferred charges, intangibles, and other assets are recorded correctly as to account, amount, and period.

- Amortization or loss in value is recorded correctly as to account, amount, and period.

- The carrying values of assets are recoverable.

POTENTIAL ERRORS AND FRAUD

- Supplies and promotional items are not inventoried and are exposed to theft.

- Expenditures are misclassified, recorded at wrong amounts, or not recorded.

- Misclassifications are used to conceal unauthorized expenditures for the benefit of employees.

- Amortization period exceeds period of benefit.

- Amortization of assets is miscalculated.

- Assets remain on the books after disposal or expiration of the benefit period.

- Intangible assets are carried in excess of value.

- Intangibles known to be worthless are not written off.

UNDERSTANDING OF ACCOUNTING SYSTEM

1. How and by whom are the transactions initiated?

   _____

   _____

   _____

2. Describe the source documents that support the transactions.

_____

_____

_____

3. Describe the computer media that is used in the processing of accounting information.

_____

_____

_____

4. Describe the documents and reports generated by the accounting system.

_____

_____

_____

5. Describe the accounting processing, records, and files (including how frequently they are updated) that are used to process the transactions, including how transactions are reflected in journals of original entry and in the general ledger.

_____

_____

_____

FURTHER UNDERSTANDING OF CONTROL ACTIVITIES

	Yes	*No*	*N/A*
1. Are all such transactions executed in accordance with management authorizations?	____	____	____
2. Is property and liability insurance coverage maintained and reviewed periodically for adequacy?	____	____	____
3. Are the unexpired amounts of premiums that were paid in advance carried as assets in prepaid expenses?	____	____	____
4. Is documentation adequate regarding intangible assets, including:			
a. Specific identity and legal title, if applicable?	____	____	____
b. Manner of acquisition (e.g., purchased, developed internally)?	____	____	____

	Yes	No	N/A
c. Basis for the capitalized amount?	___	___	___
d. Expected period of benefit?	___	___	___
e. Amortization method?	___	___	___

5. Are amortization periods and calculations approved and periodically reviewed by a responsible person?   ___ ___ ___

6. Are the carrying values of all such assets periodically reviewed for reasonableness, and are appropriate adjustments or write-downs made?   ___ ___ ___

7. Are write-downs of carrying values properly documented and approved?   ___ ___ ___

ASSESSMENT OF CONTROL RISK

(High/Maximum, Moderate, or Low)

Financial Statement Assertions

	Existence or Occurrence	Completeness	Rights and Obligations	Valuation or Allocation	Presentation and Disclosure
Assessment of control risk	___	___	___	___	___

VII. ACCOUNTS PAYABLE AND PURCHASES

INTERNAL CONTROL OBJECTIVES

- Goods or services are purchased only with proper authorization.
- Goods or services purchased represent allowable costs for reimbursement in accordance with the terms of that contract or grant agreement.
- Goods or services received are recorded correctly as to account, amount, and period.
- Recorded acquisitions are for goods and services received.
- Adjustments to vendor accounts are made in accordance with management's authorization.
- Only authorized goods and services are accepted and paid for.
- Access to purchasing, receiving, and accounts payable records is adequately controlled to prevent or detect duplicate or improper payments.

POTENTIAL ERRORS AND FRAUD

- Unauthorized purchases are incurred.
- Unallowable goods or services are purchased under a contract or grant agreement and will not be reimbursed.

- Purchases are recorded but goods or services are not received.
- Liability is incurred but not recorded.
- Purchase amount is recorded incorrectly.
- Purchase is charged to wrong account or is recorded in wrong period.
- Purchases at other than favorable terms are made to facilitate side deals for the personal benefit of employees.
- Misclassification to conceal unauthorized purchases occurs.
- Purchase discounts are taken but not recorded; amount of discounts is misappropriated.

UNDERSTANDING OF ACCOUNTING SYSTEM

1. How and by whom are the transactions initiated and authorized?

   _____

   _____

   _____

2. Describe the source documents that support the transactions.

   _____

   _____

   _____

3. Describe the computer media that are used in the processing of accounting information.

   _____

   _____

   _____

4. Describe the documents and reports generated by the accounting system.

   _____

   _____

   _____

5. Describe the accounting processing, records, and files (including how frequently they are updated) that are used to process the transactions, including how transactions are reflected in journals of original entry and in the general ledger.

   _____

   _____

   _____

FURTHER UNDERSTANDING OF CONTROL ACTIVITIES

	Yes	No	N/A
1. Does the organization have a purchasing department? If yes, is it independent of:	___	___	___
a. The accounting department?	___	___	___
b. The receiving department?	___	___	___
c. The shipping department?	___	___	___
2. Are purchases made only after the respective department heads sign purchase requisitions?	___	___	___
3. Are purchases made by means of purchase orders sent to vendors for:			
a. All purchases?	___	___	___
b. Only purchases over a predetermined dollar limit?	___	___	___
4. Do purchase orders specify:			
a. Description of items?	___	___	___
b. Quantity?	___	___	___
c. Price?	___	___	___
d. Terms?	___	___	___
e. Delivery requirements and dates?	___	___	___
5. Is a list of unfilled purchase orders maintained and reviewed periodically?	___	___	___
6. Are purchase order forms prenumbered and is the sequence accounted for periodically?	___	___	___
7. Does the client maintain an approved vendors list?	___	___	___
8. Are items purchased only after competitive bids are obtained? If yes, are competitive bids obtained for:	___	___	___
a. All purchases?	___	___	___
b. Only purchases over a predetermined dollar limit?	___	___	___
9. Is a log maintained of all receipts?	___	___	___
10. Does the receiving department prepare receiving reports for all items received? If yes, are receiving reports:	___	___	___
a. Prepared for all items?	___	___	___
b. Prepared only for items that have purchase orders?	___	___	___
c. Prenumbered?	___	___	___

Yes No N/A

11. At the time the items are received, does someone independent of the purchasing department check the merchandise before acceptance as to:

　a. Description? ___ ___ ___

　b. Quantity? ___ ___ ___

　c. Condition? ___ ___ ___

12. Are copies of receiving reports:

　a. Furnished to the accounting department? ___ ___ ___

　b. Furnished to the purchasing department? ___ ___ ___

　c. Filed in the receiving department? ___ ___ ___

13. Are receipts under blanket purchase orders monitored, and are quantities exceeding authorized total returned to vendor? ___ ___ ___

14. Are procedures adequate for the proper accounting for partial deliveries of purchase orders? ___ ___ ___

15. Are purchasing and receiving functions separate from invoice processing, accounts payable, and general ledger functions? ___ ___ ___

16. Are vendors' invoices, receiving reports, and purchase orders matched before the related liability is recorded? ___ ___ ___

17. Are invoices checked as to:

　a. Prices? ___ ___ ___

　b. Extensions and footings? ___ ___ ___

　c. Freight charges or allowances? ___ ___ ___

　d. Credit terms? ___ ___ ___

18. Are controls adequate to ensure that all available discounts are taken? ___ ___ ___

19. Are purchases recorded in a purchase register or voucher register before being processed through cash disbursements? ___ ___ ___

20. Does a responsible employee assign the appropriate general ledger account distribution to which the invoices are to be posted? ___ ___ ___

21. Are procedures adequate to ensure that invoices have been processed before payment and to prevent duplicate payment (e.g., a block stamp)? ___ ___ ___

22. Does a responsible official approve invoices for payment? ___ ___ ___

	Yes	No	N/A
23. Are procedures adequate to ensure that merchandise purchased for direct delivery to customers is promptly billed to the customers and recorded as both a receivable and a payable?	___	___	___
24. Are records of goods returned to vendors matched to vendor credit memos?	___	___	___
25. Are unmatched receiving reports, purchase orders, and vendors' invoices periodically reviewed and investigated for proper recording?	___	___	___
26. Is the accounts payable ledger or voucher register reconciled monthly to the general ledger control accounts?	___	___	___
27. Are statements from vendors regularly reviewed and reconciled against recorded liabilities?	___	___	___
28. Do adjustments to accounts payable (e.g., writing off of debit balances) require the approval of a designated official?	___	___	___
29. Are budgets used? If yes:	___	___	___
a. Are budgets approved by responsible officials?	___	___	___
b. Are actual expenditures compared with budgeted amounts and variances analyzed and explained?	___	___	___

ASSESSMENT OF CONTROL RISK

(High/Maximum, Moderate, or Low)

	Financial Statement Assertions				
	Existence or Occurrence	Completeness	Rights and Obligations	Valuation or Allocation	Presentation and Disclosure
Assessment of control risk	_____	_____	_____	_____	_____

VIII. PAYROLL AND OTHER LIABILITIES

INTERNAL CONTROL OBJECTIVES

Payroll

- Salary, wage, and benefit expenses are incurred only for work authorized and performed.

- Salaries, wages, and benefits are calculated at the proper rate.

- Salaries, wages, benefits, and related liabilities are recorded correctly as to account, contract or grant agreement, program amount, and period.

- Allocations of payroll costs to functions, programs, contracts, and grants are supported by adequate documentation.
- Employee payroll withholdings and special deductions are based on signed authorizations by employees.

Other Liabilities

- Accruals for liabilities are approved by a responsible official, and detail subsidiary records are maintained and reconciled periodically to the general ledger control accounts.

POTENTIAL ERRORS AND FRAUD

Payroll

- Unauthorized work or work not performed is accrued.
- Accrual of employee benefits (e.g., vacation pay, sick leave) is recorded but not earned.
- There are fictitious employees on the payroll.
- Employees' earnings are over-accrued or under-accrued because of improper rates or computation errors.
- Payroll costs, expenses, or related liabilities are misclassified.
- Payroll is recorded in period paid rather than in period earned.
- Time cards or reports are padded.

Other Liabilities

- Unauthorized expenses are incurred.
- Expenses and accruals are misclassified, recorded at the wrong amounts, or not recorded in the period incurred.

UNDERSTANDING OF ACCOUNTING SYSTEM

1. How and by whom are the transactions initiated?

   _____

   _____

   _____

2. Describe the source documents that support the transactions.

   _____

   _____

   _____

3. Describe the computer media that is used in the processing of accounting information.

   _____

   _____

   _____

4. Describe the documents and reports generated by the accounting system.

_____

_____

_____

5. Describe the accounting processing, records, and files (including how frequently they are updated) that are used to process the transactions, including how transactions are reflected in journals of original entry and in the general ledger.

_____

_____

_____

FURTHER UNDERSTANDING OF CONTROL ACTIVITIES

Payroll

	Yes	No	N/A
1. Are adequate controls present over timekeeping functions?	___	___	___
2. Is the payroll accounting function independent of the general ledger function?	___	___	___
3. Are changes to payroll not made unless the personnel department sends approved notification directly to the payroll department?	___	___	___
4. Are references and backgrounds checked for new hires?	___	___	___
5. Are all wage rates:			
a. Authorized in writing by a designated official?	___	___	___
b. Fixed by union contract?	___	___	___
6. Are signed authorizations on file for employees whose wages are subject to special deductions?	___	___	___
7. Are bonuses, commissions, and overtime:			
a. Approved in advance?	___	___	___
b. Reviewed for compliance with company policy?	___	___	___
8. Are sick leave, vacations, and holidays reviewed for compliance with company policy?	___	___	___
9. Are appropriate forms (e.g., W-4) completed and signed by employees to show authorization for payroll deductions and withholding exemptions?	___	___	___

	Yes	No	N/A

10. Is the payroll periodically checked against the personnel records for terminated employees, fictitious employees, etc.?

11. Does the client use a time clock for:

    a. General office workers?

    b. Factory workers?

12. If the client uses a time clock, are time cards:

    a. Punched by employees in the presence of a designated supervisor?

    b. Signed by a supervisor at the end of the payroll period?

13. Are time sheets prepared by all employees to allocate time to appropriate programs, as well as administrative and fund-raising activities?

14. Are timesheets signed by the employee and approved by his/her immediate supervisor?

15. Are payroll registers reviewed and approved, before disbursements are made, for:

    a. Names of employees?

    b. Hours worked?

    c. Wage rates?

    d. Deductions?

    e. Agreement with payroll checks?

    f. Unusual items?

16. Are all employees paid by check out of a separate bank payroll account?

17. Are payroll checks prenumbered and issued in numerical sequence?

18. Is access restricted to:

    a. Unissued payroll checks?

    b. Signature plate?

19. Are checks drawn and signed by designated officials who do not:

    a. Prepare the payroll?

    b. Have access to the accounting records?

    c. Have custody of cash funds?

	Yes	No	N/A

20. Are payroll checks distributed by someone other than the:

    a. Department head?

    b. Person who prepares the payroll?

21. Is the distribution of the payroll rotated periodically to different employees without prior notice?

22. Is the payroll bank account reconciled by a designated employee who:

    a. Is not involved in preparing the payroll?

    b. Does not sign the checks?

    c. Does not handle the check distributions?

23. Do payroll bank account reconciliation procedures include:

    a. Comparing the paid checks to the payroll?

    b. Scrutinizing canceled check endorsements?

24. Are the payroll registers reconciled to the general ledger control accounts?

25. Is a liability account set up for all wages that have remained unclaimed for a certain period of time? If yes:

    a. Have these wages been redeposited in a special bank account?

    b. Is identification required to be presented at the time of their subsequent distribution?

26. Are distributions of hours (direct and indirect) to activity or departments reviewed and approved by supervisory personnel?

27. Are actual payroll amounts reviewed and compared to budgeted amounts, and are variances analyzed regularly?

28. Do adequate procedures exist for timely and accurate preparation and filing of payroll tax returns and related taxes?

29. Are employee benefit plan contributions reconciled to appropriate employee census data?

30. Are adequate detailed records maintained of the entity's liability for vacation pay and sick pay? If yes:

    a. Are they reconciled to the general ledger control accounts periodically?

Other Liabilities

	Yes	No	N/A
1. Are accruals for liabilities approved by a responsible official?	____	____	____
2. Are detail subsidiary records maintained and reconciled periodically to the general ledger control accounts?	____	____	____

ASSESSMENT OF CONTROL RISK

(High/Maximum, Moderate, or Low)

	Financial Statement Assertions				
	Existence or Occurrence	Completeness	Rights and Obligations	Valuation or Allocation	Presentation and Disclosure
Assessment of control risk	_____	_____	_____	_____	_____

IX. DEBT AND LEASE OBLIGATIONS

INTERNAL CONTROL OBJECTIVES

- Debt and lease obligations and related expenses are authorized and recorded correctly as to account, amount, and period.

- Requirements and restrictions imposed by debt covenants and lease agreements are complied with and monitored.

- Debt retirements and modifications have been properly accounted for.

- Debt instruments and lease agreements are adequately safeguarded.

POTENTIAL ERRORS AND FRAUD

- The entity becomes obligated for debts that are not properly authorized or that are taken on at unfavorable terms.

- Long-term or short-term debt is misclassified.

- Pledged assets or collateral are not identified and disclosed; unauthorized pledging of assets occurs.

- Violations of debt covenants or lease agreements result in default.

- Capital leases are recorded as operating leases or vice versa.

- Interest expense is recorded in the wrong period or at the wrong amount, is not recorded, or is misclassified.

- Debt proceeds are used for other than business purposes.

UNDERSTANDING OF ACCOUNTING SYSTEM

1. How and by whom are the transactions initiated?

_____

_____

_____

2. Describe the source documents that support the transactions.

_____

_____

_____

3. Describe the computer media that is used in the processing of accounting information.

_____

_____

_____

4. Describe the documents and reports generated by the accounting system.

_____

_____

_____

5. Describe the accounting processing, records, and files (including how frequently they are updated) that are used to process the transactions, including how transactions are reflected in journals of original entry and in the general ledger.

_____

_____

_____

FURTHER UNDERSTANDING OF CONTROL ACTIVITIES

	Yes	No	N/A
1. Do borrowings and leases require authorization by designated personnel?	____	____	____
2. Are signatures of two or more designated officials required on all notes payable, lease agreements, and renewals?	____	____	____

	Yes	No	N/A
3. Is a notes payable register maintained by a person independent of check or note signing?	___	___	___
4. Do paid notes get canceled and returned?	___	___	___
5. Are interest charges regularly posted and reviewed?	___	___	___
6. Is compliance with loan covenants and lease agreements periodically reviewed and monitored?	___	___	___
7. Are detailed records periodically reconciled with the general ledger control accounts?	___	___	___
8. Are debt instruments and related legal documents (e.g., notes, bonds) adequately safeguarded?	___	___	___

ASSESSMENT OF CONTROL RISK

(High/Maximum, Moderate, or Low)

Financial Statement Assertions

	Existence or Occurrence	Completeness	Rights and Obligations	Valuation or Allocation	Presentation and Disclosure
Assessment of control risk	___	___	___	___	___

X. NET ASSETS

INTERNAL CONTROL OBJECTIVES

- Net asset transactions are authorized and recorded correctly as to account, net asset classification, amount, and period.
- Recorded net asset transactions and reclassifications comply with donor-imposed restrictions or board designations and are valid and properly authorized.

POTENTIAL ERRORS AND FRAUD

- Improper classification of net asset transactions.

UNDERSTANDING OF ACCOUNTING SYSTEM

1. How and by whom are the transactions initiated?

   _____

   _____

   _____

2. Describe the source documents that support the transactions.

   _____

   _____

   _____

3. Describe the computer media that is used in the processing of accounting information.

_____

_____

_____

4. Describe the documents and reports generated by the accounting system.

_____

_____

_____

5. Describe the accounting processing, records, and files (including how frequently they are updated) that are used to process the transactions, including how transactions are reflected in journals of original entry and in the general ledger.

_____

_____

_____

FURTHER UNDERSTANDING OF CONTROL ACTIVITIES

	Yes	No	N/A
1. Are net asset transactions authorized and approved in accordance with the organization's governing documents as well as documentation of donor-imposed restrictions?	___	___	___
2. Are all net asset reclassifications reviewed and approved by a member of senior management as well as a program and/or fund-raising director?	___	___	___

ASSESSMENT OF CONTROL RISK

(High/Maximum, Moderate, or Low)

	Financial Statement Assertions				
	Existence or Occurrence	Completeness	Rights and Obligations	Valuation or Allocation	Presentation and Disclosure
Assessment of control risk	_____	_____	_____	_____	_____

XI. TAX CONSIDERATIONS

INTERNAL CONTROL OBJECTIVES

- Status of pending examinations by taxing authorities is monitored.
- Maintenance of tax-exempt status is considered before new activities are undertaken.

POTENTIAL ERRORS AND FRAUD

- Required tax payments are not made.
- Requirement to maintain tax-exempt status is violated.
- Provision for unrelated business taxes and other excise taxes and assessments or the related tax liability is not reflected in the accounting records or is reflected at incorrect amounts.
- Incorrect tax or information returns are filed; subsequent audits by taxing authorities result in material unrecorded liabilities.

UNDERSTANDING OF ACCOUNTING SYSTEM

1. How and by whom are the transactions initiated?

   _____

   _____

   _____

2. Describe the source documents that support the transactions.

   _____

   _____

   _____

3. Describe the computer media that is used in the processing of accounting information.

   _____

   _____

   _____

4. Describe the documents and reports generated by the accounting system.

   _____

   _____

   _____

5. Describe the accounting processing, records, and files (including how frequently they are updated) that are used to process the transactions,

including how transactions are reflected in journals of original entry and in the general ledger.

_____

_____

_____

FURTHER UNDERSTANDING OF CONTROL ACTIVITIES

	Yes	*No*	*N/A*
1. Are current controls and procedures adequate to ensure that all tax and information returns and any related estimated payments are prepared and filed promptly?	___	___	___
2. Are procedures adequate to identify and report unrelated business income?	___	___	___
3. Are tax and information returns and financial calculations reviewed by a person independent of the preparer?	___	___	___
4. Is there a formal policy for identifying and evaluating tax exposure items such as matters which might jeopardize tax-exempt status?	___	___	___
5. Are adequate records and supporting documentation maintained in conformity with the compliance requirements of the taxing authorities?	___	___	___
6. Is access to records restricted when public access is not required?	___	___	___

ASSESSMENT OF CONTROL RISK

(High/Maximum, Moderate, or Low)

	Financial Statement Assertions				
	Existence or Occurrence	Completeness	Rights and Obligations	Valuation or Allocation	Presentation and Disclosure
Assessment of control risk	_____	_____	_____	_____	_____

XII. COMMITMENTS AND CONTINGENCIES

INTERNAL CONTROL OBJECTIVES

- Commitments and contingencies are identified and monitored.
- Commitments and contingencies are recorded or disclosed, if deemed appropriate.

- Legal and contractual matters are routed to in-house or outside legal counsel.
- Insurance coverage is adequate and is reviewed regularly.

POTENTIAL ERRORS AND FRAUD

- Provisions for losses that are probable and reasonably estimable are not recorded.
- Losses are incurred because of inadequate insurance coverage.
- Unfavorable claims, judgments, commitments, and contingencies are not disclosed.

UNDERSTANDING OF ACCOUNTING SYSTEM

1. How and by whom are the transactions initiated?

2. Describe the source documents that support the transactions.

3. Describe the computer media that is used in the processing of accounting information.

4. Describe the documents and reports generated by the accounting system.

5. Describe the accounting processing, records, and files (including how frequently they are updated) that are used to process the transactions, including how transactions are reflected in journals of original entry and in the general ledger.

FURTHER UNDERSTANDING OF CONTROL ACTIVITIES

		Yes	No	N/A
1.	Are files of contracts, legal correspondence, etc., maintained and periodically reviewed?	___	___	___
2.	Are legal and contractual matters always referred to in-house or outside legal counsel?	___	___	___
3.	Is compliance with guarantee or warranty policies reviewed by a designated official before the costs are incurred?	___	___	___
4.	Are adequate detailed records of costs incurred under product warranties maintained, and are related reserves reviewed periodically for adequacy?	___	___	___
5.	Is adequacy of insurance coverage reviewed regularly?	___	___	___
6.	Is status of litigation reviewed regularly and monitored by designated officer and consultation with legal counsel?	___	___	___
7.	Are reported claims reviewed by designated official for appropriate consideration in determining accruals for losses?	___	___	___
8.	Are provisions for losses that are probable and subject to reasonable estimation recorded promptly?	___	___	___

ASSESSMENT OF CONTROL RISK

(High/Maximum, Moderate, or Low)

	Financial Statement Assertions				
	Existence or Occurrence	Completeness	Rights and Obligations	Valuation or Allocation	Presentation and Disclosure
Assessment of control risk	___	___	___	___	___

XIII. COMPUTER CONTROLS

INTERNAL CONTROL OBJECTIVES

- Capture, process, and maintain information completely and accurately and provide it to the appropriate personnel to enable them to carry out their responsibilities and to allow the reliable preparation of financial statements.
- Computer operations use correct programs, files, and procedures.
- Program modifications are implemented correctly.
- Access is restricted to authorized personnel.

POTENTIAL ERRORS AND FRAUD

- Unauthorized access to information and programs.
- Application programs that do not meet management's objectives.
- Processing of unauthorized transactions and omitting of authorized transactions.

UNDERSTANDING OF ACCOUNTING SYSTEM

1. How and by whom are the transactions initiated?

   _____

   _____

   _____

2. Describe the source documents that support the transactions.

   _____

   _____

   _____

3. Describe the computer media that is used in the processing of accounting information.

   _____

   _____

   _____

4. Describe the documents and reports generated by the accounting system.

   _____

   _____

   _____

5. Describe the accounting processing, records, and files (including how frequently they are updated) that are used to process the transactions, including how transactions are reflected in journals of original entry and in the general ledger.

   _____

   _____

   _____

FURTHER UNDERSTANDING OF CONTROL ACTIVITIES

	Yes	No	N/A
1. Is the EDP department independent of user departments?	___	___	___
2. Is there clear segregation of duties of computer programmers and operators?	___	___	___
3. Are EDP personnel prohibited from initiating transactions and changes to master files?	___	___	___
4. Are computer operators required to take annual vacations and are their duties rotated periodically?	___	___	___
5. Is access to the computer room restricted to authorized personnel?	___	___	___
6. Are programmers prohibited from accessing production programs, job control language, and live data files?	___	___	___
7. Are computer operators prohibited from accessing source code and programming documentation?	___	___	___
8. Is testing of new or revised programs on live data files strictly prohibited?	___	___	___
9. Are utility programs adequately controlled and their use logged for subsequent management review?	___	___	___
10. Are unique and confidential passwords required to use terminals?	___	___	___
11. Are passwords changed at regular intervals and canceled for terminated employees?	___	___	___
12. Do individuals have access only to those programs or files that are necessary to perform their duties?	___	___	___
13. Are there established procedures for documenting new systems and programs, as well as modifications of existing ones?	___	___	___
14. Do system and program development procedures require active involvement by the users?	___	___	___
15. Are system and program modifications subject to appropriate testing, and are test results reviewed and approved by user and EDP management?	___	___	___
16. Are schedules prepared and adhered to for processing of computer applications?	___	___	___
17. Are adequate job setup and execution procedures in place over:			
a. Setting up of batch jobs?	___	___	___

	Yes	No	N/A

b. Loading on-line application systems? ___ ___ ___

c. Loading system software? ___ ___ ___

d. Input and output media to be used? ___ ___ ___

18. Are there appropriate procedures for identifying, reporting, and approving operator actions over:

    a. Initial loading of system and application software? ___ ___ ___

    b. System failures? ___ ___ ___

    c. Restart and recovery? ___ ___ ___

    d. Emergency situations? ___ ___ ___

    e. Any other unusual situations? ___ ___ ___

19. Are logs used to record operator activities, and are they reviewed by appropriate personnel? ___ ___ ___

20. Are there appropriate procedures for backup and storage of programs and data files? ___ ___ ___

21. Are critical data files, systems, and program libraries backed up regularly and stored off-site? ___ ___ ___

22. Have contingency plans been developed for alternative processing in the event of loss or interruption of the EDP function? ___ ___ ___

23. Has the organization studied and reviewed its automated systems to ensure Year 2000 compliance? ___ ___ ___

ASSESSMENT OF CONTROL RISK

(High/Maximum, Moderate, or Low)

	Financial Statement Assertions				
	Existence or Occurrence	Completeness	Rights and Obligations	Valuation or Allocation	Presentation and Disclosure
Assessment of control risk	_____	_____	_____	_____	_____

This Understanding of Internal Control Form has been prepared, reviewed, and updated as follows:

Prepared by _____ Date _____

Approved by _____ Date _____

Updated in subsequent years as follows:

Year	Updated by	Date

EXHIBIT 4-2
EVALUATION OF CONTROL ACTIVITIES
OVER LAWS AND REGULATIONS

For each law and regulation that has a direct and material effect on the not-for-profit organization's financial statements, control activities should be in place to provide reasonable assurance that the compliance requirement will be adhered to. For each applicable law and regulation, complete the remainder of this worksheet. Indicate whether the control is a prevention or a detection control. Each law or regulation should have one of each type of control.

LAW OR REGULATION (List or describe a specific law or regulation):

CONTROL ACTIVITIES (List or describe the prevention and/or detection controls that exist):

ARE CONTROLS EFFECTIVE?   Yes _____   No _____

If no, describe the deficiency, or the controls that should have been in existence for this client. (This should be reported as a reportable condition [and possibly a material weakness] in the internal control report.)

Information and Communication

The fourth component of internal control is information and communication. The information system relevant to financial reporting objectives, which includes the accounting system, consists of the methods and records established to record, process, summarize, and report entity transactions and to maintain accountability for the related assets, liabilities, and net assets. SAS-78 states that an information system encompasses methods and records that:

- Identify and record all valid transactions
- Describe, on a timely basis, the transactions in sufficient detail to permit proper classification of transactions for financial reporting
- Measure the value of transactions in a manner that permits recording of their proper monetary value in the financial statements
- Determine the time period in which transactions occurred to permit recording of transactions in the proper accounting period
- Present properly the transactions and related disclosures in the financial statements

Communication, which includes policy manuals, accounting, and financial reporting manuals and memoranda, involves providing an understanding of individual roles and responsibilities pertaining to internal control over financial reporting.

SAS-78 specifies that an auditor should obtain sufficient knowledge of the information system relevant to financial reporting to understand:

The classes of transactions in the entity's operations that are significant to the financial statements.
- How those transactions are initiated.
- The accounting records, supporting information, and specific accounts in the financial statements involved in the processing and reporting of transactions.
- The accounting processing involved from the initiation of a transaction to its inclusion in the financial statements, including electronic means (such as computers and electronic data interchange) used to transmit, process, maintain, and access information.
- The financial reporting process used to prepare the entity's financial statements, including significant accounting estimates and disclosures.

The auditor also needs to obtain sufficient knowledge of the means that the organization uses to communicate financial reporting roles and responsibilities and significant matters that relate to financial reporting. Exhibit 4-1 provides an example of how this information might be captured and summarized by the auditor.

Monitoring

The fifth component of internal control is monitoring. This is the process in which management monitors controls to consider whether they are operating as intended and whether controls are modified as appropriate for changing conditions. Monitoring is an assessment of internal control over a period of time, assessing the design and operation of controls on a timely basis and taking necessary corrective actions.

The auditor should obtain sufficient knowledge of the major types of activities the organization's management uses to monitor internal control over financial reporting, including how those activities lead to corrective action. Where management uses an internal audit function to perform monitoring activities, the guidance of SAS-65 (The Auditor's Consideration of the Internal Audit Function in an Audit of Financial Statements) should be used. This guidance is summarized later in this chapter.

Procedures to Obtain and Document Understanding of Internal Control

Information about internal control is generally obtained by:

- Prior experience with the not-for-profit organization
- Inquiries made of appropriate management, supervisory, and staff personnel of the organization
- Inspection of the organization's documents and records

If the auditor has not had any prior experience auditing the not-for-profit organization, he or she will need to spend more time making inquiries of the organization's personnel and inspecting its documents and records. If the auditor has prior experience with the not-for-profit organization and believes that a sufficient understanding of internal control was obtained and documented in prior years, he or she can focus the inquiries and inspections to determine what changes occurred in internal control since the last audit and to understand the changes.

The documentation that the auditor prepares for his or her understanding of internal control obtained to plan the audit will vary based on the size and complexity of the organization. For relatively small and simple organizations, a memorandum describing the control environment, the accounting system, and the related control procedures should be sufficient documentation. This memorandum should be planned to be carried forward to future years' audits and should be designed to be updated easily from year to year.

For larger not-for-profit organizations, the auditor most likely will use a combination of memoranda, questionnaires, and flowcharts to document the understanding of the internal control structure. If the auditor plans to assess control risk in some cases at below the maximum level, he or she may wish to anticipate this approach by including documentation of the control procedures on which he or she will perform tests of controls.

Consideration of Internal Control in the Assessment of Control Risk

In addition to obtaining an understanding of the internal controls for the purpose of planning the audit, the auditor must assess control risk. The auditor should assess the control risk for the assertions related to the financial statements on which he or she is opining, and as a component of the overall audit risk.

As described in SAS-31 (Evidential Matter), most of the auditor's work in forming an opinion on financial statements consists of obtaining and evaluating evidential matter on the assertions in the financial statements. These assertions—embodied in the account balance, transaction class, and disclosure components of the financial statements—are classified into the following categories:

- Existence or occurrence
- Completeness
- Rights and obligations
- Valuation or allocation
- Presentation and disclosure

The auditor considers these assertions as they relate to specific account balances and classes of transactions.

Audit risk (the risk of material misstatement in financial statement assertions) consists of:

- Inherent risk (the susceptibility of an assertion to material misstatement, assuming there are no related internal control structure policies and procedures)
- Control risk (the risk that a material misstatement will not be prevented or detected by the not-for-profit organization's internal control policies and procedures on a timely basis)

- Detection risk (the risk that the auditor will not detect a material misstatement)

Understanding the relationships among the components of audit risk as they relate to the individual assertions for account balances, classes of transactions, and disclosures is critical in developing a strategy to design and perform an audit that results in an acceptable level of audit risk. In addition, the auditor considers the risk of material misstatement of the financial statements due to fraud, which involves components of inherent risk and control risk.

A form for assessing inherent risk at the account balance and major transaction class level is shown in Exhibit 3-2 (see the chapter titled "Audit Planning"). A form for evaluating the not-for-profit organization's controls over laws and regulations that have a direct and material effect on the financial statements was shown in Exhibit 4-2.

Assessing Control Risk

Once an auditor has obtained an understanding of the not-for-profit organization's internal control, he or she may choose to assess control risk at the maximum level for some or all of the assertions of the account balances and classes of transactions. This might be necessary, for example, if the organization has no internal control policies or procedures for a particular assertion, if the policies or procedures that do exist are likely to be ineffective, or if evaluating the effectiveness of the policies and procedures would be inefficient.

> **OBSERVATION:** As a practical matter, the auditor's decision to assess control risk at the maximum level will be made by cycle, such as revenue/cash receipts or expenditures/cash disbursements. It generally is more efficient to test the controls over an entire cycle rather than to test only a few controls within a cycle. If the auditor determines that one or more controls are missing from or ineffective in the cycle being tested, it will be fairly easy to design substantive tests for the one or more assertions to compensate for the lack of these particular controls.

> **AUDIT COST-SAVING TIP:** Auditors have been successful in cutting audit hours by applying this technique of assessing controls by cycle rather than by individual control. For example, assessing controls over the disbursements cycle provides information about internal controls that affect more assertions than auditor might initially anticipate. Internal controls over disbursements may affect assertions that relate to areas such as whether additions to fixed assets are properly recorded, whether debits to prepaid accounts are properly

recorded, whether expenses are properly allocated to their proper functional classification, and whether liabilities have been appropriately decreased as a result of payment.

In an audit of financial statements, if the auditor chooses to assess control risk at the maximum level for all assertions for all account balances and classes of transactions, he or she would not consider the internal control structure further beyond obtaining an understanding of the structure to be able to plan the audit.

The auditor also may choose to assess control risk below the maximum level for some or all assertions for some or all of the account balances or classes of transactions. Assessing control risk below the maximum level involves:

- Identifying specific control relevant to specific assertions that are likely to prevent or detect material misstatements in those assertions.

- Performing tests of controls to evaluate the effectiveness of such policies and procedures.

The auditor should consider that certain controls can affect many assertions, while others may affect only one assertion for one specific account balance or class of transactions.

The controls that relate to the control environment and the information system relevant to financial reporting are likely to have a pervasive effect on many account balances and classes of transactions, thereby affecting many different assertions. A strong control environment can influence an auditor's decisions about the number of locations at which to perform audit procedures in a multi-location entity and the decision to perform certain audit procedures at an interim date. While no specific assertion about control environment can be identified in this example, it still has an impact on the nature and timing of the auditing procedures that will be performed. Both of the auditor's decisions apply to the way auditing procedures are applied to specific assertions, even though the auditor does not consider each assertion that is affected by the decision.

Other controls will have specific effects on specific account balances or classes of transactions. For example, the control procedures established to ensure that an entity's personnel are counting physical inventory and recording the results properly relate specifically to the existence assertion for physical inventory.

> **OBSERVATION:** To take this example further, the physical inventory count might provide evidence about whether the client's personnel are identifying damaged goods included in the inventory carrying amount (i.e., was the cost of these goods still included in inventory) but little direct evidence about the calculation of the original cost or valuation of the inventory.

The auditor therefore should consider the directness of the relationship between a control and an assertion. The more direct the relationship, the more effective the policy and procedure may be in reducing control risk. For example, management's review of a particular variance or performance report may be an effective control activity, but it relates only indirectly to a number of assertions that might be embodied in the account balances or classes of transactions included in the report being reviewed. Conversely, management's review and approval of a report that lists additions and deletions from the payroll master file would be more directly related to payroll expense assertions.

> **OBSERVATION:** Reviewing variance analyses provides useful but limited information about assertions, whereas reviewing additions to the payroll master file provides direct evidence about the correctness of payroll expenses (i.e., whether or not payroll expense is overstated).

As another example, the performance and supervisory review of timely bank reconciliations is a control activity that directly affects the existence assertion for the recorded cash balance. It also provides a less direct control over the completeness of the recording of revenues and disbursements through its effect on the completeness of the recording of cash receipts and disbursements.

To assess control risk for a particular assertion or group of assertions at below the maximum level, the auditor should perform tests of controls to obtain sufficient evidential matter to support the assessed level.

There are two different aspects of tests of controls as (1) procedures directed toward the design of the control and (2) procedures directed toward the operation of the control. Both types of procedures are referred to as *tests of controls.*

Tests of controls directed toward the effectiveness of the design of an internal control structure policy or procedure are concerned with whether that policy or procedure is suitably designed to prevent or detect material misstatements in specific financial statement assertions. Tests to obtain such evidential matter ordinarily include procedures such as inquiries of appropriate entity personnel, inspection of documents and reports, and observation of the application of specific internal controls. For entities with a complex internal control structure, the auditor should consider the use of flowcharts, questionnaires, or decision tables to facilitate the application of tests of design.

Tests of controls directed toward the operating effectiveness of a control are concerned with how the control was applied, the consistency with which it was applied during the audit period, and by whom it was applied. These tests ordinarily include procedures such as inquiries of appropriate personnel, inspection of documents and reports indicating performance of the control, observation of the application of the control, and reperformance of the application of the control by the auditor. In some circumstances, a specific procedure may address the effectiveness of both design and operation. However, a combination of procedures may be necessary to evaluate the effectiveness of the design or operation of an internal control.

> **OBSERVATION:** In other words, to assess control risk below the maximum level, the auditor must first understand how the particular controls are supposed to operate and then test the controls to see if they have been operating effectively during the period being audited.

Evidential Matter Relative to Control Risk Assessment

How much and what type of evidence the auditor obtains to support his or her assessment about the control risk for particular assertions are matters of professional judgment. However, the evidential matter obtained to support an assessment must be viewed in terms of the type of evidence obtained, its source, its timeliness, and the existence of other evidential matter related to the conclusions to which it leads.

Type of Evidential Matter

The type of evidence obtained from a test of controls clearly depends on the nature of the control being tested. If documentation of the control relating to the design and operation of internal controls exists, the auditor should consider inspecting it.

Some internal controls are less easily documented than others. For example, if the control involves segregation of duties, the auditor probably will need to observe this segregation in action. The auditor should, however, document his or her observations of the control in the working papers.

Source of Evidential Matter

In general, evidence the auditor obtains directly, such as through observation, provides more assurance than evidence obtained indirectly or by inference, such as through inquiry. Of course, the auditor should be aware that client personnel may perform procedures differently when the auditor is observing than when he or she is not present.

OBSERVATION: If necessary, observation procedures can be modified. For example, if the auditor is testing the control to ensure that bank reconciliations are performed, he or she will be better served by scanning a file of bank reconciliations than by watching an organization's bookkeeper perform a bank reconciliation.

There are limitations to the use of inquiry as evidence. It states that inquiry alone generally will not provide sufficient evidential matter to support a conclusion about the effectiveness of design or operation of a specific control procedure. When the auditor determines that a control procedure may have a significant effect in reducing control risk to a low level for a specific assertion, he or she ordinarily should perform additional tests to support the conclusion. While the use of the word *generally* provides some flexibility in unusual circumstances, the auditor should avoid using inquiry as the only form of evidence when testing the design or operation of a control.

OBSERVATION: In the bank reconciliation example used earlier, for the auditor to assess the control risk at less than the maximum level for the control identified, it would be appropriate to select bank reconciliations for several accounts and months and determine whether the reconciliations were properly performed.

Timeliness of Evidential Matter

Timeliness of evidential matter refers to the time when the evidential matter was obtained and the portion of the audit period to which it applies. If an auditor obtains evidence through observation, he or she should take into account that the observation is taking place at a specific point in time and may not necessarily reflect the internal control policies and procedures in place during the entire period being audited. In these circumstances, the auditor should consider supplementing the tests of controls to obtain evidential matter that reflects the entire audit period.

The auditor may use the evidence from prior audits as a starting point for obtaining evidence about controls in the current audit period. The most important evidence to carry forward usually will be concerned with the design of controls, particularly if there have been few or no changes to the design of the system from the prior year.

OBSERVATION: Generally, flowcharts and narratives describing internal control policies and procedures need only updating each year, not complete revision. Because of this, the auditor should consider automating the documentation to help carry it forward from year to year.

To evaluate the evidence from prior audits for use in the current audit, the auditor should consider the significance of the assertion involved, the specific controls evaluated during the prior audits, the degree to which the effective design and operation of those policies and procedures was evaluated, the results of the tests of controls used to make those evaluations, and the evidential matter about design or operation that may result from substantive tests performed in the current audit. The auditor also should consider that the more time that has passed since the performance of tests of controls to obtain evidential matter about control risk, the less assurance the evidence may provide. The auditor should obtain evidential matter in the current period about whether changes have occurred in the internal control structure, including changes to its policies, procedures, and personnel subsequent to the prior audits, as well as the nature and extent of any such changes.

AUDIT COST-SAVING TIP: The use of prior-year information about internal controls is an area that auditors may be overlooking as a means to increase audit efficiency. While auditors generally are good at carrying forward flowcharts, descriptive narratives, and similar items that describe internal control from one year's audit to the next, additional efficiencies may obtainable. Many not-for-profit organizations have very stable operating systems and procedures and may have very little personnel turnover in the related positions. Auditors have an opportunity to turn the "We did it this way because that's how we have done it for the last twenty years" syndrome to their advantage. Auditors should consider whether they can roll the results of their prior-year internal control tests forward by performing some limited tests in the current year to determine whether the system tested in the prior year remains unchanged and in operation in the current year being audited. While auditors may not be able to assess control risk at the minimum level using this technique, they may be able to assess control risk at a moderate level, assuming the procedures performed in the current year support the presumption that the controls remain effective. Of course, this technique has its limitations, and auditors should take care to not roll internal control tests forward for more than a few years.

If the auditor obtains evidence at an interim period, he or she should determine what additional information should be obtained for the period between the interim date and the end of the audit period. This determination is influenced by the significance of the assertion, the specific controls evaluated during the interim period, the degree to which the effective design and operation of those policies and procedures were evaluated, the results of the test of controls used to make that evaluation, the length of the remaining period, and the evidential matter about design or operation that may result from the substantive tests performed for the remaining period.

> **OBSERVATION:** The auditor should determine the most appropriate interim date, given the need to update test work for the period after the interim test work is performed. In practice, the initial interim test work should cover at least nine months of the fiscal year to be cost effective.

Interrelationship of Evidential Matter

An audit is a cumulative process whereby evidence about various assertions and other matters is obtained from a number of sources over a period of time. The auditor should consider the effects that other evidence obtained during the audit could have on the evaluation of the design and operation of internal controls.

As suggested above, the auditor may have to obtain evidence from several sources to evaluate one particular control. For example, if a control is evaluated by observation, the auditor may need to satisfy him- or herself that the control was in place and operating effectively throughout the *entire* audit period.

In addition to obtaining specific evidence about the design and operation of internal control policies and procedures, the auditor should consider evidence about the not-for-profit organization's control environment and accounting system. For example, the auditor may identify a control whereby a supervisor reviews and documents each journal entry. The auditor may decide to test and evaluate this control. However, the auditor may also have obtained evidence that the actual review and sign-off of the journal entries is done after the entries are recorded in the accounting system. The year's worth of journal entries may have been signed off a week before the audit began and backdated to the appropriate time periods. Such information about the control environment will affect the auditor's judgment about the level of assurance, if any, he or she could obtain by testing and evaluating this particular control.

Similarly, performing substantive tests may provide evidence about the appropriateness of the auditor's conclusions about a particular control. For example, on the basis of positive results obtained from testing certain internal control policies and procedures, an auditor assesses the control risk below the maximum level for one or more assertions relating to a particular account balance or class of transactions. When performing substantive tests related to those same assertions, the auditor discovers numerous misstatements that were not detected or prevented by these internal control policies and procedures. Clearly, the auditor will need to reevaluate his or her conclusion that control risk for these assertions and account balances or classes of transactions could be assessed below the maximum level.

In general, when the auditor obtains various types of evidence that support the same conclusion about the design or operation of an internal control policy or procedure, the level of assurance provided by that particular internal control policy and procedure increases. Conversely, when the auditor obtains evidence that provides conflicting information about the design and operation of a particular internal control policy and procedure, the auditor will have less assurance about that policy and procedure.

If assessing control risk below the maximum level, the auditor uses the evidential matter obtained to determine the assessed level of control risk. The lower the assessed level of control risk, the greater the assurance the evidential matter must provide that the internal control structure policies and procedures are designed and operating effectively.

The auditor uses the assessed levels of control risk and of inherent risk to determine the acceptable level of detection risk for financial statement assertions. The auditor uses the acceptable level of detection risk to determine the nature, timing, and extent of the audit procedures to be used to detect material misstatements in the financial statement assertions. Auditing procedures designed to detect such misstatements are referred to as *substantive tests*.

As the acceptable level of detection risk decreases, the assurance provided from substantive tests should increase. Consequently, the auditor may choose to make one of the following changes in the substantive tests:

- Change the nature of substantive tests from less effective to more effective procedures, such as using tests directed toward independent parties outside the entity rather than tests directed toward parties or documentation within the entity.

- Change the timing of substantive tests, such as performing them at year end rather than at an interim date.

- Change the extent of substantive tests, such as using larger sample sizes.

The auditor then bases the acceptable level of detection risk on the level of control risk and inherent risk relative to each financial statement assertion. After determining the level to which to restrict the risk of material misstatement in the financial statements and the assessed levels of inherent risk and control risk, the auditor will design and perform substantive tests to achieve an acceptable level of detection risk.

If the auditor assesses control risk at levels below the maximum, the acceptable level of detection risk increases. In other words, control risk is inversely related to detection risk. The auditor does not make a "maximum" or "minimum" determination regarding control risk. The auditor can assess control risk at one of these two extremes, or at some point in between. The auditor should have a continuum for the assessment of detection risk that corresponds in an indirect relationship to the assessment of control risk.

> **OBSERVATION:** In other words, if the auditor finds that internal controls are properly designed and operating effectively, he or she will need to perform less substantive test work for the assertions to which the control procedures pertain.

The key for the auditor in designing the most efficient audit is to anticipate whether the results of the tests of controls will permit the auditor to assess control risk at below the maximum level for assertions at the account balance or class of transactions level. If the auditor does not anticipate that he or she will be able to assess control risk at below the maximum level, there is no reason to perform tests of the controls that are known to be either ineffective or inoperative.

If the auditor assesses detection risk at a minimum level, SAS-55 required a minimum amount of substantive test work for assertions, and this requirement is unchanged by SAS-78. SAS-55 states:

> Although the inverse relationship between control risk and detection risk may permit the auditor to change the nature or the timing of substantive tests or limit their extent, ordinarily the assessed level of control risk cannot be sufficiently low to eliminate the need to perform any substantive tests to restrict detection risk for all of the assertions relevant to significant account balances or transaction classes. Consequently, regardless of the assessed level of control risk, the auditor should perform substantive tests for significant account balances and transaction classes.

This requirement does not mean that detailed tests of transactions must be performed for every significant account balance or class of transactions. Substantive analytical procedures can be used as an acceptable form of substantive test work. The auditor should use careful judgment when deciding when to use substantive analytical procedures and should follow the requirements of SAS-56 (Analytical Procedures).

Consideration of a Not-for-Profit Organization's Internal Audit Function

Many not-for-profit organizations use an internal audit function as an important element of internal control. Internal auditors may be responsible for such matters as providing analyses, evaluations, assurances, recommendations, and other information to the not-for-profit organization's management and board of directors or to others with similar authority and responsibility.

> **OBSERVATION:** When evaluating the internal audit function, the auditor should make sure that the function that he or she is considering is truly an internal audit function and not another accounting function named "Internal Audit." For instance, "internal auditors" who do nothing more than perform a pre-audit of expenditures should not be considered to be performing an internal audit function. In this example, the pre-audit function may be viewed as one aspect of the control procedures included in the not-for-profit organization's internal control structure.

The auditor performing an audit of financial statements in accordance with GAAS should obtain a sufficient understanding of the not-for-profit organization's internal control structure to be able to plan the audit. Since the internal audit function is part of the not-for-profit organization's internal control, the auditor will need to obtain an understanding of this function. If the auditor chooses to consider how the internal auditor's work might affect the nature, timing, and extent of audit procedures, the auditor should assess the competence and objectivity of the internal audit function in light of the intended effect of the internal auditor's work on the audit. The auditor also will assess the competence and objectivity of the internal audit function if the auditor requests direct assistance in performing the audit from the internal audit personnel.

SAS-65 (The Auditor's Consideration of the Internal Audit Function in an Audit of Financial Statements) provides guidance for the auditor in considering the internal audit function. SAS-65 includes the following inquiries that an auditor ordinarily would make of both management and internal audit personnel when gaining an understanding of the internal audit function to plan the audit:

- The organizational status of the internal audit function within the not-for-profit organization

- The professional standards that are used by internal auditors in the conduct of internal audits, such as those established by the Institute of Internal Auditors or the General Accounting Office

- The audit plan that the internal audit function is using and whether there are any limitations on the scope of the activities that the function would be able to perform
- The ability of internal auditors to access records and whether there are any limitations on their activities

In addition to these inquiries, the auditor can look to other sources of information about the internal audit function, such as:

- The knowledge that the auditor has about the internal audit function learned from prior years' audits
- The internal audit function's mission statement (or charter, bylaws, or other similar documents) or directions that they may have received from management or the board of directors about areas on which to concentrate efforts within their overall audit plan
- The allocation of the internal auditors' time between financial and operating areas in response to the function's risk assessment process
- Internal audit reports, which will enable the auditor to obtain detailed information about the scope of internal audit activities

If the auditor concludes, after obtaining an understanding of the internal audit function necessary to plan the audit, that the internal audit function's activities are not relevant to his or her audit of the financial statements (or if the auditor concludes that any use of the work of the internal audit function would not be cost beneficial), the auditor does not have to perform any other procedures related to the internal audit department.

> **OBSERVATION:** In the audit of a not-for-profit organization, the auditor should be careful in concluding that the work of an internal auditor is not useful to the financial statement audit, or concluding not to use directly the work of the internal audit staff in the performance of the audit. This conclusion may be viewed by management or the board of directors as not being very cost-effective. In an industry where cost containment and reduction is critical, a perceived "duplication" of audit efforts or rejection of the direct assistance of the internal auditor may be thought of poorly by both management and the board of directors.

If the auditor concludes that the activities of the internal audit function are relevant to the audit of the financial statements or that the internal auditors will provide direct assistance to the auditor, the auditor should assess the professional competence and objectivity of the internal audit function. SAS-65 provides some of the factors that the auditor should consider for both.

In assessing the competence of the internal auditors, the auditor should obtain (or update from prior years) information about such factors as:

- Educational level and professional experience of the internal auditors

- Professional certification and continuing education

- Audit policies, programs, and procedures

- Practices regarding the assignment of internal auditors

- Supervision and review of the internal auditors' activities

- Quality of working paper documentation, reports, and recommendations

- Evaluation of internal auditors' performance

In assessing the objectivity of the internal auditors, the auditor should obtain (or update from prior years) information about such factors as:

- The organizational status of the internal auditors who are responsible for the internal audit function, including such factors as:

  — Whether the internal auditors report to an officer of sufficient status to ensure broad audit coverage and adequate consideration of, and action on, the findings and recommendations of the internal auditors

  — Whether the internal auditors have direct access and reports regularly to the board of directors, the audit committee, or other such governing body or organization

  — Whether the board of directors, the audit committee, or other such governing body or organization oversees employment decisions related to the internal auditors

- Policies to maintain the internal auditors' objectivity about the areas audited, including such factors as:

  — Policies prohibiting internal auditors from auditing areas where relatives are employed in important or audit-sensitive positions

  — Policies prohibiting internal auditors from auditing areas where they were recently assigned or are scheduled to be assigned on completion of responsibilities in the internal audit function

The auditor obtains information in assessing the competency and objectivity of the internal audit function from a number of sources, such as previous experience with the internal audit function, discussions with management, and, if performed, external quality control reviews. The auditor should consider whether it is necessary to test any of the information obtained about competency and objectivity. Whether testing is necessary will be influenced by the degree to which the auditor intends to use the work of the internal audit function.

Effect of the Internal Auditors' Work on the Audit of the Financial Statements

Once the auditor is satisfied about the competence and objectivity of the internal audit function, he or she can consider how to use the work of the internal auditors. The financial statement audit will be affected by the type of procedures that the internal auditors have actually performed or plan to perform concurrently with the audit of the financial statements. Some examples where internal auditors' work may be used in the audit of the financial statements of a not-for-profit organization are as follows:

- Site visits may be performed by internal auditors throughout the year at not-for-profit organizations that have a number of local or district offices. The auditor may consider reducing the number of site visits that he or she planned to make in light of the work of the internal auditors.

- Internal auditors may perform confirmation procedures throughout the year or at year end. The auditor may reduce some of the confirmation procedures that he or she would otherwise have performed.

- The internal auditors may verify compliance with various contract and grant agreements. The auditor may consider reducing the number of contracts or grant agreements that he or she will review for compliance.

- The internal auditors may perform audit procedures to verify the existence of assets, such as physical inventories of supplies, fixed assets, equipment, or other goods or petty cash. Because these procedures are performed as of the not-for-profit organization's fiscal year end, along with a multitude of observations that may be occurring simultaneously, the use of the internal audit function to perform some of these physical observations becomes even more desirable.

- The internal auditors may have extensive documentation of two key components of the internal control structure—the accounting system and the control procedures. The auditor may be able to use this documentation to obtain an understanding of the accounting system and control procedures and to assess control risk.

- The internal auditors may have tested compliance with eligibility requirements for individuals or other organizations being serviced by the not-for-profit organization. The auditor may be able to reduce planned test work in this area after considering the internal auditors' work.

These are just a few examples for the auditor to consider. The work done by the internal auditors at the particular not-for-profit organization being audited will govern the areas where their work may affect the audit of the financial statements. The independent auditor may find it beneficial to be allowed input into the development of the internal audit function's annual work scope. In this way, the not-for-profit may benefit from reduced audit costs by using the internal auditors' work to a greater extent. In this case, however, an appropriate balance must be maintained between the auditor's use of the work of the internal audit function and the needs and concerns of management and the board of directors, which also should be addressed by the internal audit function.

Using the Internal Auditors' Work

While the work of internal auditors that is used by the auditor in the audit of financial statements can vary widely, the auditor should realize that he or she is still ultimately responsible for the audit of the financial statements—the responsibility cannot be shared with the internal auditors. The auditor also should consider that audit evidence obtained directly by the auditor is more persuasive than evidence obtained indirectly through the internal auditors. Given these factors, the auditor should always ensure that judgments about the assessments of inherent risks and control risks, the materiality of misstatements, the sufficiency of tests performed, the evaluation of significant accounting estimates, and other matters affecting the auditor's report are those of the auditor.

SAS-65 provides the following factors for the auditor to consider when making judgments about the extent of the effect of the internal auditors' work on the auditors' procedures:

- The materiality of the financial statement amounts (i.e., account balances or classes of transactions)
- The risk of material misstatement of the assertions related to these financial statement amounts, which includes both inherent risk and control risk

- The degree of subjectivity involved in the evaluation of the audit evidence gathered in support of the assertions

As the materiality, risk, and subjectivity of the nature of evidence to be obtained increases, it becomes more appropriate for the auditor, and not the internal auditors, to perform the related audit procedures. However, in instances where amounts are not material, risk is low, and the evidence to be examined is not subjective, the auditor is more likely to conclude that the related audit procedures may be performed by the internal auditors.

Evaluation of the Work Performed by Internal Auditors

SAS-65 requires that the auditor perform procedures to evaluate the quality and effectiveness of the internal auditors' work that significantly affects the nature, timing, and extent of the auditor's procedures. The auditor must use his or her professional judgment to determine the extent of evaluation procedures, in consideration of the extent of the effect of the internal auditors' work on the auditor's procedures for significant account balances and classes of transactions. In developing evaluation procedures, the auditor should consider such factors as:

- Whether the internal auditors' scope of work is appropriate to the audit objectives
- Whether the internal auditors' audit programs are adequate
- Whether the internal auditors' working papers adequately document work performed, including evidence of supervision and review
- Whether the internal auditors' conclusions are appropriate in the circumstances
- Whether the internal auditors' reports are consistent with the results of the work performed

In making the evaluation, the auditor should test some of the internal auditors' work related to the significant financial statement assertions. These tests may be accomplished either by examining some of the controls, transactions, or balances that the internal auditor examined, or by examining similar controls, transactions, or balances that were not actually examined by the internal auditors. The auditor should compare the results of his or her work to the results of the internal auditor's work to reach a conclusion about the internal auditor's work.

Direct Assistance Provided to the Auditor by the Internal Auditor

In some instances it may be useful to have internal audit staff members work under the direct supervision of the auditor. This allows the not-for-profit organization to keep audit costs down because the auditor will use fewer of his or her own staff hours to perform the audit. An additional benefit is that internal auditors may gain valuable experience working with the independent auditor, which can be applied to their own internal audit work when they have finished assisting the independent auditor.

> **OBSERVATION:** Before an auditor provides the not-for-profit organization with an audit fee estimate that reflects savings from directly using the work of internal auditors, the auditor should be fairly certain that the internal auditors' time can be used effectively. The auditor may wish to consider meeting with the individual internal auditors with whom he or she will be working to ensure that the individuals are capable of handling the assignments that the auditor intends to give them. The auditor should not spend more time training and supervising the internal auditors than he or she would have spent completing the audit work.

SAS-65 contains guidelines for auditors who receive direct assistance from internal audit staff. This guidance is summarized as follows:

- The auditor should assess the competence and objectivity of the internal auditor, similar to the manner described in the preceding sections.

- The auditor should supervise, review, evaluate, and test the work performed by the internal auditor to the extent appropriate in the circumstances.

- The internal auditors should be informed of their responsibilities; the objectives of the procedures that they are to perform; and matters that may affect the nature, timing, and extent of audit procedures, such as possible accounting and auditing issues.

- The internal auditors should be informed that all significant accounting and auditing issues identified during the audit should be brought to the auditor's attention.

Following this guidance will minimize any misunderstandings about the work to be performed by the internal auditors and will help to maximize their usefulness to the independent auditor.

SUMMARY

This chapter describes the requirements for an auditor's consideration of internal control of a not-for-profit organization in an audit of financial statements in accordance with GAAS. It also discusses the relationship of the three components of audit risk and the importance of control risk assessment when designing an audit to provide a sufficiently low level of audit risk relative to those assertions that potentially could cause the financial statements to be materially misstated. In addition, the chapter provides guidance on the independent auditor's consideration of the internal audit function of a not-for-profit organization. The internal audit function of a not-for-profit organization may be an important feature of its internal control structure. In addition, the auditor may be able to achieve certain efficiencies in conducting the audit by relying on the work performed by the internal auditors.

CHAPTER 5
STATEMENT OF FINANCIAL POSITION

CONTENTS

Chapter 5
STATEMENT OF FINANCIAL POSITION

CROSS-REFERENCES

2001 Miller Audit Procedures: Chapter 8, "Cash"; Chapter 9, "Investments"; Chapter 12, "Property, Plant, and Equipment"; Chapter 17, "Debt Obligations"

2000 Miller GAAS Guide: Section 330, "The Confirmation Process"; Section 331, "Inventories"; Section 332, "Auditing Investments"

This chapter focuses on the auditing issues an auditor should consider when auditing the most common asset, liability, and net asset accounts of a not-for-profit organization. Accounts that are more directly tied to accounts in the statement of activities (such as contributions receivable, which are directly related to contribution revenue) are discussed in the next chapter, "Statement of Activities."

The following broad categories of assets, liabilities, and net assets are discussed in this chapter:

Assets

- Cash and cash equivalents
- Investments
- Property, plant, and equipment
- Other assets, including collections

Liabilities

- Debt and other liabilities, including deferred revenue

Net Assets

- Permanently restricted net assets
- Temporarily restricted net assets
- Unrestricted net assets

This chapter explores some of the unique considerations involved in auditing these accounts in a not-for-profit organization and identifies some of the unique accounting conventions for not-for-profit organizations related to these accounts. The suggested audit procedures discussed in this chapter are included in the model audit program included on the disc accompanying this Guide. This chapter presents a general discussion of the types of audit procedures likely to be performed by an auditor. These are only *suggested* procedures. Procedures actually performed are based on the auditor's judgment and the individual client circumstances. Wherever possible, the discussion of audit procedures points out areas that auditors frequently overaudit. Alternative approaches that may be more efficient (and, in many cases, more effective), such as the use of substantive analytical procedures, are suggested wherever possible.

The following chapter, "Statement of Activities," provides similar information on accounts usually found in the statement of activities of a not-for-profit organization. That chapter also provides guidance on auditing a not-for-profit organization's compliance with FAS-116 (Accounting for Contributions Received and Contributions Made).

CASH AND CASH EQUIVALENTS

The auditing of cash and cash equivalents in a not-for-profit is similar to auditing cash and cash equivalents in a commercial enterprise. However, there are some differences in not-for-profit organizations' cash transactions that auditors should be aware of when designing audit procedures. Also, not-for-profit organizations have some unique accounting and financial reporting display issues.

The term *cash* in this section refers to cash in demand and savings accounts, currency that may be collected as part of the not-for-profit organization's fund-raising efforts, and cash maintained in petty cash funds.

Cash equivalents may be a new term to not-for-profit organizations, since many of these organizations will be preparing cash flow statements for the first time when implementing FAS-117 (Financial Statements of Not-for-Profit Organizations). FAS-117 revoked not-for-profit organizations' exemption from applying FAS-95 (Statement of Cash Flows). Since not-for-profit organizations now are required to present a statement of cash flows as part of their basic financial statements, these organizations should adopt the definition of *cash equivalents* contained in FAS-95. Cash equivalents for purposes of FAS-95 are short-term, highly liquid investments that are both:

- Readily convertible to known amounts of cash, and

- So near their maturity that they present insignificant risk of changes in value because of changes in interest rates.

Generally, only investments with original maturities (i.e., original maturity to the not-for-profit organization, which is not necessarily the same as the original maturity of the investment itself) of three months or less would qualify as cash equivalents according to the above definition.

Not-for-profit organizations sometimes have more bank accounts than similar-sized commercial organizations. In some instances, grant agreements or contracts under which assistance is obtained require that the funds received be maintained in separate bank accounts. Also, donors, such as those giving endowment funds, may request that the funds be maintained in separate bank accounts.

The not-for-profit organization also may have a number of local offices that maintain separate bank accounts. In many cases these local office accounts are deposit-only accounts, and the local office cannot write checks on or make withdrawals from these accounts. In this way, control over disbursements is maintained by a central office. Balances in deposit-only accounts are swept into the central disbursement account on a periodic (preferably daily) basis.

> **OBSERVATION:** Some not-for-profit organizations, like some commercial enterprises, are somewhat lax in closing bank accounts that are no longer needed. The auditor should assess whether the not-for-profit organization promptly closes these accounts and performs other maintenance procedures, such as removing authorized signatures from accounts when signers leave the organization or should no longer be signers. Boards of directors of not-for-profit organizations tend to appreciate management letter comments on such matters if these bank account management techniques are lacking.

In addition to having many bank accounts and many interbank transfers between the various accounts, not-for-profit organizations also may have significant activity in opening and closing bank accounts. Furthermore, some assistance contracts and grant agreements require that the funds remitted to the not-for-profit organization be maintained in interest-bearing accounts, particularly where funds are advanced to the not-for-profit before program expenditures are made. The auditor should inquire about the mechanism the not-for-profit organization uses to credit the interest earned on the account to the appropriate grant or contract.

> **AUDIT COST-SAVING TIP:** Cash is an area that auditors historically have over-audited. Cash tends to be an easy area to audit, because procedures are relatively straightforward, generally requiring less professional judgment than many other, more complex audit areas. However, just because procedures are comparatively easy does not mean the auditor will benefit from investing more audit hours than necessary in performing such procedures. The following discussion contains several

suggestions that auditors should evaluate (such as limiting the
number of bank confirmations sent or questioning whether
requesting cut-off statements is necessary) in order to determine whether cash is being audited in the most efficient
manner possible.

Audit Procedures

Audit procedures for cash and cash equivalents primarily include
the confirmation of bank balances (along with any outstanding loan
balances). The AICPA standardized bank confirmation form (Standard Form to Confirm Account Balance Information with Financial
Institutions) should be used to confirm the various bank balances.

Auditors traditionally confirmed all bank account balances, particularly since an earlier version of the standard bank confirmation
form provided information on loan balances at the financial institutions not listed on the form, compensating balance information, and
line of credit information. The confirmation was more important for
ensuring the completeness of liabilities than for determining bank
balances. Now that the information provided by the standard bank
confirmation form has been reduced, the auditor should consider
not confirming all of the bank account balances of the not-for-profit
organization. This decision will depend on the nature, activity, and
balances of the individual bank accounts under consideration. For
accounts that are not confirmed, the auditor can perform alternative
procedures, such as tracing the bank balance to the bank account
statement received from the bank.

Auditors also should consider performing cutoff audit procedures and requesting cutoff statements from banks for some or all of
the bank accounts. A sample request for a cutoff statement from a
financial institution is included on the disc accompanying this Guide
(file name: SC-01). The usefulness of cutoff procedures depends on
the individual circumstances of the not-for-profit organization being
audited. The auditor may consider requesting a cutoff statement for
the main disbursement account and not for any other accounts. If the
auditor can be satisfied that the client mailed whatever checks that it
cut before its year end within a reasonable period of time and can be
satisfied that any interbank transfers were accounted for appropriately, the auditor should consider not requesting cutoff statements
for any of the bank accounts of the not-for-profit organization. Cutoff statements generally do not provide the auditor with all of the
information needed relative to the cutoff and can disrupt the client's
bank reconciliation process. They should be used only when the
auditor cannot obtain satisfactory evidence about the cutoff from
other sources.

The auditor should consider requesting other information from
financial institutions related to cash. This could include verification
of authorized signatures on bank accounts, compensating balance

agreements, and available lines of credit. Sample confirmation letters for each of these matters are included on the disc accompanying this Guide (file names: SC-05 and SC-09).

In addition to the confirmation procedures described above, the auditor should consider tests of the bank reconciliations prepared by the not-for-profit organization. The auditor should confirm that bank reconciliations are actually being performed, on a timely basis, and that any reconciling items that require accounting entries are recorded appropriately. Performing tests of the bank reconciliations as of the year end for the major operating accounts of the organization and a sample of the reconciliations of the smaller, less active accounts may be appropriate.

Cash-on-hand is another area for which the auditor should consider performing procedures. Auditors traditionally have counted all petty cash funds as part of an audit, but recently, auditors have begun using a more risk-based approach, counting petty cash only when the results of such counts may have audit significance. However, in addition to providing information on the existence of petty cash, counting these funds provides information on unrecorded disbursements. A not-for-profit organization's management may expect the auditor to count petty cash, and these expectations may cause the auditor to count petty cash that might not have been counted based solely on an assessment of audit risk. Similarly, since there is a heightened sense of awareness of the misappropriation of donated funds at not-for-profit organizations, the auditor should consider whether any misappropriation of petty cash might cause the auditor embarrassment (or potential loss of a client).

Classification and Disclosure

In addition to completing the procedures described above, the auditor should obtain assurance about the appropriateness of the financial statement classification of cash and cash equivalents and the adequacy of the disclosures in the financial statements of matters relating to these accounts. FAS-117 requires that information about liquidity be provided in the financial statements of not-for-profit organizations by one or more of the following methods:

- Sequencing assets according to the nearness of their conversion to cash and sequencing liabilities according to the nearness of their maturity and resulting use of cash.

- Classifying assets and liabilities as current and noncurrent (following the guidance of ARB-43 [Restatement and Revision of Accounting Research Bulletins]).

- Disclosing in the notes to the financial statements relevant information about the liquidity or maturity of assets and liabilities, including restrictions on the use of particular assets.

Accordingly, cash received with donor-imposed stipulations restricting the cash's use to long-term purposes, and cash set aside for long-term purposes, should not be classified in the statement of financial position with assets that are available for current use. FAS-117 states that cash and cash equivalents restricted by donors to investments in fixed assets should not be included in the statement of financial position as "cash or cash equivalents" but as "assets restricted by donors to investment in land, buildings, and equipment." FAS-117 also states that cash and cash equivalents contributed by donors with stipulations that they be invested permanently are reported as "long-term investments." The auditor must be familiar with donor-imposed restrictions to ensure that cash and cash equivalents are appropriately classified and captioned in the statement of financial position.

The AICPA Guide notes that there may be limitations on a not-for-profit organization's ability to withdraw or use its cash and cash equivalents. Examples of such limitations are those that may be imposed by:

- Creditors and other outside parties (such as limitations imposed on cash held by financial institutions to meet compensating balance requirements; cash and cash equivalents held as collateral on debt obligations; cash received as collateral on loaned securities; and cash held for students, clients, and others under agency agreements)

- Donors who place permanent or temporary restrictions on their cash contributions (such as restricting the contributions to investments in buildings or requiring that the principal be maintained permanently or for a specific period of time)

- Governing boards, which may designate cash for investment purposes (traditionally known as "funds functioning as endowment" or "quasi-endowments" or referred to as being part of a "board-designated investment fund")

The AICPA Guide clarifies that relevant information about the nature and amount of limitations on the use of cash and cash equivalents should be included either on the face of the financial statements or in the notes to the financial statements. Any donor-imposed restrictions on the use of cash and cash equivalents should be disclosed in the net assets section of the statement of financial position or in the notes to the financial statements.

Disclosure in the notes to the financial statements also should include any unusual circumstances (such as special borrowing arrangements, requirements imposed by resource providers that cash be held in separate accounts, and known significant liquidity problems). If the not-for-profit organization has not maintained the appropriate amounts of cash and cash equivalents to comply with donor-imposed restrictions, this noncompliance should be disclosed. Donor-imposed restrictions generally apply throughout the year being audited and not just to the year-end cash balances that appear in the statement of financial position. The auditor should consider disclosing any instances of noncompliance and should consider the potential financial statement impact of any instances of noncompliance. For example, if the noncompliance is of great significance, the donor could request or demand a refund of the funds contributed.

The auditor should ensure that appropriate disclosures are made for available lines of credit and all compensating balance requirements. The definition of cash equivalents that the not-for-profit organization is using (which should be consistent with FAS-95) also should be described in the notes to the financial statements.

The auditor should consider the disclosure requirements of FAS-105 (Disclosure of Information About Financial Instruments with Off-Balance Sheet Risk and Financial Instruments with Concentrations of Credit Risk) to evaluate any required disclosures of concentrations of credit risk. The auditor should determine whether the not-for-profit organization has concentrated all of its deposits in one or more financial institutions and if the deposits exceed limits for the Federal Deposit Insurance Corporation or similar insurance. The auditor should evaluate whether there is a risk to the not-for-profit organization regarding the recovery of its deposits in the event of failure of one of these financial institutions. In addition to considering any disclosures that may be appropriate under FAS-105, the auditor may find it appropriate to suggest ways for the not-for-profit organization to reduce or eliminate this risk through better management of its cash balances.

INVESTMENTS

The auditing considerations for investments of a not-for-profit organization are similar to those of commercial enterprises. Given the significant losses by a number of organizations caused by their use of financial products known as derivatives, the area of investments has taken on increased significance in audits of both commercial and not-for-profit organizations.

In November 1995, the FASB issued Statement No. 124 (Accounting for Certain Investments Held by Not-for-Profit Organizations). FAS-124 requires that equity securities with readily determinable market values (defined more fully below) and all debt securities be reported at fair value in the statement of financial position. Gains and losses on investments are reported in the statement of activities as increases or decreases in unrestricted net assets, unless their use is temporarily or permanently restricted by explicit donor stipulations or by law. FAS-124 does not apply to investments in equity securities that are accounted for under the equity method or to investments in consolidated subsidiaries. SOP 94-3 (Reporting of Related Entities by Not-for-Profit Organizations) provides guidance for the accounting for investments by not-for-profit organizations in for-profit entities, where the for-profit organization is less than 50 percent owned by the not-for-profit organization.

According to FAS-124, an equity security is covered by the Statement if its fair value is *readily determinable*, defined as follows:

- Sales prices or bid-and-asked prices for the security are currently available on a securities exchange registered with the Securities and Exchange Commission (SEC) or in the over-the-counter market, provided that the price or quotation for the over-the-counter market is publicly reported by the NASDAQ system or the National Quotation Bureau;

- For an equity security traded only in a foreign market, the foreign market must be of a breadth and scope comparable to one of the U.S. markets described above; or

- For an investment in a mutual fund, the fair value per share or used is determined and published and is the basis for current transactions.

This definition is very broad and includes most equities, except those of closely held corporations or those with special circumstances, such as restricted stock.

FAS-124 follows the rule of FAS-117 that investment income, which would consist of dividends, interest, and other investment income (such as unrealized gains and losses), must be reported in the period earned as increases in unrestricted net assets unless the use of the assets received is limited by donor-imposed restrictions. Donor-restricted investment income should be reported as an increase in either temporarily or permanently restricted net assets, depending on the type of restriction imposed by the donor.

The classification of gains and losses on donor-restricted endowment funds can be complicated and requires careful analysis using the detailed guidance of FAS-124. As a general rule, absent an explicit donor stipulation or law that restricts their use, gains or losses on donor-restricted endowment funds are changes in unrestricted net assets. In the absence of donor stipulations or law to the contrary, losses on the investments of a donor-restricted endowment fund reduce temporarily restricted net assets to the extent that the donor-imposed temporary restrictions on net appreciation of the fund have not been met before the loss occurs. Any remaining loss is then accounted for as a reduction of unrestricted net assets.

FAS-124 requires disclosures for investments relating to both the statement of financial position and the statement of activities. These disclosures include information about the composition of investment return and the carrying amount of investments by major types and are presented in greater detail later in this chapter.

Not-for-profit organizations should not be following other guidance on the accounting and valuation of investments that applies only to commercial enterprises. For example, FAS-115 (Accounting for Certain Investments in Debt and Equity Securities) does not apply to entities that meet the definition of not-for-profit organizations included in FAS-117. In addition, FAS-117 does not provide any accounting or valuation guidance for investments. It does, however, provide guidance on displaying investments in the financial statements.

Investments Outside the Scope of FAS-124

The AICPA Guide provides clarification on the accounting treatment for investments not within the scope of FAS-124. The AICPA Guide refers to these as "other investments"—those investments that are not included in the scope of FAS-124 whose carrying amount is based on previously effective accounting rules. The examples of other investments provided by the Guide (which is not an all-inclusive list) include investments in real estate, notes, venture capital funds, partnership interests, oil and gas interests, and equity securities that do not have a readily determinable fair value.

For example, assume that previous accounting rules permitted investments to be carried at either cost or market value, provided that the same attribute is used for all investments (in other words, all investments are carried at cost, or all are carried at market, not a combination of the two.) Now assume that the not-for-profit organization adopts FAS-124 and values its equity securities with readily determinable fair values and debt securities at their fair values. The other investments of this not-for-profit organization may be carried at either cost or market, provided that all of the other investments are measured using the same attribute. In other words, this not-for-profit organization may have all of its investments measured at fair value, or it may have its equities with readily determinable fair values and its debt securities reported at their fair values and all of its "other investments" reported at cost.

The following paragraphs summarize the investment accounting requirements by type of not-for-profit organization for investments not covered by FAS-124. These paragraphs are based on the Appendix to Chapter 8 of the AICPA Guide. However, the auditor must be aware that the incorporated guidance in the proposed Audit and Accounting Guide pertains only to the "other investments" described above and not to equities with readily determinable fair values and debt securities, which are reported at their fair values in accordance with FAS-124.

Institutions of higher education, including colleges, universities, and community or junior colleges   Other investments of institutions of higher education that were acquired by purchase may be reported at cost. Contributed other investments may be reported at their fair market value or appraised value at the date of the gift, unless there has been an impairment of the value that is not considered to be temporary.

Other investments also may be reported at current market value or fair value, provided that the same attribute is used for all other investments. The financial statements or the notes to the financial statements should set forth the total performance of the investment portfolio, which is defined as investment income and realized and unrealized gains and losses.

Voluntary health and welfare organizations   Voluntary health and welfare organizations should report other investments at cost if purchased and at fair market value at the date of the contribution if contributed. If the market value of the other investments portfolio is below the recorded amount, it may be necessary to reduce the carrying amount of the portfolio to market, or to provide an allowance for decline in market value. If it can be reasonably expected that the organization will suffer a loss on the disposition of an investment, a provision for the loss should be made in the period in which the decline in value occurs. Carrying other investments at market value is also acceptable for these types of organizations. The same measurement attribute should be used for all other investments and should be disclosed.

Other not-for-profit organizations   Other not-for-profit organizations (those that are not colleges, universities, or voluntary health and welfare organizations) should report other investments at either fair value or the lower of cost or fair value. The same measurement attribute should be used for all other investments. Declines in investments carried at the lower of cost or market value should be recognized when their aggregate market value is less than their carrying amount. Recoveries of aggregate market value in subsequent periods should be recorded in those periods subject only to the limitation that the carrying amount should not exceed the original cost.

The AICPA Guide provides accounting and auditing guidance for investments relating to their initial recognition and measurement, the measurement attributes used for subsequent valuation, investment income, realized and unrealized gains and losses, and financial statement display and disclosure.

The AICPA Guide does not provide any additional guidance for the accounting for the reporting of related entities by not-for-profit organizations. Rather, it incorporates the guidance for this reporting provided by SOP 94-3 simply by reprinting SOP 94-3 within Chapter 8 of the AICPA Guide.

OBSERVATION: In addition, the Financial Accounting Standards Board (FASB) has several projects that may affect the reporting of related entities. These projects, centered around the topic of consolidations, are not moving with any great urgency within the FASB, and additional guidance may be several years away.

The following paragraphs summarize the guidance that the Guide provides for the investments included in its scope.

Initial Recognition of the Investment

Investments that are purchased by a not-for-profit organization should be recorded at their cost. The cost should be inclusive of any brokerage or other transactions fees that are incurred by the not-for-profit organization as a result of the purchase of the investment. If an investment is contributed to the not-for-profit organization, the investment should be recorded at its fair value. The contribution of the investment should be properly classified in the financial statements, which is more fully discussed in the chapter titled "Statement of Activities."

Investment Income

Investment income refers to dividends, interest, rents, royalties, and similar payments. Investment income should be recognized by the not-for-profit organization when earned. The investment income must be properly reported and classified as an increase in unrestricted, temporarily restricted, or permanently restricted net assets. The classification of the investment income depends on the donor restrictions over the investment income, if any, and not the classification of the investment that caused the income to be earned.

The auditor should determine if the not-for-profit organization is properly classifying investment income according to any donor restrictions that exist. If there are no donor restrictions, the investment income would be reported as an increase in unrestricted net assets. For example, the investments that give rise to the investment income may be invested in perpetuity (i.e., the investments are classified as part of permanently restricted net assets). The donor may specify, however, that the income from the investments be used to support a specific program. The income from these investments included in permanently restricted net assets would be recorded as an increase to temporarily restricted net assets. If the restrictions on the investment income are met, the not-for-profit organization should report in its statement of activities a reclassification from temporarily restricted net assets to unrestricted net assets. However, if the donor restrictions are met in the same reporting period as that in which the temporarily restricted investment income is recognized, the not-for-profit organization may report the investment income as unrestricted if that policy was adopted by the not-for-profit organization.

FAS-117 addresses the reporting of investment expenses. Although it requires that the statement of activities report gross revenues and expenses, it does allow investment revenues to be reported net of related expenses (such as custodial fees and investment advisory fees), provided that the amount of the expenses is disclosed either in the statement of activities or in the notes to the financial statements. Therefore, the auditor should be sure that the not-for-profit organization is able to accumulate the investment-related expenses for disclosure purposes, particularly if the organization historically has reported the investment income net of investment expenses, with no disclosure of the investment expenses. If this information is not readily available, the auditor may attempt to obtain the investment expense information as part of his or her confirmation of the investment account with the investment custodian.

Realized Gains and Losses

Not-for-profit organizations should recognize realized gains and losses when investments are sold or otherwise disposed of, which is consistent with the recognition criteria of commercial enterprises. Not-for-profit organizations should report realized gains and losses as increases or decreases in unrestricted net assets unless their use is temporarily or permanently restricted by explicit donor-imposed restrictions or by law.

> **OBSERVATION:** In December 1994, the FASB issued a special report, "Results of the Field Test of the Proposed Standards for Financial Statements of Not-for-Profit Organizations and Accounting for Contributions," which presented the results of a field test of the Exposure Drafts for FAS-116 and FAS-117. One of the areas of confusion in classifying investment income concerned whether gains and losses of the principal in a permanently restricted endowment fund was unrestricted or restricted. If the endowment agreement is silent as to gains and losses on principal, these gains and losses should be considered unrestricted in most states. Some states, however, may have statutes that govern the application of gains and losses, requiring them to be considered permanently restricted. The auditor should consult with the not-for-profit organization and its legal counsel, if appropriate, if this situation is encountered.

Some not-for-profit organizations use a spending rate formula to determine how much of the total return on their investments may be used for current operations. Total return for these purposes typically includes investment income as well as net appreciation in the investments. Auditors should remember that FAS-117 requires all investment income and recognized gains and losses to be reported on the statement of activities and classified as unrestricted unless restricted by the donor or applicable law. Therefore, the part of the total return that is available for operations does not determine that portion of investment income that will be reported as an increase to unrestricted net assets. The amount reported as an increase to unrestricted net assets will be determined by the criteria of FAS-117 as described above. The not-for-profit organization may provide information in the footnotes to the financial statements on both the total return and the spending rate. The not-for-profit organization does not have to change its operating policies over the spending rate available for operations to comply with FAS-117.

Unrealized Holding Gains and Losses

Unrealized holding gains and losses arise from changes in the fair value of investments exclusive of dividend and interest income recognized but not yet received and exclusive of any write-down of the carrying amount of investments of impairment. Whether unrealized holding gains and losses are recognized in the statement of activities depends on whether the investments are carried at fair value or whether other investments are carried at cost.

Unrealized gains and losses that are recognized should be reported as increases and decreases in unrestricted net assets unless their use is temporarily or permanently restricted by donors to a specified purpose or future period. If a donor or a relevant law requires that the not-for-profit organization retain permanently some portion of gains on investments, then the unrealized gain on the related investments should be reported as an increase in permanently restricted net assets.

> **OBSERVATION:** The guidance provided for realized gains and losses also should be considered for unrealized gains and losses where donor restrictions apply.

Because donor restrictions vary, the auditor of the not-for-profit organization should take the appropriate measures to ensure that both realized gains and losses and recognized unrealized gains and losses are properly classified as increases or decreases in the correct net asset category. The relevant facts of the circumstance, including the specific donor restrictions or any law that may be relevant, should be considered. The auditor also should ensure that the not-for-profit organization staff making decisions about the classification of these gains and losses has an adequate understanding of the individual donor restrictions and laws to make the proper decisions.

Investment Income on Endowment Funds

Auditors need to pay special attention to the accounting and reporting for investment income relating to endowment funds. Valuing investments at fair value raises questions on reporting the net appreciation and net depreciation in the fair values of these assets.

In a typical endowment fund, the donor stipulates that the gift be invested in perpetuity. Donors (or relevant law) may require that the not-for-profit organization permanently retain some portion of gains or losses (i.e., net appreciation) on the donor-restricted endowment funds. Unless net appreciation on the donor-restricted endowment funds is temporarily or permanently restricted by the donor's explicit stipulation or by laws that extend a donor's restriction to donor-restricted endowment funds, net appreciation on donor-restricted endowment funds should be reported as a change in unrestricted net assets. Thus, the absence of donor stipulations, laws to the contrary, or donor restrictions on the use of income of an endowment fund also extends to the net appreciation on the endowment fund.

FAS-124 provides guidance on recording losses on endowment fund assets. In the absence of donor stipulations or laws to the contrary, losses on the investments of a donor-restricted endowment fund reduce temporarily restricted net assets to the extent that donor-imposed temporary restrictions on net appreciation of the fund are not met before a loss occurs. Any remaining loss should reduce unrestricted net assets.

If losses reduce the assets of a donor-restricted endowment fund below the level required by donor stipulation or law, gains that restore the fair value of the assets of the endowment fund to the required level should be classified as increases in unrestricted net assets. After the fair value of the assets of the endowment fund equals the required level, gains that are restricted by the donor should be classified as increases in temporarily restricted net assets or permanently restricted net assets, depending on the donor's restrictions on the endowment fund.

Investment Pools

A not-for-profit organization may have investments from a number of different donors that must be accounted for separately to ensure proper reporting to the donor. However, for purposes of investing these funds, the not-for-profit organization may find it beneficial to pool all or part of its investments. Pooling can result in less recordkeeping, lower investment management fees, higher returns, and reduced investment risk to the portfolio. The number and nature of the pools varies from organization to organization depending on the needs of each individual not-for-profit organization.

At the time a pool is established, ownership interests are assigned (such as through a unit value type method) to the various pool categories (which are sometimes referred to as *participants*) based on the market value of the cash and securities placed in the pool by each participant. Current market value is used to determine the number of units allocated to any additional assets placed in the pool and to value withdrawals from the pool. Investment income and realized gains and losses (as well as any unrecognized gains and losses) are allocated equitably based on the number of units assigned to each participant.

Financial Statement Disclosures

The AICPA Guide and FAS-124 require various disclosures for investments of not-for-profit organizations.

For each period for which a statement of financial position is presented, a not-for-profit organization should disclose the following:

- The aggregate carrying amount of investments by major types (e.g., equity securities, U.S. Treasury securities, corporate debt securities, mortgage-backed securities, oil and gas, and real estate)

- The basis for determining the carrying value for investments other than equity securities with readily determinable fair values and all debt securities

- The method of methods and significant assumptions used to estimate the fair values of investments other than financial instruments if those other investments are reported at fair value

- The aggregate amount of the deficiencies for all donor-restricted endowment funds for which the fair value of the assets at the reporting date is less than the level required by donor stipulations or law

For each period for which a statement of activities is presented, a not-for-profit organization should disclose the following:

- The composition of the investment return including, at a minimum, investment income, realized gains and losses on investments reported at other than fair value, and net gains or losses on investments reported at fair value

- A reconciliation of investment return to amounts reported in the statements of activities if some, but not all, of the investment return is included within a measure of operations, together with a description of the policy used to determine the portion of the return that is included in the measure of operations and a discussion of circumstances leading to a change, if any, in that policy

Significant amounts of information regarding the investments of a not-for-profit organization must be disclosed, primarily in the notes to the financial statements. The auditor should make sure that the appropriate individuals at the not-for-profit organization are familiar with these requirements, so that the detailed information that is required can be accumulated and reported.

The auditor should assess the not-for-profit organization's ability to accumulate this information accurately. This assessment will affect the auditor's procedures regarding concluding on whether the information is fairly presented. The lower the assessment by the auditor that the not-for-profit organization can accumulate the information in an accurate manner, the more likely the auditor is to include some or all of the information in confirmation requests to the custodians of the investments to obtain an independent assessment of the information.

> **OBSERVATION:** The disclosures described above should be considered as minimum disclosures, of course governed by the individual items that are being considered for disclosure. If the auditor believes other important or unique instances should be disclosed, he or she should insist that these additional disclosures be included in the financial statements.

When determining the adequacy of not-for-profit organizations' disclosures regarding investments, auditors should also consider all of the disclosure and other requirements applicable to commercial organizations.

The following summarizes the applicability and requirements of the more important FASB Statements that should be considered in auditing the investment area:

- FAS-105 (Disclosures of Information about Financial Instruments with Off-Balance Sheet Risk and Financial Instruments with Concentrations of Credit Risk)—This Statement requires disclosures to be made about risk relating to financial instruments that might not be apparent from the balance sheet or might be the result of risk being concentrated in counter parties to financial instruments having similar activities or having similar economic instruments. (This Statement will be superceded by FAS-133 when that Statement becomes effective.) However, FAS-133 will amend FAS-107 to include the disclosure requirements of FAS-105 about the concentration of credit risk in FAS-107.

- FAS-107 (Disclosures about Fair Value of Financial Instruments)—This Statement requires entities to disclose the fair value of financial instruments, both assets and liabilities recognized and not recognized in the statement of financial position, for which it is practicable to estimate fair value. However, in December 1996, the FASB issued FAS-126 (Exemption from Certain Disclosure Requirements about Financial Instruments for Certain Nonpublic Entities). FAS-126 makes optional the disclosures about the fair values of financial instruments required by FAS-107 if all of the following criteria are met:

— The entity is a nonpublic entity.

— The entity's total assets are less than $100 million on the date of the financial statements.

— The entity has not held or issued any derivative financial instruments, as defined in FAS-119 (see below).

FAS-126, which is effective for fiscal years ending after December 15, 1996, is likely to make the FAS-107 disclosure requirements optional for most not-for-profit organizations.

- FAS-115 (Accounting for Certain Investments in Debt and Equity Investments)—This Statement is not applicable to not-for-profit organizations. Some of its definitions and other principles were considered by the FASB when it issued FAS-124, which applies specifically to not-for-profit organizations.

- FAS-119 (Disclosure about Derivative Financial Instruments and Fair Value of Financial Instruments)—This Statement requires disclosures about derivative financial instruments, such as futures, forward contracts, options, swaps, or other financial instruments with similar characteristics. (This Statement will be superceded by FAS-133 when that Statement becomes effective.)

- FAS-133 (Accounting for Derivative Instruments and Hedging Activities)—In June 1998, the FASB issued FAS-133, which is a long-anticipated and quite controversial Statement providing accounting guidance for derivative instruments and hedging activities. FAS-133 was originally effective for all fiscal quarters of fiscal years beginning after June 15, 1999. However, FAS-137 (Accounting for Derivative Instruments and Hedging Activities—Deferral of the Effective Date of FASB Statement No. 133) defers the effective date of FAS-133 to all fiscal quarters of all fiscal years beginning after June 15, 2000. Earlier application of FAS-133 is encouraged, but is permitted only as of the beginning of any fiscal quarter that begins after the issuance of the Statement.

FAS-133 will require that entities recognize all derivatives as either assets or liabilities in the statement of financial position and that they measure those instruments at fair value. Under FAS-133, not-for-profit organizations will recognize the change in the fair value of derivatives as a change in net assets in the period of the change. Not-for-profit organizations will not be permitted special hedge accounting for derivatives used to hedge forecasted transactions.

Audit Procedures

In December 1996 the Auditing Standards Board of the AICPA issued Statement on Auditing Standards No. 81 (Auditing Investments) (SAS-81) to provide guidance to auditors auditing investments. SAS-81 became effective for audits of financial statements for periods ending on or after December 15, 1997.

For auditors of not-for-profit organizations, SAS-81 provides guidance in the following areas:

- Nature of audit procedures
- Valuation and presentation of investments
- Investments accounted for under the equity method (SAS-81 also provides guidance on auditing the appropriateness of the classification of investments under FAS-115. These procedures would not be applicable to not-for-profit organizations, which are not included in the scope of FAS-115.)
- Nature of audit procedures

The procedures that are performed to obtain evidence about the existence, ownership, and completeness of investments vary depending on the type of investment being audited and the assessment of audit risk. SAS-81 specifies, however, that audit procedures should include one or more of the following:

- Physical inspection
- Confirmation with the issuer
- Confirmation with the custodian
- Confirmation of unsettled transactions with the broker-dealer
- Confirmation with the counter party
- Reading executed partnership or similar agreements

In addition, the guidance of SAS-70 (Reports on the Processing of Transactions by Service Organizations) should be considered if the not-for-profit organization obtains either or both of the following services from another organization:

- Execution of investment transactions and maintenance of the related accountability

- Recording of investment transactions and processing of the related data

> **OBSERVATION:** Clearly, SAS-81 reaffirms the importance of using confirmation with an independent third party as an important source of audit evidence when auditing investments.

- Valuation and presentation of investments

Most investments for not-for-profit organizations are recorded at fair value, although the preceding discussion of accounting for investments describes certain circumstances where cost would still be used for certain investments. SAS-81 provides the following guidance for obtaining evidence about the cost and fair value of investments:

- Cost

The audit procedures performed to obtain evidence about cost may include inspection of documentation indicating the purchase price of the security, confirmation with the issuer or custodian, and recomputation of discount or premium amortization.

SAS-81 also provides certain factors that an auditor would consider in evaluating whether an other-than-temporary impairment exists where fair value of the investment is below cost. The factors are designed for evaluating certain conditions under FAS-115, which would not apply to not-for-profit organizations. However, where a not-for-profit organization is carrying "other investments" (described in the preceding section on the accounting for investments not covered by FAS-124), where fair value is below cost, the auditor should consider the following factors in determining whether there is an impairment in the value of an investment:

- Fair value is significantly below cost.

- The decline in fair value is attributable to specific adverse conditions affecting a particular investment.

- The decline in fair value is attributable to specific conditions, such as conditions in an industry or in a geographic area.

- Management does not possess both the intent and the ability to hold the investment for a period of time sufficient to allow for any anticipated recovery in fair value.
- The decline in fair value has existed for an extended period of time.
- A debt security has been downgraded by a rating agency.
- The financial condition of the issuer has deteriorated.
- Dividends have been reduced or eliminated, or scheduled interest payments on debt securities have not been made.
- Fair value

Most of a not-for-profit organization's investments are carried at fair value. For equity securities, only those with a readily determinable fair value are reported at fair value. SAS-81 confirms that quoted market prices obtained from financial publications, or from national exchanges or the National Association of Securities Dealers Automated Quotations System (NASDAQ), are considered to provide sufficient evidence about the fair value of investments.

For auditing debt securities, fair value does not have to be readily determinable for reporting at fair value. All debt securities are reported at fair value. Therefore, other provisions of SAS-81 would be considered for these securities (as well as any other "other investments" that are reported at fair value.)

In the case of investments where a valuation model is used, the auditor should assess the reasonableness and appropriateness of the model. The auditor should determine whether the market variables and assumptions that are used are reasonable and appropriately supported. The auditor should also determine whether the appropriate disclosures about the methods and significant assumptions used to estimated fair value were made. In some circumstances, the auditor may consider it necessary to involve a specialist in assessing fair value estimates or estimation models.

- Investments accounted for under the equity method

SAS-81 provides that financial statements of an investee generally constitute sufficient evidential matter as to the equity in the underlying net assets and the results of operations of the investee, if such statements have been audited by an auditor whose report is satisfactory, for this purpose, to the investor's auditor. Unaudited financial statements, reports issued on examination by regulatory bodies and taxing authorities, and similar data do not, by themselves, provide sufficient evidential matter for purposes of recording the applicable portion of the net assets and results of operations of an investee. If the financial statements of the investee are not audited, the auditor should apply (or request that the investor arrange with the investee to have performed) appropriate auditing procedures to the unaudited financial statements, considering the materiality of the investment in relation to the financial statements of the investor.

If the carrying amount of an investment reflects factors that are not recognized in the investee's financial statements (such as goodwill or other intangibles) or reflects fair values of assets that are materially different from the investee's carrying amounts, the auditor should consider obtaining current valuations of these amounts.

SAS-81 also prescribes that when a time lag exists between an investee's fiscal year end and an investor's fiscal year end, the time lag should be consistent from year to year. If a change in the time lag occurs that has a material effect on the investor's financial statements, an explanatory paragraph should be added to the auditor's report because of the change in the reporting period.

The auditor should consider the following additional points:

- To address subsequent events and transactions of the investee (after the date of the investee's financial statements, but before the investor's financial statements are issued), the auditor should read available interim financial statements of the investee and make appropriate inquiries as to the existence of any material subsequent events or transactions.

- Evidence relating to material transactions between the investor and the investee should be obtained to evaluate the propriety of the elimination of unrealized intercompany profits and losses and the adequacy of the disclosure about material related-party transactions.

The basic auditing procedures that an auditor employs for investments of a not-for-profit organization are essentially the same as those that would be used for a commercial enterprise. Consistent with SAS-81, the primary procedure is confirmation with the custodian of the investment. Where the not-for-profit organization has physical custody of securities, the auditor will apply physical inspection procedures to obtain assurance about existence and ownership. The auditor may use the sample forms for confirmation of investments that are included on the disc accompanying this Guide (file names: SC-02 and SC-03). The sample letter can be modified to fit the specific circumstances. In some instances, the auditor will be auditing investments that are reported at market value with disclosure of cost. In other instances, the auditor will be auditing investments that are reported at cost, with disclosure of market value. The auditor should consider the need for these two reported amounts in confirming investments with the investment holders.

The auditor should ascertain whether the not-for-profit organization has properly classified investments (and related investment income and realized and recognized but unrealized gains and losses) into the three categories of net assets—unrestricted, temporarily restricted, and permanently restricted. When designing procedures to test this classification, the auditor should consider his or her potential legal exposure if the investments are misclassified. Just as it is usually worse to overstate an asset and understate a liability, the auditor is exposed to more legal liability when restricted net assets (either temporarily or permanently) are included in unrestricted net assets than when unrestricted net assets are included in either temporarily or permanently restricted net assets. The auditor should design any detailed test work accordingly, including testing transactions that are recorded as unrestricted to make sure that they are, in fact, unrestricted.

> **OBSERVATION:** Auditors will need to be prepared to address the accounting for derivatives that will be required by FAS-133. Not-for-profit organizations that invest in derivatives may have been disclosing the fair value of these instruments under FAS-107 or FAS-119. Under FAS-133, derivatives will be reported in the statement of financial position at fair value. This will require the auditor to determine whether the fair value reported is appropriate. In addition, the auditor will need to pay special attention that derivatives covered by FAS-133 are actually reported on the statement of financial position.

The auditor also should consider testing some of the transactions for purchases and sales or maturities of investments during the year. In the case of sales, the proper calculation and classification (among unrestricted, temporarily restricted, or permanently restricted net assets) of the realized gain or loss should be tested. The auditor also may test the calculation of any recognized, but unrealized, gains and losses, which basically includes testing the differences between cost and market values of investments.

The auditor should be able to test other types of investment income (such as dividends, interest, rents, and royalties) by performing analytical procedures. If considered necessary, the auditor may perform detailed tests of transactions. In the past, auditors performed a great deal of detailed test work on investment income. For a more efficient audit, the auditor should try to limit the audit procedures to substantive analytical procedures, particularly if there are few or no issues regarding the classification of investment income.

Derivatives

The auditor must be aware of recent financial losses suffered by not-for-profit organizations, commercial enterprises, and governments as a result of investments in financial instruments known as *deriva-*

tives. These financial instruments have resulted in some very newsworthy and, in some cases, significant losses to both public and private organizations.

Derivatives often are designed to produce a leveraged effect on the investment, which can result in magnified losses when an investor makes a wrong "bet" on some financial barometer (e.g., rising or falling interest rates). In addition to market risks, an investor needs to understand the credit risks and counterparty risks before making derivative investments.

For auditors, the primary considerations are to ensure that the proper valuations and disclosures are made for any derivative investment financial products included in the not-for-profit organization's portfolio.

The auditor also should be cognizant of the not-for-profit organization's risk management controls related to derivative financial products and to investments in general. A reliable system of providing valuation information should exist, and personnel should have the appropriate level of expertise for the complexity of the investments that the not-for-profit organization holds. In addition, the auditor should determine whether the not-for-profit organization has appropriate controls over the authorization of investment transactions so that the appropriate levels of approval are obtained before any investment transaction is made. A periodic and systematic review of all investment transactions should be used to view investment trading activities, especially if there is a great deal of trading activity.

There is currently a heightened sense of awareness about investments, particularly derivatives. This is a particularly sensitive issue at not-for-profit organizations where the level of investment experience and sophistication of the individuals making investment decisions may be lower than at comparable commercial organizations. Adding to the sensitivity is the pressure on not-for-profit organizations to continue their existence and, in most cases, increase the level of services that they provide. Pressure to earn a higher rate of return, which would increase the funding available for the not-for-profit organization's programs, may lead the organization's investment managers to accept more risk in an investment portfolio than otherwise would be warranted. In addition, any losses incurred on investments, particularly derivatives, where the corpus of the investment was received as a donation is a particularly sensitive issue.

The auditor may easily be embarrassed (at best) or sued (at worse) for not being prudent when examining the investment area. Particularly in the area of derivatives, where the risks have been well-publicized and well-analyzed, the auditor simply cannot afford to be unknowledgeable about the risks of, and the not-for-profit organization's accounting for and controls over, these types of investments.

PROPERTY, PLANT, AND EQUIPMENT

The auditing considerations for the property, plant, and equipment of a not-for-profit organization are similar to those of a commercial enterprise. Like commercial enterprises, the size a not-for-profit organization's investment in property, plant, and equipment depends on the nature of its program activities. For example, a college or university will have a much greater investment in property, plant, and equipment than will a local soccer association.

The AICPA Guide lists the following as some of the typical types of property, plant, and equipment held by not-for-profit organizations:

- Land used as a building site not subject to depreciation
- Land improvements, buildings and building improvements, equipment, furniture and office equipment, library books, motor vehicles, and similar depreciable assets
- Leased property and equipment that has been capitalized in accordance with FAS-13 (Accounting for Leases)
- Improvements to leased property
- Construction in progress
- Contributed use of facilities and equipment that have been capitalized in accordance with FAS-116

The following paragraphs discuss some of the unique accounting considerations with which the auditor should be familiar before conducting an audit of a not-for-profit organization.

Most of the transactions that a not-for-profit organization records relating to its property, plant, and equipment are similar to those of a commercial organization. For example, not-for-profit organizations may purchase, construct, or lease assets that comprise its property, plant, and equipment. Not-for-profit organizations record the transactions in the same manner as commercial enterprises, including the recognition of depreciation, where applicable.

Contributions of Property, Plant, and Equipment

Not-for-profit organizations may receive some of their property, plant, and equipment through contributions. Although the accounting for contributions is more fully discussed in the chapter titled "Statement of Activities," the more pertinent requirements for accounting for contributions relating to property, plant, and equipment are discussed in the following paragraphs.

Contributions of property, plant, and equipment should be recognized at their fair value at the date of the contribution. Unconditional promises to give property and equipment should be recognized as receivables in the same manner. (Unconditional promises to give are discussed more fully in the chapter titled "Statement of Activities.")

Depending on donor restrictions and the not-for-profit organization's accounting policy, these contributions should be included in the appropriate class of net assets—permanently restricted, temporarily restricted, and unrestricted.

- If the donor stipulates how or how long the contributed property, plant, and equipment must be used by the not-for-profit organization, the contribution should be reported as either permanently restricted or temporarily restricted support, as is proper in the circumstances.

- If the not-for-profit organization has an accounting policy of implying a time restriction on the use of such assets that expires over the assets' useful life, the not-for-profit organization should record the contributed asset as restricted support.

- If there are no donor restrictions on the contributed asset and the not-for-profit organization does not have an accounting policy of implying a time restriction, the contributed property, plant, and equipment should be recorded as unrestricted support.

A not-for-profit also may acquire property, plant, and equipment in an exchange transaction. *Exchange transactions* are those in which the not-for-profit organization and the counterparty have an "exchange" in value as a result of the transaction (i.e., unlike a donor, the counterparty to the transactions receives something equivalent from the not-for-profit organization in return). In some exchange transactions, the not-for-profit organization receives assets or, more commonly, funding to purchase assets that consist of property, plant, and equipment under the terms of a contract or grant to provide services. Contracts entered into under federal awards programs would be considered in this instance to be exchange transactions.

Property, plant, and equipment used in exchange transactions in which the resource provider retains legal title during the term of the arrangement should be capitalized by the not-for-profit organization only if it is probable that the organization will be permitted to keep the assets when the arrangement terminates. The terms of these types of arrangements should be disclosed in the notes to the financial statements.

Depreciation

FAS-93 (Recognition of Depreciation by Not-for-Profit Organizations) requires all not-for-profit organizations to recognize depreciation for all property and equipment, except land used as a building site and similar assets and collections. Since commercial enterprises also do not depreciate land, the substantive difference in recording depreciation between a not-for-profit organization and a commercial enterprise relates to collections, which FAS-93 does not require to be depreciated.

FAS-93 defines and clarifies this exception as follows:

> Consistent with the accepted practice for land used as a building site, depreciation need not be recognized on individual works of art or historical treasures whose economic benefit or service potential is used up so slowly that their estimated useful lives are extraordinarily long. A work of art or historical treasure shall be deemed to have that characteristic only if verifiable evidence exists demonstrating that (a) the asset individually has cultural, aesthetic, or historical value that is work preserving perpetually and (b) the holder has the technological and financial ability to protect and preserve essentially undiminished the service potential of the asset and is doing that.

Depreciation should be recorded for property, plant, and equipment that is contributed, as well as for property, plant, and equipment acquired and recorded in exchange transactions. Depreciation expense should be recorded in the statement of activities as a decrease in unrestricted net assets.

When contributed property, plant, and equipment is recorded as temporarily restricted support, the assets should be reclassified over a period of time as unrestricted net assets in the statement of activities. The reclassification is necessary to reflect the fact that the donor's temporary restrictions will expire during the asset's useful life. Reclassifications are also necessary if the not-for-profit organization has adopted an accounting policy that implies a time restriction on contributions of property, plant, and equipment that expires over the useful life of the contributed assets.

The amount reclassified is reported in the statement of activities as "net assets released from restrictions" and may or may not equal the amount of the related depreciation. The amount reclassified should be based on the length of time indicated by the donor-imposed restrictions, whereas the amount of depreciation should be based on the useful economic life of the asset. The donor restrictions may expire over a period of time that is shorter than the remaining economic useful life of the donated asset.

Gains or Losses on Dispositions of Property, Plant, and Equipment

Any gains or losses on the disposition of assets comprising property, plant, and equipment should be classified in the statement of activities as increases or decreases in unrestricted net assets, unless there are explicit donor stipulations or laws that require their use to be temporarily or permanently restricted. In these cases, gains or losses should be classified as increases or decreases in temporarily restricted or permanently restricted net assets.

Impairment of Long-Lived Assets

In auditing the area of property, plant and equipment, auditors should also be cognizant of the requirements of FAS-121 (Accounting for the Impairment of Long-Lived Assets and for Long-Lived Assets to Be Disposed Of). FAS-121 requires that long-lived assets and certain identifiable intangibles be reviewed for impairment whenever events or changes in circumstances indicate that the carrying amount of an asset may not be recoverable. In performing reviews for recoverability, not-for-profit organizations should estimate the future cash flows expected to result from the use of the asset and its eventual disposition. If the sum of the expected future cash flows (undiscounted and without interest charges) is less than the carrying amount of an asset, an impairment loss is recognized. Measurement of an impairment loss for long-lived assets and identifiable intangibles that an organization expects to hold and use is based on the fair value of the asset.

In addition, long-lived assets and certain intangibles to be disposed of are reported at the lower of carrying amount or fair value less cost to sell (or in some cases, at the lower of the carrying amount or net realizable value).

Auditors should inquire as to the possible situations where impairment of a long-lived asset has occurred and determine if the not-for-profit organization has made the appropriate calculations and has recorded losses where required at appropriate amounts.

Financial Statement Disclosures

The AICPA Guide lists a number of disclosures that should be made, where applicable, for a not-for-profit organization's property, plant, and equipment. The statement of financial position should include the balances of each major class of property and equipment. The basis of valuations (for example, cost for purchased assets and fair value for contributed assets) also should be disclosed. Separate disclosures should be made of the following items:

- Nondepreciable assets
- Property and equipment not held for use in operations (e.g., items held for sale or for investment purposes or construction in process)
- Assets restricted by donors to investment in property and equipment
- Improvements to leased facilities
- Assets (related obligations) recognized under capital leases in conformity with FAS-13
- Capitalized interest (in conformity with FAS-34 [Capitalization of Interest Cost] and FAS-62 [Capitalization of Interest Cost in Situations Involving Tax-Exempt Borrowings and Certain Gifts and Grants])
- Significant accounting policies concerning property, plant, and equipment, such as the following:
  — Capitalization policy adopted
  — Whether time restrictions are implied on the use of contributed long-lived assets (and contributions of assets restricted to purchase them) received without donor stipulations concerning how long the contributed assets must be used
  — Whether donor-restricted contributions of long-lived assets are reported as unrestricted or restricted support when restrictions are satisfied in the same reporting period in which the contributions are received
- Accumulated depreciation, either of each major class of property, plant, and equipment or in total
- The amount of depreciation expense for the period and the method or methods used to compute depreciation for the major classes of property, plant, and equipment
- Depreciation methods used
- Disclosures concerning the liquidity of the not-for-profit organization's property, plant, and equipment, including information about limitations on their uses, such as:
  — Property, plant, and equipment pledged as collateral or otherwise subject to lien

— Property, plant, and equipment acquired with restricted assets where title may revert to another party, such as a resource provider

— Donor or legal restrictions on the use of or proceeds from the disposal of property and equipment

The auditor should obtain an understanding about whether the not-for-profit organization has adequate records to be able to prepare these disclosures. If the not-for-profit organization is unable to obtain this information, the auditor may consider obtaining the information for these disclosures directly from outside parties, such as through direct confirmation with the donors of contributed assets.

Audit Procedures

The auditor of a not-for-profit organization should consider the sources of the property, plant, and equipment recorded by the organization when designing an effective audit strategy. The auditor should review the "roll-forward" of the property, plant, and equipment from the end of the prior year to the end of the current year to understand the extent of asset additions and dispositions. Additions to property, plant, and equipment can then be segregated between assets that were purchased by the not-for-profit organization and assets that were donated to it or acquired in exchange transactions.

Property, plant, and equipment that is purchased by the not-for-profit organization should be audited in a manner that is the most similar to that of commercial enterprises. If significant, the auditor may perform detailed tests of transactions relating to the purchase and sale of these types of assets. The auditor should determine whether the appropriate costs related to acquisitions of property, plant, and equipment, such as freight charges and installation costs, have been capitalized. Costs being capitalized for assets that are being constructed and capitalized interest costs also should be tested. The usual skepticism of the auditor regarding the propriety of costs capitalized as property, plant, and equipment also would pertain to not-for-profit organizations, particularly when these costs would otherwise be charged to unrestricted net assets. Similarly, where the costs of acquisition or construction are being borne by a donor, the auditor's skepticism should focus on determining whether only the appropriate costs are being capitalized and claimed for reimbursement by the donor.

The auditor's concerns for contributed property, plant, and equipment are different from his or her concerns for purchased assets. The auditor should determine if the not-for-profit organization is recording these assets at fair value and should determine the basis used to determine fair value.

For significant contributions, the auditor should review the documentation of fair value that was obtained by the not-for-profit organization when recording the contribution. The auditor also should review documentation to determine what restrictions, if any, the donor may have imposed on the use or disposition of the donated property, plant, and equipment. The documentation may consist of correspondence with the donor, a specific contract with the donor, or other documents associated with individual contribution transactions. Board of directors meeting minutes also may provide evidence of discussion of donor restrictions applicable to significant property, plant, and equipment donations. This documentation is important for determining whether the contributed asset has been recorded in the proper class of net assets.

The auditor should determine whether other property, plant, and equipment transactions are accounted for properly (e.g., ensuring that property, plant, and equipment not used in the operations of the not-for-profit organization is reported separately). In addition, the auditor should determine if the not-for-profit organization has properly calculated the transfer of temporarily restricted net assets to unrestricted net assets, either in recognition of the passage of time relating to temporary donor restrictions or where an accounting policy recognizes that otherwise unrestricted property, plant, and equipment is temporarily restricted to the not-for-profit organization since its benefit is realized with the passage of time. In addition, a review for impairment of long-lived assets should be performed.

The auditor should determine if assets acquired through exchange transactions and recorded as property, plant, and equipment will have to be returned to the party that funded their purchase. If it appears that the assets will have to be returned to the counterparty, the auditor should question the propriety of recording the costs as part of the not-for-profit organization's property, plant, and equipment.

The auditor also should perform procedures to ascertain whether depreciation has been calculated properly and recorded as a decrease in unrestricted net assets in the statement of activities. The auditor should review the depreciation methods and estimated useful lives used to determine whether the depreciation calculations conform to generally accepted accounting principles. Although it is possible to perform detailed audit tests of the not-for-profit organization's depreciation calculations, the auditor may find it more efficient to perform substantive analytical procedures.

Depending on the extent of property, plant, and equipment recorded by the not-for-profit organization and the nature of the assets, the auditor should consider whether a physical observation of some or all of the assets is warranted. For example, a college or university may have acquired a building during the year being audited. The auditor can obtain more reliable evidence about the building's ownership and existence by reviewing the closing documents from the purchase transaction. Physical observation may indicate that the building is standing, but it adds little, if any, evidence that the college or university owns it. Conversely, the same college or university may have a significant, material investment in research equipment or other equipment that is very movable and has a high per-unit cost. The auditor may find it prudent at least to test check the existence of this equipment to verify the accuracy of the recorded property, plant, and equipment.

The auditor's decision about whether to perform physical observations will be influenced by any problems noted in this area in prior-year audits and the extent that the not-for-profit organization itself performs physical observations of property, plant, and equipment.

OTHER ASSETS, INCLUDING COLLECTIONS

Other asset accounts commonly found at not-for-profit organizations include inventories, prepaid expenses, and deferred charges. With the issuance of FAS-116, a not-for-profit must consider additional guidance when recording collections as assets on the statement of financial position.

Inventory

The sale of inventory usually is not one of the primary activities of not-for-profit organizations, but some not-for-profit organizations will sell merchandise as an ancillary activity to their exempt function. These activities might include the sale of books by a college or university or sales of memorabilia, such as T-shirts or coffee mugs, by a museum. The tax implications of such activities are discussed in the chapter titled "Tax Considerations."

The inventory procedures for a not-for-profit organization are similar to the procedures performed at a commercial organization, but the extent of the procedures should be tempered by the relative significance of the merchandising activities to the overall activities of the not-for-profit. For example, if the merchandising activities are a relatively small part of the not-for-profit's activities, the auditor may wish to eliminate, or significantly reduce, physical observation procedures, which normally would be performed in the audit of a commercial enterprise.

Contributions of inventory to a not-for-profit organization should be valued at fair value as of the date of the contribution. If the inventory contribution has no value (such as used clothing that cannot be resold) the not-for-profit organization should not recognize a contribution for these items.

Inventory that is purchased should be valued using the same method as would be used in a commercial enterprise. The auditor should be concerned with the existence of any obsolete items or damaged or unusable goods that may be appropriate to write-off or value at a lower amount.

Prepaid Expenses and Deferred Charges

The prepaid expenses and deferred charges of not-for-profit organizations are similar to those of commercial enterprises. Depending on the materiality of the accounts, the auditor should perform some detailed tests to ensure that the amounts recorded as assets are reasonable. In some cases, the auditor may find it more efficient to use substantive analytical procedures. These procedures should be used whenever feasible to eliminate unnecessary detailed test work, particularly with accounts that are not significant.

One aspect of not-for-profit organizations that was different from commercial enterprises is the deferral of costs relating to a fund-raising campaign. A not-for-profit organization may conduct a fund-raising campaign annually or in longer time increments (such as once every five or ten years). Shorter-duration campaigns are used more for operating purposes, while longer-duration campaigns are used more to raise capital funds, such as a five-year campaign to raise funds to construct a new building.

Not-for-profit organizations incur significant costs for these campaigns before they receive any funds or pledges. If the costs are incurred in the fiscal year being audited and the resulting revenues will not be received until subsequent years, it had been an acceptable practice for the not-for-profit organization to record the campaign costs as a deferred charge.

The auditor should approach such deferrals with a degree of skepticism and should perform sufficient procedures to ensure that the costs being deferred are not fund-raising costs. The AICPA Guide specifically states that fund-raising costs should be expensed when received, even if the related revenue will not be received until future years.

During 1998 the AICPA issued SOP 98-1 (Accounting for the Costs of Computer Software Developed or Obtained for Internal Use). This SOP requires that, upon meeting certain conditions, entities capitalize certain internal-use software costs. SOP 98-1 is effective for financial statements for fiscal years beginning after December 15, 1998, with earlier application encouraged.

Also in 1998, the AICPA issued SOP 98-5 (Reporting on the Costs of Start-Up Activities). This SOP requires that organizations expense the cost of start-up activities and organization costs as received. Prior practice resulted in many of those costs being capitalized. SOP 98-5 is effective for fiscal years beginning after December 15, 1998, with earlier adoption encouraged.

Collections

The accounting and financial reporting relating to collections has been clarified by FAS-116, which defines a *collection* as works of art, historical treasures, or similar assets that are:

- Held for public exhibition, education, or research in furtherance of public service rather than financial gain;
- Protected, kept unencumbered, cared for, and preserved; and
- Subject to an organizational policy that requires the proceeds of items that are sold to be used to acquire other items for collections.

The not-for-profit organization must decide whether to capitalize its collections. If the not-for-profit organization elects to capitalize its collections, it must decide how to value its existing collections when initially adopting FAS-116.

FAS-116 permits a prospective application of its provisions relating to collections. Therefore, the not-for-profit organization can elect to capitalize only those collection items acquired after the initial adoption of FAS-116. FAS-116 also permits a retroactive application of its provision relating to collections. In this case, a not-for-profit organization would capitalize its collections not previously capitalized and acquired before the initial adoption of FAS-116. For purposes of retrospective application, the not-for-profit may value the collections at their cost or fair value at the date of their acquisition, current cost, or current value, whichever is deemed most practical.

Although FAS-116 does not require not-for-profit organizations to capitalize collections, it does encourage them to capitalize retroactively collections acquired in years before its adoption or to capitalize collections on a prospective basis. FAS-116 precludes not-for-profit organizations from capitalizing only selected collections or items within a collection.

The AICPA Guide includes disclosures that should be included in the financial statements of a not-for-profit organization with collections. The disclosures depend on the capitalization policy adopted. If the not-for-profit organization adopts a policy of either prospectively or retrospectively capitalizing collections that meet the definition in FAS-116, the statement of financial position should include the total amount capitalized on a separate line item titled "Collections" or "Collection Items." The amount capitalized for works of art, historical treasures, and similar assets that meet the definition should be disclosed separately on the face of the statement of financial position.

A not-for-profit organization that does not recognize and capitalize its collections should report the following on the face of its statement of activities, separately from revenues, expenses, gains, and losses:

- Costs of collection items purchased as a decrease in the appropriate class of net assets
- Proceeds from sales of collection items as an increase in the appropriate class of net assets
- Proceeds from insurance recoveries for lost or destroyed collection items as an increase in the appropriate class of net assets

Similarly, a not-for-profit organization that capitalizes its collections prospectively should report proceeds from sales and insurance recoveries of items not previously capitalized separately from revenues, expenses, gains, and losses.

A not-for-profit that does not recognize and capitalize its collections or that capitalizes collections prospectively should describe its collections, including their relative significance, and its accounting and stewardship policies for collections. If collection items not capitalized are deaccessed during that period, the not-for-profit organization should (1) describe the items given away, damaged, destroyed, lost, or otherwise deaccessed during the period or (2) disclose their fair value. In addition, a line item should be shown on the face of the statement of financial position that refers to the disclosures just described.

Some of the auditing procedures the auditor should consider performing for capitalized or noncapitalized collections are listed below.

Noncapitalized Collections

- Review the policies and procedures used by the not-for-profit organization to determine what assets are categorized as collections, and determine the appropriateness of the classification of assets as noncapitalized collections.
- Determine the appropriateness of the display and disclosures in the financial statements for noncapitalized collections.
- Review the not-for-profit organization's procedures for controlling and physically inspecting collections.
- Consider whether to physically observe the collections, and consider whether, based on the adequacy of the not-for-profit organization's procedures and the relative size of the collection, to use the work of a specialist during the observation of the collection.
- Review management's follow-up on any discrepancies noted by the not-for-profit organization after conducting its own physical observation of the collection(s).
- Review the documentation supporting accessions and deaccessions of collection items.

- Review minutes of the board of directors meetings for authorization of major accessions or deaccessions.
- Inquire of curatorial personnel about accessions or deaccessions.

Capitalized Collections

- Review the not-for-profit organization's procedures for controlling collections and performing physical inspections of them.
- Consider whether to observe the physical inspection of the collection, and consider whether, based on the adequacy of the not-for-profit organization's procedures and the relative size of the collection, to use the work of a specialist during the observation.
- Review management's follow-up on any discrepancies noted by the not-for-profit organization after conducting its own physical observation of the collection(s).
- Review the documentation supporting accessions and deaccessions on collection items.
- Review minutes of the board of directors meetings for authorization of major accessions or deaccessions, evidence of current-period purchases and contributions, and any donor restrictions imposed on the not-for-profit organization relative to contributed collections.
- Inquire of curatorial personnel about accessions or deaccessions.
- Review documentation and procedures supporting the determination of cost (for purchases) or fair value (for contributions).
- Review donor correspondence to determine the presence or absence of restrictions.
- Determine whether specific collection items are restricted, and review collection item transactions for propriety of use and disposition.
- Review documentation underlying collection items for propriety of classification.

Collections Capitalized Retroactively Before FAS-116 Implementation

- Review documents and procedures supporting the determination of cost or fair value at date of acquisition or current cost or current market value at date of initial recognition.
- Review donor correspondence to determine the presence or absence of donor restrictions.
- Review minutes of the board of directors meetings for evidence of restrictions on the collections.

- Review the documentation underlying contributed collection items for propriety of classification.

- Consider the need to use the work of a specialist in conjunction with determining the reliability of the carrying values of the collection.

In all instances where the not-for-profit organization is reflecting activity relating to collections care must be taken to ensure that the transactions are reflected in (or disclosed parenthetically in) the appropriate classes of net assets. This is particularly important in the initial year of adoption of both FAS-116 and FAS-117 for not-for-profit organizations choosing retroactive capitalization because of the many first-time classification decisions that will need to be made.

DEBT AND OTHER LIABILITIES, INCLUDING DEFERRED REVENUE

Liabilities of not-for-profit organizations closely track those of commercial organizations. An auditor of a not-for-profit organization would expect to find the same types of accounts payable and accrued expenses at a not-for-profit organization as would be found at a commercial enterprise. Accounting for these liabilities is the same as the accounting for a commercial enterprise. However, the amount of accounts payable at a not-for-profit organization will be less than would be expected at a commercial enterprise, because not-for-profit organizations probably will have few, if any, accounts payable attributable to merchandise inventory purchased for resale. Not-for-profit organization accrued expenses generally include typical accrued expenses, such as telephone and utility expenses. However, a not-for-profit organization's payroll expenses are usually a significant part of its overall expenses, and the auditor should determine whether the not-for-profit organization has calculated an appropriate accrual for salary and related fringe benefit expenses as of the end of the organization's fiscal year.

When auditing accounts payable, the auditor may consider performing a search for unrecorded liabilities by reviewing disbursements after the fiscal year-end date and determining whether the disbursements should have been recorded as liabilities as of the fiscal year-end date. When the auditor believes there are serious problems with accounts payable, he or she may consider confirming the accounts with some of the major vendors or vendors with frequent activity during the year but with zero balances at year end. For accrued expenses, the auditor should consider reperforming some of the not-for-profit organization's calculations to determine their propriety. The auditor also may consider selecting some expenses that he or she believes should have been accrued and determining whether the organization made the appropriate accrual.

Long- and Short-Term Debt and Other Borrowings

Some liabilities are unique to not-for-profit organizations and require special attention, such as long- and short-term debt and other borrowings. Not-for-profit organizations are capable of incurring long-term debt including mortgages and other borrowings. They also may incur short-term debt to finance seasonal borrowing needs. The short-term borrowing may be in the form of a line of credit that the not-for-profit organization accesses as cash is required.

In some cases a state or local governmental financing authority may issue tax-exempt debt to finance some of the activities of a not-for-profit organization. Since the not-for-profit organization is responsible for the repayment of the debt, the debt should be recorded as a liability on the not-for-profit organization's statement of financial position.

For all types of borrowings, the auditor should consider reviewing the underlying agreements or notes to understand the terms of the borrowing. This is important in determining whether the liquidity information provided by the not-for-profit organization in its financial statements as required by FAS-117 is properly stated. These documents also will provide information about interest rates, assets pledged, or other restrictions and terms that need to be disclosed in the financial statements.

Auditors generally use confirmation procedures for these types of borrowings, including instances where the organization has a line of credit with no balance outstanding. Where restrictions are placed on the operation of the not-for-profit organization in the various debt covenants governing its debt, the auditor should ensure compliance with restrictions. Failure to comply with certain features of debt covenants may cause otherwise long-term debt to become due and payable immediately, which obviously would be of concern to the auditor, unless the not-for-profit organization obtained a waiver from the lender.

Auditors should also be aware that FAS-125 (Accounting for Transfers and Servicing of Financial Assets and Extinguishment of Liabilities) eliminated the use of "in-substance" defeasances of debt. Under FAS-125 a liability is derecognized if and only if either (a) the debtor pays the creditor and is relieved of its obligation for the liability or (b) the debtor is legally released from being the primary obligor under the liability, either judicially or by the creditor. Thus, a liability is not considered extinguished by an in-substance defeasance.

FAS-125 is effective for extinguishment of liabilities occurring after December 31, 1996. The FASB issued FAS-127 (Deferral of the

Effective Date of Certain Provisions of FASB Statement No. 125), which deferred the effective date of some of the provisions of FAS-125. However, the provisions of FAS-125 relating to the extinguishment of liabilities were not deferred by FAS-127 and are currently effective.

Deferred Revenues

The AICPA Guide provides guidance on the recording of deferred revenue, including the recording of advances from third parties. A not-for-profit organization may receive resources in exchange transactions from customers, patients, and other service beneficiaries for specific projects, programs, or activities that have not yet taken place. To the extent that the earnings process has not been completed, the not-for-profit organization should record these resources as a liability. The example in the proposed Audit and Accounting Guide is a theater that receives resources from the advance sale of season tickets. Revenue from these advance sales should be deferred and then recognized as the performances are held (i.e., as the revenues are earned).

A not-for-profit organization may receive advances from third parties, such as government agencies and private foundations, based on the estimated cost of providing services to constituents, or they may receive resources from third parties to be used to make loans to the not-for-profit organization's constituents. Advances from third parties for services not yet performed, as well as refunds due to third parties for amounts previously received under such agreements, should be included as liabilities on the statement of financial position.

When the auditor is aware of advances or revenue received in advance of the earnings process being completed, he or she should perform at least some detailed tests of revenues to ensure that all revenue recorded has been earned. Performing tests of the deferred revenue account will provide the auditor with evidence that what has been recorded as deferred revenue is appropriate and has been properly calculated; however, these procedures will not provide evidence of the completeness of the deferred revenue account.

Annuity Obligations and Agency Transactions

In the course of obtaining contributions from donors, not-for-profit organizations sometimes find themselves parties to complicated transactions involving the sharing of various rights and obligations. These types of arrangements, sometimes referred to as *split-interest agreements*, are more fully described in the chapter titled "Statement of

Activities." Split-interest agreements may consist of interest in charitable gift annuity contracts and charitable remainder and lead trusts, and they may impose upon the not-for-profit organization obligations to make future payments to others.

The AICPA Guide states that annuity obligations arising from split-interest gifts should be recognized by the not-for-profit organization as liabilities. They should be measured at the present value of the actuarially determined obligation. Periodic evaluations of these liabilities most likely will result in changes in the value of split-interest agreements, and the changes in value should be reported as changes in net assets in the statement of activities.

The auditor should inquire about the existence of these agreements and should review the not-for-profit organization's calculation of the recorded liability, including a review of the calculation to determine the present value of the obligation, noting that the interest-rate assumption used is reasonable and that the time period used is correct. The auditor should determine whether the not-for-profit organization performs periodic revaluations of these liabilities and should use procedures similar to those just described to determine whether the revaluations were performed properly.

Not-for-profit organizations also may receive resources from *agency transactions*, which are described more fully in the chapter titled "Statement of Activities." When auditing liabilities, the auditor should ensure that amounts that must be remitted to other entities pursuant to such transactions are reported as liabilities of the not-for-profit organization in its statement of financial position.

NET ASSETS

FAS-117 made significant changes in the way not-for-profit organizations report the difference between their assets and liabilities. Before FAS-117 these organizations typically reported "fund balances" in categories such as current unrestricted, current restricted, endowment, and plant funds. The terminology used differed between types of not-for-profit organizations, depending on which AICPA Accounting and Auditing Guide (or SOP 78-10) was used.

FAS-117 eliminates the differences between the various types of not-for-profit organizations. It also simplifies these organizations' financial statements, since the statement of financial position displays all of the organization's assets and liabilities combined and only segregates net assets into its three categories in the net asset section of the statement.

Although the auditor really audits the amount of total net assets when auditing the assets and liabilities of the not-for-profit organization, he or she should determine whether the organization has properly classified net assets into its three components and also should ensure that the not-for-profit organization follows the display and disclosure requirements contained in FAS-117.

FAS-117 requires that the net assets of a not-for-profit organization be classified into the following classifications—permanently restricted net assets, temporarily restricted net assets, and unrestricted net assets. FAS-117 defines *permanently restricted net assets* as:

> The part of the net assets of a not-for-profit organization resulting (a) from contributions and other inflows of assets whose use by the organization is limited by donor-imposed stipulations that neither expire by passage of time nor can be fulfilled or otherwise removed by actions of the organization, (b) from other asset enhancements and diminishments subject to the same kinds of stipulations, and (c) from reclassifications from (or to) other classes of net assets as a consequence of donor-imposed stipulations.

FAS-117 defines a *donor-imposed restriction* as:

> A donor stipulation that specifies a use for a contributed asset that is more specific than broad limits resulting from the nature of the organization, the environment in which it operates, and the purposes specified in its articles of incorporation or bylaws or comparable documents for an unincorporated association. A restriction on an organization's use of the asset contributed may be temporary or permanent.

Permanently restricted net assets must be maintained by the not-for-profit organization in perpetuity. The use of the asset or its economic benefit neither expires with the passage of time nor can be removed by the organization's meeting certain requirements.

Examples of permanently restricted net assets include capitalized collections that the donor stipulates must be maintained permanently in the organization's collections and cash or investments contributed to a not-for-profit organization as a permanent endowment fund. While the not-for-profit organization will most likely be able to use the investment income from these funds either for its operating purposes or for a donor-specified purpose, the principal of the permanent endowment fund must be invested in perpetuity.

FAS-117 defines *temporarily restricted net assets* as:

> The part of the net assets of a not-for-profit organization resulting (a) from contributions and other inflows of assets whose use by the organization is limited by donor-imposed stipulations that either expire by passage of time or can be fulfilled and removed by actions of the organization pursuant to those stipulations, (b) from other asset enhancements and diminishments subject to the same kinds of stipulations, and (c) from reclassifications to (or from) other classes of net assets as a consequence of do-

nor-imposed stipulations, their expiration by passage of
time, or their fulfillment and removal by actions of the
organization pursuant to those stipulations.

Temporarily restricted net assets include those assets having donor
restrictions that must be met either through some specific actions of
the not-for-profit organization (such as spend this money on a specific program) or by the passage of time (such as spend one-fifth of
this money in each of the next five years).

In addition to donor-imposed stipulations, the not-for-profit organization may adopt an accounting policy that recognizes purchases or donations of long-lived assets (absent any donor-imposed
stipulations) as part of temporarily restricted net assets to reflect that
the benefit of the asset will be realized by the organization with the
passage of time.

FAS-117 defines *unrestricted net assets* as:

> The part of net assets that is neither permanently re-
> stricted nor temporarily restricted by donor-imposed stipu-
> lations.

Unrestricted net assets include those assets that may be restricted
by the not-for-profit organization's board of directors (such as a
board-designated investment fund) and those that are limited in
their use by a contract entered into as an exchange transaction.
Exchange transactions are more fully discussed in the chapter titled
"Statement of Activities." However, the auditor must understand
the distinction between limits on the use of assets imposed by donors (which would be reported as permanently or temporarily restricted net assets), and assets whose use is limited because the not-
for-profit organization must fulfill some part of a contract in an
exchange transaction (which would be reported as unrestricted net
assets).

During any year audited, there will be reclassifications of net
assets caused by events that happened during the year or by the
passage of time. Reclassifications are recorded in circumstances such
as the following:

- The not-for-profit organization fulfills the purposes for which
  the net assets were restricted.
- The donor-imposed restrictions expire with the passage of time
  or with the death of an annuity beneficiary.
- The donor withdraws, or court action removes, previously
  imposed restrictions.

The auditor should review the not-for-profit organization's methodology for reclassifying net assets and should perform some test
checks of reclassifications that have been made. The area of greater
audit exposure is restricted net assets reported as unrestricted rather

than unrestricted net assets reported as restricted. The auditor should consider this when determining the extent of audit procedures that will be performed on the classification of net assets. The audit procedures performed also should include testing expenditures to determine whether restricted net assets were used for their restricted purpose. The chapter titled "Statement of Activities" discusses additional considerations for classification of net assets in the discussion of the recording of contributions.

The AICPA Guide provides guidance on the disclosures regarding net asset classifications that should be included in a not-for-profit organization's financial statements. The not-for-profit organization's statement of financial position should include the total amounts of net assets and of each of the three classifications of net assets. The statement of activities should include the total changes in net assets and changes in each net asset class. Reclassifications of amounts between net asset classes should be reported separately from other transactions in the statement of activities. Specific changes in each net asset class should be aggregated into reasonably homogenous groups.

The following information should be shown on the face of the financial statements or in the notes to the financial statements:

- Different kinds of permanent restrictions, such as those related to collection items and other specific assets to be held in perpetuity and those related to assets that have been contributed by donors with stipulations that they be invested in perpetuity

- Different kinds of temporary restrictions, such as those concerning the support of specific operating activities, use in specific future periods, or acquisition of long-term assets

Separate disclosure of significant limitations other than those imposed by donors, such as those imposed by governing boards, are permitted to be made on the face of the financial statements or in the notes to the financial statements.

SUMMARY

This chapter provides information to auditors for accounts generally found on not-for-profit organizations' statements of financial position. The unique accounting aspects of these accounts was summarized and a general audit approach was presented for each of these accounts. The general audit approaches presented are reflected in the audit program and other checklists included on the disc accompanying this Guide. Accounts that appear on the statement of financial position but are more closely related to accounts in the statement of activities (such as contributions receivable) are discussed in the chapter titled "Statement of Activities."

CHAPTER 6
STATEMENT OF ACTIVITIES

CONTENTS

CHAPTER 6
STATEMENT OF ACTIVITIES

CROSS-REFERENCES

2001 MILLER NOT-FOR-PROFIT ORGANIZATION AUDITS: Chapter 17, "Compliance and Subrecipient Considerations"

2001 MILLER AUDIT PROCEDURES: Chapter 19, "Revenues and Expenses"

This chapter addresses some of the unique accounting and auditing considerations for revenue and expense accounts of a not-for-profit organization. It provides a brief description of the types of audit procedures the auditor should consider when testing these accounts. These procedures are detailed in the audit program included on the disc accompanying this Guide. The revenue and expense accounts and issues discussed in this chapter include the following:

Revenues and Support

- Contributions, including contributions receivable and split-interest agreements
- Agency transactions
- Exchange transaction revenues, including related receivables

Expenses

- Expense recognition and reporting
- Joint cost allocations
- Payroll expenses
- Indirect cost allocation plans

CONTRIBUTIONS

FAS-116 (Accounting for Contributions Received and Contributions Made) provides significant guidance to not-for-profit organizations and their auditors on the accounting for and reporting of contributions. This guidance relates not only to existing accounting practices, but also to new standards for accounting for contributions pledged but not yet made. Additional information relating to contributions is provided by the AICPA Guide, including additional guidance on distinguishing contributions from agency and exchange transactions (which is also the topic of a FASB Interpretation to FAS-116). The AICPA Guide also provides guidance on the recording of split-interest agreements.

FAS-116 defines a *contribution* as follows:

> A contribution is an unconditional transfer of cash or other assets to an entity or a settlement or cancellation of its liabilities in a voluntary nonreciprocal transfer by another entity acting other than as an owner. Other assets include securities, land, buildings, use of facilities or utilities, materials and supplies, intangible assets, services, and unconditional promises to give those items in the future.

A key term in this definition is *nonreciprocal transfer,* which FAS-116 defines as a "transaction in which an entity incurs a liability or transfers an asset to another entity (or receives an asset or cancellation of a liability) without directly receiving (or giving) value in exchange." In other words, the donor does not receive something of equivalent value in consideration for his or her contribution.

Another important term in the definition of contributions is *unconditional promise to give,* which FAS-116 defines as "a promise to give that depends only on passage of time or demand by the promisee for performance." This terminology is significant because unconditional promises to give are included as part of the "other assets" included in the definition of contributions. Therefore, unconditional promises to give should be recognized as contributions and recorded as receivables. Other factors that need to be considered before unconditional promises to give are recorded as contributions and receivables are discussed later in this chapter.

When recording contributions, the not-for-profit organization and its auditor need to distinguish between contributions from agency transactions and exchange transactions. How a transfer of resources to an organization is recorded depends on whether it is a contribution, an agency transaction, or an exchange transaction.

DISTINGUISHING CONTRIBUTIONS FROM OTHER TYPES OF TRANSACTIONS

Before determining the proper accounting treatment for contributions, it is important for a not-for-profit organization and its auditor to be able to distinguish whether the transfer of assets to the not-for-profit organization represents an agency transaction, an exchange transaction, or a contribution.

Agency Transactions

Resources received in transactions in which a not-for-profit organization is acting as an agent, trustee, or intermediary for a resource provider should be reported as increases in assets and liabilities. Distributions to third parties are reported as decreases in asset and liability accounts; i.e., they are not reflected in the statement of activities.

The key factor in determining whether the transfer of resources is an agency transaction and not a contribution is the extent of discretion that the not-for-profit organization has in the use of the assets received. In September 1996 the FASB issued Interpretation No. (FIN)-42 (Accounting for Transfers of Assets in Which a Not-for-Profit Organization Is Granted Variance Power), an interpretation of FAS-116 that provides specific guidance in this area. FIN-42 is effective for financial statements issued for fiscal years ending after September 15, 1996, with earlier application encouraged.

FIN-42 provides the following:

> A recipient organization that is directed by a resource provider to distribute the transferred assets, income from those assets, or both to a specified third-party beneficiary acts as a donee and a donor, rather than an agent, trustee or intermediary, if the resource provider explicitly grants the recipient organization the unilateral power to redirect the use of the transferred assets to another beneficiary. In that situation, *explicitly grants* means that the recipient organization's unilateral power to redirect the use of assets is referred to in the instrument transferring the assets, and *unilateral power* means that the recipient organization can override the resource provider's instructions without approval from the resource provider, specified third-party beneficiary, or any other interested party.

In June 1999 the FASB issued Statement No. 136, "Transfers of Assets to a Not-for-Profit Organization or Charitable Trust That Raises or Holds Contributions for Others" (FAS-136). In addition to new guidance, FAS-136 incorporates without reconsideration the guidance of FIN-42 described above. FAS-136 is effective for financial statements issued for fiscal years beginning after December 15, 1999, except for the provisions of FIN-42, which would continue to be effective as they are currently. Earlier application is encouraged. FAS-136 may be applied either by restating the financial statements of all years presented or by recognizing the cumulative effect of the change in accounting principle in the year of change.

This Statement applies to transactions in which an entity (the donor) makes a contribution by transferring assets to another not-for-profit organization (the recipient organization), which accepts the assets from the donor and agrees to use those assets on behalf of another organization (the beneficiary) or transfers those assets, the return on investment on those assets, or both to the beneficiary.

Basically, if a recipient organization accepts cash or other financial assets from a donor and agrees to disburse them to a specified beneficiary, the recipient organization should recognize the value of those assets as a liability to the specified beneficiary concurrent with recognizing those assets it received from the donor. However, if the donor grants the recipient organization variance power or if the recipient organization and the specified beneficiary have a relationship that is characterized by one organization having an ongoing economic interest in the net assets of the other, the recipient organization would be required to recognize the fair value of any assets it receives as a contribution received. Similarly, a specified beneficiary would recognize its right to the assets held by a recipient organization as an asset, unless the donor has explicitly granted the recipient organization variance power. The rights are recognized as an interest in the net assets of the recipient organization, a beneficial interest, or a receivable.

In the case of a beneficiary and a recipient organization one of which has an ongoing economic interest in the net assets of the other, the beneficiary would recognize its interest in the net assets of the recipient organization and adjust that interest for its share of the changes in the net assets of the recipient organization, similar to the equity method for accounting for investments in common stock. On the other hand, if the recipient organization has variance power, the beneficiary should not recognize its potential interest in the assets held by the recipient organization.

FAS-136 also describes four circumstances in which a transfer of assets to a recipient organization is accounted for as a liability by the recipient organization and as an asset by the resource provider because the resource provider is revocable or reciprocal. These circumstances are as follows:

- The transfer is subject to the resource provider's unilateral right to redirect the use of the assets to another beneficiary.

- The transfer is accompanied by the resource provider's conditional promise to give or is otherwise revocable or repayable.

- The resource provider controls the recipient organization and specifies an unaffiliated beneficiary.

- The resource provider specifies itself or its affiliate as the beneficiary, and the transfer is not an equity transaction.

FAS-136 also contains ten examples of transactions to assist financial statement preparers and their auditors in applying its guidance.

OBSERVATION: During the initial years of implementation of FAS-136, auditors must be alert for circumstances where organizations that raise funds for others are improperly recording contribution revenue (and the corresponding contribution expense) for transfers that should be treated only as assets and liabilities. In addition, determining whether such organizations are financially interrelated will require a significant degree of professional judgment. Auditors should be aware that organizations that raise funds for others would generally rather record contribution revenue (and the corresponding contribution expense), since eliminating these transfers from the statement of activities often eliminates a substantial part of their operations from this statement. In addition, financial performance ratios, such as the ratio of fund-raising expenses to contributions received, are negatively impacted by the treatment of these types of transfers as "balance sheet only" transactions.

EXCHANGE TRANSACTIONS

Exchange transactions are reciprocal transfers in which each party receives and sacrifices something of approximately equal value. These are the types of transactions typically found in audits of commercial enterprises. A buyer of goods or services compensates the seller of the goods or services with cash, another asset, forgiveness of a liability, or a promise to pay in the future.

Not-for-profit organizations typically enter into a number of exchange transactions as well. Salaries paid to employees or costs for utilities are clear examples of exchange transactions. Similarly, on the revenue side, the payment of tuition to a college or university (barring any unusual instances or conditions) is an exchange transaction. Something of value (in this case, education credits) is obtained for something of approximately equal value (cash).

The more difficult transactions for a not-for-profit organization and its auditor to classify are those that contain elements of both contributions and exchange transactions. The classification of asset transfers as exchange transactions or contributions may require the exercise of judgment concerning whether a reciprocal transaction has occurred. A reciprocal transaction in this context means that the recipient not-for-profit organization has given up assets, rights, or privileges of approximately equal value to the assets, rights, or privileges received. Value should be assessed from both the recipient's and the resource provider's points of view. It can be affected by a wide variety of factors, such as the resource provider retaining the right to share in the use of, or income from, an asset provided to the not-for-profit organization.

The AICPA Guide contains a list of indicators not-for-profit organizations should use to determine whether a transaction is a contribution or an exchange transaction. This table is reproduced in Exhibit 6-1.

EXHIBIT 6-1
INDICATORS USEFUL IN DISTINGUISHING CONTRIBUTIONS
FROM EXCHANGE TRANSACTIONS

Indicator	Contribution	Exchange Transaction
Recipient not-for-profit organization's (NPO's) intent in soliciting the asset	Recipient NPO asserts that it is soliciting the asset as a contribution.	Recipient NPO asserts that it is seeking resources in exchange for specified benefits.
Expressed intent about the purpose of the asset to be provided by recipient NPO	Resource provider asserts that it is making donations to support the NPO's programs.	Resource provider asserts that it is transferring resources in exchange for specified benefits.
Method of delivery	The time or place of delivery of the asset to be provided by the recipient NPO to third-party recipients is at the discretion of the NPO.	The method of delivery of the asset to be provided by the recipient NPO to third-party recipients is specified by the resource provider.
Method of determining amount of payment	The resource provider determines the amount of the payment.	Payment by the resource provider equals the value of the cost of the assets to be provided by the recipient NPO, or the asset's cost plus markup; the total payment is based on the quantity of assets delivered.
Penalties assessed if NPO fails to make timely delivery of assets	Penalties are limited to the delivery of assets already produced and the return of the unspent amount. (The NPO is not penalized for nonperformance.)	Provisions for economic penalties exist beyond the amount of payment. (The NPO is penalized for nonperformance.)
Delivery of assets to be provided by the recipient NPO	Assets are to be delivered to individuals or organizations other than the resource provider.	Assets are to be delivered to the resource provider or to individuals or organizations closely connected to the resource provider.

Membership dues is an area that typically requires judgments about whether to record the transactions as contributions or exchange transactions, or as a combination of both. The AICPA Guide contains a list of indicators for determining the contribution and exchange portions of membership dues. This table is reproduced in Exhibit 6-2. The AICPA Guide uses the following example to demonstrate a split of membership dues into contributions and revenue from an exchange transaction.

Example: A not-for-profit organization has annual membership dues of $100. The only benefit received by members is a monthly newsletter valued at $25 per year. Twenty-five dollars of the annual membership dues should be considered revenue from an exchange transaction and should be recognized as the revenue is earned. Therefore, the not-for-profit organization should record 1/12 of the $25 each month as the newsletter is published and distributed. The remaining $75 should be recorded as a contribution. The contribution should be recorded as a contribution when received.

Grants, awards, and sponsorships, both governmental and nongovernmental, can be difficult to classify as contributions or exchange transactions. For example, a not-for-profit organization may have a contract with a local government to provide day care services for a certain number of children for a fixed number of hours per day for a fixed period of time. Assuming that the rate paid per hour per child is reasonable, this would seem to be an exchange transaction.

In another example, the day care center receives a grant from a private foundation to study the effect of leaving children in day care centers on the children's future performance in school. The results of the study may be published by the day care center. This transaction appears more like a contribution since the resource provider is not expecting something of equal value in return for its resources.

The table presented in Exhibit 6-1 should be used to distinguish between contributions and exchange transactions in various grants, contracts, awards, cooperative agreements, or similar types of agreements or contracts.

It is important to determine the correct classification of transactions as revenues or contributions beyond simply the presentation on the statement of activities. First, the recognition principles for recording an increase in net assets from a contribution differ from those for recording an increase from an exchange transaction. Contributions, in general, are recorded when received. Revenues from exchange transactions are recorded when the revenue is earned, which is not always the same as when contributions are earned. Therefore, total net assets are affected by the distinction between these two types of transactions.

EXHIBIT 6-2
INDICATORS USEFUL FOR DETERMINING THE
CONTRIBUTION AND EXCHANGE PORTIONS
OF MEMBERSHIP DUES

Indicator	Contribution	Exchange Transaction
Recipient NPO's expressed intent concerning purpose of dues payment	The request describes the dues as being used to provide benefits to the general public or to the not-for-profit organ-ization's (NPO's) service beneficiaries.	The request describes the dues as providing economic benefits to members or to other organizations or individuals designated by or related to the members.
Extent of benefits	The benefits to members are negligible.	The substantive benefits to members (for example, publications, admissions, educational programs, and special events) may be available to nonmembers for a fee.
NPO's service efforts	The NPO provides service to members and nonmembers.	The NPO benefits are provided only to members.
Duration of benefits	The duration is not specified.	The benefits are provided for a defined period; additional payment of dues is required to extend benefits.
Expressed agreement concerning refundability of the payment.	The payment is not refundable to the resource provider.	The payment is fully or partially refundable if the resource provider withdraws from membership.
Qualifications for membership	Membership is available to the general public.	Membership is available only to individuals who meet certain criteria (for example, requirements to pursue a specific career or to live in a certain area.

Second, the classification of the two types of transactions into the appropriate net assets class (permanently restricted, temporarily restricted, and unrestricted) may be affected by the classification of transactions as contributions or exchange transactions. Exchange transactions should always be classified as revenues that are increases to unrestricted assets. This is true even if the resource provider has imposed limitations on the use of the resources. The following considerations should be made:

- If there are limitations on the use of the resources, the not-for-profit organization and its auditor should ensure that the resources have been used in a manner consistent with the limitations and that the earnings process is complete for the resources.

- If the not-for-profit has not expended the resources in accordance with limitations imposed by the resource provider, the auditor should consider whether there is a real or contingent liability for returning the resources to the resource provider.

- If the earnings process has not been completed, the auditor should ensure that the not-for-profit organization has performed and recorded an appropriate calculation of deferred revenue.

- If the transaction is a contribution, the contribution and increase in net assets may be made to any one of the three classifications of net assets. The classification and recognition depends on a number of factors, including the existence of donor-imposed conditions or limitations. The accounting and auditing concerns for recognizing contributions are discussed in the following section.

RECOGNIZING AND CLASSIFYING CONTRIBUTIONS

FAS-116 provides a significant amount of guidance on accounting for contributions and will require all not-for-profit organizations that receive contributions to evaluate their past practices for accounting for contributions. In many cases, not-for-profit organizations will have to make changes in their accounting for contributions to be in compliance with FAS-116. The AICPA Guide also contains a significant amount of guidance related to accounting for contributions.

To understand the proper principles for recognizing and classifying contributions, the not-for-profit organization and its auditor must understand two terms defined in FAS-116: *donor-imposed condition* and *donor-imposed restriction*.

Donor-Imposed Conditions

A *donor-imposed condition* is a donor stipulation that specifies a future and uncertain event whose occurrence or failure to occur (1) gives the promisor a right of return of the assets it has transferred or (2) releases the promisor from its obligation to transfer its assets. Thus, donor-imposed conditions create uncertainty about whether the not-for-profit organization will ultimately receive or be able to keep the contribution. Because of this uncertainty, the not-for-profit organization should substantially meet all donor-imposed conditions before recognizing the receipt of the assets (including the "receipt" of a contribution receivable) as a contribution. Transfers of assets with donor-imposed conditions should be reported as refundable advances until the conditions have been substantially met.

However, transfers of assets on which resource providers have imposed conditions should be recognized as contributions if the likelihood of not meeting the conditions is remote. For example, if the donor requires the not-for-profit organization to meet some administrative requirements, such as filing an annual financial report, the likelihood that the not-for-profit organization will not meet this administrative requirement is remote, so this condition should not delay the recognition of contribution revenue.

In some cases, the donor-imposed conditions will be met over a period of time or in stages. In these cases, the not-for-profit organization should recognize contribution revenue in stages as the conditions are met. For example, a donor matches contributions raised by a not-for-profit organization dollar for dollar, up to a maximum dollar amount. As the not-for-profit organization raises the funds that will be matched, it would be appropriate for the organization to recognize the equivalent amount for the matching grant, up to the maximum dollar amount that has been set by the donor.

Of course, if the contribution has no donor-imposed conditions (i.e., the contribution is unconditional), it should be recognized as contribution revenue in the period received. Although the kind of benefit received by the not-for-profit organization may vary, contributions should be recognized as increases in assets (such as cash, securities, contributions receivable, property and equipment, and capitalized collections), decreases in liabilities (such as notes payable or accounts payable forgiven) or what would otherwise be an expense (such as a contribution of legal or accounting services).

Donor-Imposed Restrictions

Not-for-profit organizations and their auditors sometimes will encounter circumstances where it is unclear whether the contribution is conditional or unconditional with restrictions. FAS-116 defines a *donor-imposed restriction* as a donor stipulation that specifies a use for the contributed asset that is more specific than broad limits resulting from the nature of the organization, the environment in which it operates, and the purposes specified in its articles of incorporation, bylaws, or comparable documents for an unincorporated association. A restriction on an organization's use of the asset contributed may be temporary or permanent.

A donor-imposed restriction does not establish conditions that must be met for the not-for-profit organization to receive the contribution. Instead, it is a specific restriction on the *use* of the assets. The following summarizes the accounting for contributions with donor-imposed restrictions:

- Unconditional contributions received without donor-imposed restrictions should be reported as unrestricted support that increases unrestricted net assets.

- Unconditional contributions received with donor-imposed restrictions should be reported as restricted support that increases either permanently restricted or temporarily restricted net assets, depending on the nature of the restriction.

If the contribution is unconditional, donor-imposed restrictions result only in a change in the classification of the contribution revenue from that which increases unrestricted net assets to that which increases either permanently restricted or temporarily restricted net assets, depending on the nature of the restriction. The restrictions do not affect the timing of the recognition of the contribution revenue.

The donor may impose one or more conditions and one or more restrictions on the same contribution. In these cases, meeting the conditions will govern *when* the contribution is recognized and the restrictions will govern *how* it is recognized (i.e., what net asset classification should be increased by this contribution).

The types of restrictions imposed by donors can vary widely, and the not-for-profit organization and its auditor often may find that judgment is required to determine the proper classification of the contribution. Restrictions must be specific and must restrict the contribution to more than the stated purpose of the not-for-profit organization.

For example, a donor may make a contribution to a not-for-profit organization whose mission is to help the homeless. The donor can assume that its contribution will be used in the various functions the not-for-profit organization performs to provide services to the homeless. The auditor would not consider this donation to have donor-imposed restrictions that restrict the use of the funds to the provision of services to the homeless, because service to the homeless is part of the overall mission of this particular not-for-profit organization. On the other hand, if the donor stipulates that the contribution be used to purchase playground equipment for a day camp for homeless children, the contribution would be reported as restricted contribution revenue and an increase to temporarily restricted net assets, assuming that the restriction is not satisfied within the fiscal year for which the financial statements are being prepared.

In the example used above, the donor-imposed restriction relates to a specific purpose for which the contribution is to be used. The restriction also may be related to the passage of time. For example, the donor may stipulate that the not-for-profit organization cannot use the contribution until the passage of a period of time, or that the not-for-profit organization must use the contribution over a certain period of time. The donor-imposed restriction may consist of both a purpose restriction and a time restriction. The donor-imposed restrictions may be stipulated explicitly by the donor in a written or oral communication accompanying the contribution or may result implicitly from the circumstances surrounding receipt of the contributed asset. For example, if a donor makes a contribution to a capital campaign being run by the not-for-profit to construct a building, the contribution is implicitly restricted to be used for the construction of the building for which the capital campaign is being run.

Once a contribution is determined to be unrestricted or restricted, the not-for-profit organization must classify the restricted contributions as either permanently restricted or temporarily restricted. The permanently restricted classification should be used if the limits imposed on the used of the contributed assets are permanent. Examples of permanently restricted contributions include contributions of cash or investments that must be invested in perpetuity or a contribution of a collection that must be maintained in perpetuity.

The temporarily restricted classification is used for restricted contributions if the limitations are temporary. Examples of temporarily restricted contributions include contributed assets that may be used only at some future dates or for some specific program.

The not-for-profit organization also must have a system for recording transfers from the restricted net assets classification to the unrestricted net assets class. According to FAS-116, if an organization meets the donor-imposed restrictions on all or a portion of the amount contributed in the same reporting period in which the contribution is received, the contribution (to the extent that the restrictions have been met) may be reported as an unrestricted contribution that increases unrestricted net assets. If the not-for-profit organization uses this policy, it must follow the policy consistently for *all* transactions in the category, and the policy must be disclosed in the notes to the financial statements.

The expiration of donor-imposed restrictions should be reported in the period (or periods if the restrictions expire in more than one reporting period) in which:

- A donor-stipulated time has elapsed, or

- A donor-stipulated purpose for which the contribution was restricted has been fulfilled by the not-for-profit organization.

If two or more donor-imposed restrictions are stipulated by the donor, the expiration of the restriction should be reported in the period in which the last remaining restriction is satisfied. Expirations of donor-imposed restrictions should be reported in the statement of activities as reclassifications, decreasing temporarily restricted assets and increasing unrestricted net assets. These reclassifications would by definition affect only temporarily restricted net assets, not permanently restricted net assets (unless the donor removed permanent restrictions).

Unconditional Promises to Give

As mentioned in previous sections, an unconditional promise to give is considered an "other asset" that may be contributed to a not-for-profit organization causing the recognition of contribution revenue. FAS-116 defines an *unconditional promise to give* as a promise to give that depends only on the passage of time or demand by the promisee for performance.

When a not-for-profit organization enters into a written or oral agreement with a donor regarding a future, nonreciprocal transfer of cash, other assets, or services, the not-for-profit organization must determine if it is appropriate to recognize contribution revenue and a related receivable as a result of the agreement. If the agreement is in substance an unconditional promise to give, it should be reported as contribution revenue and a related receivable in the period in which the promise is received, even if the promise is not legally enforceable. If the agreement is a conditional promise to give cash or other assets, contribution revenue and the related receivable should be recognized when the conditions are substantially met.

Based on the donor's intentions for the use of the assets at the time the unconditional promise is made, the not-for-profit organization should classify the contribution revenue and related receivable as an increase in one of the three classifications of net assets. For example, if the donor promises to give cash or securities that must be invested in perpetuity, an increase in permanently restricted net assets is appropriate.

The AICPA Guide provides additional guidance for not-for-profit organizations and their auditors in determining whether unconditional promises to give have enough substance to require them to be recorded. Before a promise to give can be recognized, sufficient verifiable evidence should exist documenting that a promise was made by the donor and received by the not-for-profit organization. Such evidence may be included in written or verifiable oral communications including:

- Written agreements
- Pledge cards
- Oral promises documented by tape recordings, written contemporaneous registers, follow-up written confirmations, and other measures that permit subsequent verification of the oral communications

A communication that does not indicate clearly whether it is a promise is considered an unconditional promise to give if it indicates an unconditional willingness to give that is legally enforceable. The legally enforceable requirement applies regardless of whether the not-for-profit organization chooses to enforce this ability. For example, a letter received from a donor that merely suggests an intention to consider giving will not be considered a promise to give unless, for some reason, it is legally enforceable, which, in this case, is unlikely. Promises to give that do not discuss the specific time or place for the contribution but that are otherwise clearly unconditional in nature should be considered unconditional promises to give.

Not-for-profit organizations may receive communications from donors that are *intentions* to give, rather than *promises* to give. The AICPA Guide provides the example of an individual including a not-for-profit organization as a beneficiary in the individual's will. This would not be considered an unconditional promise to give because the individual retains the ability to modify the will up until the time of death. In this case, the intention to give would not be recognized in the financial statements until the individual dies and the will is declared valid, assuming there were no conditions included in the will that were dependent on future or uncertain events.

> **OBSERVATION:** In certain circumstances, not-for-profit organizations and their auditors will find the nature of donor-imposed conditions and restrictions concerning promises to give difficult to judge. The AICPA Guide provides that if such a determination is unclear, promises to give should be considered conditional and, accordingly, should not be recognized until the promise is clearly unconditional.

When recording receivables for unconditional promises to give, auditors must consider the valuation of the receivable. The best example for this consideration is the receipt by the not-for-profit organization of pledge cards in a fund-raising campaign, which generally relate to a large number of relatively small contributions. While a signed pledge card may appropriately qualify the pledge as an unconditional promise to give and accordingly warrant that contribution revenue be recognized and a receivable be recorded, the not-for-profit organization's past experience may indicate that not all pledges are received. In this case, the valuation of the pledge receivable recorded should be recorded only at the estimate of the amount of the pledges expected to be collected. Similarly, donors of significant unconditional promises to give that have been recorded may become unable to fulfill their commitments. For example, the bankruptcy of a corporation may affect its ability to fulfill unconditional promises to give to a not-for-profit organization. The auditor must be aware of these valuation issues to ensure that the net amount of contributions receivable recorded by the not-for-profit organization is not overstated. This consideration is particularly important if the receivables for unconditional promises to give are significant to the not-for-profit organization and are likely to be considered by lenders to the not-for-profit organization as sources of future cash flows.

Recognition of Contributed Services

According to FAS-116, contributions of services should be recognized only if certain conditions are met. These conditions are clarified by the AICPA Guide, and as a result, contributed services should be reported as contribution revenue and as assets or expenses only if the services create or enhance a nonfinancial (i.e., nonmonetary) asset or if *all* of the following conditions are met:

- The not-for-profit organization typically would need to purchase the services if they had not been provided by the contribution.
- The services require specialized skills.
- The services are provided by individuals with those specialized skills. Specialized skills include accounting, financial, construction, educational, electrical, legal, medical, and other services provided by accountants, investment advisers, contractors, teachers, electricians, lawyers, doctors, and other professionals and craftspeople.

In addition, contributed services (and the related assets and expenses) should be recognized if the employees of separately governed affiliated organizations regularly perform services (in other than an advisory capacity) for and under the direction of the recipient not-for-profit organization and the recognition criteria for contributed services are met.

> **OBSERVATION:** Using the criteria described above, it would appear that if a not-for-profit organization's auditor is performing the audit without charge, the not-for-profit organization

should record the fair value of the audit as contribution revenue and an equivalent amount as audit fee expenses. FAS-116, in paragraphs 195–206, presents additional examples of contributed services that both do and do not qualify for recognition as contributions. These examples may prove helpful to not-for-profit organizations and their auditors in determining whether recognition of services as a contribution is appropriate.

To determine whether a not-for-profit organization has properly recorded contributions of services, the auditor must determine whether the services in a particular instance should be recognized and also must determine whether the value of the contributed services is appropriate. The auditor should review the sources of the fair values of the services that were obtained by the not-for-profit organization and review them for reasonableness. If the value of contributed services is significant enough to the financial statements, or if there are questions about some of the fair values used, the auditor should obtain some of his or her own estimates of fair values of services and compare them to the amounts recorded by the not-for-profit organization.

The notes to the financial statement should describe the programs or activities for which the contributed services were used. The nature and extent of contributed services received for the periods presented and the amount recognized as revenues also should be disclosed for the periods presented. FAS-116 also encourages not-for-profit organizations to disclose the fair value of contributed services received even if it is not recorded in the financial statements, if it is practicable to make such a disclosure.

Split-Interest Agreements

Not-for-profit organizations sometimes enter into trust or other arrangements under which they receive benefits that are shared (i.e., split) with other beneficiaries. Split-interest agreements are agreements in which a donor makes an initial gift to a trust or directly to a not-for-profit organization, in which the not-for-profit organization has a beneficial interest but is not the sole beneficiary. Some of these agreements do not allow donors to revoke their gifts, while others may permit donors to revoke the agreements in certain situations. The time period covered by the agreement is expressed as a specific number of years, in perpetuity, or as the remaining life of an individual or individuals designated by the donor. The assets covered by the agreement are invested and administered by the not-for-profit organization, a trustee, or a fiscal agent. Distributions are made to a beneficiary or beneficiaries during the term of the agreement. At the end of the agreement's term, the remaining assets covered by the agreement are distributed either to the not-for-profit organization or another beneficiary or beneficiaries.

Irrevocable Split-Interest Agreements

Not-for-profit organizations should account for irrevocable split-interest agreements as part contribution and part exchange agreement. Assets received under the agreement should be recorded at their fair value. The portion of the agreement that represents the unconditional transfer of assets in a voluntary, nonreciprocal transfer represents the contribution and should be recognized as revenue. Liabilities that are incurred in the exchange portion of the agreement also should be recognized. The liabilities typically represent an agreement to pay an annuity to the donor.

Revocable Split-Interest Agreements

Revocable split-interest agreements should be accounted for as conditional promises to give. Assets received by not-for-profit organizations under revocable split-interest agreements should be recognized at fair value and as refundable advances. Income earned on assets held under revocable split-interest agreements that is not available for the not-for-profit organization's unconditional use should be recognized as an adjustment to assets and as a refundable advance. Contribution revenue should be recognized by the not-for-profit organization when revocable split-interest agreements become irrevocable or when assets are distributed to the not-for-profit organization for its unconditional use.

Disclosures

The AICPA Guide provides guidance for disclosure of split-interest agreements in the not-for-profit organization's financial statements. Assets and liabilities recognized under split-interest agreements should be disclosed separately from the other assets and liabilities in a statement of financial position or in the related notes to the financial statements. Contribution revenue and changes in the value of split-interest agreements recognized under such agreements should be disclosed as separate line items in a statement of activities or in the related notes.

The notes to the financial statements should include the following disclosures:

- A description of the general terms of existing split-interest agreements

- The basis used for recognized assets (e.g., cost, lower of cost or market, or fair market value)
- The discount rates and actuarial assumptions used to calculate present values

Types of Split-Interest Agreements

The following summaries of split-interest agreements are presented to assist the auditor in identifying these types of agreements, not to provide detailed legal descriptions. The auditor will need to review the aspects of each specific agreement being audited. Each may have certain provisions that affect the accounting treatment. The auditor should work closely with the not-for-profit organization's finance, fund-raising, and legal staffs to determine the appropriate accounting treatment for these types of agreements.

Charitable lead trust   A *charitable lead trust* is an arrangement in which a donor establishes and funds a trust with specific distributions to be made to a designated not-for-profit organization over a specified period. The not-for-profit organization's use of the assets distributed may be restricted by the donor. The distributions may be a fixed dollar amount or a fixed percentage of the trust fund's fair market value, determined annually. Upon termination of the trust, the remainder of the trust assets is paid to the donor or to the beneficiaries designated by the donor.

Perpetual trust held by a third party   A *perpetual trust held by a third party* is an arrangement in which a donor establishes and funds a perpetual trust administered by an individual or organization other than the not-for-profit organization that is the beneficiary. Under the terms of the trust, the not-for-profit organization has the irrevocable right to receive the income earned on the trust assets in perpetuity, but never receives the assets held in trust. Distributions received by the not-for-profit organization may be restricted by the donor.

Charitable remainder trust   A *charitable remainder trust* is an arrangement in which a donor establishes and funds a trust with specified distributions to be made to a designated beneficiary or beneficiaries over the trust's term. Upon termination of the trust, a not-for-profit organization may ultimately have unrestricted use of those assets, or the donor may place permanent or temporary restrictions on their use. The distributions to the beneficiaries may be for a fixed dollar amount or for a specified percentage of the trust's fair market value as determined annually.

Charitable gift annuity   A *charitable gift annuity* is an arrangement between a donor and a not-for-profit organization in which the donor contributes assets to the organization in exchange for a promise by the organization to pay a fixed amount for a specified period of time to the donor or to individuals or organizations designated by the donor. The agreements are similar to charitable remainder annuity trusts except that no trust exists. The assets received are held as general assets of the not-for-profit organization, and the annuity liability is a general obligation of the organization.

Pooled or life income fund Not-for-profit organizations may form, invest, and manage *pooled or life income funds*. These funds are divided into units, and contributions of many donors' life income gifts are pooled and invested as a group. Donors are assigned a specific number of units based on the proportion of the fair value of their contributions to the total fair value of the pooled income fund on the date of the donor's entry to the pooled fund. Until a donor's death, the donor (or the donor's designated beneficiary or beneficiaries) is paid the actual income (as defined under the arrangement) earned on the donor's assigned units. Upon the donor's death, the value of these assigned units reverts to the not-for-profit organization.

Auditing Split-Interest Agreements

When auditing split-interest agreements, the auditor must ensure that these agreements have been accounted for properly. The following paragraphs discuss some specific auditing concerns and procedures relating to split-interest agreements. However, the overall auditing concerns for contributions apply to split-interest agreements as well.

The auditor should first obtain copies of any split-interest agreements that the not-for-profit has entered into as well as any correspondence with the donors or trustees participating in these agreements. The auditor also may gain information about split-interest agreements entered into by reading the minutes of board of directors meetings.

Based on the reviews of these documents and inquiries of various personnel of the not-for-profit organization (including fund-raising and legal staffs), the auditor should determine whether all unconditional split-interest agreements are recognized and whether the income under split-interest agreements is recorded.

The auditor should perform some detailed test work of the recorded split-interest agreements as well, such as comparing the income distribution terms of the agreements with the periodic reports and remittances received from the trustees and agreeing these amounts to the cash receipts records. For determining the appropriateness of the recorded assets and liabilities, the auditor should again look to reports from the trustees that support the determination of fair values of assets and revenues as well as future liabilities.

Since some of these calculations will involve actuarial calculations, the auditor should not only review and test these calculations, but should also consider using the work of an actuary as a specialist to review the assumptions used and calculations performed.

Auditors must be satisfied that the assets, revenues, and liabilities under these agreements have been properly classified into the appropriate classification of net assets, and the auditor must determine whether the not-for-profit organization has made the appropriate reclassifications on the statement of activities to reflect assets distributed to it and restrictions that have expired or been satisfied. The auditor should obtain information on these classification issues by reviewing the terms of the agreements that have been recorded during the year being audited and by using the information obtained about existing agreements to test whether reclassifications that would be expected to have taken place actually have and whether the reclassifications have been properly recorded.

> **OBSERVATION:** For a further discussion of the details of split-interest agreements and more information on the accounting considerations for these types of agreements, the auditor should refer to Chapter 6 of the AICPA Guide, which provides a more complete discussion of these aspects of these agreements.

AUDITING REVENUES AND SUPPORT

To design an audit strategy for revenue and support and the related asset and liability accounts, the auditor must address some basic auditing considerations (applicable to one or more of the types of revenue and support). The following section completes the discussion of auditing considerations by addressing some of the basic, but unique, auditing considerations an auditor must make when auditing all types of revenues and support received by a not-for-profit organization, specifically cash contributions, fee-for-service revenues, and receivables testing. The basic disclosure requirements for revenue and support also are addressed.

Cash Contributions

A majority of the revenue and support received by most not-for-profit organizations is in the form of currency and checks. One of the auditor's important considerations is to determine whether all of the cash received by the not-for-profit organization is actually deposited into the organization's bank accounts and recorded on its books and records.

In a commercial environment, audit trails are generated to determine the completeness of the recording of cash receipts. A commercial enterprise can relate the vast majority of its cash receipts to transactions. For example, a local ice cream store may receive currency as payment for an ice cream cone. Although this is a small transaction in which currency is received as payment, accountability still can be maintained. Some ice cream store chains require their clerks to account for the number of cones used during their shift as part of the process to prove that all cash transactions have been recorded. Similarly, stores with signs that state your purchase is free if you don't get a receipt are more concerned with the clerk recording your sale than with whether you obtain a receipt.

Collections of receivables resulting from credit sales can be controlled relatively easily by commercial enterprises, since each collection relates to a specific receivable. While clerks receiving these checks (or clerks crediting customer accounts) may find ways to steal checks, eventually these schemes end because ultimately there are customers who have paid their bills who will hold the commercial enterprise accountable for the payment that has been remitted.

Not-for-profit organizations, on the other hand, receive currency and checks as contributions completely at the discretion of their donors. There generally is no clear-cut, direct way for the not-for-profit to make sure that every donor's contribution has been properly received and recorded.

For example, if the not-for-profit organization sends a direct mail solicitation for funds, it cannot precisely quantify the dollar amount of cash receipts that will be received. Based on its past experience, the not-for-profit organization will be able to estimate a range of response rates and the average dollar amount of each response. However, this range would be much too broad to be considered as an effective control over cash receipts. An individual could steal a significant amount of funds before the missing funds would be noticed by the not-for-profit organization's monitoring of response levels.

Not-for-profit organizations usually rely on indirect internal control procedures to ensure that all receipts are deposited and recorded. The not-for-profit organization's auditor will need to understand these control procedures and determine if they are being used. Some guidance on the reliance on internal controls over the completeness of cash receipts is contained in an Interpretation of SAS-31 (Evidential Matter). The question addressed by this Interpretation is whether management's written representations and the auditor's assessment of control risk constitute sufficient audit evidence about the completeness assertion. The last paragraph of the Interpretation states:

> The extent of substantive tests of completeness may properly vary in relation to the assessed level of control risk. Because of the unique nature of the completeness assertion, an assessed level of control risk below the maximum

level may be an effective means for the auditor to obtain evidence about that assertion. Although an assessed level of control risk below the maximum is not required to satisfy the auditor's objectives with respect to the completeness assertion, the auditor should consider that for some transactions (e.g., revenues that are received primarily in cash, such as those of a casino or of some charitable organizations) it may be difficult to limit audit risk for those assertions to an acceptable level without an assessed level of control risk below the maximum.

OBSERVATION: The auditor of a not-for-profit organization that receives a significant number of cash contributions should plan on assessing control risk at less than the maximum level for the assertion of completeness over the recording of cash receipts. Therefore, the auditor should identify these controls and test their effectiveness. The auditor may perform detailed tests of controls over transactions or may use inquiry and observation techniques. Because the controls are attempting to capture all of the transactions that should be captured, inquiries and observation of the not-for-profit organization's controls over the completeness of cash receipts generally is the best approach. However, the auditor should not assess control risk at the minimum level solely because of inquiries and observations.

The not-for-profit organization may adopt various internal control policies and procedures to ensure the completeness of the recording of cash receipts. The techniques used should be based on the types of solicitations for contributions made and the individual circumstances of the not-for-profit organization being audited. Some examples of internal control procedures over the completeness of the recording of cash receipts are as follows:

- Solicitations sent by direct mail should request that contributions be mailed directly to a bank or other institution lockbox. The bank lockbox will then present an accounting of the cash receipts received on a daily or weekly basis.

- For direct canvassing, such as door-to-door solicitations, the not-for-profit organization should use maps and other guides to divide the area canvassed into accountable units. Those individuals doing the soliciting should be required to prepare an accounting of the area that they have covered and the amount of contributions they have received. These reports should be reconciled to the areas covered to make sure that all of the reports (and all of the contributions) for the areas covered have been remitted to the not-for-profit organization. Wherever possible, the use of supervisors or team captains in the field as solicitors simultaneously canvassing various areas also may present an appearance of control and may discourage theft of contributions.

- The not-for-profit organization should use prenumbered documents, such as receipts, donation envelopes, and other materials in direct solicitors and should account for sequences of these numbers. Prenumbered documents may discourage thefts, although the limitations of this technique should be recognized. When prenumbered documents are used in connection with cash receipts, having separate individuals open or collect the receipts and record the accounting transactions is an important additional control.

- The not-for-profit organization should deposit any funds collected in a timely manner and should reconcile deposits and deposit tickets to cash receipts recorded on the books of the not-for-profit organization.

- If the not-for-profit organization receives direct mail contributions directly, it should segregate the functions of opening the mail and recording cash receipts transactions into the accounting system. Wherever possible, mail received should be opened in the presence of two individuals, who should independently list cash receipts. The work of each individual should then be test checked.

- The not-for-profit organization may use physical collection devices that are constructed to discourage theft. Prenumbered collection canisters, for instance, that can accept contributions of currency, but cannot be easily opened and/or resealed, may discourage theft.

- Some contributions may be considered part exchange transactions and may be associated with evidence that can verify their completeness. The not-for-profit organization should establish controls to check this evidence. For example, a not-for-profit organization holding a fund-raising dinner should have procedures in place to ensure that the tickets sold for the dinner have been collected and recorded. This should be part of the not-for-profit organization's procedures; the organization should not leave such reconciliations to the auditor for performance during the audit, but should perform these types of reconciliations on a timely basis, with appropriate follow-up on any discrepancies noted.

Auditors should perform at least inquiry and observation techniques to ensure that the not-for-profit organization actually is using the controls over cash receipts and that its official policies are being followed. The audit procedures used are affected by the individual circumstances of the solicitation. For example, certain fund-raising procedures may occur throughout the year on a consistent basis, allowing the not-for-profit organization the opportunity to design and implement a series of internal control procedures to be used throughout the year.

On the other hand, some fund-raising events may occur only once a year and may be performed with staff "borrowed" from various other functions within the not-for-profit organization. These infrequent events sometimes are much less controlled than the routine events because the staff members working on the event are unfamiliar with the procedures and controls and because of the great deal of time pressure associated with special events, which often results in controls being ignored or overridden. The auditor should be aware of these influences and should adjust the extent of procedures performed to test the controls over cash receipts accordingly.

Although the auditor is concerned with material misstatements in the financial statements caused by the theft of cash collections, his or her main concern is the negative publicity that can result from the theft of cash contributions, particularly theft by the not-for-profit organization's staff. Even if the theft does not cause the not-for-profit organization's financial statements to be materially misstated, it may affect the not-for-profit organization's ability to maintain its reputation and may damage its future fund-raising operations.

Of course, the nature of the circumstances and the seriousness of the abuses will affect the amount of harm done to the organization. One isolated instance in a district fund-raising office of a national organization may not have a significant impact. On the other hand, disclosures that serious internal control weaknesses and lack of adequate supervision by management routinely allowed 10 percent of all cash contributions to be stolen could be devastating to an organization.

The auditor must be in a position to defend the extent of his or her audit work in the area of cash contributions. The auditor also should realize that even if the amount of audit work performed was appropriate in terms of the professional standards and sound auditor judgment, the auditor will be exposed to (at best) negative publicity and (at worse) negative publicity and legal liability if significant amounts of contributions have been stolen and the auditor has never brought control weaknesses to the attention of management or the board of directors.

Fee-for-Service Revenue

The auditor of fee-for-service revenue has similar concerns to that of an auditor of a commercial enterprise. Just as in commercial enterprises, the variety of types of revenues that may be earned by a not-for-profit organization is extensive. Some examples that show the diversity of these revenues are:

- Tuition for colleges, universities, elementary schools, and secondary schools
- Day care services provided by a not-for-profit child care center
- Subscriptions to an educational organization's magazine
- Membership dues of clubs, associations, unions, and similar organizations
- Merchandise sales for memorabilia of various types of not-for-profit organizations
- Admission fees for concerts, museums, sporting events, performing arts events, etc.
- Car wash revenues from a weekend car wash sponsored by a local church or other not-for-profit organization

The auditor's primary concern for fee-for-service activities is to determine if all revenue earned has been recorded, and to determine if all revenue recorded has been earned. In general, not-for-profit organizations earn fees for services in small, high-volume units. They usually do not build and sell aircraft engines, mainframe computers, or office buildings. When the number of transactions is low but each has a dollar volume, the actual service provided may be broken down into a large number of small dollar amount transactions. For example, a day care center may send a monthly billing to a local government for providing day care services. Although the monthly billing may be large, the service fee revenue can be broken down into the number of days or hours of service provide to a certain number of children during the month.

The auditor probably will not be able to audit a few large transactions to be satisfied with the recording of service fee revenue. Rather, the auditor is more likely to attempt to assess internal control risk over the assertions in service fee revenue at below the maximum level and then perform substantive analytical procedures to produce an acceptable level of detection risk. Sampling for achieving an acceptable level of detection risk usually is not an effective audit technique for service fee revenue at not-for-profit organizations because of the nature of the transactions. In addition, many of these types of revenue result in the receipt of payment immediately for the service provided, resulting in a disproportionately lower level of receivables than for, say, credit sales of merchandise. Therefore, the evidence obtained about service fee revenue as a result of testing the related receivables generally is not that strong, and the substantive analytical procedures performed by the auditor for service fee revenue should be strong enough to reduce detection risk to an appropriately low level. This is not to imply that the auditor should never consider performing detailed tests of transactions for revenue. It is suggesting, however, that detailed tests of transactions be performed only when there is compelling evidence that substantive analytical procedures are not effective and, for example, when the auditor assesses inherent risk as high and control risk at the maximum level.

The following are examples of substantive analytical procedures for several different types of service fee revenues. These examples will help the auditor design procedures for whatever type of service fee revenue that he or she is auditing. In all cases, differences between the estimate calculated by the auditor and the amounts recorded by the client should be investigated and the auditor's estimates modified, if appropriate. The chapter titled "Concluding the Audit" provides information on evaluating the unresolved differences between an auditor's estimates from substantive analytical procedures and the amounts recorded by the not-for-profit organization.

- Voluntary health and welfare organizations typically provide services for various people in need, such as homeless individuals, children in foster care, and home care services to the elderly or disabled. The auditor should determine an estimate of the number of units of service provided during the year and, using an average of the rate received by the not-for-profit organization, compare the expected service fee revenue with that recorded by the not-for-profit organization. To estimate the units of service provided (such as the total number of days of day care provided), the auditor should review the various reports prepared by the not-for-profit organization for the funding agency on a monthly, quarterly, or annual basis. The auditor should determine whether these reports are reasonable, based on his or her knowledge of the operations of the day care center.

  If the center has five classes of ten children and operates five days per week, the auditor would not expect more than 250 units of service to be billed in any week. In fact, the auditor should probably factor in some absence estimates and estimates of cases where classes may not be filled to capacity to determine the most reasonable estimate of the units of service provided.

  In determining the rate per day per child in this case, the auditor should determine the contractual rates in effect during the year being audited. Further fine-tuning for differences in rates due to the ages of the children cared for and whether any special rates are received for special classes of children can be made to make the auditor's calculation closer to a real expectation of what the service fee revenue would be.

- Tuition fees, whether at the college or university level or at the primary or secondary school level, are service fee revenues for which the use of substantive analytical procedures is very appropriate, using the same unit of service (credit hour, number of students, etc.) and fee per unit of service as described in the preceding example.

- Revenue from a concert or other artistic performance can be analytically reviewed using the number of tickets sold and ticket cost.

- Revenue from magazine or professional journal subscriptions can be analytically reviewed by obtaining the number of subscribers (which can be verified for reasonableness with a fulfillment organization or through analysis of postal or printing costs) and multiplying it by the subscription rate. Of course, the deferred revenue recorded at the beginning and end of the year for subscriptions received but not yet earned also should be reviewed as part of these procedures.

Although it is not exactly a substantive analytical procedure, if a not-for-profit organization has a cost-reimbursement type of contract to provide some type of service, testing the expenses charged to this contract will provide evidence about the revenue earned on the contract. That is, the revenue should be equal to the allowable costs charged to the contract up to the maximum amount of the contract.

Receivables

When designing an audit strategy for receivables, the auditor should consider whether it is appropriate (or required by generally accepted auditing standards) to confirm accounts receivable. To determine whether the confirmation of accounts receivable is required by GAAS, the auditor should look to the guidance of SAS-67 (The Confirmation Process).

SAS-67 discusses the auditor's use of confirmation procedures in general and accounts receivable confirmations in particular. It defines *accounts receivable* as:

> An entity's claims against customers that have arisen from the sale of goods or services in the normal course of business, and, a financial institution's loans.

SAS-67 states that it is generally presumed that the evidence obtained from third parties will provide the auditor with higher-quality audit evidence than is available from within the entity. Thus, SAS-67 presumes that the auditor will request the confirmation of accounts receivable during an audit unless one of the following is true:

- Accounts receivable are immaterial to the financial statements.

- The use of confirmations would be ineffective. (For example, if, based on prior years' audit experience or on experience with similar engagements the auditor concludes that response rates to properly designed confirmation requests will be inadequate, or if responses are known or expected to be unreliable, the auditor may determine that the use of confirmations will be ineffective.)

- The auditor's combined assessment of inherent and control risk is low, and the assessed level, in conjunction with the evidence expected to be provided with analytical procedures or other substantive tests of details, is sufficient to reduce audit risk to an acceptably low level for the applicable financial statement assertions. In many situations, both confirmation of accounts receivable and other substantive tests of details are necessary to reduce audit risk to an acceptably low level for the applicable financial statement assertions.

An auditor who has not requested confirmations in the examination of accounts receivable should document how he or she overcame the presumption that confirmations are necessary.

The auditor of a not-for-profit organization can conclude that contributions receivable do not meet the SAS-67 definition of accounts receivable and that there is no presumption that these receivables will be confirmed. Accounts receivable resulting from providing services for fees, however, do appear to meet the definition of SAS-67, and there is a presumption that these accounts receivable will be confirmed.

Auditors must consider these requirements when designing the audit strategy for a not-for-profit organization's receivables. However, the individual circumstances of the not-for-profit organization being audited must be considered. The following paragraphs describe some of the considerations that the auditor should make when designing audit procedures for a not-for-profit organization's receivables.

Contributions Receivable

While confirmation of contributions receivable is not required by SAS-67, it may be an effective audit technique. In some cases, the auditor may be unsure that a donor has made an unconditional promise to give that has been recorded by the not-for-profit organization as a receivable. Confirmation of the receivable with the donor can be a useful method for obtaining evidence about the existence and validity of the receivable.

In addition, the auditor may find it beneficial to confirm with the donor contribution receivables that are individually significant. The auditor should be concerned with these types of receivables and should understand why the actual cash contribution is not being made. In some cases, there simply may be timing issues. For example, the not-for-profit organization may have a fiscal year end of June 30, and it may conduct a fund-raising drive to obtain pledges before its year end. However, from a donor's point of view, particularly if the contribution is of a significant size, the cash contribution can be made any time during a calendar year to obtain the tax deduction. In the example, the donor may delay the actual cash contribution to the latter part of December in the year contributed. However, if the donor's pledge extends beyond such an explainable type of delay, the auditor may find that confirmation is an appropriate technique to determine the existence and validity of the receivable.

Large numbers of small contributions receivable, usually obtained through a specific fund-raising drive or technique, such as a telephone solicitation, probably are best audited by reviewing cash collections subsequent to year end to determine the existence, validity, and collectibility of the receivables. When large numbers of receivables are involved, the auditor's use of review of subsequent cash collections, combined with knowledge of the collection experience in prior years, can be a very effective technique. For example, the not-for-profit organization's experience may be that it receives collections for 50 percent of its pledges in the month following the receipt of the pledges, an additional 25 percent in the next month, etc. The auditor can use this information to determine whether the recorded receivable balance is reasonable given the collection experience of the not-for-profit organization subsequent to year end and prior to the auditor's completion of fieldwork.

If the auditor decides to test other contribution receivables, but does not confirm them and has not received subsequent cash collections before the end of the audit fieldwork, the auditor should review documentation received by the not-for-profit organization from the donor informing the not-for-profit organization of the donor's unconditional promise to give. The auditor also may find the acknowledgment letter from the not-for-profit organization to the donor useful, although, since this letter is generated within the not-for-profit organization, its use as audit evidence should be limited accordingly.

As for all receivables, the auditor should review the valuation of the contributions receivable recorded by the not-for-profit organization. Significant receivables that have become old should be reviewed in detail to ensure that their collectibility has not become impaired. When the not-for-profit organization has a large number of small balances receivable, an appropriate allowance should be set up to account for uncollectibility, based on the prior history of collections by the organization and the rate of collection in the current year.

Receivables from Fee-for-Service Revenues

Receivables from revenue earned by not-for-profit organizations from activities similar to those of a commercial enterprise meet the definition of accounts receivable included in SAS-67. Accordingly, there is a presumption that these receivables will be confirmed. In the not-for-profit environment, these activities often are incidental to the operations of the not-for-profit organization, and the exception to the SAS-67 presumption to confirm based on the immateriality of the accounts receivable balance often can be used (and documented) to avoid using confirmation techniques. However, in other cases, such as educational institutions or voluntary health and welfare organizations performing most of their services under one or two primary contracts, the accounts receivable balance may be significant.

When confirming, the auditor is generally best-served by stratifying the accounts receivable population. Confirmations should be sent to the smaller number of accounts that represent a significant part of the overall accounts receivable balance. For the remaining balance, which in general will consist of a large number of smaller balances, the auditor may send confirmations to a sample of accounts or may audit this portion of the balance through subsequent cash collections or substantive analytical procedures.

When the auditor does not receive responses to confirmations (even after second requests are sent and telephone inquiries are made), the auditor should use subsequent cash collections (documentation received by the not-for-profit organization that supports the receivable) as an alternative procedure, or as a last resort. In the case of fee-for-service receivables, the auditor often can determine whether a receivable is valid by determining whether the service to which the receivable relates actually was provided. For example, the registrar of a college, university, or other educational institution will have evidence on whether a student actually was registered for the class to which the receivable relates. Similarly, a day care center will have some form of documentation of the number of days of child-care service that it has provided under the terms of a contract, which will support the amount of a receivable.

When the fee-for-service receivables result from a contract (or contracts) under which the not-for-profit organization receives a large portion of its funding, the auditor should consider confirming additional information about the contract that might be useful in other parts of the audit. This additional information also may help the contractor respond to the confirmation. For example, the auditor may find it useful to confirm the following information about a contract:

- Time period covered by the contract
- Original amount of the contract

- Amended amount of the contract (if any)
- Total billings to date (year end) under the contract
- Cash remitted to date (year end) under the contract (specific payments and their dates may be listed if they are not too voluminous)
- Receivable amount at year end under the contract
- Expenditures charged to date (year end) under the contract (for cost-reimbursable contracts)
- Any special terms and conditions of the contract

The auditor may find this additional information useful for disclosures in the notes to the financial statements as well as other audit areas, such as revenue and expenses related to the particular contract. Having the additional information on the confirmation also may make the reconciliation of any discrepancies noted easier, since more of the detailed information is available.

As with contributions receivables (and any other receivable recorded by the not-for-profit organization), the auditor must consider the collectibility of the receivable to ensure that it is properly valued. The auditor should review the agings of receivables prepared by the not-for-profit organization for its fee-for-service receivables. Agings may not be as useful for contributions receivable because these receivables may not have specific due dates. Fee-for-service receivables, however, should have specific due dates. The auditor should discuss with the not-for-profit whether an allowance for doubtful accounts should be established and the amount of the allowance that would be appropriate. As with contributions receivable, cash collections after the year-end date but before the completion of the auditor's fieldwork provide valuable evidence for determining the valuation of the recorded fee-for-service receivables.

EXPENSE RECOGNITION AND REPORTING

Expense recognition for not-for-profit organizations is similar to the expense recognition for commercial organizations. *Expenses*, as defined in FASB Concepts Statement No. 6 (Elements of Financial Statements), are outflows or other using up of assets or incurrence of liabilities (or a combination of both) from delivering or producing goods, rendering services, or carrying out other activities that constitute the entity's ongoing major or central operations. Concepts Statement No. 6 applies equally to commercial enterprises and not-for-profit organizations. Expenses are different from losses, which are decreases in an organization's net assets from peripheral or incidental transactions. Expenses are always reported as decreases in the unrestricted net assets of a not-for-profit organization.

The AICPA Audit Guide summarizes some of the types of expenses that an auditor of a not-for-profit organization may encounter and their recognition:

- Some expenses are recognized simultaneously with revenues that result directly and jointly from the same transactions or other events or expenses. Examples of such expenses are costs of goods sold, where the cost of an item sold is recognized at the same time that the revenue from the sale is recognized, and expenditure-driven revenue from cost-reimbursable programs or contracts, where the recognition of revenue and expense is simultaneous, up to the maximum amount of the program or contract.

- Some expenses are recognized when cash is spent or liabilities are incurred for goods or services that are used up either simultaneously with acquisition or shortly thereafter. Examples of expenses recognized in this manner include salaries, rent, and utilities.

- Some expenses are allocated by systematic and rational procedures to the periods during which the related assets are expected to provide services. Examples of expenses recognized in this manner are depreciation of fixed assets and amortization of leasehold improvements.

- An expense or loss also is recognized if it becomes evident that the previously recognized future economic benefits of an asset have been reduced or eliminated, or that a liability has been incurred or increased, with associated economic benefits. Examples of these expenses include the write-offs of receivables (assuming there is no allowance for doubtful accounts) or the recognition of a liability incurred as a result of the loss of a lawsuit.

The recognition of expenses by not-for-profit organizations follows generally accepted accounting principles and is little different from commercial enterprises. The remaining paragraphs of this section focus on the classification of the different types of expenses that are incurred by not-for-profit organizations and the reporting considerations and requirements an auditor must consider when determining whether the financial statement reporting of expenses is adequate and appropriate.

A not-for-profit organization classifies its expenses into two broad categories: program service expenses and supporting service expenses. *Program service expenses* are the costs related to the not-for-profit organization's provision of its program or social service. FAS-117 defines *program services* as the activities that result in goods and services being distributed to beneficiaries, customers, or members that fulfill the purposes or mission for which the organization exists. That is, program services represent the reason that the not-for-profit organization exists. In tax terms, this is similar to the organization's exempt function or functions.

Program Services

Not-for-profit organizations may have one or more classifications of program services for financial reporting purposes. Usually, not-for-profit organizations have more than one classification of program services that should be considered major classes of programs and should be reported separately for financial reporting purposes. The AICPA Guide offers some examples of not-for-profit organizations that have multiple classifications of program services:

- A large university may have programs for student instruction, research, and public service, among others.
- A health and welfare organization may have programs for health and family services, research, disaster relief, and public education, among others.

The number of classifications used depends on the operations of the not-for-profit organization and should assist in providing meaningful information to users. Too many classifications can be just as confusing as too few classifications.

Supporting Services

FAS-117 defines *supporting services* as all activities of the not-for-profit organization other than program services. It also identifies the following activities as the three components of supporting services: management and general, fund-raising, and membership development.

Management and General Activities

Management and general activities include oversight, business management, general record keeping, budgeting, financing, and related administrative activities, and all management and administration except for direct conduct of program services and fund-raising activities. The costs of soliciting funds other than contributions, including exchange transactions (whether program-related or not) and funds other than contributions solicited from governments, should be classified as management and general expenses.

Management and general activities may include advertising costs. The accounting for advertising costs is discussed in the AICPA Guide, which reflects the guidance of SOP 93-7 (Reporting on Advertising Costs). *Advertising* is defined as the promotion of an industry, an entity, a brand, a product name, or specific products or services to create or stimulate a positive entity image or to create or stimulate a desire to buy the entity's products or services. Advertising for a not-for-profit organization also includes activities to create or stimulate a desire to use the organization's products or services that are provided without charge. Depending on the nature of the advertising, the costs may be classified as management and general activities or fund-raising activities.

The AICPA Guide includes guidance on the accounting for advertising costs. Advertising costs should be expensed either as incurred or the first time the advertising takes place, except for direct-response advertising that results in probable future benefits.

Direct-response advertising should be capitalized if it is expected to result in future benefits, such as if sales resulting from direct-response advertising are in excess of future costs to be incurred in realizing those revenues. If no future revenues are anticipated, however, because the products or services advertised are being provided by the organization without charge, there is no basis for capitalizing the costs of direct-response advertising beyond the first time the advertising takes place.

Fund-Raising Activities

Fund-raising activities include publicizing and conducting fund-raising campaigns; maintaining donor mailing lists; conducting special fund-raising events; preparing and distributing fund-raising manuals, instructions, and other materials; and conducting other activities involved with soliciting contributions from individuals, foundations, government agencies, and others.

The AICPA Guide provides guidance on the accounting for fund-raising costs that may change the way not-for-profit organizations recognize these expenses. Fund-raising costs, including the cost of special fund-raising events, are incurred to induce potential donors to make contributions to an organization and should be expensed when incurred. Fund-raising costs incurred in one year, such as those made to obtain bequests, compile a mailing list of prospective contributors, or solicit contributions in a direct-response activity, may result in contributions that will be received in future years. These costs should be expensed as incurred, however, because of the difficulty in assessing their ultimate recoverability. Under prior guidance, these costs could be deferred in certain circumstances. The election to defer these types of costs is no longer an option for not-for-profit organizations. Fund-raising costs will have to be expensed when incurred.

Some not-for-profit organizations conduct fund-raising activities, including special social and educational events (such as symposia, dinners, dances, and theater parties), in which the attendee receives a direct benefit. FAS-117 requires the reporting of the gross amounts of revenues and expenses from special events and other fund-raising activities, but permits (but does not require) reporting net amounts if the receipts and related costs result from special events that are peripheral or incidental activities (i.e., that result in gains or losses). The frequency of the events and the significance of the gross revenues and expenses distinguish major or central events from peripheral or incidental events.

FAS-117 requires all not-for-profit organizations to report expenses by their functional classification (program services by major program, management and general, fund-raising, and membership development) either in the statement of activities or in the notes to the financial statements.

In addition to the functional classification, voluntary health and welfare organizations are required to provide information about expenses by their natural classification, such as salaries, rent, electricity, interest expense, depreciation, awards and grants to others, and professional fees, in a matrix format in a separate financial statement. FAS-117 encourages, but does not require, other not-for-profit organizations to provide information about expenses by their natural classification.

Membership-Development Activities

Membership-development activities include soliciting for prospective members and membership dues, membership relations, and similar activities. If there are no significant benefits or duties connected with membership, however, the substance of membership-development activities may, in fact, be fund-raising and the related costs should be reported as fund-raising costs.

Functional Reporting

Given the importance placed on the classification and reporting of expenses of not-for-profit organizations as described in the preceding paragraphs, auditors should pay more attention to the proper classification of expenses than they might ordinarily in the audit of a commercial enterprise.

The ratio of program expenses to total expenses of a not-for-profit organization is a key performance statistic for a not-for-profit organization. This ratio shows (perhaps in the most overly simplistic terms) how much of each dollar that a donor contributes actually goes to the program services of the organization. Obviously, the higher this ratio, the better. Donors feel that more of their contribution is going for the purpose to which they want to contribute, rather than just supporting the administration and fund-raising of the not-for-profit organization itself.

In addition, readers of not-for-profit organization financial statements (as well as the organization's management) should be interested in the expenses incurred in fund-raising compared with the actual amount of contributions recognized. Not only does this give an indication of the success of the fund-raising efforts, it also gives the donors information on how much of their contributions will be spent on additional fund-raising efforts.

In many cases, auditors will assess control risk over expenses at less than the maximum level to reduce the extent of substantive procedures, perhaps even limiting the audit of expenses to substantive analytical procedures. This is likely to be an effective strategy for auditing expenses. There are several particular considerations for a not-for-profit organization that the auditor should address when designing the test work for this area:

- In testing controls, auditors frequently include a procedure that tests the control over the proper classification of the expenses. The auditor should make sure that the individual staff auditors are aware of the classification issues described above so that they can properly test this control. In addition, the control should pertain not only to classification of the expenses into their natural classification, but also to their correct functional classification.

- Some of a not-for-profit organization's expenses are expended under contracts with various compliance requirements, which may be either contractual or legal. If any of the funding for these expenditures originates with the federal government, additional audit procedures and reporting are required by *Government Auditing Standards* and Office of Management and Budget (OMB) Circular A-133. These requirements are further discussed in the chapter titled "Preplanning Audit Activities." The auditor must consider whether noncompliance with these compliance requirements would have a direct and material effect on the financial statements of the not-for-profit organization. Where there is a risk of such an effect of noncompliance, the auditor should design procedures to reduce control risk and/or detection risk to an acceptable level as it relates to compliance with these terms and conditions. This compliance testing probably will not be accomplished through the use of substantive analytical procedures. Some detail tests of transactions (either for tests of controls or as a substantive test) should be performed where contract compliance is an important audit issue.

JOINT COST ALLOCATIONS UNDER SOP 98-2

In March 1998, the AICPA issued Statement of Position (SOP) 98-2 (Accounting for Costs of Activities of Not-for-Profit Organizations and State and Local Governmental Entities That Include Fund Raising). SOP 98-2 presents guidance for instances where costs are incurred for activities that have some program activities and management and general activities along with some fund-raising aspects. SOP 98-2 is effective for financial statements for years beginning on or after December 15, 1998, with earlier application encouraged in fiscal years for which financial statements have not been issued. Implementation of SOP 98-2 is likely to lower that amount of joint costs that has historically been allocated to program activities. Its criteria are designed to be restrictive in allowing such allocations.

SOP 98-2 specifies criteria that it calls purpose, audience, and content.

- If all of these three criteria are met, the costs of joint activities that are identifiable with a particular function should be charged to that function, and joint costs should be allocated between fund-raising and the appropriate program or management and general function.

- If any one of these three criteria is *not* met, all costs of the joint activity should be reported as fund-raising costs, regardless of whether these costs might have been considered program costs or management and general costs if they had been incurred in a different activity. An exception to this rule is that costs of goods or services provided in exchange transactions that are part of joint activities (such as costs of direct donor benefits of a special event—say, the cost of a meal provided at a fund-raising dinner) should not be reported as fund-raising.

The three criteria are described generally in SOP 98-2 as follows:

Purpose

The purpose criterion is met if the purpose of the joint activity includes accomplishing program functions or management and general functions.

- *Program activities* To accomplish program functions, the activity should call for specific action by the audience that will help accomplish the entity's mission. (For example, if the purpose of the not-for-profit organization is to encourage good health, and the organization mails a brochure to an audience encouraging them to stop smoking, lose weight, etc., with suggestions as to how to go about these changes, then the call-to-action requirement is met and the considerations in the following bullet should be examined.

- *Program and management and general activities*   For program activities that meet the call-to-action requirement (see preceding bullet) and for any management and general activity, whether the purpose criterion has been met should be determined based on the following considerations. (SOP 98-2 lists these factors in their order of importance, as follows.)

  1. Whether compensation or fees for performing the activity are based on contributions received. The purpose criterion is *not* met if a majority of compensation or fees for any party's performance of any component of the discrete joint activity is based on contributions raised for that discrete activity.

  2. Whether a similar program activity or management and general activity is conducted separately and on a similar or greater scale. The purpose criterion is met if either of the following two conditions is met:

     a. Condition 1

        i. The program component of the joint activity calls for a specific action by the recipient that will help accomplish the entity's mission, and

        ii. A similar program component that is conducted without the fund-raising component uses the same medium and is conducted on a scale that is similar to or greater than the scale on which the program component is conducted with fund-raising.

     b. Condition 2

        A management and general activity that is similar to the management and general component of the joint activity, but without the fund-raising component being accounted for, is conducted using the same medium and on a scale that is similar to or greater than the scale on which the management and general activity is conducted with the fund-raising.

  3. Other evidence, if the factors discussed above do not determine whether the purpose criterion is met. All available evidence, both positive and negative, should be considered.

Audience

SOP 98-2 presumes that the audience criterion is not met if the audience includes prior donors or if the audience is otherwise selected based on its ability or likelihood to contribute to the not-for-profit organization. This presumption can be overcome if the audience is also selected for one or more of the reasons listed below.

The following reasons may be used to satisfy the audience criteria where the audience includes no prior donors and is not chosen on the basis of its ability or likelihood to contribute to the not-for-profit organization (these factors may also be used to rebut the audience presumption described in the preceding paragraph):

- The audience needs to use the specific action called for by the program component of the joint activity or has reasonable potential for use of the specific action.
- The audience has the ability to take specific action to assist the not-for-profit organization in meeting the goals of the program component of the joint activity.
- The not-for-profit organization is required to direct the management and general component of the joint activity to the particular audience, or the audience has reasonable potential for use of the management and general component.

> **OBSERVATION:** The audience criterion may be very difficult for not-for-profit organizations to meet. Prior donors are usually a key target audience for joint activities, and SOP 98-2's audience presumption is likely to be a major hurdle to get over.

Content

The content criteria is met if the joint activity supports program functions or management or general functions as follows:

- *Program* The joint activity calls for specific action by the recipient that will help accomplish the not-for-profit organization's mission. If the need for and benefits of the action are not clearly evident, information describing the action and explaining the need for and benefits of the action should be provided.
- *Management and general* The joint activity fulfills one or more of the not-for-profit organization's management responsibilities through a component of the joint activity.

SOP 98-2 is very specific about when joint costs can be allocated for joint activities. In fact, Appendix E of SOP 98-2 provides seventeen specific examples that should be used in applying the purpose, audience, and content criteria to individual circumstances. Although implementation of the new SOP by a majority of not-for-profit organizations is being done only now, it is anticipated that there will be fewer opportunities to allocate joint costs under the SOP than there are under the previous, somewhat more generous requirements.

OBSERVATION: Of course, auditors should be aware that not-for-profit organizations that desire to allocate costs are likely to begin to modify, where possible, their joint activities so that the three criterion of the SOP will be met. Early discussion with not-for-profit organization auditees as to their plans for joint cost allocations under the future requirements will help to alleviate some implementation issues that are likely to develop. There is often a significant lag between the time when these types of activities are planned and the time when the activities actually take place and significant costs are incurred. Accordingly, not-for-profit organizations may currently be working on designs of brochures and other materials constituting joint activities that will be in use when the requirements of the SOP become effective.

Allocation Methods

While SOP 98-2's discussion of *when* joint costs may be allocated is quite rigid, its discussion of *how* to allocate joint costs is more flexible. The allocation methodology that is used must be rational and systematic, resulting in a reasonable allocation that is applied consistently across similar facts and circumstances. Appendix F of the SOP describes some commonly used allocation methods, but does not require that any particular one of the methods presented be used.

Incidental Activities

Provided its criteria are met, SOP 98-2 makes allocating joint costs optional in circumstances where a fund-raising, program, or management and general activity is conducted in conjunction with another activity and is incidental to the other activity. However, SOP 98-2 warns that in circumstances where the program activity or management and general activity is incidental to the fund-raising activities, the SOP's conditions for allocating joint costs are not likely to be met.

OBSERVATION: In auditing an organization's compliance with the criteria of SOP 98-2, auditors should anticipate that they will need to evaluate client representations and assertions about whether all of the criteria are met that may be unfamiliar to the auditor, such as whether the call-to-action component of the purpose criterion for program activities is met. Auditors will need to consider how these representations and assertions will be evaluated, and they should discuss with the not-for-profit organization what types of evidence will be needed. These discussions should take place in the planning phase of the audit.

PAYROLL EXPENSES

Payroll expenses for not-for-profit organizations should be accounted for and audited in the same manner as payroll expenses for commercial organizations. However, the auditor should pay close attention to the payroll of a not-for-profit organization for two reasons:

1. Payroll usually constitutes a significant part of the total expenses of a not-for-profit organization and, as such, should receive an appropriate level of audit attention.

2. Payroll costs (salaries and fringe benefits) often are used as an allocation basis for indirect cost allocation plans. The proper recording and allocation of payroll costs therefore can affect the total costs charged to each of the classifications of the not-for-profit organization's activities—program services, management and general, fund-raising, and membership development—as well as to specific programs and contracts that are funded on a cost–reimbursement basis.

The audit procedures performed for payroll should be similar to those performed in a commercial organization. If the workforce is fairly stable, the auditor should be able to audit payroll expenses effectively through the use of substantive analytical procedures. Comparing payroll costs from one year to the next, after consideration of changes in the workforce and increases in pay rates, often will provide the auditor with sufficient evidence to reduce detection risk to an acceptably low level. In most cases, to use substantive analytical procedures alone to reduce detection risk, the auditor should assess control risk at something less than the maximum level. This will require some tests of controls, such as tests of details or inquiry and observation techniques.

In the past, auditors routinely performed a payroll test where individual paychecks were selected and a complete gross pay to net pay calculation was performed, including recalculation of the withholding amounts for taxes and other purposes. Since the value of this test in reducing audit risk increasingly has been seen as small, many auditors are now reducing or eliminating this test.

> **AUDIT COST-SAVINGS TIP:** Payroll is an area that is subject to "overauditing." Auditors should review the planned procedures for payroll expenses and liabilities to ensure that their audit objectives are being met effectively. For example, in the payroll area, the "gross to net pay" recalculations referred to above generally do not provide evidence that is as valuable as effective substantive analytical procedures may be.

For an audit of a not-for-profit organization, a more effective methodology is to determine how the organization controls the charging and allocations of payroll costs to each expense classification, and if appropriate, to individual contracts or grants. The auditor should find that these controls center on the use of time sheets, completed by employees and approved by their supervisors, which capture their time charges to categories of expenses that act as cost centers. These controls can be tested by inquiry and observation techniques or by testing a few transactions or individuals to see if the controls are operating effectively.

For example, if there is a fund-raising department, the auditor may test check some of the time charges of that department to make sure its employees' time is being charged to fund-raising activities and not to programs. The auditor also may inquire about and observe how some of the administrative departments, such as accounting, human resources, and data processing, charge their time, whether these charges are consistently applied, and whether the procedures in place to control the charging of these expenses are appropriate. The auditor should also enquire whether the not-for-profit organization uses the work of consultants, who might be determined under audit by the Internal Revenue Service to be employees rather than independent contractors.

The author believes that performing these types of procedures will result in audit evidence much more "usable" than that obtained from a mechanical recalculation of payroll. Assuming that these tests of controls support the assessment of control risk at below the maximum level, the auditor may then rely on substantive analytical procedures to obtain an acceptable level of detection risk.

The auditor should be aware of the not-for-profit organization's accounting and reporting for fringe benefit costs. Many organizations have been redesigning their fringe benefit packages in recent years to provide more flexibility in benefits, while also reducing costs. Not-for-profit organizations historically have offered generous fringe benefit packages to their employees, so they are even more susceptible to the need to reign in these types of costs.

In addition, the not-for-profit organization should have recently adopted two relatively new accounting standards that will need to be audited: FAS-106 (Employers' Accounting for Postretirement Benefits Other Than Pensions) and FAS-112 (Employers' Accounting for Postemployment Benefits). Not-for-profit organizations that offer postretirement and postemployment benefits to their employees and retirees will need to perform (or more likely hire an actuary to perform) calculations of the liabilities and periodic expenses that must be recognized under Statements 106 and 112. The auditor should determine whether he or she should use the work of a specialist (an actuary and perhaps a benefits specialist) to audit the amounts recorded by the not-for-profit organization.

Relief from Certain Disclosures about Pensions and Other Postretirement Benefits

In February 1998, the FASB issued Statement No. 132 (Employers' Disclosures about Pensions and Other Postretirement Benefits) (FAS-132). This Statement is effective for fiscal years beginning after December 15, 1997, with earlier application encouraged. Restatement of disclosures for earlier periods provided for comparative purposes is required—unless the information is not readily available, in which case the notes to the financial statements should include all available information, plus a description of information that is not available.

FAS-132 supersedes the disclosure requirements of FAS-87 (Employers' Accounting for Pensions), FAS-88 (Employers' Accounting for Settlements and Curtailments of Defined Benefit Pension Plans and for Termination Benefits), and FAS-106 (Employers' Accounting for Postretirement Benefits Other Than Pensions). FAS-132's objective is to provide financial statement readers with more usable information about pension plans and other postretirement benefits. The changes in these disclosure requirements are reflected in the disclosure checklist that is provided as part of this Guide.

FAS-132 also provides some disclosure relief for nonpublic entities with respect to pensions and other postretirement benefits. FAS-132 defines *nonpublic entity* as "…any entity other than one (a) whose debt or equity securities trade in a public market either on a stock exchange (domestic or foreign) or in the over-the-counter market, including securities quoted locally or regionally, (b) that makes a filing with a regulatory agency in preparation for the sale of any class of debt or equity securities in a public market, or (c) that is controlled by an entity covered in (a) or (b)." The Statement permits nonpublic entities to present reduced disclosures as to pensions and postretirement benefits, which should alleviate some of these burdensome disclosure requirements for many not-for-profit organizations. These reduced disclosures for nonpublic entities are also presented in the disclosure checklist that is provided as part of this Guide.

INDIRECT COST ALLOCATION PLANS

Not-for-profit organizations often use indirect cost allocation plans. The purpose of these plans is to allocate costs that are not directly attributable to individual functions to all functions in a manner that is consistently and reasonably applied.

At a minimum, the not-for-profit should have an indirect cost allocation plan to allocate indirect costs to its major program service activities, management and general activities, fund-raising activities, and membership-development activities. This plan also should address the not-for-profit organization's policies for allocating joint costs to these expense classifications. If the not-for-profit organization has specific contracts or grants that are funded on a cost-reimbursable basis, the organization also will need an indirect cost allocation plan to allocate indirect costs to these contracts and grants.

The complexity of the indirect cost allocation plan used by a not-for-profit organization should be governed by the extent of indirect costs that need to be allocated and the number and nature of the programs and other cost centers to which costs need to be allocated. A typical indirect cost allocation plan has a basis on which indirect costs will be allocated. The basis represents costs (or other factors) that can be specifically identified with individual programs or activities. The basis can be expressed in dollar terms (such as directly charged salary or personnel costs) or other terms (such as the number of staff of the not-for-profit working directly on specific projects or activities). An indirect cost pool is developed that consists of these costs that cannot be specifically identified with a program or an activity. Typically, the indirect cost pool includes such costs as rent, utilities, professional fees, and payroll costs of administrative personnel not working directly on programs or activities, such as the executive director of the not-for-profit organization. The total indirect cost pool is then allocated to the programs and activities in proportion to the extent of each individual program or activity's percentage of the total basis. For example, if indirect costs were allocated on the basis of payroll costs and an individual program had 20 percent of the directly charged payroll costs charged to it, this program would be allocated 20 percent of the indirect cost pool.

As a practical matter, not-for-profit organizations typically establish indirect cost rates that estimate the additional percentage of indirect costs that will be allocated to programs and activities. To continue the above example, based on a current-year budget or a prior year's actual results, the not-for-profit organization may determine that for each dollar of directly charged personnel cost, an amount equal to 20 percent of directly charged personnel costs will be charged to the program representing the program's indirect cost allocation. Using the percentage method enables the not-for-profit organization to prepare reports and, if applicable, bill for cost-reimbursements using the estimate of indirect costs. When the books are closed and audited at the end of a fiscal year, the actual indirect cost rate can be calculated for use in reporting amounts in the financial statements and for adjusting any interim billings under cost-reimbursable contracts.

The auditor's concern for indirect cost allocation plans is twofold:

1. The auditor should determine whether the indirect cost allocation plan provides a reasonable allocation of costs for presentation of functional classification of expenses in the financial statements.

2. The auditor should determine whether the indirect cost allocation plan provides for an allocation of indirect costs that is acceptable for the cost-reimbursable contracts for which the not-for-profit organization is using the plan to allocate indirect costs. If the plan is not acceptable and results in an overallocation of costs to these cost-reimbursable contracts, the not-for-profit organization may have the excess costs charged disallowed. These disallowances may have a direct and material impact on the financial statements if the not-for-profit organization must refund the overcharges to the contractor.

Auditors should inquire about how the not-for-profit organization being audited allocates indirect costs and should obtain an understanding of the methodology used. Based on the extent that the not-for-profit organization uses such a plan and is subject to the risks described above, the auditor should design an appropriate level of detailed test work to determine that the actual cost allocations are being performed in accordance with the procedures in the indirect cost allocation plan. In addition, the auditor should ensure that any costs not allowable under certain cost-reimbursable contracts are excluded from the indirect cost pool that is allocated to these contracts. For example, certain contracts may prohibit the charging of salaries over a certain level, or may prohibit certain types of expenses (such as advertising or alcohol served at social functions).

SUMMARY

This chapter describes the general auditing procedures an auditor should consider when auditing the most significant accounts usually found in a not-for-profit organization's statement of activities. The unique accounting and operating conventions used by not-for-profit organizations are discussed to enable the auditor to identify those areas where audit procedures might deviate from those normally performed in an audit of a commercial enterprise.

The chapter titled "Tax Considerations" will describe the issues an auditor needs to address regarding the tax-exempt status of not-for-profit organizations.

CHAPTER 7
EXTENT OF AUDIT PROCEDURES AND SAMPLING

CONTENTS

EXTENT OF AUDIT PROCEDURES AND SAMPLING

CROSS-REFERENCES

2000 MILLER GAAS GUIDE: Section 350, "Audit Sampling"

Once the auditor decides what audit procedures to apply (i.e., *nature* of tests to be performed), and when to apply them (i.e., *timing* of the tests), a decision must be made about how many items to apply the procedures to (i.e., the *extent* of testing).

This section discusses the relationship between these professional standards on audit risk and materiality (SAS-47) (Audit Risk and Materiality in Conducting an Audit) and those on audit sampling (SAS-39) (Audit Sampling). SAS-39 defines *audit sampling* as follows:

> The application of an audit procedure to less than 100 percent of the items within an account balance or class of transactions for the purpose of evaluating some characteristic of the balance or class.

According to SAS-39, audit sampling is a necessary and acceptable way to gather evidence to support the auditor's assessment of control risk. There are several reasons for sampling in the audit process. Audits are performed to provide reasonable, but not absolute, assurance about the financial statements. This process entails a level of uncertainty. The assurance related to the internal control is that the auditor's judgment about the assessed level of control risk is correct. Therefore, audit sampling may be used to effectively reduce the risk of misjudgment about the level of control risk to a reasonable level.

According to SAS-39, the following three conditions must be met to constitute audit sampling:

1. Less than 100% of the population must be examined.

2. The sample results must be projected as population characteristics.

3. The projected sample results must either (a) be compared to an existing client-determined account balance to determine whether to accept or reject the client's balance or (b) be used to assess control risk.

Numerous situations exist in an audit when the auditor does not use audit sampling. The following are examples of audit procedures that do not constitute audit sampling:

- Inquiry and observation (e.g., completing an internal control questionnaire)
- Performing a 100% examination of an account or transaction balance because the auditor is not willing to accept sampling risk for the balance
- Performing a walkthrough of the client's accounting system to gain an understanding of how transactions are processed
- Testing individually significant dollar amounts in an account balance and not testing the remaining balance because of immateriality
- Performing analytical review procedures

DETERMINING WHETHER AUDIT SAMPLING IS NECESSARY

The auditor can follow the following three steps to determine whether audit sampling is necessary:

1. Identify individually significant items to be examined.
2. Determine whether the extent of evidential matter obtained from examining the individually significant items in Step 1 above is sufficient. Generally, if the auditor can accept the evidence obtained as sufficient, there is no need to apply audit sampling.
3. If the extent of evidential matter gathered in Step 2 is not sufficient, consider the contribution of other audit procedures and determine whether the resulting evidence is sufficient. Generally, if the auditor can accept such evidence as sufficient, there is no need to apply audit sampling.

If the extent of evidential matter obtained from examining individually significant items (Step 2) and the contribution of other audit procedures (Step 3) is not considered sufficient, it would be appropriate for the auditor to apply audit sampling. Each of the three steps will be discussed in detail below and a worksheet will be provided to assist the auditor in determining whether audit sampling is necessary.

Step 1. Identify Individually Significant Items to Be Examined

The first step in selecting specific individually significant items to audit is to identify any transactions or accounts that are individually important because of their size or that the auditor believes have a high likelihood of misstatement. To establish a cutoff amount for individually significant items to be tested 100%, a common rule of thumb is to divide tolerable misstatement (see the chapter titled "Audit Planning") by a factor ranging from three to six, depending on how much reliance is placed on the audit procedures being applied. Because an individual item within an account balance or class of transactions that exceeds tolerable misstatement is likely to be important or significant, the auditor should consider using the cutoff amount (i.e., tolerable misstatement divided by a factor from three to six) in defining individually significant items. The auditor should also apply professional judgment in determining which additional individual items in an account balance or class of transactions need to be examined. In determining individually significant items to be examined 100%, the auditor should consider, in addition to the size of the item, factors such as the following:

- Transactions involving estimates and requiring highly subjective judgments (e.g., allowance for uncollectible pledges receivable accounts, reclassifying assets from temporarily restricted to unrestricted classifications)
- Large or unusual transactions recorded as of or near the end of the client's year end (e.g., significant contributions receivable just before or after year end)
- Old items (e.g., past due receivables)
- Transactions having a high degree of management involvement (e.g., related-party transactions)
- Other large or unusual items

Any items the auditor has decided to test 100% are not subject to sampling.

Exhibit 7-1 provides an example of how the auditor can identify individually significant items to be examined.

As discussed above, sometimes examining individually significant items may provide sufficient coverage so that there is little risk that the remaining items contain a material misstatement. In these

---

EXHIBIT 7-1
IDENTIFYING INDIVIDUALLY SIGNIFICANT ITEMS

Assume that the auditor has established the following in connection with the audit of a not-for-profit organization as of and for the year ended June 30, 20XX:

Planning materiality	$ 150,000	
Tolerable misstatement	$ 75,000	(50% of planning materiality)
Individually significant items	$ 25,000	(1/3 of tolerable misstatement)

The auditor reviews the contributions receivable trial balance and determines the composition of those receivable to be as follows:

Number of Accounts	Account Balances	Total Accounts
5	over $100,000	$ 582,000
8	$25,000–99,999	326,000
74	$1–24,999	313,000
87		$ 1,221,000

Based on the above, the auditor determines that there are 13 (5 + 8) individually significant items (i.e., accounts with a balance greater than 1/3 of tolerable misstatement, or $25,000) with an aggregate balance of $908,000 ($582,000 + $326,000). In this case, if the 13 largest accounts are confirmed by the auditor, 74% ($908,000 divided by $1,221,000) of the accounts receivable balance is supported. Also, the auditor may decide to confirm contribution receivable balances that have unusual characteristics (e.g., receivables that are very delinquent).

> **OBSERVATION:** When auditing receivables of a commercial enterprise, an auditor may choose individual invoices as the sampling unit or may choose customer balances (that is, an aggregate of the invoices for each customer) as the sampling unit. When auditing contributions receivable for a not-for-profit organization, it is likely to be more effective to use the aggregate of all contributions receivable from a particular donor as the sampling unit (that is, the donor's "account balance"). This will not only uncover situations where the not-for-profit organization may have recorded the same pledge as a contribution receivable more than once, but will also serve to further substantiate the acknowledgment by the donor that the donor intends to honor the pledge.

cases, no further testing may be necessary. Generally, a coverage of two-thirds or higher of the total population would be considered sufficient. However, the auditor should use professional judgment and consider the factors discussed in Step 2 in determining whether the extent of evidential matter obtained is sufficient.

Generally, there is no need to sample the remaining population if the following conditions are met:

- The auditor has examined a substantial number of individually significant items (e.g., obtained a coverage of two-thirds or higher of the entire population).
- The auditor observed no evidence of problems from other audit procedures performed.
- The remaining population totals less than an amount that would be considered material to the financial statements.

Step 2. Determine Whether the Extent of Evidential Matter Obtained from Examining the Individually Significant Items in Step 1 Is Sufficient

SAS-39 identifies certain factors in evaluating the sufficiency of evidential matter obtained in tests of details for a particular account balance or class of transactions. These include:

- The importance and significance of the individual items examined. If the items examined account for a high percentage of the total population, the auditor may be reasonably assured that there is an acceptably low risk of an undetected misstatement in the remaining population. The auditor should consider whether the dollar amount of the remaining population is equal to or greater than an amount that would be material to the financial statements. If the auditor believes that the remaining population is not material, he or she may decide that no additional testing by sampling is necessary.
- The nature and cause of the misstatements. If the auditor detects misstatements during the course of the audit, he or she should evaluate them to determine if they are (1) caused by differences in accounting principles or application thereof, (2) errors or irregularities, (3) caused by misunderstanding of instructions, or (4) resulting from carelessness.
- Possible effect and relationship of the misstatements to other phases of the audit. For example, if the auditor determines that the misstatement is an irregularity or fraud, this would require a broader consideration of the possible implications than would the discovery of an error.

- The characteristics of the sample compared to the population. The auditor may obtain some knowledge of the types of items in the population if the characteristics in the sample are similar in nature and the same internal controls are followed for processing the transactions. The auditor should consider the degree of risk involved (i.e., how susceptible the account is to misstatement and whether there have been problems with this area in prior audits).

> **OBSERVATION:** There are qualitative factors relating to populations being sampled that should be considered. For example, the auditor may not only be interested in the extent of a contribution receivable, but might also need evidence as to whether there are donor restrictions that would affect the net asset classification of the contribution revenue and receivable.

Step 3. Consider the Contribution of Other Audit Procedures

The auditor should consider whether other evidence obtained contributes to conclusions regarding the account balance or class of transactions. The auditor often considers the contribution of other procedures at the same time the extent of evidential matter obtained from examining individual items is considered.

When assessing control risk at the maximum level, the auditor usually would rely primarily on analytical procedures and substantive tests of details to support an opinion on the financial statements. In deciding whether other audit procedures make a contribution, the auditor should consider whether they support the audit objectives in the area, whether they indicate a potential problem, and whether the evidence is consistent with the previous evidence obtained. Therefore, the auditor should use professional judgment in determining whether an unqualified opinion can be given without performing additional tests in the form of audit sampling.

STATISTICAL VERSUS NONSTATISTICAL SAMPLING

Guidance regarding audit sampling and its application is found in:

- SAS-39 (Audit Sampling)
- The AICPA Audit and Accounting Guide, *Audit Sampling*

Once a decision is made that audit sampling is necessary, the auditor's only choice is between a statistical and nonstatistical approach. Both statistical and nonstatistical sampling are satisfactory sampling methods. Both approaches require that the auditor use professional judgment in planning, performing, and evaluating a sample, and in relating the evidential matter produced by the sample to other evidential matter when forming a conclusion about the related account balance or class of transactions.

Statistical sampling is the use of mathematical measurement techniques to calculate formal statistical results and is based on probability concepts. Statistical sampling is highly technical (i.e., the sample must be statistically selected in such a way that each item in the sample must have a known probability of selection), and the sample results must be quantitatively or mathematically evaluated. The primary benefit of statistical methods is the quantification of sampling risk. The primary disadvantages of statistical sampling are that (1) the auditor must thoroughly understand its selection and evaluation techniques and (2) it is not efficient unless the population being sampled is large.

Nonstatistical sampling includes all other sampling selection and evaluation techniques. In nonstatistical sampling, the auditor does not quantify sampling risk; instead, conclusions are reached about populations on a more judgmental basis.

SAS-39 recognizes that from a conceptual perspective, statistical sampling and nonstatistical sampling are very similar. In fact, SAS-39 discusses sampling in general and makes few references to concepts or procedures unique to either statistical or nonstatistical sampling.

Types of Statistical Sampling Models

There are two broad categories of statistical sampling:

1. Classical statistical sampling models: attribute, discovery, and variable

    a. *Attribute sampling*—Attribute sampling is a statistical sampling method used to estimate the rate (percentage) of occurrence of a specific quality (attribute) in a population. Attribute sampling is used primarily for tests of controls.

    b. *Discovery sampling*—Discovery sampling is a special kind of attribute sampling typically used when the auditor expects very few or no deviations. Discovery sampling is typically used for substantive testing in situations where few misstatements are expected.

    c. *Variable sampling*—Variable sampling is a statistical technique applied when the auditor desires to reach a dollar or a quantitative conclusion about a population. Variable sampling is used primarily for substantive testing.

2. *Probability-proportionate-to-size (PPS) sampling*—PPS sampling enables the auditor to make dollar conclusions about the total dollar amount of misstatement in a population. Whereas the classical sampling techniques focus on physical units of the population, PPS sampling focuses on the dollar units of a population. That is to say, instead of the auditor viewing a $100,000 contribution receivable population as containing 500 individual customer balances, the auditor considers the population as 100,000 individual dollar units from which to draw a sample. In PPS sampling, each dollar is a sampling unit. Therefore, individual accounts with larger balances have a proportionally higher chance of being selected in a sample because they contain more sampling units, hence the name probability-proportionate-to-size sampling.

PPS sampling is used by auditors for both tests of controls and substantive tests. In practice, PPS sampling goes under a variety of different labels, such as:

- Dollar unit sampling
- Monetary unit sampling
- Cumulative monetary amount sampling
- Combined attribute-variables sampling

Audit Sampling for Substantive Tests and Tests of Controls

Once the auditor decides to use audit sampling, he or she must decide whether to use statistical or nonstatistical sampling and whether to use audit sampling for substantive tests, for tests of controls, or for both. There are five steps involved in applying audit sampling to both substantive tests and to tests of controls:

1. *Plan the sample.* The purposes of planning the sample are to make sure that the audit tests are performed in a manner to provide the desired sampling risk (e.g., 95% confidence level provides a 5% sampling risk) and to minimize the likelihood of nonsampling error.

2. *Determine the sample size.* This step involves predefining the various factors that affect the sample size (e.g., tolerable rate, expected population deviation rate).

3. *Select the sample.* This step involves deciding how to select sample items from the population. The auditor should select a sample size that is adequate, giving consideration to materiality, audit risk, and population characteristics.

4. *Perform the tests.* This step primarily involves the examination of documents and performing other audit procedures.

5. *Evaluate the sample results.* This step involves drawing conclusions about the likely effect on the total population based on the audit tests of the sample.

The remainder of this chapter discusses the application of audit sampling to substantive tests and tests of controls.

AUDIT SAMPLING APPROACH
FOR SUBSTANTIVE TESTS

Most not-for-profit organizations have special characteristics that make the application of nonstatistical sampling for substantive tests much more cost-effective and efficient than statistical sampling. While some accounts of a not-for-profit organization may support statistical sampling because of their large size and volume (such as pledges receivable for a nationwide fund-raising event or student accounts at a large university), most auditors of not-for-profit organizations find that the size of the population typically sampled is not sufficient to achieve the full benefits of statistical sampling. This section focuses on the use of nonstatistical sampling for substantive tests and explains an effective approach for most organizations, particularly small ones.

The approach discussed in this section is adapted from the AICPA *Audit Sampling Guide.* This approach is based on the nonstatistical sampling model in the *Sampling Guide*, which is based on the statistical theory underlying probability-proportionate-to-size (PPS) sampling. Therefore, the auditor should recognize that this approach is essentially an application of statistical theory to nonstatistical samples, and the factors presented for determining sample sizes are based on certain judgments and may differ, as auditors' judgments differ, depending on the circumstances. The following steps are involved in applying audit sampling to substantive tests:

Planning the Sample

1. Determine the audit objective of the test. The auditor should decide whether the dollar value assigned by management to an account balance or group of transactions is reasonable (i.e., whether the population is fairly stated).

2. Define the population.
   a. Define the sampling unit (e.g., individual pledges receivable).

b. Consider the completeness of the population (e.g., determine that the receivable aged trial balance agrees with the general ledger, or if items are numerically sequenced, account for the numerical sequence of items in the population before selecting the sample from that sequence).

c. Consider variations within the population. This is primarily to determine if the sample size selected is representative of the population. For example, a contributions receivable trial balance may be composed of a few large balances, several medium balances, and numerous smaller balances. The auditor may review the accounts receivable trial balance or prior years' workpapers to determine the extent of variations within the population.

d. Identify individually significant items (e.g., large dollar items or delinquent accounts receivable). As discussed above, the cutoff amount for individually significant dollar items can be any amount up to tolerable misstatement and may include items that the auditor considers significant due to their nature.

e. Determine the sampling population. The auditor determines the sampling population by deducting any items that have been determined to be significant and that will be examined 100% from the total amount of the account balance or transaction class.

Determining the Sample Size

1. Consider the risk of *incorrect acceptance*. This is the risk that the results of a sample will lead the auditor to conclude that the recorded account balance is not materially misstated when in fact it is. If the auditor places greater reliance on internal accounting controls, analytical procedures, and other substantive tests, the auditor can accept a greater risk of incorrect acceptance for the planned substantive test and can decrease the desired degree of audit assurance from the planned substantive test. The *desired degree of audit assurance* is the complement of the risk of incorrect acceptance. Therefore, if the auditor places little or no reliance on internal controls, analytical procedures, and other substantive tests, the desired degree of audit assurance increases and therefore the appropriate sample size increases. The primary factors affecting the auditor's decision about the desired degree of audit assurance are the combined assessments of inherent risk and control risk (discussed in the audit risk model in the chapter titled "Audit Planning"). When internal controls are effective, control risk can be assessed at below the maximum, which reduces the likelihood of material

misstatement in the account balance or transaction class. The relationship between the likelihood of material misstatement, discussed in the audit risk model in the chapter titled "Internal Control Considerations," and the desired degree of audit assurance is illustrated in Exhibit 7-2. While nonstatistical audit sampling does not allow the auditor to measure the desired degree of audit assurance achieved, the relationship between the sample size and the desired degree of audit assurance still applies as is illustrated in Exhibit 7-3. The desired degree of audit assurance is expressed in terms of high, moderate, or low. The lower the desired degree of audit assurance, the smaller the sample size. Conversely, the higher the desired degree of audit assurance, the larger the sample size.

2. Determine tolerable misstatement. As discussed above, tolerable misstatement relates to and is based on the auditor's assessment of planning materiality. There is an inverse relationship between tolerable misstatement and the required sample size. Therefore, as the tolerable misstatement decreases, the required sample size increases.

3. Assess the expected misstatement likely to exist in the sampling population. The *expected misstatement* is the auditor's best estimate of misstatements in the remaining population from which the sample is selected (sometimes referred to as "expected projected misstatement"). The expected misstatement does not include adjustments that the client expects the auditor to make (e.g., adjustments to accruals or prepaids).

   There is a direct relationship between expected misstatement and the required sample size. The required sample size increases as the auditor's estimate of the expected amount of misstatement in the population increases. The assessment of the expected misstatement likely to exist in the population is a matter of professional judgment; however, it is based on the following factors: (a) understanding of the client's business, (b) previous experience and prior years' tests of the population, (c) results of any tests of controls, and (d) knowledge of the population.

   In general, as the expected amount of misstatement in the sampling population approaches the tolerable misstatement established by the auditor, there is a need for more precise information from the sample. Therefore, the auditor should select a larger sample size as the expected amount of misstatement in the sampling population increases. Sampling generally is not appropriate if the amount of expected misstatement is likely to exceed 1/3 of tolerable misstatement. If the amount of expected misstatement is likely to exceed 1/3 of tolerable misstatement, the population should be corrected before sampling can be performed.

EXHIBIT 7-2
RELATIONSHIP BETWEEN THE LIKELIHOOD OF
MATERIAL MISSTATEMENT AND THE DESIRED DEGREE
OF AUDIT ASSURANCE

Likelihood of Material Misstatement	Desired Degree of Audit Assurance
High	High
Moderate	Moderate
Low	Low

EXHIBIT 7-3
MODEL APPROACH FOR DETERMINING SAMPLE SIZE

	Assurance Factors	
Desired Degree of Audit Assurance	Little or No Error Is Expected	Some Error Is Expected
High	3	6
Moderate	2.3	4
Low	1.5	3

A high desired degree of audit assurance generally indicates that little or no reliance is placed on internal accounting controls or other related substantive procedures.

A moderate desired degree of audit assurance generally indicates that some reliance is placed on internal accounting controls or other related substantive procedures.

A low desired degree of audit assurance generally indicates that considerable reliance is placed on internal accounting controls or other related substantive procedures.

---

4. Calculate the sample size. The sample size is calculated as follows:

$$\frac{\text{Sampling Population}}{\text{Tolerable Misstatement}} \times \begin{array}{c}\text{Assurance}\\\text{Factor}\end{array} = \begin{array}{c}\text{Initial}\\\text{Sample}\\\text{Size}\end{array}$$

When sample sizes are selected nonstatistically, on the basis of some statistical theory such as PPS, it is assumed that the sample units are every dollar in the population, each of which should have an equal opportunity to be selected for testing. Therefore, the sampling population should be stratified, with the total required sample units allocated among the dollar amount of the strata, so that all dollars have an approximately equal chance of being tested. The model approach discussed herein assumes that the population to be sampled will be stratified.

A common stratification technique is to select 1/3 of the sample from items with values less than the population average value and 2/3 of the sample from items with values equal to or greater than the population average value. If it is impractical for the auditor to stratify, the sample size should be increased.

The AICPA *Audit Sampling Guide* offers no guidance on the increase in sample size required if it is impractical for the auditor to stratify. Factors used to expand the initial sample size vary widely in practice (i.e., ranging from 10% to 100%) and are primarily a function of the auditor's professional judgment. However, an expansion factor from 1.2 to 1.5 generally can be used to compensate for the lack of stratification. For example, if the overall engagement risk or the likelihood of potential misstatements is relatively high, the auditor should select an expansion factor close to 1.5. Once the auditor decides on an expansion factor to compensate for the lack of stratification, an adjusted sample size can be calculated as follows:

$$\begin{array}{c}\text{Initial}\\\text{Sample}\\\text{Size}\end{array} \times \begin{array}{c}\text{Sampling Risk}\\\text{Expansion Factor}\\\text{(A factor of 1.2 to 1.5)}\end{array} = \begin{array}{c}\text{Adjusted}\\\text{Sample}\\\text{Size}\end{array}$$

Selecting the Sample

SAS-39 merely requires that the sample be selected in such a way that it is expected to be representative of the population; it does not require that random-sampling selection methods be used. Simple random sampling generally means that each item in the population has an equal opportunity (probability) of being selected. One way to draw a random sample from an accounting population is to assign a different number to each item in the population, write these numbers on small pieces of paper, place the pieces in a hat, thoroughly mix, draw a piece, and so on. Although this method would result in a random sample, it is time-consuming and difficult to document adequately. In practice, auditors use several techniques to select random samples. Common representative random-sampling methods used by auditors include systematic selection, random-number selection, and haphazard selection. Each of these methods is discussed below.

Systematic selection   Systematic sampling consists of determining a uniform interval and selecting throughout the population one item at each of the uniform intervals from the starting point (i.e., every nth item). The following steps should be observed when systematic sampling selection is used:

- Determine the population (N).
- Determine the sample size (n).
- Compute the interval size by dividing N by n.
- Select a random start (a random-number table can be used to determine the starting point). The starting point should be less than the interval size.
- Determine the sample items selected by successively adding the interval to the random starting point.

Exhibit 7-4 illustrates the application of systematic selection.

Random-number selection   Random-number selection methods commonly used in selecting audit samples are random-number tables and computer-generated random numbers. *Random-number tables* are published tables of numbers that are subjected to statistical tests to ensure randomness. A well-known random-number table publication is the "Tables of 105,000 Random Decimal Digits," published by the U.S. Interstate Commerce Commission, Bureau of Transport Economics and Statistics. To manually select a random sample from a random-number table, the auditor can follow the following four steps:

1. Establish correspondence between the sampling units in the population and the digits in the random-number table.
2. Select a starting point. A random stab into the table can identify the starting point.
3. Select a route through the table. Random-number tables can be read in any direction (up or down columns or across rows) and any portion and combination of the digits can be used, as long

EXHIBIT 7-4
APPLYING SYSTEMATIC SELECTION

Assume the auditor wants to select a sample of four contributions receivable balances for confirmation from a population of twelve receivables totalling $529,920. A breakdown of the accounts receivable population, including cumulative totals, is provided in the table below.

Customer	Recorded Amount	Cumulative Balance
1	$ 35,251	$ 35,251
2	127,298	162,549
3	5,518	168,067
4	55,987	224,054
5	8,210	232,264
6	14,566	246,830
7	142,953	389,783
8	24,071	413,854
9	13,982	427,836
10	39,977	467,813
11	31,985	499,798
12	30,122	529,920
	$ 529,920	

The interval size is calculated to be 132,480 ($529,920 divided by 4). A starting point between zero and 132,479 is selected by the use of a random-number table (assume it is 11,271), and the interval is added. The random numbers are therefore 11,271; 143,751 (11,271 + 132,480); 276,231 (143,751 + 132,480); and 408,711 (276,231 + 132,480). Accordingly, the sample items selected are customers 1, 2, 7, and 8.

---

as the conventions are consistently followed. The auditor should document the route selected.

4. Record the selection and the stopping point. It is important that the auditor record the stopping point so that the sample can be reconstructed or additional items selected, should either become necessary. In recording the selection, it will be necessary for the auditor to discard numbers in the table that are not in the population.

A more efficient way to generate random numbers is to use time-sharing programs, audit software, or personal computers, all of which create random numbers according to user specifications. Use of a computer is highly preferable to manual determination of random numbers because manual determination is a very tedious and time-consuming process. Furthermore, the advantages of computer-generated random numbers are that (1) workpapers are automatically produced and (2) the potential for human error (nonsampling risk) in the sample selection process is greatly reduced.

Haphazard selection   A *haphazard selection* consists of a selection that is made without any special reason for including or excluding a given item from the sample. For example, the auditor may select disbursement vouchers from a client's file cabinet, without consideration to the size or location of such vouchers. Haphazard samples cannot be used in statistical sampling because they are not selected based on defined probability concepts. However, the auditor may find it useful, and is permitted, to use haphazard selection in non-statistical sampling, as long as the auditor expects the selected sample to be representative of the population.

Performing the Tests

Once the sample has been selected, the auditor should apply appropriate audit procedures. If the auditor is unable to perform an audit procedure on a sampling unit selected for testing, alternative auditing procedures should be considered. If the sampling unit does not have an effect on the conclusion reached by the auditor concerning the acceptability of the population, alternative audit procedures do not have to be applied, and the sampling unit may be treated as an error for evaluation purposes. In addition, the auditor should determine whether the inability to apply an audit procedure has an effect on (1) the planned reliance on internal control or (2) the assessment of risk on representation made by the client.

Evaluating the Sample Results

SAS-39 states, "The auditor should project the misstatement results of the sample to the items from which the sample was selected." The AICPA *Audit Sampling Guide* presents two methods to project the sample error to the population: (1) ratio of population dollars to sample dollars and (2) ratio of population items to sample items.

Ratio of population dollars to sample dollars   The ratio of population dollars to sample dollars method projects the amount of error found in the sample by using the following formula:

Population Value
Less Individually   Amount of
$$\frac{\text{Significant Items}}{\text{Sample Dollars}} \quad \text{x} \quad \begin{array}{c} \text{Misstatement} \\ \text{in the Sample} \end{array} \quad = \quad \begin{array}{c} \text{Projected} \\ \text{Misstatement} \end{array}$$

Ratio of population items to sample items The ratio of population items to sample items method projects the amount of error found in the sample by using the following formula:

Population Items
Less Individually   Amount of
$$\frac{\text{Significant Items}}{\text{Sample Items}} \quad \text{x} \quad \begin{array}{c} \text{Misstatement} \\ \text{in the Sample} \end{array} \quad = \quad \begin{array}{c} \text{Projected} \\ \text{Misstatement} \end{array}$$

Exhibit 7-5 provides an example of projecting the error results of the sample to the population using the methods described above.

These two methods will give identical results if the fraction represented by the proportion of population items to sample items is the

---

EXHIBIT 7-5
ILLUSTRATION OF PROJECTING ERROR RESULTS
OF A SAMPLE TO THE POPULATION

Assume that the auditor has gathered the following information about the population and the sample tested in connection with the audit of contributions receivable, and there are no individually significant items:

	Dollar Amount	*Number of Items*
Population	$1,000,000	500
Sample tested	$ 400,000	175
Sample misstatement	$ 25,000	10

The projected error calculation based on ratio of population dollars to sample dollars is $62,500, calculated as follows:

$$\frac{\$1,000,000}{\$400,000} \quad \text{x} \quad \$25,000 \quad = \quad \$62,500$$

The projected error calculation based on ratio of population items to sample items is $71,429, calculated as follows:

$$\frac{500}{175} \quad \text{x} \quad \$25,000 \quad = \quad \$71,429$$

same as the fraction represented by the proportion of population dollars to sample dollars. If the errors relate closely to the size of the item, the auditor ordinarily should use the first approach (i.e., ratio of population dollars to sample dollars). On the other hand, if the errors are relatively constant for all items, the auditor ordinarily should use the second approach (i.e., ratio of population items to sample items). For example, assume that if in the audit of accounts receivable, as illustrated in Exhibit 7-5, the misstatements noted are unrelated to the size of the receivable, the auditor should use the second approach. On the other hand, if the misstatements noted vary in size depending on the size of the receivable (i.e., larger account receivables have larger misstatements), then the auditor should use the first approach. Generally, the first approach is more appropriate since it is very unlikely that the misstatements will be the same dollar amount regardless of the size of the item.

If the auditor designed the sample by separating the items subject to sampling into groups (i.e., stratified sampling), the auditor should separately calculate the projected misstatement for each individual group or strata sampled. The projected misstatement of such groups should then be added to the actual misstatement found in the individually significant items that were examined 100%. The total is the projected misstatement for the account balance or transaction class.

A Step-by-Step Summary Approach to Audit Sampling for Substantive Tests

The following is a step-by-step summary approach for applying the audit sampling model for substantive tests discussed above:

1. Identify the population.
2. Calculate tolerable misstatement.
3. Identify individually significant items within the population to be tested 100%.
4. Calculate the sampling base.
5. Determine the desired degree of audit assurance.
6. Assess the expected error in the population from which the sample is selected and choose an appropriate assurance factor.
7. Determine the appropriate sample size and select the sample.
8. Evaluate the sampling results.

Audit Sampling Worksheet for Substantive Tests

The auditor can use the "Audit Sampling Worksheet for Substantive Tests," on the accompanying disc, to assist in planning, performing, and evaluating a nonstatistical sample for substantive tests.

ILLUSTRATION OF AUDIT SAMPLING APPROACH FOR SUBSTANTIVE TESTS

The practical implementation of the audit sampling approach for substantive tests described above and the use of the related worksheet is illustrated in this section.

The auditor gathered the following financial information of Sample Not-for-Profit Organization, Inc., as of and for the year ended June 30, 20XX:

Current assets	$ 4,200,000
Other assets	1,100,000
Total assets	$ 5,300,000
Total liabilities	3,100,000
Net assets	$ 2,200,000
Support and revenue	$ 17,700,000
Total expenses	$ 17,442,000
Increase in net assets	$ 258,000
Contributions receivable	$ 900,000
Number of individual donors	425

Step 1. Identify the Population

The auditor determines that there are 425 individual donors with contributions receivable aggregating $900,000.

Step 2. Calculate Tolerable Misstatement

The auditor's firm policy is to estimate tolerable misstatement at 50% of planning materiality. The auditor calculates planning materiality to be $75,000, using the worksheet discussed in the chapter titled "Audit Planning."

Tolerable misstatement is calculated as follows:

Planning materiality	$ 75,000
	x .50
Tolerable misstatement	$ 37,500

Step 3. Identify Individually Significant Items within the Population to Be Tested 100%

The auditor's firm policy is to divide tolerable misstatement by three to establish a cutoff amount for individually significant items to be tested 100%. The cutoff amount for individually significant items is calculated as follows:

Tolerable misstatement	$ 37,500
Divided by	3
Cutoff amount	$ 12,500

Using this cutoff amount, the auditor identifies eight accounts totalling $200,000 greater than the cutoff amount. Three accounts are over $25,000 (totalling $100,000), and five accounts are between $15,000 and $25,000 (totalling $100,000). The next largest account is $7,500.

Step 4. Calculate the Sampling Base

The *sampling base* is the total population value less the total amount of individually significant items to be tested 100%. The auditor calculates it to be $700,000, as follows:

Population value (Step 1)	$ 900,000
Less: Total amount of individually significant items (Step 3)	(200,000)
Sampling base	$ 700,000

Step 5. Determine the Desired Degree of Audit Assurance

The auditor desires to select a sample that will provide her with only a moderate risk that the sample results would support the account balance if it were materially misstated. The auditor's decision to accept a moderate risk of incorrect acceptance (or achieve a moderate degree of audit assurance) is based on her evaluation of internal accounting controls and analytical review procedures related to the same objective. This is based on the result of the combined assessment of inherent risk and control risk, which resulted in a moderate likelihood of material misstatement. The desired degree of audit assurance is derived from Table 1 in Exhibit 7-6, which is based on the model discussed in this chapter and summarized in Exhibit 7-2.

EXHIBIT 7-6
AUDIT SAMPLING WORKSHEET
FOR SUBSTANTIVE TESTS

Client Name: _____

Date of Financial Statements: _____

Audit Area: _____

INSTRUCTIONS

This worksheet is designed to assist the auditor in planning, performing, and evaluating a nonstatistical sample for substantive tests. This worksheet implements the discussion in the chapter titled "Extent of Audit Procedures and Sampling," with respect to (1) planning the sample, (2) determining the sample size, (3) selecting the sample, (4) performing the tests, and (5) evaluating the sample results. Therefore, before completing this worksheet, the auditor should become familiar with the concepts discussed in Chapter 6.

1. Describe the audit objective of the test.

   _____

   _____

   _____

   _____

   _____

2. Describe the sampling unit.

   _____

   _____

   _____

   _____

   _____

3. Nature of substantive test:

   _____

   _____

   _____

4. Population characteristics (e.g., many small items, few large amounts, even distribution):

   _____

   _____

   _____

5. Describe how the completeness of the population was considered.

   _____

   _____

   _____

6. Determining individually significant items coverage:

   a. Population value .... $ _____

   b. Number of items in population .... _____

   c. Planning materiality (from "Planning Materiality Calculation Form," Chapter 4) .... $ _____

   d. Tolerable misstatement, usually 50%–75% of planning materiality in 6c .... $ _____

   e. Individually significant item cutoff amount (tolerable misstatement in 6d divided by a factor of 3 to 6) .. $ _____

   f. Total amount of individually significant items .... $ _____

   g. Number of individually significant items .... _____

   h. Individually significant items coverage (6f divided by 6a) .... _____

    i. Sampling base (6a – 6f) (if sample is stratified,
provide sampling base for each strata) $ _____

        Strata 1 $ _____

        Strata 2 $ _____

7. Is individually significant items coverage percentage in
6h above considered adequate coverage? (Generally,
if the percentage in 6h covers 2/3 [67%] or more of the
population, the coverage is considered adequate.)   Yes __ No __
    If the answer is "Yes," do not complete the rest of this
form. Sampling generally would not be considered necessary in this case, as long as the auditor observed no
evidence of problems from other audit procedures performed and the remaining population in 6i totals less
than an amount that would be considered material to
the financial statements.
    If the answer is "No," complete the rest of this form.

8. Calculating the sample size and selection technique:

    a. Likelihood of material misstatement (from chapter
titled "Audit Planning")   _____

    b. Desired degree of audit assurance (from Table 1
below)   _____

    c. Expected errors   _____

    d. Assurance factor (from Table 2 below)   _____

    e. Initial sample size [(6i/6d) x 8d]   _____

    f. Will the sample be stratified?   Yes __ No __

    g. Sampling risk expansion factor for lack of stratifica-
tion (a factor of 1.2 to 1.5 if 8f is "No"; N/A if 8f is
"Yes")   _____

    h. Adjusted sample size (8e x 8g if 8f is "No"; same as
8e if 8f is "Yes")   _____

    i. Selection technique (choose Systematic, Random,
or Haphazard)   _____

9. Summary of test results and total misstatement (if
sample is not stratified enter applicable amounts on
line "No Stratification"; if stratified, enter applicable
amounts on lines "Strata 1" and "Strata 2"):

    a. Amount of misstatement in the sample tested:

        (1) No Stratification $ _____

        (2) Strata 1 $ _____

        (3) Strata 2 $ _____

b. Total dollar amount of sample items selected in 8h above:

(1) No Stratification $ _____

(2) Strata 1 $ _____

(3) Strata 2 $ _____

c. Projected misstatement (use the first approach if the errors relate closely to the size of the item; use the second approach if the errors are unrelated to the size of the items; and check the appropriate method):

  __X__ Ratio of population dollars to sample dollars [(6i/9b) x 9a]

  _____ Ratio of population items to sample items {[(6b – 6g)/8h] x 9a}

(1) No Stratification $ _____

(2) Strata 1 $ _____

(3) Strata 2 $ _____

d. Known misstatement (the amount of misstatement found in the individually significant items that were examined 100% for the items in 6g) $ _____

e. Total misstatement (9c + 9d) $ _____

10. Conclude on the acceptability of test results and any modifications to the audit plan:

_____

_____

_____

_____

_____

_____

_____

_____

_____

_____

Prepared by: _____ Date: _____

Approved by: _____ Date: _____

Table 1: Relationship Between the Likelihood of
Material Misstatement and the Desired Degree
of Audit Assurance

Likelihood of Material Misstatement	Desired Degree of Audit Assurance
High	High
Moderate	Moderate
Low	Low

Table 2: Model Approach for Determining Sample Size

Desired Degree of Audit Assurance	Assurance Factors	
	Little or No Error Is Expected	Some Error Is Expected
High	3	6
Moderate	2.3	4
Low	1.5	3

A *high desired degree of audit assurance* generally indicates that little or no reliance is placed on internal control or other related substantive procedures.

A *moderate desired degree of audit assurance* generally indicates that some reliance is placed on internal control or other related substantive procedures.

A *low desired degree of audit assurance* generally indicates that consider-able reliance is placed on internal control or other related substantive procedures.

Step 6. Assess the Expected Error in the Population from Which the Sample Is Selected and Choose an Appropriate Assurance Factor

Because the Sample Not-for-Profit Organization had only moderately effective internal accounting controls over the processing of contributions receivable, the auditor believes that some errors might have existed in the receivable balances. However, the auditor did not expect any errors to exist in the items to be tested 100% and expected the total error in the population not to exceed $10,000.

To determine an appropriate assurance factor, the auditor uses Table 2 in Exhibit 7-6, which is based on the model discussed in this chapter and summarized in Exhibit 7-3. An assurance factor of 4 is selected because the auditor desires a moderate degree of audit assurance and some errors are expected.

Step 7. Determine the Appropriate Sample Size and Select the Sample

The auditor calculates the initial sample size to be 75, using the following formula:

$$\text{Sample Size} = \frac{\text{Population Value} - \text{Individually Significant Items}}{\text{Tolerable Misstatement}} \times \text{Assurance Factor}$$

$$\frac{\$900,000 \text{ (Step 1)} - \$200,000 \text{ (Step 3)}}{\$37,500 \text{ (Step 2)}} \times 4 \text{ (Step 6)} = 75$$

Because the sample will not be stratified, the auditor expands the initial sample size from 75 to 97, using the following formula:

Initial Sample Size		Sampling Risk Expansion Factor (A factor of 1.2 to 1.5)		Adjusted Sample Size
	x		=	
75	x	1.3	=	97

The auditor selects an expansion factor of 1.3 because the auditor assessed the likelihood of material misstatement as moderate. The auditor uses random selection to select the 97 sample items, which totalled $480,000.

A total of 105 confirmations will be mailed as follows:

Individually significant items (Step 3)	8
Sample items (Step 7)	97
Total confirmations	105

Step 8. Evaluate the Sample Results

The auditor mailed confirmation requests to each of the 105 donors whose balances were selected. Of the 105 confirmation requests, 85 were returned to the auditor. The auditor is able to obtain reasonable assurance through alternative procedures that the 20 customer balances that were not confirmed are valid receivables and are not misstated. Of the 85 responses received, only 4 indicated that their balances were overstated. The auditor investigates these balances further and concludes that they are indeed misstated as a result of the donors indicating that their pledges were not unconditional. The sampling results are summarized as follows:

	Recorded Amount of Sample	Audit Amount of Sample	Amount of Overstatement
Items tested 100%	$ 200,000	$ 199,516	$ 484
Sample items	$ 480,000	$ 475,125	$ 4,875

The auditor considers the errors found and concludes that the amount of error in the population is more likely to correlate to total dollar amount of items in the population than to the number of items in the population. Therefore, the auditor projects the amount of error of $4,875 found in the sample items to be $7,109, using the following formula:

$$\frac{\text{Population Value Less Individually Significant Items}}{\text{Sample Dollars}} \times \begin{array}{c}\text{Amount of}\\\text{Misstatement}\\\text{in the Sample}\end{array} = \begin{array}{c}\text{Projected}\\\text{Misstatement}\end{array}$$

$$\frac{\$900,000 - \$200,000}{\$480,000} \times \$4,875 = \$7,109$$

Because the items tested 100% were not subject to sampling, the related amount of the overstatement in those receivable balances should be added to the projected misstatement to come up with the total misstatement. Therefore, the total misstatement is $7,593 ($7,109 + $484).

The auditor compares the total misstatement of $7,593 with the tolerable misstatement of $37,500 (Step 2) and decides that there was a relatively low risk that she would have accepted the sample results if the recorded amount of the contributions receivable balance was misstated by more than the tolerable misstatement of $37,500. In other words, even the addition of a reasonable allowance for sampling risk to projected error would not be likely to result in a total misstatement exceeding tolerable misstatement.

The auditor concludes that the sample results supported the recorded amount of the contributions receivable balance. However, the total misstatement will be included with other relevant audit evidence to evaluate whether the financial statements taken as a whole may be materially misstated.

The steps discussed above with respect to the audit sampling exercise were documented in the audit sampling worksheet shown in Exhibit 7-6.

AUDIT SAMPLING APPROACH FOR TESTS OF CONTROLS

As discussed earlier in this chapter, there are five steps involved in applying audit sampling (statistical or nonstatistical) to tests of controls: (1) planning the sample, (2) determining the sample size, (3) selecting the sample, (4) performing the tests, and (5) evaluating the sample results.

Planning the Sample

1. Determine the audit objective of the test. The objective of tests of controls is to provide the auditor with assurances about whether internal controls are operating effectively. For example, to determine whether disbursements have been authorized, the auditor could examine payment vouchers to determine if the authorized client personnel signed the payment voucher before processing.

2. Define the population.

   a. Define the sampling unit. A sampling unit may be, for example, a document, an entry, or a line item. If the objective of the test is to determine whether disbursements have been authorized and the prescribed control procedure requires an authorized signature on the voucher before processing, the sampling unit might be defined as the voucher. On the other hand, if one voucher pays several invoices and the prescribed control procedure requires each invoice to be authorized individually, the line item on the voucher representing the invoice might be defined as the sampling unit.

   b. Consider the completeness of the population. The population represents the body of data about which the auditor wishes to generalize. For example, in performing tests of recorded sales transactions, the auditor generally defines the population as all recorded sales for the year. If the auditor randomly samples from only one month's transactions, it is invalid to draw conclusions or generalizations about the sales for the entire year. To consider the completeness of the population, the auditor scans the sales journal for the year to account for the numerical sequence of invoice numbers issued.

c. Define the period covered by the test. Tests of controls may be applied to transactions executed throughout the period under audit (e.g., the entire year) or during the period from the beginning of the year to an interim date. If the auditor decides to define the period covered by the test as less than the period under audit, the auditor might use audit sampling to reach a conclusion about compliance with the prescribed activity for the period up to the interim date. In this situation, the auditor should obtain reasonable assurance regarding the remaining period by performing additional procedures. The extent of these procedures depends on factors such as (1) the results of the tests during the interim period, (2) the length of the remaining period, (3) responses to inquiries concerning the remaining period, and (4) evidence of compliance within the remaining period obtained from substantive tests performed.

If the auditor defines the population to include transactions from the entire period under audit but performs testing during an interim period, the auditor should estimate the number of transactions to be executed in the population for the remaining period. Transactions selected for testing that were not executed before the interim period would be examined during the completion of the audit. For example, assume that in the first ten months of the year, the entity issued 10,000 checks for disbursements numbered from 10,001 to 20,000. Based on the entity's business cycle, the auditor might estimate that 2,000 checks will be issued in the last two months of the year. Therefore, the auditor will use the numerical sequence of 10,001 to 22,000 for selecting the desired sample. Checks with numbers between 10,001 and 20,000 that are selected would be examined during the interim work, and the remaining sampling units would be examined during the completion of the audit.

3. Define the deviation conditions. A *deviation* in tests of controls is a departure from the prescribed internal control activity. The auditor must make a precise statement of what constitutes a deviation so that the staff performing the audit procedure will have specific guidelines for identifying deviations. For example, for purposes of auditing sales, the auditor might identify the related internal control activities and define the corresponding deviation conditions as shown in Exhibit 7-7.

EXHIBIT 7-7
ILLUSTRATION OF DEVIATION CONDITIONS
RELATING TO CERTAIN INTERNAL CONTROL
ACTIVITIES FOR SALES

Internal Control Activity	*Deviation Condition*
Program manager approves direct purchases to be charged to a government assistance contract.	Lack of program manager's initials indicating approval.
Fund-raising director verifies that donor contributions recorded as receivables are unconditional.	Lack of fund-raising director's initials indicating approval.
Vendor invoices are stamped "paid" when vouchered.	A vouchered vendor invoice is not stamped "paid."

Determining the Sample Size

1. Consider the acceptable risk of overreliance on internal accounting control (also sometimes referred to as the risk of assessing control risk too low). This is the risk that the sample supports the auditor's planned degree of reliance on the control when the true compliance rate for the population does not justify such reliance. Choosing the appropriate acceptable risk of overreliance on internal accounting control in a particular audit area is a decision in which the auditor must use his or her best judgment. Since the risk of overreliance on internal accounting control is a measure of the level of risk that the auditor is willing to take, the main consideration is the extent to which the auditor plans to reduce the assessed level of control risk. If the auditor plans to reduce the assessed level of control risk below the maximum as a basis for reducing substantive tests, a lower acceptable risk of overreliance on internal accounting control is desirable. For example, if an auditor selects a 10% risk of overreliance, the auditor has a 10% chance of assessing the level of control risk as low or moderate when control is ineffective given a certain tolerable deviation rate from a prescribed control procedure. Conversely, a 10% risk of overreliance means that the auditor has a 90% reliability level, or probability, of being right. Most major public accounting firms consider the maximum acceptable risk of overreliance on internal accounting control to be 10%.

There is an inverse relationship between the risk of overreliance on internal accounting control and sample size. If the auditor is willing to accept only a low risk of overreliance, the sample size ordinarily would be larger than if a higher risk were acceptable. Although consideration of risk is implicit in all audit sampling applications, the auditor should explicitly state an acceptable risk of overreliance for an audit sampling application of tests of controls. However, this risk does not need to be quantified, and the auditor may assess it in qualitative terms such as low, moderate, or high.

2. Consider the tolerable rate. The tolerable rate is the maximum rate of deviation from a prescribed control activity that the auditor is willing to accept without altering the planned assessed level of control risk. There is an inverse relationship between the tolerable rate and the sample size (i.e., the lower the tolerable rate, the larger the sample size). If, after performing the sampling application, the auditor finds that the rate of deviation from the prescribed control activity is close to, or exceeds, the tolerable rate, the auditor might decide that there is an unacceptably high sampling risk that the deviation rate for the population exceeds the tolerable rate. Under these circumstances, the auditor should modify planned reliance on the prescribed control.

   In assessing the tolerable rate, the auditor should consider that although deviations from pertinent control activities increase the risk of material errors in the accounting records, such deviations do not necessarily result in errors. A recorded disbursement that does not show evidence of required approval might nevertheless be a transaction that is properly authorized and recorded. Therefore, a tolerable rate of 5% does not necessarily imply that 5% of the dollar amounts are in error.

3. Consider the expected population deviation rate. This is also referred to as the "expected error rate" or the "expected rate of occurrence." It is common for the auditor to use the results of the preceding year's audit to make an estimate of the expected population deviation rate. If prior year's results are not available, the auditor considers other factors, such as his or her assessment of the overall control environment. There is a direct relationship between the expected population deviation rate and the sample size (i.e., the higher the expected population deviation rate, the larger the sample size).

   As the expected population deviation rate approaches the tolerable rate, the need for more precise information from the sample arises. However, the expected population deviation rate should not equal or exceed the tolerable rate. If the auditor believes that the actual expected population deviation rate is higher than the tolerable rate, the auditor generally should omit the tests of controls of the particular control activity and design substantive tests without relying on that particular control activity.

4. Consider the effect of population size. In most circumstances, the size of the population has little or no effect on the determination of the required sample size. The *Audit Sampling Guide* concludes that a population size of 5,000 sampling units or greater will have practically no effect on the size of the sample. However, as the population size decreases from 5,000 sampling units, the effect of the population size on the sample size increases.

A practical approach for determining sample size for tests of controls   The approach adopted in this Guide is a variation of a statistical method called "attributes sampling." Three primary factors determine the sample size for attributes sampling: (1) acceptable risk of overreliance on internal accounting control, (2) tolerable rate, and (3) expected population deviation rate.

The effect of changing any of these three factors on the determination of the sample size can be summarized as follows:

Factor	*Effect on Sample Size*
Increase acceptable risk of overreliance on internal accounting control	Decrease
Increase the tolerable rate	Decrease
Increase the expected population deviation rate	Increase

Attributes sampling is the most common statistical method used in practice for performing tests of controls. The methodology suggested in this chapter does not require the same degree of formality and precision in specifying sampling planning decisions and conclusions as does attributes sampling. Therefore, this approach is efficient and does not require specialized knowledge in statistical sampling. This approach, which is commonly used in practice, is summarized as follows:

Planned Assessed Level of Control Risk	*Assurance Desired from Sample Tests of Controls*	*Risk of Overreliance on Internal Accounting Control*	*Tolerable Rate*
Low	High	5%	2–5%
Moderate	Moderate or Low	10%	6–10%
High	None	N/A	Omit Test

Exhibit 7-8 provides a matrix for determining sample size for tests of controls, which is based on the approach described above.

Sample size of 25 or less   Note that the minimum sample size in this approach is 25. As noted earlier, the risk of drawing improper conclusions from a representative sample varies inversely with the sample size; that is, the more items examined, the smaller the risk. Professional auditing literature suggests that a representative sample should include at least 25 items to provide a basis for relying on the sample results. This minimum sample size also is appropriate only when both of the following conditions exist:

1. No deviations are expected that would affect the auditor's conclusion about the population.

2. The tests to be performed are only one of the bases for the auditor's conclusion (i.e., direct tests of balances, including analytical procedures, provide corroborative evidence that internal control activities are functioning and/or account balances are not materially misstated).

EXHIBIT 7-8
MATRIX FOR DETERMINING SAMPLE SIZE FOR TESTS OF CONTROLS

Planned Assessed Level of Control Risk	Number of Expected Deviations			
	0	1	2	3
Low[1]	60	*	*	*
Moderate[2]	25	40	60	*
High[3]	N/A	N/A	N/A	N/A

[1] When the planned assessed level of control risk is low, the degree of assurance desired from the sample tests of controls is high. Therefore, the auditor allows for a low level of sampling risk (i.e., 5%) and a tolerable rate not in excess of 5%.

[2] When the planned assessed level of control risk is moderate, the degree of assurance desired from the sample tests of controls is moderate or low. Therefore, the auditor allows for a higher level of sampling risk (i.e., 10%) and a tolerable rate not in excess of 10%.

[3] When the assessed level of control risk is high (i.e., at the maximum level), tests of controls would be inefficient and the auditor would perform primarily substantive tests.

* Sample size is too large to be cost-effective for most audit applications.

Tests of 1, 2, 5, 10, or 12 items are merely walk-throughs and should be considered only as part of the review of the system documentation. While the auditor may learn something about the internal control from these procedures, sample sizes of less than 25 are not large enough to draw conclusions about the population or to limit other procedures. If a sample of 25 seems like too much work, the auditor may be able to identify a better way to achieve the audit objective. The key questions the auditor should ask are:

- What is the purpose of the test and what is the auditor trying to accomplish?
- If 25 is too many, is the test worth performing at all?
- Can the procedures on another sample be extended to cover the purpose of the test?

The use of one sample to accomplish several purposes can be particularly efficient. For example, the auditor may want to consider using a sample of shipping documents for testing credit approval, processing of sales, and recording of cash receipts. This way the auditor can use the same sample to test the transaction from its inception to its consummation.

If no errors are detected in a representative sample of 25 items, the auditor can conclude with 90% reliability that the risk of assessing control risk too low is not greater than 10% and that the deviation rate in the population is not greater than 10%. This conclusion is appropriate even if the number of items in the population is very large. However, it is not necessary to state this conclusion separately, as these results should be combined with the corroborative evidence obtained from other audit procedures. Then, the auditor can conclude that internal controls are functioning to provide reasonable assurance that specific internal control objectives are being achieved and recorded amounts are properly stated.

Sample size of more than 25   If errors are found in the initial sample size of 25, the auditor should increase the sample size from the minimum of 25 items. As an example, if one error is found, the sample should be increased by 15 items to a total of 40. When no errors are found in the additional 15 items, the test results support the same conclusion as finding no errors in a sample of 25 items (i.e., moderate level of control risk). However, before the auditor expands the initial sample, the auditor should challenge his or her expectation that no additional deviations will be found. When the auditor decides that this is not a reasonable expectation, he or she should challenge whether the internal controls tested are functioning and effective.

Selecting the Sample

As discussed earlier, sample items should be selected in such a way that the sample can be expected to be representative of the population. Therefore, all items in the population should have an opportunity to be selected. In practice, auditors use several techniques to select random samples. Common representative random-sampling methods used by auditors include systematic selection, random-number selection, and haphazard selection. Each of these methods was discussed earlier in this chapter.

Performing the Tests

Once the sample has been selected, the auditor should apply appropriate audit procedures. If the auditor is unable to perform an audit procedure on a sampling unit selected for testing, alternative auditing procedures should be considered. If the sampling unit does not have an effect on the conclusion reached by the auditor concerning the acceptability of the population, alternative audit procedures do not have to be applied, and the sampling unit may be treated as an error for evaluation purposes. In addition, the auditor should determine whether the inability to apply an audit procedure has an effect on the planned reliance on internal control or the assessment of risk on representation made by the client.

Audit procedures should be applied to each sampling unit to determine whether there has been a deviation from the established internal control activity. Usually a deviation occurs if the auditor is unable to perform an audit procedure or apply alternative audit procedures to a sampling unit. As a general rule, sampling units that are selected but are not examined, such as voided transactions or unused documents, should be replaced with new sampling units. Voided or unused documents are not considered errors if the established procedure of accounting for these items has been properly followed.

If the auditor has defined the population to include the entire period under audit, but plans to perform a portion of the sampling procedure before the end of the period, the auditor may find it necessary to estimate the population size and numbering sequence before the documents have been used. If the auditor overestimates the population size and numbering sequence, any numbers that are selected as part of the sample and that exceed the actual numbering sequence used would be treated as unused documents. Such numbers should be replaced by matching extra random numbers with appropriate documents.

Evaluating the Sample Results

After the audit procedures have been applied to each sampling unit, and the deviations, if any, from the prescribed internal control activities have been summarized, the results of the sampling must be evaluated. Whether the sample is statistical or nonstatistical, the auditor should exercise professional judgment in evaluating the results and reaching an overall conclusion. When the auditor uses nonstatistical sampling, such as the approach discussed in this chapter, the sampling risk cannot be measured directly and, therefore, cannot be quantified. However, it is generally appropriate for the auditor to assume that the sample results do not support the planned assessed level of control risk if the rate of compliance deviation identified in the sample exceeds the expected deviation rate used in designing the sample. In that case, there is likely to be an unacceptably high risk that the true deviation rate in the population exceeds the tolerable rate. The following generalizations should be observed when the auditor evaluates the results of nonstatistical sampling:

- The auditor may rely on the internal controls when the auditor's best estimate of the population deviation rate (based on the sample results) is equal to, or less than, the expected population deviation rate.
- The auditor cannot rely on the internal controls when the auditor's best estimate of the population deviation rate is greater than the expected population deviation rate.

To illustrate this evaluation process, assume that the auditor, in testing the internal control activity that quantities shipped agree to quantities billed, uses a sample of 25 items. Using the matrix in Exhibit 7-8, the auditor selects a sample of 25 because the auditor plans an assessed level of control risk as moderate and no deviations are expected in the sample selected. If the test results reveal one exception (i.e., one actual deviation), the test results would not provide the auditor with a basis for assessing control risk as moderate. Therefore, the auditor should select an additional 15 items (i.e., a total of 40) to be able to support an assessed level of control risk of moderate, as long as no additional deviations are found in the 15 items. If the auditor does not wish to increase the sample size to 40, then the auditor should assess control risk as high.

Exhibit 7-9 provides a form that will assist the auditor in documenting these considerations in a test of controls. The auditor also should consider the qualitative aspects of each deviation. The nature and cause of each deviation should be analyzed and deviations should be classified into errors or irregularities. A determination should be made as to whether the deviation resulted from a misunderstanding of instructions, from carelessness, from intentional failure to perform procedures, or from other factors. The discovery of an

EXHIBIT 7-9
AUDIT SAMPLING WORKSHEET
FOR TESTS OF CONTROLS

Client Name: _____

Date of Financial Statements: _____

Audit Area: _____

INSTRUCTIONS

This worksheet is designed to assist the auditor in planning, performing, and evaluating audit sampling for tests of controls. This worksheet implements the discussion in this chapter with respect to (1) planning the sample, (2) determining the sample size, (3) selecting the sample, (4) performing the tests, and (5) evaluating the sample results. Therefore, before completing this worksheet, the auditor should become familiar with the concepts discussed in Chapter 6.

1. Describe the audit objective(s) of the test.

   _____

   _____

   _____

2. Describe the internal control activities being tested.

   _____

   _____

   _____

3. Define the sampling unit.

   _____

   _____

   _____

4. Describe how the completeness of the population was considered.

_____

_____

_____

_____

5. Define the period covered by the test.

_____

_____

_____

_____

6. Define the deviation conditions.

_____

_____

_____

_____

7. Indicate the expected number of deviations. (Note: If the expected number of deviations is more than 2, STOP; the sample size would be relatively large to be cost-effective for most audit applications. The auditor should challenge whether the internal control procedures are functioning and effective and modify the planned audit procedures accordingly.)   0 __ 1 __ 2 __

8. Indicate the planned assessed level of control risk (Low, Moderate, or High).   _____

9. Determine the sample size and selection technique:

   a. Sample size (use matrix in Table 1 below)   _____

   b. Selection technique (Systematic, Random, or Haphazard)   _____

10. Describe the tests of controls to be performed.

_____

_____

_____

_____

_____

_____

_____

_____

Evaluation of Sample Results and Overall Conclusions

11. Specify the number and type of deviations noted and the reasons for such deviations.

_____

_____

12. Summarize the final assessment of control risk (Low, Moderate, or High). _____

13. Conclude on the acceptability of test results and any modifications to the audit plan.

_____

_____

Prepared by: _____ Date: _____

Approved by: _____ Date: _____

Table 1: Matrix for Determining Sample Size for Tests of Controls

Planned Assessed Level of Control Risk	Number of Expected Deviations			
	0	1	2	3
Low[1]	60	*	*	*
Moderate[2]	25	40	60	*
High[3]	N/A	N/A	N/A	N/A

[1] When the planned assessed level of control risk is low, the degree of assurance desired from the sample tests of controls is high. Therefore, the auditor allows for a low level of sampling risk (i.e., 5%) and a tolerable rate not in excess of 5%.

[2] When the planned assessed level of control risk is moderate, the degree of assurance desired from the sample tests of controls is moderate or low. Therefore, the auditor allows for a higher level of sampling risk (i.e., 10%) and a tolerable rate not in excess of 10%.

[3] When the assessed level of control risk is high (i.e., at the maximum level), tests of controls would be inefficient and the auditor would perform primarily substantive tests.

* Sample size is relatively large to be cost-effective for most audit applications.

irregularity generally would require more attention from the auditor than the discovery of an error.

In addition to the sample results of tests of controls, the auditor should consider the following factors in determining whether the overall audit approach supports the planned reliance on internal control:

- Results of inquiries about controls that do not leave an audit trail

- Results of observations concerning control activities that are based on the segregation of responsibilities

Professional judgment is required in reaching a conclusion on the way the results of the tests of controls will affect the nature, timing, and extent of the subsequent substantive tests.

> **OBSERVATION:** The preceding discussion is a "classical" discussion of tests of controls that will be very effective for auditing large populations where assessing control risk as low will be very cost-effective because of the reduction in related substantive procedures.

Applying the sample sizes in this discussion to Circular A-133 audits testing internal control over compliance with laws, regulations, contracts, and grant agreements at the major federal program level may prove problematic. In the Circular A-133 audit, the procedures and extent of test must be designed as if a low level of control risk were to be obtained. (This is discussed more fully in the chapter titled "Internal Controls over Federal Awards.") This would result in a sample size for all tests of controls of at least 60 items for each control attribute tested.

To avoid overtesting, auditors should consider other evidence about internal control over compliance that they obtain in other aspects of the audit, including inquiry and observation techniques. In addition, in testing for compliance, auditors should consider using dual tests (which test both controls and balances). These tests would likely reduce the total sample items that would be tested.

In addition, Circular A-133 does not require testing of controls when the control is not effective, as long as the ineffectiveness is reported in the schedule of findings and questioned costs. The auditor can make this determination during the testing. For example, assume an auditor designs a test that will be performed for 60 sample items. After testing 10 items, the auditor finds two deviations. The control can be judged to be ineffective because it is not being performed; the test should be stopped and a finding reported in the schedule of findings and questioned costs. Of course, the impact of this finding on the extent of substantive testing of the related compliance requirements must then be taken into account in light of the ineffective control.

AUDIT SAMPLING AND THE SMALL ORGANIZATION

Small not-for-profit organizations typically have limited segregation of duties. Therefore, for effectiveness and efficiency, the auditor frequently chooses to assess control risk at the maximum level. Accordingly, the auditor of a small organization generally will not have to consider tests of controls, including sampling of documentary evidence, to determine if controls are working as prescribed. For substantive testing, small businesses frequently have small populations of accounting data in both account balances and classes of transactions. Consequently, sampling may not be as useful, since there may not be large populations of accounting data.

In determining the extent of testing, consider alternatives to using audit sampling. Other alternatives, which would eliminate the requirements of SAS-39, may provide a more effective and efficient audit approach for small business engagements. Alternative approaches include:

- Applying procedures to 100% of certain groups of transactions or balances
- Testing unusual items without applying procedures to the remainder of the population
- Performing tests that involve application of procedures to less than 100% of the items in the population without drawing a conclusion about the entire account or class of transactions

SUMMARY

Included in the concept of "reasonable assurance" is the understanding that the auditor does not review every transaction of a not-for-profit organization when performing an audit of financial statements. This chapter addressed the extent of audit procedures required for an audit in generally accepted auditing standards. It also provided an effective sampling methodology that may be used for auditing accounts of not-for-profit organizations where sampling is required.

CHAPTER 8
TAX CONSIDERATIONS

CONTENTS

CHAPTER 8
TAX CONSIDERATIONS

CROSS-REFERENCES

2000 MILLER NOT-FOR-PROFIT REPORTING: Chapter 13, "Tax Reporting Requirements"

An effective audit of a not-for-profit organization should include consideration of the tax status of the organization and a determination about whether appropriate provision has been made in the financial statements of the organization for any taxes that may be due. The auditor should include consideration of the following in the audit of a not-for-profit organization's financial statements:

- The tax-exempt status of the not-for-profit organization, including obtaining and maintaining tax-exempt status
- Business income earned by the not-for-profit organization from an unrelated trade or business that is subject to taxation
- Reporting of tax information to donors

These considerations are the primary concern for an auditor since either loss of its exempt status or earning unrelated business income may have direct consequences to the not-for-profit organization in terms of liability for federal income tax payments. This chapter is devoted to these two concerns.

Two other areas of tax compliance that are less likely to have a direct and material effect on the financial statements are the requirements for payroll taxes and sales taxes.

PAYROLL TAXES

Generally, a not-for-profit organization is subject to the same payroll tax requirements of a commercial organization. Only some not-for-profit organizations, however, which are classified as *private founda-*

tions, are subject to federal unemployment taxes. There are no special requirements for not-for-profit organizations regarding payment of Social Security and Medicare withholdings and tax deposit rules. Therefore, the auditor should obtain assurance that the organization is complying with these rules and not subjecting itself to penalties or incurring liabilities for not depositing payroll taxes as required.

The not-for-profit organization is required to file the same reports as a commercial enterprise (with the federal unemployment exception described above), such as quarterly reports and Forms W-2 and 1099 at the calendar year end.

Not-for-profit organizations tend to be large users of independent contractors. The Internal Revenue Service has recently emphasized auditing not-for-profit organizations' classification of workers between true independent contractors and employees. The auditor should obtain some assurances that this is not a significant tax exposure area for the not-for-profit organization. If, based on an audit, the Internal Revenue Service determines that an independent contractor actually is an employee, the not-for-profit organization may be liable for Social Security and Medicare taxes (both employee and employer shares) and withholding taxes that would have been withheld had the individual been classified as an employee. These facts could lead to a significant potential liability to the not-for-profit organization.

SALES TAXES

Sales tax requirements are determined by states or localities that impose such taxes on transactions within their individual jurisdictions. Accordingly, this issue is raised in this chapter only to alert the auditor to these taxes. The facts and circumstances of the states and localities where the specific not-for-profit organization being audited operates will need to be considered.

In many instances, not-for-profit organizations are exempt from paying sales taxes on goods and services they purchase. However, in many locations, the not-for-profit organization may be subject to collecting and remitting sales tax on the goods or services that it is providing to third parties as a result of a trade or business activity that it conducts. The auditor should inquire about these requirements and obtain assurance that the not-for-profit organization is complying with the state and/or local government requirements.

OVERVIEW

This chapter is not intended to be a comprehensive tax manual for certified public accountants providing tax services to not-for-profit

1organizations. Auditors who are engaged by a not-for-profit organization to prepare or review tax filings with the Internal Revenue Service and/or a state regulatory body may need to consult other authoritative sources to be able to provide such services. This chapter is intended to make an auditor aware of certain tax issues that he or she should address in the audit of a not-for-profit organization's financial statements. Auditors also may need to refer to other authoritative sources for tax information that relates to the activities of the specific not-for-profit organizations they are auditing.

TAX-EXEMPT STATUS

A not-for-profit organization's status as an entity that is exempt from federal income taxes is not automatic. Once a not-for-profit organization is organized (in the vast majority of cases, incorporated) under the laws of a state, it will apply to the Internal Revenue Service for tax-exempt status.

For most not-for-profit organizations, the application is made on IRS Form 1023, "Application for Recognition of Exemption Under Section 501(c)(3) of the Internal Revenue Code." (A copy of this form is provided in Appendix B.) Form 1024, "Application for Recognition of Exemption Under Section 501(a) or for Determination Under Section 120 of the Internal Revenue Code." Additional forms, such as Form 872-C, to request a ruling that the not-for-profit organization be treated as a publicly supported organization for short initial tax years, and Form 8718, to remit the user fee for an exempt-organization determination letter request, also may be required.

An organization may request tax-exempt status under several subsections of Internal Revenue Code Section 501(c). Section 501(c)(3) covers a corporation (and any community chest, fund, or foundation) organized and operated exclusively for religious, charitable, scientific, testing of public safety, literary or educational purposes, or to foster national or international amateur sports competition, or for the prevention of cruelty to animals.

Examples of commonly used sections of the Internal Revenue Code for other types of not-for-profit organizations are as follows:

- *Section 501(c)(4)*   Civic league, an organization not organized for profit but operated exclusively for the promotion of social welfare, or a local association of employees
- *Section 501(c)(6)*   Business league, chamber of commerce, real estate board, board of trade, or professional football league
- *Section 501(c)(7)*   Club organized for pleasure, recreation, and other not-for-profit purposes (social and recreation clubs)

- *Section 501(c)(8)*   Fraternal beneficiary society, order, or association
- *Section 501(c)(9)*   Voluntary employees' beneficiary organization
- *Section 501(c)(10)*   Domestic fraternal society or association
- *Section 501(c)(19)*   Post or organization of past or present members of the U.S. Armed Forces
- *Section 501(c)(23)*   Political organization

An auditor is most likely to encounter Section 501(c)(3) organizations. Two limitations on the operations of not-for-profit organizations exempt under Section 501(c)(3) are as follows:

1. No part of the earnings of the not-for-profit organizations can benefit (i.e., inure) any individual or private shareholder. This does not preclude the organizations from having an excess of revenues over expenses. However, an excess of revenues over expenses cannot benefit an individual or group of individuals.

2. The Internal Revenue Service regulates transactions between a not-for-profit organization and insiders. The AICPA Guide provides guidance on understanding these transactions. Insiders are individuals with a personal or private interest in the organization, such as board members, officers, certain employees, and substantial contributors. Transactions between insiders and not-for-profit organizations are permitted, but the not-for-profit organization must be able to satisfy the Internal Revenue Service that the transaction was reasonable, was adequately documented, had independent approval, and did not violate any law or regulation. Employee compensation can create an inurement problem if it is judged to be unreasonably high.

The concept of private benefit prohibits a not-for-profit organization from benefiting the private interests of any specific individual or group—both insiders and outsiders. The not-for-profit organization should have sound policies for transactions with insiders and outsiders, and these policies should document that the transactions were appropriate and were approved by disinterested parties.

These rules are designed to ensure that the not-for-profit organization isn't really a commercial enterprise set up in the format of a not-for-profit organization. The rules affect the organization when it is applying for its tax-exempt status. In addition, the rules can affect the not-for-profit organization after it is granted tax-exempt status, since the Internal Revenue Service can revoke an organization's tax exemption.

In 1996 the Taxpayer Bill of Rights was enacted into law. This law permits the Internal Revenue Service to impose significant penalties on insiders and managers of section 501(c)(3) and 501(c)(4) organizations in certain circumstances related to excess benefit transactions. (An excess benefit transaction is a transaction in which an economic benefit is provided to an individual in which the value of the economic benefit provided by the organization exceeds the value of the consideration received by the organization.) Auditors should consider whether the not-for-profit organization has implemented procedures to identify potential excess benefit transactions before they occur.

Engaging in commercial activities does not disqualify the not-for-profit organization from its tax exemption. In fact, many not-for-profit organizations conduct commercial activities at some level. However, when the commercial activities becomes the primary activity of the organization, its tax-exempt status is at risk. Some not-for-profit organizations form for-profit subsidiaries, which will enter into and record the commercial transactions. This helps not-for-profit organizations avoid the gray area of determining exactly when an organization's commercial activities become its primary activity.

Additional factors may cause an organization either to be denied a tax-exempt status initially or to lose its tax-exempt status. These conditions are addressed in the AICPA Guide and are summarized below:

- The not-for-profit organization cannot have as a substantial part of its activities the carrying on of propaganda or other attempts to influence legislation. In addition, there should be no participation or intervention in any political campaigns.

  The prohibition against lobbying prohibits activities that are a "substantial part" of the not-for-profit organization's activities. The not-for-profit organization may elect to be governed by a defined limitation to lobbying expenses instead of being governed by a subjective definition of the "substantial part" of the organization's activities.

  All political campaign activity is prohibited, even insignificant amounts of activity. Prohibited political activities include contributing to candidates or political organizations, including in-kind contributions of services, publicity, advertising, paid staff time, facilities, and office space. Also prohibited are evaluating candidates, and their positions on specific issues and encouraging voter registration for a specific political group. A not-for-profit organization is not prohibited from participating in nonpartisan get-out-the-vote campaigns. For example, the IRS revoked a church's tax exemption because the church took out an newspaper advertisement that attacked the views of a candidate. This revocation was upheld in court.

- The Internal Revenue Service may revoke a not-for-profit organization's tax-exempt status if it determines that the percentage of its income from commercial activities unrelated to its specific exempt purposes is too large. There is no specific percentage of unrelated business income that can be designated as too large and, therefore, not permissible. The facts and individual circumstances of the not-for-profit organization must be considered when determining whether this is a particular risk for an entity. Further discussion of unrelated business income is provided later in this chapter.

- Under the Internal Revenue Service's "commensurate test," the scope of the not-for-profit organization's programs must be commensurate with its financial resources. The charitable program that is run by the not-for-profit organization must be real and substantial, taking into consideration the particular organization's financial resources and other circumstances. This means that the organization's fund-raising expenses and administrative expenses should not be an excessive portion of the total expenses of the organization. Again, the Internal Revenue Service does not provide a specific percentage for determining what would be considered excessive; the facts of the individual circumstances must be considered, although low levels of program activity may encourage scrutiny by the Internal Revenue Service. Such circumstances also may encourage state charities registration departments to scrutinize a particular not-for-profit organization, which may later bring additional scrutiny by the Internal Revenue Service.

The Internal Revenue Service can revoke a not-for-profit organization's tax exemption at any time. In addition, the not-for-profit organization may lose its exemption from state income tax from the state in which it is incorporated and from any other states in which it does business.

The Internal Revenue Service may revoke a not-for-profit organization's tax-exempt status retroactively. While these instances are not common, there are three cases where a retroactive revocation of tax-exempt status might occur. These instances are as follows:

1. The not-for-profit organization omitted or misstated a material fact in the process of acquiring the tax exemption.

2. The not-for-profit organization operated in a matter materially different from that which was originally represented.

3. The not-for-profit organization engaged in a prohibited transaction, which is one in which the not-for-profit organization entered for the purpose of diverting substantial corpus or income from its exempt purpose.

A retroactive revocation of a not-for-profit organization's tax exemption clearly would be detrimental to the organization. Its ability to raise funds in the future would be eliminated. In addition, the deductibility of the contributions from donors during the time period to which the retroactive revocation applies would be eliminated. Certainly, donors would demand refunds of those contributions, not to mention the expenses theoretically incurred by donors for filing amended income tax returns to restate the amount of charitable contributions that they claimed as deductions. Clearly, auditors need to be cognizant of the ramifications of not-for-profit organizations conducting activities that could result in loss of tax-exempt status. The loss of tax-exempt status would likely have a material impact on an organization's financial statements and might even impair the organization's ability to continue as a going concern.

Distinguishing Public Charities and Private Foundations

Not-for-profit organizations that are charitable organizations and their auditors must determine whether the organization is a public charity or a private foundation. Private foundations are subject to different rules than public charities, so this is an important distinction.

A not-for-profit organization is considered a charitable organization if it qualifies for its tax-exempt status under Section 501(c)(3) of the Internal Revenue Code. The Internal Revenue Service considers all organizations that are tax-exempt under Section 501(c)(3) to be private foundations unless they qualify as public charities under one of several tests contained in the Internal Revenue Code. These tests can be quite complex. Whether the charitable not-for-profit organization is a public charity or a private foundation should be resolved as part of the initial application for tax exemption. However, changes in the organization and operation of the not-for-profit organization may affect its classification as a public charity or a private foundation.

Some of the types of organizations that qualify as public charities are as follows:

- Public institutions, such as churches, educational organizations, and medical care and research organizations

- Publicly supported organizations, such as those organizations that receive their revenue from either donations or fee-for-service activities that are related to their exempt function

- Service-providing organizations, such as those that are responsive to the general public, as opposed to the private interests of a limited number of donors or other individuals

- Supporting organizations, such as those not-for-profit organizations that may not fall into one of the categories described above but that support and are closely related to one or more other organizations that do fall into one of the above categories

Private foundations are subject to more restrictive rules than public charities, such as prohibitions against self-dealing and excess business holdings. In addition, private foundations are subject to an excise tax on their investment income. They also are required to make annual distributions of 5 percent of the average market value of their noncharitable-use assets for charitable, educational, scientific, and similar purposes. Noncharitable-use assets are assets that are not used or held for use directly in carrying on the organization's exempt purpose. Private foundations also are required to publish on an annual basis a notice that their annual reports are available for inspection, and are subject to federal unemployment taxes.

Auditors should be aware of the classification of the charitable organization so that they can evaluate compliance with the appropriate Internal Revenue Code provisions that could have a direct and material effect on the financial statements. For example, if an organization is a private foundation and not a public charity, the auditor should determine whether the excise taxes on the organization's investment income have been paid and whether the appropriate accruals for this liability have been made.

ANNUAL REPORTING REQUIREMENTS

Not-for-profit organizations exempt from federal income tax still must file a tax return with the Internal Revenue Service. Almost all not-for-profit organizations, with the exception of churches and certain other not-for-profit organizations with gross receipts of less than $25,000, are required to file annual information returns with the Internal Revenue Service. These returns are due on the 15th day of the fifth month after the not-for-profit organization's fiscal year end. For example, a not-for-profit organization with a calendar year end of December 31, would be required to file the return by May 15.

> **OBSERVATION:** More than one not-for-profit organization has misinterpreted the filing date as five and one-half months after year end. This is incorrect. The deadline is the 15th day of the fifth month.

Most not-for-profit organizations file Form 990, "Return of Organization Exempt from Income Tax," or Form 990-EZ, "Short Form Return of Organization Exempt from Income Tax." Form 990-EZ may be used by not-for-profit organizations that ordinarily would file Form 990, but have gross receipts of less than $100,000 and total assets (at year end) of less than $250,000. Certain filers [including organizations exempt under Section 501(c)(3)] also must file Schedule A of Form 990 and Form 990-EZ. This Schedule requires additional information to be provided on the not-for-profit organization's activities, lobbying activities, and compensation of the five highest paid employees. See Appendix A at the end of this Guide.

In addition to these forms, tax-exempt organizations with gross unrelated business income of at least $1,000, and certain organizations that are subject to a proxy tax on lobbying expenditures, must file Form 990-T, "Exempt Organization Business Income Tax Return."

Finally, Form 990-PF, "Return of Private Foundation," is filed by all private foundations.

Not-for-profit organizations that are private foundations or that are exempt under IRC Sections 501(c) and 501(d) are required to make copies of their annual information returns (excluding certain information, such as donor lists) available to the public for inspection at the location of the not-for-profit organization. Under the Taxpayer Bill of Rights 2, enacted in July 1996, 501(c) and 501(d) exempt organizations are required to provide copies of their information returns to the public without charge, except for any reproduction or mailing costs. If the request is made in person, the copies must be provided immediately. If the request is made in writing, the copies must be provided in 30 days. These regulations became effective in June 1999. The Tax and Trade Relief Extension Act of 1998 will extend these regulations to private foundations when the IRS issues regulations to implement the requirements. Private foundations will be required to provide a list of their contributors.

Auditors should inquire as to whether their audit clients are complying with these requirements. Failure to provide copies of any annual information return subjects the organization to a $5,000 fine.

The not-for-profit organization more than likely will have to file annual reports with one or more state department(s) that supervise charities within each state. The not-for-profit organization may have to file in the state in which it is incorporated, the state(s) in which it has its business office(s), and the states in which it solicits funds. Often these filings require financial statements and compilation, review, or audit reports, depending on the size of the particular not-for-profit organization and the requirements of the various states.

The auditor should review the controls the not-for-profit organization has established to ensure compliance with the various Internal Revenue Code requirements and the controls established to ensure that all of the federal, state, and local annual reporting requirements are met. The auditor should review copies of the federal and state filings to gain some assurance that these returns reflect the actual facts and circumstances of the particular not-for-profit organization as they are understood by the auditor.

The size of the not-for-profit organization will most likely determine the level of tax expertise that the organization possesses. Smaller not-for-profit organizations may engage the auditor to prepare the required annual filings. In this case, the auditor should gain an understanding of whether the appropriate personnel of the not-for-profit organization are cognizant of the various limitations under which the organization must operate. Staff members of larger not-for-profit organizations may have a good level of tax expertise and may routinely handle the annual filing and reporting requirements. The larger the not-for-profit organization, however, the more complex the tax issues may be, so the auditor needs to make sure that he or she spends an adequate amount of time understanding the tax issues that the organization may be addressing. The auditor should obtain some assurance that these matters are being addressed properly and that reasonable conclusions are being reached.

UNRELATED BUSINESS INCOME

A not-for-profit organization may earn income from an unrelated trade or business activity. An unrelated trade or business activity is any trade or business whose conduct is not substantially related to the performance or exercise of the not-for-profit organization's exempt purpose.

Determining whether income from a trade or business activity is related to the organization's exempt function can be difficult. The focus of the determination is not on what the not-for-profit organization does with the income. For example, if the not-for-profit organization performs a trade or business activity (such as selling T-shirts, and coffee mugs) to generate funds for its exempt purpose (such as feeding homeless people), the selling of merchandise is still considered an unrelated activity. A detailed discussion of the various Internal Revenue Service Regulations, Private Letter Rulings, and court decisions that have defined *unrelated* is beyond the scope of this Guide.

Some categories of income should not be considered unrelated business income, including dividends, interest, royalties, and gains on the sale of property, unless the property was used in an unrelated trade or business. Unrelated business income also does not include income from activities in which substantially all of the work is done by volunteers, income from the sale of donated merchandise, and rents from real property.

The amount of unrelated business income is determined as the gross income from the unrelated trade or business, less expenses directly connected with the unrelated trade or business, certain operating losses, and qualified charitable contributions. Unrelated business income is subject to federal corporate taxes on income, including the alternative minimum tax. The first $1,000 of unrelated business income is excluded from taxation. Various rules pertaining to tax credits and the use of operating losses, including offsetting of losses from one activity against profits of another activity apply and must be considered when calculating the tax due. As stated above, not-for-profit organizations with at least $1,000 of unrelated business income must file Form 990-T to report the activity and calculate the tax due.

Auditors should consider the same audit objectives, control procedures, and auditing procedures in designing an audit strategy for the tax provision for taxes on unrelated business income as they would for commercial enterprises. The auditor should consider reviewing tax returns and related correspondence for tax years that are still subject to audit by the Internal Revenue Service. If applicable, the auditor should review any revenue agent reports for any audits conducted by the Internal Revenue Service to determine whether unrecorded liabilities exist.

The auditor also should review the calculation of the tax provision on unrelated business income, the assumptions used for determining what has been considered by the not-for-profit organization as an unrelated business activity, and the reasonableness of the expenses deducted from gross unrelated business income to determine taxable income. If considered necessary, detailed testing of the revenue amounts and the expenses deducted may be performed, depending on the size and significance of these accounts and the tax provision to the financial statements.

In addition, auditors of not-for-profit organizations that have no provision for unrelated business income should obtain assurance that there is no unrelated business income for which taxes should have been provided.

REPORTING TAX INFORMATION TO DONORS

Not-for-profit organizations must provide certain information to their donors.

Information on the Amount of Contributions in Excess of the Value of Goods and Services Received

Donors may deduct charitable contributions for income tax purposes only to the extent that the contribution's value exceeds the value of any goods or services that the donor receives in return. In many cases the donor receives a benefit in return for the contribution in the form of goods and services of lesser value than the contribution itself.

For example, a ticket to a fund-raising dinner may cost $500, but the value of the meal received may be $75. The contribution in this case would be $425.

While the Internal Revenue Service has in the past strongly encouraged charities to voluntarily provide their donors with an estimate of the fair market value of the goods or services provided in exchange for the contribution, charities are now required to provide this information when the amount of the total payment received is more than $75. In the above example, the not-for-profit organization would be required to report to the donor the value of the meal of $75, since the total payment of $500 exceeds the $75 threshold. If the ticket price was $75 and the value of the meal was $65, the not-for-profit organization would be strongly encouraged, but not required, to report to the donor the value of the meal provided.

In reporting the amount of the meal to the donor, the not-for-profit organization should provide a written statement to the donor either as part of the solicitation or as part of the receipt for the contribution. The written statement should include the following information:

- An explanation that the amount of the deductible contribution for federal income tax purposes is the excess of the amount of the money or value of any property over the value of the goods or services provided by the not-for-profit organization
- The estimate made in good faith by the not-for-profit organization of the value of the goods or services that are provided to the donor

The Internal Revenue Service has provided for exceptions to the above rules when the goods and services received by the donor are of nominal value.

Written Acknowledgment of Contributions

Donors *must* receive a written acknowledgment of the donation from the not-for-profit organization in order to be permitted to deduct contributions of $250 and more. The donor's canceled check will no longer be considered adequate support to substantiate these contributions. Not-for-profit organizations must have the appropriate systems in place to be able to provide this written acknowledgment. Clearly, the impact on the organizations will depend on the volume of contributions over the $250 threshold.

The auditor of the not-for-profit organization should inquire about how the organization is complying with this requirement. While the burden to obtain the documentation actually rests with the donor, a not-for-profit organization that is unable to provide these receipts will certainly have difficulty maintaining its contributions. Donors will not be inclined to contribute to an organization that does not enable the donor to adequately support the contribution.

SUMMARY

A number of complex tax issues can affect a not-for-profit organization. These issues center around the organization's ability to obtain and keep its status as a tax-exempt organization. Failure to maintain tax-exempt status can have an extremely detrimental effect on the organization and can call into question its ability to continue as a going-concern.

A not-for-profit organization must pay tax on its earnings from a trade or business that is unrelated to its exempt function. The determination of which earnings are subject to this tax and the calculation of the tax on the net amount of the gross revenues less direct expenses also results in a number of areas for which the correct tax treatment may not be clear. This will have a direct impact on the financial statements of the not-for-profit organization since it affects the tax provision that is provided for these earnings.

Given these important and significant issues, the auditor of a not-for-profit organization should give the appropriate level of attention to the tax considerations described in this chapter.

CHAPTER 9
CONCLUDING THE AUDIT

CONTENTS

CHAPTER 9
CONCLUDING THE AUDIT

CROSS-REFERENCES

2001 MILLER NOT-FOR-PROFIT ORGANIZATION AUDITS: Chapter 19, "Concluding the A-133 Audit"

2001 MILLER AUDIT PROCEDURES: Chapter 7, "Analytical Procedures"; Chapter 20, "General Auditing Procedures"; Chapter 21, "Concluding the Audit"

2000 GAAS GUIDE: Section 329, "Analytical Procedures"; Section 333, "Management Representations"; Section 341, "The Auditor's Consideration of an Entity's Ability to Continue as a Going Concern"; Section 560, "Subsequent Events"

Before issuing an audit opinion on the financial statements of a not-for-profit organization, the auditor should perform certain procedures and considerations as part of the conclusion or wrap-up of the audit. These procedures involve completing and concluding on work performed for specific account balances and classes of transactions, reviewing and concluding on some general audit areas, and evaluating the results of all audit procedures performed to ensure that the appropriate audit report is issued. This chapter discusses the following specific areas:

- Obtaining a client representation letter.
- Performing final analytical procedures.
- Identifying any events subsequent to year end that might need to be reflected in the financial statements.
- Identifying commitments and contingencies, including correspondence with the not-for-profit organization's attorney(s).
- Considering the not-for-profit organization's ability to continue as a going concern.
- Summarizing and evaluating passed audit adjustments.
- Completing the final review and completing the audit working papers.

CLIENT REPRESENTATION LETTER

An auditor performing an audit in accordance with generally accepted auditing standards is required to obtain certain written representations from management. These representations are obtained in a document that is commonly referred to as a *representation letter*.

In November 1997, the Auditing Standards Board of the AICPA issued SAS-85 (Management Representations) which superseded SAS-19 and provides additional guidance on obtaining written management representations. SAS-85 is effective for audits of financial statements for periods ending on or after June 30, 1998. The guidance on representation letters contained in this chapter incorporates the guidance and requirements of SAS-85.

In addition to providing a revised example of a representation letter that has been updated, fo r example, to reflect the requirements of SAS-82 representation letters where certain conditions exist, SAS-85 provides a sample letter to update management's representations through a later date. In addition, SAS-85 requires a predecessor auditor to obtain a representation letter from management, in addition to the representation letter from the successor auditor, before reissuing a report that was previously issued on financial statements of a prior period.

SAS-85 provides the following additional guidance as to obtaining written representation from management:

- Written representations should be obtained for all financial statements presented by the auditor's report. For example, if comparative financial statements are reported on, the written representations obtained at the completion of the most recent audit should address all periods that are being reported upon.

- Representations may be limited to matters that are considered either individually or collectively to the financial statements, provided management and the auditor have reached an agreement on materiality for this purpose. Materiality considerations would not apply to those representations that are not directly related to amounts included in the financial statements, such as representations concerning fraud involving management or employees who have significant roles in internal control.

- The representation letter should be dated no earlier than the date of the auditor's report and should be signed by those members of management with overall responsibility for financial and operating matters whom the auditor believes are responsible for and knowledgeable about financial and operating matters. Signers would normally include the chief executive and chief financial officers.

SAS-85 discusses the general representations that should be obtained and provides a sample representation letter. They also require that the representations obtained reflect the nature of the individual circumstances and the basis of presentation of the financial statements. Accordingly, an auditor should consider the following additional representations for inclusion in the standard representation letter obtained from a not-for-profit organization:

- Maintenance of an appropriate composition of assets in amounts needed to conform with all donor restrictions, as well as compliance with all other donor restrictions
- Tax-exempt status and taxation
- Reasonableness of the allocation of functional expenses
- Inclusion in the financial statements of all assets and liabilities under the not-for-profit organization's control
- Adequacy of internal controls over the receipt and recording of contributions
- Propriety of reclassifications between net asset classes
- Identification of all direct and indirect governmental financial assistance

> **OBSERVATION:** The auditor may also find it useful to obtain information about management remediation efforts regarding the Year 2000 Issue. Sample language is provided in note 5 of Exhibit 9-1. This language may still need to be considered subsequent to January 1, 2000, as Year 2000 problems may not reveal themselves until well into the year 2000.

The sample representation letter shown in Exhibit 9-1 allows the auditor to meet the requirements of SAS-85 and should be modified to include any of the applicable matters listed above and any additional matters that are appropriate in the auditor's judgment. A sample letter to update a representation letter is provided as Exhibit 9-2.

FINAL ANALYTICAL PROCEDURES

SAS-56 (Analytical Procedures) provides guidance on the use of analytical procedures in the planning phase of an audit, as substantive tests and as part of the overall review of the audit. The use of analytical procedures as substantive tests depends on the judgment of the auditor, but SAS-56 requires analytical procedures to be applied in the planning and final review phases of an audit performed in accordance with generally accepted auditing standards.

EXHIBIT 9-1
REPRESENTATION LETTER

[Date of auditor's report]

To *[name of independent auditor]*:

We are providing this letter in connection with your audit of the statement of financial position as of *[year end]* and the statements of activities and cash flows for the year then ended of *[name of not-for-profit organization]* for the purpose of expressing an opinion as to whether the financial statements referred to present fairly, in all material respects, the financial position, changes in net assets, and cash flows of *[name of not-for-profit organization]* in conformity with generally accepted accounting principles.

Certain representations in this letter are described as being limited to matters that are material. Items are considered material, regardless of size, if they involve an omission or misstatement of accounting information that, in the light of surrounding circumstances, makes it probable that the judgment of a reasonable person relying on the information would be changed or influenced by the omission or misstatement.

We confirm, to the best of our knowledge and belief, the following representations made to you during your audit:

1. The financial statements referred to above are presented in conformity with generally accepted accounting principles.

2. We have made available to you all—

   a. Financial records and related data.

   b. Minutes of the meetings of the board of trustees and committees of the board of trustees, or summaries of actions of recent meetings for which minutes have not yet been prepared.

3. There have been no communications from regulatory agencies concerning noncompliance with, or deficiencies in, financial reporting practices.

4. We have no plans or intentions that may materially affect the carrying value or classification of assets and liabilities.

5. The following have been properly recorded or disclosed in the financial statements:

   a. Related-party transactions and related receivables or payables, including sales, support, or other revenue, purchases, loans, transfers, leasing arrangements, and guarantees.

   b. Arrangements with financial institutions involving compensating balances or other arrangements involving restrictions on cash balances and line-of-credit or similar arrangements.

   c. Guarantees, whether oral or written, under which the organization is contingently liable.

    d. Significant estimates and material concentrations known to management that are required to be disclosed in accordance with the AICPA's Statement of Position 94-6 (Disclosures of Certain Significant Risks and Uncertainties).

    e. Agreements to repurchase assets previously sold.

6. There are no:

    a. Violations or possible violations of laws and regulations whose effects should be considered for disclosure in the financial statements or as a basis for recording a loss contingency.

    b. Unasserted claims or assessments that our lawyer has advised us are probable of assertion and must be disclosed in accordance with Statement of Financial Accounting Standards No. 5.

    c. Other liabilities or gain or loss contingencies that are required to be accrued or disclosed by Statement of Financial Accounting Standards No. 5.

7. There has been no:

    a. Fraud involving management or employees who have significant roles in internal control

    b. Fraud involving others that could have a material effect on the financial statements.

8. There are no material transactions that have not been properly recorded in the financial statements.

9. Provision, when material, has been made to reduce excess or obsolete inventories to their net realizable value.

10. The organization has satisfactory title to all owned assets, and there have been no liens or encumbrances on such assets nor has any asset been pledged.

11. We have complied with all aspects of contractual agreements that would have a material effect on the financial statements in the event of noncompliance.

12. We acknowledge that:

    a. Management is responsible for [*name of not-for-profit organization*]'s compliance with laws and regulations applicable to it.

    b. Management has identified and disclosed to you all laws and regulations that have a direct and material effect on the determination of financial statement amounts.

13. No events have occurred subsequent to the date of the statement of financial position that would require adjustment to, or disclosure in, the financial statements.

[*Name of chief executive officer and title*]

[*Name of chief financial officer and title*]

Notes:

1. The letter should be signed by the chief executive and financial officers. In a not-for-profit organization, these individuals are typically referred to as the executive director or president and the vice president for finance or director of finance, although titles with certainly vary from organization to organization. The auditor should consider having any other appropriate individual sign the letter. For example, if the vice president for finance of a not-for-profit organization has very little dealing with the accounting and financial reporting of the not-for-profit organization, it might be appropriate to have the controller or accounting director sign the letter as well.

2. The sample letter assumes that there are no matters to disclose to the auditor or reflect in the financial statements. If there are such matters, the letter should be modified to so indicate by listing these matters following the representation, by reference to accounting records or the financial statements, or by other similar means.

3. If volunteers are used, consider referencing them in paragraphs 3a, 3b, and 7a.

4. If the not-for-profit organization does not have a lawyer, paragraph 6b should be changed to read, "There are no unasserted claims or assessments that must be disclosed in accordance with Statement of Financial Accounting Standards No. 5, and we have not consulted with an attorney regarding unasserted claims or assessments."

5. The auditor should also consider including the following representations relating to the Year 2000 Issue (These representations should be considered, with appropriate modification, subsequent to January 1, 2000, in order to cover problems already known to have arisen as well as problems that may still arise subsequent to January 1, 2000.):

   [*Name of not-for-profit organization*] has considered the impact of Year 2000 issues on its computer systems and applications and has developed remediation plans. Conversion activities are in process, and conversion and testing is expected to be completed during calendar year 1999. Further, we confirm that:

   - Systems that we considered to be mission-critical have been identified and are being addressed in the remediation plans.
   - Timely completion of its Year 2000 project is a priority of [*name of not-for-profit organization*].
   - The estimated timetable is based on assumptions that management believes are reasonable and appropriate. Management is committing and will continue to commit necessary human and financial resources to complete its remediation plans on a timely basis.
   - Management has no information indicating that a significant vendor, service provider, or revenue provider may be unable to sell goods or provide services or revenues to [*name of not-for-profit organization*] because of Year 2000 issues.
   - Management does not expect Year 2000 issues to have a material adverse effect on [*name of not-for-profit organization*]'s operation or financial results in 1999.

6. In December 1999 the AICPA issued Statement on Auditing Standards No. 89, "Audit Adjustments," which is effective for audits of financial statements for periods beginning on or after December 15, 1999, with earlier application permitted. In addition to its requirements for communicating audit adjustments to audit committees, SAS-89 adds a representation as to the effect of unrecorded audit adjustments to the financial statements to the list of matters that should be addressed in a representation letter in connection with a financial statement audit. Accordingly, the following would be added to the representation letter when SAS-89 is implemented:

   > We believe that the effects of the uncorrected financial statement misstatements summarized in the accompanying schedule are immaterial, both individually and in the aggregate, to the financial statements taken as a whole.

   A schedule of unrecorded audit adjustments would be added to the representation letter. However, if management believes that certain of the identified items are not misstatements, management's belief may be acknowledged by adding to the representation, for example, "We do not agree that items XX and XXX constitute misstatements because [*description of reasons*]."

EXHIBIT 9-2
UPDATING MANAGEMENT REPRESENTATION LETTER

[*Date*]

To [*Name of independent auditor*]:

In connection with your audit(s) of the statement of financial position as of [*year-end*] and the statements of activities and cash flows for the year then ended of [*name of not-for-profit organization*] as of [*dates*] and for the [*periods*] for the purpose of expressing an opinion as to whether the financial statements present fairly, in all material respects, the financial position, changes in net assets, and cash flows of [*name of not-for-profit organization*] in conformity with generally accepted accounting principles, you were previously provided with a representation letter under date of [*date of previous representation letter*]. No information has come to our attention that would cause us to believe that any of those previous representations should be modified.

To the best of our knowledge and belief, no events have occurred subsequent to [*date of latest balance sheet reported on by the auditor*] and through the date of this letter that would require adjustment to or disclosure in the aforementioned financial statements.

[*Name of Chief Executive Officer and Title*]

[*Name of Chief Financial Officer and Title*]

The purpose of analytical procedures in the final review phase is to help the auditor assess the conclusions reached during the course of the audit and to evaluate the overall financial statement presentation. The review generally consists of reviewing the financial statements, including the footnotes, to assess the adequacy of evidence gathered in response to unusual or unexpected balances identified in planning the audit or in the course of the audit and any unusual or unexpected balances that were not previously identified. The final overall analytical review may indicate that the auditor should obtain more audit evidence if he or she concludes that sufficient evidence for these unusual or unexpected balances was not obtained during the course of the audit.

Thus, the overall final analytical procedures give the auditor the opportunity to step back from the financial statement presentation and assess his or her understanding of unusual or unexpected balances and determine whether sufficient audit evidence was obtained for those fluctuations. Auditors automatically may perform such an overall review once the audit is complete. However, to meet the requirements of SAS-56, the auditor must document the performance of these procedures.

The extent of procedures performed is left to the judgment of the auditor. Common procedures include comparing current-year and prior-year balances for the statement of financial position and the statement of changes in net assets. In addition, comparisons between internal relationships within the financial statements, such as a comparison of contributions receivable to total support for the period under audit, should be performed as necessary.

> **OBSERVATION:** Often, auditors of not-for-profit organizations are asked to present the audited financial statements to senior management and the board of directors or trustees and discuss the financial highlights of the statements. Completing overall analytical procedures is a valuable way for the auditor to prepare for such a presentation because it forces the auditor to confirm his or her knowledge of the various interrelationships and variances from the prior year that will likely be of interest to these groups.

SUBSEQUENT EVENTS

The financial statements of a not-for-profit organization and the accompanying auditor's report are issued at some date subsequent to the date of the statement of financial position. Events may occur between the year-end date on the statement of financial position and the date of the auditor's report that have a material effect on the financial statements and therefore require adjustment or disclosure in the financial statements. These events are commonly referred to as *subsequent events*.

Generally accepted auditing standards define two types of subsequent events that require consideration by management and evaluation by the auditor. The first type of subsequent events consists of those events that provide additional evidence with respect to conditions that existed at the date of the statement of financial position and affect the estimates inherent in the financial statements. Any information that becomes available before the financial statements are issued should be used in the evaluation of the estimates. For these type of subsequent events, the financial statements should be adjusted for any changes in estimates resulting from the use of such evidence.

The second type of subsequent events consists of those events that provide evidence with respect to conditions that did not exist at the date of the statement of financial position but arose subsequent to this date. These events do not require adjustment of the financial statements. However, disclosure of these events may be required to keep the financial statements from being misleading.

Examples of subsequent events that would result in disclosure in the financial statements, but not adjustment of financial statement amounts, include:

- Issuance or incurrence of a material amount of debt
- Notice of a loss of a significant funding source
- Notice of the disallowance of a material amount of grant or contract revenue and expenses
- Settlement of litigation when the event giving rise to the claim occurred subsequent to the date of the statement of financial position
- Loss of a facility as a result of fire or flood
- Losses on contribution or other receivables resulting from conditions (such as the loss of a major donor or a catastrophe) arising subsequent to the date of the statement of financial position

Subsequent events affecting the realization of assets such as receivables or the settlement of estimated liabilities ordinarily will require adjustment of the financial statements, because these types of events typically represent the culmination of conditions that existed over a relatively long period of time.

The period subsequent to the date of the statement of financial position and through the date of the auditor's report is known as the "subsequent period" in generally accepted auditing standards. The auditor typically tests some transactions during this period to aid in the evaluation of assets and liabilities as of the date of the statement of financial position. For example, the auditor may examine cash collections on receivables during the period subsequent to the date of the statement of financial position to provide evidence about those receivables. In addition to these types of procedures, generally accepted auditing standards prescribe other procedures with respect to the subsequent period that the auditor should perform at or near the completion of fieldwork. These procedures are as follows:

- Read the latest available interim financial statements and ask about any significant differences with the financial statements being reported upon.
- Inquire of and discuss with officers and other executives having responsibility for financial and accounting matters about:
  - Whether any substantial contingent liabilities or commitments existed at the date of the statement of financial position being reported on or at the date the inquiry is made.
  - Whether any changes in the capital and debt structure or working capital occurred during the subsequent period.

—The current status of matters in the financial statements being reported on that were accounted for on the basis of tentative, preliminary, or inconclusive data.

—Whether any unusual adjustments had been made during the subsequent period.

- Read the available minutes of meetings of the board of trustees and its committees. If minutes are not available for the most recent meetings, ask about the matters discussed at the meetings.

- Review the client representation letter and responses received from inquiry letters from the not-for-profit organization's attorneys, which also will provide information about the subsequent period.

Any matter that the auditor notes while performing the above procedures should be followed up to determine whether it should be considered a subsequent event. In addition, the auditor should perform any additional procedures that he or she feels are appropriate in the particular circumstances. The length of the subsequent period can vary from weeks to years. Clearly, the auditor should modify his or her procedures for the subsequent period based on the length of time of the period.

COMMITMENTS AND CONTINGENCIES

The auditor should perform procedures to ensure that any required disclosures or accruals in the financial statements relating to commitments and contingencies are properly made. *Commitments* are contractual obligations for the future expenditure of resources. They may include:

- Commitments to purchase large quantities of goods, sometimes at prices in excess of market prices prevailing at the date of the statement of financial position

- Commitments to other not-for-profit organizations for grant funds

- Building or construction commitments to expand or rehabilitate facilities

- Commitments to acquire investments or other long-term assets

- Long-term leases with fixed payments for a number of years

Contingencies are existing conditions that may create a legal obligation in the future but that arise from past transactions or events (i.e., events that have taken place at or prior to the date of the statement of financial position). Examples of contingencies are:

- Financial arrangements where guarantees or endorsements have been given

- Litigation, claims, and assessments, including those pending, threatened, or unasserted

- Possible claims for reimbursement of funds received under grants or contracts for noncompliance with the terms of those grants or contracts

- Potential exposure for income taxes, based on challenges to the not-for-profit organization's tax-exempt status, classification of income as taxable unrelated business income, or any other tax matters.

The auditor will need to identify commitments and contingencies throughout the course of the audit. In many instances, commitments and contingencies are not recorded in the accounting records, so the auditor's procedures will be less direct than tests performed for other specifically recorded assets and liabilities. For example, if the auditor becomes aware that the not-for-profit organization paid significant architectural fees that were capitalized during the year, he or she may suspect the existence of a construction commitment that would require disclosure. If the not-for-profit organization paid significant fees to attorneys during the year, significant litigation may exist and may have to be disclosed or accrued as a liability in the financial statements.

> **OBSERVATION:** The chapter of this Guide titled "Audit Planning" describes how auditors should consider the Year 2000 Issue during the planning phase of the audit. The conclusions reached with regard to these procedures should be taken into account when the auditor addresses whether any commitments or contingencies need to be considered relating to the Year 2000 Issue.

The auditor should consider performing the following procedures for identifying commitments and contingencies:

- Inquire of management about the existence of any unrecorded commitments or contingencies. These inquiries should be with both financial and nonfinancial staff of the not-for-profit organization.

- Read the minutes of the meetings of the board of trustees and its committees.

- Read and analyze the requirements of contracts and grants that are sources of funding for the not-for-profit organization. Review any correspondence from these funding sources relating to potential disallowances of expenses or activities charged to these agreements.

- Read any other contracts, including loan agreements, bond indentures, and leases.

- Test transactions after the date of the statement of financial position. For example, significant disbursements during the subsequent period should be tested to determine if the disbursements have been properly accrued in the financial statements, where appropriate.

- Analyze legal expenses to determine if the not-for-profit organization has engaged attorneys because of litigation that should be analyzed for disclosure or accrual.

> **OBSERVATION:** Not-for-profit organizations often are successful in obtaining pro bono legal services, so auditors should not assign more importance to a lack of legal fees than is warranted in determining whether there is outstanding litigation. At the same time, auditors should determine if donated legal services, if any, are treated properly in accordance with FAS-116 (Accounting for Contributions Received and Contributions Made).

- Send a letter of inquiry to the not-for-profit organization's legal counsel.

The auditor should perform any other procedures he or she thinks are necessary, given the specific circumstances of the not-for-profit organization being audited.

SAS-79 (Amendment to Statement on Auditing Standards No. 58, Reports on Audited Financial Statements) eliminates the requirement that, when certain conditions are met, the auditor add an uncertainties explanatory paragraph to the auditor's report. SAS-79 is explained more fully in the chapter titled "Reporting."

Attorney Letters

One of the most important audit procedures for determining the proper recognition or disclosure of contingencies in the financial statements is obtaining a response to a letter of inquiry sent to the not-for-profit organization's attorney(s). Not-for-profit organizations are subject to the same litigious environment in which commercial enterprises operate. This means that auditors should give the same high level of consideration to this procedure as they would in the audit of a commercial enterprise.

The procedures for making inquiries of an auditee's attorneys are governed by SAS-12 (Inquiry of a Client's Lawyer Concerning Litigation, Claims, and Assessments). According to SAS-12, auditors should obtain the following evidential matter with respect to litigation, claims, and assessments:

- The existence of a condition, situation, or set of circumstances indicating an uncertainty about the possible loss to a not-for-profit organization arising from litigation, claims, and assessments
- The period in which the underlying cause for legal action occurred
- The degree of probability of an unfavorable outcome
- The amount or range of potential loss

The letter of audit inquiry to an auditee's attorney is the auditor's primary means of obtaining corroboration of the information furnished by management concerning litigation, claims, and assessments. Evidential matter obtained from the client's in-house general counsel or legal department may provide the auditor with the necessary corroboration, although SAS-12 states that evidential matter obtained from inside counsel is *not* a substitute for information outside counsel refuses to furnish.

> **OBSERVATION:** Auditor's judgment is important in determining the use of inquiry letters. However, in most audits of not-for-profit organizations, the auditor should use inquiry letters rather than rely on the representations of in-house counsel, unless it can be determined that the outside counsel performed services that clearly did not relate to litigation, such as a real estate closing. Auditors should also be sensitive to a practical problem that sometimes occurs when the only service performed by an attorney is to respond to an audit inquiry letter, resulting in the payment of a legal fee, which results in an audit inquiry letter in the following year. These situations, which do arise, should be avoided.

The matters that should be covered in a letter of audit inquiry are described in SAS-12 and include, but are not limited to, the following:

1. Identification of the not-for-profit organization and any affiliated organizations included in the financial statements and the date of the audit.
2. A list prepared by management (or a request by management that the attorney prepare a list) that describes and evaluates

pending or threatened litigation, claims, and assessments with respect to which the attorney has been engaged and to which he or she has devoted substantive attention on behalf of the not-for-profit organization in the form of legal consultation or representation.

3. A list prepared by management that describes and evaluates unasserted claims and assessments that management considers to be probable of assertion, and that, if asserted, would have at least a reasonable possibility of an unfavorable outcome, with respect to which the attorney has been engaged and to which he or she has devoted substantive attention on behalf of the not-for-profit organization in the form of legal consultation or representation.

4. As to each of the matters identified in (2) above, a request that the attorney furnish the following information or comment on those matters on which his or her views may differ from those stated by management, as appropriate:

   a. A description of the nature of the matter, the progress of the case to date, and the action that the not-for-profit organization intends to take, such as protesting the matter vigorously or seeking an out-of-court settlement.

   b. An evaluation of the likelihood of an unfavorable outcome and an estimate, if one can be made, of the amount or range of the potential loss.

   c. If the list is prepared by management, an identification of the omission of any pending or threatened litigation, claims, and assessments or a statement that the list of such matters is complete.

5. As to each matter listed in item (3) above, a request that the attorney comment on those matters on which his or her views concerning the description or evaluation of the matter may differ from those stated by management.

6. A statement by the not-for-profit organization that it understands that whenever the attorney, in the course of performing legal services for the not-for-profit organization with respect to a matter recognized to involve an unasserted possible claim or assessment that may call for financial statement disclosure, has formed a professional conclusion that the not-for-profit organization should disclose or consider disclosing such possible claims or assessment, the attorney, as a matter of professional responsibility to the not-for-profit organization, will so advise the not-for-profit organization and will consult with the not-for-profit organization concerning the question of such disclosure and the applicable requirements of FAS-5 (Accounting for Contingencies).

7.   A request that the attorney confirm whether the understanding described in item (6) is correct.

8.   A request that the attorney specifically identify the nature of and reasons for any limitations on his or her response.

A sample letter that may be used for making the above inquiries and requests to an attorney is included in Exhibit 9-3.

The most difficult part of making inquiries of a client's attorney is obtaining a response that is acceptable to the auditor. Attorneys often refer to the American Bar Association's "Statement of Policy Regarding Lawyers' Responses to Auditors' Request for Information," which explains concerns lawyers have in responding to audit inquiry letters and the nature of the limitations placed on them.

An attorney may limit his or her response to matters to which he or she has given substantive attention in the form of legal consultation. An attorney's response also may be limited to matters that are considered individually or collectively material to the financial statements, provided the attorney and auditor have reached an understanding of the limits of materiality for this purpose. These two limitations are not considered to be limitations on the scope of the audit.

However, other limitations in the responses of attorneys may be considered limitations on the scope of the audit that would be sufficient to preclude an unqualified opinion on the financial statements. An attorney's refusal to furnish the information described above in an inquiry letter either in writing or orally would be considered a scope limitation that would preclude the issuance of an unqualified opinion.

In addition, the attorney may be unable to respond concerning the likelihood of an unfavorable outcome of litigation, claims, and assessments or the amount or range of potential loss because of inherent uncertainties. A number of factors may preclude an attorney from reaching conclusions on matters in the inquiry letter, such as a lack of historical experience of the not-for-profit with similar litigation, and the experience of similar organizations may not be readily available. In such circumstances, the auditor ordinarily will conclude that the financial statements are affected by an uncertainty concerning the outcome of a future event that is not susceptible to reasonable estimation and will consider the adequacy of disclosing the uncertainty in the financial statements.

An Interpretation of SAS-12 was issued in January 1997. The Interpretation, titled "Use of Explanatory Language Concerning Unasserted Possible Claims or Assessments in Lawyers' Responses to Audit Inquiry Letters," addresses a concern that the inclusion of certain explanatory comments in responses by lawyers to audit inquiry letters may result in letters not being deemed acceptable to avoid a limitation in the scope of the audit.

EXHIBIT 9-3
ILLUSTRATIVE AUDIT INQUIRY LETTER TO
CLIENT LEGAL COUNSEL IF MANAGEMENT HAS PROVIDED
DETAILS OF LEGAL ACTIONS[1]

[Prepared on client's letterhead]
[Date]
[Name and address of lawyer]

In connection with an audit of our financial statements as of *[insert date of statement of financial position]* and for the *[insert period]* then ended, we have prepared and furnished to our independent auditors *[insert name and address of auditors]* a description and evaluation of certain contingencies, including those set forth below, involving matters with respect to which you have been engaged and to which you have devoted substantive attention on behalf of the Organization *[and any of its subsidiaries, if applicable]* in the form of legal consultation or representation. These contingencies are regarded by us as material for this purpose if they involve claims amounting to more than *[insert materiality dollar amount]*, individually or in the aggregate.

Pending or Threatened Litigation, Asserted Claims, and Assessments

[The client should prepare a list describing all material pending or threatened litigation, asserted claims, and assessments. Ordinarily, such information would include (1) the nature of the matter, including (a) the proceedings, (b) the amount of monetary damages sought, or if no amounts are indicated, a statement to that effect, (c) the extent to which potential damages are covered by insurance, and (d) the objectives sought by the plaintiff other than monetary or other damages, if any; (2) the progress of the matter to date; (3) how management is responding or intends to respond (e.g., to contest the case vigorously or to seek an out-of court settlement); and (4) an evaluation of the likelihood of an unfavorable outcome and an estimate, if one can be made, of the amount or range of potential loss.]

Please furnish to our auditors such explanation, if any, that you consider necessary to supplement the foregoing information, including an explanation of those matters for which your views differ from those stated, and an identification of the omission of any pending or threatened litigation, claims, and assessments, or a statement that the list of such matters is complete. If you cannot express an opinion on the outcome of certain litigation, please so state, together with your reasons for that position.

Unasserted Claims and Assessments (considered by us to be probable of assertion, and, if asserted, to have at least a reasonable possibility of an unfavorable outcome)[2]

[The client should prepare a list describing all such material contingencies. Ordinarily, management's information would include (1) the nature of the matter, (2) how management intends to respond if the claim is asserted, and

(3) an evaluation of the likelihood of an unfavorable outcome and an estimate, if one can be made, of the amount or range of potential loss.]

Please furnish to our auditors an explanation, if any, that you consider necessary to supplement the foregoing information, including an explanation of those matters for which your views differ from those stated.

We understand that whenever, in the course of performing legal services for us with respect to a matter recognized to involve an unasserted possible claim or assessment that may call for financial statement disclosure, you have formed a professional conclusion that we should disclose or consider disclosure concerning such possible claim or assessment, as a matter of professional responsibility to us, you will so advise us and will consult with us concerning the question of such disclosure and the applicable requirements of Statement of Financial Accounting Standards No. 5 (excerpts of which can be found in the ABA's Auditor's Letter Handbook). Please specifically confirm to our auditors that our understanding is correct.

We have represented to and assured our auditors that the unasserted claims and assessments mentioned in this letter include all unasserted claims and assessments that you have advised us are probable of assertion and must be disclosed in accordance with Statement of Financial Accounting Standards No. 5.

Other Matters[3]

[The auditor may request the client to inquire about additional matters (e.g., specified information on certain contractually assumed obligations of the Organization, such as guarantees of indebtedness of others).]

Response[4]

Your response should include matters that existed as of *[insert date]* and additional information about those matters or new matters that arose during the period from that date to the effective date of your response.

Please specifically identify the nature of and reasons for any limitation on your response.

We expect to have our audit completed about *[insert expected completion date]*. Therefore, we appreciate receiving your reply by that date with a specified effective date no earlier than *[insert date]*.[5]

Your response will not be quoted or referred to in the Organization's financial statements without prior consultation with you.

Please send your response directly to our auditors, with a copy to me.

Thank you for your anticipated timely cooperation with this request.

Respectfully,
[Name of client]

[Client's authorized signature and title]

---

[1] This letter generally should be used if the client prepares an audit inquiry letter that includes a list describing and evaluating all material pending or threatened litigation, asserted claims, and assessments. Therefore, the letter is sent to the client legal counsel to obtain corroboration of information furnished by management to the auditor.

[2] This letter assumes that the client specifies certain unasserted claims and assessments. If management believes that there are no unasserted claims or assessments to be specified to the lawyer for comment that are probable of assertion and that, if asserted, would have a reasonable possibility of an unfavorable outcome, the unasserted claims and assessments section should be replaced in its entirety by the following:

Unasserted Claims and Assessments

We have represented to our auditors that there are no unasserted possible claims or assessments that you have advised us are probable of assertion and must be disclosed in accordance with Statement of Financial Accounting Standards No. 5 (excerpts of which can be found in the ABA's Auditor's Letter Handbook).

We understand that whenever, in the course of performing legal services for us with respect to a matter recognized to involve an unasserted possible claim or assessment that may call for financial statement disclosure, you have formed a professional conclusion that we should disclose or consider disclosure concerning such possible claim or assessment, as a matter of professional responsibility to us, you will so advise us and will consult with us concerning the question of such disclosure and the applicable requirements of Statement of Financial Accounting Standards No. 5. Please specifically confirm to our auditors that our understanding is correct.

[3] The auditor may wish to confirm with legal counsel the amount owed by the client for legal services. Accordingly, language similar to the following would be appropriate:

"Please indicate the amount owed to you for services and expenses, billed and unbilled, as of [*insert date of statement of financial position*]."

[4] In some cases, to emphasize the preservation of the attorney–client privilege or the attorney work-product privilege, clients have included language similar to the following in the audit inquiry letter to legal counsel:

"We do not intend that either our request to you to provide information to our auditor or your response to our auditor should be construed in any way to constitute a waiver of the attorney–client privilege or the attorney work-product privilege."

The explanatory language about the attorney–client privilege or the attorney work-product privilege does not result in a limitation on the scope of the audit. Such language simply makes explicit what has always been implicit: that the client's request does not constitute an expression of intent to waive such privileges.

[5] Ordinarily, a two-week period should be allowed between the specified effective date of the lawyer's response and the expected completion date of the audit.

Lawyers sometimes include explanatory comments in their responses to audit inquiry letters that are intended to emphasize the preservation of the attorney–client privilege with respect to unasserted possible claims or assessments. An example of these comments is as follows:

> It would be inappropriate for this firm to respond to a general inquiry relating to the existence of unasserted possible claims or assessments involving the organization.

The Interpretation states that the inclusion of this or similar wording in a lawyer's response does not result in a limitation on the scope of the audit. The Interpretation also reaffirms to auditors the requirement of SAS-12 to obtain the lawyer's acknowledgment of his or her responsibility to advise and consult with the client concerning financial statement disclosure obligations with respect to unasserted possible claims or assessments.

> **OBSERVATION:** A significant exposure for an auditor in the area of attorney inquiry letters is to accept as appropriate a response to an inquiry letter that has not provided the information required by SAS-12. The auditor should read every line of the response carefully to ensure that the attorney has not avoided responding to one or more of the inquiries through the use of clever qualifying language. Wherever necessary, the auditor should obtain, at a minimum, oral clarification of any qualifications. It is even more desirable to have the attorney reissue any response that, in the judgment of the auditor, is unacceptable. In the not-for-profit environment, it is sometimes more difficult to obtain acceptable attorney responses, particularly where legal services are being provided by the attorney on a pro bono basis, and the attorney is attempting to minimize his or her risk by limiting the response.

GOING-CONCERN CONSIDERATIONS

As part of the audit of the financial statements of a not-for-profit organization, the auditor should evaluate the not-for-profit organization's ability to continue as a going concern. The considerations that should be made and other audit requirements are specified in SAS-59 (The Auditor's Consideration of an Entity's Ability to Continue as a Going Concern). According to SAS-59, an auditor should assume an organization will continue as a going concern unless there is significant information to the contrary. To significantly contradict the going-concern assumption, information obtained would relate to a not-for-profit organization's inability to continue to meet its obligations as they become due without substantial disposition of assets outside the ordinary course of business, restructuring of debt, externally forced revisions, or similar actions.

SAS-59 states that any auditor has a responsibility to evaluate whether substantial doubt exists about an entity's ability to continue as a going concern for a reasonable period of time (not to exceed one year beyond the date of the financial statements being audited). This requirement can be particularly significant for not-for-profit organizations that rely on one or a few grants or contracts to provide a majority of their funding. If the renewal of these grants or contracts is in doubt, substantial doubt may exist about a not-for-profit organization's ability to continue as a going concern.

When evaluating an entity's ability to continue as a going concern for a reasonable period of time, the auditor should consider whether the results of procedures performed in planning, gathering evidential matter relative to the various audit objectives, and completing the audit identify conditions and events that, when considered in the aggregate, indicate substantial doubt exists about the not-for-profit organization's ability to continue as a going concern for a reasonable period of time. The auditor may find it necessary to obtain additional information about such conditions and events, as well as the appropriate evidential matter to support information that mitigates the auditor's doubt.

It is not necessary to design audit procedures solely to identify conditions and events that, when considered in the aggregate, indicate substantial doubt exists about a not-for-profit organization's ability to continue as a going concern. The results of audit procedures already performed to meet other audit objectives should be sufficient for that purpose.

> **OBSERVATION:** The chapter of this Guide titled "Audit Planning" addresses when going-concern considerations may arise because of the Year 2000 Issue.

Examples of audit procedures that may identify conditions and events that may indicate substantial doubt about an organization's ability to continue as a going concern include:

- Analytical procedures
- Review of subsequent events
- Review of compliance with the terms of debt and loan agreements
- Reading of minutes of meetings of the board of trustees and its committees

- Inquiry of the not-for-profit organization's legal counsel about litigation, claims, and assessments
- Confirmation with related and third parties of the details of arrangements to provide or maintain financial support

When performing these audit procedures, the auditor may identify conditions or events that, when considered in the aggregate, indicate that substantial doubt may exist about a not-for-profit organization's ability to continue as a going concern. The following are examples of these conditions and events:

- Negative trends, such as recurring excesses of expenditures over revenues, negative cash flows, and adverse key financial ratios
- Other indications of possible financial difficulties, such as defaults on loan or similar agreements, denial of usual trade credit from suppliers, need to seek new sources or methods of financing or to dispose of substantial assets, or recurring emergency transfers from investment funds designated by the board of trustees
- Internal matters, such as work stoppages or other labor difficulties, substantial dependence on the success of a particular project, uneconomic long-term commitments, or the need to significantly revise operations
- External matters, such as legal proceedings, legislation, or similar matters that might jeopardize a not-for-profit organization's ability to operate, loss of a principal contractor or grantor or supplier, uninsured or underinsured catastrophe, such as a drought, earthquake, or flood
- Insufficient unrestricted revenues to provide supporting services to activities funded by restricted contributions
- A high ratio of fund-raising expenses to contributions received or a low ratio of program expenses to total expenses
- Insufficient resources to meet donor's restrictions, particularly when restricted net assets are used for purposes that do not satisfy the donor's restrictions
- Activities that could jeopardize the not-for-profit organization's tax-exempt status and thus endanger current contribution levels
- Concerns expressed by governmental authorities regarding alleged violations of state laws governing a not-for-profit organization's maintenance or preservation of certain assets, such as collection items
- A loss of key governing board members or volunteers

- Events that could affect donors' motivations to continue to contribute
- Decrease in revenues contributed by repeat donors
- A loss of a major funding source
- Impact of the Year 2000 Issue on the not-for-profit organization, including donors, customers, and vendors.

If the auditor believes that substantial doubt exists about the not-for-profit organization's ability to continue as a going concern for a reasonable period of time, he or she should:

- Obtain information about management's plans that are intended to mitigate the effect of such conditions or events, and
- Assess the likelihood that such plans can be effectively implemented.

When evaluating management's plans, the auditor may consider the following factors that might affect management's plans:

- Plans to dispose of assets
- Restrictions on the disposal of assets, such as covenants limiting such transactions in loan or similar agreements or encumbrances against assets, both of which may be the result of donor-imposed restrictions
- Apparent marketability of assets that management plans to sell
- Possible direct or indirect effects of the disposal of assets
- Plans to borrow money or restructure debt
- Availability of debt financing, including existing or committed credit arrangements, such as lines of credit or arrangement for factoring receivables or the sale-leaseback of assets
- Existing or committed arrangements to restructure or subordinate debt or to guarantee loans to the not-for-profit
- Possible effects on management's borrowing plans of existing restrictions on additional borrowing or the sufficiency of available capital
- Plans to reduce or delay expenditures
- Apparent feasibility of plans to reduce overhead or administrative expenditures, to postpone maintenance or research and development projects, or to lease rather than purchase assets
- Possible direct or indirect effects of reduced or delayed expenditures
- Plans to increase the not-for-profit organization's capital

- Apparent feasibility of plans to increase capital, such as the anticipated success of capital fund-raising campaigns
- Apparent feasibility of for-profit subsidiaries' existing or committed arrangements to accelerate cash distributions to the not-for-profit organization

After the auditor has evaluated management's plans, he or she should determine whether he or she has substantial doubt about the not-for-profit organization's ability to continue as a going concern for a reasonable period of time. If the auditor concludes substantial doubt exists, he or she should:

- Consider the adequacy of disclosure about the not-for-profit organization's possible inability to continue as a going concern for a reasonable period of time, and
- Include an explanatory paragraph (following the opinion paragraph) in his or her report to reflect the conclusion.

SAS-77 [Amendments to Statements on Auditing Standards No. 22 (Planning and Supervision), SAS-59 (The Auditor's Consideration of an Entity's Ability to Continue as a Going Concern), and SAS-62 (Special Reports)] modified the acceptable language that an auditor may use in an explanatory paragraph of an auditor's report to emphasize a going-concern problem.

SAS-77 precludes an auditor from using conditional language in the auditor's conclusion about the organization's ability to continue as a going concern in a going concern explanatory paragraph. SAS-77 provides examples of acceptable and unacceptable language:

Acceptable conclusion language

- The accompanying financial statements have been prepared assuming that the Company will continue as a going concern. As discussed in Note X to the financial statements, the Company has suffered recurring losses from operations and has a net capital deficiency that raises substantial doubt about its ability to continue as a going concern. Management's plans in regard to these matters are also described in Note X. The financial statements do not include any adjustments that might result from the outcome of this uncertainty.

Unacceptable conclusion language

- If the Company continues to suffer recurring losses from operations and continues to have a net capital deficiency, there may be substantial doubt about its ability to continue as a going concern.

or

- The Company has been unable to renegotiate its expiring credit agreements. Unless the Company is able to obtain financial support, there is substantial doubt about its ability to continue as a going concern.

The auditor should note that the explanatory paragraph included in his or her report is not considered a departure from the standard report in terms of uncertainties or departures from generally accepted accounting principles.

The auditor may conclude that the not-for-profit organization has not made adequate disclosures in its financial statements of circumstances that indicate substantial doubt about the organization's ability to continue as a going concern. The auditor may consider this lack of disclosure to be a departure from generally accepted accounting principles, and may include this departure in the "except for" report format or may issue an adverse opinion.

The auditor should clearly document any of the considerations made in the working papers. In addition, where the auditor has no reason to believe that substantial doubt exists about the not-for-profit organization's ability to continue as a going concern and does not perform any additional procedures, the working papers should document that the auditor considered the going-concern assumptions when performing standard audit procedures.

SUMMARIZING AND EVALUATING RESULTS

SAS-47 (Audit Risk and Materiality in Conducting an Audit) includes guidance for evaluating audit findings. The auditor should aggregate misstatements that the not-for-profit organization has not corrected in a way that enables him or her to consider whether, in relation to individual amounts, subtotals, or totals in the financial statements, they materially misstate the financial statements taken as a whole. Qualitative considerations also influence an auditor in reaching a conclusion on whether misstatements are material.

The auditor should consider both known and projected misstatements. *Known misstatements* are misstatements the auditor has specifically identified. *Projected misstatements* are those misstatements an auditor estimates. For example, analytical procedures that indicate a potential misstatement may result in the auditor projecting what the misstatement might be rather than calculating a precise amount. Similarly, where an auditor uses sampling and discovers misstatements in the items tested, two components of misstatement exist: (1) the actual errors in the sample items tested are known misstatements and (2) the projection of the known misstatements of the sample items to the entire population from which the sample items were selected is a projected misstatement. Similarly, where accounting estimates are included in the not-for-profit organization's accounts, differences in the auditor's estimate of an account and the recorded amount are considered projected misstatements.

The auditor should consider both types of misstatements when evaluating the results of the audit and determining whether the financial statements of the not-for-profit organization are fairly presented in accordance with generally accepted accounting principles. In addition, the auditor should consider the known and projected misstatements from the prior year that would affect the current year's financial statements.

> **OBSERVATION:** For example, if the allowance for uncollectible pledges receivable was projected by the auditor to be misstated by the same amount in both the prior and current year, with no adjustment to the allowance account being made by the not-for-profit organization in either year, the statement of changes in net assets would not be misstated in the current year.

If the auditor determines that the likely misstatement of the financial statements (the likely misstatement is the combination of the known and projected error) is material, the auditor may take one of several actions, including:

- Request that the not-for-profit organization record adjustments to the financial statements at least to the extent that the auditor's calculation of likely misstatement is reduced to an amount acceptable to the auditor. Auditors generally are more successful convincing not-for-profit organizations to record known misstatements rather than projected misstatements.

- In areas where there are projected misstatements, the auditor may perform additional audit procedures to fine-tune the projections, which may result in the projected (and likely) levels of misstatement being reduced to an acceptable level.

For example, if there is a possibility that the results of an audit sample are not representative of the population, additional sample items may be tested to reevaluate the projection of the known error to the entire population. If the not-for-profit organization and the auditor disagree on the amount of the allowance for uncollectible pledges receivable, the auditor may expand his or her audit procedures for subsequent cash collections of these pledges to provide more evidence about the appropriate amount of the allowance account.

- If resolution of an unacceptable level of likely misstatement in the financial statements cannot be obtained, the auditor should issue either an opinion qualified for a departure from generally accepted accounting principles or, if the likely misstatement is of greater significance, an adverse opinion.

The evaluation of audit findings also includes considering the adequacy and appropriateness of the disclosures in the financial statements. However, where the auditor and the not-for-profit organization disagree on the accounting treatment of a particular item, the auditor should not to try to "cure" the problem by having the not-for-profit organization expand the disclosure of the accounting treatment in the financial statements. Additional disclosures do not resolve departures from generally accepted accounting principles.

FINAL REVIEW AND COMPLETION OF THE WORKING PAPERS

Near the conclusion of the audit fieldwork, the auditor should begin to identify open items that must be resolved to complete the audit fieldwork and issue his or her report in accordance with generally accepted auditing standards. It is almost impossible to complete an audit without missing some form of documentation or overlooking some audit procedures. In fact, it is more efficient during the fieldwork phase not to delay proceeding until an open item has been cleared.

Some typical open items that are not resolved until the final stages of the audit fieldwork are the following:

- Documents that could not be located during the course of the audit that must be read and/or tested

- Inquiries of client personnel that could not be completed because of their unavailability during the course of the audit fieldwork

- Confirmations, such as confirmations of bank balances and receivables, that have not been received

- Letters of inquiry to the recipient organization's attorneys that either have not been received or have been received in a format that is not satisfactory to the auditor

- Final audit reports or representations that have not been received from other auditors participating in the audit of the recipient organization or its affiliated organizations

- Copies of the minutes of the board of directors and its various committee meetings, particularly the minutes of the meetings closest to the last day of fieldwork of the audit

This is only a brief listing of possible open items. Numerous other items may remain open at the end of the audit. The auditor should have a good control listing of open items that must be cleared and completed before the required reports can be issued.

The control list of open items facilitates the review of the audit working papers, because the reviewer will be able to review a section of the audit even though several items may still be open. If the reviewer is satisfied that the open items are recorded on a control listing, the reviewer will be able to check the open items after the initial review is completed.

The review procedures and methodology for an audit of a not-for-profit organization should be fairly consistent with those for an audit of a commercial enterprise in accordance with generally accepted auditing standards. The following provides a brief outline of the structure of the review procedures and policies that should be employed.

Audit working papers should be reviewed by the senior accountant in charge of the audit fieldwork. This review should be done promptly as the work progresses so the accountant preparing the working papers can address the review comments as soon as possible. A prompt review also will inform the in-charge accountant of any problems, difficulties, or findings that have been discovered during the course of the test work. The in-charge accountant can then make an initial assessment of their potential impact on the planned audit strategy. The in-charge accountant should document his or her review by initialing each individual working paper reviewed.

An individual senior to the in-charge accountant should perform a second-level review of the working papers. If the audit engagement or audit firm is large enough, the second review is often assigned to an audit manager. The second-level review should be performed after the in-charge accountant's review comments have been cleared by the individual preparing the working papers. If it is a small engagement or a small audit firm, the individual signing the accountant's reports (i.e., either a partner in the audit firm or the sole practitioner) should perform the second review. Again, this review of each of the working papers should be documented by having the reviewer initial each working paper reviewed.

If the second-level review is performed by an audit manager, then the partner (or sole practitioner) who will sign the accountant's reports should perform an additional review of the audit working papers. This individual may determine that he or she does not need to review every audit working paper. However, the individual should review working papers related to the critical or significant audit areas and the general working papers related to matters such as responses of the recipient organization's attorneys to letters of inquiry and the client representation letter received. This review should be clearly documented in the working papers, such as by the preparation of a memorandum, supplemented by the initialing of individual working papers that have been reviewed.

Most audit firms also have the accountant's reports, financial statements, and key working papers reviewed by a second partner not otherwise associated with the audit engagement. This type of "cold review" is meant not only to address reporting issues and presentations, but also to provide an additional check that the audit firm's quality control procedures have been adhered to and to ensure that the significant and critical audit areas have been adequately addressed. Documentation of the review by the second partner is most frequently accomplished through the preparation of a brief memorandum to be included in the audit working papers.

A sole practitioner performing audits of not-for-profit organizations in accordance with generally accepted auditing standards will not have a second partner to complete the cold review. Many sole practitioners have the accountant's reports and financial statements reviewed by another certified public accountant before their issuance. This second review is highly recommended, and it gives the sole practitioner an opportunity to discuss any difficult decisions that were made during the course of the audit or the drafting of the reports. These discussions can make the sole practitioner more comfortable with the decisions that he or she has already made or can highlight areas where changes might be appropriate.

> **OBSERVATION:** Reviewers should make sure that their comments have been addressed adequately before accountant's reports are released. Reviewers should make sure that the working papers have been changed to address the comments and questions raised by the reviewer.

At the conclusion of all of the reviews, any lists of review comments and questions should be destroyed, so that the working papers stand alone as the auditor's evidence of performing the audit. Lists of review comments, even if they contain only questions or comments that have been adequately addressed, can provide a road map of audit difficulties useful to hostile parties who, in the future, may review the working papers. Such parties will include litigants if the audit is challenged in court.

In addition, a recent court finding of various audit working paper "clean-up" procedures that were performed well after the issuance of the auditor's report may prove to be an expensive oversight for that auditor in not completing the working papers before the issuance of the auditor's opinion on the financial statements.

SUMMARY

Performing audit procedures relating to client representations, commitments, contingencies, subsequent events, and consideration of an organization's ability to continue as a going concern are important audit matters that should be given the appropriate high level of attention by the auditor. In addition, the auditor should make sure that he or she has adequately summarized, reviewed, and concluded on the results of his or her audit findings. This consideration, and the final review and wrap-up of the audit working papers, should be completed before the auditor's opinion is issued.

CHAPTER 10
REPORTING

CONTENTS

CHAPTER 10
REPORTING

CROSS-REFERENCES

2001 MILLER NOT-FOR-PROFIT ORGANIZATION AUDITS: Chapter 18, "Reporting Under Circular A-133"

2001 MILLER AUDIT PROCEDURES: Chapter 22: "Auditor's Reports"

2000 MILLER GAAS GUIDE: Section 380, "Communication with Audit Committees"; Section 508, "Reports on Audited Financial Statements"; Section 530, "Dating of the Independent Auditor's Report"; Section 532, "Restricting the Use of an Auditor's Report"; Section 543, "Part of Audit Performed by Other Independent Auditors"; Section 544, "Lack of Conformity with Generally Accepted Accounting Principles"

The reporting for an audit of a not-for-profit organization is the same as that for a commercial enterprise. The auditing standards and reporting examples are derived from the same standards.

For convenience, the report examples contained in this chapter have been tailored wherever possible to make them easier to use for audits of not-for-profit organizations. For example, the statements listed in the sample audit reports conform with statement names applicable to not-for-profit organizations.

The three aspects of reporting on the audit of the financial statements of a not-for-profit organization are as follows:

1. Auditor's report on the financial statements (and supplementary information, if applicable)

2. Reporting of required information to the board of trustees of the not-for-profit organization

3. Preparation of an effective management letter for communicating the auditor's suggestions for improvement of operations or controls and, if applicable, reportable conditions and material weaknesses in internal control

AUDITOR'S REPORT

The primary authoritative source of guidance for reporting on the financial statements of a not-for-profit organization is SAS-58 (Reports on Audited Financial Statements). SAS-58 applies to auditor's reports issued in connection with audits of historical financial statements that are intended to present financial position, results of operations, and cash flows in conformity with generally accepted accounting principles.

A secondary authoritative source of guidance is SAS-62 (Special Reports). SAS-62 applies to auditor's reports issued in connection with the following:

- Financial statements that are prepared in conformity with a comprehensive basis of accounting other than generally accepted accounting principles

- Specified elements, accounts, or items of a financial statement

- Compliance with aspects of contractual agreements or regulatory requirements related to audited financial statements

- Financial presentations to comply with contractual agreements or regulatory provisions

- Financial information presented in prescribed forms or schedules that require a prescribed form of auditor's report

In addition, an Interpretation of SAS-62 (Reports on the Financial Statements Included in Internal Revenue Form 990, "Return of Organizations Exempt from Income Tax") provides guidance and a report example for use when an auditor is requested to express an opinion on financial statements presented on Form 990.

The following reporting guidance also reflects SAS-77 (Amendments to Statement on Auditing Standards No. 22, "Planning and Supervision," No. 59, "The Auditor's Consideration of an Entity's Ability to Continue as a Going Concern," No. 62, "Special Reports"), which modifies the language permitted for an explanatory paragraph regarding going concern considerations and SAS-87 (Restricting the Use of an Auditor's Report). SAS-79 eliminates the requirement that, when certain conditions are met, the auditor add an uncertainties explanatory paragraph to the auditor's report.

The following reports will be discussed in this chapter, along with reporting examples:

Unqualified Opinions

- Unqualified opinion on financial statements

- Unqualified opinion on comparative financial statements

- Unqualified opinion on financial statements of a voluntary health and welfare organization that include a statement of functional expenses.

- Unqualified opinion on financial statements that refer to the report(s) of other auditor(s)

- Unqualified opinion on financial statements with an explanatory paragraph

Auditor's Reports with Modifications

- Qualified opinion on financial statements because of a departure from generally accepted accounting principles

- Qualified opinion on financial statements because of a scope limitation

- Adverse opinion on financial statements for departures from generally accepted accounting principles

- Disclaimer of opinion on financial statements for scope limitations

Other Auditor's Reports

- Reporting on a comprehensive basis of accounting other than generally accepted accounting principles

  — Report on a cash basis of accounting

  — Report on financial statements included in Form 990

- Reporting on condensed financial information in a client-prepared document

Unqualified Opinion on Financial Statements

An unqualified opinion on financial statements states that the financial statements of the not-for-profit organization present fairly, in all material respects, the organization's financial position, results of activities, and cash flows in conformity with generally accepted accounting principles. This opinion should be expressed only when the audit has been performed in accordance with generally accepted auditing standards. The form of the auditor's standard report on the financial statements of a not-for-profit organization is shown in Exhibit 10-1.

EXHIBIT 10-1
UNQUALIFIED OPINION ON FINANCIAL STATEMENTS

Independent Auditor's Report

To Board of Trustees

[*Name of not-for-profit organization*]

We have audited the accompanying statement of financial position of [*name of not-for-profit organization*] as of [*date of statement of financial position*], and the related statements of activities and cash flows for the year then ended. These financial statements are the responsibility of [*name of not-for-profit organization*]'s management. Our responsibility is to express an opinion on these financial statements based on our audit.

We conducted our audit in accordance with generally accepted auditing standards. Those standards require that we plan and perform the audit to obtain reasonable assurance about whether the financial statements are free of material misstatement. An audit includes examining, on a test basis, evidence supporting the amounts and disclosures in the financial statements. An audit also includes assessing the accounting principles used and significant estimates made by management, as well as evaluating the overall financial statement presentation. We believe that our audit provides a reasonable basis for our opinion.

In our opinion, the financial statements referred to above present fairly, in all material respects, the financial position of [*name of not-for-profit organization*] as of [*date of statement of financial position*], and the changes in its net assets and its cash flows for the year then ended in conformity with generally accepted accounting principles.

[*Signature of Firm*]

[*Name of City, State*]

[*Date of the completion of fieldwork*]

Notes to the auditor's report:
1. The title of the report should include the word "independent."
2. The report is addressed to the governing board, in the sample report, to the board of trustees. The report could be addressed to the organization itself.

Unqualified Opinion on Comparative Financial Statements

Before the adoption of FAS-117, not-for-profit organizations often did not present comparative financial statements. Because of the usually cumbersome columnar presentations previously made of fund information, prior-year information generally was presented only in total amounts that were derived from the basic financial statements.

With the adoption of FAS-117, comparative financial statements with complete information for the prior year will be clearer and easier to present, and comparative statements most likely will become the normal reporting format for not-for-profit organizations.

The sample report shown in Exhibit 10-2 would be used to report on the comparative financial statements of a not-for-profit organization in the years subsequent to the initial adoption of FAS-117.

Unqualified Opinion on Financial Statements of a Voluntary Health and Welfare Organization That Include a Statement of Functional Expenses

FAS-117 requires not-for-profit organizations that are voluntary health and welfare organizations to provide information about expenses by their natural classification, such as salaries, rent, electricity, interest expense, depreciation, awards and grants to others, and professional fees. This information is in addition to information about expenses by their functional classification, such as major classes of program services and supporting services, and should be presented in a matrix format in a separate financial statement. Not-for-profit organizations that are *not* voluntary health and welfare organizations are encouraged, but not required, to present this information.

The auditor should use the auditor's report shown in Exhibit 10-3 when the not-for-profit organization presents the information as one of the basic financial statements.

Unqualified Opinion on Financial Statements of a Not-for-Profit Organization That Voluntarily Includes Information on Functional Expenses as Supplemental Information

Not-for-profit organizations that are not voluntary health and welfare organizations are encouraged, but not required, to present information on natural expense classifications. Many of the not-for-profit organizations that elect to provide such information will do so by providing the same information found in a statement of functional

---

EXHIBIT 10-2
UNQUALIFIED OPINION ON
COMPARATIVE FINANCIAL STATEMENTS

Independent Auditor's Report

To Board of Trustees
[*Name of not-for-profit organization*]

We have audited the accompanying statements of financial position of [*name of not-for-profit organization*] as of [*dates of statements of financial position for the two years presented*], and the related statements of activities and cash flows for the years then ended. These financial statements are the responsibility of [*name of not-for-profit organization*]'s management. Our responsibility is to express an opinion on these financial statements based on our audits.

We conducted our audits in accordance with generally accepted auditing standards. Those standards require that we plan and perform the audit to obtain reasonable assurance about whether the financial statements are free of material misstatement. An audit includes examining, on a test basis, evidence supporting the amounts and disclosures in the financial statements. An audit also includes assessing the accounting principles used and significant estimates made by management, as well as evaluating the overall financial statement presentation. We believe that our audits provide a reasonable basis for our opinion.

In our opinion, the financial statements referred to above present fairly, in all material respects, the financial position of [*name of not-for-profit organization*] as of [*dates of statements of financial position for the two years presented*], and the changes in its net assets and its cash flows for the years then ended in conformity with generally accepted accounting principles.

[*Signature of Firm*]

[*Name of City, State*]

[*Date of the completion of fieldwork*]

Notes to the auditor's report:
1. The title of the report should include the word "independent."
2. The report is addressed to the governing board, in the sample report, to the board of trustees. The report could be addressed to the organization itself.
3. The report on comparative financial statements refers to the audits performed in the plural form, since there were two separate audits of the financial statements (i.e., one audit for each year presented). However, only one opinion is being presented, which is why the reference to the opinion is singular.

EXHIBIT 10-3
UNQUALIFIED OPINION ON FINANCIAL STATEMENTS OF A VOLUNTARY HEALTH AND WELFARE ORGANIZATION THAT INCLUDE A STATEMENT OF FUNCTIONAL EXPENSES

Independent Auditor's Report

To Board of Trustees
[*Name of not-for-profit organization*]

We have audited the accompanying statement of financial position of [*name of not-for-profit organization*] as of [*date of statement of financial position*], and the related statements of activities, functional expenses, and cash flows for the year then ended. These financial statements are the responsibility of the [*name of not-for-profit organization*]'s management. Our responsibility is to express an opinion on these financial statements based on our audit.

We conducted our audit in accordance with generally accepted auditing standards. Those standards require that we plan and perform the audit to obtain reasonable assurance about whether the financial statements are free of material misstatement. An audit includes examining, on a test basis, evidence supporting the amounts and disclosures in the financial statements. An audit also includes assessing the accounting principles used and significant estimates made by management, as well as evaluating the overall financial statement presentation. We believe that our audit provides a reasonable basis for our opinion.

In our opinion, the financial statements referred to above present fairly, in all material respects, the financial position of [*name of not-for-profit organization*] as of [*date of statement of financial position*], and the changes in its net assets and its cash flows for the year then ended in conformity with generally accepted accounting principles.

[*Signature of Firm*]

[*Name of City, State*]

[*Date of the completion of fieldwork*]

Notes to the auditor's report:
1. The title of the report should include the word "independent."
2. The report could be addressed to the organization itself.

expenses in a schedule that is provided as supplementary information. The auditor should report on this schedule in relation to the basic financial statements. The sample auditor's report shown in Exhibit 10-4 may be used in these circumstances.

The auditor also may choose to report on the schedule of functional expenses as supplemental information through the use of a stand-alone report that precedes the actual schedule of functional expenses, and that refers to the auditor's report on the basic financial statements. An example of such a stand-alone report is shown in Exhibit 10-5.

Unqualified Opinion of Financial Statements That Refers to the Report(s) of Other Auditor(s)

An auditor may be requested to opine on the financial statements of a not-for-profit organization that include certain net assets and changes in net assets that have been audited by other auditors. As described more fully in Statement of Position (SOP) 94-3 (Reporting of Related Entities by Not-for-Profit Organizations), a not-for-profit organization may have for-profit subsidiaries and affiliated not-for-profit organizations whose financial statements are consolidated with those of the not-for-profit organization. The financial statements of these for-profit subsidiaries or affiliated not-for-profit organizations may be audited by other auditors. In addition, there may be other divisions, branches, or components of the not-for-profit organization that are audited by other auditors.

When other auditors have audited one or more components of the not-for-profit organization on which the auditor is reporting, the audit should make several considerations.

First, the auditor should reaffirm whether it is appropriate to serve as principal auditor. If significant parts of the audit have been performed by other auditors, the auditor must decide whether his or her participation is sufficient to enable him or her to serve as the principal auditor and to report as such on the financial statements. In deciding this question, the auditor should consider, among other things, the following:

- The materiality of the portion of the financial statements he or she has audited in comparison with the portion audited by other auditors

- The extent of his or her knowledge of the overall financial statements

- The importance of the components he or she audited in relation to the not-for-profit organization as a whole

EXHIBIT 10-4
UNQUALIFIED OPINION ON FINANCIAL STATEMENTS
OF A NOT-FOR-PROFIT ORGANIZATION THAT VOLUNTARILY
INCLUDE INFORMATION ON FUNCTIONAL EXPENSES AS
SUPPLEMENTAL INFORMATION

Independent Auditor's Report

To Board of Trustees
[*Name of not-for-profit organization*]

We have audited the accompanying statement of financial position of [*name of not-for-profit organization*] as of [*date of statement of financial position*], and the related statements of activities and cash flows for the year then ended. These financial statements are the responsibility of [*name of not-for-profit organization*]'s management. Our responsibility is to express an opinion on these financial statements based on our audit.

We conducted our audit in accordance with generally accepted auditing standards. Those standards require that we plan and perform the audit to obtain reasonable assurance about whether the financial statements are free of material misstatement. An audit includes examining, on a test basis, evidence supporting the amounts and disclosures in the financial statements. An audit also includes assessing the accounting principles used and significant estimates made by management, as well as evaluating the overall financial statement presentation. We believe that our audit provides a reasonable basis for our opinion.

In our opinion, the financial statements referred to above present fairly, in all material respects, the financial position of [*name of not-for-profit organization*] as of [*date of statement of financial position*], and the changes in its net assets and its cash flows for the year then ended in conformity with generally accepted accounting principles.

Our audit was conducted for the purpose of forming an opinion on the basic financial statements taken as a whole. The schedule of functional expenses on page [X] is presented for purposes of additional analysis and is not a required part of the basic financial statements. Such information has been subjected to the auditing procedures applied in the audit of the basic financial statements and, in our opinion, is fairly stated in all material respects in relation to the basic financial statements taken as a whole.

[*Signature of Firm*]

[*Name of City, State*]

[*Date of the completion of fieldwork*]

Notes to the auditor's report:

1. The title of the report should include the word "independent."

2. The report is addressed to the governing board, in the sample report, to the board of trustees. The report could be addressed to the organization itself.

EXHIBIT 10-5
STAND-ALONE REPORT ON
SUPPLEMENTAL INFORMATION

Independent Auditor's Report

To Board of Trustees
[*Name of not-for-profit organization*]

Our report on our audit of the basic financial statements of [*name of not-for-profit organization*] appears on page [X]. We conducted our audit in accordance with generally accepted auditing standards for the purpose of forming an opinion on the basic financial statements taken as a whole. The schedule of functional expenses on page [X] is presented for purposes of additional analysis and is not a required part of the basic financial statements. Such information has been subjected to the auditing procedures applied in the audit of the basic financial statements and, in our opinion, is fairly stated, in all material respects, in relation to the basic financial statements taken as a whole.

[*Signature of Firm*]

[*Name of City, State*]

[*Date of the completion of fieldwork*]

Notes to the auditor's report:

1. The title of the report should include the word "independent."

2. The report is addressed to the governing board, in the sample report, to the board of trustees. The report could be addressed to the organization itself.

3. The report in this case indicates that the schedule of functional expenses is not a required part of the basic financial statements. Presently this information as supplemental information would be appropriate only for not-for-profit organizations that are not voluntary health and welfare organizations.

Once the auditor decides that it is appropriate to serve as the principal auditor, he or she must decide whether to make reference to the other auditor or auditors in the auditor's report.

If the auditor decides to assume responsibility for the work of the other auditor as it relates to the auditor's expression of an opinion on the financial statements taken as a whole, no reference should be made to the other auditor's work or report. SAS-1 (Codification of Auditing Standards and Procedures) and SAS-64 (Omnibus Statement on Auditing Standards—1990) contain the guidance for auditors in this area. The auditor may be able to reach a decision not to refer to the work of the other auditor after considering the following conditions:

- Part of the audit is performed by another independent auditor from an associated or correspondent firm and whose work is acceptable to the principal auditor based on his or her knowledge of the professional standards and competence of the firm.
- The other auditor was retained by the principal auditor and the work was performed under the principal auditor's guidance and control.
- The principal auditor, whether or not he or she selected the other auditor, nevertheless takes steps he or she considers necessary to be satisfied about the audit performed by the other auditors and is satisfied about the reasonableness of the accounts for the purpose of inclusion in the financial statements on which the auditor is opining.
- The portion of the financial statements audited by the other auditor is not material to the financial statements covered by the principal auditor's opinion.

Based on the above considerations, the auditor may decide not to refer to the other auditor in the audit report. On the other hand, the auditor may conclude that reference to the other auditor or auditors is appropriate. Should the auditor reach that conclusion, the report sample shown in Exhibit 10-6 may be used to make the reference.

Regardless of whether the principal auditor decides to refer to the other auditor, generally accepted auditing standards prescribe certain procedures and inquiries concerning the professional reputation and independence of the other auditor. The auditor may consider:

- Making inquiries about the professional reputation and standing of the other auditor to one or more of the following:
  - The AICPA, the applicable state society of certified public accountants, and/or the local chapter, or in the case of a foreign auditor, his or her corresponding professional organization.

— Other practitioners.

— Bankers and other grantors.

— Other appropriate sources.

- Obtaining a representation from the other auditor that he or she is independent under AICPA requirements.

- Ensuring through communication with the other auditor the following:

  — That the other auditor is aware that the financial statements of the component he or she is to audit are to be included in the financial statements on which the principal auditor will report, and that the other auditor's report thereon will be relied on (and, where applicable, referred to) by the principal auditor.

  — That the other auditor is familiar with generally accepted accounting principles and with generally accepted auditing standards promulgated by the AICPA and will conduct his or her audit and report in accordance with those principles and standards.

  — That the other auditor has knowledge of the relevant financial reporting requirements for statements and schedules to be filed with regulatory agencies.

  — That a review will be made of matters affecting elimination of intercompany transactions and accounts and, if appropriate in the circumstances, the uniformity of accounting practices among the components included in the financial statements.

EXHIBIT 10-6
UNQUALIFIED OPINION OF FINANCIAL STATEMENTS THAT REFERS TO THE REPORT(S) OF OTHER AUDITOR(S)

Independent Auditor's Report

To Board of Trustees
[*Name of not-for-profit organization*]

We have audited the accompanying statement of financial position of [*name of not-for-profit organization*] as of [*date of statement of financial position*], and the related statements of activities and cash flows for the year then ended. These financial statements are the responsibility of the [*name of not-for-profit organization*]'s management. Our responsibility is to express an opinion on these financial statements based on our audit. We did not audit the financial statements of [*name of affiliated organization*], an affiliated organization, whose statements reflect total assets of $[XX,XXX] as of [*date of statement of financial position*], and total support and revenues of $[XX] for the year then ended. Those statements were audited by other auditors whose report has been furnished to us, and our opinion, insofar as it relates to amounts included for [*name of affiliated organization*], is based solely on the report of other auditors.

We conducted our audit in accordance with generally accepted auditing standards. Those standards require that we plan and perform the audit to obtain reasonable assurance about whether the financial statements are free of material misstatement. An audit includes examining, on a test basis, evidence supporting the amounts and disclosures in the financial statements. An audit also includes assessing the accounting principles used and significant estimates made by management, as well as evaluating the overall financial statement presentation. We believe that our audit provides a reasonable basis for our opinion.

In our opinion, based on our audit and the report of other auditors, the financial statements referred to above present fairly, in all material respects, the financial position of [*name of not-for-profit organization*] as of [*date of statement of financial position*], and the changes in its net assets and its cash flows for the year then ended in conformity with generally accepted accounting principles.

[*Signature of Firm*]

[*Name of City, State*]

[*Date of the completion of fieldwork*]

Notes to the auditor's report:

1. The title of the report should include the word "independent."

2. The report is addressed to the governing board, in the sample report, to the board of trustees. The report could be addressed to the organization itself.

3. This report refers to "financial statements." Depending on the nature of the organization that is included in the financial statements of the not-for-profit organization, these financial statements may be referred to as "combined" or "consolidated," and the language in the above sample opinion should be modified accordingly.

4. If the other auditor's report is not unqualified, the auditor should refer to the report modification and evaluate whether the departure from the standard report of the other auditor involved a matter significant enough to affect the principal auditor's opinion.

OBSERVATION: While some of the considerations of generally accepted auditing standards that relate to foreign auditors
may seem more applicable to multinational corporations than
to not-for-profit organizations, this is not necessarily true. For
example, a significant number of not-for-profit organizations
are conduits for U.S. government aid to Third World countries.
These organizations sometimes have significant operations outside of the United States, and the services of a local auditing
firm are sometimes required to audit these branch locations.

Unqualified Opinion on Financial Statements with an Explanatory Paragraph

Certain circumstances, while not affecting the auditor's unqualified
opinion, may require the auditor to add an explanatory paragraph
(or other explanatory language) to his or her standard report. SAS-
58, as amended by SAS-79, provides a list of these circumstances,
which include, in addition to referring to the work of another auditor, the following:

- To prevent the financial statements from being misleading
  because of unusual circumstances, the financial statements contain a departure from an accounting principle promulgated by
  a body designated by the AICPA Council to establish such
  principles.

- There is substantial doubt about the entity's ability to continue
  as a going concern.

- There has been a material change between periods in accounting principles or in the method of their application.

- Certain circumstances relating to reports or comparative financial statements exist.

- Supplementary information required by the GASB or FASB has
  been omitted or is materially misstated, or the auditor is unable
  to complete prescribed procedures with respect to such information.

- Other information in a document containing audited financial
  statements is materially inconsistent with information appearing in the financial statements.

The explanatory information included in the auditor's report may
be included before or after the opinion paragraph of the report,
although presenting the information after the opinion paragraph is
the more common presentation.

Going-Concern Explanatory Paragraph

SAS-77 clarifies the way in which an auditor may use an explanatory paragraph in an auditor's report to refer to a going-concern conclusion. SAS-59 requires an auditor to reach a conclusion in every audit about whether there is substantial doubt about an organization's ability to continue as a going concern for a reasonable period of time. Experience with auditors' wording of these going-concern explanatory paragraphs indicates that auditors were not making clear in the explanatory paragraphs whether they had actually reached this conclusion.

SAS-77 was issued to amend SAS-59 to preclude the use of conditional language in the auditor's conclusion about the organization's ability to continue as a going concern in a going-concern explanatory paragraph.

The following is an example of acceptable language for a going-concern explanatory paragraph using the guidance of SAS-77:

Uncertainty About Ability to Continue as a Going Concern

As discussed in note [X] to the financial statements, [*name of not-for-profit organization*] has sustained significant reductions in the level of revenues earned under a contract for services with a local government and has a deficiency in its net assets that raise substantial doubt about its ability to continue as a going concern. Management's plans regarding these matters are also described in note [X]. The financial statements do not include any adjustments that might result from the outcome of this uncertainty.

Uncertainty Explanatory Paragraph

SAS-58 originally included guidance for an explanatory paragraph to an auditor's report when the financial statements were affected by uncertainties concerning future events, the outcomes of which were not susceptible to reasonable estimation at the date of the auditor's report.

SAS-79 amended SAS-58 to eliminate the requirement that, when criteria are met, the auditor add an uncertainty explanatory paragraph to the auditor's report. SAS-79 states that conclusive evidential matter concerning the ultimate outcome of uncertainties cannot be expected to exist at the time of an audit, because the outcome and the related evidential matter are prospective. In these circumstances, management is responsible for estimating the effect of future events on the financial statements or determining that a reasonable estimate cannot be made and making the required disclosures, in accordance with generally accepted accounting principles. The audit includes an assessment of whether the evidential matter is sufficient to support management's analysis. The absence of the existence of information related to the outcome of the uncertainty does not necessarily lead to a conclusion that the evidential matter supporting management's assertion is not sufficient. The auditor's judgment regarding the sufficiency of the evidential matter is based on the evidential matter that is, or should be, available. If the auditor considers the existing conditions and available evidence, he or she may conclude that sufficient evidential matter supports management's assertion about the nature of a matter involving an uncertainty and its presentation or disclosure in the financial statements, and an unqualified opinion would ordinarily be appropriate.

If the auditor cannot obtain sufficient evidential matter to support management's assertion about the nature of a matter involving an uncertainty and its presentation or disclosure in the financial statements, the auditor should consider the need to express a qualified opinion or disclaimer of opinion because of a scope limitation.

SAS-79 provides guidance to the auditor to differentiate between a scope limitation related to an uncertainty and an instance where an auditor is able to conclude that the financial statements are materially misstated due to departures from generally accepted accounting principles related to uncertainties. Departures from generally accepted accounting principles may be caused by inadequate disclosure concerning the uncertainty, by the use of inappropriate accounting principles, or by the use of unreasonable accounting estimates.

SAS-79 categorizes departures from generally accepted accounting principles involving risks or uncertainties into the following categories:

- *Inadequate disclosure*   If the auditor concludes that a matter involving a risk or an uncertainty is not adequately disclosed in the financial statements in conformity with generally accepted accounting principles, the auditor should express a qualified or adverse opinion. Materiality judgments involving risks or uncertainties are made in light of the surrounding circumstances. The auditor should evaluate the materiality, both individually and in the aggregate, of reasonably possible losses that may be incurred upon the resolution of uncertainties. This evaluation of reasonably possible losses is made without regard to the evaluation of materially known and likely misstatements of the financial statements.

- *Inappropriate accounting principles*   FAS-5 (Accounting for Contingencies) describes situations where the inability to make a reasonable estimate about a loss contingency may raise questions about the appropriateness of the accounting principles used. If, in those or other situations, the auditor concludes that the accounting principles used cause the financial statements to be materially misstated, a qualified or adverse opinion should be expressed.

- *Unreasonable accounting estimates* If the auditor concludes that management's estimate of a loss is unreasonable and has caused the financial statements to be materially misstated, a qualified or adverse opinion should be expressed.

AUDITOR'S REPORTS WITH MODIFICATIONS

The following discussion of reporting focuses on situations in which the auditor needs to modify the standard auditor's report. The basic modifications are qualified reports for departures in the financial statements from generally accepted accounting principles or for limitations on the scope of the audit. In addition, this section discusses adverse opinions for departures from generally accepted accounting principles and disclaimers of opinion for limitations on the scope of the audit that do not allow the auditor to complete the audit.

Qualified Opinion on Financial Statements Because of a Departure from Generally Accepted Accounting Principles

Financial statements of a not-for-profit organization may be materially misstated because of a departure from generally accepted accounting principles. This misstatement may be the result of many different departures from generally accepted accounting principles, such as:

- Not recording transactions or valuation accounts that should have been recorded, such as not providing a valuation account for pledges receivable or not recording contributions for which there is an unconditional promise to pay from the donor.
- Omitting a required disclosure or a required financial statement, such as the many required disclosures normally contained in the notes to the financial statements or a statement of functional expenses for voluntary health and welfare organizations.
- Misclassifying or misrecording transactions, such as recording a contribution receivable as an increase in unrestricted net assets, when it should be recorded as an increase in permanently restricted net assets.
- Recording transactions that should not have been recorded, such as recording a contribution receivable when a donor has made only a conditional promise to give.

These are only examples of the types of misstatements that an auditor may encounter in the audit of the financial statements of a not-for-profit. Countless other misstatements may occur, including all of the departures from generally accepted accounting principles normally encountered in an audit of a commercial enterprise.

An auditor first must determine that a misstatement (assuming, of course, that the not-for-profit organization refuses to correct the misstatement or disagrees with the auditor's application of an accounting principle) in the financial statements is material. This is part of the audit conclusion process discussed in the chapter titled "Concluding the Audit." If a misstatement is material, the auditor generally will issue a qualified audit opinion. If the misstatement is so pervasive that the auditor concludes that the financial statements do not present the financial position, changes in net assets, and cash flows in accordance with generally accepted accounting principles, then the auditor would issue an adverse opinion on the financial statements.

The sample audit report in Exhibit 10-7 is a report qualified for a departure from generally accepted accounting principles. Following the report, sample paragraphs that would be inserted into the report for departures from generally accepted accounting principles that might be found in the audit of a not-for-profit organization are presented.

Qualified Opinion on Financial Statements Because of a Scope Limitation

An auditor may issue an unqualified opinion only when his or her audit has been conducted and completed in accordance with generally accepted auditing standards, and any procedures considered necessary were able to be performed and completed. Restrictions may be imposed on the auditor, either by the not-for-profit organization being audited or by the circumstances in which the auditor is conducting the audit. For example, the timing of the audit procedures being performed, the inability to obtain sufficient, competent evidence, or the inadequacy of the accounting records are all factors that may contribute to circumstances that do not permit an auditor to complete the necessary audit procedures to perform the audit in accordance with generally accepted auditing standards.

Generally accepted auditing standards provide guidance to the auditor in determining the effect, if any, on the audit opinion if certain audit procedures cannot be performed. The auditor's decision to qualify the audit opinion (or disclaim an audit opinion, as discussed below) depends on an assessment of the importance of the omitted procedure or procedures to the ability to form an opinion on the financial statements that are being audited. This assessment is affected by the nature and magnitude of the potential effects of the matters in question and by their significance to the financial

EXHIBIT 10-7
QUALIFIED OPINION ON FINANCIAL STATEMENTS
BECAUSE OF A DEPARTURE FROM GENERALLY
ACCEPTED ACCOUNTING PRINCIPLES

Independent Auditor's Report

To Board of Trustees

[*Name of not-for-profit organization*]

We have audited the accompanying statement of financial position of [*name of not-for-profit organization*] as of [*date of statement of financial position*], and the related statements of activities and cash flows for the year then ended. These financial statements are the responsibility of [*name of not-for-profit organization*]'s management. Our responsibility is to express an opinion on these financial statements based on our audit.

We conducted our audit in accordance with generally accepted auditing standards. Those standards require that we plan and perform the audit to obtain reasonable assurance about whether the financial statements are free of material misstatement. An audit includes examining, on a test basis, evidence supporting the amounts and disclosures in the financial statements. An audit also includes assessing the accounting principles used and significant estimates made by management, as well as evaluating the overall financial statement presentation. We believe that our audit provides a reasonable basis for our opinion.

[*Insert a paragraph that describes the departure from generally accepted accounting principles.*]

In our opinion, except for the effects of [*phrase that briefly describes the departure from generally accepted accounting principles*] as discussed in the preceding paragraph, the financial statements referred to above present fairly, in all material respects, the financial position of [*name of not-for-profit organization*] as of [*date of statement of financial position*], and the changes in its net assets and its cash flows for the year then ended in conformity with generally accepted accounting principles.

[*Signature of Firm*]

[*Name of City, State*]

[*Date of the completion of fieldwork*]

Notes to the auditor's report:
    1. The title of the report should include the word "independent."

2. The report is addressed to the governing board, in the sample report, to the board of trustees. The report could be addressed to the organization itself.

3. The following are sample paragraphs (along with sample phrases for the opinion paragraph) that might be used by the auditor:

Failure to Record a Contribution Receivable

[*Name of not-for-profit organization*] does not record unconditional promises to give from donors as contributions receivable as required by generally accepted accounting principles. The unrecorded contributions receivable, net of a provision for uncollectible receivables, as of [*date of statement of financial position*] is $[XX,XXX], which results in an understatement of net assets and changes in net assets of $[X,XXX], $[X,XXX], and $[X,XXX] in unrestricted net assets, temporarily restricted net assets, and permanently restricted net assets, respectively.

Phrase for opinion paragraph of report: "Except for the effects of not recording contributions receivable, as discussed in the preceding paragraph...."

Omission of a Statement of Functional Expenses by a Voluntary Health and Welfare Organization

[*Name of not-for-profit organization*] declined to present a statement of functional expenses for the year ended [*date of statement of financial position*]. Presentation of such statement, which provides information on the functional and natural classification of expenses, is required by generally accepted accounting principles.

Phrase for opinion paragraph of report: "Except that the omission of a statement of functional expenses results in an incomplete presentation, as described in the preceding paragraph...."

Misclassification of a Contribution Received

[*Name of not-for-profit organization*] recorded a contribution received from a donor in the amount of $[X,XXX] as an increase in unrestricted net assets. Because the donor that made this contribution to [*name of not-for-profit organization*] placed a restriction on the use of these funds, which will be satisfied within the next five years, generally accepted accounting principles require that this contribution be recorded as an increase in restricted net assets. Accordingly, unrestricted net assets and the changes in unrestricted net assets are overstated by this amount, and restricted net assets and changes in restricted net assets are understated by this amount.

Phrase for opinion paragraph of the report: "Except for the effect of the misclassification of contributions described in the preceding paragraph...."

statements. If the potential effects relate to many financial statement items, this significance is likely to be greater than if only a limited number of items is involved.

One of the more common reasons for qualifying an opinion on financial statements is the inability of the auditor to observe physical inventories. In audits of not-for-profit organizations, physical inventories may be nonexistent or of only minor significance to the not-for-profit organization, so this qualification probably will be rare. However, other types of scope limitations, such as an inability to confirm receivables or a failure to audit financial statements of a foreign or domestic affiliated organization, may present situations in which qualification for a scope limitation is appropriate. (Generally accepted auditing standards have a presumption that receivables will be confirmed. However, for a not-for-profit organization, this presumption would be applicable to receivables related to fees for services that have been performed by the not-for-profit organization.) In addition, the accounting system and controls over currency collected by the not-for-profit organization may be so inadequate that the auditor is unable to complete adequate auditing procedures on the completeness of the recording of contribution revenue.

> **OBSERVATION:** If the auditor cannot obtain sufficient competent evidence about disclosures that the not-for-profit organization includes in its financial statements, a scope limitation may be required. This is discussed more fully in the chapter titled "Audit Planning."

Auditors of not-for-profit organizations whose audits have been restricted by scope limitations may use the sample report in Exhibit 10-8. The notes to the sample report provide some examples of paragraphs that may be found in reports that are qualified because of a scope limitation.

Adverse Opinion on Financial Statements for Departures from Generally Accepted Accounting Principles

An adverse opinion states that the financial statements do not present fairly the financial position, changes in net assets, or cash flows in conformity with generally accepted accounting principles. When there are departures from generally accepted accounting principles, an auditor must decide whether to issue a qualified opinion for the departure or an adverse opinion. The auditor should consider a number of factors, with the primary factor being the nature of the departure from generally accepted accounting principles.

For example, if a not-for-profit organization declines to present a statement of cash flows, this is a departure from generally accepted

---

EXHIBIT 10-8
QUALIFIED OPINION ON FINANCIAL STATEMENTS
BECAUSE OF A SCOPE LIMITATION

Independent Auditor's Report

To Board of Trustees

[*Name of not-for-profit organization*]

We have audited the accompanying statement of financial position of [*name of not-for-profit organization*] as of [*date of statement of financial position*], and the related statements of activities and cash flows for the year then ended. These financial statements are the responsibility of [*name of not-for-profit organization*]'s management. Our responsibility is to express an opinion on these financial statements based on our audit.

Except as discussed in the following paragraph, we conducted our audit in accordance with generally accepted auditing standards. Those standards require that we plan and perform the audit to obtain reasonable assurance about whether the financial statements are free of material misstatement. An audit includes examining, on a test basis, evidence supporting the amounts and disclosures in the financial statements. An audit also includes assessing the accounting principles used and significant estimates made by management, as well as evaluating the overall financial statement presentation. We believe that our audit provides a reasonable basis for our opinion.

[*Insert a paragraph that describes the nature of the scope limitations.*]

In our opinion, except for the effects of such adjustments, if any, as might have been determined to be necessary had we been able to [*briefly mention the nature of the scope limitations described in the preceding paragraph*], the financial statements referred to above present fairly, in all material respects, the financial position of [*name of not-for-profit organization*] as of [*date of statement of financial position*], and the changes in its net assets and its cash flows for the year then ended in conformity with generally accepted accounting principles.

[*Signature of Firm*]

[*Name of City, State*]

[*Date of the completion of fieldwork*]

Notes to the auditor's report:

1. The title of the report should include the word "independent."

2. The report is addressed to the governing board, in the sample report, to the board of trustees. The report could be addressed to the organization itself.

3. The following are some sample paragraphs that may be inserted in the auditor's report to describe some scope limitations:

   Scope limitation if audit is unable to audit currency collections

   [*Name of not-for-profit organization*] does not maintain any accounting controls over its collection of currency as contributions before the initial entry of these contributions into its accounting system. Accordingly, it was not practicable to extend auditing procedures of such currency receipts beyond auditing the amounts actually recorded in the accounting system.

   Phrase for use in the opinion paragraph report: "Except for the effects of such adjustments, if any, as might have been determined to be necessary had the collection of contributions in the form of currency been susceptible to the application of sufficient audit procedures...."

   Foreign affiliated not-for-profit organization not audited

   We were unable to obtain audited financial statements supporting [*name of not-for-profit organization*]'s supporting amounts included in the financial statements for the inclusion of a foreign affiliated not-for-profit organization with net assets of $[X,XXX], $[X,XXX], and $[X,XXX], or changes in net assets of $[X,XXX], $[X,XXX], and $[X,XXX], classified as unrestricted net assets, temporarily restricted net assets, and permanently restricted net assets, respectively, as described in Note [X] to the financial statements, nor were we able to satisfy ourselves as to the amounts recorded in the financial statements by other auditing procedures.

   Phrase for use in opinion paragraph of the report: "Except for the effects of such adjustments, if any, as might have been determined to be necessary had we been able to examine evidence regarding the amounts included in the financial statements relating to the foreign affiliated organization...."

accounting principles. In this instance, a qualified opinion would be appropriate, particularly since the lack of a statement of cash flows does not affect whether the information presented in the statement of financial position or the statement of activities is fairly presented.

On the other hand, if a not-for-profit organization does not prepare financial statements to conform with the requirements of FAS-117 (to classify its net assets and changes in net assets into the three categories required by FAS-117) and there are material amounts in each of these three categories of net assets, an adverse opinion on the financial statements probably would be more appropriate. The impact of this departure is pervasive, and the statements would not presently fairly the financial position or changes in net assets in accordance with the recently changed generally accepted accounting principle.

SAS-58 provides guidance on this decision by instructing the auditor to consider not only the dollar value effect on the financial statements of the departure from generally accepted accounting principles, but also the qualitative factors of materiality. The significance of the item to a particular entity (for example, contributions to a not-for-profit organization), the pervasiveness of the misstatement (such as whether it affects the amounts and presentation of numerous financial statement items), and the effect of the misstatement on the financial statements taken as a whole are all factors to be considered when making a judgment regarding materiality.

A sample report that expresses an adverse opinion on the financial statements of a not-for-profit organization is shown in Exhibit 10-9.

Disclaimer of Opinion on Financial Statements for Scope Limitations

A disclaimer of opinion states that the auditor does not express an opinion on the financial statements. This report is used when the auditor has not performed an audit sufficient in scope to enable an opinion to be expressed on the financial statements. A disclaimer of opinion should not be expressed because the auditor believes, on the basis of his or her audit, that there are material departures from generally accepted accounting principles.

The auditor will need to exercise professional judgment when determining whether to issue a qualified opinion for a scope limitation, as described earlier, or to issue a disclaimer of opinion. The judgment is one involving the significance of the procedures that the auditor was not able to perform. In addition, the pervasiveness of any misstatements that might have been detected by the audit procedures that the auditor was not able to perform should be considered in determining whether to issue a qualified opinion with a scope limitation or a disclaimer of opinion.

EXHIBIT 10-9
ADVERSE OPINION ON FINANCIAL STATEMENTS
FOR DEPARTURES FROM GENERALLY ACCEPTED
ACCOUNTING PRINCIPLES

Independent Auditor's Report

To Board of Trustees
[*Name of not-for-profit organization*]

We have audited the accompanying statement of financial position of [*name of not-for-profit organization*] as of [*date of statement of financial position*], and the related statements of activities and cash flows for the year then ended. These financial statements are the responsibility of [*name of not-for-profit organization*]'s management. Our responsibility is to express an opinion on these financial statements based on our audit.

We conducted our audit in accordance with generally accepted auditing standards. Those standards require that we plan and perform the audit to obtain reasonable assurance about whether the financial statements are free of material misstatement. An audit includes examining, on a test basis, evidence supporting the amounts and disclosures in the financial statements. An audit also includes assessing the accounting principles used and significant estimates made by management, as well as evaluating the overall financial statement presentation. We believe that our audit provides a reasonable basis for our opinion.

[*Insert a paragraph to explain the reason for issuing an adverse opinion.*]

In our opinion, because of the effects of the matters discussed in the preceding paragraph, the financial statements referred to above do not present fairly, in conformity with generally accepted accounting principles, the financial position of [*name of not-for-profit organization*] as of [*date of statement of financial position*], and the changes in its net assets and its cash flows for the year then ended.

[*Signature of Firm*]

[*Name of City, State*]

[*Date of the completion of fieldwork*]

Notes to the auditor's report:
1. The title of the report should include the word "independent."
2. The report is addressed to the governing board, in the sample report, to the board of trustees. The report could be addressed to the organization itself.
3. The following is an example of an explanatory paragraph that might be used to explain the reasons for the report qualification.

[*Name of not-for-profit organization*] has not implemented the financial reporting requirements of Statement of Financial Accounting Standards No. 117 (Financial Statements of Not-for-Profit Organizations), which is required by generally accepted accounting principles. Accordingly, [*name of not-for-profit organization*] has reported the difference between its assets and liabilities as a single amount entitled "Fund Balance." In addition, the activities of the organization have been reported as the revenues and expenses, the net of which is reported as a single amount that affects the reported fund balance. Generally accepted accounting principles require that the net assets of a not-for-profit organization be categorized as unrestricted net assets, temporarily restricted net assets, and permanently restricted net assets. In addition, the changes in each of these three categories must be presented in a statement of activities. Because [*name of not-for-profit organization*] did not record transactions throughout the year to correspond with the three categories of net assets described above, the effect of this departure from generally accepted accounting principles cannot be reasonably determined.

When the auditor believes that, on the basis of the audit performed, there are material departures from generally accepted accounting principles in the financial statements, he or she should not use the disclaimer of opinion. Although the not-for-profit organization client might feel this method is more palatable (i.e., the auditor didn't finish the audit instead of the financial statements are not in accordance with generally accepted accounting principles), the use of the disclaimer for this purpose is prohibited by generally accepted auditing standards. This prohibition was re-emphasized by SAS-79.

A sample of a report that the auditor may use to disclaim an opinion on financial statements is shown in Exhibit 10-10.

EXHIBIT 10-10
DISCLAIMER OF OPINION ON FINANCIAL STATEMENTS
FOR SCOPE LIMITATIONS

Independent Auditor's Report

To Board of Trustees

[*Name of not-for-profit organization*]

We were engaged to audit the accompanying statement of financial position of [*name of not-for-profit organization*] as of [*date of statement of financial position*], and the related statements of activities and cash flows for the year then ended. These financial statements are the responsibility of [*name of not-for-profit organization*]'s management.

[*Insert a paragraph to explain the reason for issuing a disclaimer of opinion.*]

[*Phrase that refers to the reasons in the preceding paragraph for issuing a disclaimer of opinion*], the scope of our work was not sufficient to enable us to express, and we do not express, an opinion on these financial statements.

[*Signature of Firm*]

[*Name of City, State*]

[*Date of the completion of fieldwork*]

Notes to the auditor's report:

1. The title of the report should include the word "independent."

2. The report is addressed to the governing board, in the sample report, to the board of trustees. The report could be addressed to the organization itself.

3. The following is an example of an explanatory paragraph and related phrase for the last paragraph of the report:

   Explanatory paragraph: "[*Name of not-for-profit organization*] requested that we not request confirmation of pledges receivable, which aggregated $[XX,XXX] as of [*date of statement of financial position*] by direct correspondence with the donors."

   Phrase for last paragraph of report: "Since we did not request confirmation of pledges receivable by direct correspondence with donors and we were not able to apply other auditing procedures to satisfy ourselves as to the recorded amount of pledges receivable...."

OTHER AUDITOR'S REPORTS

Restricting the Use of an Auditor's Report

The preceding discussion of auditor's reports on financial statements pertains to general-purpose reports of financial statements that are prepared in accordance with generally accepted accounting principles. The following discussion of other types of audit reports includes some reports that are intended only for specific parties. During 1998, the AICPA issued SAS-87 (Restricting the Use of an Auditor's Report), which provides guidance to auditors on when and how to restrict the use of an auditor's report. SAS-87 is effective for reports issued after December 31, 1998.

SAS-87 describes the following three situations in which an auditor should restrict the use of his or her report:

- The subject matter of the report or the presentation being reported on is based on contractual provisions or regulatory requirements that are not in accordance with generally accepted accounting principles or an other comprehensive basis of accounting (OCBOA).

- The accountant's report is based upon procedures that are specifically designed and performed to satisfy the needs of specified parties who accept the responsibility for the sufficiency of the procedures. (This is commonly referred to as an agreed-upon procedures engagement.) An auditor may agree to add other parties as specified parties to this type of report, based upon the identity of the other parties and their intended use of the report. However, if the auditor does agree to add other parties, the auditor should have the other parties acknowledge (ordinarily in writing) their understanding of the nature of the engagement, the measurement or disclosure criteria used in the engagement, and the related report.

- The auditor's reports are a by-product of a financial statement audit and are based solely on the audit procedures the auditor performed in order to express an opinion on the financial statements. In other words, the auditor did not perform special procedures to provide assurance on the subject matter of the report. SAS-87 provides the following examples of these "by-product" reports:

  — The auditor is reporting reportable conditions under SAS-60 (Communication of Internal Control Related Matters in an Audit).

  — The auditor is communicating to the audit committee or similarly situated body in accordance with SAS-61 (Communications with Audit Committees).

  — The auditor is reporting on compliance with aspects of contractual agreements or regulatory requirements related to audited financial statements in accordance with SAS-62 (Special Reports).

  The use of the by-product report should be restricted to an organization's audit committee, board of directors, management, others within the organization, specified regulatory agencies, and, in the case of reports on compliance with aspects of contractual agreements, the parties of the contractual agreement. SAS-87 states that an auditor should not agree to add other parties as specified parties in a by-product report.

SAS-87 specifies that an auditor's report that is restricted should include a special paragraph at the end of the report that contains the following elements:

- A statement indicating that the report is intended solely for the information and use of the specified parties
- An identification of the specified parties to whom the report's use is restricted
- A statement that the report is not intended to be and should not be used by anyone other than the intended parties

The example paragraph provided by SAS-87 is as follows:

> This report is intended solely for the information and use of [the specified parties] and is not intended to be and should not be used by anyone other than these specified parties.

The report examples included in the remaining section of this chapter have been updated to reflect the restriction language contained in SAS-87.

Reporting on a Comprehensive Basis of Accounting Other Than Generally Accepted Accounting Principles

Auditors of not-for-profit organizations often are asked to report on financial statements prepared on bases of accounting different from generally accepted accounting principles. Reporting requirements for other comprehensive bases of accounting are prescribed by SAS-62. For purposes of applying the requirements of SAS-62, a *comprehensive basis of accounting* is defined as:

- A basis of accounting that the not-for-profit organization uses to comply with the regulatory requirements or financial reporting provisions of a governmental regulatory agency to whose jurisdiction the organization is subject.
- A basis of accounting that the not-for-profit organization uses or expects to use to file its income tax return for the period covered by the financial statements.
- The cash receipts and disbursements basis of accounting, and modifications of the cash basis having substantial support, such as recording depreciation on fixed assets or accruing income taxes.
- A definite set of criteria having substantial support that is applied to all material items appearing in financial statements, such as the price-level basis of accounting.

Of the different comprehensive bases of accounting described above, the two most common situations the auditor may encounter for a not-for-profit organization are reporting on financial statements prepared on the cash basis of accounting and reporting on financial statements included in the federal annual information return, Form 990. (This form is reproduced in Appendix A.)

During 1998 the Auditing Issues Task Force of the AICPA issued an auditing Interpretation (Evaluating the Adequacy of Disclosure in Financial Statements Prepared on the Cash, Modified Cash, or Income Tax Basis of Accounting) of SAS-62 (Special Reports). The Interpretation concludes (1) that the discussion of the basis of accounting needs to include only the significant differences of the accounting basis from generally accepted accounting principles and (2) that these differences do not have to be quantified.

In addition, if the financial statements prepared on these accounting bases contain elements, accounts, or items for which generally accepted accounting principles would require disclosure, the financial statements should either:

- Provide the relevant disclosure that would be provided under generally accepted accounting principles, or
- Provide information that communicates the substance of that disclosure.

Qualitative information may be substituted for some of the quantitative information required in a presentation in accordance with generally accepted accounting principles. In addition, disclosure requirements under generally accepted accounting principles that are not relevant to the measurement of the element, account, or item need not be considered.

Report on a cash basis of accounting A sample report for reporting on the financial statements of a not-for-profit organization prepared on the cash basis of accounting is shown in Exhibit 10-11.

Report on financial statements included on Form 990 In some cases, the state agency that monitors the activities of not-for-profit organizations permits these organizations to file federal Form 990 (Return of Organization Exempt from Income Tax) as the required annual information return with the state agency. An Interpretation of SAS-62 provides specific guidance to auditors who are asked to provide an opinion on whether the financial statements included in Form 990 are presented fairly in conformity with generally accepted accounting principles. In some cases, Form 990 is used primarily to satisfy statutory requirements, but the regulatory authorities may make the financial statements and auditor's report a matter of public record.

The auditor first should consider whether the financial statements (including appropriate footnotes) are in conformity with generally accepted accounting principles. If they are, the auditor can express an unqualified opinion.

EXHIBIT 10-11
AUDITOR'S OPINION ON FINANCIAL STATEMENTS
PREPARED IN ACCORDANCE WITH THE
CASH BASIS OF ACCOUNTING

Independent Auditor's Report

To Board of Trustees

[*Name of not-for-profit organization*]

We have audited the accompanying statement of assets, liabilities, and net assets of [*name of not-for-profit organization*] as of [*date of statement of financial position*], and the related statements of support and revenue collected and expenses paid for the year then ended. These financial statements are the responsibility of [*name of not-for-profit organization*]'s management. Our responsibility is to express an opinion on these financial statements based on our audit.

We conducted our audit in accordance with generally accepted auditing standards. Those standards require that we plan and perform the audit to obtain reasonable assurance about whether the financial statements are free of material misstatement. An audit includes examining, on a test basis, evidence supporting the amounts and disclosures in the financial statements. An audit also includes assessing the accounting principles used and significant estimates made by management, as well as evaluating the overall financial statement presentation. We believe that our audit provides a reasonable basis for our opinion.

As described in note [X], these financial statements were prepared on the basis of cash receipts and disbursements, which is a comprehensive basis of accounting other than generally accepted accounting principles.

In our opinion, the financial statements referred to above present fairly, in all material respects, the assets and liabilities arising from cash transactions of [*name of not-for-profit organization*] as of [*date of statement of financial position*], and its support and revenue collected and expenses paid for the year then ended on the basis of accounting described in note [X].

[*Signature of Firm*]

[*Name of City, State*]

[*Date of the completion of fieldwork*]

Notes to the auditor's report:

1. The title of the report should include the word "independent."

2. The report is addressed to the governing board, in the sample report, to the board of trustees. The report could be addressed to the organization itself.

3. The report should state the basis of accounting in accordance with which the financial statements were prepared, refer to a footnote in the financial statements that describes the basis of accounting, and describe the basis of accounting as a comprehensive basis of accounting other than generally accepted accounting principles.

4. The titles of the financial statements are modified to reflect the cash basis of accounting and to make clear that they do not represent financial statements prepared in accordance with generally accepted accounting principles.

However, if the financial statements are not in conformity with generally accepted accounting principles, the auditor should consider the distribution of the report to determine whether it is appropriate to issue a special report on a regulatory basis of accounting. Reports for financial statements prepared on a regulatory basis are, by definition, intended solely for the purpose of the regulatory authority. If the not-for-profit organization's financial statements on Form 990 are subject to public inspection, the Interpretation of SAS-62 states that this form of reporting is appropriate even though by law or regulation the auditor's report may be a matter of record. Therefore, the form of report illustrated in Exhibit 10-12 may be used if the Form 990 report is made a matter of public record. If the report is publicly distributed (i.e., the Form 990 is mailed to all of the organization's donors), then the reporting on a regulatory basis of accounting is not appropriate and a qualified report for a departure from generally accepted accounting principles or an adverse opinion is appropriate.

These requirements may become less significant as reporting by not-for-profit organizations is standardized under FAS-117 and as the Internal Revenue Service implements revisions to Form 990. Not-for-profit organizations and their auditors should expect more Form 990s to be presented in accordance with generally accepted accounting principles, permitting the issuance of a standard unqualified report by the auditor and eliminating some of the confusion and disparities noted above. Until that time, the sample report in Exhibit 10-11 may be used for financial statements presented on Form 990 that are not in accordance with generally accepted accounting principles, but are prepared in accordance with a regulatory basis, and are a matter of public record, but are not publicly distributed.

EXHIBIT 10-12
AUDITOR'S OPINION ON FINANCIAL STATEMENTS
PREPARED IN ACCORDANCE WITH A REGULATORY
BASIS OF ACCOUNTING

Independent Auditor's Report

To Board of Trustees
[*Name of not-for-profit organization*]

We have audited the accompanying balance sheet (Part V) of [*name of not-for-profit organization*] as of [*date of statement of financial position*], and the related statements of support, revenue and expenses and changes in fund balances (Part I) and statement of functional expenses (Part II) for the year then ended included in the accompanying Internal Revenue Service Form 990. These financial statements are the responsibility of [*name of not-for-profit organization*]'s management. Our responsibility is to express an opinion on these financial statements based on our audit.

We conducted our audit in accordance with generally accepted auditing standards. Those standards require that we plan and perform the audit to obtain reasonable assurance about whether the financial statements are free of material misstatement. An audit includes examining, on a test basis, evidence supporting the amounts and disclosures in the financial statements. An audit also includes assessing the accounting principles used and significant estimates made by management, as well as evaluating the overall financial statement presentation. We believe that our audit provides a reasonable basis for our opinion.

As described in note [X], these financial statements were prepared in conformity with the accounting practices prescribed by the Internal Revenue Service and the Office of the State of [state], which is a comprehensive basis of accounting other than generally accepted accounting principles.

In our opinion, the financial statements referred to above present fairly, in all material respects, the assets, liabilities, and fund balances of [*name of not-for-profit organization*] as of [*date of statement of financial position*], and its support, revenue and expenses, and changes in fund balances for the year then ended on the basis of accounting described in note [X].

Our audit was made for the purpose of forming an opinion on the above financial statements taken as a whole. The accompanying information on pages [X] to [X] is presented for purposes of additional analysis and is not a required part of the above financial statements. Such information, except for that portion marked "Unaudited," on which we express no opinion, has been subjected to the audit procedures applied in the audit of the above financial statements, and, in our opinion, the information is fairly stated in all material respects in relation to the financial statements taken as a whole.

This report is intended solely for the information and use of the board of trustees and management of [*name of not-for-profit organization*] and for filing with the Internal Revenue Service and the Office of the State of [state] and is not intended to be and should not be used by anyone other than these specified parties.

[*Signature of Firm*]

[*Name of City, State*]

[*Date of the completion of fieldwork*]

Notes to the auditor's report:

1. The title of the report should include the word "independent."

2. The report is addressed to the governing board, in the sample report, to the board of trustees. The report could be addressed to the organization itself.

3. As included in the above sample report, the report should state the basis of accounting in accordance with which the financial statements were prepared, refer to a footnote in the financial statements that describes the basis of accounting, and describe the basis of accounting as a comprehensive basis of accounting other than generally accepted accounting principles.

4. The titles of the financial statements are modified to reflect the related parts of Form 990 and to make clear that they do not represent financial statements prepared in accordance with generally accepted accounting principles.

5. This report refers to the appropriate state office that is requiring the Form 990 information to be audited. The Internal Revenue Service does not require that Form 990 be audited.

6. SAS-77 states that the auditor may use this form of report only if the financial statements and report are intended solely for filing with one or more regulatory agencies to whose jurisdiction the organization is subject.

Reporting on Condensed Financial Information in a Client-Prepared Document

A not-for-profit organization may choose to present condensed financial information in its annual report or other material that it distributes to its donors or other interested parties. If the document or the condensed financial statements do not make reference to the auditor, the auditor has no responsibility to report on the condensed financial information. On the other hand, if the condensed financial statements or the document in which they are contained makes reference to the auditor, the auditor should issue a report on those condensed financial statements. Since condensed financial statements are an incomplete presentation of what is required under generally accepted accounting principles, the report issued by the auditor is essentially an adverse opinion. Exhibit 10-13 shows an example of a report that may be issued on condensed financial statements.

REPORTING REQUIRED INFORMATION TO THE BOARD OF TRUSTEES

SAS-61 (Communication with Audit Committees) establishes requirements for auditors to communicate certain matters to those who have responsibility for the oversight of the financial reporting process. For purposes of SAS-61, the recipient of the information is referred to as an *audit committee,* although the communication can be with an equivalent group.

The communications of SAS-61 are actually required only for entities that have an audit committee or a group equivalent to an audit committee, such as a finance or budget committee, or when the audit is performed as part of an engagement for a filing with the Securities and Exchange Commission. However, even if the auditor of a not-for-profit organization reports only to a general board of trustees on the results of his or her audit and can avoid the requirements of SAS-61, it is good practice to communicate these matters.

The communications required by SAS-61 may be oral or written. If the information is communicated orally, the auditor should document the communication by memorandum or notations in the working papers. When the auditor communicates in writing, the report should indicate that it is intended solely for the use of the audit committee or board of directors and, if appropriate, management. It is considered a restricted-use report under SAS-87.

The auditor has some flexibility in reporting these matters. For example, if the auditor is convinced that management has communicated certain information to the audit committee already, the auditor is not required to repeat the information. In addition, to the extent that some of the information to be communicated is repetitive, the auditor may elect not to repeat recurring information each year, but to report it only periodically or as circumstances, such as the rotation of individuals on the committee, deem such communication to be appropriate.

> **OBSERVATION:** The auditor may wish to communicate that an audit in accordance with generally accepted audit standards does not provide any assurance with respect to the Year 2000 Issue.

EXHIBIT 10-13
REPORTING ON CONDENSED FINANCIAL INFORMATION
IN A CLIENT-PREPARED DOCUMENT

Independent Auditor's Report

To Board of Trustees
[*Name of not-for-profit organization*]

We have audited the statement of financial position of [*name of not-for-profit organization*] as of [*date of statement of financial position*], and the related statements of activities and cash flows for the year then ended (not presented herein). These financial statements are the responsibility of [*name of not-for-profit organization*]'s management. Our responsibility is to express an opinion on these financial statements based on our audit.

We conducted our audit in accordance with generally accepted auditing standards. Those standards require that we plan and perform the audit to obtain reasonable assurance about whether the financial statements are free of material misstatement. An audit includes examining, on a test basis, evidence supporting the amounts and disclosures in the financial statements. An audit also includes assessing the accounting principles used and significant estimates made by management, as well as evaluating the overall financial statement presentation. We believe that our audit provides a reasonable basis for our opinion.

The condensed statement of financial position [*date of statement of financial position*], and the related statements of activities and cash flows for the year then ended, presented on pages [X] to [X], are presented as a summary and therefore do not include all of the disclosures required by generally accepted accounting principles.

In our opinion, because of the significance of the omission of the information referred to in the preceding paragraph, the financial statements referred to above do not present fairly, in conformity with generally accepted accounting principles, the financial position of [*name of not-for-profit organization*] as of [*date of statement of financial position*], and the changes in its net assets and its cash flows for the year then ended.

[*Signature of Firm*]

[*Name of City, State*]

[*Date of the completion of fieldwork*]

Notes to the auditor's report:

    1. The title of the report should include the word "independent."

2. The report is addressed to the governing board, in the sample report, to the board of trustees. The report could be addressed to the organization itself.

3. This sample report assumes that the year being reported on is *not* the initial year of implementation of FAS-117.

4. The report should be dated with the same date as the report on the financial statements in accordance with generally accepted accounting principles.

OBSERVATION: In December 1999, SAS-89 (Audit Adjustments) was issued. It is effective for audits of financial statements for periods beginning on or after December 15, 1999, with earlier application encouraged. SAS-89 requires the auditor to inform the audit committee about uncorrected misstatements aggregated by the auditor during the current year's audit for the latest financial statement period presented that were determined by management to be immaterial, both individually and in the aggregate, to the financial statements taken as a whole. In addition, the section currently titled "Significant Audit Adjustments" is to be retitled "Audit Adjustments." Effectively, auditors will be communicating the amount of passed audit adjustments.

According to SAS-61, the auditor has flexibility in terms of the level of the communication that is presented. For example, the communication can reflect the experience of the individual committee members in the level of detail communicated. The following paragraphs list the requirements, if applicable, of SAS-61. These should not be interpreted as a limit on what the auditor should communicate to the audit committee. The auditor should communicate any other matters that he or she thinks are appropriate or that would be helpful to the audit committee in fulfilling its responsibilities to oversee the financial reporting process. A sample communication is provided in Exhibit 10-14.

Auditor's Responsibility Under Generally Accepted Auditing Standards

The auditor should inform the audit committee of the level of responsibility assumed for matters such as the internal control structure and whether the financial statements are free of material misstatement under generally accepted auditing standards. The audit committee should understand that an audit conducted in accordance with generally accepted auditing standards is designed to obtain reasonable, but not absolute, assurance about the financial statements.

EXHIBIT 10-14
EXAMPLE OF WRITTEN COMMUNICATION
WITH AUDIT COMMITTEE

To the Board of Trustees
[*Name of not-for-profit organization*]

We have audited the financial statements of [*Name of not-for-profit organization*] for the year ended [*date of statement of financial position*], and have issued our report thereon dated [*date of auditor's report*]. Professional standards require that we provide you with the following information related to our audit.

Our Responsibility Under Generally Accepted Auditing Standards

Our responsibility, as described by professional standards, is to plan and perform our audit to obtain reasonable, but not absolute, assurance about whether the financial statements are free of material misstatement. Because of the concept of reasonable assurance and because we did not perform a detailed examination of all transactions, there is a risk that material errors, or illegal acts, including fraud and defalcations, may exist and not be detected by us.

As part of our audit, we considered the internal control of [*Name of not-for-profit organization*]. Such considerations are solely for the purpose of planning our audit procedures and not to provide any assurance about internal control.

An audit of financial statements conducted in accordance with generally accepted auditing standards is not designed to detect whether an organization is Year 2000 ready. Further, we have no responsibility with regard to [*name of not-for-profit organization*]'s effort to make its systems, or any other systems, such as those of [*name of not-for-profit organization*]'s vendors, service providers, or any other third parties, Year 2000 ready or provide assurance on whether the [*name of not-for-profit organization*] has addressed or will be able to address all of the affected systems on a timely basis. These are responsibilities of [*name of not-for-profit organization*]'s management.

As part of obtaining reasonable assurance about whether the financial statement are free of material misstatement, we performed tests of [*name of not-for-profit organization*]'s compliance with certain provisions of laws, regulations, contracts, and grants. However, the objective of our tests was not to provide an opinion on compliance with such provisions.

Significant Accounting Policies

Management has the responsibility for selection and use of appropriate accounting policies. In accordance with the terms of our engagement letter, we will advise management about the appropriateness of accounting policies and their application. The significant accounting policies used by [*Name of not-for-profit organization*] are described in Note X to the financial statements. We noted no transactions entered into by [*Name of not-for-profit organization*] during the year that were both significant and unusual, and of which, under professional standards, we are required to inform you, or transactions for which there is a lack of authoritative guidance or consensus.

Accounting Estimates

Accounting estimates are an integral part of the financial statements prepared by management and are based on management's current judgments. Certain accounting estimates are particularly sensitive because of their significance to the financial statements and because of the possibility that future events affecting them may differ significantly from management's current judgments.

Significant Audit Adjustments

For purposes of this letter, professional standards define a significant audit adjustment as a proposed correction of the financial statements that, in our judgment, may not have been detected except through our auditing procedures. These adjustments may include those proposed by us but not recorded by [*Name of not-for-profit organization*] that could potentially cause future financial statements to be materially misstated, even though we have concluded that such adjustments are not material to the current financial statements. We proposed no significant audit adjustments as defined by professional standards.

Note: In December 1999, the AICPA issued Statement on Auditing Standards No. 89, "Audit Adjustments," which is effective for audits of financial statements for periods beginning on or after December 15, 1999, with earlier application permitted. SAS-89 addresses communicating of audit adjustments to audit committees. It removes the word *significant* from this communication.

Other Information in Documents Containing Audited Financial Statements

The financial statements referred to above that were audited by us are included in the annual report prepared by [*Name of not-for-profit organization*], Our responsibility under professional standards does not extend beyond the financial statements covered by our auditor's report, and we have no obligation to corroborate other information contained in the annual report or other documents in which the financial statements are included. We have only read this information to consider whether it was materially inconsistent with the financial statements.

Disagreements with Management

For purposes of this letter, professional standards define a disagreement with management as a matter, whether or not resolved to our satisfaction, concerning a financial accounting, reporting, or auditing matter that could be significant to the financial statements or the auditor's report, including management's judgments about accounting estimates. No such disagreements arose during the course of our audit.

Consultations with Other Independent Accountants

In some cases, management may decide to consult with other accountants about auditing and accounting matters. To our knowledge, there were no such consultations with other accountants.

Issues Discussed Prior to Retention of Independent Auditors

There were no issues discussed with management that were a condition to our retention.

Difficulties Encountered in Performing the Audit

We encountered no difficulties in dealing with management in performing our audit.

This report is intended solely for the information and use of the audit committee, board of directors, management, and others within the organization and is not intended to be and should not be used by anyone other than the specified parties.

[*Signature of Firm*]

[*Name of City, State*]

[*Date*]

Notes to the auditor's report:

1. This sample communication report assumes that there are no matters to report to the Board of Trustees or its Audit Committee. Appropriate modifications should be made where there are matters to report.

2. This communication should address certain minimum requirements, which the above sample does address. However, auditors should feel free to customize this communication to provide additional information that would be relevant or useful.

Significant Accounting Policies

The auditor should ensure that the audit committee is informed about the initial selection of and changes in significant accounting policies or their application. The auditor also should ensure that the audit committee is informed about the methods used to account for significant unusual transactions and the effect of significant accounting policies in controversial or emerging areas for which there is a lack of authoritative guidance or consensus.

Management Judgments and Accounting Estimates

The auditor should ensure that the audit committee is informed about the process used by management to formulate particularly sensitive accounting estimates and about the basis for the auditor's conclusions regarding the reasonableness of those estimates.

Significant Audit Adjustments

The auditor should inform the audit committee about adjustments arising from the audit that, in the auditor's judgment, either individually or in the aggregate, have a significant effect on the not-for-profit organization's financial reporting process. For purposes of this communication, an audit adjustment, whether or not recorded by the not-for-profit organization, is a proposed correction of the financial statements that, in the auditor's judgment, may not have been detected except through the auditing procedures performed.

Other Information in Documents Containing Audited Financial Statements

The audit committee often considers information prepared by management that accompanies the audited financial statements. The auditor should discuss with the audit committee the auditor's responsibility for other information in documents containing audited financial statements, any procedures performed, and the results.

Disagreements with Management

The auditor should discuss with the audit committee any disagreements with management about matters that individually or in the aggregate could be significant to the not-for-profit organization's financial statements or the auditor's report, and whether these disagreements were satisfactorily resolved. Disagreements do not include differences of opinion based on incomplete facts or preliminary information that are later resolved.

Consultation with Other Accountants

If the auditor becomes aware that management has consulted with other accountants about accounting or auditing matters, he or she should discuss with the audit committee his or her own views about significant matters that were the subject of such consultation.

Major Issues Discussed with Management Before Retention

The auditor should discuss with the audit committee any major issues that were discussed with management in connection with the initial or recurring retention of the auditor including, among other matters, any discussions regarding the application of accounting principles and auditing standards.

Difficulties Encountered When Performing the Audit

The auditor should inform the audit committee of any serious difficulties encountered in dealing with management related to the performance of the audit. This may include, among other things, unreasonable delays by management in permitting the commencement of the audit or in providing needed information, and whether the timetable set by management was unreasonable under the circumstances. The auditor also should consider informing the audit committee of other matters, if considered significant, such as the unavailability of client personnel or the failure of client personnel to complete client-prepared schedules on a timely basis.

PREPARING AN EFFECTIVE MANAGEMENT LETTER

The management letter traditionally has been an important means for the auditor to communicate to the client his or her recommendations for improvements to the operations or internal controls. Management letters in the not-for-profit environment probably have more importance than they have in the commercial enterprise environment for several reasons.

First, boards of trustees (or if applicable, the audit committees of the boards of trustees) of not-for-profit organizations are likely to appreciate the comments and recommendations that the auditor can provide. The management letter gives boards of trustees greater insights into the operations of the not-for-profit organization and helps them better understand the progress that management is making in improving the internal controls and operations of the organization. From the auditor's perspective, the more constructive and useful information that he or she can provide to the board of trustees, the greater the value that the board will place on his or her services.

Second, management of the not-for-profit organization may appreciate comments that the auditor makes in a management letter about operations and internal controls. While criticizing an individual's own area of responsibility may meet with resistance, a president or executive director of a not-for-profit organization who does not have an extensive background in financial management may view the management letter as a tool for better management of the finance department. Comments in a management letter also may give support to additional resources that may be needed in financial personnel or in financial management and accounting systems.

When preparing a management letter, the auditor should determine whether the letter is meeting the needs of the not-for-profit organization's management. In addition, the auditor should ensure that the management letter is in accordance with generally accepted auditing standards as they relate to informing the board of trustees of reportable conditions, and reportable conditions that are considered material weaknesses in internal controls, that were discovered during the audit.

The auditor first should decide whether to issue a management letter based on the audit of financial statements in accordance with generally accepted auditing standards. If the auditor identifies no matters that he or she considers to be reportable conditions (including reportable conditions that are considered to be material weaknesses in internal controls), then no management letter is required. (The definition of *reportable conditions* is provided below.) If the auditor identifies reportable conditions, GAAS require the auditor to report these matters to the audit committee or, if no audit committee exists, to the individuals with a level of authority and responsibility equivalent to an audit committee. Usually reportable conditions are reported through the management letter. If reportable conditions are included in the overall management letter, they should be clearly identified as such.

The not-for-profit organization may request that reportable conditions be reported in a separate letter. Either method is acceptable, although if separate letters are issued, a reference to the separate letter issued to management should be included in the letter reporting the reportable conditions.

SAS-60 defines *reportable conditions* as those matters that come to the auditor's attention that, in his or her judgment, should be communicated to the audit committee because they represent significant deficiencies in the design or operation of the internal control structure, which could adversely affect the organization's ability to record, process, summarize and report financial data consistent with the assertions of management in the financial statements. Such deficiencies may involve aspects of the internal control elements.

When determining which matters are reportable conditions, the auditor should consider various factors relating to the not-for-profit organization, such as its size, complexity and diversity of activities, organizational structure, and ownership characteristics.

> **OBSERVATION:** According to SAS-60, the auditor's objective in an audit of financial statements is to form an opinion on the financial statements taken as a whole. The auditor is not obligated to search for reportable conditions.

SAS-60 includes a list of examples of matters that might be considered reportable conditions. This list, which is reproduced below, is still subject to the auditor's judgment, in consideration of the individual circumstances of the not-for-profit organization.

Deficiencies in Design of Internal Controls

- Inadequate overall design of internal controls
- Absence of appropriate segregation of duties consistent with appropriate control objectives
- Absence of appropriate reviews and approvals of transactions, accounting entries, or systems output
- Inadequate procedures for appropriately assessing and applying accounting principles
- Inadequate provisions for the safeguarding of assets
- Absence of other control techniques considered appropriate for the type and level of transaction activity
- Evidence that a system fails to provide complete and accurate output that is consistent with objectives and current needs because of design flaws

Failures in the Operation of the Internal Control

- Evidence of failure of identified controls in preventing or detecting misstatements of accounting information
- Evidence that a system fails to provide complete and accurate output consistent with the entity's control objectives because of the misapplication of control procedures
- Evidence of failure to safeguard assets from loss, damage, or misappropriation
- Evidence of intentional override of the internal control by those in authority to the detriment of the overall objectives of the system
- Evidence of failure to perform tasks that are part of the internal control, such as reconciliations not prepared or not timely prepared
- Evidence of willful wrongdoing by employees or management
- Evidence of manipulation, falsification, or alteration of accounting records or supporting documents
- Evidence of intentional misapplication of accounting principles
- Evidence of misrepresentation by client personnel to the auditor
- Evidence that employees or management lack the qualifications and training to fulfill their assigned functions

Others

- Absence of a sufficient level of control consciousness within the organization
- Failure to follow up on and correct previously identified internal control deficiencies
- Evidence of significant or extensive undisclosed related-party transactions
- Evidence of undue bias or lack of objectivity by those responsible for accounting decisions

The auditor may issue various reports for reportable conditions and related matters. Several are illustrated in Exhibits 10-15 through 10-19 on the following pages.

These reports have been updated to include the new language on the restriction of the use of these reports that is contained in SAS-87.

In addition to these matters, the auditor may also wish to communicate information obtained about the organization's progress in its Year 2000 efforts. The auditor must not imply that he or she is providing assurance on Year 2000 readiness. The AICPA's Year 2000 Task Force Report, titled *The Year 2000 Issue—Current Accounting and Auditing Guidance,* provides a sample management letter comment that is included in the sample management letter contained in Exhibit 10-19.

SUMMARY

This chapter discusses the reporting aspects of an audit of the financial statements of a not-for-profit organization. It covers the various reports on financial statements that an auditor may issue and discusses the required communications to audit committees and preparation of management letters, which may include reportable conditions and material weaknesses in internal control.

EXHIBIT 10-15
MANAGEMENT LETTER COMMENTS

No Reportable Conditions; No Material Weaknesses in Internal Control

To Board of Trustees
[*Name of not-for-profit organization*]

In planning and performing our audit of the financial statements of [*name of not-for-profit organization*] as of and for the year ended [*date of statement of financial position*], we considered its internal control to determine our auditing procedures for the purpose of expressing our opinion on the financial statements and not to provide assurance on internal control. Our consideration of internal control would not necessarily disclose all matters in internal control that might be material weaknesses under standards established by the American Institute of Certified Public Accountants. A *material weakness* is a condition in which the design or operation of one or more of the specific internal control components does not reduce to a relatively low level the risk that errors or irregularities in amounts that would be material in relation to the financial statements being audited may occur and not be detected within a timely period by employees in the normal course of performing their assigned functions. We noted no matters involving internal control and its operations that we consider to be material weaknesses as defined above. We did, however, note certain matters involving internal control that are presented in the attachment to this letter for your consideration. These comments and recommendations, all of which have been discussed with the appropriate members of management, are intended to improve the internal control structure or result in other operating efficiencies.

This report is intended solely for the information and use of the board of trustees, management, and others within the organization and is not intended to be and should not be used by anyone other than these specified parties.

[*Signature of Firm*]

[*Name of City, State*]

[*Date of the completion of fieldwork*]

Notes:
1. This report (which is really the cover letter to the management letter) should be used to communicate comments that are not considered reportable conditions. Note that the letter should *not* include a positive statement that there are no reportable conditions for the not-for-profit organization as a result of the audit of financial statements.
2. The comments may be included in separate paragraphs of the body of the letter if that is a more convenient format.
3. The following is a sample management letter comment adapted from the AICPA's Year 2000 Task Force Report titled *The Year 2000 Issue— Current Accounting and Auditing Guidelines.* Auditors should consider whether this comment is still appropriate given (1) the known impact of

the Year 2000 Issue on the not-for-profit organization and (2) the potential for additional Year 2000 effects that the not-for-profit organization has not yet encountered:

The Year 2000 Issue results from a computer's inability to process year-date data accurately beyond the year 1999. Except in recent years, computer programmers consistently have abbreviated dates by eliminating the first two digits of the year, with the assumption that these two digits would always be 19. Thus, January 1, 1965, became 01/01/65. Unless corrected, this shortcut is expected to create widespread problems when the clock strikes 12:00:01 A.M. on January 1, 2000. On that date, some computer programs may recognize the date as January 1, 1900, and process data inaccurately or stop processing altogether. Additionally, the use of abbreviated dates may cause failures when systems currently attempt to perform calculations into the year 2000.

The Year 2000 Issue presents another challenge: The algorithm used in some computers for calculating leap years is unable to detect that the year 2000 is a leap year. Therefore, systems that are not Year 2000 ready may not register the additional day, and date calculations may be incorrect. Furthermore, some software programs use several dates in the year 1999 to mean something other than the date. Examples of such dates are 01/01/99, 09/09/99, and 12/31/99. As systems process information using these dates, they may produce erratic results or stop functioning.

We recommend that you take the necessary actions to remediate or replace, and to test all systems that may be negatively affected by the Year 2000 Issue, particularly mission-critical systems. This project should be monitored closely to ensure completion before mission-critical systems begin to fail. Such failures may be evident before January 1, 2000. If [*name of not-for-profit organization*] fails to take timely and appropriate action, it may experience costly and significant application-program failures that could prevent it from performing its normal processing activities. Depending on the extent of system failures, noncompliance could have catastrophic consequences for [*name of not-for-profit organization*].

Also, [*name of not-for-profit organization*] should implement additional verification procedures to test the accuracy of information received from its vendors, service providers, bankers, customers, and other third-party organizations with whom it exchanges date-dependent information, because these organizations also must become Year 2000 ready. [*Name of not-for-profit organization*] also should satisfy itself that vendors, service providers, bankers, customers, and other third-party organizations will not experience problems relating to the Year 2000 Issue that could the affect [*name of not-for-profit organization*]'s operations or cash flows.

EXHIBIT 10-16
NO MANAGEMENT LETTER COMMENTS

No Reportable Conditions; No Material Weaknesses in Internal Control

To Board of Trustees
[*Name of not-for-profit organization*]

In planning and performing our audit of the financial statements of [*name of not-for-profit organization*] as of and for the year ended [*date of statement of financial position*], we considered its internal control to determine our auditing procedures for the purpose of expressing our opinion on the financial statements and not to provide assurance on internal control. Our consideration of internal control would not necessarily disclose all matters in internal control that might be material weaknesses under standards established by the American Institute of Certified Public Accountants. A *material weakness* is a condition in which the design or operation of one or more of the internal control components does not reduce to a relatively low level the risk that errors or irregularities in amounts that would be material in relation to the financial statements being audited may occur and not be detected within a timely period by employees in the normal course of performing their assigned functions. However, we noted no matters involving internal control and its operations that we consider to be material weaknesses as defined above.

This report is intended solely for the information and use of the board of trustees, management, and others within the organization and is not intended to be and should not be used by anyone other than these specified parties.

[*Signature of Firm*]
[*Name of City, State*]
[*Date*]

Notes:
1. If the auditor does not intend to issue a management letter because he or she has no management letter comments, reportable conditions, or material weaknesses in internal control to report, the not-for-profit organization may request that the auditor issue a letter indicating that there are no material weaknesses in internal control. The following sample report may be used for this purpose. Note that a report cannot state that there are no reportable conditions.

EXHIBIT 10-17
MANAGEMENT LETTER COMMENTS

Reportable Conditions Reported; No Material Weaknesses;
No Statement on Material Weaknesses Requested by the
Not-for-Profit Organization

To Board of Trustees
[*Name of not-for-profit organization*]

In planning and performing our audit of the financial statements of [*name of not-for-profit organization*] as of and for the year ended [*date of statement of financial position*], we considered its internal control to determine our auditing procedures for the purpose of expressing our opinion on the financial statements and not to provide assurance on internal control. However, we noted certain matters involving internal control and its operation that we consider to be reportable conditions under standards established by the American Institute of Certified Public Accountants. *Reportable conditions* involve matters coming to our attention relating to significant deficiencies in the design or operation of internal control that, in our judgment, could adversely affect the organization's ability to record, process, summarize, and report financial data consistent with the assertions of management in the financial statements.

[*Include paragraphs to describe the reportable conditions noted, or refer to an attachment.*]

This report is intended solely for the information and use of the board of trustees, management, and others within the organization and is not intended to be and should not be used by anyone other than these specified parties.

[*Signature of Firm*]

[*Name of City, State*]

[*Date*]

Notes to the auditor's report:
1. This sample report may be used when the auditor has discovered reportable conditions that must be reported, but none of the reportable conditions are considered material weaknesses in internal control and the not-for-profit organization has not requested the auditor (and the auditor does not choose) to make a statement that none of the reportable conditions are material weaknesses.
2. Note 3 of Exhibit 10-15 provides a sample management letter comment regarding the Year 2000 Issue.

EXHIBIT 10-18
MANAGEMENT LETTER COMMENTS

Reportable Conditions Reported; No Material Weaknesses Noted;
Statement That There Are No Material Weaknesses
Requested by the Not-for-Profit Organization

To Board of Trustees
[*Name of not-for-profit organization*]

In planning and performing our audit of the financial statements of [*name of not-for-profit organization*] as of and for the year ended [*date of statement of financial position*], we considered its internal control to determine our auditing procedures for the purpose of expressing our opinion on the financial statements and not to provide assurance on internal control. However, we noted certain matters involving internal control and its operation that we consider to be reportable conditions under standards established by the American Institute of Certified Public Accountants. *Reportable conditions* involve matters coming to our attention relating to significant deficiencies in the design or operation of internal control that, in our judgment, could adversely affect the organization's ability to record, process, summarize, and report financial data consistent with the assertions of management in the financial statements.

[*Include paragraphs to describe the reportable conditions noted, or refer to an attachment.*]

A *material weakness* is a reportable condition in which the design or operation of one or more of the internal control components does not reduce to a relatively low level the risk that errors or irregularities in amounts that would be material in relation to the financial statements being audited may occur and not be detected within a timely period by employees in the normal course of performing their assigned functions.

Our consideration of internal control would not necessarily disclose all matters in internal control that might be reportable conditions and, accordingly, would not necessarily disclose all reportable conditions that are also considered to be material weaknesses as defined above. However, none of the reportable conditions described above is believed to be a material weakness.

This report is intended solely for the information and use of the board of trustees, management, and others within the organization and is not intended to be and should not be used by anyone other than these specified parties.

[*Signature of Firm*]

[*Name of City, State*]

[*Date*]

Notes to the auditor's report:

1. This sample report may be used when the auditor has discovered reportable conditions that must be reported but are not considered material weaknesses in internal control and the not-for-profit organization has requested the auditor to make a statement that none of the reportable conditions are material weaknesses.

2. Note 3 of Exhibit 10-15 provides a sample management letter comment regarding the Year 2000 issue.

EXHIBIT 10-19
MANAGEMENT LETTER COMMENTS

Material Weaknesses in Internal Control Reported

To Board of Trustees
[*Name of not-for-profit organization*]

In planning and performing our audit of the financial statements of [*name of not-for-profit organization*] as of and for the year ended [*date of statement of financial position*], we considered its internal control to determine our auditing procedures for the purpose of expressing our opinion on the financial statements and not to provide assurance on internal control. Our consideration of internal control would not necessarily disclose all matters in the internal control structure that might be material weaknesses under standards established by the American Institute of Certified Public Accountants. A *material weakness* is a condition in which the design or operation of one or more of the specific internal control components does not reduce to a relatively low level the risk that errors or irregularities in amounts that would be material in relation to the financial statements being audited may occur and not be detected within a timely period by employees in the normal course of performing their assigned functions. We noted the following matters involving internal control and its operation that we consider to be material weaknesses as defined above.

[*Include paragraphs to describe the material weaknesses in internal control noted, or refer to an attachment.*]

This report is intended solely for the information and use of the board of trustees, management, and others within the organization and is not intended to be and should not be used by anyone other than these specified parties.

[*Signature of Firm*]

[*Name of City, State*]

[*Date*]

Notes to the auditor's report:
1. This sample report may be used when the auditor has discovered material weaknesses in internal control that must be reported.
2. Note 3 of Exhibit 10-15 provides a sample management letter comment regarding the Year 2000 issue.

PART II
SINGLE AUDITS
UNDER OMB CIRCULAR A-133

CHAPTER 11
INTRODUCTION TO
CIRCULAR A-133 AUDITS

CONTENTS

CHAPTER 11
INTRODUCTION TO
CIRCULAR A-133 AUDITS

CROSS-REFERENCES

2001 MILLER SINGLE AUDITS: Chapter 1, "Introduction to the Single Audit"

The audit requirements for not-for-profit organizations that receive federal financial assistance have undergone significant changes over the past several years. These changes have transformed audits that were once thought to be simple, routine, and straightforward into audits that are extraordinarily complex.

Complexity of Audits

The complexity of audits of not-for-profit organizations receiving federal awards can be traced to a number of areas, but these stand out as particularly important:

1. Newness of standards
2. Authoritative sources
3. Changing requirements

Newness of standards The standards for audits of not-for-profit organizations that receive federal funds are relatively new. The original version of OMB Circular A-133 (Audits of Institutions of Higher Education and Other Nonprofit Organizations) (hereinafter "original Circular A-133") applied to audits for fiscal years that began on or after January 1, 1990. Recently, a major revision to Circular A-133 significantly changed many of the ways that these audits are performed.

Compare this with the slow evolution of auditing standards promulgated by the AICPA. The Auditing Standards Committee of the
AICPA issued Statement on Auditing Standards (SAS) No. 1 (Codification of Auditing Standards and Procedures) in November 1972,
almost twenty-five years ago. SAS-1 provided a codification of previous Statements on Auditing Procedures, which were issued even
earlier. Since that time, on average fewer than three Statements on
Auditing Standards have been issued per year, some dealing with
very specific, narrowly focused topics. Comparatively, not-for-profit
organizations and their auditors are in the infancy of the process of
implementing Circular A-133 audits.

Authoritative sources   The second factor adding complexity to the
performance of Circular A-133 audits is the number of authoritative
sources with which an auditor must be familiar to properly meet all
of the requirements. The AICPA provides the auditor with Statements on Auditing Standards, Statements of Position, and Audit
Guides. The GAO provides the "Yellow Book," which specifies the
requirements for government auditing standards. The OMB provides, in addition to Circular A-133 itself, a Compliance Supplement
covering compliance requirements and suggested audit procedures.
OMB has also issued guidance on the impact of the Year 2000 Issue
on audits performed in accordance with Circular A-133. Further,
OMB establishes separate cost principles for educational institutions
and other not-for-profit organizations. The President's Council on
Integrity and Efficiency (PCIE) provides guidance to federal cognizant agencies through its Position Statements and checklists for
performing desk reviews of Single Audit reports.

Recently, the Federal Clearinghouse, which receives completed
Single Audit reports, has imposed yet another obstacle to be overcome in successfully completion and filing of a Single Audit report.

Compounding the complexity that results from so many interested parties to the standards-setting process, each of these organizations is continuously modifying and fine-tuning its requirements as
implementation issues arise and as policy decisions are made. The
time frames for document revisions often overlap, so that the specific
requirements an auditor is attempting to meet are almost always in a
state of change.

In addition to examining the formal guidance available to the
auditor, the auditor and recipient organization can review the scope
of the work to be performed during the Circular A-133 audit with the
federal cognizant agencies. Interaction with the cognizant agency is
likely to increase under the revised Circular A-133. Cognizant agencies also may choose to conduct an after-the-fact review of the scope
of work that was performed.

The auditor also must be familiar with the specific grants, contracts, or cooperative agreements that the auditee has signed with
one or many of the federal agencies. The types and sizes of programs

under which an auditee may receive federal funding are extremely varied.

Changing audit requirements   Performing audits of not-for-profit organizations receiving federal awards presents the auditor with a constantly changing set of requirements. On July 5, 1996, the President of the United States signed into law the Single Audit Act Amendments of 1996. This law (and subsequent guidance provided by the Office of Management and Budget in the revision to Circular A-133) have far-reaching effects on the performance of single audits of not-for-profit organizations that receive federal awards.

Many detailed changes and two broad changes will affect when and how single audits of federally funded not-for-profit organizations will be performed.

First, the original Single Audit Act of 1984 did not include not-for-profit organizations within its scope. Single audit requirements were imposed on not-for-profit organizations by regulation, namely, the original Circular A-133. The Single Audit Act Amendments of 1996 includes not-for-profit organizations within its scope, so the single audit requirements for not-for-profit organizations are now imposed by law and not regulation.

Second, because the requirements of the Single Audit Act Amendments of 1996 apply to state and local governments and not-for-profit organizations, the single audit requirements for these two broad categories of entities are now the same. Circular A-128 has been rescinded, and both state and local governments and not-for-profit organizations are now included in the scope of Circular A-133.

The new single audit requirements are effective July 1, 1996, and apply to audits of fiscal years ending on or after June 30, 1997. One exception to this effective date relates to the restriction that an auditor who prepares an indirect cost proposal or allocation plan for an organization may not perform that organization's single audit when the indirect costs recovered by the organization exceed $1 million during the prior year. This restriction is not effective until audits of fiscal years ending on or after June 30, 1999.

The following list briefly summarizes the changes to the single audit that have resulted from the Single Audit Act Amendments of 1996. This summary provides only an overview and key features of the new requirements. Not-for-profit organizations and their auditors should refer to specific chapters which cover in detail each of these changes in requirements. This Guide fully incorporates the new single audit requirements.

- The threshold for when a single audit is required has been raised to $300,000 of expenditures in a year.

- Organizations that expend federal awards under only one federal program (except research and development programs) may elect to have a program-specific audit, provided that the federal program's laws, regulations, and grant agreements do not require a financial statement audit of the organization.

- Single audits are required to be performed annually, with minimal exception.

- The identification of major federal programs has been changed to a risk-based approach. After categorizing federal programs into two categories based on size, an auditor determines which large programs are low risk and which small programs are high risk in order to determine what programs will be considered major programs. Expenditures under federal programs audited as major programs must aggregate at least 50% of the total federal expenditures. Certain organizations may qualify as "low-risk auditees," in which case the 50% requirement will be reduced to 25%.

- The auditor must plan the testing of internal control over major programs to support a low assessed level of control risk for the assertions relevant to the compliance requirements for each major program. The auditor must also perform testing of internal controls over major programs as planned to support a low assessed level of control risk for the assertions relevant to the compliance requirements for each major program.

- After a transition period, the single audit reports will be due nine months after the fiscal year end.

- A data collection form, to be completed by the organization's management and its auditor, will be required to be filed. The form summarizes the particulars of the organization's single audit for the year.

- Questioned costs need to be reported only when the known or "likely" amount of questioned costs for a compliance requirement of a major program exceeds $10,000.

- Reports on compliance with "general" requirements and on compliance testing for nonmajor programs have been eliminated.

- Guidance is provided to auditors in reporting on the follow-up on prior audit comments.

There are a number of interpretations and definitions that are important in fully understanding these changes. This information is provided throughout the remaining chapters of this Guide.

Other Changes in Requirements

In addition to the pervasive changes to the Single Audit requirements described above, this year's edition of the Guide also incorporates the following recent, specific changes to the Single Audit requirements and/or updates to authoritative resources that underlie the Single Audit process:

- Amendment No. 1 to *Government Auditing Standards*, "Documentation Requirements When Assessing Control Risk at Maximum for Controls Significantly Dependent Upon Computerized Information Systems"

- Amendment No. 2 to *Government Auditing Standards*, "Auditor Communication"

- Amendment dated September 30, 1999, to OMB Circular A-110, "Uniform Administrative Requirements for Grants and Agreements with Institutions of Higher Education, Hospitals and Other Non-Profit Organizations." This amendment relates primarily to public access to research information developed by not-for-profit organizations under federal research and development programs and grants.

- 1999 revision to the OMB Circular A-133 Compliance Supplement

- OMB guidance issued for the impact of the Year 2000 Issue on audits performed in accordance with Circular A-133

Purpose of This Audit Guide

The information provided in Part II (Single Audits Under OMB Circular A-133) gives auditors one source that can guide them through a Circular A-133 audit and refer them to the specific additional documents and sources that they might need. The Guide is structured in the same way that an auditor would perform an audit—from planning through reporting. In addition, electronic workpapers, including a model audit program, are included on the accompanying disc. These tools will make audits of not-for-profit organizations much more efficient. Specific information particularly affecting not-for-profit organizations will also be included. This Guide is designed only to include information relative to Single Audits of not-for-profit organizations. It should not be used to perform a Single Audit of a state or local governmental entity.

CHAPTER 12
TECHNICAL RESOURCES FOR
A-133 AUDITS

CONTENTS

CHAPTER 12
TECHNICAL RESOURCES FOR A-133 AUDITS

CROSS-REFERENCES

2001 MILLER NOT-FOR-PROFIT ORGANIZATION AUDITS: Chapter 13, "Government Auditing Standards"; Chapter 17, "Compliance and Subrecipient Considerations"

2001 MILLER SINGLE AUDITS: Chapter 3, "Government Auditing Standards"

To effectively perform single audits in accordance with Circular A-133, auditors must be familiar with a number of important documents. Auditors also must understand the context of the guidance they are following and the impact of the reports they will issue to meet the requirements of Circular A-133.

Single audit standards are composed of three levels—Applicable AICPA auditing standards and other guidance, *Government Auditing Standards*, and requirements issued by the Office of Management and Budget (OMB).

APPLICABLE AICPA AUDITING STANDARDS

The 1994 Yellow Book states that "for financial statement audits, generally accepted government auditing standards (GAGAS) incorporate AICPA Statements on Auditing Standards that interpret its standards of fieldwork and provide additional requirements for compliance auditing." In addition, the Yellow Book states that any AICPA Statements concerning fieldwork and compliance auditing are automatically incorporated into *Government Auditing Standards* unless specifically excluded by the GAO.

Auditors performing audits in accordance with Circular A-133 and *Government Auditing Standards* must be fully cognizant of the requirements of generally accepted auditing standards (GAAS) for fieldwork and reporting. These standards are fully assessed in Part I (Financial Statement Audits) of this Guide. The auditor may find him- or herself in the position of issuing reports referring to either *Government Auditing Standards* or GAAS, or to both. In an audit report submitted to comply with a requirement for an audit in accordance with *Government Auditing Standards*, the auditor must state that the audit was performed in accordance with *Government Auditing Standards*. The report may refer to GAAS as well. In audit reports submitted for purposes other than complying with a requirement for an audit in accordance with *Government Auditing Standards*, the auditor may refer only to *Government Auditing Standards* or only to GAAS. The Yellow Book encourages the auditor to refer to *Government Auditing Standards* in all audit reports issued, including audit reports covering only the financial statements. However, the Yellow Book does not preclude the auditor, having met all of the requirements of *Government Auditing Standards*, from referring only to GAAS in the audit report.

Therefore, auditors should comply with all of the requirements of GAAS when performing audits in accordance with *Government Auditing Standards*. This will give the auditor the flexibility to issue an audit report solely on the financial statements referring only to GAAS.

> **OBSERVATION:** The auditor also must consider the fact that the perception (and probably the assumption) of readers relying on the auditor's report is that the audit has been conducted in accordance with GAAS even if that is not stated in the report. This is particularly important in the environment of not-for-profit organizations, where the stewardship of and accountability for donated resources is extremely important. Additionally, the auditor should be aware of any requirements of the state in which the not-for-profit is incorporated or the states in which the not-for-profit conducts operations, particularly fundraising activities. Frequently, these requirements specify the need for an audit in accordance with GAAS.

A number of AICPA Statements on Auditing Standards and Statements of Position have particular relevance for audits performed in accordance with *Government Auditing Standards*. Two that are particularly important are:

- SAS-74: Compliance Auditing Considerations in Audits of Governmental Entities and Recipients of Governmental Financial Assistance

- SOP 98-3: Audits of States, Local Governments, and Not-for-Profit Organizations Receiving Federal Awards

SAS-74: Compliance Auditing Considerations in Audits of Governmental Entities and Recipients of Governmental Financial Assistance

The Auditing Standards Board of the AICPA issued SAS-74 in February 1995. SAS-74 addresses both governmental and nongovernmental recipients of governmental assistance. However, the discussion in this Guide focuses on those matters important to auditors of nongovernmental organizations.

Effects of laws on financial statements SAS-74 addresses violations of laws and regulations that have a direct and material effect on the determination of financial statement amounts in audits of governmental and other recipients of governmental financial assistance.

Entities accepting governmental assistance (which includes both federal and nonfederal financial assistance) may be subject to laws and regulations that have a direct and material effect on the determination of amounts in their financial statements. The auditor should design the audit to provide reasonable assurance that the financial statements are free of material misstatements resulting from violations of laws and regulations that have a direct and material effect on the determination of financial statement amounts.

According to SAS-74, auditors should perform the following steps to meet these requirements:

- Obtain an understanding of the possible effects on financial statements of laws and regulations that are generally recognized by auditors as having a direct and material effect on the determination of net income.
- Assess whether management has identified such laws and regulations and obtain an understanding of the possible effects on the financial statements of such laws and regulations.
- Consider performing the following procedures to assess such laws and regulations and to obtain an understanding of their possible effects on the financial statements:
  — Consider knowledge about such laws and regulations obtained from prior years' audits.
  — Discuss such laws and regulations with the entity's chief financial officer, legal counsel, or grant administrators.
  — Obtain written representations from management regarding the completeness of management's identification.
  — Review the relevant portions of any directly related agreements, including those related to grants and loans.
  — Inquire of the office of the federal, state, or local auditor or other appropriate audit oversight organization about the

laws and regulations applicable to entities within their jurisdiction, including statutes and uniform reporting requirements.

— Review information about compliance requirements, such as the information included in the Compliance Supplements (described later in this chapter), the Catalog of Federal Domestic Assistance, and state and local policies and procedures.

Government Auditing Standards   SAS-74 requires auditors to follow *Government Auditing Standards* when required to do so by law, regulation, agreement, contract, or policy. This makes the auditor's responsibility to follow *Government Auditing Standards* when performing Circular A-133 audits a part of GAAS.

Federal audit requirements   SAS-74 reviews the basic elements of audits of recipients of federal financial assistance and prescribes that, when planning the audit, the auditor should determine and consider the specific federal audit requirements applicable to the engagement, including the issuance of separate reports.

SAS-74 provides guidance on the evaluation of the results of compliance audit procedures. When evaluating whether the recipient organization has complied with laws and regulations that, if not complied with, could have a direct and material effect on each major federal awards program, the auditor should consider the effect of identified instances of noncompliance on each such program. The auditor should consider:

- Frequency of noncompliance identified
- Adequacy of the primary recipient's system for monitoring subrecipients and the possible effect on the program of any noncompliance identified by the primary recipient or the auditors of the subrecipients
- Whether any instances of noncompliance resulted in questioned costs and, if they did, whether questioned costs are material to the program

When auditors are evaluating the effect of questioned costs on the opinion on compliance, they should consider the best estimate of total questioned costs for each major federal awards program (defined as *likely questioned costs*), not just the questioned costs specifically identified (defined as *known questioned costs*). Therefore, when using audit sampling, the auditor should project the amount of known questioned costs identified in the sample to the items in the major federal awards program from which the sample was selected. Note that only known questioned costs are required to be reported; the auditor is not required to report likely questioned costs.

OBSERVATION: Circular A-133 contains specific guidance for considering and reporting questioned costs.

Auditors also should consider the likely questioned costs in their report on compliance in accordance with *Government Auditing Standards* and in their opinion on the financial statements.

Communication regarding applicable audit requirements   According to SAS-74, auditors should exercise due professional care in ensuring that they and client management understand the type of engagement to be performed. Where contracts, proposals, engagement letters, etc., are used, the auditor should consider including a statement about the type of engagement and whether it is intended to meet specific audit requirements.

SAS-74 requires that, if during the course of an audit of financial statements in accordance with GAAS the auditor becomes aware that the entity is subject to an audit requirement that may not be encompassed in the terms of the engagement, the auditor should communicate to management and the audit committee (or others with equivalent authority and responsibility) that an audit in accordance with GAAS may not satisfy the relevant legal, regulatory, or contractual commitment. This communication may be oral or written, although if oral, the communication should be documented in the working papers. The auditor should consider management's actions (such as not arranging for an audit that meets the applicable requirements) in relation to the guidance provided in SAS-54.

This is only a brief introduction to the requirements of compliance auditing. They will be covered much more extensively in the chapter titled "Compliance Considerations."

SOP 98-3: Audits of States, Local Governments, and Not-for-Profit Organizations Receiving Federal Awards

In March 1998, the AICPA issued SOP 98-3 (Audits of States, Local Governments, and Not-for-Profit Organizations Receiving Federal Awards) to provide guidance for auditors in meeting the requirements of Circular A-133. It supersedes SOP 92-9 (Audits of Not-for-Profit Organizations Receiving Federal Awards), which had provided guidance under the original Circular A-133 and had grown seriously outdated and irrelevant. The SOP is effective for audits of fiscal years beginning after June 30, 1996, in which the related fieldwork commences on or after March 1, 1998.

SOP 98-3 incorporates the guidance found in the Single Audit Amendments Act of 1996, Circular A-133 (including its Compliance Supplement), and the 1994 Yellow Book (described more fully in the chapter titled "Government Auditing Standards").

A separate, extensive discussion of each of the topics covered by SOP 98-3 is not provided in this Guide. Its guidance is incorporated throughout this Guide. However, for reference purposes, the following are the general areas that are covered by SOP 98-3:

- Overview of an auditor's responsibility in an audit of federal awards
- Description of the applicability of the Single Audit Amendments Act of 1996 and Circular A-133
- Description of the auditor's responsibility for testing and reporting on the schedule of expenditures of federal awards
- Description of the auditor's responsibility for considering internal control and for performing tests of compliance with applicable laws, regulations, and program compliance requirements under GAAS and *Government Auditing Standards.*
- Description of reporting responsibilities and sample reports required by Circular A-133 and *Government Auditing Standards.*
- Description of considerations made for federal pass-through awards
- Description of the requirements for program-specific audits

Clearly, SOP 98-3 filled a very important gap in the professional literature for performing audits in accordance with Circular A-133.

GOVERNMENT AUDITING STANDARDS

The auditor must be familiar with *Government Auditing Standards* issued by the U.S. General Accounting Office (GAO). These standards are established by the Comptroller General of the United States, and Circular A-133 specifically requires that audits performed in accordance with the circular be performed in accordance with *Government Auditing Standards.* The document is commonly referred to as the Yellow Book. The most recent edition was issued in June 1994 and was effective for single audits beginning after January 1, 1995. Two amendments to the Yellow Book were issued during 1999. The guidance, which covers audits performed under Circular A-133, also may be required for any audits of federal awards.

The requirements and guidance of the Yellow Book are extensive and should be understood and carefully followed. In addition to broad guidance for auditing and reporting, the Yellow Book includes specific guidance on continuing education and quality control review requirements for auditors performing audits in accordance with *Government Auditing Standards* and on reporting internal control and compliance findings. The chapter titled "Government Auditing Standards" details the Yellow Book requirements and describes the two recent amendments to the Yellow Book. Auditors should study these before undertaking any Circular A-133 audit. The chapter titled "Preplanning for a Circular A-133 Audit" provides information on several revisions that are being contemplated to the Yellow Book.

SINGLE AUDIT STANDARDS

OMB Circular A-133: Audits of Institutions of Higher Education and Other Nonprofit Organizations

OMB Circular A-133 contains a number of requirements for audits of not-for-profit organizations that receive federal awards. These requirements relate to the following areas:

- Performing a risk analysis to determine which federal programs will be tested as major programs.
- Testing of internal controls over the administration of federal financial assistance.
- Opining on the recipient organization's compliance with laws and regulations for each of its major federal awards programs.
- Reporting on additional internal control and compliance test work performed as well as reporting on a supplemental schedule to the financial statements, which reports on the financial activities of all federal awards programs.

These requirements are discussed in detail throughout the remaining chapters of this Guide.

Position Statements of the President's Council on Integrity and Efficiency

The President's Council on Integrity and Efficiency (PCIE) was created in 1981 to identify fraud, waste, and abuse in programs funded by federal financial assistance. As such, it has played an important role in the development of the single audit concept and the fine-tuning of single audit requirements.

The Standards Committee of the PCIE issued six Position Statements that addressed specific implementation and performance issues for single audits. One of the most important documents issued by the PCIE was Position Statement No. 6 (Q&A—OMB Circular A-133). PCIE Position Statement No. 6 was applicable to audits under the original Circular A-133. Much of the guidance from this Position Statement has been incorporated into the revised Circular A-133. Position Statement No. 6 should not be used as a primary source of guidance for audits under the current Circular A-133.

PCIE had also published "Federal Cognizant Agency Audit Organization Guidelines." These guidelines contained a checklist titled "Uniform Desk Review for Single Audits" that, while designed for cognizant audit agencies, was in fact used by others, including pass-through entities, as a checklist for determining whether the basic requirements of a Single Audit had been met. This checklist was used in desk reviews, meaning that the checklist was completed using the Single Audit report, rather than using a detailed review of auditor working papers.

During 1999, PCIE issued the "Guide for Initial Review of A-133 Audit Reports" and the "Guide for Quality Control Review for A-133 Audits." As these titles suggest, the Initial Review Guide is less detailed than the Quality Review Guide and is designed to be used by federal agencies and others to perform an initial review of a federal award recipient's Single Audit report in order to select reports that should be subject to the more comprehensive Quality Review Guide. These two reports completely update the PCIE's checklist to incorporate the significant recent changes to the Single Audit requirements that are described throughout this Guide.

These PCIE guides may be valuable to a not-for-profit organization that is serving as a "pass-through entity" (explained more fully later in this Guide), meaning that the organization receives a federal award directly from a federal agency (or other not-for-profit organization or state or local governmental entity) and passes some or most of this award to other not-for-profit organizations, often called subrecipients. As will be described later in this Guide, the pass-through entity has certain responsibilities to make sure that its subrecipients use these funds in accordance with the requirements of the federal award program—including, when certain requirements are met, ascertaining whether the subrecipients have had an audit conducted in accordance with the Single Audit requirements. The PCIE guides may be very helpful to the organization in monitoring subrecipients to determine their compliance with these requirements.

> **AUDIT COST-SAVINGS TIP:** Encouraging a not-for-profit organization client to establish a formal monitoring system of subrecipients using these types of tools may help an auditor to trim audit hours in determining compliance with subrecipient monitoring requirements. The auditor also needs to be concerned with whether the organization's subrecipients are complying with the federal program requirements. Disallowances of costs charged to the federal programs by subrecipients may result in a financial statement impact to the auditor's client if

the client must itself reimburse the federal agency for disallowed costs.

OMB Circular A-110: Uniform Administrative Requirements for Grants and Agreements with Institutions of Higher Education, Hospitals, and Other Non-Profit Organizations

OMB Circular A-110 establishes standards for the administration of federal grants to and agreements with not-for-profit organizations that receive federal financial assistance (e.g., property management and reporting requirements). A revised version of the Circular was issued by the Office of Management and Budget on November 19, 1993, and amended as of August 29, 1997. A further revision of Circular A-110 was issued on September 30, 1999.

It is important for an auditor to understand the basic requirements of this Circular because they make up one of the "regulations" that the auditor will be testing for and reporting on compliance. It is a source of many of the compliance requirements contained in the Compliance Supplement. These requirements are applicable to not-for-profit organizations, including colleges and universities and hospitals. They are not applicable to state or local governments. Awareness of these requirements is important because auditors designing and performing test work on compliance with these requirements often have only general audit training and are not familiar with the level of detail contained in these requirements.

> **OBSERVATION:** OMB Circular A-110 is included on the disc accompanying this Guide.

> **OBSERVATION:** The financial management of recipient organizations should be very familiar with the A-110 requirements. This circular contains accounting and reporting requirements (e.g., requirements for the regular reporting of financial information to grantor agencies) that, in many cases, will result in a fair amount of additional work for recipient organizations.

The Circular is divided into four subparts:

- Subpart A—General requirements
- Subpart B—Pre-award requirements
- Subpart C—Post-award requirements
- Subpart D—After-the-award requirements

It also contains an appendix of standard contract provisions that all contracts (including small purchases) awarded by a recipient of federal financial assistance covered by the Circular must contain.

The auditor must fully understand the requirements of A-110 to effectively perform an audit in accordance with Circular A-133. Familiarity with this document will help the auditor identify the many requirements that are imposed on the recipients of federal funds, which may or may not be specifically included in the contract, grant, or cooperative agreement under which the not-for-profit organization receives federal financial assistance.

For example, Circular A-110 contains a number of very specific requirements regarding property management. These standards apply to property that is purchased and used by the not-for-profit organization but paid for by the federal government through a federal financial assistance program. The standards are very specific and usually would not be considered in an audit performed in accordance with GAAS. Examples of the requirements are as follows:

- The recipient organization must maintain the same insurance coverage on assets purchased with federal funds as on any of the other assets the organization owns.

- The recipient organization's equipment records for assets acquired with federal funds must include a description of the equipment, the serial number or other identification number, the source of the equipment including the award number, whether the title of the equipment vests with the federal government or the recipient organization, the acquisition date of the property, the percentage of federal ownership (if applicable), the location and condition of the equipment, the unit acquisition cost of the equipment, and the ultimate disposition data of the equipment.

- The recipient is required to perform a physical inventory of the equipment every two years and reconcile the count of the equipment to the equipment records.

This is not a complete list of the Circular A-110 property management requirements, and property management is not the only area subject to Circular A-110 administrative requirements. The list is presented only to give the auditor an understanding of the specificity of the requirements imposed on recipient organizations.

> **OBSERVATION:** Financial managers of recipient organizations may find it helpful to prepare a working paper that lists each requirement of Circular A-110 with an explanation of, and cross-reference to, how the recipient organization complies with the requirement. This type of document would be extremely helpful to the recipient organization's auditor.

The auditor must be in a position to understand the nature of these requirements and consider them when establishing an overall audit plan for evaluating the controls established by the recipient organization to ensure compliance with the requirements. The auditor also must be in a position to test the recipient organization's compliance with these requirements.

The post-award requirements in Subpart C of Circular A-110 contain the substance of the circular's guidance for the day-to-day administration of federal financial assistance programs. In addition to the property standards in the example above, Subpart C also includes requirements for financial and program management, procurement standards, reports and records, and termination and enforcement. Listed below are the general areas that are covered for each of these topics. The auditor must carefully consider all of the requirements contained in the circular when designing an effective audit program and should therefore read Circular A-110 in its entirety.

Financial and program management The financial and program management standards provide the requirements that recipients of federal financial assistance must use relating to financial management and reporting, cost accounting, and program management. The financial and program management standards provide specific requirements in the following areas:

- Financial management systems and their ability to provide accurate financial and performance data, effective control over financial resources, and the processes for recipient organizations to obtain advances or reimbursement of expenditures

- Cost sharing or matching provided by the recipient organizations, including cash and in-kind cost sharing or matching

- Uses of income generated by a program, such as whether it would be applied to increase the size of a federal program, or whether it would be used to reduce the federal financial assistance provided to a particular program

- Revision of budget and program plans for construction and nonconstruction projects including flexibility within budget line items and changes to the programmatic nature or requirements of a program

- Nonfederal audits area, which identifies the types of audits performed for recipients of federal funds, such as Circular A-133

- Definition of the allowable costs that can be charged to federal financial assistance programs (This definition is provided by reference to the OMB circular that describes the cost principles for various types of recipients of federal financial assistance. For example, not-for-profit organizations are subject to the cost principles of OMB Circular A-122 [Cost Principles for Non-profit Organizations], and OMB Circular A-21 [Cost Principles of Educational Institutions], which are described later in this chapter.)

- Period that the federal funds are available for use

Procurement standards   The procurement standards provide the requirements that recipients of federal financial assistance must use when procuring goods and services with federal funds. The procurement standards provide specific requirements in the following areas:

- The responsibility for accountability of the federal funds rests with the recipient organization, which is not relieved of its contractual requirements by passing these requirements along to subrecipients or vendors.

- The recipient is required to maintain written codes of conduct concerning the performance and actions of the recipient's employees who are responsible for the award and administration of contracts.

- Procurement transactions should provide for open and free competition for contracts or awards to the maximum extent possible.

- Written procurement standards should be maintained and should cover certain topics, including the avoidance of unnecessary purchases, the analysis of purchasing and leasing decisions, specific requirements that should be contained in purchasing solicitations, and additional considerations that the recipient organizations should make during the procurement process.

- A documented cost and price analysis should be made for each procurement.

- The requirements for the documentation that must be maintained for purchases other than small purchases.

- The establishment and operation of an effective contract administration system to ensure contractor compliance with the terms and conditions of contracts and to provide for timely follow up when instances of noncompliance are noted.

- Specific provisions that should be included in procurement contracts should be established and documented.

Reports and records   The reports and records requirements provide minimum standards for reporting and records that will allow the federal awarding agency to evaluate the financial and programmatic results of the program. These requirements cover:

- The monitoring of and reporting on program reports (The type of report and frequency of reporting should be governed by the contract under which the federal funds are awarded.)

- The methods and forms for financial reporting, including the Financial Status Report (Form SF-269 or SF-269A), the Request for Advance (Form SF-270), and the Report of Federal Cash Transactions (Form SF-272)

- The record retention requirements that recipients should follow, along with guidelines about access to the records maintained

Termination and enforcement   The termination and enforcement requirements describe the procedures and reasons for terminating a contract or invoking enforcement actions against a recipient organization, including:

- Termination of the contract by the federal awarding agency for material noncompliance with the terms and conditions of an award, or termination with the mutual consent of both parties or when requested by the recipient organization.

- The various enforcement remedies available to the federal awarding agency in instances of material noncompliance with the terms and conditions of an award. These enforcement actions include temporarily withholding cash payments, disallowing certain expenditures that were charged to the federal financial assistance program, suspending or partially terminating the award, withholding future awards to the project or program, or other legal remedies that may be available.

> **OBSERVATION:** Recipient organizations may find auditors' comments and suggestions on deficiencies in the administration of federal programs to be helpful, although the financial and program management of recipient organizations would be expected to be much more familiar with the implementation of and compliance with these requirements than auditors.

Although they have a less significant effect on the day-to-day administration of federal financial assistance, the other subparts of the circular should not be ignored. Subpart A defines many of the terms used in Circular A-110. It also gives the OMB the authority to grant exceptions to the circular, although it clearly emphasizes that, in the interest of uniformity, exceptions should be rare. Subpart A also clarifies that requirements of the circular flow through to subrecipients of federal financial assistance when those subrecipients are institutions of higher education, hospitals, or other not-for-profit organizations. Subrecipients that are state and local governmental units should follow the guidance of OMB Circular A-102 (Grants and Cooperative Agreements to State and Local Governments).

Subpart B of OMB Circular A-110 discusses the process for applying for a federal award. It provides guidance on the three main legal formats used to provide federal financial assistance: grants, cooperative agreements, and contracts. Subpart B provides guidance to federal agencies on how to design a federal award and provides guidance to potential recipients on the appropriate application process.

Of particular interest to recipient organizations, Subpart B allows recipient organizations that do business with a federal agency on a recurring basis to make the standard certifications and representations annually to the federal agency. This saves the recipient organization the sometimes excruciating process of completing the boilerplate forms every time a proposal or application is made.

Subpart D describes the procedures for the closeout of a federal financial assistance agreement and the handling of adjustments and disallowances after closeout. Subpart D requires recipient organizations to complete all reports (financial and performance reports as well as any other required reports) within 90 days after the date of the completion of the award. Other information to be furnished by the recipient organization to the federal awarding agency is also specified. The duties of the federal awarding agency and the right of the agency to extend deadlines are also specified.

Subpart D reserves the rights of the federal awarding agency to recover funds from recipient organizations when audits performed subsequent to the closeout of the agreement uncover disallowances. The procedures for the return of funds to the federal awarding agency also are discussed.

The administrative requirements of Circular A-110 are far-reaching and impose a significant amount of responsibility on the recipient organization. It is essential for the auditor to have a clear understanding of these administrative requirements to properly consider them during the audit process.

In September 1999, OMB issued a revision to Circular A-110 that focused on the area of publicly funded research activities. Basically, Congress directed federal agencies to ensure that data produced under publicly funded research programs would be available to the public. Considering the large number of federally funded research projects conducted by colleges and universities and not-for-profit hospitals, as well as many other types of not-for-profit organizations, this is a very important issue.

> **OBSERVATION:** The following numbers may help the reader understand just how important this issue is: OMB reports that it received over 9,000 comment letters on its original proposed changes, and over 3,000 additional comment letters on its amended proposed changes.

OMB amended Circular A-110 to explicitly state that the federal government has the right to:

- Obtain, reproduce, publish, or otherwise use the data first produced under a federal award, and
- Authorize others to receive, reproduce, publish, or otherwise use such data for federal purposes.

In addition, in response to a Freedom of Information Act (FOIA) request for research data relating to published research findings that were produced under an award and that then were used by the federal government in developing an agency action that has the force and effect of law, the federal awarding agency may request the not-for-profit organization award recipient to provide the research data within a reasonable period of time so that the data can be made available to the public through the procedures established under the FOIA.

Circular A-110 also describes certain research data that would not be subject to these requirements, such as trade secrets, commercial information, materials that must be kept confidential prior to publication, and personnel or medical information the publication of which would be an invasion of privacy.

OMB Circular A-122: Cost Principles for Nonprofit Organizations

OMB Circular A-122 was originally issued in July 1980 to provide some standardization of the cost principles used by not-for-profit organizations to charge costs to federal financial assistance programs. Previously, cost principles used by recipient not-for-profit organizations were the result of varying requirements among the federal awarding agencies. Circular A-122 was further amended on May 8, 1987, and August 29, 1997, with legislative lobbying and political activities. A revision to Circular A-122 in September 1995 allowed federal agencies with cost negotiation cognizance to increase the threshold for capitalization of equipment from $500 to $5,000. This revision does not extend to certain not-for-profit organizations subject to certain specific cost accounting standards. The not-for-profit organization should clear this change with its cognizant agent before increasing the threshold. OMB issued another revision to Circular A-122 that became effective on June 1, 1998.

The effect of this latest revision is to:

1. Amend the definition of *equipment* by increasing the capitalization threshold to the lesser of the amount used for financial statement purposes or $5,000.

2. Require that major not-for-profit organizations (that is, those receiving more than $10 million in direct federal funding) report indirect cost rates by two major component categories:

   - *Facilities*—defined as depreciation and use allowances on buildings, equipment, and capital improvement; interest on debt associated with certain buildings, equipment, and capital improvements; operations and maintenance expenses

   - *Administration*—defined as general administration and general expenses such as the director's office, accounting, personnel, library expenses, and all other types of expenditures not specifically identified as a part of the facilities category

3. Modify the multiple allocation base (MAB) method for computing indirect costs to be consistent with OMB Circular A-21 (see following section on Circular A-21). MAB is one of three available methodologies for computing indirect costs.

4. Clarify the treatment of the following cost items to make them consistent with Circular A-21 and the Federal Acquisition Regulations (where applicable):

   - Alcoholic beverages

   - Advertising and public relations costs

   - Organization-furnished automobiles

   - Defense and prosecution of criminal and civil proceedings, claims, appeals, and patent infringements

   - Housing and living expenses

   - Insurance

   - Memberships

   - Selling or marketing of goods and services

   - Severance pay for foreign nationals

> **OBSERVATION:** The latest revision to Circular A-122 might be better known for the costs principles it did not change than for the changes it did make. Specifically, OMB was considering restricting the allowability of trustees' travel expenses at not-for-profit organizations. It did not implement these restrictions. In addition, OMB was considering an upper limit on the payment of administrative expenses (limiting administrative expenses to 26% of total expenses). However, OMB has deferred implementing any such limits until it collects better data on indirect costs at not-for-profit organizations.

The goal of the circular is to make sure that the federal programs are not the only programs of the recipient organization that are directly charged. This prevents the recipient organizations from including these other activities as indirect costs that are allocated to programs, usually on a basis that is related to direct cost charges.

> **OBSERVATION:** Auditors will find that the recipient organization's noncompliance with these cost principles can be a significant source of questioned costs. This is because certain costs, which may be part of a recipient organization's normal operating costs, might not be chargeable to a federal financial assistance program under Circular A-122. The recipient organization should set up separate general ledger accounts to accumulate these nonallowable costs. This will help ensure that nonallowable costs are not charged to a federal program either directly or indirectly through the allocation of overhead. The existence of these accounts also demonstrates that the recipient organization is making a good faith effort to identify and segregate nonallowable costs.

> **OBSERVATION:** OMB Circular A-122 is included on the disc accompanying this Guide.

OMB Circular A-122 is divided into three attachments:

- Attachment A—General Principles
- Attachment B—Selected Items of Cost
- Attachment C—Not-for-Profit Organizations Not Subject to This Circular

Attachment A Attachment A identifies the general principles a recipient organization must use when designing a cost strategy to charge only allowable costs to federal financial assistance programs. This Attachment addresses five main groups of considerations:

1. Basic considerations for determining appropriate, allowable costs
2. Discussion of direct costs
3. Discussion of indirect costs
4. Allocation of indirect costs to programs and the determination of indirect cost rates
5. Negotiation and approval of rates

Basic considerations for determining appropriate, allowable costs Recipient organizations (and their auditors) must consider certain basic facts when determining costs to be charged to federal financial assistance programs. These basic considerations are as follows:

- The total cost of a program consists of the sum of its direct costs and its allocable share of indirect costs, less any applicable credits.

- The allowability of costs is affected by a number of factors including whether the cost is allowed under the specific federal financial assistance program; whether the cost is reasonable, documented, and determined in accordance with generally accepted accounting principles; and, perhaps most importantly, whether the cost is treated in a manner consistent with that used for other costs. The cost must also not be used to meet cost-sharing requirements of any other federal program.

- The cost must be *reasonable*, which means that a prudent person would reasonably be expected to incur the same cost given the same set of circumstances.

- The cost is properly allocable to the particular federal financial assistance program (i.e., it is both allowable under the program and necessary for the overall operation of the program).

- The costs charged to the program are net of any applicable credits. Any purchase discounts, rebates, or allowances obtained by a recipient organization on costs charged to a federal financial assistance program must be passed along to the federal awarding agency.

- If it is unclear whether certain costs are allowable, the recipient organization is encouraged to reach an advance understanding regarding allowability with the federal awarding agency.

Direct costs The principle regarding direct costs regulates which costs may be charged directly to federal financial assistance programs and which should be charged to other programs of the recipient organization. Different not-for-profit organizations have different policies regarding the costs they charge directly to programs, including federal programs, and the costs they include as indirect costs, which are then allocated to programs.

Although it allows recipient organizations some flexibility to design cost accounting systems, Circular A-122 makes it clear that activities such as fund raising and investment management are considered programs that should be directly charged with their applicable costs.

Indirect costs Indirect costs are costs incurred for the common or joint benefit of the entire recipient organization; they cannot be charged to a specific program of the recipient organization.

Indirect costs typically include rent or occupancy costs, personnel costs related to the organization's senior management, and accounting and finance costs. Some organizations, however, treat these costs as direct costs. For instance, some accounting and finance personnel are able to allocate their time to specific programs. A particular accountant might devote all of his or her time to the approval of payment vouchers relating to a specific program. All of the personnel costs relating to that individual might be directly charged to that specific program. This is appropriate only if *all* of the significant programs of the organization are charged directly for the time and expense of accounting personnel. If they are not, then all of the personnel costs relating to accounting and finance personnel should be treated as indirect costs.

Indirect cost allocation The cost principle regarding indirect cost allocation regulates the allocation of indirect costs to programs and the development and use of indirect cost rates. Circular A-122 is fairly detailed in terms of the acceptable methods of allocating indirect costs to programs.

Recipients of federal financial assistance should establish an acceptable basis for spreading indirect costs to each program, depending on the relative benefit each individual program receives from the indirect costs. Typically, the recipient organization will choose direct costs or some component of direct costs to allocate indirect costs. The allocation basis might be total direct costs, total direct administrative costs (i.e., exclusive of direct program costs), direct personnel costs (including fringe benefits), or directly charged salaries. These bases involve amounts that are expressed in dollars, but a nonmonetary basis, such as the square footage of office space occupied by personnel or the actual head count of personnel, also may be appropriate. The more common bases for not-for-profit organizations are those that can be expressed in terms of monetary value.

Circular A-122 describes the processes and procedures required to use an "indirect cost rate" in charging indirect costs to programs. For example, an organization might use salary expenses as its basis for allocation and may determine that indirect costs equate to 40 percent of directly charged salary expense. Therefore, for every dollar of salary expenses charged to programs, an additional forty cents is charged to cover indirect costs.

The Circular provides guidance for recipient organizations in developing indirect cost allocation plans and obtaining approval of the rates used from their cognizant audit agencies. The use of a simplified allocation method and a multiple allocation base is descried, along with the direct allocation method.

Negotiation and approval of indirect cost rates This section describes the uses of predetermined, fixed, provisional, and final indirect cost rates.

> **OBSERVATION:** Auditing indirect cost allocation plans may be a new experience for auditors. Auditors should ensure that

the consideration of the indirect cost allocation plan is included as an integral part of their audit programs.

Attachment B   Attachment B of Circular A-122 lists 56 individual costs and discusses their allowability as costs charged to federal financial assistance programs. These costs are listed in Exhibit 12-1. This discussion is meant to provide only an overview of the Circular, but to illustrate the Circular's contents we will examine one of the 56 costs: advertising costs.

Circular A-122 defines *advertising costs* as media advertising (e.g., magazines, newspapers, television) and the related costs. The circular states that only certain types of advertising costs are allowable under federal programs: advertising to recruit personnel, advertising to procure goods and services, and generally, advertising for the disposal of excess material acquired in the performance of the program, and advertising specifically required by the federal program. No other advertising costs are allowable charges to a federal financial assistance program.

As this example illustrates, the requirements under which the recipient must operate are very specific. If the recipient organization and its auditor are not familiar with the cost principles discussed in Circular A-122, the recipient organization is likely to charge unallowable costs to a federal financial assistance program and the auditor may not identify the particular item as an unallowable cost.

Attachment C   Attachment C lists more than 30 not-for-profit organizations that are not subject to the requirements of the circular. It also lists "other not-for-profit organizations as negotiated with awarding agencies." The vast majority of not-for-profit organizations, however, are subject to the requirements of Circular A-122.

OMB Circular A-21: Cost Principles for Educational Institutions

OMB Circular A-21, originally issued in 1979, establishes cost principles applicable to research and development, training, and other sponsored work performed by colleges and universities under grants, contracts, and other agreements with the federal government. It is the equivalent of Circular A-122 for educational institutions. A significant revision of Circular A-21 was made in April 1996, with subsequent revision. The currently effective version of Circular A-21 is dated October 27, 1998. The Guide incorporates the revised material, where applicable.

Circular A-21 is divided into sections A–K. The following discussion is meant to provide some general information on the contents of these sections. Auditors engaged to perform A-133 audits of educa-

EXHIBIT 12-1
OMB CIRCULAR A-122 COST CATEGORIES

The cost categories addressed by OMB Circular A-122 are:

1. Advertising and public relations costs
2. Alcoholic beverages
3. Bad debts
4. Bid and proposal costs (reserved)
5. Bonding costs
6. Communication costs
7. Compensation for personal services
8. Contingency provisions
9. Contributions
10. Defense and prosecution of criminal and civil proceedings, claims, appeals, and patent infringement
11. Depreciation and use allowances
12. Donations
13. Employee morale, health, and welfare costs and credits
14. Entertainment costs
15. Equipment and other capital expenditures
16. Fines and penalties
17. Fringe benefits
18. Goods and services for personal use
19. Housing and personal living expenses
20. Idle facilities and idle capacity
21. Independent research and development (reserved)
22. Insurance and indemnification
23. Interest, fund-raising, and investment management costs
24. Labor relations costs
25. Lobbying
26. Losses on other awards
27. Maintenance and repair costs
28. Materials and supplies
29. Meetings and conferences
30. Membership, subscription, and professional activity costs
31. Organization costs
32. Overtime, extra-pay shift, and multi-shift premiums
33. Page charges in professional journals
34. Participant support costs
35. Patent costs
36. Pension plans
37. Plant security costs
38. Pre-award costs
39. Professional service costs
40. Profits and losses on disposition of depreciable property of their capital assets
41. Publication and printing costs
42. Rearrangement and alteration costs
43. Reconversion costs
44. Recruiting costs
45. Relocation costs
46. Rental costs
47. Royalties and other costs for use of patents and copyrights
48. Selling and marketing
49. Severance pay
50. Specialized service facilities
51. Taxes
52. Termination costs
53. Training and education costs
54. Transportation costs
55. Travel costs
56. Trustees

tional institutions should carefully review Circular A-21 and incorporate its requirements into the audit programs they develop.

> **OBSERVATION:** OMB Circular A-21 is included on the disc accompanying this Guide.

Section A of Circular A-21 discusses the document's purpose and scope, including its objective, general policy guidelines, and application. The circular requires the sound application of accounting practices by colleges and universities, allowing these institutions to accumulate costs in accordance with generally accepted accounting principles and to adequately document these costs.

Section B provides definitions for the following terms:

- Major functions of an institution
- Sponsored agreement
- Allocation
- Facilities and administrative costs

Section C discusses basic cost considerations. Costs of a *sponsored agreement* (which is defined in Section B as any grant, contract, or other agreement between the institution and the federal government) are defined as the allowable direct costs incident to the performance of the sponsored agreement, plus the allocable portion of the allowable indirect costs of the institution, net of any applicable credits. Section C analyzes each of the following factors.

To be allowable, costs:

- Must be reasonable.
- Must be allocable to sponsored agreements under the principles and methods provided with Circular A-21.
- Must be given consistent treatment through application of those generally accepted accounting principles appropriate in the circumstances.
- Must conform to any limitations or exclusions set forth in the cost principles of Circular A-21 or in the sponsored agreement as to types or amounts or cost items.

Section D of Circular A-21 analyzes the types of costs that would be charged directly to a particular sponsored activity or any other activity of the college or university. Examples of direct costs include compensation expenses for the individuals performing work under the sponsored agreement (which may include fringe benefit costs, if these costs are consistently treated as direct costs), costs of materials consumed or expended in the performance of the work (whether they are purchased or provided through some type of internal service department of the college or university), extraordinary utility consumption, and any other items that can be specifically attributable to the work performed under the sponsored agreement.

Sections E through H discuss indirect costs and indirect cost allocation plans now referred to as "facilities and administrative (F&A) costs." Section E covers some general concepts relating to F&A costs. As defined by the Circular, F&A costs are "those costs that are incurred for common or joint objectives and therefore cannot be identified readily and specifically with a particular sponsored project, an institutional activity, or any other institutional activity." Section F of Circular A-21 offers the following examples of indirect costs of colleges and universities:

- Depreciation and use allowances
- Interest
- Operation and maintenance expenses
- General administration and general expenses
- Departmental administration expenses
- Sponsored projects administration expenses
- Library expenses
- Student administration and services

Section F also discusses the need for cost groupings, the selection of a distribution method, and the order of distribution of F&A costs.

Section G discusses the determination and application of F&A cost rates. This section covers the establishment of F&A cost pools and their distribution basis. Also discussed are the use of negotiated lump sums for F&A costs, predetermined fixed rates for F&A costs, negotiated fixed rates and carry-forward provisions for adjustment of over- or underrecovery of F&A costs for prior years, and limitations on the reimbursement of administrative costs.

> **OBSERVATION:** OMB is considering developing a standardized format for submitting and reviewing F&A cost proposals. If such a standardized format is developed, it will be incorporated into the requirements of Circular A-21.

Section H provides a simplified procedure for determining allowable indirect costs for colleges and universities that may be used when the total direct cost for work covered by Circular A-21 does not exceed $10 million in a fiscal year.

Section J (Section I is not applicable) establishes the principles used to determine the allowability of 50 specific cost items. Some of the specific items listed are also covered by Circular A-122, but a number of items in this section relate specifically to costs incurred by colleges and universities.

The principles and rules in OMB Circular A-21 apply equally to direct and F&A costs. For example, Section J specifically states that the costs of alcoholic beverages are unallowable. Therefore, not only would alcoholic beverages be unallowable as an F&A cost, they also would be unallowable as a cost included in an F&A cost pool. This is significant since the individuals charging their time and expenses to sponsored programs will probably be familiar with many of the cost principles described in this circular and the particular grants or contracts underlying the sponsored programs. However, the administrative person who prepares and codes the check requisition to pay for the department's holiday party may not be at all familiar with these cost principles, resulting in an incorrect charge to the federal financial assistance program. Appendixes A and B include cost accounting standards and cost accounting disclosure statements, as well as their applicability.

Compliance Supplement

The Compliance Supplement has been prepared and issued by OMB to assist auditors in performing audits in accordance with Circular A-133. The current version of the Compliance Supplement, which was issued in April 1999 updates the previous "Provisional" Compliance Supplement, which was issued by OMB in June 1997.

> **OBSERVATION:** A copy of the Compliance Supplement is included in the disc accompanying this Guide. Because of its large size, auditors may find it easier to order a copy of the Compliance Supplement from the Government Printing Office at 202-512-1800, stock number 041-001-00522-6.

The following sections describe the contents of the Compliance Supplement and some of the significant audit implications of the document. It also highlights some of the more important areas where the April 1999 version differs from the June 1998 Compliance Supplement.

The Compliance Supplement is divided into the following parts:

1. Background, purpose, and applicability
2. Matrix of compliance requirements
3. Compliance requirements
4. Agency program requirements
5. Clusters of programs

6. Internal control

7. Guidance for auditing programs not included in the Compliance Supplement

Part 1—Background, Purpose, and Applicability

The April 1999 Compliance Supplement updates and supersedes the June 1998 Compliance Supplement. While the Compliance Supplement is designed to assist auditors in performing audits in accordance with Circular A-133, auditors should still perform reasonable procedures to ensure that compliance requirements are current. These procedures might include inquiries of management and review of contract and grant agreements for major programs to determine whether the compliance requirements for these programs that are included in the Compliance Supplement are current and whether there are any additional provisions of contract and grant agreements that should be covered by an audit under the Single Audit Amendments Act of 1996 or that update or augment the requirements of the Compliance Supplement. If auditors perform these procedures, the Compliance Supplement may be considered a "safe harbor" for identification of compliance requirements to be tested for programs that are included in the Compliance Requirement. Auditors should not consider the Compliance Supplement to be a "safe harbor" for identifying the audit procedures to apply in a particular engagement.

Part 2—Matrix of Compliance Requirements

The Compliance Supplement includes a matrix that lists all of the CFDA numbers for the programs included in the Compliance Supplement vertically and each of the 14 compliance requirements (to be discussed later) horizontally. The check-box for each compliance requirement will either (a) contain a "Y," which indicates that the compliance requirement may apply to that program, or (b) be shaded, which indicates that the program normally does not have activity that is subject to this type of compliance requirement.

If a Y is indicated, the auditor should use Parts 3 and 4 (described below) in planning and performing tests of compliance. Part 3 would provide overall guidance on testing the compliance requirement and Part 4 would provide information on the compliance requirements pertaining to a particular program. In addition, the auditor would consult Part 6 in assessing control risk and in designing tests of internal control with respect to each applicable compliance requirement.

The April 1999 update to the Compliance Supplement brings to over 100 the number of federal programs now covered by the Compliance Supplement. Important to auditors of not-for-profit organizations, these programs include many of those typically awarded to not-for-profit organizations, including those administered by the following:

- U.S. Agency for International Development (new for 1999)
- Department of Housing and Urban Development
- Department of Labor
- National Endowment for the Humanities (new for 1999)
- Department of Education
- Department of Health and Human Services
- Corporation for National and Community Service

Part 3—Compliance Requirements

This part of the Compliance Supplement contains those compliance requirements that are generic to federal programs. Administrative requirements unique to a single program or to a cluster of programs are discussed in Part 4.

The compliance requirements relating to the administrative requirements for not-for-profit organizations are derived primarily from Circular A-110. The cost principles inherent in these compliance requirements are derived from Circulars A-122 and A-21. Both of these Circulars were described earlier in this chapter and are included in electronic format in the disc accompanying this Guide.

For each of the 14 compliance requirements, Part 3 provides the following:

- General description of the compliance requirement
- Audit objectives relative to the compliance requirement
- Suggested audit procedures

The suggested audit procedures are provided to assist auditors in planning and performing tests of compliance. Auditor judgment is required to determine whether the suggested procedures are sufficient to achieve the stated audit objective and whether additional or alternative audit procedures are needed.

> **OBSERVATION:** As mentioned above, it is clear that auditors are required to take responsibility for the sufficiency of their audit procedures and not simply rely on the Compliance Supple-

ment to provide a "safe-harbor" listing of audit procedures to be performed.

The compliance requirements included in Part 3 are as follows:

- Activities allowed or unallowed
- Allowable costs/cost principles
- Cash management
- Davis–Bacon Act
- Eligibility
- Equipment and real property management
- Matching, level of effort, earmarking
- Period of availability of federal funds
- Procurement and suspension and debarment
- Program income
- Real property acquisition and relocation assistance
- Reporting
- Subrecipient monitoring
- Special tests and provisions

The April 1999 update to the Compliance Supplement added compliance requirements, audit objectives, and suggested audit procedures for testing large research facilities' construction costs, consistent with revisions to OMB Circular A-21. Suggested audit procedures were augmented with advice to the auditor consulting with the not-for-profit organization that is being audited. One area of discussion was the most efficient way to audit indirect cost rate proposals.

Part 4—Agency Program Requirements

This part of the Compliance Supplement provides compliance information about specific federal programs to assist auditors in testing compliance for each major federal program. Part 4 describes each of the objectives of the included program as well as some of the important procedures of the program. Part 4 also lists, for each applicable compliance requirement, audit objectives and suggested audit procedures for the included programs.

There are five specific types of compliance requirements that, when applicable to a program included in Part 4, will always provide specific program information in Part 4. These compliance requirements are:

- Activities allowed or unallowed
- Eligibility
- Matching, level of effort, earmarking
- Reporting
- Special tests and provisions

The other nine types of compliance requirements generally are not specific to a program and usually are not included in Part 4. However, when one of these other nine types of compliance requirements has information specific to a program, that specific information will be included in Part 4.

Thus, when developing the audit procedures to test compliance for a major federal program, the auditor should first look in Part 2 to identify which of the compliance requirements are applicable, and then use both Part 3 and Part 4 to determine the details of the requirements.

The April 1999 update to the Compliance Supplement, under "Special Tests and Provisions," confirms that auditors are not expected to plan and perform audit procedures to determine whether the recipient complied with contractual requirements relating to the Year 2000 Issue. However, auditors need to consider the effect of Year 2000 Issues when performing tests of compliance. These considerations will be discussed later in this Guide.

Part 5—Clusters of Programs

OMB Circular A-133 provides that in certain circumstances programs may be audited as clusters of programs. Programs with different CFDA numbers could be defined as a *cluster of programs* if they are so closely related that they share common compliance requirements.

Part 5 lists a number of programs that are to be treated as clusters of programs. Of the programs on this list, Part 5 includes specific requirements for only two: Student Financial Aid and Research and Development. Thus, for these two program clusters auditors should use the compliance requirements and suggested audit procedures in Part 5 in the same way that they use the specific requirements of individual programs in Part 4. For program clusters other than the two whose requirements have been included, auditors should use the guidance of Part 7 (described below) for auditing compliance when a program is not included in the Compliance Supplement.

Part 6—Internal Control

This part of the Compliance Supplement provides guidance to auditors in meeting their responsibilities to test internal controls over major federal awards programs. It describes each compliance requirement, the objectives of internal control, and certain characteristics of internal control that, when present and operating effectively, may ensure compliance with program requirements.

Part 6 describes certain characteristics of each of the five components of internal control that should reasonably assure compliance with the requirements of federal laws, regulations, and program compliance requirements. Part 6 also provides a description of the components of internal control and examples of characteristics common to the 14 types of compliance requirements. While these listings are not a checklist, Part 6 of the Compliance Supplement has served to broaden the auditor's consideration of internal control, because the internal control characteristics that it is providing to auditors as guidance are quite specific.

Part 7—Guidance for Auditing Programs Not Included in the Compliance Supplement

Part 7 provides guidance to auditors in designing tests to check compliance and then auditing the compliance of a major federal program when the program is not included in the Compliance Supplement or when a cluster of programs listed in Part 5 is not included in the Compliance Supplement.

Basically, the auditor is responsible for determining the applicable compliance requirements. The compliance requirements that the auditor must identify are those that may have a direct and material effect on the program.

Part 7 provides some detailed steps relating to each of the following questions, which will serve as a guide for determining what compliance requirements to test:

- What are the program objectives, program procedures, and compliance requirements for a specific program?
- Which of the compliance requirements could have a direct and material effect on the program?
- Which of the compliance requirements are susceptible to testing by the auditor?
- Into which of the 14 types of compliance requirements does each compliance requirement fall?
- For special tests and provisions, what are the applicable audit objectives and audit procedures?

SUMMARY

The guidance and requirements of the documents discussed in this chapter have been incorporated throughout Part II of this Guide.

CHAPTER 13
GOVERNMENT AUDITING STANDARDS

CONTENTS

Chapter 13
GOVERNMENT AUDITING STANDARDS

CROSS-REFERENCES

2001 Miller Not-for-Profit Organization Audits: Chapter 3, "Audit Planning"; Chapter 4, "Internal Control Considerations"; Chapter 18, "Reporting Under Circular A-133"

2001 Miller Single Audits: Chapter 3, "Government Auditing Standards"

OVERVIEW

Audits performed in accordance with OMB Circular A-133 also must be performed in accordance with *Government Auditing Standards*. These standards also are sometimes referred to as generally accepted government auditing standards (GAGAS) and are issued by the U.S. General Accounting Office (GAO) in a document frequently referred to as the "Yellow Book" (because of its bright yellow cover). *Government Auditing Standards* were first issued in 1972 and have been revised periodically. In 1999, the GAO issued two amendments to the 1994 version of the Yellow Book that make some relatively minor changes to the Yellow Book requirements, as well as update its terminology to conform with recently issued AICPA Statements on Auditing Standards.

Amendment No. 1, "Additional Documentation Requirements When Assessing Control Risk at Maximum for Computer-Related Controls" (A-GAGAS-1), prescribes additional documentation requirements for (1) the assessment of control risk at maximum for assertions that are significantly dependent on computer applications and (2) the basis for concluding that resulting audit procedures are designed to effectively achieve audit objectives and appropriately reduce audit risk to an acceptable level.

The second amendment, "Auditor Communication" (A-GAGAS-2), requires specific communication with the organization being audited, including its audit committee, as to the scope of compliance and internal control work performed under *Government Auditing Standards*. It also requires that the report on the financial statements emphasize the importance of the reports on compliance with laws and regulations and internal control over financial reporting when these reports are issued separately from the report on the financial statements.

The revisions to *Government Auditing Standards* resulting from A-GAGAS-1 are effective for financial statement audits of periods ending on or after September 15, 1999. The revisions resulting from A-GAGAS-2 are effective for financial statement audits of periods ending on or after January 1, 2000.

The Yellow Book provides standards for audits of government organizations, programs, activities, and functions and of government assistance received by contractors, not-for-profit organizations, and other nongovernmental organizations. The standards pertain to the auditor's professional qualifications, the quality of audit effort, and the characteristics of professional and meaningful audit reports.

The Yellow Book covers both financial and performance audits. It is organized as follows:

- Chapter 1—Introduction
- Chapter 2—Types of Government Audits
- Chapter 3—General Standards
- Chapter 4—Fieldwork Standards for Financial Audits
- Chapter 5—Reporting Standards for Financial Audits
- Chapter 6—Fieldwork Standards for Performance Audits
- Chapter 7—Reporting Standards for Performance Audits

This Guide discusses Chapters 1–5 of the Yellow Book, which cover the standards applicable to audits performed in accordance with Circular A-133. The Yellow Book is organized to follow the AICPA's organization of GAAS: general standards, fieldwork standards, and reporting standards. Each section of the Yellow Book indicates the extent to which it incorporates the corresponding GAAS.

> **OBSERVATION:** Auditors should not ignore Chapters 6 and 7 of the Yellow Book. There are several cross-references to these chapters in the first five chapters of the Yellow Book, and the reporting guidance in Chapters 6 and 7 is helpful in drafting findings relating to a recipient organization's internal controls and compliance with laws and regulations.

> **OBSERVATION:** The 1994 Yellow Book and the two amendments described above are included on the disc accompanying this Guide.

INTRODUCTION

Chapter 1 of the Yellow Book discusses the purpose and applicability of *Government Auditing Standards*. It calls attention to the fact that the resources used by governments at various levels must be properly accounted for by the officials and employees that manage the resources and the related public programs. Because of this accountability, more information about government programs and services is needed. This includes those government programs that are carried out by not-for-profit organizations.

The Yellow Book establishes auditing standards to provide accountability and to assist public officials and employees in carrying out their responsibilities. The standards not only codify the current practices, but also include concepts and audit areas that are still evolving, which are vital to the accountability objectives in audits of governments and their programs and services.

> **OBSERVATION:** OMB Circular A-133 audits are performed in the public spotlight. Auditors must consider this when designing and executing audit programs.

> **OBSERVATION:** Audit reports of not-for-profits generally are subject to public inspection. This is another issue auditors should consider when designing audits and drafting findings. Public reports also make managers of the recipient organizations particularly sensitive to the reporting of findings by auditors.

Chapter 1 of the Yellow Book also addresses the procurement of audit services. Although it does not establish a standard that must be followed, it lists criteria in addition to price that an organization should consider when procuring audit services. These criteria include the responsiveness of the bidder to the request for proposal, the experience of the bidder, the availability of bidder staff with professional qualifications and technical abilities, and the results of the bidder's external quality control reviews.

The Yellow Book encourages recipient organizations to consider the above factors (and other factors that might be applicable to the particular circumstances) in addition to price when selecting an auditor. This is particularly important for A-133 audits and audits in accordance with GAAS, because not all independent auditors have the skills or qualifications needed to perform these types of audits. In almost all cases, the recipient organization is under financial pressure and is looking for the lowest cost audit available; this may lead to lower quality audits.

TYPES OF AUDITS

Chapter 2 of the Yellow Book defines, and distinguishes between, financial audits and performance audits.

Financial Audits

Financial audits include financial statement audits and financial related audits. Financial statement audits provide reasonable assurance about whether the financial statements of an audited entity present fairly the entity's financial position, results of operations, and cash flows in conformity with generally accepted accounting principles. Financial statement audits also include audits of financial statements prepared in conformity with any of several other bases of accounting discussed in auditing standards issued by the AICPA.

In a financial related audit, the auditor determines whether:

- Financial information is presented in accordance with established or stated criteria,
- The entity has adhered to specific financial compliance requirements, or
- The entity's internal control structure over financial reporting and/or the safeguarding of assets is suitably designed and implemented to achieve the control objectives.

Financial related audits may include audits of the following items:

- Segments of financial statements; financial information (e.g., statement of revenue and expenses, statement of cash receipts and disbursements, statement of fixed assets); budget requests; and variances between estimated and actual financial performance
- Internal controls over compliance with laws and regulations, such as those governing the bidding for, accounting for, and reporting on grants and contracts, including proposals, amounts billed, amounts due on termination of claims, and so forth
- Internal controls over financial reporting and/or the safeguarding of assets, including controls using computer-based systems
- Compliance with laws and regulations and allegations of fraud

Performance Audits

A *performance audit* is an objective and systematic examination of evidence for the purpose of providing an independent assessment of the performance of a government organization, program, activity, or function. The assessment should provide information to improve public accountability and facilitate decision making by parties with responsibility to oversee or initiate corrective action. Performance audits include economy and efficiency audits and program audits.

> **AUDIT COST-SAVINGS TIP:** Audits performed in accordance with Circular A-133 are financial audits. However, this certainly doesn't preclude auditors performing A-133 audits from conducting performance audits for clients as an augmentation of the A-133 audits. In fact, the knowledge obtained by the auditor in the A-133 audit places him or her in a good position to determine which areas warrant a performance audit.
>
> For example, when auditing the results of a particular federal program, the auditor may discover that the program did not meet its objectives. The auditor may then suggest further study of the program (a performance audit) to obtain more information about the program's performance and to develop solutions to the problems discovered. Additionally, performance audits may be performed for not-for-profit organizations that pass federal awards through to subrecipients. Auditors can assist such clients in monitoring subrecipients by auditing their performance on federal award programs. This may be a significant new practice area for auditors to develop.

GENERAL STANDARDS

Chapter 3 of the Yellow Book prescribes general standards for conducting financial and performance audits. These standards relate to the qualifications of the staff, the audit organization's and the individual auditor's independence, the exercise of due professional care in conducting the audit and in preparing related reports, and the presence of quality controls.

Qualifications of the Audit Staff

The first general standard states:

> The staff assigned to conduct the audit should collectively possess adequate professional proficiency for the tasks required.

This standard makes the audit organization responsible for ensuring that audits are conducted by staff members who collectively have the knowledge and skills necessary for that audit. These skills should include a thorough knowledge of government auditing and of the specific or unique environment in which the auditee operates. This standard applies to the knowledge and skills of the audit organization as a whole and not necessarily to the knowledge and skills of each individual auditor. The Yellow Book acknowledges that an audit organization may need to employ personnel or hire outside consultants knowledgeable in such areas as accounting, statistics, law, engineering, audit design and methodology, automated data processing, public administration, economics, social sciences, or actuarial sciences.

As part of its discussion of the first general standard, the Yellow Book includes a discussion of continuing education requirements and staff qualifications.

Continuing education requirements   The continuing education requirements contained in the 1988 Yellow Book had a significant effect on the audit community. Auditors were required to meet certain requirements, including the specification of the acceptable types of educational areas. This increased the time and financial commitments of auditors conducting audits in accordance with the Yellow Book. The 1994 revision of the Yellow Book carries forward these requirements essentially unchanged. In fact, the 1994 revision of the Yellow Book refers to a document issued by the GAO in April 1991 that provides guidance on applying the 1988 Yellow Book requirements. Thus, auditors can continue to look to the *Interpretation of Continuing Education and Training Requirements* when seeking guidance on continuing education requirements

> **OBSERVATION:** *GAO's Interpretation of Continuing Education and Training Requirements* is included on the disc accompanying this Guide.

Each auditor responsible for planning, directing, conducting, or reporting on audits under these standards should complete, every two years, at least 80 hours of continuing education and training that contributes to the auditor's professional proficiency. At least 20 hours should be completed in any one year of the two-year period. Individuals responsible for planning or conducting an audit, conducting substantial portions of the fieldwork, or reporting on the audit under these standards should complete at least 24 of the 80 hours of continuing education and training in subjects directly related to the government environment and government auditing. If the audited entity operates in a specific or unique environment, auditors also should receive training related to that environment.

> **OBSERVATION:** Specific or unique environment training will become increasingly prevalent. As auditors gain increasing experience performing Yellow Book audits for longer periods

of time, the basic and intermediate level governmental auditing courses will no longer provide sufficient information. Experienced auditors will not want to invest their time and money in these low-level courses.

The continuing education and training courses applied to the 80-hour requirement may cover topics such as current developments in audit methodology, accounting, assessment of internal controls, principles of management or supervision, financial management, statistical sampling, evaluation, design, and data analysis. They also may cover subjects related to the auditor's fieldwork, such as public administration, public policy and structure, industrial engineering, economics, social sciences, or computer science.

The Yellow Book notes two exceptions to the above requirements:

1. External consultants and internal experts and specialists should be qualified and should maintain professional proficiency in their areas of expertise or specialization. However, they are not required to meet the stated continuing education and training requirements.

2. Auditors performing nonaudit activities and services are not required to meet the stated continuing education and training requirements.

> **OBSERVATION:** Auditors should refer to *Interpretation of Continuing Education and Training Requirements* for additional guidance on the application of Yellow Book requirements to individual auditors and for a discussion of the allowability of certain continuing education topics.

To meet the Yellow Book's continuing education requirements, an audit organization should establish a program to ensure that its staff maintains professional proficiency through continuing education and training. The organization should maintain adequate documentation of the education and training completed.

Staff qualifications The Yellow Book addresses the broader issue of staff qualifications by prescribing a list of skills and their applicability to certain audit situations. Qualifications for staff members conducting audits include:

- Knowledge of the methods and techniques applicable to government auditing and the education, skills, and experience to apply such knowledge to the audit being conducted

- Knowledge of government organizations, programs, activities, and functions
- Skills to communicate clearly and effectively both orally and in writing
- Skills appropriate for the audit work being conducted:
  — If the work requires use of statistical sampling, the staff or consultants to the staff should include persons with statistical sampling skills.
  — If the work requires extensive review of computerized systems, the staff or consultants to the staff should include persons with computer audit skills.
  — If the work involves review of complex engineering data, the staff or consultants to the staff should include persons with engineering skills.
  — If the work involves the use of nontraditional audit methodologies, the staff or consultants to the staff should include persons with skills in those methodologies.
- For financial audits that lead to an expression of an opinion the following qualifications:
  — Auditors should be proficient in the appropriate accounting principles and in *Government Auditing Standards*.
  — Public accountants engaged to conduct audits should be (1) licensed certified public accountants or persons working for a licensed certified public accounting firm or (2) public accountants licensed on or before December 31, 1970, or persons working for a public accounting firm licensed on or before December 31, 1970.

Independence

The second Yellow Book general standard states:

> In all matters relating to the audit work, the audit organization and the individual auditors, whether government or public, should be free from personal and external impairments to independence, should be organizationally independent, and should maintain an independent attitude and appearance.

OBSERVATION: All audit firms, but particularly larger ones, should be careful when partners or other employees serve on the boards of directors or as trustees of recipient organizations that are potential audit clients. Such participation may preclude the audit organization from serving as auditors to these potential clients.

Personal impairments, which would cause the auditor to lose the perception of independence, include, but are not limited to, the following:

- Official, professional, personal, or financial relationships that might cause an auditor to limit the extent of the inquiry, to limit disclosure, or to weaken or slant audit findings in any way
- Preconceived ideas about individuals, groups, organizations, or objectives of a particular program that could bias the audit
- Previous responsibility for decision making or managing an entity that would affect current operations of the entity or program being audited
- Biases, including those induced by political or social convictions, that result from employment in, or loyalty to, a particular group, organization, or level of government
- Subsequent performance of an audit by the same individual who, for example, had previously approved invoices, payrolls, claims, and other proposed payments of the entity or program being audited
- Concurrent or subsequent performance of an audit by the same individual who maintained the official accounting records
- Financial interest that is direct, or is substantial though indirect, in the audited entity or program

External factors are those factors external to the audit organization that may restrict the audit or interfere with an auditor's ability to form independent and objective opinions and conclusions. The Yellow Book provides the following circumstances, in which an audit may be adversely affected and an auditor may not have complete freedom to make an independent and objective judgment:

- External interference or influence that improperly or imprudently limits or modifies the scope of an audit
- External interference with the selection or application of audit procedures or in the selection of transactions to be examined
- Unreasonable restrictions on the time allowed to complete an audit
- Interference external to the audit organization in the assignment, appointment, and promotion of audit personnel
- Restrictions on funds or other resources provided to the audit organization that would adversely affect the audit organization's ability to carry out its responsibilities
- Authority to overrule or influence the auditor's judgment regarding the appropriate content of an audit report

- Influences that jeopardize the auditor's continued employment for reasons other than competency or the need for audit services

The Yellow Book also includes a discussion of organizational independence, targeted at governmental auditors' independence. For example, the independence of a governmental internal audit department could be affected by its place within the structure of the government entity. Its independence also could be affected by the individual to whom the department reports and by whether it is auditing internally or externally.

In addition to the requirement stated in the second general standard, public accountants should follow the AICPA Code of Professional Conduct, the code of professional conduct of the state board with jurisdiction over the practice of the public accountant and the audit organization, and the guidance on personal and external impairments in these standards.

Due Professional Care

The third Yellow Book general standard states:

> Due professional care should be used in conducting the audit and in preparing related reports.

Exercising due professional care means using sound judgment in establishing the scope, selecting the methodology, and choosing tests and procedures for the audit. The same sound judgment should be applied when conducting the tests and procedures and when evaluating and reporting the audit results.

Auditors should use sound professional judgment when determining the standards that apply to the work to be conducted. In cases where the auditor determines that certain standards do *not* apply to the audit, the determination should be documented in the working papers.

The due professional care standard places responsibility on the auditor and the audit organization to exercise due professional care in the performance of an audit assignment. It does not imply unlimited responsibility for the auditor, nor does it imply infallibility on the part of either the individual auditor or the audit organization.

> **OBSERVATION:** It may be difficult for auditors to explain the difference between how they exercise due professional care during audits in accordance with the Yellow Book and how they exercise due professional care during audits in accordance with GAAS.

Quality Control

The fourth Yellow Book general standard states:

> Each audit organization conducting audits in accordance with these standards should have an appropriate internal quality control system in place and undergo an external quality control review.

Auditors should keep in mind that the fourth general standard is twofold. Audit organizations must (1) establish and maintain an internal quality control system and (2) undergo an external quality control review.

Internal quality control system   The internal quality control system should provide reasonable assurance to the audit organization that it has adopted and is following applicable auditing standards and that it has established and is following adequate audit policies and procedures. The systems established by individual organizations and the extent of their documentation will vary depending on a number of factors, including the size of the audit organization, the degree of operating autonomy allowed its personnel and its audit offices, the nature of its work, its organizational structure, and appropriate cost–benefit considerations.

> **OBSERVATION:** Sole practitioners and very small firms should **not** ignore this requirement. Standards for workpaper preparation, maintenance of a professional library, etc., are elements of a quality control system that should be considered regardless of the size of the audit firm.

External quality control review   Organizations conducting audits in accordance with *Government Auditing Standards* should have an external quality control review at least once every three years. The review should be conducted by an organization not affiliated with the firm being reviewed, and its objective should be to determine whether the audit organization's internal quality control system is in place and operating effectively to provide reasonable assurance that established policies and procedures and applicable auditing standards are being followed. The Yellow Book prescribes the following requirements for external quality control reviews performed under this general standard:

- Reviewers should be qualified and should have current knowledge of the type of work to be reviewed and the applicable auditing standards. For example, individuals reviewing government audits should have a thorough knowledge of the government environment and government auditing relative to the work being reviewed.

- Reviewers should be independent (as defined in the Yellow Book) of the audit organization being reviewed, its staff, and the auditees whose audits are selected for review. An audit organization is *not* permitted to review the organization that conducted its most recent external quality control review.

- Reviewers should use sound professional judgment when conducting and reporting the results of the external quality control review.

- Reviewers should use one of the following two approaches for selecting audits for review:

  — Select audits that provide a reasonable cross section of the audits conducted in accordance with the Yellow Book standards.

  — Select audits that provide a reasonable cross section of the organization's audits, including one or more audits conducted in accordance with the Yellow Book standards.

- The review should include a review of the audit reports, working papers, and other necessary documents (e.g., correspondence and continuing education documentation) as well as interviews with the reviewed organization's professional staff.

- The reviewer should prepare a written report communicating the results of the external quality control review.

> **OBSERVATION:** Auditors are already familiar with quality reviews through programs such as that administered by the AICPA. Performing these reviews has become the primary work source for a number of firms. Audit organizations performing A-133 audits should ensure that the firms they engage to perform quality reviews understand the requirements of the Yellow Book and Circular A-133 as they relate to not-for-profit organizations. This gives the audit organization additional comfort that its practices are appropriate.

According to the 1994 Yellow Book, "Audit organizations seeking to enter into a contract to perform an audit in accordance with these standards should provide their most recent external quality control review report to the party contracting for the audit. Information in the external quality control review report often would be relevant to decisions on procuring audit services."

> **OBSERVATION:** The term *report* does not include separate letters of comment.

The Yellow Book also states that external quality review reports should be made available to other auditors using the reviewed organization's work and to appropriate oversight bodies. The Yellow Book also recommends that the report be made available to the public.

FIELDWORK STANDARDS FOR FINANCIAL AUDITS

Chapter 4 of the Yellow Book establishes fieldwork standards for financial statement and financial related audits. For financial statement audits, the Yellow Book incorporates the three standards of fieldwork found in GAAS, which are as follows:

1. The work must be adequately planned and assistants, if any, must be properly supervised.
2. A sufficient understanding of the internal control structure must be obtained to plan the audit and to determine the nature, timing, and extent of tests to be performed.
3. Sufficient competent evidential matter must be obtained through inspection, observation, inquiries, and confirmations to afford a reasonable basis for an opinion regarding the financial statements under audit.

The Yellow Book incorporates any Statement on Auditing Standard that interprets the AICPA standards of fieldwork. In fact, the Yellow Book incorporates any new AICPA standard relevant to financial statement audits unless excluded by the GAO by formal announcement.

The Yellow Book fieldwork standards for financial audits include additional standards relating to:

- Auditor communication
- Audit follow-up
- Noncompliance other than illegal acts
- Documentation of the assessment of control risk for assertions significantly dependent upon computerized information systems
- Working papers

They provide additional guidance on three key aspects of financial statement audits:

1. Materiality
2. Fraud and illegal acts
3. Internal controls

Auditor Communication

Amendment 2 to the Yellow Book imposes an additional fieldwork standard for audits in accordance with *Government Auditing Standards*. The new standard relates to communication with the organization being audited, including both the individuals who contract for or request audit services and the audit committee. Auditors must communicate information regarding the nature and extent of planned testing and reporting on compliance with laws and regulations and internal control over financial reporting.

The purpose of this communication is to reduce the likelihood that the organization being audited will misinterpret the extent of planned testing and reporting compliance with laws and regulations and internal control over financial reporting. Since the Yellow Book does not impose more testing on compliance and internal control than would have been performed in a financial statement audit (the Yellow Book reports on compliance and internal control address matters that would be material to the financial statements), there is the risk that the user of the Yellow Book reports on compliance and internal control may assume that additional audit procedures are being performed. Users may over-rely on the reports or may use them for inappropriate purposes.

The required auditor communication attempts to prevent this over-reliance. During the planning stages of the audit, the auditor should communicate his or her responsibility in a financial statement audit, including the responsibility for testing and reporting on compliance with laws and regulations and on internal control over financial reporting. The communication should also describe the nature of any additional testing of compliance and internal control that is required by laws and regulations, or that otherwise has been requested. Further, it should state whether the auditor plans to issue opinions on compliance with laws and regulations and internal control over financial reporting. For audits performed in accordance with Circular A-133, the communication should make reference to the additional compliance and internal control procedures required in Circular A-133. The auditor should also communicate that the needs of report users may still not be met by these additional tests required by laws and regulations and that, in such instances, the auditor could be engaged to perform additional agreed-upon procedures, or the examination could be expanded to result in an auditor's opinion.

The Yellow Book prefers, but does not require, that the required communication be in writing, although from a practical perspective it makes sense to include this information in writing. An effective vehicle for the communication is the engagement letter, which is further discussed in the chapter of this Guide titled "Preplanning for a Circular A-133 Audit."

Audit Follow-Up and Materiality

The Yellow Book adds the following standard for financial statement audits:

> Auditors should follow up on known material findings and recommendations from previous audits.

To help the auditor apply this standard, the Yellow Book provides additional guidance on materiality. The Yellow Book confirms that materiality is a matter of professional judgment and should be considered in light of surrounding circumstances. The Yellow Book states that materiality involves both quantitative and qualitative considerations. It also, however, provides additional information and guidance for performing an audit in accordance with generally accepted government auditing standards:

> In an audit of the financial statements of a government entity or an entity that receives government assistance, auditors may set lower materiality levels than in audits in the private sector because of the public accountability of the auditee, the various legal and regulatory requirements, and the visibility and sensitivity of government programs, activities, and functions.

The auditor performing an audit in accordance with Circular A-133 should consider this guidance on materiality when planning the audit, designing an audit strategy, and evaluating the results of the audit procedures performed. The guidance usually results in auditors performing more audit procedures in these types of audits. The impact of materiality considerations on the design of an audit strategy and assessment of audit risk is fully discussed in the chapter titled "Planning for a Circular A-133 Audit." Part I of this Guide describes the various considerations that auditors need to take into account in auditing not-for-profit organizations because many of their funds are "public" funds. The Yellow Book standards described above pertain to funds that are "public" in that they originate with the federal government. Whether funds are obtained from the federal government or from individual donors, auditors of not-for-profit organizations need to be aware that many of these organizations operate in the public spotlight because of the source of their funds; auditors need to be careful to consider this fact in determining planning materiality.

> **OBSERVATION:** The A-133 auditor will have to make additional materiality decisions, particularly regarding materiality

at the major federal award program level. These decisions should be considered when establishing overall materiality at the financial statement level.

As background for its additional requirements of follow-up of prior-year material findings and recommendations, the Yellow Book points out that the real benefit from the audit work is not in the identification and reporting of findings and recommendations, but in the resolution of the findings and recommendations by the management of the auditee. This is the reasoning behind the requirements to follow up on known material findings and recommendations from previous audits that could affect the financial statement audit. Auditors should do this to determine whether the recipient organization has taken timely and appropriate corrective actions. Auditors should report on the status of uncorrected material findings and recommendations from prior audits that affect the financial statement audit.

Fraud, Illegal Acts, and Noncompliance Other than Illegal Acts

The Yellow Book incorporates the AICPA standards relating to fraud and illegal acts. These standards require the following:

- Auditors should design the audit to provide reasonable assurance of detecting fraud that is material to the financial statements.

- Auditors should design the audit to provide reasonable assurance of detecting material misstatements resulting from direct and material illegal acts.

- Auditors should be aware of the possibility that indirect illegal acts may have occurred. If specific information comes to the auditors' attention that provides evidence concerning the existence of possible illegal acts that could have a material indirect effect on the financial statements, the auditors should apply audit procedures specifically developed to ascertain whether an illegal act has occurred.

> **OBSERVATION:** The requirements of SAS-82 (Consideration of Fraud in a Financial Statement Audit) would also apply to, and update, the guidance provided by the Yellow Book.

The Yellow Book contains the following additional compliance standards for financial statement audits:

- Auditors should design the audit to provide reasonable assurance of detecting material misstatements resulting from noncompliance with provisions of contracts or grant agreements that have a direct and material effect on the determination of financial statement amounts. If specific information comes to the auditors' attention that provides evidence concerning the existence of possible noncompliance that could have a material indirect effect on the financial statements, auditors should apply audit procedures specifically developed to ascertain whether that noncompliance has occurred.

- The term *noncompliance* has a broader meaning than *illegal acts;* it includes not only illegal acts but also the violations of provisions of contracts or grant agreements. GAAS promulgated by the AICPA do not discuss the auditor's responsibility for detecting noncompliance other than illegal acts. Therefore, the Yellow Book addresses this specific issue and gives auditors the same responsibilities for detecting material misstatements arising from other types of noncompliance as they have for detecting those from illegal acts.

The Yellow Book provides definitions and additional guidance to auditors in applying this additional standard. *Direct and material noncompliance* is noncompliance having a direct and material effect on the determination of financial statement amounts. Auditors should design the audit to provide reasonable assurance of detecting material misstatements resulting from direct and material noncompliance with provisions of contracts or grant agreements.

Indirect noncompliance is noncompliance having material but indirect effects on the financial statements. A financial statement audit provides no assurance that indirect noncompliance with provisions of contracts and grant agreements will be detected. However, if specific information comes to the auditors' attention that provides evidence concerning the existence of possible noncompliance that could have a material indirect effect on the financial statements, auditors should apply audit procedures specifically developed to ascertain whether that noncompliance has occurred.

Auditors performing audits in accordance with Circular A-133 generally will not have to perform additional procedures relating to federal awards programs to implement this additional standard. The auditor in an A-133 audit is already considering compliance with the contracts and grant agreements relating to major federal awards programs. However, if specific information comes to the auditor's attention that provides evidence of possible noncompliance that could have a material indirect effect on the financial statements, the auditor must consider those indirect effects. In addition, the Yellow Book does not define contracts and grants as solely those from federal awards programs. Therefore, the auditor also must consider the direct and indirect effects of noncompliance with contracts and grants outside of the federal awards programs.

Internal Controls

The 1994 Yellow Book did not prescribe any additional internal control standards for financial statement audits. It did, however, provide additional guidance on the following four aspects of internal control:

- Safeguarding controls
- Controls over compliance with laws and regulations

Amendment No. 2 to the Yellow Book does establish additional requirements when control risk is assessed at the maximum level when financial statement assertions are significantly dependent on computerized information systems. These requirements are also described in this section.

The following discussion summarizes the additional guidance provided by the Yellow Book. A more detailed discussion is provided in the chapter titled "Internal Controls over Federal Awards."

Safeguarding controls The Yellow Book provides an extensive discussion of safeguarding controls. These controls relate to the prevention or timely detection of unauthorized transactions and unauthorized access to assets that could result in losses material to the financial statements. Safeguarding controls are not limited to preventing or detecting misappropriation. They also help prevent or detect other material losses that could result from the unauthorized acquisition, use, or disposition of assets.

Because preventing or detecting material misappropriation is an objective of safeguarding controls, understanding those controls can be essential to planning the audit. Understanding these safeguarding controls can help auditors assess the risk that financial statements could be materially misstated.

> **OBSERVATION:** The Yellow Book adds to what is normally thought of as safeguarding controls. For instance, assets are not safeguarded when an unauthorized acquisition results in a recipient organization acquiring something that it did not need or want or in a recipient organization not getting the most favorable price or terms for the goods or services acquired.

Controls over compliance with laws and regulations As stated above, auditors should design the audit to provide reasonable assurance that the financial statements are free of material misstatements resulting from violations of laws and regulations that have a direct and material effect on the determination of financial statement amounts. Auditors should have an understanding of internal controls relevant to financial statement assertions affected by those laws and regulations. Auditors should use that understanding to identify types of potential misstatements, consider factors that affect the risk of material misstatement, and design substantive tests.

Control risk assessments relating to computerized information systems Amendment No. 2 to the Yellow Book imposes a documentation requirement on auditors regarding internal control assessment in a particular circumstance—that is, one in which the auditor plans to assess control risk at the maximum level for assertions related to material account balances, transaction classes, and disclosure components of financial statements when such assertions are significantly dependent upon computerized information systems. In this circumstance, the auditor is required to document:

- The basis for this assessment, including:
  — The ineffectiveness of the design and/or operation of the controls, or
  — The reason why it would be inefficient to test the controls
- The consideration that the planned procedures are designed to achieve audit objectives and to reduce audit risk to an acceptable level. The documentation should include:
  — The rationale for determining the nature, timing, and extent of planned audit procedures;
  — The kinds and competence of available evidential matter produced outside a computerized information system; and
  — The effect on the auditor opinion or report if evidential matter to be gathered during the audit does not afford a reasonable basis for the auditor's opinion on the financial statements.

OBSERVATION: This is a documentation requirement, not a requirement for auditors to assess control risk at less than the maximum level. There are many reasons why a not-for-profit organization's auditor may assess control risk at a maximum level even when there is significant computer processing. For example, the auditor of a school with a computerized student financial system may be able to obtain sufficient evidence about the revenues recorded using analytical techniques (number of students, credit hours, number of classes, faculty members, etc.) and confirmation of receivables for there being no reason to plan to assess control risk at less than the maximum level because of the strength of the substantive procedures.

Working Papers

The Yellow Book contains the following additional standard relating to working papers:

> Working papers should contain sufficient information to enable an experienced auditor having no previous connection with the audit to ascertain from them the evidence that supports the auditors' significant conclusions and judgments.

The working papers for an audit performed in accordance with *Government Auditing Standards* should contain:

- The objectives, scope, and methodology, including any sampling criteria used
- Documentation of the work performed to support significant conclusions and judgments, including descriptions of transactions and records examined that would enable an experienced auditor to examine the same transactions and records
- Evidence of supervisory reviews of the work performed

Auditors can meet the above documentation requirements by listing voucher numbers, check numbers, or other means of identifying specific documents they examined. Auditors are not required to include in the working papers copies of documents they examined, nor are they required to list detailed information from those documents.

As an additional requirement, arrangements should be made so that working papers are available, upon request, to other auditors. To facilitate reviews of audit quality and reliance by other auditors on the auditor's work, contractual arrangements for audits to be performed in accordance with *Government Auditing Standards* should provide for access to working papers.

Financial Related Audits

The Yellow Book incorporates certain AICPA standards that address specific types of financial related audits. In addition, and in a manner similar to its treatment of AICPA standards relating to financial statement audits, the Yellow Book incorporates into *Government Auditing Standards* any new AICPA standards relevant to financial related audits unless excluded by GAO through a formal announcement.

The AICPA standards specifically incorporated into the Yellow Book (as updated by Amendment No. 2) are as follows:

a. SAS No. 75, *Engagements to Apply Agreed-Upon Procedures to Specific Elements, Accounts, or Items of a Financial Statement;*

b. SAS No. 62, *Special Reports,* for auditing specified elements, accounts, or items of a financial statement;

c. SAS No. 74, *Compliance Auditing Considerations in Audits of Governmental Entities and Recipients of Governmental Financial Assistance,* for testing compliance with laws and regulations applicable to federal financial assistance programs;

d. SAS No. 70, *Reports on the Processing of Transactions by Service Organizations,* for examining descriptions of internal control of service organizations that process transactions for others;

e. Statement of Standards for Attestation Engagements (SSAE) No. 1, *Attestation Standards,* as amended by SSAE No 9, *Amendments to Statement on Standards for Attestation Engagements Nos. 1, 2, and 3,* for examining or reviewing an entity's assertions about financial related matters not specifically addressed in other AICPA standards;

f. SSAE No. 2, *Reporting on an Entity's Internal Control Over Financial Reporting,* as amended by SSAE No. 9, *Amendments to Statement on Standards for Attestation Engagements Nos. 1, 2, and 3,* for examining an entity's assertions about its internal control over financial reporting and/or safeguarding assets;

g. SSAE No. 3, *Compliance Attestation,* as amended by SSAE No. 9, *Amendments to Statement on Standards for Attestation Engagements Nos. 1, 2, and 3,* for (1) examining or applying agreed-upon procedures to an entity's assertions about compliance with specified requirements or (2) applying agreed-upon procedures to an entity's assertions about internal control over compliance with laws and regulations; and

h. SSAE No. 4, *Agreed-Upon Procedures Engagements,* for applying agreed-upon procedures to (1) an entity's assertions about internal control over financial reporting and/or safeguarding of assets or (2) an entity's assertions about financial related matters not specifically addressed in other AICPA standards.

For financial related audits, auditors should follow the Yellow Book's fieldwork standards for audit follow-up and working papers and should apply or adapt the other fieldwork standards and guidance as appropriate in the circumstances. For financial related audits not previously described, auditors should follow the Yellow Book's fieldwork standards for performance audits.

REPORTING STANDARDS
FOR FINANCIAL AUDITS

The Yellow Book incorporates the generally accepted auditing standards for reporting. These four standards are as follows:

1. The report shall state whether the financial statements are presented in accordance with generally accepted accounting principles.

2. The report shall identify those circumstances in which such principles have not been consistently observed in the current period in relation to the preceding period.

3. Informative disclosures in the financial statements are to be regarded as reasonably adequate unless otherwise stated in the report.

4. The report shall contain either an expression of opinion regarding the financial statements, taken as a whole, or an assertion to the effect that an opinion cannot be expressed. When an overall opinion cannot be expressed, the reasons therefor should be stated. In all cases where an auditor's name is associated with financial statements, the report should contain a clear-cut indication of the character of the auditor's work, if any, and the degree of responsibility the auditor is taking.

The Yellow Book prescribes additional reporting standards in the following areas:

- Reporting compliance with *Government Auditing Standards*
- Reporting on compliance with laws and regulations and on internal control over financial reporting
- Privileged and confidential information
- Report distribution

Reporting Compliance with Government Auditing Standards

The Yellow Book's first additional reporting standard for financial statement audits states:

> Audit reports should state that the audit was made in accordance with generally accepted government auditing standards.

When the report on the financial statements is submitted to comply with a legal, regulatory, or contractual requirement for an audit in accordance with *Government Auditing Standards* (e.g., required by Circular A-133), it should specifically cite generally accepted government auditing standards. The report on financial statements may cite GAAS as well.

The Yellow Book permits (but does not encourage) the auditor to refer to GAAS only in certain circumstances. It states that the auditee may need a financial statement audit for purposes other than to comply with requirements calling for an audit in accordance with *Government Auditing Standards*. The Yellow Book does not prohibit auditors from issuing a separate report on the financial statements conforming only to the requirements of the AICPA under GAAS; however, according to the Yellow Book, it may be advantageous to use a report issued in accordance with *Government Auditing Standards* for these other purposes because it provides information on compliance with laws and regulations and internal controls that is not contained in a report issued in accordance with AICPA standards.

Reporting on Compliance with Laws and Regulations and on Internal Control over Financial Reporting

The second additional reporting standard promulgated by the Yellow Book is:

> The report on the financial statements should either (1) describe the scope of the auditors' testing of compliance with laws and regulations and internal control over financial reporting and present the results of those tests or (2) refer to separate reports containing that information. In presenting the results of those tests, auditors should report fraud, illegal acts, other material noncompliance, and reportable conditions in internal controls. In some circumstances, auditors should report fraud and illegal acts directly to parties external to the audited entity.

Specific reporting examples under the Yellow Book are included in the chapter titled "Reporting under Circular A-133."

Reporting of fraud and illegal acts When auditors conclude, based on evidence obtained, that fraud or an illegal act either has occurred or is likely to have occurred, they should report relevant information. Auditors need not report information about fraud or an illegal act that is clearly inconsequential. Thus, auditors should report the same fraud and illegal acts that they report to audit committees under AICPA standards. Auditors should also report other noncompliance (i.e., a violation of a contract provision) that is material to the financial statements.

The Yellow Book also specifies that, when reporting material fraud, illegal acts, or other noncompliance, the auditor should place his or her findings in proper perspective. To give the report reader a basis for judging the prevalence and consequences of the conditions noted, the instances should be related to the universe or the number of cases examined and be quantified in terms of dollar value, if appropriate.

Audit findings often are regarded as containing the elements of criteria, condition, and effect, plus cause when problems are found. However, the elements needed for a finding depend entirely on the objectives of the audit. Reportable conditions and noncompliance found by the auditor may not always have all of these elements fully developed, given the scope and objectives of the specific financial audit. However, auditors should identify at least the condition, criteria, and possible asserted effect. This provides information to federal, state, and local officials, allowing them to determine the effect and cause of the finding and to take prompt and proper corrective action.

> **OBSERVATION:** The auditor should expect all A-133 audits to be desk reviewed by the federal cognizant agency or primary federal grantor agency. Therefore, the auditor's comments and findings should conform to these requirements to prevent rejection of the A-133 audit report. (Federal cognizant agencies are discussed in detail in the chapter titled "Planning for a Circular A-133 Audit.")

The Yellow Book requires the auditor to directly report fraud or illegal acts to outside parties in the following two circumstances:

1. The recipient organization may be required by law or regulation to report certain fraud or illegal acts to specified external parties, such as a federal inspector general or state attorney general. If the recipient organization fails to report the fraud or illegal acts after the auditor has communicated them to the recipient organization, the auditor should communicate his or her awareness of that failure to the recipient organization's governing body. If the recipient organization does not make the required report as soon as practicable after the auditor's communication with the governing body, the auditor should report the fraud or illegal acts directly to the external party specified in the law or regulation.

2. Management is responsible for taking timely and appropriate steps to remedy fraud or illegal acts that the auditor reports. When fraud or an illegal act involves assistance received directly or indirectly from a government agency, auditors may have a duty to report it directly to the agency if management fails to take remedial steps. If the auditor concludes that such failure is likely to cause him or her to depart from the standard report on the financial statements or to resign from the audit, the auditor should communicate that conclusion to the recipient organization's governing body. Then, if the recipient organization does not report the fraud or illegal act to the entity that provided the government assistance, the auditor should report the irregularity or illegal act directly to that entity.

These requirements are in addition to any legal requirements for direct reporting of fraud or illegal acts. These requirements should be met even if the auditor has resigned or been dismissed from the audit.

In both of these situations, the auditor should obtain sufficient, competent, and relevant evidence (e.g., evidence obtained through confirmation with outside parties) to corroborate assertions by management that it has reported fraud and illegal acts. If the auditor is unable to do so, he or she should report the fraud or illegal acts directly to the funding agency as discussed above.

The Yellow Book reminds auditors that under some circumstances laws, regulations, or policies may require them to promptly report indications of certain types of fraud or illegal acts to law enforcement or investigatory authorities. When auditors conclude that this type of fraud or illegal act either has occurred or is likely to have occurred, they should ask those authorities and/or legal counsel if reporting certain information about that fraud or illegal act would compromise investigative or legal proceedings. Auditors should limit their reporting to matters that would not compromise those proceedings, perhaps by reporting only information that is already a part of the public record.

In any of the circumstances described above, the auditor should consider consulting with his or her legal counsel. This is highly recommended given the sensitivity and the severity of reporting directly to outside parties.

> **OBSERVATION:** Auditors should thoroughly understand the complete facts of any of these types of circumstances and should exercise a great deal of care to avoid incorrectly making such reports to outside parties.

Deficiencies in internal control The Yellow Book provides examples of internal control deficiencies that might be reportable conditions under AICPA standards. A list of these examples is provided in the chapter titled "Internal Controls over Federal Awards."

Privileged and Confidential Information

The Yellow Book's third additional reporting standard for financial statement audits states:

> If certain information is prohibited from general disclosure, the audit report should state the nature of the information omitted and the requirement that makes the omission necessary.

Before reporting under the criteria of this additional standard, the auditor should obtain assurance that a valid requirement for the omission exists and, when appropriate, consult with legal counsel.

Report Distribution

The Yellow Book's fourth additional reporting requirement for financial statement audits is:

> Written audit reports are to be submitted to the appropriate officials of the auditee and to the appropriate officials of the organizations requiring or arranging for the audits, including external funding organizations, unless legal restrictions prevent it. Copies of the reports should also be sent to other officials who have legal oversight authority or who may be responsible for acting on audit findings and recommendations and to others authorized to receive such reports. Unless restricted by laws or regulations, copies should be made available for public inspection.

Audit reports should be distributed in a timely manner to officials interested in receiving the results. However, if the subject of the audit involves material that is classified for security purposes or that is not releasable to particular parties or the public for other valid reasons, the auditor may limit the report distribution.

Financial Related Audits

The Yellow Book incorporates the same AICPA standards in the reporting standards section as in the fieldwork standards. These are covered in the section above titled "Fieldwork Standards for Financial Audits."

SUMMARY

The Yellow Book provides additional requirements and guidance for auditors performing audits in accordance with *Government Auditing Standards*. It clarifies some of the language of previous Yellow Books and presents additional requirements.

The Yellow Book changes the auditor's reports that must be issued in accordance with *Government Auditing Standards*; however, it does not provide specific report examples. Report examples are provided in the chapter titled "Reporting under Circular A-133," along with other detailed instructions.

CHAPTER 14
PREPLANNING FOR A
CIRCULAR A-133 AUDIT

CONTENTS

CHAPTER 14
PREPLANNING FOR A CIRCULAR A-133 AUDIT

CROSS-REFERENCES

2001 MILLER NOT-FOR-PROFIT ORGANIZATION AUDITS: Chapter 2, "Preplanning Audit Activities"

2001 MILLER SINGLE AUDITS: Chapter 2, "Preplanning"

Before an auditor begins planning an audit in accordance with OMB Circular A-133, he or she should address several considerations that are unique to this type of audit. Similarly, a not-for-profit organization should understand its obligation to comply with the requirements of Circular A-133 and should have a good working understanding of the nature of the audit that it will "purchase" from an independent auditor. The responsibility for obtaining an audit in accordance with Circular A-133 is that of the not-for-profit organization.

The primary activities that should take place before the planning phase of a Circular A-133 audit are as follows:

- The not-for-profit organization should determine if a Circular A-133 audit is required. The requirements of the new Circular A-133 are significantly different from those of the original.

- The not-for-profit organization should select an independent auditor, and an auditor should accept the engagement.

- The not-for-profit organization should formalize the audit engagement in an engagement letter.

DETERMINING IF A CIRCULAR A-133
AUDIT IS REQUIRED

The recent revision to Circular A-133 made two significant changes from previous requirements in determining when an audit in accordance with the Circular is required. First, it increased the threshold of when an audit is required. Second, the threshold is applied to federal awards expended during the year—rather than to assistance received during the year.

Circular A-133 requires that not-for-profit organizations that expend $300,000 or more in a year in federal awards have a single audit or a program-specific audit performed in accordance with the requirements of the Circular.

Not-for-profit organizations that expend less than $300,000 in a year in federal awards are exempt from the federal audit requirements in that year, but must make records available for review or audit by appropriate officials of federal agencies, pass-through entities, and the United States General Accounting Office.

All organizations that receive federal awards (whether they have a single audit, a program-specific audit, or are exempt from federal audit requirements) are subject to additional federal audit requirements. Circular A-133 explicitly states that it does not limit the authority of federal agencies or the General Accounting Office to conduct or arrange for additional audits. Any additional audits (whether financial audits, performance audits, evaluations, inspections, or reviews) should be planned in such a way to build upon work performed by other auditors.

Program-Specific Audits

In certain, limited circumstances, a not-for-profit organization may elect to have a program-specific audit performed in lieu of a single audit. This election is available if the not-for-profit organization expends federal awards under only one federal program (excluding research and development) and the federal program's laws, regulations, or grant agreements do not require a financial statement audit of the not-for-profit organization. A program-specific audit may not be elected for research and development unless all expenditures are for federal awards received from the same federal agency or the same pass-through entity. In addition, the federal agency, or pass-through entity in the case of a subrecipient, must approve the program-specific audit in advance.

The exception to the program-specific audit rule described above is an important one for not-for-profit colleges and universities and healthcare providers. For purposes of applying the provisions of Circular A-133 to research and development, the Circular defines *research and development* as "... all research activities, both basic and applied, and all development activities that are performed by a non-Federal entity." *Research* is defined as a systematic study directed toward fuller scientific knowledge or understanding of the subject studied. The term *research* also includes activities involving the training of individuals in research techniques where such activities utilize the same facilities as other research and development activities and where such activities are not included in the instruction function. *Development* is the systematic use of knowledge and understanding gained from research directed toward the production of useful materials, devices, systems, or methods, including design and development of prototypes and processes.

Circular A-133 also provides guidance to auditors on performing program-specific audits. See Exhibit 14-1 for a synopsis of the guidance in Circular A-133 for performing program-specific audits.

Not-for-Profit Organizations Covered by Circular A-133

Circular A-133 defines *not-for-profit organization* as any corporation, trust, association, cooperative, or other organization that (1) operates primarily for scientific, educational, service, charitable, or similar purposes in the public interest; (2) is not organized primarily for profit; and (3) uses its net proceeds to maintain, improve, and/or expand its operations. The term includes not-for-profit institutions of higher education and hospitals.

Question 13 of PCIE Position Statement No. 6 provides additional guidance on organizations *affiliated* with not-for-profit organizations.

The determination of affiliated organizations is important because it affects which organizations will be included in the scope of the Circular A-133 audit. Examples of affiliated organizations are university athletic associations, not-for-profit organizations that create other not-for-profit organizations to perform specific functions or missions, and national not-for-profit organizations with local chapters under the national umbrella organization. Generally, when an affiliated organization receives federal awards it is subject to the requirements of Circular A-133, whether it is a prime recipient or a subrecipient.

The Circular A-133 is silent on determining affiliated organizations included in its scope. A not-for-profit organization and its auditor may consider earlier guidance for single audits when implementing the revised Circular A-133. To be excluded from the requirements for an audit under the prior Circular A-133, the affiliated organization have met *all* of the following criteria:

- The affiliated organization does not receive direct or indirect federal awards.

EXHIBIT 14-1
PROGRAM-SPECIFIC AUDITS

The guidance contained in Circular A-133 relates to program-specific audits that address two conditions under which an auditor may be asked to perform a program-specific audit: (1) where a program-specific audit guide is available and (2) where a program-specific audit guide is not available.

Program-Specific Audit Guide Available

In a number of cases, federal agencies provide program-specific audit guides to assist auditors with respect to internal control, compliance requirements, suggested audit procedures, and audit reporting requirements for specific programs. The auditor should contact the Inspector General's Office of the federal agency sponsoring the program to determine whether a program-specific audit guide is available. If a current, program-specific audit guide is available, the auditor should follow the guide and *Government Auditing Standards* when performing the program specific audit.

Program-Specific Audit Guide Not Available

When a program-specific audit guide is not available, a not-for-profit organization and its auditor have the same responsibilities for the federal program as they would have for an audit of a major program in a single audit.

The not-for-profit organization should prepare financial statements for the federal program that include, at a minimum:

- A schedule of the federal program's expenditures
- Notes to the schedule that describe the significant accounting policies used to prepare the schedule
- A summary schedule of prior audit findings (consistent with the requirements for the same schedule in a single audit)
- A corrective action plan (consistent with the requirements for a corrective action plan in a single audit)

Circular A-133 lists the following audit requirements for an auditor in a program-specific audit:

- Audit the financial statement of the federal program in accordance with *Government Auditing Standards*.
- Obtain an understanding of internal control and perform tests of internal control over the federal program consistent with the single audit requirements for a major program.
- Perform procedures to determine whether the not-for-profit organization complied with laws, regulations, and the provisions of contracts or

grant agreements that could have a direct and material effect on the federal program, consistent with the single audit requirements for a major program.

- Follow up on prior-year audit findings; perform procedures to assess the reasonableness of the summary schedule of prior audit findings prepared by the not-for-profit organization; and report, as a current-year audit finding, if it is concluded that the summary schedule of prior-year audit findings materially misrepresents the status of any prior-year audit finding in accordance with the single audit requirements.

Reporting

The auditor's report should state that the audit was performed in accordance with Circular A-133 and should include the following:

- An opinion as to whether the financial statement of the federal program is fairly presented in all material respects in accordance with the stated accounting policies
- A report on internal control related to the federal program, describing the scope of testing of internal control and the results of the tests
- A report on compliance that includes an opinion as to whether the not-for-profit organization complied with laws, regulations, and the provisions of contracts and grant agreements that could have a direct and material effect on the federal program
- A schedule of findings and questioned costs for the federal program, consistent with the single audit requirements, including a summary of the auditor's results applicable to the audit of the federal program, consistent in format with the single audit requirements

Reports for program-specific audits must be submitted within nine months after the end of the audit period, or 30 days after receipt of the auditor's report, whichever is earlier. (Note: For fiscal years beginning on or before June 30, 1998, the audit shall be completed and the required reporting submitted within the earlier of 30 days after receipt of the auditor's report, or 13 months after the end of the audit period, unless a longer period is agreed to in advance by the federal agency that provided the funding or a different period is specified in a program-specific audit guide.)

When a program-specific audit guide is available, the not-for-profit organization submits to the central clearinghouse one copy of the data collection form, consistent with the single audit requirements, but as applicable to program-specific audits, as well as an archival copy of the reporting required by the program-specific audit guide. The not-for-profit organization should also submit to the federal awarding agency or pass-through entity the reporting required by the program-specific audit guide.

When a program-specific audit guide is not available, the reporting package should contain in addition to the data collection form, the financial statement of the federal program, a summary schedule of prior-year audit findings, a corrective action plan, and the auditor's reports, as described above. One copy of the reporting package is submitted to the central clearinghouse. When the schedule of findings and questioned costs discloses audit findings or the summary schedule of prior audit findings reports the status of any audit findings, the not-for-profit organization should submit one copy of the reporting package to the central clearinghouse on behalf of the federal awarding agency or directly to the pass-through entity in the case of a subrecipient.

Additional information on report submission is contained in the chapter of this guide on reporting in accordance with Circular A-133.

- The affiliated organization is not included in the not-for-profit organization's indirect cost plan.

- The not-for-profit organization does not provide the affiliated organization with payments or benefits paid out of federal awards.

Non-U.S.-Based Entities

Circular A-133 does not apply to non-U.S.-based entities expending federal awards received either directly as recipients or indirectly as subrecipients. This is a particularly important area for not-for-profit organizations, since the programs of many organizations involve foreign aid programs or other programs where federal funds are expended outside of the United States. SOP 98-3 addresses this issue by providing some examples:

- A federal agency provides financial assistance to an orphanage operated by a foreign government. Circular A-133 would not apply.
- A university based in the United States receives a federal award to send a researcher to a foreign country for three months to perform research. Circular A-133 would apply to the travel and related costs incurred by the researcher.
- A hospital receives a federal award to perform medical research in a foreign country. The research is conducted in the hospital's research laboratory based in a foreign country. Circular A-133 would apply.

Definition of Federal Awards

The not-for-profit organization and its auditor must be very precise when determining the amount of federal awards because this determination will determine if the organization is required to be audited in accordance with Circular A-133. The recipient organization, therefore, must carefully interpret what is meant by the term *federal award*.

Circular A-133 defines *federal awards* to include federal financial assistance and federal cost-reimbursement contracts that non-federal entities receive directly from pass-through entities. It does not include procurement contracts, vendor grants or contracts, used to buy goods or services from vendors. (Audits of such vendors are covered by the terms and conditions of the contract.) The focus for the not-for-profit organization in detailing the amount of federal awards should be on understanding *federal financial assistance.* Circular A-133 defines this term to include:

- Grants
- Cooperative agreements
- Donated surplus property
- Food commodities
- Loans
- Loan guarantees
- Interest subsidies
- Insurance
- Property
- Direct appropriations
- Other assistance

It does not matter whether the federal financial assistance is received directly from the federal government or indirectly by subrecipients who receive awards identified as federal funds by the recipient organizations. The recipient organization is responsible for identifying the source of the funds to the subrecipient.

> **OBSERVATION:** For purposes of this discussion, a *recipient organization* is a not-for-profit or other organization that receives federal financial assistance directly from the federal grantor agency. A *subrecipient* is a not-for-profit or other organization that receives federal funds as pass-through funds from a recipient organization. Note that a not-for-profit may be a recipient organization and a subrecipient simultaneously; it can receive both direct and indirect federal financial assistance at the same time.

The requirements of Circular A-133 do not apply to individuals who receive direct cash assistance from the federal government.

Several layers of subrecipients may exist. A not-for-profit may receive a federal award from a federal grantor agency and pass some or all of the award through to one or more subrecipients. The subrecipients could pass through these awards further to additional subrecipients, and so on. The audit requirements are determined for each subrecipient depending on each subrecipient's total federal awards. The criteria described above for recipients also apply to subrecipients.

A not-for-profit organization passing federal awards through to a subrecipient is responsible for monitoring the subrecipient. Monitoring activities are discussed in the chapter titled "Subrecipient Considerations."

> **OBSERVATION:** The financial management of recipient organizations should make sure that contracts with subrecipient organizations include appropriate language requiring the subrecipient to meet any applicable requirements of Circular A-133.

The amount of federal awards *expended* determines whether an audit in accordance with Circular A-133 is required.

Determining when an award is expended is based upon when the activity related to the award occurs. Generally, the activity pertains to events that require the not-for-profit organization to comply with laws, regulations, and the provisions of contracts or grant agreements. Examples of these activities included in Circular A-133 are:

- Expenditures/expense transactions associated with grants, cost-reimbursement contracts, cooperative agreements, and direct appropriations
- The disbursement of funds passed through to subrecipients
- The use of loan proceeds under loan and loan guarantee programs
- The receipt of property
- The receipt of surplus property
- The receipt or use of program income
- The distribution or consumption of food commodities
- The disbursement of amounts entitling the not-for-profit organization to an interest subsidy
- The period of when insurance is in force

The following pages provide guidance in determining the amount of federal awards expended for these types of federal assistance that may be received by a not-for-profit organization.

Contracts, grants, and cooperative agreements Not-for-profit organizations receive federal awards in different legal forms. The terms *contract*, *grant*, and *cooperative agreement* describe these legal agreements and are sometimes used interchangeably, but they actually are quite different. Each type of agreement is in the form of a legal "contract," but each results in a different level of responsibility for the parties involved.

In a contract, including a cost-reimbursement contract, the federal awarding agency is specifying in the greatest level of detail the activities that will be performed by the recipient organization. Contracts usually are very specific about the services the not-for-profit will perform. For example, a contract may specify the number of participants that will be served by the program, the number of meals that will be served, and the responsibilities of any subrecipients that receive pass-throughs of federal awards under the contract.

Grants usually are less specific about the activities that will be performed by the recipient. Grants to perform a study or some type of research by necessity cannot be as specific as a contract regarding the output expected from a federal award. The recipient of a grant has more latitude in the day-to-day activities that will be performed than does the recipient receiving funds under a contract.

A cooperative agreement falls somewhere between a contract and a grant. While some deliverables can be specified as in a contract, other deliverables cannot. The total dollars that may be expended over the life of the cooperative agreement may not be known at the inception of the agreement, although a funding ceiling usually is established. The recipient organization and the federal grantor agency agree to "cooperate" over the life of the agreement to define the program and its deliverables. Cost estimates probably will be needed over the life of the agreement for projects and modifications of projects that the grantor and the recipient mutually agree will be performed.

Loans, loan guarantees, and interest subsidies Circular A-133 states that loans and loan guarantees are to be considered as federal awards for purposes of determining whether the audit threshold has been met. This form of federal assistance is typically very important to colleges and universities that administer student financial assistance programs. The difficulty in applying this requirement involves determining what value to place on loans and loan guarantees.

Circular A-133 calculates the value of the federal awards under loans and loan guarantees as the sum of (1) the value of new loans made or received during the year, (2) the balance of loans from previous years for which the federal government imposes continuing compliance requirements, and (3) any interest subsidies and cash or administrative cost allowances received.

Determining the value of loans and loan guarantees under student loan programs for students of institutions of higher education is slightly more complicated.

If the student loan is made by a banking institution or a service organization, such as in a guaranteed student loan program, the institution of higher education does not make the loan. The value of the federal award is computed as the value of the loans made during the year being audited. Past loans would *not* be taken into consideration when calculating the value of federal awards expended for the year. In this way, the institution of higher education's participation in the process (determination of eligibility) is what governs the value of the federal award because it is based on the year that the loan is actually made.

For other types of loan and loan guarantee programs, the focus on determining whether prior year loans or loan guarantees should be considered as part of federal awards expended depends on whether there are continuing compliance requirements. Where the loan proceeds were received and expended in prior years and the laws, regulations, and the provisions of contracts or grant agreements pertaining to such loans impose no continuing compliance requirements other than to repay the loans, the loan should not be considered as part of federal awards expended in the current year.

Endowment funds   The cumulative balance of federal awards for endowment funds that are federally restricted are considered awards expended in each year in which the funds are still restricted.

Medicare   Medicare payments to a not-for-profit organization for providing patient care services to medicare eligible individuals are not considered federal awards expended.

Medicaid   Medicaid payments to a not-for-profit organization for providing patient care services to Medicaid eligible individuals are not considered federal awards expended unless a State requires the funds to be treated as federal awards expended because reimbursement is on a cost-reimbursement basis.

Property and other noncash awards   The fair value—or the assessed value provided by the federal agency—of property and other noncash forms (such as food stamps, food commodities, donated property, or donated surplus property) of federal awards should be included in the total federal awards expended when determining whether an audit in accordance with Circular A-133 is required. Value generally should be determined using fair market value at the time of receipt or the assessed value provided by the federal agency.

Free rent   If the recipient organization receives free rent by itself from the federal awarding agency, it is not considered as a federal award expended. If free rent is received as part of an award to carry out a federal program, then the fair value of the free rent received should be considered as part of a federal award expended.

National Credit Union Administration loans Loans made from the National Credit Union Share Insurance Fund and the Central Liquidity Facility that are funded by contributions from insured institutions are not considered federal awards expended.

> **OBSERVATION:** Although the above guidelines provide additional guidance for recipient organizations and their auditors for determining whether a Circular A-133 audit is required, circumstances that fall outside of these guidelines can arise. If recipient organizations and their auditors cannot reach a reasonable conclusion on how to value federal awards, they should consult with the federal grantor agencies for resolution of the items in question.

DETERMINING REQUIREMENTS FOR THE FREQUENCY OF AUDITS

Circular A-133 requires that single audits be performed annually. However, a not-for-profit organization may undergo its audits biennially if it had biennial audits for all biennial periods ending between July 1, 1992, and January 1, 1995.

PROCURING THE SERVICES OF AN INDEPENDENT AUDITOR FOR A CIRCULAR A-133 AUDIT

The following pages discuss special consideration that a not-for-profit organization should make in procuring services for an audit in accordance with Circular A-133. Exhibit 14-2 identifies some specific requirements contained in Circular A-133. Auditors may be asked to assist their clients in meeting these requirements. This section provides some general guidance that might be shared with clients concerning procurement of audit services. It may also benefit auditors who wish to encourage "fair" competition for the performance of these types of services.

Once a not-for-profit organization determines that it is required to have an audit performed in accordance with Circular A-133 (or when it makes such a determination after consulting with its current auditor), the services of an independent auditor must be procured. Many not-for-profit organizations naturally have their current auditors expand the scope of the financial statement audit to encompass the requirements of Circular A-133. Retaining the current auditor and increasing the audit scope to conform with Circular A-133 has several advantages:

EXHIBIT 14-2
AUDITOR SELECTION REQUIREMENTS
OF CIRCULAR A-133

Circular A-133 specifies that not-for-profit organizations should follow the requirements of OMB Circular A-110 (Uniform Requirements for Grants and Agreements with Institutions of Higher Education, Hospitals and Other Non-Profit Organizations) or applicable Federal Acquisition Requirements. Accordingly, obtaining audit services for a Circular A-133 audit should follow the not-for-profit organization's policies and procedures for procurement that comply with these requirements; i.e., it should be treated as any other purchase. Requests for proposal should clearly set forth the objectives and scope of the audit.

Circular A-133 also specifies that whenever possible, not-for-profit organizations should make positive efforts to utilize small businesses, minority-owned firms, and women's business enterprises in procuring audit services.

In addition, in evaluation of proposals to provide audit services, not-for-profit organizations should consider the responsiveness of the proposal to the request for proposal, relevant experience, availability of staff with professional qualifications and technical abilities, the results of external quality control reviews, and price.

Restrictions on Auditors Preparing Indirect Cost Proposals

Frequently, a not-for-profit organization's auditor prepares the indirect cost proposal or cost allocation plan for the not-for-profit organization, which is a key component in determining what costs are charged to federal awards. Circular A-133 specifies that an auditor who prepares the indirect cost proposal or cost allocation plan may not also be selected to perform the A-133 audit when the indirect costs recovered by the not-for-profit organization during the prior year exceeded $1 million.

This restriction applies to the base year used in the preparation of the indirect cost proposal or cost allocation plan and any subsequent years in which the resulting indirect cost agreement or cost allocation plan is used to recover costs.

To minimize the disruption of current contracts for audit services, this provision applies to audits of fiscal years beginning after June 30, 1998.

- The initial year of a Circular A-133 audit requires a significant amount of work for the auditor to obtain an understanding of the various compliance requirements that will be tested and of the related control systems in place to ensure compliance. This requires the auditor to expand his or her understanding of the organization's controls over its federal awards and to understand the requirements of the federal awards themselves. An auditor who already has a high level of knowledge of a recipient organization will be much further along on the learning curve and should be more efficient in designing an effective audit plan.

- The current auditor will be able to more readily perform the risk assessments now required by Circular A-133.

- The current auditor may have already performed additional procedures relating to federal awards in accordance with specific audit guides, such as the audit guide published by the Department of Health and Human Services. This will make it even more efficient for the auditor to expand his or her scope to incorporate the requirements of Circular A-133.

- The current auditor may have a good rapport with the recipient organization's board of directors, senior management, and financial staff. This familiarity and rapport may prove quite helpful to these individuals in the recipient organization in understanding the additional requirements of Circular A-133.

- Changing auditors often results in additional burdens placed on the staff of the recipient organization, particularly on the financial and accounting staff. Adding the first-time requirements of implementing Circular A-133 to the burdens caused by changing auditors may overextend the abilities of accounting and financial personnel to be responsive to auditors' requests and inquiries while still maintaining their normal work flow.

While these factors are persuasive, the recipient organization also should consider the advantages of changing auditors before making a decision. Some of these advantages are as follows:

- The current auditor may not have the appropriate level of expertise specifically relating to the performance of audits in accordance with Circular A-133. Performing these types of audits is a specialized area, and not all auditors familiar with not-for-profit auditing are familiar with the audit requirements for not-for-profit organizations receiving federal funds. At a minimum, the recipient organization should determine through inquiry whether its current auditor meets or will meet the continuing education and quality control review requirements contained in the Yellow Book.

- The current auditor may just add the additional procedures required by Circular A-133 to the usual procedures for a financial statement audit. A new auditor will design an audit approach "from the ground up" and may integrate the Circular A-133 required procedures into the audit in a more efficient manner. This could result not only in a lower overall cost, but also in less recurring wear and tear on the recipient organization's accounting and finance staff.

- A new auditor will give the recipient organization a fresh look at how it conducts its business, and how it administers its federal awards programs. A new auditor may be able to provide the recipient organization with constructive suggestions on how to improve these functions and may be more anxious than an incumbent auditor to impress the board of directors and management with constructive and meaningful suggestions. In addition, the board of directors and management may be more receptive to the comments of a new auditor because it will confirm their wisdom in deciding to change auditors.

- Obtaining proposals from several different auditors may result in the auditors being more price conscious in their proposals. This will result in a lower audit cost to the recipient organization.

- Depending on how the recipient organization intends to recoup the audit costs relating to Circular A-133, it may determine that it should periodically solicit proposals from audit firms to perform its Circular A-133 audit. The first time that an organization is required to have a Circular A-133 audit may be the most appropriate time to begin the practice of periodically soliciting proposals.

Retaining the Current Auditor

If a decision is made to retain the current auditor to perform the Circular A-133 audit, the process of engaging the auditor becomes somewhat easier. The auditor should supply a cost estimate to the recipient organization for the additional procedures and reporting requirements that will be required under a Circular A-133 audit.

> **OBSERVATION:** Auditors should be realistic in assessing the additional costs of performing a Circular A-133 audit. Additional audit costs of 30–50 percent for the additional Circular A-133 requirements may result, largely because of additional internal control and compliance considerations and tests that must be made. As discussed below, however, the auditor will consider a number of circumstances when determining a fee estimate.

The auditor must carefully consider all of the Circular A-133 requirements when preparing a cost estimate. Obviously, the number and magnitude of the federal awards received by the recipient organization relative to its entire operations must be considered. In addition, the number and types of federal agencies providing awards should be considered, as each agency will have its own requirements. The greater the number of different federal awards programs involved, the greater the effort that will be required to design audit procedures.

The types of programs that a recipient organization may administer for federal agencies varies widely. If an auditor will have to understand a broad variety of programs administered by the recipient organization, he or she can expect to spend additional hours obtaining an understanding of the programs, the compliance requirements, and the controls over the administration of each type of federal award program. The auditor also should consider his or her own experience with the individual federal agencies, since familiarity with an agency from other audits will be a significant help in performing a Circular A-133 audit of an organization that also receives federal awards from that agency.

In determining a cost estimate for the Circular A-133 audit, the auditor should consider the extent to which the recipient organization passes funds through to subrecipients. The greater the number of recipient organizations, the greater the amount of time that will be spent auditing the recipient organization's monitoring of the subrecipients. The auditor also should consider the characteristics of the subrecipients. As a general rule, the larger and more sophisticated the subrecipients, the easier it will be for the recipient organization to monitor them, probably resulting in the auditor spending less time auditing subrecipient monitoring. On the other hand, if the subrecipients are small, struggling not-for-profit organizations that are not familiar with the requirements of Circular A-133 and other applicable documents, the recipient organization (and its auditor) will spend additional time monitoring (and auditing the monitoring of) the subrecipient.

When subrecipients are located outside of the United States, the auditors of the recipient organization will need to obtain a good understanding of the extent to which they will able to rely on the work of non-U.S. accountants. The extent to which the auditor will need to expand his or her procedures to include audit coverage for foreign subrecipients will affect audit costs.

The issues and complexities related to both foreign and domestic subrecipients are discussed in greater detail in the chapter titled "Subrecipient Considerations."

Once the terms of the audit, including its scope and cost, have been agreed to, the agreement should be formalized in an engagement letter, which is discussed later in this chapter.

Performing Client Acceptance/Retention Procedures

The AICPA Statement on Quality Control Standards (SQCS) No. 2, "System of Quality Control for a CPA Firm's Accounting and Auditing Practices," requires that audit firms design and maintain policies and procedures to minimize the likelihood of accepting a client, or continuing a client, whose management lacks integrity. SQCS-2 provides some general guidance to CPA firms for accepting and continuing client relationships, in addition to the usual communication with the predecessor auditor, as required by SAS-7 (Communication Between Predecessor and Successor Auditors).

SQCS-2 provides that CPA firms should also establish policies and procedures that provide reasonable assurance that the CPA firm:

- Undertakes only those engagements that the firm can reasonably expect to be completed with professional competence
- Appropriately considers the risks associated with providing professional services in the particular circumstances

Individual certified public accountants or firms of certified public accountants should establish procedures to be performed before the acceptance or continuation of an audit engagement. These procedures for Circular A-133 audits should be similar to or the same as those employed for audits of financial statements in accordance with GAAS.

However, when evaluating the potential risk of accepting a client or continuing a relationship with a client, the auditor should consider the risks associated with auditing a not-for-profit organization that receives federal awards. Just as an auditor might assign a greater risk to an engagement of a client whose stock or debt is publicly traded than to one for a privately held organization, a not-for-profit organization receiving federal awards may be a greater risk than a privately held organization that does not receive federal awards.

Although the amount of risk for a not-for-profit organization receiving federal funds is probably far less than the risk for a publicly traded company, all other things being equal, the auditor should consider the special environment in which these organizations operate to properly assess the risk of accepting or retaining a Circular A-133 audit engagement.

The environment of not-for-profit organizations receiving federal awards is influenced to a great extent by the fact that these organizations often operate in the public eye. This means that events concerning these organizations are subject to greater scrutiny by the press and other organizations than events concerning the typical privately held company. Not-for-profit organizations use public funds (federal, and perhaps state and local, government aid) as well as donor contributions. The public expects the not-for-profit to maintain a high level of stewardship over these funds, and a high level of criticism is levied when that stewardship is not provided.

Not-for-profit organizations frequently engage in advocacy activities for certain groups or constituencies and provide services to individuals or organizations that are in some way disadvantaged or in need of assistance. If any of these activities is mismanaged, financially or otherwise, not-for-profit organizations can be subjected to intense scrutiny and public debate about their management practices. The scrutiny intensifies if the not-for-profit organization receives voluntary contributions from the general public, and maybe even more so if it receives involuntary contributions from taxpayers in the form of federal awards.

Auditors should understand that the public scrutiny of not-for-profit organizations can extend to the organization's auditors. The auditor of a not-for-profit organization whose program or financial management activities are criticized also may be criticized. This is true particularly if the alleged management failures have not been communicated in the form of management letters or reports on internal control. However, auditors may be criticized even if some or all of the problems had been brought to the attention of management.

Although actual financial liability of the auditor probably would be similar to that in audits of privately held organizations, the real risk to the auditor is the damage to his or her reputation.

In addition to the unique risk factors discussed above, the auditor should consider other, more typical factors before formally accepting an engagement to perform a Circular A-133 audit. These factors include:

- The reputation and capabilities of the recipient organization's management and the individuals who make up the board of directors or other oversight body
- The auditor's independence with respect to the organization, including an evaluation of any board of director positions that individual auditors may hold
- The expected users of the financial statements, including the reliance thereon of creditor organizations and federal grantor agencies
- The likelihood that the recipient organization has suitable accounting systems and internal control to properly account for and control its financial activities
- Any anticipated limitations on the scope of the auditor's procedures
- The professional capabilities of the auditor, especially when deciding to accept or retain a Circular A-133 audit engagement because of the Yellow Book's continuing professional education and quality control review requirements

ENGAGEMENT LETTER

Once a recipient organization selects an auditor, formalizing the terms of the audit engagement becomes important to both the recipient organization and the auditor. Sometimes the terms are formalized through the negotiation of a contract, but more often they are formalized in an engagement letter signed by both the auditor and the recipient organization.

An engagement letter protects the interests of both the auditor and the recipient organization by defining the responsibilities of each party and minimizing confusion between the two.

If the engagement letter contains very specific information relating to audit scope or if it is tailored in some unique or extraordinary way, the recipient organization and the auditor may deem it appropriate to discuss the engagement letter with the cognizant audit agency. (The definition and description of *cognizant agencies* are expanded in the chapter titled "Planning for a Circular A-133 Audit.")

Discussing the engagement letter with the cognizant audit agency is not required. Such discussions, however, would protect the recipient organization and the auditor from the cognizant audit agency taking exception to the scope of the audit after the audit has been completed and the reports issued. Such consultations should be the exception rather than the rule.

SOP 98-3 (Audits of States, Local Governments, and Not-for-Profit Organizations Receiving Federal Awards) contains a list of items pertaining to Circular A-133 that an auditor should consider including in the representation letter. The example in Exhibit 14-3 includes these items and has also been updated to reflect changes resulting from SAS-83 (Establishing an Understanding with the Client). This example contains certain minimum information, and the auditor (and to some extent the recipient organization) should make appropriate modifications to the letters to tailor them to the individual circumstances of the engagement. The engagement letter is addressed to the recipient organization. An appropriate official of the recipient organization responsible for the management of the audit should sign a copy of the letter and return it to the auditor as acknowledgment that the terms of the letter have been accepted.

OTHER AUDITOR CONSIDERATIONS

In many instances, auditors of organizations that receive federal awards may find themselves performing the audits in conjunction with other independent auditors.

Frequently, audits in conjunction with other independent auditors involve sharing audit work with minority- or woman-owned CPA firms. A common practice is for the recipient organization to

EXHIBIT 14-3
SAMPLE ENGAGEMENT LETTER—
CIRCULAR A-133[1]

[Addressee—Not-for-Profit Organization]

This letter sets forth our understanding of the terms and objectives of our engagement, the nature and scope of the services we will provide, and the related fee arrangements.

We will audit the organization's financial statements as of and for the year ended *[date]*, in accordance with generally accepted auditing standards, the standards for financial audits contained in *Government Auditing Standards* issued by the Comptroller General of the United States, and the provisions of Office of Management and Budget Circular A-133.[2] The management of *[name of organization]* has responsibility for the financial statements and all assertions and representations contained therein. Management also has responsibility for the adoption of sound accounting policies and the implementation of record keeping and internal control to maintain the reliability of the financial statements and to provide reasonable assurance against the possibility of misstatements that are material to the financial statements. In conducting the audit, we will perform tests of the accounting records and such other procedures as we consider necessary in the circumstances to provide a reasonable basis for our opinion on management's financial statements. We also will assess the accounting principles used and significant estimates made by management, as well as evaluate the overall financial statement presentation.

Our report will be addressed to the Board of Trustees of *[name of organization]*. We cannot provide assurance that an unqualified opinion will be rendered. Circumstances may arise in which it is necessary for us to modify our report or withdraw from the engagement. In such circumstances, our findings or reasons for withdrawal will be communicated to you and the Board of Trustees.

Management of *[name of organization]* is responsible for establishing and maintaining internal control. To fulfill this responsibility, estimates and judgments by management are required to assess the expected benefits and related costs for internal control policies and procedures. The objectives of internal control are to provide management with reasonable, but not absolute, assurance that assets are safeguarded against loss from unauthorized use or disposition, and that transactions are executed in accordance with management's authorization and recorded properly to permit the preparation of financial statements in accordance with generally accepted accounting principles. Because of inherent limitations in any system of internal control, errors or irregularities may nevertheless occur and not be detected. Also, projection of any evaluation of internal control to future periods is subject to the risk that procedures may become inadequate because of changes in conditions, or that the effectiveness of the design and operation of policies and procedures may deteriorate.

As part of our financial statement audit, we will consider [*name of organization*]'s internal control and assess control risk, as required by *Government Auditing Standards,* for the purpose of establishing a basis for determining the nature, timing, and extent of auditing procedures necessary for expressing our opinion on the financial statements and not to provide assurance on internal controls. Furthermore, our audit, including the limited inquiries we will make in connection with Year 2000 issues, is not designed to, and does not, provide any assurance that Year 2000 issues that may exist will be identified, on the adequacy of [*name of organization*]'s Year 2000 remediation plans with respect to operational or financial systems, or on whether [*name of organization*] is or will become Year 2000 compliant on a timely basis. Year 2000 compliance is the responsibility of management. However, we may communicate matters that come to our attention relating to the Year 2000 issue which, in our judgment, may be of benefit to management.

We will prepare a written report on our understanding of [*name of organization*]'s internal control and the assessment of control risk made as part of the financial statement audit. Our report will include (1) the scope of our work in obtaining an understanding of internal control and in assessing control risk and (2) the reportable conditions, including the identification of material weaknesses, identified as a result of our work in understanding and assessing the control risk for the financial statement audit.

In accordance with *Government Auditing Standards,* we are informing you that tests of compliance with laws and regulations and internal control over financial reporting in a financial statement audit contribute to the evidence supporting our opinion on the financial statements. However, they generally do not provide a basis for opining on compliance or internal control over financial reporting. To meet certain audit report users' needs, laws and regulations sometimes prescribe testing and reporting on compliance and internal control over financial reporting to supplement the financial statement audit's coverage of theses areas. The results of additional tests of compliance and internal control over financial reporting required by laws and regulations may still not meet some reasonable needs of report users. These needs may be met by performing further tests of compliance and internal control in either of two ways: (1) supplemental (or agreed-upon) procedures or (2) examination, resulting in an opinion.

A financial statement audit is designed to provide reasonable assurance about whether the financial statements are free of material misstatement, whether caused by error or fraud. *Fraud* is defined as purposeful acts that may cause a material misstatement of the financial statements and can include misstatements that arise from fraudulent financial reporting as well as misstatements arising from misappropriation of assets. Management is responsible for the prevention and detection of fraud. Our audit will include procedures designed to provide reasonable, but not absolute, assurance of detecting material misstatements. As you are aware, however, there are inherent limitations in the auditing process. For example, audits are based on the concept of selective testing of the data being examined and are, therefore, subject to the limitations that such matters, if they exist, may not be detected. Also, because of the characteristics of irregularities, including attempts at concealment through collusion, forgery, and fraud, a properly designed and executed audit of financial statements may not detect a material irregularity. Also, an audit is not designed to detect matters that are immaterial to the financial statements.

To the extent that they come to our attention, we will inform management about any material error and any instances of fraud or illegal acts. Further, to the extent that they come to our attention, we will inform the Board of Trustees about fraud and illegal acts that involve senior management, fraud that in our judgment causes a material misstatement of the financial statements of [*name of organization*], and illegal acts, unless clearly inconsequential, that have not otherwise been communicated to the committee.

Compliance with laws, regulations, contracts, and grants that govern federal awards programs is the responsibility of management. We will perform the tests of [*name of organization*]'s compliance with certain specific provisions of laws, regulations, contracts, and grants we determine to be necessary based on OMB's Compliance Supplement and report whether in our opinion the organization complied, in all material respects, with the laws and regulations applicable to its major federal financial awards programs. The procedures outlined in the Compliance Supplement are those suggested by each federal agency and do not cover all areas of regulations governing each program. Program reviews by federal agencies may identify additional instances of noncompliance.

In summary, in accordance with OMB Circular A-133, we will issue a report which (1) provides our opinion on the schedule of expenditures of federal awards in relation to the financial statements taken as a whole, (2) provides our opinion on [*name of organization*]'s compliance with laws, regulations, contracts, and grant agreements that have a direct and material effect on a major federal award program, and (3) communicates our consideration of internal control over federal awards programs.

In addition to OMB Circular A-133 requirements to maintain internal control and comply with laws, regulations, contracts, and grants that govern federal award programs as discussed above, OMB Circular A-133 requires [*name of organization*] to prepare a:

- Schedule of expenditures of federal awards,
- Summary schedule of prior audit findings,
- Corrective action plan, and
- Data collection form.

While we may assist you in the preparation of these items, preparation is, and must remain, the responsibility of [*name of organization*].

Certain provisions of Circular A-133 allow a granting agency to request that a specific program be selected as a major program provided that the federal granting agency is willing to pay the incremental cost of such a selection. [*Name of organization*] agrees to notify us of any such request by a granting agency and to work with us to modify the terms of this letter as necessary to accommodate such requests.

Other Engagement Issues

[*Name of organization*] is also responsible for following up and taking corrective action on audit findings and submitting the reporting package in accordance with the instructions of Circular A-133.

[*Name of organization*] agrees that all records, documentation, and information we request in connection with our audit will be made available to us, that all material information will be disclosed to us, and that we will have the full cooperation of [*name of organization*]'s personnel. As required by *Government Auditing Standards*, we will make specific inquiries of management about the representations embodied in the financial statements, the effectiveness of the internal control, any known instances of fraud; including fraudulent financial reporting and misstatements arising from misappropriation of assets, that could have a material effect on the financial statements, and [*name of organization*]'s compliance with laws and regulations, and obtain a representation letter from management about these matters. The responses to our inquiries, the written representations, and the results of audit tests comprise the evidential matter we will reply upon in forming an opinion on the financial statements.

It is our responsibility to ensure that the Board of Trustees are informed of any significant illegal acts that become aware of during our audit. If an illegal act involves funds from governmental entities, it is [*name of organization*]'s responsibility to inform the governmental entities of these acts. If [*name of organization*]'s management and Board of Trustees are involved in an illegal act or do not report it to the appropriate governmental entities on a timely basis, we as auditors, will be obligated to report the illegal acts to these governmental entities.

Circular A-133 requires that auditors retain working papers and reports for a minimum of three years after the date of issuance of the report, unless the auditor is notified in writing by the cognizant agency for audit, the oversight agency for audit, or the pass-through entity to extend the retention period. However, if we are aware that a federal awarding agency, a pass-through entity, or [*name of organization*] is contesting an audit finding, we will contact the parties contesting the audit finding for guidance prior to the destruction of the working papers and reports.

Pursuant to *Government Auditing Standards*, we are required to make certain working papers available to federal regulatory agencies upon request for their reviews of audit quality and use by their auditors. Access to the requested working papers will be provided to the regulators under supervision of personnel of our firm.

For your information, we have attached a copy of our firm's most recent peer review report.[3]

We understand that our report on internal control and compliance with laws and regulations, both as part of the financial audit, is intended for the information and use of the Board of Trustees, management, and federal awarding agencies and pass-through agencies and is not intended to be and should not be used by anyone other than these specified parties.

At the conclusion of the engagement, [*name of organization*]'s management will provide to us a representation letter that, among other things, will confirm management's responsibility for the preparation of the financial statements in conformity with generally accepted accounting principles; the availability of financial records and related data; compliance with provisions of laws, regulations, contracts, and grants that govern federal programs; the completeness and availability of all minutes of board of directors (and committee) meetings; and the absence of irregularities involving management or those employees who have significant roles in the control structure.

Our fees for the audit will be [*describe fee arrangement*]. We anticipate completing the engagement by [*describe timetable*], unless unexpected factors are encountered. This timetable has been discussed with and agreed to by your [*internal audit and*] accounting department[s], which will provide assistance to us in the audit. Should circumstances prevent [*name of organization*] from providing this assistance, our timetable and fee are likely to be affected.[4] [*On fixed-fee engagements, the auditor may include wording indicating that he or she may have to revise the fee estimate and timetable for unexpected factors of which he or she becomes aware after the engagement has begun.*]

We would be pleased to discuss this letter with you.

[*Signature*]

[*Date*]

Accepted:

[*Name of not-for-profit organization*]

By: _____ Date: _____

---

[1] In December 1999, the AICPA issued Statement on Auditing Standards No. 89, "Audit Adjustments," which is effective for audits of financial statements for periods beginning on or after December 15, 1999, with earlier application permitted. In addition to its requirement for communicating audit adjustments to audit committees and for obtaining management's representation as to the effect of unrecorded audit adjustments, SAS-89 adds the following to the list of matters that are generally included in the understanding with the client:

> Management is responsible for adjusting the financial statements to correct material misstatements and for affirming to the auditor in the representation letter that the effects of any uncorrected misstatements aggregated by the auditor during the current engagement and pertaining to the latest period presented are immaterial, both individually and in the aggregate, to the financial statements taken as a whole.

[2] The auditor should be aware of the constantly changing requirements related to performing audits in accordance with generally accepted auditing standards, *Government Auditing Standards*, and Circular A-133. These changes should be incorporated into the engagement letter when appropriate.

[3] *Government Audit Standards* requires that the auditor make available to the auditee a copy of the firm's most recent peer review report. A convenient way to demonstrate compliance with the requirement is to transmit the Peer Review Report along with the engagement letter.

[4] In the areas of assistance provided or to be provided by the client, the timing of the audit procedures, the fee arrangements, and any other appropriate area, the auditor should feel free to

expand on the brief descriptions provided in the sample letter. It may also be in the best interests of the recipient organization to be as specific as possible regarding what assistance it will provide to the auditor, the timing of the audit, and the details of the fee arrangements that are agreed to with the auditor. Reaching a clear understanding of the responsibilities of the recipient organization and documenting these responsibilities will eliminate misunderstandings later on and will encourage the recipient organization to be aware of its commitments and deadlines for providing assistance to the auditor. This will help the auditor complete the engagement within the agreed-upon time frame.

---

engage an auditor to perform an audit and request (or require) that a certain percentage of the audit be performed by a minority- or woman-owned firm. The percentages can vary widely, although 25 percent of the audit (which can be defined by the recipient organization as audit hours, audit fee, or both) is typical.

In other cases, auditors may perform audits in conjunction with the independent auditors engaged by affiliated organizations or subsidiary corporations that are part of the reporting entity on which the primary auditor will opine. The recipient organization may choose to have an affiliated organization audited by a different auditor.

In some cases, the primary auditors may request that certain work be performed by other auditors, often because of geographical considerations or the particular expertise of another audit firm.

The actual circumstances of these audits vary widely and take many forms. For example, a minority- or woman-owned audit firm performing 25 percent of an audit may jointly sign the auditor's reports with the primary auditor, or it may provide some other form of assurance to the primary auditor and have the primary auditor as the only signatory to the audit report. The selection of either of these options affects the manner in which the audit work is divided between the two firms, the level of supervisory review that will be performed, and many other practical considerations. The option chosen also can affect the legal obligations of the firms.

Several considerations concerning these types of auditor relationships should be taken into account during the preplanning phase of an audit, and some are particularly important when performing audits in accordance with Circular A-133. The considerations that relate specifically to A-133 audits include confirming and appropriately documenting the following:

- The other auditor must meet the independence requirements contained in the Yellow Book.

- The individuals the other audit firm assigns to the audit must meet the requirements, where applicable, of the Yellow Book as they relate to continuing professional education.

- The other auditor must meet the Yellow Book quality control review requirements.

- The other auditor must comply with all of the other appropriate requirements of generally accepted government auditing standards.

Clearly establishing and documenting the responsibilities and requirements of each auditor during the preplanning stage benefits all of the auditors. Clearly defining these relationships (and confirming the terms with the recipient organization) allows the audit to progress in an orderly fashion with fewer surprises caused by weak communication between (or among) the auditors.

SUMMARY

Both the auditor and the recipient organization will benefit greatly by considering the procedures outlined in this chapter during the preplanning stage of the engagement. These administrative procedures should be completed before the auditor even begins to plan the audit.

Taking the time and making the effort to perform these administrative tasks before planning the audit gives the auditor and the recipient organization a clear understanding of the expectations for the audit and assurance that the requirements of Circular A-133 are achievable. This is a firm footing on which to move into the planning phase of the audit.

Chapter 15
PLANNING FOR A
CIRCULAR A-133 AUDIT

CONTENTS

Chapter 15
PLANNING FOR A
CIRCULAR A-133 AUDIT

CROSS-REFERENCES

2001 MILLER NOT-FOR-PROFIT ORGANIZATION AUDITS: Chapter 3, "Audit Planning"; Chapter 18, "Reporting Under Circular A-133"

2001 MILLER SINGLE AUDITS: Chapter 6, "Planning the Single Audit"

BENEFITS OF PLANNING

The effectiveness of the planning phase of an audit engagement will determine whether the audit is performed in accordance with professional standards, on a timely basis, and in a manner that will be profitable to the auditor. It will also increase the likelihood that the organization being audited will receive efficient, high-quality service.

In performing a Circular A-133 audit of a not-for-profit organization, planning is essential to ensure that those procedures performed for the Circular A-133 aspect of the engagement are well-coordinated with those procedures performed as part of the audit of the financial statements. Timelines and audit efficiency both depend on proper planning.

OVERVIEW

This chapter provides a guide to the planning considerations necessary for performing an audit in accordance with Circular A-133. Some of these considerations are in addition to, or overlap, the planning procedures normally performed for an audit of financial statements in accordance with GAAS and are meant to supplement the normal planning procedures. Planning procedures should be tailored to individual client circumstances, and therefore, the auditor should exercise good judgment when determining which procedures are required during the planning phase of an audit engagement.

An audit planned in accordance with Circular A-133 should include the following components:

- Obtaining an understanding of the not-for-profit organization and the environment in which it operates.
- Considering the requirements of the federal cognizant audit agency.
- Identifying all federal awards and subrecipients of federal awards programs.
- Identifying major federal awards programs.
- Determining materiality levels.
- Completing the initial audit risk assessment and developing an audit strategy.
- Considering the specific requirements of *Government Auditing Standards*.
- Following up on prior-year audit report findings.
- Reviewing the reporting requirements of Circular A-133.
- Documenting the planning phase in a planning memorandum.

OBTAINING AN UNDERSTANDING OF THE NOT-FOR-PROFIT ORGANIZATION AND THE ENVIRONMENT IN WHICH IT OPERATES

To properly design an audit approach for an audit in accordance with Circular A-133, the auditor must have a reasonably comprehensive understanding of the not-for-profit organization and its operating environment. This understanding should include how the organization operates its affairs and its administrative structure. The auditor should review an organization chart of the entire not-for-profit organization, and the finance department in particular.

The auditor should have a general understanding or assessment of the extent to which the organization is conscious and supportive of internal controls and of the strength of its financial management. Although the auditor will expand this understanding when assessing the organization's control environment, a preliminary assessment of the control environment is useful during the planning phase of the audit and will be necessary in designing a preliminary audit strategy.

The auditor should obtain a general understanding of the following operating characteristics of the recipient organization as they relate to federal awards for use in designing an audit strategy:

- Extent to which accounting and financial systems are computerized, including the type of computers (mainframe, workstations, networks, or stand-alone personal computers)
- Existence of an internal audit group or department, whether the independent auditor can rely on its work, and whether staff from the internal audit group or department will be available to assist the independent auditor
- Extent of the management of federal awards and the individuals in the organization responsible for managing those awards
- The manner in which indirect costs are accumulated and allocated to the various programs and activities of the recipient organization
- The manner in which any subrecipients of federal awards are monitored and the individuals in the recipient organization responsible for the monitoring procedures
- The extent of financial experience and acumen of the program management and other top management individuals who do not have direct responsibility for the financial affairs of the recipient organization

> **OBSERVATION:** Obviously, the considerations listed above are important during the first year an auditor is engaged to perform a Circular A-133 audit. It is just as important, however, for the auditor to update his or her understanding of these considerations every year. As the auditor's knowledge of the recipient organization builds from year to year, he or she will derive more and more benefit from being able to review these matters.

Not-for-profit organizations operate in a variety of fields and serve numerous constituencies and purposes. The operating environment issues that affect a major college or university are different from those affecting a human service organization providing meals to the indigent. The college or university may have as a significant concern or exposure area the tax status of revenues obtained by its football team in a corporate-sponsored bowl game. The human service organization may be concerned with having its operations judged efficient, thereby putting the five- and ten-dollar contributions it receives to the fullest use and advantage. Similarly, these organizations may receive federal funding for completely different purposes. For example, it may take years before research performed by the university shows results. The human service organization, on the other hand, may provide daily sustenance to people and have an immediate effect. Federal award programs often change in nature, source of funding, and program requirements. Not-for-profit organizations must have a sufficient grants-monitoring process in place to track these changes and to ensure that important sources of revenues are not lost.

The auditor must identify the issues affecting the organization under audit and determine what their implications might be to an audit in accordance with Circular A-133.

The auditor should consider many factors of the operating environment, including:

- The outlook for the continued solicitation of unrestricted revenues, such as through fund-raising activities, annual giving, bequests, special events, and fee-for-service activities

- The size of the federal awards programs and their importance to the recipient organization, the status of multiyear contracts or grants, and the prospects for obtaining new federal awards to replace expiring ones; the outlook for increasing or decreasing federal awards programs in the areas in which the not-for-profit organization operates

- The appropriateness of the resources and experience of the administrative staff and capabilities of the not-for-profit organization, given the outlook for its revenue growth or shrinkage

- The environmental factors that affect the operating expenses of the not-for-profit organization, such as employee health care costs, technology changes, and other factors affecting the delivery of services by the organizations

> **OBSERVATION:** Environmental factors affecting not-for-profit organizations include many of the same environmental factors facing commercial enterprises (e.g., personnel and payroll matters, purchasing and procurement, cash management, and facilities management). Auditors should not overlook these environmental/institutional factors when planning their audits.

Review of Prior-Year Audit

In attempting to understand the not-for-profit organization and its operating environment, the auditor should first consult the prior-year audit report and the prior-year working papers. This is an easy step for recurring audit engagements, because the auditor will already have the working papers.

For organizations that were previously audited by another auditor, the current auditor should obtain the prior auditor's working papers. To comply with the AICPA's ethics requirements for confidentiality, the client should approve the auditor's request to review the predecessor auditor's working papers.

The requirements covering communications between predecessor and successor auditors are discussed in full in the chapter titled "Preplanning Audit Activities."

Information obtained from prior reports and working papers (whether the auditor's own or a predecessor's) can be quite valuable in planning for the current-year audit, even if the prior-year audit was not performed in accordance with the requirements of Circular A-133.

The prior-year audit report should focus first on any comments regarding internal control, whether they identify material weaknesses in the internal control, reportable conditions, or simply items included in a comment letter to management. The second area of focus is any instance of noncompliance with laws, regulations, or contracts relating to federal awards. These may be categorized as material instances of noncompliance or may be included in a schedule of findings and questioned costs.

The prior-year audit also should contain the predecessor auditor's assessment of the internal control, including (1) whether the auditor tested the internal control to reduce the extent of substantive testing performed and (2) the number and dollar magnitude of the adjustments the auditor proposed to the financial statements, including the dollar amount of the adjustments the recipient organization recorded and the amount of the proposed adjustments the auditor waived.

The existence and extent of control deficiencies and instances of noncompliance with laws, regulations, and other contracts in prior years will provide the auditor with background information when approaching the current-year audit. The auditor should review any test work that proved to be problematic in the prior year (because it did not provide the evidence that the auditor thought it would or because the evidence was difficult to obtain) and should anticipate modifying this particular test work in the current year to make the audit procedures more efficient.

> **OBSERVATION:** For the auditor to obtain full benefit from prior-year working papers, the working papers must have been prepared properly. Full use of narratives and supporting commentaries and conclusions are helpful to subsequent audits, particularly when different individuals are performing the audit planning. These narratives should be prepared in a computerized format so that they may be carried forward easily from year to year.

A checklist for recording the status of prior-year reportable conditions, material weaknesses in internal control, and instances of noncompliance is shown in Exhibit 15-1.

Follow-up on prior-year audit findings has special implications under Circular A-133. The responsibility for determining the status

EXHIBIT 15-1
STATUS OF PRIOR-YEAR FINDINGS

This form should be used to document the status findings included in prior-year audit reports. Comments relating to conditions that have been corrected in the year by the recipient organization should be reviewed and evaluated. If the comments have not been cleared, or have not been cleared satisfactorily, the comment should be repeated again this year. Modify the comment as appropriate for any actions taken by the recipient organization or other developments this year.

Last Year's Comments	Status of Findings This Year	Disposition	Status of Prior-Year Audit Findings*
1.	1.	1.	1.
2.	2.	2.	2.
3.	3.	3.	3.
4.	4.	4.	4.
5.	5.	5.	5.
6.	6.	6.	6.

* Indicate by "Yes" or "No" if the status has been properly reported by the client in the Schedule of the Status of Prior-Year Audit Findings. If "No," cross-reference to the related current-year audit finding.

of prior-year findings shifts from the auditor to the not-for-profit organization. The not-for-profit organization is responsible for preparing a summary schedule of prior audit findings. This summary schedule reports the status of all audit findings included in prior audits' schedule of findings and questioned costs. Additional information on the summary schedule of prior audit findings is provided in the chapter of this Guide titled "Reporting under Circular A-133."

In planning an audit in accordance with Circular A-133, the auditor should consider that he or she will need to examine this schedule to determine the veracity of the information provided by the not-for-profit organization. If the auditor disagrees with any of the information provided by management in the summary schedule, a compliance exception results will need to be reported by the auditor.

Discussions with Management and Planning Meetings

After reviewing the prior year's audit, the auditor should meet with the senior management of the not-for-profit organization. Here the auditor's relationship with management will influence the breadth and depth of information the auditor can obtain. If the auditor has a good working relationship with management, the quality of the information obtained most likely will be excellent. When management views the auditor as a business adviser as well as an auditor, it usually will share information openly, since the quality and depth of the auditor's understanding of the organization will affect his or her ability to provide valuable comments to management about the organization's operations.

In a planning discussion between the auditor and management, fundamental areas to be discussed include:

- Status of federal awards, including new awards programs obtained and previous award programs lost or expired
- Existence of any ongoing audits by federal grantor agencies and the status of any such audits
- Monitoring of subrecipients and identification of any new subrecipients
- Changes in key personnel, both in senior management and in financial management
- Significant changes in the revenues and expenses of the organization that would have an impact on its operating characteristics
- Any new litigation with which the organization is involved and the status of any new or proposed significant federal, state, or local legislation

- Any financial concerns or areas of focus about which the board of directors or top management is particularly concerned
- Status of banking relationships, including new loans or credit lines obtained during the year
- Any significant changes in the financial accounting systems from the prior year and, if there are changes, management's understanding of the progress of implementing the new systems
- Status of the organization's use of the Internet for donation solicitation and/or procurement of goods and services
- Status of the investment of endowment funds, including whether any significant losses were incurred during the year
- Overall changes to the organization's legal structure (i.e., changes in the corporate structure, any new entities incorporated, and any changes that might affect the organization's tax-exempt status)
- Confirmation of management's plan to prepare a summary schedule of prior audit findings.

Performing a Preliminary Analytical Review

Auditors should refer to SAS-56 (Analytical Procedures) for detailed information on performing analytical review procedures during the planning phase of the engagement. SAS-56 requires that analytical procedures be applied to some extent to help the auditor plan the nature, timing, and extent of other auditing procedures.

The value of these procedures is discussed in the chapter titled "Audit Planning."

CONSIDERING THE REQUIREMENTS OF THE FEDERAL COGNIZANT AUDIT AGENCY

Circular A-133 describes the role of the federal cognizant audit agencies in considerable detail. In terms of the assignment of cognizant agencies, only not-for-profit organizations expending more than $25 million a year in federal awards are assigned a cognizant audit agency. The cognizant agency is to be the federal awarding agency that provides the not-for-profit organization with the predominant amount of direct funding. The determination of a cognizant agency is made every five years beginning in 1995 (thereafter 2000, 2005, etc.). For example, a federal agency that provides a not-for-profit organization with its predominant amount of funding in 1995 will be the cognizant agency for that not-for-profit organization from 1996 through 2000.

The responsibilities of the cognizant agency for audit are provided in Circular A-133 as follows:

- Provide technical audit advice and liaison to auditees and auditors.

- Consider auditee requests for extensions to the report submission due dates of Circular A-133. The cognizant agency may grant extensions for audit for good cause.

- Obtain or conduct quality control reviews of selected audits made by non-federal auditors and provide the results, where appropriate, to interested organizations.

- Promptly inform other affected federal agencies and appropriate federal law enforcement officials of any fraud or illegal acts directly reported by the not-for-profit organization or its auditor, as required by *Government Auditing Standards* or laws and regulations.

- Advise the auditor and, where appropriate, the not-for-profit organization of any deficiencies found in the audits when the deficiencies require that the auditor take corrective action.

- Coordinate, where practical, audits or reviews made by or for federal agencies that are in addition to the audits made pursuant to this part, so that the additional audits or reviews build upon audits performed in accordance with Circular A-133.

- Coordinate a management decision for audit findings that affect the federal programs of more than one agency.

- Coordinate the audit work and reporting responsibilities among auditors to achieve the most cost-effective audit.

When a not-for-profit organization is not assigned a cognizant agency, because it has not met the $25 million expenditure threshold described above, assistance is provided by what is called an *oversight agency for audit*. The role of the oversight agency for audit is to:

- Provide technical advice to auditees and auditors as requested

- Assume all or some of the responsibilities normally provided by a cognizant agency for audit.

> **OBSERVATION:** Not-for-profit organizations and their auditors should expect the level of involvement of the cognizant agency in the audit process to vary widely. Factors affecting the involvement include the size of the not-for-profit organization, the amount of the federal financial assistance in relation to the total revenues of the not-for-profit organization, which federal grantor agency serves as the cognizant agency, and which

regional office of the cognizant agency handles the audit relationship.

Once the cognizant or oversight agency (hereinafter referred to as the cognizant agency for simplicity) has been identified, the recipient organization and its auditor should discuss whether to request a planning meeting with the cognizant agency for audit and what benefits might result from such a meeting. Clearly, the auditor should first hold a planning meeting with not-for-profit organization personnel and should discuss meeting with the cognizant agency.

Usually, single audit requirements have been met in the past with the cognizant agency playing no active role in the audit process and raising no significant questions about the scope of the audit or the resolution of internal control weaknesses and compliance deviations disclosed in prior-year audits. If this is the case, the recipient organization and its auditor may choose not to request an audit planning meeting with the cognizant audit agency.

In rare instances, a planning meeting with the cognizant agency before the start of the audit may prove very helpful. This might be the case if the cognizant agency has been actively involved in reviewing the scope of prior-year audits or if there has been significant interaction with the cognizant agency regarding the recipient organization's action plans to correct serious internal control weaknesses or compliance deviations noted in past audits.

A planning meeting also might be beneficial if the not-for-profit organization's operations have changed or if new federal awards have been received that were not considered in previous audits. If the auditor or the recipient organization is unclear about whether certain activities should be in the scope of the audit, or if there is considerable uncertainty about what procedures are appropriate in a particular circumstance relating to subrecipients, a planning meeting might be appropriate.

The benefits of holding a planning meeting with the cognizant agency are that potential differences in opinion about the scope of the audit can be resolved before the audit, when they can be resolved with a minimum of additional cost and work for the recipient organization or the auditor. The meeting also gives the auditor an opportunity to learn what the cognizant agency believes are the important aspects of the audit, information that may prove valuable in the audit planning process.

An understanding of the progress of the not-for-profit organization in resolving internal control weaknesses or compliance deviations usually can be obtained more easily in a face-to-face meeting than from written documents. Circular A-133 specifically recommends coordinating various audits being performed at a recipient organization to maximize efficiency and minimize audit costs. If multiple audits are being performed, the only realistic way to achieve such coordination is to meet with the cognizant agency before starting the Circular A-133 audit so that reliance on some or all of the other audits being performed can be discussed.

Holding such a meeting does have risks, however. The cognizant agency may interpret issues about which existing audit literature or federal guidelines are unclear in a way that will actually increase the scope of the audit, resulting in additional work for the auditor and additional cost for the recipient organization. In the end, however, it may be more costly to resolve these scope issues after the Circular A-133 audit reports are issued than to resolve them before beginning and to incorporate the additional procedures into the rest of the audit.

If a planning meeting seems appropriate and the cognizant agency agrees to such a meeting, certain topics should be covered, including any items the cognizant agency wishes to include on the agenda. Potential topics include:

- The overall audit plan prepared by the auditor
- Status of prior-year findings, comments, and questioned costs
- Identification of major federal awards programs (particularly under Circular A-133, where there is subjectivity in determining major programs)
- Planned audit strategy of the auditor, including a discussion of risk assessment
- Methodology to be used for testing the monitoring of subrecipients and any problems expected in obtaining Circular A-133 audit reports from subrecipients, where required
- New or expanded federal awards programs administered by the recipient organization
- Review of the reports expected to be issued by the auditor
- Any items of special interest to the cognizant agency of which the recipient organization and the auditor should be aware
- The expected activities of the cognizant agency in fulfilling its responsibilities under Circular A-133
- Any problems the auditor expects to encounter during the audit or any areas of particular concern to the auditor (problems or areas of concern may be highlighted by the cognizant agency, the auditor, or the recipient organization)
- Whether the not-for-profit organization will be considered a low-risk auditee

The planning meeting provides an excellent opportunity for the cognizant agency, the auditor, and the recipient organization to agree on the benefits and necessity of holding additional planning or other meetings and, if appropriate, to set dates and times for such future meetings.

IDENTIFYING ALL FEDERAL AWARDS AND SUBRECIPIENTS OF FEDERAL AWARDS PROGRAMS

As part of performing planning procedures, the auditor should ask the recipient organization to prepare a list of all its federal awards programs. The auditor should confirm, generally through inquiry and observation, that the list is complete.

> **OBSERVATION:** The best approach is for the recipient organization to prepare the list described above. This will establish the recipient organization's responsibility for maintaining this information and will provide additional assurance that the list is complete, since the auditor will spend time verifying the list rather than preparing it.

Failure to identify all of the federal awards programs that should be covered in the audit of a recipient organization for a given fiscal year can have a significant effect on whether the audit meets the requirements of Circular A-133. The consequences of failing to identify a federal awards program can be even more significant if the overlooked program is considered a major program, as discussed below.

Identification of the federal awards programs of a not-for-profit organization at first seems to be a fairly simple task. If the recipient not-for-profit organization only has one federal award program that is received directly from the federal awarding agency, it *is* a fairly simple task.

In larger recipient organizations, however, and even in more moderate-sized organizations, identifying the federal awards programs can be a complex process. The more federal awards programs there are to administer, the more likely it is that the awards programs will be managed by several different departments of the organization, and the more difficult these programs may be to identify.

If the not-for-profit organization is a subrecipient of a federal award the difficulties increase, because the organization may not even be aware that the funds it is receiving for a particular program originate with a federal grantor agency. In fact, funds may pass through a number of organizations before reaching the recipient organization, further obscuring their original federal source.

A final complication is that not all federal awards programs result in the transfer of funds to recipient organizations. Awards may take the form of noncash assistance, such as free rent or loan guarantees.

The identification of federal awards should not be considered to be a more difficult process than it actually is, however. There are a number of checks and balances and reporting requirements that, when operating properly, will result in the clear identification of federal awards. Because there are significant consequences if these checks and balances and reporting requirements fail, the auditor should obtain adequate evidence that all of the federal awards programs have been identified. Procedures the auditor might perform include the following:

- Obtain the schedule of expenditures of federal awards from the prior year and ensure that all of the awards that have not expired are still included in the current-year list of federal awards programs.

- For prior-year programs that have expired during the year, inquire if each of the programs has been replaced by another federal awards program or whether the terms of the grant or contract have been extended.

- Ask the personnel who manage the recipient organization's programs about the existence of grants and contracts and about the sources of the funds or other forms of assistance that are received under those grants and contracts.

- Review the quarterly and/or monthly financial status reports and cash status reports the recipient organization files with the federal grantor agencies to make sure that all of the federal awards on these documents are accounted for on the schedule.

- For programs whose source of funding is a state or local government or another not-for-profit organization, inquire whether the recipient organization being audited has received communications from the grantor government or not-for-profit organization about whether the source of the award program is a federal agency. If necessary, review the files for these programs for any indication of the responsibilities of the recipient organization as a subrecipient of funds. Also if necessary, the recipient organization or the auditor can correspond with the grantor government or not-for-profit organization to confirm whether the source of the awards program is a federal grantor agency.

- Obtain, as part of the representation letter, the written acknowledgment of management that it has disclosed to the auditor all of the federal awards programs the recipient organization has received from all federal grantor agencies and all pass-through funds whose origin is with a federal grantor agency.

It will be more difficult to identify all of a recipient organization's federal awards programs in the first year that an auditor audits a particular recipient organization or in the first year that the single audit requirements are being met. Once a master list of federal awards programs is developed and the auditor becomes more familiar with the recipient organization, monitoring additions to and deletions from the master list becomes easier.

A checklist for identifying federal awards is shown in Exhibit 15-2.

IDENTIFYING MAJOR FEDERAL PROGRAMS

In order to focus more audit effort on programs thought to be more problematic, Circular A-133 requires what is referred to as a *risk-based* approach to determine major programs. The approach is a combination of consideration of a program's size and its risk characteristics. Complete discussions of both of these approaches is provided in the following pages.

Once all of the federal awards programs have been identified, the recipient organization—with the assistance of the auditor, if necessary—needs to place all of the programs into two categories: major programs and all other programs. The scope of audit work and the reporting requirements for the internal controls used in administering, and in complying with laws, regulations, and other contract provisions for major programs are significantly different from the scope and reporting requirements for federal programs that are not major programs.

Circular A-133 requires the auditor to determine which federal programs are to be treated as major programs using a risk-based approach. The risk-based approach gives consideration to a federal program's current and prior audit experience, oversight of federal agencies and pass-through entities, and the inherent risk of the federal program.

> **OBSERVATION:** A small exception to the requirement for a risk-based approach is provided for the first year that the revised Circular A-133 is applied and the first year a new auditor performs the single audit. An explanation of this exception is provided at the end of this section.

Circular A-133 provides a series of steps that an auditor should use to determine which programs are considered major programs. Chapter 7 of SOP 98-3 also provides information on determining major programs. The following steps are consistent with Circular A-133 and SOP 98-3. Exhibit 15-3 (see page 589) can be used to facilitate this classification.

Step 1 Federal programs are categorized as Type A programs and Type B programs. A *federal program* is defined as all federal awards

EXHIBIT 15-2
FEDERAL OR FEDERAL PASS-THROUGH
AWARD INTERVIEW CHECKLIST

Use this checklist to interview the appropriate personnel in the recipient organization about the existence of any type of federal or pass-through awards received or applied for this year, or any other awards of which the personnel may be aware.

List the personnel interviewed including their position in the organization:

Name	Position/Responsibility
1.	
2.	
3.	
4.	
5.	
6.	
7.	
8.	
9.	
10.	

Were any of the following types of federal or federal pass-though awards applied for or awarded during the year, or were expenditures made under them during the year?

GRANTS:

1.   Applied for:

2.   Awarded during the year:

3.   Expenditures during the year:

CONTRACTS:

1. Applied for:

2. Awarded during the year:

3. Expenditures during the year:

COOPERATIVE AGREEMENTS:

1. Applied for:

2. Awarded during the year:

3. Expenditures during the year:

LOANS OR LOAN GUARANTEES:

1. Applied for:

2. Awarded during the year:

3. Expenditures during the year:

PROPERTY AND OTHER NON-CASH ASSISTANCE:

1. Applied for:

2. Awarded during the year:

3. Expenditures during the year:

INTEREST SUBSIDIES OR INSURANCE:

1. Applied for:

2. Awarded during the year:

3. Expenditures during the year:

Any other forms of federal or federal pass-through awards received directly or indirectly (including affiliated organizations):

For any grants, contracts, cooperative agreements, loans, loan guarantees, property and other non-cash awards, interest subsidies, insurance, or any other form of award noted above, obtain a copy of the award agreement and other relevant data, including copies of award reports, correspondence, and compliance requirements.

---

under the same CFDA number, with the exception of research and development, student financial aid, and a cluster of programs. The cluster is treated as a combined category of programs.

- The Type A (i.e., the larger) programs are federal programs with federal expenditures during the audit period exceeding the larger of:
  — $300,000 or 3% of total federal expenditures in the case of a not-for-profit organization for which total federal expenditures equal or exceed $300,000 but are less than or equal to $100 million.
  — $3 million or .3% of total federal expenditures in the case of a not-for-profit organization in which total federal expenditures exceed $100 million but are less than or equal to $10 billion.
  — $30 million or .15% of total federal expenditures in the case of a not-for-profit organization in which total federal expenditures exceed $10 billion.

In performing these calculations, Circular A-133 provides a special caution to auditors concerning large loan and loan guarantee programs. The inclusion of these large programs should not result in the exclusion of other programs as Type A programs. When a federal program providing loans or loan guarantees significantly affects the number or size of Type A programs, the auditor should consider this federal program as a Type A program and exclude its value in determining other Type A programs. According to SOP 98-3, determining whether including these programs "significantly affects" the number or size of Type A programs is a matter of the auditor's professional judgment.

Any federal program that does not meet the above criteria to be considered a Type A program is to be considered a Type B program.

Step 2 The auditor identifies the Type A programs which are considered low-risk. For a Type A program to be considered low-risk, it had to have been audited as a major program in at least one of the two most recent audit periods and, in the most recent audit period, have had no audit findings reported in the schedule of findings and

EXHIBIT 15-3
MAJOR PROGRAM DETERMINATION FORM

CFDA Number[1]	Grantor Agency	Pass-Through Grantor's No.	Grant Award Amount	Expenditures Recognized (or other non-cash awards)	Type A or B Program	Low-Risk Type A or High-Risk Type B	Major Program (Yes or No)	Reference to Internal Control Procedures	Reference to Compliance Test Work
1.									
2.									
3.									
4.									
5.									
6.									
7.									
8.									
9.									
10.									
11.									
TOTALS									

Total Expenditures Recognized _____ (A)
Total Expenditures—Major Programs _____ (B)
(B) ÷ (A) _____
50% Test Met (25% for low-risk auditee) _____ Yes or No[2]

[1] Only one CFDA number per line, as major program dollar criteria are applicable to only a single CFDA number.
[2] If no, identify additional major programs to meet the test.

questioned costs. In applying the second part of the criteria (no audit findings in the most recent audit period), the auditor is permitted some judgment. Not all findings and questioned costs would preclude the program from being considered low-risk. After using the appropriate judgment in considering risk factors (described below), an auditor is not precluded from considering a Type A program from being low-risk for the following types of findings:

- Known questioned costs which are greater than $10,000.

- Known fraud affecting a federal award, fraud being a type of illegal act that involves obtaining something of value through willful misrepresentation.

- Instances where the results of audit follow-up procedures disclosed that the summary schedule of prior audit findings prepared by the recipient organization materially misrepresents the status of any prior audit finding.

In determining whether a program could still be considered low-risk despite having one or more of the above findings, Circular A-133 instructs an auditor to consider the following risk factors:

- Oversight exercised by federal agencies and pass-through entities. Recent monitoring or other reviews performed by an oversight entity which disclosed no significant problems would indicate lower risk. However, monitoring which disclosed significant problems would indicate higher risk.

- The inherent risk of the federal program. Circular A-133 provides the following examples:

  — The nature of the federal program may indicate risk. Consideration should be given to the complexity of the program and the extent to which the federal program contracts for goods and services. For example, federal programs that disburse funds through third-party contracts or have eligibility criteria may be of higher risk. Federal programs primarily involving staff payroll costs may have a high risk for time and effort reporting, but otherwise be at low risk.

  — The phase of a federal program in its life cycle at the federal agency may indicate risk. For example, a new federal program with new or interim regulations may have higher risk than an established program with time-tested regulations. In addition, significant changes in federal programs, laws, regulations, or the provisions of contracts or grant agreements may increase risk.

  — The phase of a federal program in its life cycle at the recipient organization may indicate risk. For example, during the first and last years that a not-for-profit organization participates in a federal program, the risk may be higher because of start-up or close-out of program activities and staff.

— The results of audit follow-up.

— Whether any changes in personnel or systems affecting the Type A program have significantly increased risk.

— The application of professional judgment in determining whether a Type A program is low-risk.

Before moving on to Step 3, there is one more consideration for the auditor in Step 2. The OMB may approve a federal awarding agency's request that a Type A program at certain recipient organizations may not be considered low-risk. At least 180 days before the end of the fiscal year to be audited, the federal agency should notify the recipient organization and, if known, the auditor who the OMB has given its approval.

Step 3 Using professional judgment and Circular A-133's criteria for federal program risk, the auditor should identify Type B programs that are high-risk. These criteria are as follows:

1. *General discussion and approach* The auditor's determination of risk should be based on an overall evaluation of the risk of noncompliance occurring that could be material to the federal program. The auditor uses judgment and other criteria, including the following specific discussion, to identify risk in federal programs. As part of the risk analysis, the auditor may wish to discuss a particular federal program with the recipient organization's management and the federal agency or pass-through entity.

2. *Current and prior audit experience*

   • Weaknesses in internal control over federal programs would indicate higher risk. Consideration should be given to the control environment over federal programs and to such factors as the expectation that management will adhere to applicable laws and regulations and the provisions of contracts and grant agreements and the competence and experience of personnel who administer the federal programs.

     — A federal program administered under multiple internal control structures may have higher risk. When assessing risk in a large single audit, the auditor should consider whether weaknesses are isolated in a single operating unit (such as one college campus) or are pervasive throughout the entity (such as an entire university).

     — When significant parts of a federal program are passed through to subrecipients, a weak system for monitoring subrecipients would indicate higher risk.

— The extent to which computer processing is used to administer federal programs, as well as the complexity of that processing, should be considered by the auditor in assessing risk. New or recently modified computer systems may also indicate risk.

- Prior audit findings would indicate higher risk, particularly when the situations identified in the audit findings could have a significant impact on a federal program or have not been corrected.

- Federal programs not recently audited as major programs may be of higher risk than federal programs recently audited as major programs without audit findings.

- Oversight exercised by federal agencies or pass-through entities could indicate risk. Recent monitoring or other reviews performed by an oversight entity that disclosed no significant problems would indicate lower risk. However, monitoring that disclosed significant problems would indicate higher risk.

- Federal agencies, with the concurrence of the OMB, may identify federal programs which are higher risk.

3. *Inherent risk of the federal program*

Circular A-133 provides the following examples:

- The nature of the federal program may indicate risk. Consideration should be given to the complexity of the program and the extent to which the federal program contracts for goods and services. For example, federal programs that disburse funds through third-party contracts or have eligibility criteria may be of higher risk. Federal programs primarily involving staff payroll costs may have a high risk for time and effort reporting, but otherwise be at low risk.

- The phase of a federal program in its life cycle at the federal agency may indicate risk. For example, a new federal program with new or interim regulations may have higher risk than an established program with time-tested regulations. In addition, significant changes in federal programs, laws, regulations, or the provisions of contracts or grant agreements may increase risk.

- The phase of a federal program in its life cycle at the recipient organization may indicate risk. For example, during the first and last years that a not-for-profit organization participates in a federal program, the risk may be higher because of start-up or close-out of program activities and staff.

- Type B programs with larger expenditures would be of higher risk than programs with substantially smaller expenditures.

Circular A-133 specifies that, with the exception of the following, a single risk criteria (described above) would seldom cause a Type B program to be consider high-risk. The exceptions are:

- Known reportable conditions in internal control
- Known compliance problems with regard to the following:

  — Weaknesses in internal control over federal programs would indicate higher risk. Consideration should be given to the control environment over federal programs and to such factors as the expectation that management will adhere to applicable laws and regulations and the provisions of contracts and grant agreements and the competence and experience of personnel who administer the federal programs.

  — A federal program administered under multiple internal control structures may have higher risk. When assessing risk in a large single audit, the auditor should consider whether weaknesses are isolated in a single operating unit or are pervasive throughout the entity.

  — When significant parts of a federal program are passed through to subrecipients, a weak system for monitoring subrecipients would indicate higher risk.

  — The extent to which computer processing is used to administer federal programs, as well as the complexity of that processing, should be considered by the auditor in assessing risk. New or recently modified computer systems may also indicate risk.

  — Prior audit findings would indicate higher risk, particularly when the situations identified in the audit findings could have a significant impact on a federal program or have not been corrected.

  — Oversight exercised by federal agencies or pass-through entities could indicate risk. Recent monitoring or other reviews performed by an oversight entity that disclosed no significant problems would indicate lower risk. However, monitoring that disclosed significant problems would indicate higher risk.

Circular A-133 specifies that its requirements are not meant to cause relatively small federal programs to be audited as major programs. Therefore, it provides some relief (in quantifiable terms) to small Type B programs which do not have to be assessed to determine if they are high-risk. An auditor is required to perform risk assessments of only those Type B programs that exceed the larger of:

- $100,000 or .3% of total federal expenditures when the recipient organization has less than or equal to $100 million in total federal expenditures.
- $300,000 or .03% of total federal expenditures when the recipient organization has more than $100 million in total federal expenditures.

Step 4 At this point, the auditor is ready to determine what programs, at a minimum, will need to be audited as major programs. The auditor should audit all of the following as major programs:

- All Type A programs, except that the auditor may exclude those considered low-risk.
- High risk Type B programs identified under one of the following two options:
  - **Option 1:** At least one half of the Type B programs identified as high-risk, except that the auditor is *not* required to audit more high-risk Type B programs than the number of Type A programs identified as low-risk.
  - **Option 2:** One high-risk Type B program for each Type A program identified as low- risk.

> **OBSERVATION:** Circular A-133 encourages the auditor, in making the choice between Option 1 and Option 2, to choose the approach that provides an opportunity for different high-risk type B programs to be audited as major over a period of time.

Any additional programs that need to be audited as major programs to meet the 50 percent rule. The *50 percent rule* is that the auditor must audit as major programs federal programs with expenditures that, in the aggregate, encompass at least 50 percent of total federal expenditures. If the recipient organization meets the criteria of being a "low-risk auditee" (discussed below), the auditor need only audit as major programs federal programs with expenditures that, in the aggregate, encompass at least 25% of total federal expenditures.

Circular A-133 specifies the criteria that a recipient organization must meet for the 50 percent rule to be reduced to 25 percent. A recipient organization that meets all of the following conditions for each of the preceding two years qualifies as a low-risk auditee:

- The audits were performed annually in accordance with the provisions of Circular A-133.

- The auditor's opinions on the financial statements and the schedule of expenditures of federal awards were unqualified. However, the cognizant or oversight agency for audit may judge that an opinion qualification does not affect the management of federal awards and may consequently provide a waiver.

- No deficiencies in internal control were identified as material weaknesses under the requirements of *Government Auditing Standards*. However, the cognizant or oversight agency for audit may judge that the material weaknesses do not affect the management of federal awards and may consequently provide a waiver.

- None of the Type A programs had audit findings from any of the following:

  — Internal control deficiencies which were identified as material weaknesses.

  — Noncompliance with the provisions of laws, regulations, contracts, or grant agreements which have a material effect on the Type A program, or

  — Known or likely questioned costs that exceed 5 percent of total expenditures for a Type A program during the year.

Consideration of the Year 2000 Issue

In August 1999, OMB issued guidance as to the effect of the Year 2000 Issue on audits in accordance with Circular A-133, specifically the effect on major program determination. The following is the relevant portion of the guidance that was issued:

> As with any other issue affecting an auditee's ability to comply with requirements related to Federal awards, auditors must consider the effect of the Y2K Issue when conducting audits in accordance with OMB Circular A-133, including applying the risk-based approach to selecting major programs (paragraph .520 of OMB Circular A-133). However, the auditor is not expected to plan and perform procedures to determine whether an auditee is Y2K compliant or has made specified program towards becoming Y2K compliant.
>
> When applying the risk-based approach to selecting major programs, paragraph .520(c)(1) of OMB Circular A-133 states that "The auditor shall consider . . . whether any changes in personnel or systems affecting a Type A program have significantly increased risk. . . ." The Y2K Issue poses a greater risk for Federal awards that rely

heavily on data processing systems to administer such awards. Auditors should specifically assess the risk associated with Y2K for large Federal programs (i.e., Type A programs) and document this assessment as part of the risk-based approach.

Documentation of Risk Analysis

Circular A-133 requires that auditors document in the working papers the risk analysis process used in determining major programs. Auditors should find the practice aid material in this Guide helpful in meeting this requirement.

Circular A-133 also provides that an auditor's judgment in determining major programs is presumed to be correct, provided the determination was performed and documented as required above. Challenges by federal agencies or pass-through entities should be made only for clearly improper use of the guidance provided above. This does not preclude, however, federal agencies and pass-through entities from providing auditors with guidance about the risk of a particular program. The auditor must consider this guidance in determining major programs in audits not yet completed.

Exception to Requirement for a Risk-Based Approach to Determining Major Programs

The above discussion of Circular A-133's requirements for using a risk-based approach makes clear that a significant amount of judgment is required of the auditor. While specific guidance about how to make these judgments is provided, experience with working with the Circular on recurring audit engagements will clearly be necessary for the auditor to be fully comfortable with some or many of the judgments that are required to be made.

Circular A-133 provides two exceptions that could delay the implementation of a risk-based approach. For first-year audits, the auditor may elect to determine major programs as all Type A programs, plus any Type B programs as necessary to meet the 50 percent rule. A *first-year audit* is defined as the first year a recipient organization is audited under Circular A-133 or the first year of a change of auditors.

To ensure that frequent changes of auditors will not preclude the audit of high-risk Type B programs, the election for first-year audits may not be used by a recipient organization more than once every three years.

DETERMINING MATERIALITY LEVELS

During the planning phase of an audit in accordance with Circular A-133, the auditor must address significant considerations when setting a level of materiality that are in addition to the considerations addressed in a financial statement audit. The determinations of materiality in an audit in accordance with Circular A-133 are subject to the same high level of professional judgment required in an audit of financial statements.

Materiality at the Financial Statement Level

The auditor's first step in determining materiality is to make his or her usual determination of materiality for the audit of the financial statements of the recipient organization. The chapter of this Guide titled "Audit Planning" presents a complete description of determining materiality at the financial statement level.

Materiality at the Major Federal Program Level

In addition to establishing materiality at the financial statement level, as is normally done for an audit of financial statements in accordance with GAAS, the auditor must establish a level of planning materiality at the major program level.

Planning materiality is established for each major federal program because the auditor must test and opine on the recipient organization's compliance for each major program. Circular A-133 clearly states that the auditor should determine whether "the institution has complied with laws and regulations that may have a direct and material effect on its financial statement amounts and on each major federal program."

The auditor should consider both qualitative and quantitative characteristics for determining whether an instance of noncompliance would be a material instance of noncompliance.

SOP 98-3 lists the following as factors that affect materiality: (1) the nature of the compliance requirements, which may or may not be quantifiable in monetary terms; (2) the nature and frequency of noncompliance identified, with an appropriate consideration of sampling risk; and (3) qualitative considerations, such as the needs and expectations of federal agencies and pass-through entities.

Qualitative factors indicating immaterial compliance are (1) a low risk of public or political sensitivity, (2) a single exception with a low risk of being pervasive, and (3) the auditor's judgment and experience that federal agencies or prime recipients normally would not need to resolve the finding or take follow-up action, or that the cost of recovery would exceed the amount of the finding. Decisions on these criteria are based on the auditor's professional judgment. However, for a not-for-profit organization that is a recipient of federal awards, the materiality level and/or threshold of acceptable risk may be lower than in similar type audits in the private sector because of the public accountability of the entity, the various legal and regulatory requirements, and the visibility and sensitivity of federal programs, activities and functions.

> **OBSERVATION:** The auditor should consider similar qualitative factors for materiality determinations at the financial statement level.

Materiality Determination

As stated earlier, existence of a quantifiable level of materiality at the major federal program level should be determined during the planning phase of the engagement in order to appropriately balance audit risk and materiality in the design of an overall audit strategy.

Determining a level of planning materiality at the major federal program level is as important as determining planning materiality at the financial statement level. However, for determining a basis on which to apply a percentage to calculate materiality, the options are somewhat more limited.

For the most part federal awards programs are expected to have no excess of revenues over expenses, so a "net income" approach does not work. Because there is no "net income," a net asset approach also cannot be used. In addition, federal awards programs often have very few significant assets or liabilities that are recorded by the recipient organizations. Frequently, the largest asset is a receivable from the federal grantor agency for unreimbursed program expenditures, which can vary significantly with the timing of receipts from the federal grantor agency and would somewhat distort the level of planning materiality that would be determined if total assets, or some other balance sheet amount, were used as a basis.

> **OBSERVATION:** Total program expenditures becomes almost by default the basis on which to determine planning materiality. The percentage to be applied against the basis is clearly a matter of professional judgment given all of the factors that go into determining materiality discussed in this section. All things being equal, however, assigning 5 percent of total major program expenditures to each of the major programs would be a reasonable approach for determining planning materiality.

OBSERVATION: Auditors should recognize that this level of materiality may result in significant sample sizes for testing expenditures for each major program. Techniques such as stratification of the population should be considered to limit sample sizes while maintaining an effective audit. For example, the auditor may decide to test all transactions over a certain dollar amount for a given population, and then sample from the remaining items whose amounts are lower than the selected dollar threshold.

ASSESSING INITIAL AUDIT RISK AND DEVELOPING AN AUDIT STRATEGY

Audit risk is defined by SAS-47 as "the risk that the auditor may unknowingly fail to appropriately modify his opinion on financial statements that are materially misstated." SAS-47 further discusses the inverse relationship that exists between audit risk and materiality. The risk that an account balance or class of transactions and its related assertions could be materially misstated by a large amount might be considered low, whereas the risk that it could be misstated by a small amount might be considered high. The consideration of materiality and the determination of an acceptable level of audit risk must be made by considering both possibilities.

Audit risk comprises three individual, independent risks:

- *Inherent risk*
- *Control risk*
- *Detection risk*

An additional risk that is cross-cutting to these components of audit risks is fraud risk.

The auditor should ensure that the audit strategy he or she employs will result in an appropriately low level of risk for his or her audit of financial statements in accordance with GAAS. The design of an audit strategy is discussed in the chapter of this Guide titled "Audit Planning." For audits performed in accordance with Circular A-133, consideration of risk includes an assessment of the risk that the recipient organization did not comply with laws and regulations and that such instances of noncompliance may have a direct and material effect on each major federal awards program. Exhibit 15-4 provides a form that may be used to facilitate this inherent risk assessment.

The audit strategy for a Circular A-133 audit includes the same principles as an audit of financial statements in accordance with GAAS. However, a Circular A-133 audit has additional requirements. These relate, in particular, to the required testing of the

EXHIBIT 15-4
INHERENT RISK ASSESSMENT FORM—
SINGLE AUDIT LEVEL

Name of Client: _____

Major Federal Program Name: _____

CFDA Number: _____

Complete this form for each major federal award program by indicating the degree of inherent risk for each item below (H–high, M–moderate, L–low):

	H	M	L
SIZE OF PROGRAM:			
1. Amount of expenditures for the year relative to total expenditures for the entire organization and expenditures of all major federal programs?	___	___	___
ACTIVITY LEVEL:			
1. Volume of disbursement transactions? (high volume indicates higher risk)	___	___	___
2. Seasonal activity? (consistent level indicates lower risk)	___	___	___
COMPLEX TRANSACTIONS:			
1. Construction type of award? (may indicate higher risk)	___	___	___
2. Need to determine eligibility of individuals? (usually indicates higher risk)	___	___	___
3. Requires many steps to complete?	___	___	___
SUSCEPTIBILITY TO FRAUD:			
1. Is program deemed high risk?	___	___	___
2. Compliance requirements are specifically defined?	___	___	___
3. Level of monitoring by grantor agency?	___	___	___
4. Can be easily reconciled to other records?	___	___	___

	H	M	L
EXTENT OF JUDGMENT BY CLIENT:			
1. Are client personnel required to use much judgment?			
2. Degree of oversight over judgments made by other individuals?			
PRIOR-YEAR FINDINGS:			
1. Types of findings from prior years?			
2. Types of findings from grantor agency this year?			
Overall Assessment of Inherent Risk for This Program:			

recipient organization's internal controls over its administration of federal awards and to the auditor's reporting on the recipient organization's compliance with laws and regulations.

The auditor begins to design an audit strategy by assessing control risk for each of the assertions inherent in the financial statements and the detail accounts. *Assertions* are defined by SAS-31 (Evidential Matter) as:

> Representations by management that are embodied in the financial statement components. They can be either explicit or implicit and can be classified according to the following broad categories:
>
> - Existence or occurrence
> - Completeness
> - Rights and obligations
> - Valuation or allocation
> - Presentation and disclosure

An auditor designs a Circular A-133 audit strategy to obtain sufficient competent evidential matter for each of management's assertions about compliance with laws and regulations related to the federal awards programs. To obtain evidence relevant to the assertions, the auditor must develop audit objectives for each material account and class of transactions and then design audit procedures to obtain the evidence that will enable him or her to meet those audit objectives. These audit procedures will be compiled into an audit program, which will guide the auditor's performance of procedures throughout the audit and will ensure that the audit objectives for each assertion for all material accounts, classes of transactions, and major federal awards programs are met.

When determining the audit procedures, the auditor must assess audit risk for *each* assertion relative to *each* material account, class of transactions, and major federal awards program. To do so, the auditor considers the three components of audit risk: inherent risk, control risk, and detection risk.

For inherent risk, the auditor assesses the susceptibility of each assertion to material misstatement. To illustrate, the auditor's assessment of the assertion for the existence of cash is quite different from the assessment of the existence of a building. The rights of the holder a $100 bill are fairly clear—the holder of the bill is likely the owner of the bill and has the right to the bill. On the other hand, the occupant of a building may not be its owner. The building may be leased, or there may be liens against the building that preclude the named owner of the building from having clear title.

> **OBSERVATION:** The inherent risk assessment may be considered somewhat easier to make in Circular A-133 audits than in financial statement audits, because the auditor is dealing with expenditures of assistance under federal awards programs and the assertions may appear to be readily identifiable. However, auditors of recipient organizations that have a variety of procedures for various programs should evaluate inherent risk for each type of expenditure under each type of program. For example, a university's federal research and development activities may be administratively processed completely separately from its federal student financial assistance programs. Similarly, a voluntary health and welfare organization's food program may be administered separately from its employment program.

To assess audit risk properly, the auditor should determine the inherent risk for each assertion for each material account balance and class of transactions. This can be a difficult and cumbersome task. However, to be in compliance with SAS-47, the auditor should consider the requirements carefully and adequately document the action taken.

The second component of audit risk is control risk. This is the risk that a material misstatement could occur and not be prevented or detected by the recipient organization's internal control on a timely basis. Again, the auditor must assess control risk for each assertion as it relates to each material account balance and class of transactions.

> **OBSERVATION:** Although the emphasis in Circular A-133 audits typically seems to fall on expenditures, risk is assessed in

other areas as well, such as claims filed to obtain federal financial assistance and the consideration of the revenues that the recipient organization receives as a result.

Based on his or her understanding of the internal control of the recipient organization, the auditor may choose to assess control risk at the maximum level for each assertion as it relates to material account balances and classes of transactions. The auditor may believe that the controls in place are inadequate or are not being performed effectively. The auditor also may believe that it would be more efficient to assess control risk at the maximum and increase the amount of substantive test work that is performed. This has the effect of decreasing detection risk, enabling the auditor to assess control risk at the maximum level while still maintaining an acceptable level of audit risk. (The chapter on *Government Auditing Standards* describes certain documentation that is required when control risk is assessed at the maximum level and the controls relate to information processed by computer applications.)

If the auditor's initial understanding of the internal control indicates that controls are properly designed and are being properly performed, the auditor may choose to assess control risk below the maximum. Assessing control risk below maximum allows the auditor to accept a greater level of detection risk and to perform less substantive test work.

When deciding whether to assess control risk at the maximum level or at less than the maximum level, the auditor should keep in mind that Circular A-133 requires certain testing of controls over the administration and management of major federal awards programs. The decision whether to assess control risk at or below the maximum level will be affected by this required internal control test work. In other words, if certain tests are required it may be more efficient to try to incorporate this test work into a strategy that allows the auditor to assess control risk at below the maximum and accept a higher level of detection risk. This means the auditor would have to do less substantive test work.

A complete discussion of the test work the auditor is required to perform under Circular A-133 and its effect on the design of an efficient audit strategy is included in the chapter titled "Internal Controls Over Federal Awards."

Finally, an acceptable level of detection risk must be determined for each assertion for each material account balance or class of transactions. This determination is affected, as described above, by the auditor's assessment of inherent risk and control risk for each assertion for each material account balance and class of transactions. The auditor's determination of planning materiality is also a consideration in determining the detection risk.

The considerations involved in determining an acceptable level of detection risk for compliance with laws and regulations for the major federal awards programs are discussed fully in the chapter titled "Compliance Considerations."

After assessing audit risk and its three components for all assertions, the auditor develops an overall audit strategy. This includes determining audit objectives for the significant account balances and classes of transactions (including compliance with laws and regulations for the major federal awards programs) and incorporating the risk assessment decisions into the design of audit procedures.

The audit procedures developed are clearly affected by the audit strategy. For example, if the auditor chooses to assess control risk at below the maximum level, the audit program will have to reflect the test work the auditor performs on the internal control procedures. Conversely, if the auditor chooses to assess control risk at the maximum level, the audit program will have to include enough substantive test work for the auditor to obtain sufficient evidence about the account balances or classes of transactions and thus reduce detection risk to an acceptable level.

CONSIDERING THE SPECIFIC REQUIREMENTS OF GOVERNMENT AUDITING STANDARDS

During the planning phase of the audit, the auditor must be aware of the specific requirements of *Government Auditing Standards*. The Yellow Book has requirements relating to independence, continuing professional education, and quality control review with which the auditor must comply and for which the auditor must prepare adequate documentation of compliance.

In addition, the Yellow Book has guidance and requirements for financial audits relating to general, fieldwork, and reporting standards. These requirements are discussed in detail in the chapter titled "Government Auditing Standards" and are incorporated in the requirements discussed throughout this Guide. The auditor should make a special effort to consider these requirements and document that consideration during the planning phase of the engagement.

> **OBSERVATION:** The auditor should make sure that his or her compliance with the Yellow Book requirements is clearly documented in the audit working papers. This is most effectively done during the planning phase of the engagement, since any areas of noncompliance will be identified very early in the engagement.

Failure to follow *Government Auditing Standards* can be a serious matter for an auditor. AICPA Ethics Ruling No. 501-3 discusses the failure to meet the Yellow Book requirements in government audits:

Engagements for audits of government grants, government units or other recipients of government moneys typically require that such audits be in compliance with government audit standards, guides, procedures, statutes, rules and regulations, in addition to generally accepted auditing standards. If a member has accepted such an engagement and undertakes an obligation to follow specified government audit standards, guides, procedures, statutes, rules and regulations, in addition to generally accepted auditing standards, he is obligated to follow such requirements. Failure to do so is an act discreditable to the profession in violation of Rule 501, unless the member discloses in his report the fact that such requirements were not followed and the reasons therefor.

Clearly, when planning a Circular A-133 audit, the auditor must consider the requirements of not only the Yellow Book, but also the other professional and government-issued literature (including Circular A-133). Failure to do so can have significant professional consequences.

FOLLOWING UP ON PRIOR-YEAR AUDIT REPORT FINDINGS

When planning the audit strategy and procedures, the auditor must consider his or her responsibility to follow up and report on the resolution of prior-year findings, including both internal control-related materials and instances of noncompliance with laws and regulations. Circular A-133 requires that the auditor report on the status of known but uncorrected significant material findings and recommendations from prior audits that affect the current audit objectives as specified in *Government Auditing Standards.*

Government Auditing Standards provide guidance on the follow-up of prior-year comments. If auditors know of any material findings and recommendations from previous audits that could affect the financial statement audit, they should follow up to determine whether the auditee has taken timely and appropriate corrective actions and they should report any uncorrected material findings or recommendations.

The Yellow Book states that follow-up is important because much of the benefit of audit work is not in the findings reported or the recommendations made, but in their effective resolution. The Yellow Book states further that auditee management is responsible for resolving audit findings and recommendations. Having a process to track their status can help management fulfill this responsibility; if management does not have such a process, auditors may wish to establish one. Continued attention to material findings and recommendations can help auditors assure that the benefits of their work are realized.

> **OBSERVATION:** Although the primary emphasis of the federal cognizant agencies and other grantor agencies may be to track and address uncorrected findings from the prior year, the auditor should also comment on **corrected** findings from the prior year.

During the planning phase of the audit, the auditor should read the findings reported in the prior-year audit report and determine which of them should be reported as having been corrected by management. The auditor should perform this step even if the prior-year report was issued by a different auditor.

> **OBSERVATION:** If a prior-year finding clearly is not relevant to the current year, the auditor does not have to report on its status. For example, the auditor would not need to follow up on a prior-year finding regarding a program that has expired or is inactive during the current year, provided the finding does not relate to any of the recipient organization's other programs. However, the number of prior-year findings that are not relevant to the current year probably will be low, and the auditor should expect to follow up on most prior-year findings.

Once the auditor has determined which prior-year findings will be followed up, he or she should make sure that the planned procedures will provide enough information to report appropriately on the status of each finding. The auditor should do this early in the planning phase, since some of the follow-up information can be obtained during the planning discussions held with the recipient organization's management.

REVIEWING THE REPORTING REQUIREMENTS UNDER CIRCULAR A-133

The reporting requirements of Circular A-133 are quite complex and will be described in detail in the chapter titled "Reporting Under Circular A-133." Reporting requirements are considered throughout this Guide as well, since they have such a clear impact on the audit work that is required to be performed, particularly in the areas of internal controls and compliance with laws and regulations.

During the planning phase, however, it is important for the auditor to identify the types of reports to be issued so that he or she can properly and fully plan for the audit and can design an audit strategy that provides a basis on which to issue the required opinions and reports. The auditor also should review any changes and revisions to the documents on which the reporting requirements of Circular

A-133 are based to determine whether the contents or formats of any of the required reports and opinions have changed.

A complete discussion of these reporting requirements is contained in the chapter titled "Reporting under Circular A-133."

DOCUMENTING THE PLANNING PHASE IN A PLANNING MEMORANDUM

The planning procedures described above are an integral part of an audit in accordance with GAAS and Circular A-133. The auditor should ensure that his or her working papers properly document the planning process that has been performed.

Certain assessments and conclusions are easily documented in checklists or matrices. For example, in assessing the inherent, control, and detection risks for each assertion for material account balances and classes of transactions, the auditor should use a somewhat standardized worksheet. This is the most efficient way to accomplish such a detailed analysis, enabling the auditor to spend more time on the assessment process itself than on the documentation of the process.

In addition, the assessment of the risk components will be referenced to audit objectives and audit procedures contained in the programs the auditor develops. Such correlation in and of itself adequately documents the effect the auditor's risk assessment has on audit objectives and procedures.

Certain considerations, however, do not lend themselves to formatted workpapers or standardized audit programs. These considerations, as well as other information that the auditor may wish to document for convenience, should be documented in a planning memorandum.

The planning memorandum is the part of the documentation that indicates that appropriate planning procedures have been performed. Its format can vary greatly and usually depends on the individual style of the auditor or of the firm with which he or she is affiliated. Some auditors, for example, have general guidelines for the contents of planning memoranda and leave the writing to the individual auditor in charge of the audit engagement. Other auditors use a standardized form with a "fill-in-the-blank" approach that encourages efficiency and completeness, but does not encourage the incorporation of information that is not required but would be useful.

Similarly, the length of planning memoranda can vary widely. While a half-page boilerplate memorandum will in almost all circumstances be inadequate, a 50-page tome for a small to medium-sized recipient organization may signal that too much time is being spent on form over substance. A two- to five-page document will generally provide adequate content and detail.

The planning memorandum for a Circular A-133 audit engagement should expand on the planning memorandum typically prepared for audits of financial statements in accordance with GAAS. Some general suggestions for content, with an emphasis on the requirements of a Circular A-133 audit, are as follows:

- State clearly that the audit will be performed in accordance with GAAS, *Government Auditing Standards,* and the requirements of Circular A-133. Documenting the amount of federal awards expended also would be appropriate if it is not documented elsewhere.

- Identify the major federal programs or refer to a supporting working paper.

- Identify the recipient organization that will be audited (including or excluding affiliated/consolidated organizations) and the period that will be covered by the audit.

- Describe planned reliance on the work of other auditors and the coordination of work and/or reporting requirements with other auditors.

- Outline the time plan needed to complete the audit, including audit hours by critical or significant audit areas and the deadline for submission of the final report to the client.

- Supply names, titles, telephone numbers, etc., of key client personnel and, if applicable, of contacts at other audit firms.

- Supply specific information about the assistance the recipient organization plans to provide, as well as the auditor's expected role in actual financial statement preparation.

- Refer to the documentation with which all individual auditors working on the audit engagement should be familiar, such as the Yellow Book, Circular A-133, and the Compliance Supplement.

- Briefly describe the recipient organization's operations, including the types of programs it administers, with an expanded discussion of any programs or activities initiated during the period being audited.

- Discuss any specific areas where the auditor expects to assess control risk at below the maximum level for financial statement reporting purposes.

- Indicate the approach the auditor will use to document and test internal controls over the administration of federal awards. Indicate the planned effect of testing these controls on the test work to be performed on compliance with laws and regulations, including compliance with the documentation requirements of *Government Auditing Standards* when control risk is assessed at the maximum level for processes that include significant computer processing.

- Document the audit approach that will be taken with regard to any subrecipients of federal awards.
- Analyze planning materiality, including a calculation of planning materiality levels at the financial statement level and for each major federal awards program.
- Refer to the planning analytical procedures that were performed and the plan for addressing any unusual findings as a result of those procedures.
- Analyze the effect, if any, of any new pronouncements on accounting, auditing, and the performance of audits in accordance with Circular A-133.
- Document that the individual auditors and the audit firm have complied with appropriate independence, continuing professional education, and quality control requirements.
- Discuss any significant follow-up activities that will need to be performed to report on the status of prior-year findings.
- Identify the staff to be assigned to the audit engagement, including any specialists.

Upon completion of the planning memorandum, all of the auditors who will work on the engagement should acknowledge in writing that they have read and understand the planning memorandum.

The above suggestions are a guide that should be tailored to the individual audit. Effective use of planning memoranda helps satisfy the GAAS and *Government Auditing Standards* documentation requirements. It also helps the auditor understand the overall approach to the audit, and it identifies many of the issues that will be encountered during the course of the audit so they can be resolved early.

SUMMARY

There are a number of benefits to planning a Circular A-133 audit appropriately, and auditors should devote a sufficient amount of time and effort to planning procedures. This effort will highlight potential problems early in the audit engagement and help to ensure that the audit is performed efficiently and in compliance with professional and other standards.

CHAPTER 16
INTERNAL CONTROL
OVER FEDERAL AWARDS

CONTENTS

CHAPTER 16
INTERNAL CONTROLS
OVER FEDERAL AWARDS

CROSS-REFERENCES

2001 MILLER NOT-FOR-PROFIT ORGANIZATION AUDITS: Chapter 4, "Internal Control Considerations"; Chapter 7, "Extent of Audit Procedures and Sampling"; Chapter 17, "Compliance and Subrecipient Considerations"

2001 MILLER SINGLE AUDITS: Chapter 8, "Internal Controls"

2001 MILLER AUDIT PROCEDURES: Chapter 5, "Internal Controls"

The preceding chapter on planning a Circular A-133 audit provides an overview of the issues the auditor should consider regarding a not-for-profit organization's internal control when designing an audit strategy for an audit in accordance with Circular A-133. This chapter focuses on what an auditor needs to consider when performing an audit in accordance with both Circular A-133 and *Government Auditing Standards*.

For testing internal control used in managing and administering major federal programs, Circular A-133 has requirements that go beyond GAAS. Therefore, the auditor must have an understanding of the internal control requirements contained in Circular A-133 and in *Government Auditing Standards*. To fulfill the Circular A-133 internal control requirements, the auditor will "build on" the GAAS requirements.

CONSIDERATION OF INTERNAL CONTROL
FOR AN AUDIT OF FINANCIAL STATEMENTS

The concepts and requirements for understanding internal control in an audit of financial statements are covered in the chapter of this Guide titled "Internal Control Considerations." The discussions in this chapter tailor these considerations for audits of financial statements where a Circular A-133 audit is performed. However, since a Circular A-133 audit includes a financial statement audit, all of the guidance in the chapter titled "Internal Control Considerations" will be relevant to the auditor performing a Circular A-133 audit.

SOP 98-3 refers to these types of controls as "internal control over financial reporting." The following elements of a control environment may influence the auditor's assessment of control risks:

- Significant pass-through of funds to subrecipients

- Management's awareness, or lack of awareness, of relevant laws and regulations

- Requirement to include only allowable and allocable costs in amounts claimed for reimbursement

- Organization policy regarding such matters as acceptable operating practices and codes of conduct

- Assignment of responsibility and delegation of authority for dealing with such matters as organizational goals and objectives, operating functions, and regulatory requirements

- A mixture of volunteers and employees participating in operations (Depending on the size and other features of an organization, day-to-day operations sometimes are conducted by volunteers instead of employees. The manner in which responsibility and authority are delegated varies among organizations, and may affect the control over financial transactions, particularly with respect to authorization.)

- A limited staff, which may be too small to provide for appropriate segregation of duties

- A volunteer governing board, many of whose members serve for limited terms

- A budget approved by the governing board (The budget may serve as authorization for management to carry out activities to achieve an organization's program objectives. Many not-for-profit organizations prepare budgets for both operating and capital expenditures.)

CONSIDERATION OF INTERNAL CONTROL OVER FEDERAL PROGRAMS REQUIRED BY CIRCULAR A-133

Circular A-133 states that its definition of *internal control* is the same as that used in generally accepted auditing standards. (Internal control in an audit of financial statements in accordance with generally accepted auditing standards is discussed in the chapter titled "Internal Control Considerations.") Circular A-133 defines *internal control over federal programs* as a process effected by an entity's management and other personnel designed to provide reasonable assurance regarding the achievement of the following objectives for federal programs:

- Transactions are properly recorded and accounted for:
  - — Permit the preparation of reliable financial statements and federal reports,
  - — Maintain accountability over assets, and
  - — Demonstrate compliance with laws, regulations, and other compliance requirements.
- Transactions are executed in compliance with:
  - — Laws, regulations, and the provisions of contracts or grant agreements that could have a direct and material effect on a federal program, and
  - — Any other laws and regulations that are identified in the Compliance Supplements, and
- Funds, property, and other assets are safeguarded against loss from unauthorized use or disposition."

These controls are part of the larger internal control framework addressed by SAS-55 and SAS-78. In other words, the internal control over federal awards may overlap the organization's internal controls over financial reporting. For example, assume that a not-for-profit organization has effectively designed and operating internal control policies and procedures in place over cash disbursements. Cash disbursements for the federal programs are made using the same internal controls. These controls ensure that cash disbursements are made only for valid purposes and are properly recorded. In addition, the internal control policies and procedures require the not-for-profit organization's personnel to verify that federal program disbursements are in conformity with the applicable laws, regulations, and requirements.

The internal control over federal awards includes all of the policies and procedures for ensuring that disbursements are valid and conform with the laws, regulations, and other requirements of the applicable federal program. The internal control over federal awards includes the internal control policies and procedures the recipient organization uses for *all* cash disbursements, even those not charged directly or indirectly to a federal awards program.

Circular A-133 requires the auditor to obtain an understanding of, assess control risk for, and perform tests of controls on the policies and procedures designed to provide reasonable assurance that the recipient organization is managing federal awards in compliance with applicable laws, regulations, and contract terms and that the recipient safeguards federal funds. Internal control policies and procedures include the not-for-profit organization's system for monitoring subrecipients and the controls in effect to ensure that direct and indirect costs are properly computed and billed. These controls make up the internal control over federal programs. The auditor is required to test controls related to the internal control over the administration of federal programs.

> **OBSERVATION:** The auditor should recognize that he or she may be able to benefit from the test work (i.e., assess internal control risk at below the maximum level for the applicable assertion).

When obtaining an understanding of and assessing internal controls, the auditor also should consider the requirements of OMB Circular A-110 (Uniform Administrative Requirements for Grants and Agreements with Institutions of Higher Education, Hospitals, and Other Non-Profit Organizations) and other federal pronouncements, such as program handbooks and guides, which specify uniform administrative requirements for grants and agreements with not-for-profit organizations. These administrative requirements include requirements over cash depositories, bonding and sharing, matching, financial reporting, monitoring and reporting of program performance, payment requirements, revisions of financial plans, closeout procedures, suspensions and terminations, applications for federal assistance, and standards for property management and procurement.

The auditor must gain an understanding and test the operation of the internal control policies and procedures over the assertions that relate to these administrative requirements. Because of the wide range of administrative requirements, the types of internal control policies and procedures present will vary and may be different from the policies and procedures to which the auditor is accustomed. Internal control policies and procedures over administrative requirements encompass more than financial information.

> **OBSERVATION:** Auditing the recipient organization's compliance with the administrative requirements listed above is covered in the chapter titled "Compliance Considerations." This chapter addresses only the internal control policies and procedures the recipient organization has designed and placed into operation to ensure compliance with these requirements.

> **OBSERVATION:** The auditor is testing different assertions when dealing with administrative requirements. The ownership as-

sertion, for example, clearly does not apply to testing controls over the administrative requirements related to cash depositories.

One internal control over the monitoring and reporting of program performance is a "contracts administrator" who oversees the submission of required program reports to the federal agencies. The contracts administrator is usually responsible for knowing the report format requirements and due dates. He or she requests information from the manager of each specific program; reviews the information for accuracy, completeness, and conformity to the reporting requirements; and submits the information to the federal agency in accordance with the required reporting deadlines.

Contrast this control policy and procedure with a not-for-profit organization having no centralized control over the submission of program performance reports. This recipient relies on a number of program personnel to submit their own reports to the applicable federal grantor agencies. Program personnel often overlook the reporting deadlines and rush to develop information in some marginally acceptable format.

Clearly, the first recipient organization has better internal control over program performance reporting. Even though this information is not financial in nature, the auditor is still able to understand the internal control procedure and meet the testing requirements of Circular A-133. A form for evaluating a recipient organization's information system and control activities for its major federal programs is shown in Exhibit 16-1. A form for evaluating the control activities of a *decentralized* accounting system for federal awards is shown in Exhibit 16-2 (see page 624).

The auditor may test the internal control over administrative requirements as part of the audit of the financial statements in accordance with GAAS, particularly when federal awards are significant to the financial statements. Other internal control policies and procedures go beyond those the auditor might consider during the financial statement audit, such as the distribution of salaries among programs.

The Compliance Supplement of Circular A-133 provides guidance for auditors as to their understanding of internal control over federal awards programs. Part 6 of the Compliance Supplement is devoted exclusively to these internal control considerations.

> **OBSERVATION:** Circular A-133's internal control "requirements" is one area that results in significant additional audit work and, accordingly, additional audit costs.

Part 6 of the Compliance Supplement is designed to assist auditors in complying with the internal control requirements of Circular

EXHIBIT 16-1
EVALUATION OF THE ACCOUNTING
INFORMATION SYSTEM FOR MAJOR FEDERAL PROGRAMS

Part I.   Establish the Type of Accounting Information System Used in Each Award Program

For each of the key areas below, identify whether it is part of the centralized accounting system. This will pertain to each award program. See also Part III.

	Centralized [1]	Decentralized [2]	Comments
Cash Receipts			
Cash Disbursements			
Payroll			
Property & Equipment			
Accounts Receivable			
Accounts Payable			

[1] These award programs were included in the overall documentation of the accounting information system.

[2] Documentation of the accounting information system for these decentralized award programs is found in separate workpapers.

Part II.   Document an Overall Summary of the Decentralized Accounting Information System Used by the Award Programs

The following information must be documented for award programs that are accounted for in a decentralized accounting system.

	Yes	No	N/A	Comments
1. Is the accounting system automated by personal computer, minicomputer, mainframe computer, or local or wide area network?				
2. Is the accounting system maintained manually in a set of ledgers?				
3. Are journals and appropriate subsidiary ledgers (e.g., cash receipts journal) used?				
4. Are books and records posted on a current basis?				

	Yes	No	N/A	Comments

5. Are the books and records kept and filed in a neat and orderly manner?

6. Is there an adequate segregation of duties between the person keeping the books and the person who has custody over the assets (e.g., cash and accounts receivable)?

7. Are the books, journal entries, and other records reviewed/approved by a person in a position higher than the person recording the transactions, such as a supervisor?

8. Are periodic reconciliations done by someone other than the person who is recording the transactions in the records?

9. Are personnel adequately trained and supervised?

10. Are personnel experienced and knowledgeable?

11. Are personnel adequately bonded?

12. Is there a current accounting policy and/or procedure manual in use?

13. Are there adequate safeguards over the manual records, such as storing them in a safe when not in use?

14. Are there adequate safeguards over computerized records, such as restricting access and storing backups offsite?

15. Are records kept in accordance with approved record retention levels?

Part III. Document the Details of Each Type of Transaction Identified in Part I

For each major federal program using a decentralized accounting information system, document the details of each of the six transaction categories below:

1. Program cash receipts

2. Program cash disbursements

3. Program payroll

4. Program property and equipment

5. Program accounts receivable

6. Program accounts payable

Record this information on the sheets that follow, or prepare flowcharts.

Cash Receipts

A. How are the transactions initiated, reviewed, and approved, and by whom?

B. Describe the processing of the transaction from the initial step until the transaction is recorded in the general ledger.

C. List and describe any supporting documents that are used and/or generated in the process above. For cost-reimbursable grants, describe how cost information is accumulated for claiming purposes.

D. List and describe any journal or subsidiary ledger used in the recording process.

E. List and describe any computer reports or other output data that are used in the recording process (answer only D or E, depending on the accounting system in use).

Cash Disbursements

A. How are the transactions initiated, reviewed, and approved, and by whom?

B. Describe the processing of the transaction from the initial step until the transaction is recorded in the general ledger.

C. List and describe any supporting documents that are used and/or generated in the process above.

D. List and describe any journal or subsidiary ledger used in the recording process.

E. List and describe any computer reports or other output data that are used in the recording process (answer only D or E, depending on the accounting system in use).

F. Describe how costs that are chargeable to federal programs are accumulated in total and for each separate program.

G. Describe the indirect cost allocation plan and the process for charging indirect costs to programs.

Payroll Transactions

A. How are the transactions initiated, reviewed, and approved, and by whom?

B. Describe the processing of the transaction from the initial step until the transaction is recorded in the general ledger.

C. List and describe any supporting documents that are used and/or generated in the process above.

D. List and describe any journal or subsidiary ledger used in the recording process.

E. List and describe any computer reports or other output data that are used in the recording process (answer only D or E, depending on the accounting system in use).

Property and Equipment

A. How are the transactions initiated, reviewed, and approved, and by whom?

B. Describe the processing of the transaction from the initial step until the transaction is recorded in the general ledger.

C. List and describe any supporting documents that are used and/or generated in the process above.

D. List and describe any journal or subsidiary ledger used in the recording process.

E. List and describe any computer reports or other output data that are used in the recording process (answer only D or E, depending on the accounting system in use).

F. Describe how payroll costs (including fringe benefits) that are chargeable to federal programs are determined.

Accounts Receivable

A. How are the transactions initiated, reviewed, and approved, and by whom?

B. Describe the processing of the transaction from the initial step until the transaction is recorded in the general ledger.

C. List and describe any supporting documents that are used and/or generated in the process above.

D. List and describe any journal or subsidiary ledger used in the recording process.

E. List and describe any computer reports or other output data that are used in the recording process (answer only D or E, depending on the accounting system in use).

Accounts Payable

A. How are the transactions initiated, reviewed, and approved, and by whom?

B. Describe the processing of the transaction from the initial step until the transaction is recorded in the general ledger.

C. List and describe any supporting documents that are used and/or generated in the process above.

D. List and describe any journal or subsidiary ledger used in the recording process.

E. List and describe any computer reports or other output data that are used in the recording process (answer only D or E, depending on the accounting system in use).

EXHIBIT 16-2
ACCOUNTING CONTROL PROCEDURES
FOR DECENTRALIZED MAJOR FEDERAL PROGRAMS

Significant Account Balance/Transaction Class _____

Document an Overall Summary of the Control Procedures Used in Each Decentralized Award Program Documented in the Evaluation of the Accounting Information System for Major Federal Programs

	Yes	No	N/A	Comments
1. Are the individual items making up the account balance or transaction class properly controlled at the time of receipt to prevent loss, theft, or misappropriation?	___	___	___	_____
2. Are transactions properly approved before they are entered into the accounting system?	___	___	___	_____
3. Have transactions relating to laws and regulations affecting the entity (federal, state, and local) been properly reviewed and approved as being in compliance?	___	___	___	_____
4. Are transactions relating to federal awards reviewed and approved by someone who is knowledgeable about federal laws and regulations?	___	___	___	_____
5. Is there a proper segregation of duties relating to receipt of the item, custody of the item, recording of the item, and reconciliation of the item to the general ledger, subsidiary ledgers, or other records?	___	___	___	_____
6. Is the item properly safeguarded from the time of receipt, as long as it remains with the entity?	___	___	___	_____
7. Is access to this item restricted to those personnel that should have access?	___	___	___	_____
8. Is this item prenumbered, and if so, are the numbers accounted for and reconciled periodically by someone not involved in the daily custody?	___	___	___	_____
9. Should this item be prenumbered for control purposes?	___	___	___	_____

Yes No N/A Comments

10. Are voided transactions properly approved and controlled to prevent reuse and/or misappropriation? ___ ___ ___ _____

11. Is a periodic inventory performed for this account balance, as necessary? ___ ___ ___ _____

12. If this item is processed by the computer, are adequate checks in place to verify that the computer processed this account/transaction properly? ___ ___ ___ _____

Describe, in the space provided below, any deficiencies that you observed or any recommendations to improve the control procedures for this account balance or transaction class. If the deficiency noted is significant, then a reportable condition, and possibly a material weakness, also should be reported as a finding and/or noncompliance item.

_____

_____

_____

_____

_____

A-133. The requirement for not-for-profit organizations to maintain internal control over federal programs is found in Circular A-110 (Uniform Administrative Requirements for Grants and Agreements with Institutions of Higher Education, Hospitals and Other Non-Profit Organizations). Circular A-110 requires not-for-profit organizations to establish and maintain internal controls designed to reasonably ensure compliance with federal laws, regulations, and program compliance requirements. The Circular A-133 audit requirements (which are described in the following section of this chapter) require auditors to:

- Obtain an understanding of the not-for-profit organization's internal control over federal programs sufficient to plan the audit to support a low assessed level of control risk for major programs.

- Plan the testing of internal control over major programs to support a low assessed level of control risk for the assertions relevant to the compliance requirements for each major program.

- Unless internal control is likely to be ineffective, perform testing of internal control as planned.

Compliance requirements for major federal programs are described in the following chapter of this Guide. There are 14 compliance requirements. The Compliance Supplement provides a matrix to assist in determining which compliance requirements are applicable to each federal award program included in the Compliance Supplement. The 14 compliance requirements are as follows:

- Activities allowed or unallowed
- Allowable costs/cost principles
- Cash management
- Davis–Bacon Act
- Eligibility
- Equipment and real property management
- Matching, level of effort, earmarking
- Period of availability of federal funds
- Procurement and suspension debarment
- Program income
- Real property acquisition and relocation assistance
- Reporting
- Subrecipient monitoring

For each type of compliance requirement, Part 6 of the Compliance Supplement describes the following:

- The objectives of internal control for each compliance requirement
- Certain characteristics of internal control that, when present and operating effectively, may ensure compliance with program requirements

The characteristics of internal control for each compliance requirement are presented in the context of the framework of internal control provided by SAS-78 (Consideration of Internal Control in a Financial Statement Audit). Accordingly, for each compliance requirement listed above, the Compliance Supplement lists internal control characteristics for each of the following components of internal control:

- Control environment
- Risk assessment
- Control activities

- Information and communication
- Monitoring

The Compliance Supplement indicates that its lists of internal control characteristics should not be considered to be checklists of required internal control characteristics. It acknowledges that entities may have implemented internal control in different ways and may have adequate internal control even if some or all of the characteristics included in Part 6 are not present. In addition, there could be other characteristics of internal control that are not included in Part 6. Professional judgement is required of the entity and its auditor to determine the most appropriate and cost-effective internal control in a given environment or circumstance to provide reasonable assurance of compliance with federal awards program requirements.

Exhibit 16-3 provides, in a checklist format, the internal control characteristics contained in the Compliance Supplement. This checklist permits the auditor to supplement the internal control characteristics and to cross-reference the relevant controls that are being tested to the related internal control test work. Where controls are considered ineffective and are not tested, the form provides for a cross-reference to the related finding that is included in the schedule of findings and questioned costs.

Requirements of Circular A-133

Circular A-133 increases the amount of testing of internal control over federal programs that auditors are required to perform. It does this by requiring an auditor to perform procedures to obtain an understanding of internal control over federal programs sufficient to plan the audit to achieve a *low* level of control risk for major programs and to perform testing of internal controls (except as provided below) as planned.

When an auditor assesses control risk at below the maximum level, he or she should obtain sufficient evidential matter to support that assessed level. In a Circular A-133 audit, the planned level of risk assessment for internal controls over compliance laws, regulations, and program requirements for federal awards programs is required to be "low." Materiality for the overall consideration of audit risk must be determined for each major federal award program.

Accordingly, the auditor needs to consider the requirements of SAS-55, as amended by SAS-78, to determine whether he or she would obtain sufficient evidential matter to assess control risk at a low level. The evidential matter that is sufficient to support a specific assessed level of control risk is a matter of the auditor's judgment.

(text continues on page 660)

EXHIBIT 16-3
EVALUATION OF CONTROLS OVER MAJOR FEDERAL PROGRAMS

Name of Major Federal Program: _____

CFDA Number: _____

Fiscal Period: _____

Part 6 of the OMB Compliance Supplement provides a description of the characteristics of internal control relating to each of the five components of internal control that should reasonably assure compliance with the requirements of federal laws, regulations, and program compliance requirements.

Auditors should use this exhibit as a guide to identify the internal controls that a recipient organization has in place over compliance with laws, regulations, and program compliance requirements. This is not a checklist of required internal control characteristics. The Compliance Supplement acknowledges that a recipient organization could have effective internal controls even though some or all of the characteristics listed below are not present. However, the characteristics of internal control described in the Compliance Supplement are quite specific and should convey to the auditor the degree of detailed consideration of internal control that is suggested by the Compliance Supplement.

How to Use This Form

Auditors should complete this checklist for each major federal award program. Where major federal awards programs have common internal controls, the same checklist may be used for multiple major federal awards programs. Where necessary, a description of compensating or additional internal controls that will be tested by the auditor should be included in this checklist.

A. ACTIVITIES ALLOWED OR UNALLOWED and

B. ALLOWABLE COSTS/COST PRINCIPLES

Control Objectives

To provide reasonable assurance that federal awards are expended only for allowable activities and that the costs of goods and services charged to federal awards are allowable and in accordance with the applicable cost principles.

Control Environment

- Management sets reasonable budgets for federal and non-federal programs so that no incentive exists to miscode expenditures.   ___ ___ ___ _____

- Management enforces appropriate penalties for misappropriation or misuse of funds.   ___ ___ ___ _____

- Organization-wide cognizance of need for separate identification of allowable federal costs.   ___ ___ ___ _____

- Management provides personnel approving and pre-auditing expenditures with a list of allowable and unallowable expenditures.   ___ ___ ___ _____

- Description of alternative or compensating controls:

  _____

  _____

  _____

  _____

Risk Assessment

- Process in place for assessing risks resulting from changes to cost accounting systems.   ___ ___ ___ _____

- Key manager has a sufficient understanding of staff, processes, and controls to identify where unallowable activities or costs could be charged to a federal program and not be detected.   ___ ___ ___ _____

- Description of alternative or compensating controls:

  _____

  _____

  _____

  _____

	Yes	No	N/A	*Working Paper Reference*

Control Activities

- Accountability provided for charges and costs between federal and non-federal activities. ___ ___ ___ _____

- Process in place for timely updating of procedures for changes in activities allowed and cost principles. ___ ___ ___ _____

- Computations checked for accuracy. ___ ___ ___ _____

- Supporting documentation compared to list of allowable and unallowable expenditures. ___ ___ ___ _____

- Adjustments to unallowable costs made where appropriate and follow-up action taken to determine the cause. ___ ___ ___ _____

- Adequate segregation of duties in review and authorization of costs. ___ ___ ___ _____

- Accountability for authorization is fixed in an individual who is knowledgeable of the requirements for determining activities allowed and allowable costs. ___ ___ ___ _____

- Description of alternative or compensating controls:

_____

_____

_____

_____

Information and Communication

- Reports, such as a comparison of budget to actual, provided to appropriate management for review on a timely basis. ___ ___ ___ _____

- Internal and external communication channels on activities and costs allowed are established. ___ ___ ___ _____

- Training programs, both formal and informal, provide knowledge and skills necessary to determine activities and costs allowed. ___ ___ ___ _____

- Interaction occurs between management and staff regarding questionable costs. ___ ___ ___ _____

- Grant agreements (including referenced program laws, regulations, handbooks,

	Yes	No	N/A	Working Paper Reference

etc.) and cost principles Circulars available to staff responsible for determining activities allowed and allowable costs under federal awards. ___ ___ ___ _____

- Description of alternative or compensating controls:

_____

_____

_____

_____

Monitoring

- Management reviews supporting documentation of allowable cost information. ___ ___ ___ _____

- Flow of information from federal agency to appropriate management personnel is sufficient. ___ ___ ___ _____

- Comparisons are made with budget and expectations of allowable costs. ___ ___ ___ _____

- Analytical reviews (e.g., comparison of budget to actual or prior year to current year) and audits performed. ___ ___ ___ _____

- Description of alternative or compensating controls:

_____

_____

_____

_____

C. CASH MANAGEMENT

Control Objectives

To provide reasonable assurance that the draw-down of federal cash is only for immediate needs, organizations comply with applicable Treasury agreements, and recipients limit payments to subrecipients to immediate cash needs.

Control Environment

- Appropriate assignment of responsibility for approval of cash draw-downs and payments to subrecipients. ___ ___ ___ _____

- Budgets for draw-downs are consistent with realistic cash needs. ___ ___ ___ _____

- Description of alternative or compensating controls:

_____

_____

_____

_____

	Yes	No	N/A	Working Paper Reference

Risk Assessment

- Mechanisms exist to anticipate, identify, and react to routine events that affect cash needs. ___ ___ ___ _____

- Routine assessment of adequacy of sub-recipient cash needs. ___ ___ ___ _____

- Management has identified programs that receive cash advances and is aware of cash management requirements. ___ ___ ___ _____

- Description of alternative or compensating controls:

_____

_____

_____

_____

Control Activities

- Cash flow statements by program are prepared to determine essential cash flow needs. ___ ___ ___ _____

- Accounting system is capable of scheduling payments for accounts payable and requests for funds from Treasury to avoid time lapse between draw-down of funds and actual disbursements of funds. ___ ___ ___ _____

- Appropriate level of supervisory review of cash management activities. ___ ___ ___ _____

- Written policy that provides:
  - Procedures for requesting cash advances as close as is administratively possible to actual cash outlays, ___ ___ ___ _____
  - Monitoring of cash management activities, and ___ ___ ___ _____
  - Repayment of excess interest earnings where required. ___ ___ ___ _____

	Yes	No	N/A	Working Paper Reference

- For programs subject to a Treasury–recipient agreement, a written policy exists that includes:

  — Programs covered by the agreement, ⎯ ⎯ ⎯ ⎯⎯⎯

  — Methods of funding to be used, ⎯ ⎯ ⎯ ⎯⎯⎯

  — Method used to calculate interest, and ⎯ ⎯ ⎯ ⎯⎯⎯

  — Procedures for determining check-clearing patterns (if applicable for the funding method). ⎯ ⎯ ⎯ ⎯⎯⎯

- Description of alternative or compensating controls:

_____

_____

_____

_____

Information and Communication

- Variance reporting of expected versus actual cash disbursements of federal awards and draw-downs of federal funds. ⎯ ⎯ ⎯ ⎯⎯⎯

- Established channel of communication between pass-through entity and sub-recipients regarding cash needs. ⎯ ⎯ ⎯ ⎯⎯⎯

- Description of alternative or compensating controls:

_____

_____

_____

_____

Monitoring

- Periodic independent evaluation (e.g., by internal audit, top management) of entity cash management, budget and actual results, repayment of excess interest earnings, and federal draw-down activities. ⎯ ⎯ ⎯ ⎯⎯⎯

- Subrecipients requests for federal funds are evaluated. ⎯ ⎯ ⎯ ⎯⎯⎯

- Review of compliance with Treasury–recipient agreements. ⎯ ⎯ ⎯ ⎯⎯⎯

- Description of alternative or compensating controls:

_____

_____

_____

_____

D. DAVIS–BACON ACT

Control Objectives

To provide reasonable assurance that contractors and subcontractors paid prevailing wage rates for projects covered by the Davis–Bacon Act.

	Yes	No	N/A	*Working Paper Reference*

Control Environment

- Management understands and communicates to staff, contractors, and subcontractors the requirements to pay wages in accordance with the Davis–Bacon Act. ___ ___ ___ _____
- Management understands its responsibility for monitoring compliance. ___ ___ ___ _____
- Description of alternative or compensating controls:

_____

_____

_____

_____

Risk Assessment

- Mechanisms in place to identify contractors and subcontractors most at risk of not paying the prevailing wage rates. ___ ___ ___ _____
- Management identified how compliance will be monitored and the related risks of failure to monitor for compliance with Davis–Bacon Act. ___ ___ ___ _____
- Description of alternative or compensating controls:

_____

_____

_____

_____

	Yes	No	N/A	Working Paper Reference

Control Activities

- Contractors informed in the procurement documents of the requirements for prevailing wage rates. ___ ___ ___ _____

- Contractors and subcontractors required to submit certifications and copies of payrolls which meet the requirements to pay prevailing wage rates. ___ ___ ___ _____

- Contractors' and subcontractors' payrolls monitored for compliance with prevailing wage rates. ___ ___ ___ _____

- Description of alternative or compensating controls:

_____

_____

_____

_____

Information and Communication

- Prevailing wage rates are appropriately communicated. ___ ___ ___ _____

- Reports provide sufficient information to determine if requirements are being met. ___ ___ ___ _____

- Channels are established for staff, contractors, and workers to report mis-classifications or failure to pay prevailing wages. ___ ___ ___ _____

- Description of alternative or compensating controls:

_____

_____

_____

_____

Monitoring

- Management reviews to ensure that contractors and subcontractors are being required to pay prevailing wage rates. ___ ___ ___ _____

- On-site visits are performed to monitor classifications and wage rates. ___ ___ ___ _____

- Monitoring reports from contractors are compared to independent checks. ___ ___ ___ _____

- Description of alternative or compensating controls:

_____

_____

_____

_____

E. ELIGIBILITY

Control Objectives

To provide reasonable assurance that only eligible individuals and organizations receive assistance under federal award programs, that subawards are made only to eligible subrecipients, and that amounts provided to or on behalf of eligibles were calculated in accordance with program requirements.

	Yes	No	N/A	Working Paper Reference

Control Environment

- Staff size and competence provides for proper making of eligibility determinations.
- Realistic caseload/performance targets established for eligibility determinations.
- Lines of authority clear for determining eligibility.
- Description of alternative or compensating controls:

_____

_____

_____

_____

Risk Assessment

- Identification of risk that eligibility information prepared internally or received from external sources could be incorrect.
- Conflict-of-interest statements are maintained for individuals who determine eligibility.
- Process for assessing risks resulting from changes to eligibility determination systems.

- Description of alternative or compensating controls:

_____

_____

_____

_____

*Working
Paper*
Yes   No   N/A   Reference

Control Activities

- Written policies provide direction for making and documenting eligibility determinations.

_____

- Procedures to calculate eligibility amounts consistent with program requirements.

_____

- Eligibility objectives and procedures clearly communicated to employees.

_____

- Authorized signatures (manual or electronic) on eligibility documents periodically reviewed.

_____

- Access to eligibility records limited to appropriate persons.

_____

- Manual criteria checklists or automated process used in making eligibility determinations.

_____

- Process for periodic eligibility re-determinations in accordance with program requirements.

_____

- Verification of accuracy of information used in eligibility determinations.

_____

- Procedures to ensure the accuracy and completeness of data used to determine eligibility requirements.

_____

- Description of alternative or compensating controls:

_____

_____

_____

_____

Information and Communication

- Information system meets needs of eligibility decisionmakers and program management.

_____

	Yes	No	N/A	Working Paper Reference
• Processing of eligibility information subject to edit checks and balancing procedures.	——	——	——	————
• Training programs inform employees of eligibility requirements.	——	——	——	————
• Channels of communication exist for people to report suspected eligibility improprieties.	——	——	——	————
• Management receptive to suggestions to strengthen eligibility determination process.	——	——	——	————
• Documentation of eligibility determinations in accordance with program requirements.	——	——	——	————

• Description of alternative or compensating controls:

———————————————————————————

———————————————————————————

———————————————————————————

———————————————————————————

Monitoring

	Yes	No	N/A	Working Paper Reference
• Periodic analytical reviews of eligibility determinations performed by management.	——	——	——	————
• Program quality control procedures performed.	——	——	——	————
• Periodic audits of detailed transactions.	——	——	——	————

• Description of alternative or compensating controls:

———————————————————————————

———————————————————————————

———————————————————————————

———————————————————————————

F. EQUIPMENT AND REAL PROPERTY MANAGEMENT

Control Objectives

To provide reasonable assurance that proper records are maintained for equipment acquired with federal awards, equipment is adequately safeguarded and maintained, disposition or encumbrance of any equipment or real property is in accordance with federal requirements, and the federal awarding agency is appropriately compensated for its share of any property sold or converted to non-federal use.

	Yes	No	N/A	*Working Paper Reference*

Control Environment

- Management committed to providing proper stewardship for property acquired with federal awards.   —— —— —— ————
- No incentives exist to under-value assets at time of disposition.   —— —— —— ————
- Sufficient accountability exists to discourage temptation of misuse of federal assets.   —— —— —— ————
- Description of alternative or compensating controls:

————————————————————

————————————————————

————————————————————

————————————————————

Risk Assessment

- Procedures to identify risk of misappropriation or improper disposition of property acquired with federal awards.   —— —— —— ————
- Management understands requirements and operations sufficiently to identify potential areas of noncompliance (e.g., decentralized locations, departments with budget constraints, transfers of assets between departments).   —— —— —— ————

Control Activities

- Accurate records maintained on all acquisitions and dispositions of property acquired with federal awards.   —— —— —— ————
- Property tags are placed on equipment.   —— —— —— ————
- A physical inventory of equipment is periodically taken and compared to property records.   —— —— —— ————
- Property records contain description (including serial number or other identification number), source, who holds title, acquisition date and cost, percentage of federal participation in the cost, location, condition, and disposition data.   —— —— —— ————
- Procedures established to ensure that the federal awarding agency is appropriately reimbursed for dispositions of property acquired with federal awards.   —— —— —— ————

	Yes	No	N/A	Working Paper Reference

- Policies and procedures in place for responsibilities of recordkeeping and authorities for disposition. ___ ___ ___ _____

- Description of alternative or compensating controls:

_____

_____

_____

_____

Information and Communication

- Accounting system provides for separate identification of property acquired wholly or partly with federal funds and with non-federal funds. ___ ___ ___ _____

- A channel of communication exists for people to report suspected improprieties in the use or disposition of equipment. ___ ___ ___ _____

- Program managers are provided with applicable requirements and guidelines. ___ ___ ___ _____

- Description of alternative or compensating controls:

_____

_____

_____

_____

Monitoring

- Management reviews the results of periodic inventories and follows up on inventory discrepancies. ___ ___ ___ _____

- Management reviews dispositions of property to ensure appropriate valuation and reimbursement to federal awarding agencies. ___ ___ ___ _____

- Description of alternative or compensating controls:

_____

_____

_____

_____

G. MATCHING, LEVEL OF EFFORT, EARMARKING

Control Objectives

To provide reasonable assurance that matching, level of effort, or earmarking requirements are met using only allowable funds or costs which are properly calculated and valued.

	Yes	*No*	*N/A*	*Working Paper Reference*

Control Environment

- Commitment from management to meet matching, level of effort, and earmarking requirements (e.g., adequate budget resources to meet a specified matching requirement or maintain a required level of effort).

- Budgeting process addresses/provides adequate resources to meet matching, level of effort, or earmarking goals.

- Official written policy exists outlining:

  — Responsibilities for determining required amounts or limits for matching, level of effort, or earmarking.

  — Methods of valuing matching requirements, e.g., "in-kind" contributions of property and services, calculations of levels of effort.

  — Allowable costs that may be claimed for matching, level of effort, or earmarking.

  — Methods of accounting for and documenting amounts used to calculate amounts claimed for matching, level of effort, or earmarking.

- Description of alternative or compensating controls:

  _____

  _____

  _____

  _____

Risk Assessment

- Identification of areas where estimated values will be used for matching, level of effort, or earmarking.

	Yes	No	N/A	Working Paper Reference

- Management has sufficient understanding of the accounting system to identify potential recording problems. ___ ___ ___ _____
- Description of alternative or compensating controls:

_____

_____

_____

_____

Control Activities

- Evidence obtained such as a certification from the donor, or other procedures performed to identify whether matching contributions:

  — Are from non-federal sources. ___ ___ ___ _____

  — Involve federal funding, directly or indirectly. ___ ___ ___ _____

  — Were used for another federally assisted program. ___ ___ ___ _____

Note: Generally, matching contributions must be from a non-federal source and may not involve federal funding or be used for another federally assisted program.

- Adequate review of monthly cost reports and adjusting entries. ___ ___ ___ _____
- Description of alternative or compensating controls:

_____

_____

_____

_____

Information and Communication

Accounting system capable of:

- Separately accounting for data used to support matching, level of effort, or earmarking amounts or limits or calculations. ___ ___ ___ _____
- Ensuring that expenditures or expenses, refunds, and cash receipts or revenues are properly classified and recorded only once as to their effect on matching, level of effort, or earmarking. ___ ___ ___ _____

- Documenting the value of "in-kind" contributions of property or services, including:

    — Basis for local labor market rates for valuing volunteer services.　＿＿　＿＿　＿＿　＿＿＿＿

    — Payroll records or confirmation from other organizations for services provided by their employees.　＿＿　＿＿　＿＿　＿＿＿＿

    — Quotes, published prices, or independent appraisals used as the basis for donated equipment, supplies, land, buildings, or use of space.　＿＿　＿＿　＿＿　＿＿＿＿

- Description of alternative or compensating controls:

_____

_____

_____

_____

Monitoring

- Supervisory review of matching, level of effort, or earmarking activities performed to assess the accuracy and allowability of transactions and determinations, e.g., at the time reports on federal awards are prepared.　＿＿　＿＿　＿＿　＿＿＿＿

- Description of alternative or compensating controls:

_____

_____

_____

_____

H. PERIOD OF AVAILABILITY OF FEDERAL FUNDS

Control Objectives

To provide reasonable assurance that federal funds are used only during the authorized period of availability.

Control Environment

- Management understands and is committed to complying with period of availability requirements.　＿＿　＿＿　＿＿　＿＿＿＿

*Working
Paper*
Yes No N/A Reference

- Entity's operations are such that it is unlikely there will be federal funds remaining at the end of the period of availability.   ___ ___ ___ _____

- Description of alternative or compensating controls:

  _____

  _____

  _____

  _____

Risk Assessment

- The budgetary process considers period of availability of federal funds as to both obligation and disbursement.   ___ ___ ___ _____

- Identification and communication of period of availability cut-off requirements as to both obligation and disbursement.   ___ ___ ___ _____

- Description of alternative or compensating controls:

  _____

  _____

  _____

  _____

Control Activities

- Accounting system prevents obligation or expenditure of federal funds outside of the period of availability.   ___ ___ ___ _____

- Review of disbursements by person knowledgeable of period of availability of funds.   ___ ___ ___ _____

- End of grant period cut-offs are met by such mechanisms as advising program managers of impending cut-off dates and review of expenditures just before and after cut-off date.   ___ ___ ___ _____

- Cancellation of unliquidated commitments at the end of the period of availability.   ___ ___ ___ _____

- Description of alternative or compensating controls:

  _____

  _____

  _____

  _____

Working
Paper
Yes   No   N/A   Reference

Information and Communication

- Timely communication of period of availability requirements and expenditure deadlines to individuals responsible for program expenditure, including automated notifications of pending deadlines.   ___   ___   ___   _____

- Periodic reporting of unliquidated balances to appropriate levels of management and follow up.   ___   ___   ___   _____

- Description of alternative or compensating controls:

_____

_____

_____

_____

Monitoring

- Periodic review of expenditures before and after cut-off date to ensure compliance with period of availability requirements.   ___   ___   ___   _____

- Review by management of reports showing budget and actual for period.   ___   ___   ___   _____

- Description of alternative or compensating controls:

_____

_____

_____

_____

I. PROCUREMENT AND SUSPENSION DEBARMENT

Control Objectives

To provide reasonable assurance that procurement of goods and services are made in compliance with the provisions of OMB Circular A-110, and that no subaward, contract, or agreement for purchases of goods or services is made with any debarred or suspended party.

Control Environment

- Existence and implementation of codes of conduct and other policies regarding acceptable practice, conflicts-of-interest, or expected standards of ethical and moral behavior for making procurements.   ___   ___   ___   _____

	Yes	No	N/A	*Working Paper Reference*

- Procurement manual that incorporated federal requirements. ___ ___ ___ _____

- Absence of pressure to meet unrealistic procurement performance targets. ___ ___ ___ _____

- Management's prohibition against intervention or overriding established procurement controls. ___ ___ ___ _____

- Board or governing body oversight required for high dollar, lengthy, or other sensitive procurement contracts. ___ ___ ___ _____

- Adequate knowledge and experience of key procurement managers in light of responsibilities for procurements for federal awards. ___ ___ ___ _____

- Clear assignment of authority for issuing purchasing orders and contracting for goods and services. ___ ___ ___ _____

- Description of alternative or compensating controls:

_____

_____

_____

_____

Risk Assessment

- Procedures to identify risks arising from vendor inadequacy, e.g., quality of goods and services, delivery schedules, warranty assurances, user support. ___ ___ ___ _____

- Procedures established to identify risks arising from conflicts-of-interest, e.g., kickbacks, related party transactions, bribery. ___ ___ ___ _____

- Management understands the requirements for procurement and suspension and debarment, and, given the organization's staff, departments, and processes, has identified where noncompliance could likely occur. ___ ___ ___ _____

- Conflict-of-interest statements are maintained for individuals with responsibility for procurement of goods or services. ___ ___ ___ _____

- Description of alternative or compensating controls:

_____

_____

_____

_____

	Yes	No	N/A	Working Paper Reference

Control Activities

- Job descriptions or other means of defining tasks that comprise particular procurement jobs.

- Contractor's performance with the terms, conditions, and specifications of the contract is monitored and documented.

- Establish segregation of duties between employees responsible for contracting and accounts payable and cash disbursing.

- Procurement actions appropriately documented in the procurement files.

- Supervisors review procurement and contracting decisions for compliance with federal procurement policies.

- Procedures established to verify that vendors providing goods and services under the award have not been suspended or debarred by the federal government.

- Official written policy for procurement and contracts establishing:

  — Contract files that document significant procurement history.

  — Methods of procurement, authorized including selection of contract type, contractor selection or rejection, and the basis of contract price.

  — Verification that procurements provide full and open competition.

  — Requirements for cost or price analysis, including for contract modifications.

  — Obtaining and reacting to suspension and debarment certifications.

	Yes	No	N/A	*Working Paper Reference*

— Other applicable requirements for procurements under federal awards are followed. ___ ___ ___ _____

- Official written policy for suspension and debarments that:

— Contains or references the federal requirements; ___ ___ ___ _____

— Prohibits the award of a subaward, covered contract, or any other covered agreement for program administration, goods, services, or any other program purpose with any suspended or debarred party; and ___ ___ ___ _____

— Requires staff to obtain certifications from entities receiving subawards (contract and subcontract) over $100,000, certifying that the organization and its principals are not suspended or debarred. ___ ___ ___ _____

- Description of alternative or compensating controls:

_____

_____

_____

_____

Information and Communication

- A system in place to assure that procurement documentation is retained for the time period required by the A-102 Common Rule, OMB Circular A-110, award agreements, contracts, and program regulations. Documentation includes:

— The basis for contractor selection; ___ ___ ___ _____

— Justification for lack of competition when competitive bids or offers are not obtained; and ___ ___ ___ _____

— The basis for award cost or price. ___ ___ ___ _____

- Employees' procurement duties and control responsibilities are effectively communicated. ___ ___ ___ _____

- Procurement staff are provided a current *List of Parties Excluded from Fed-*

	Yes	No	N/A	*Working Paper Reference*

eral Procurement or Nonprocurement Programs, issued by the General Services Administration, or have on-line access.

___ ___ ___ _____

- Channels of communication are provided for people to report suspected procurement and contracting improprieties.

___ ___ ___ _____

- Description of alternative or compensating controls:

_____

_____

_____

_____

Monitoring

- Management periodically conducts independent reviews of procurements and contracting activities to determine whether policies and procedures are being followed as intended.

___ ___ ___ _____

- Description of alternative or compensating controls:

_____

_____

_____

_____

J. PROGRAM INCOME

Control Objectives

To provide reasonable assurance that program income is correctly earned, recorded, and used in accordance with the program requirements.

Control Environment

- Management recognizes its responsibilities for program income.

___ ___ ___ _____

- Management's prohibition against intervention or overriding controls over program income.

___ ___ ___ _____

- Realistic performance targets for the generation of program income.

___ ___ ___ _____

- Description of alternative or compensating controls:

_____

_____

_____

_____

Working
Paper
Yes No N/A Reference

Risk Assessment

- Mechanisms in place to identify the risk of unrecorded or miscoded program income. _____

- Variances between expected and actual income analyzed. _____

- Description of alternative or compensating controls:

_____

_____

_____

_____

Control Activities

- Pricing and collection policies procedures clearly communicated to personnel responsible for program income. _____

- Mechanism in place to ensure that program income is properly recorded as earned and is deposited in the bank as collected. _____

- Policies and procedures provide for correct use of program income in accordance with federal program requirements. _____

- Description of alternative or compensating controls:

_____

_____

_____

_____

Information and Communication

- Information systems identify program income collections and usage. _____

- A channel of communication for people to report suspected improprieties in the collection or use of program income. _____

- Description of alternative or compensating controls:

_____

_____

_____

_____

	Yes	No	N/A	*Working Paper Reference*

Monitoring

- Internal audit of program income. _____

- Management compares program income to budget and investigates significant differences. _____

- Description of alternative or compensating controls:

_____

_____

_____

K. REAL PROPERTY ACQUISITION AND RELOCATION ASSISTANCE

Control Objectives

To provide reasonable assurance of compliance with the real property acquisition, appraisal, negotiation, and relocation requirements.

Control Environment

- Management committed to ensuring compliance with the Uniform Relocation Assistance and Real Property Acquisition Policies Act of 1970, as amended (URA). _____

- Written policies exist for handling relocation assistance and real property acquisition. _____

- Description of alternative or compensating controls:

_____

_____

_____

_____

Risk Assessment

- Identification of risk that relocation will not be conducted in accordance with the URA, e.g., improper payments will be made to individuals or businesses that relocate. _____

- Description of alternative or compensating controls:

				Working
				Paper
	Yes	*No*	*N/A*	*Reference*

Control Activities

- Employees handling relocation assistance and real property acquisition have been trained in the requirements of the URA.

- Review of expenditures pertaining to real property acquisition and relocation assistance by employees knowledgeable in the URA.

- Description of alternative or compensating controls:

Information and Communication

- A system is in place to adequately document relocation assistance and real property acquisition.

- Description of alternative or compensating controls:

Monitoring

- Management monitors relocation assistance and real property acquisition for compliance with the UFA.

- Description of alternative or compensating controls:

L. REPORTING

Control Objectives

To provide reasonable assurance that reports of federal awards submitted to the federal awarding agency or pass-through entity include all activity of the reporting period, are supported by underlying accounting or performance records, and are fairly presented in accordance with program requirements.

	Yes	No	N/A	*Working Paper Reference*

Control Environment

- Persons preparing, reviewing, and approving the reports possess the required knowledge, skills, and abilities. ___ ___ ___ _____

- Management's attitude toward reporting promotes accurate and fair presentation. ___ ___ ___ _____

- Appropriate assignment of responsibility and delegation of authority for reporting decisions. ___ ___ ___ _____

- Description of alternative or compensating controls:

_____

_____

_____

_____

Risk Management

- Mechanisms exist to identify risks of faulty reporting caused by such items as lack of current knowledge of, inconsistent application of, or carelessness or disregard for standards and reporting requirements of federal awards. ___ ___ ___ _____

- Identification of underlying source data or analysis for performance or special reporting that may not be reliable. ___ ___ ___ _____

- Description of alternative or compensating controls:

_____

_____

_____

_____

Working
Paper
Yes No N/A Reference

Control Activities

- Written policy exists that establishes responsibility and provides the procedures
  for periodic monitoring, verification, and
  reporting of program progress and accomplishments. ___ ___ ___ _____
- Tracking system that reminds staff when
  reports are due. ___ ___ ___ _____
- The general ledger or other reliable
  records are the basis for the reports. ___ ___ ___ _____
- Supervisory review of reports performed
  to assure accuracy and completeness
  of data and information included in the
  reports. ___ ___ ___ _____
- The required accounting method is used
  (e.g., cash or accrual). ___ ___ ___ _____
- Description of alternative or compensating controls:

  _____

  _____

  _____

  _____

Information and Communication

- An accounting or information system that
  provides for the reliable processing of
  financial and performance information
  for federal awards. ___ ___ ___ _____
- Description of alternative or compensating controls:

  _____

  _____

  _____

  _____

Monitoring

- Communications from external parties
  corroborate information included in the
  reports for federal awards. ___ ___ ___ _____
- Periodic comparison of reports to supporting records. ___ ___ ___ _____
- Description of alternative or compensating controls:

  _____

  _____

  _____

  _____

M. SUBRECIPIENT MONITORING

Control Objectives

To provide reasonable assurance that federal award information and compliance requirements are identified to subrecipients, subrecipient activities are monitored, subrecipient audit findings are resolved, and the impact of any subrecipient noncompliance on the pass-through entity is evaluated. Also, the pass-through entity should perform procedures to provide reasonable assurance that the subrecipient obtained required audits and takes appropriate corrective action on audit findings.

	Yes	No	N/A	Working Paper Reference

Control Environment

- Establishment of "tone at the top" of management's commitment to monitoring subrecipients.
- Management's intolerance of overriding established procedures to monitor subrecipients.
- Entity's organizational structure and its ability to provide the necessary information flow to monitor subrecipients is adequate.
- Sufficient resources dedicated to subrecipient monitoring.
- Knowledge, skills, and abilities needed to accomplish subrecipient monitoring tasks defined.
- Individuals performing subrecipient monitoring possess knowledge skills and abilities required.
- Subrecipients demonstrate that:
  - They are willing and able to comply with the requirements of the award and
  - They have accounting systems, including the use of applicable cost principles, and internal control systems adequate to administer the award.
  - Appropriate sanctions taken for subrecipient noncompliance.
- Description of alternative or compensating controls:

_____

_____

_____

_____

	Yes	No	N/A	*Working Paper Reference*

Risk Assessment

- Key managers understand the subrecipient's environment, systems, and controls sufficiently to identify the level and methods of monitoring required. ___ ___ ___ _____

- Mechanisms exist to identify risks arising from external sources affecting subrecipients, such as risks related to:

  — Economic conditions. ___ ___ ___ _____

  — Political conditions. ___ ___ ___ _____

  — Regulatory changes. ___ ___ ___ _____

  — Unreliable information. ___ ___ ___ _____

- Mechanisms exist to identify and react to changes in subrecipients, such as:

  — Financial problems that could lead to diversion of grant funds. ___ ___ ___ _____

  — Loss of essential personnel. ___ ___ ___ _____

  — Loss of license or accreditation to operate program. ___ ___ ___ _____

  — Rapid growth. ___ ___ ___ _____

  — New activities, products, or services. ___ ___ ___ _____

  — Organizational restructuring. ___ ___ ___ _____

- Description of alternative or compensating controls:

_____

_____

_____

_____

Control Activities

- Identify to subrecipients the federal award information (e.g., CFDA title and number, award name, name of federal agency, amount of award) and applicable compliance requirements. ___ ___ ___ _____

- Include in agreements with subrecipients the requirement to comply with the compliance requirements applicable to the federal program, including the audit requirements of OMB Circular A-133. ___ ___ ___ _____

	Yes	*No*	*N/A*	*Working Paper Reference*

- Subrecipient's compliance with audit requirements monitored using techniques such as the following:

  — Determining by inquiry and discussions whether subrecipient met thresholds requiring an audit under OMB Circular A-133. ___ ___ ___ _____

  — If an audit is required, assuring that the subrecipient submits the report, the report package, or the documents required by OMB Circulars and/or recipient's requirements. ___ ___ ___ _____

  — If a subrecipient was required to obtain an audit in accordance with OMB Circular A-133 but did not do so, following up with the subrecipient until the audit is completed. ___ ___ ___ _____

  — Taking appropriate actions such as withholding further funding until the subrecipient meets the audit requirements. ___ ___ ___ _____

- Subrecipient's compliance with federal program requirements monitored using such techniques as the following:

  — Issuing timely management decisions for audit and monitoring findings to inform the subrecipient whether the corrective action planned is acceptable. ___ ___ ___ _____

  — Maintain a system to track and follow up on reported deficiencies related to programs funded by the recipient, and ensure that timely corrective action is taken. ___ ___ ___ _____

  — Regular contacts with subrecipients and appropriate inquiries concerning the federal program. ___ ___ ___ _____

  — Reviewing subrecipient reports and following up on areas of concern. ___ ___ ___ _____

  — Monitoring subrecipient budgets. ___ ___ ___ _____

  — Performing site visits to subrecipient to review financial and programmatic records and observe operations. ___ ___ ___ _____

  — Offering subrecipients technical assistance where needed. ___ ___ ___ _____

	Yes	No	N/A	*Working Paper Reference*

- Official written policies and procedures exist establishing:
  - Communication of federal award requirements to subrecipients. — — — ———
  - Responsibilities for monitoring subrecipients. — — — ———
  - Process and procedures for monitoring. — — — ———
  - Methodology for resolving findings of subrecipient noncompliance or weaknesses in internal control. — — — ———
  - Requirements for and processing of subrecipient audits, including appropriate adjustment of pass-through entity's accounts. — — — ———
- Description of alternative or compensating controls:

_____

_____

_____

_____

Information and Communication

- Standard award documents used by the non-federal entity contain:
  - A listing of federal requirements that the subrecipient must follow. Items can be specifically listed in the award document, attached as an exhibit to the document, or incorporated by reference to specific criteria. — — — ———
  - The description and program number for each program as stated in the Catalog of Federal Domestic Assistance (CFDA). If the program funds include pass-through funds from another recipient, the pass-through program information should also be identified. — — — ———
  - A statement signed by an official of the subrecipient, stating that the subrecipient was informed of, understands, and agrees to comply with the applicable compliance requirements. — — — ———

Working
Paper
Yes No N/A Reference

- A recordkeeping system is in place to assure that documentation is retained for the time period required by the recipient. ____ ____ ____ _____

- Procedures are in place to provide channels for subrecipients to communicate concerns to the pass-through entity. ____ ____ ____ _____

- Description of alternative or compensating controls:

_____

_____

_____

_____

Monitoring

- Establish a tracking system to assure timely submission of required reporting, such as: financial reports, performance reports, audit reports, on-site monitoring reviews of subrecipients, and timely resolution of audit findings. ____ ____ ____ _____

- Supervisory reviews performed to determine the adequacy of subrecipient monitoring. ____ ____ ____ _____

- Description of alternative or compensating controls:

_____

_____

_____

_____

SOP 98-3 prescribes that assessing control risk at below the maximum level involves (a) identifying specific controls relevant to specific assertions that are likely to prevent or detect material misstatements in those assertions and (b) performing tests of controls to evaluate the effectiveness of such controls. However, evidential matter varies substantially in the assurance that it provides to the auditor as he or she develops an assessed level of control risk. The assurance that is obtained from evidential matter is affected by the following factors:

- *Type of evidential matter*—For some controls, documentation of the design or operation of controls may exist, while for other controls such documentation may not exist.

- *Source of evidential matter*—Generally, evidence the auditor obtains directly by observation provides more assurance than evidential matter obtained by inquiry. In fact, SAS-55, as amended, specifically states that inquiry alone generally will not provide sufficient evidential matter to support a conclusion about the effectiveness of design or operation of a specific control. Accordingly, when an auditor determines that a specific control may have a significant effect in reducing control risk to a low level for a specific assertion, he or she ordinarily needs to perform additional tests to obtain sufficient evidential matter to support the conclusion about the effectiveness of the design or operation of that control.

  > **OBSERVATION:** Auditors performing Circular A-133 audits should consider this requirement carefully, since it generally limits the ability of auditors to use only inquiries as evidence to reduce control risk to a low level.

- *Timeliness of evidential matter*—Evidence from some tests of controls, such as observation, pertains only to the point in time at which the auditing procedure is performed. As a result, such evidential matter may be insufficient to evaluate the effectiveness of the design or operation of controls for the period that is not observed, and the auditor may consider supplementing this test with other audit procedures. In addition, when evidence about controls is obtained at an interim period, the auditor should determine what additional evidential matter should be obtained for the remaining period being audited—that is, from the end of the interim period to the end of the fiscal year.

- *Interrelationships of evidential matter*—In evaluating the adequacy of evidential matter obtained about an internal control, the auditor should consider other types of evidence that have been obtained about the same assertion and should consider the evidence in total that results from all procedures.

The Circular A-133 requirements have two major impacts:

1. Sample sizes for tests of controls will increase. For example, to plan for control risk slightly below the maximum (as under the former Circular A-133), an auditor may have examined a sample of 5 items. To plan for control risk at a low level, this sample size would need to increase to perhaps as many as 25 items, depending on the audit approach used by individual auditors and auditing firms. (See the chapter titled "Extent of Audit Procedures and Sampling" for a discussion of audit sampling.)

2. Using inquiry and observation techniques to test controls to achieve control risk at slightly below the maximum level was a fairly common practice. Inquiry techniques only would generally not be acceptable to reduce control risk to a low level for many types of internal controls. In addition, where observation techniques are used the auditor will need to determine whether an observation at a particular point in time represents sufficient evidence as to the functioning of a control throughout the year.

> **OBSERVATION:** Auditors should note carefully that the requirement of the Circular A-133 is to plan the procedures to obtain a low level of control risk. The auditor does not have to actually achieve a low level of control risk. Therefore, if an auditor encounters an unacceptable number of exceptions in a sample of items selected to achieve a low level of control risk, the auditor does not have to test additional items to actually achieve the low level of control risk.

Circular A-133 provides an exception to the requirement to test internal controls for ineffective controls. When internal control over some or all of the compliance requirements for a major program are likely to be ineffective in preventing or detecting noncompliance, the planning and testing described above are not required for those compliance requirements. However, the auditor should report a reportable condition or a material weakness in internal control, assess the related control risk at the maximum level, and consider whether additional compliance tests are required because of ineffective internal control over the major program.

Circular A-133 requires auditors to test internal controls over the administration of federal awards. Auditors used to the requirements of generally accepted auditing standards (auditors can choose *not* to test controls under generally accepted auditing standards) may overlook this Circular A-133 requirement. The auditor must look at the three components of audit risk—inherent risk, control risk, and detection risk—when testing for material noncompliance with laws, regulations, and terms of awards. If, after performing tests of internal control policies and procedures, the auditor is able to assess control risk at below the maximum amount for one or more assertions, he or she can then increase the tolerable amount of detection risk for those assertions and still maintain an acceptably low level of audit risk. This is an important link between the requirements of generally accepted auditing standards and the Circular A-133 internal control requirements.

> **OBSERVATION:** The auditor makes similar assessments of control risk for internal controls over the administration of federal awards programs and of internal controls relating to the accumulation of accounting information for financial statement preparation purposes.

Increasing the acceptable level of detection risk decreases the amount of substantive test work that must be performed when the auditor tests for compliance. (A complete discussion of compliance testing and reporting is provided in the chapter titled "Compliance Considerations.") Therefore, in designing the overall strategy for a Circular A-133 audit, the auditor should seek to increase the efficiency of the audit by considering the results of the tests of controls over the administration of federal awards programs when determining the extent of the tests of controls and the substantive tests of compliance.

For example, a small not-for-profit organization may have too few employees for effective separation of duties. The auditor should report the lack of separation of duties as a reportable condition or material weakness. Alternatively, the auditor may determine that there are compensating controls that can be tested. In this case, a reportable condition may not exist. The auditor does not have to test (or in the absence of a control, report as a reportable condition) every conceivable control over federal awards programs. The auditor will determine which controls to test while obtaining an understanding of the internal control policies and procedures. For example, if there are duplicate or overlapping controls, the auditor should test the control that is the most effective and may choose not to test the less effective, duplicate control.

> **OBSERVATION:** The auditor should exercise care when deciding not to test duplicate or overlapping controls, because some internal control policies and procedures affect a number of assertions. The auditor must consider **all** of the assertions relating to the impact of a particular control before deciding not to test it.

The requirements make it fairly difficult for the auditor to make an assessment that the internal control policies and procedures for a particular area are ineffective. Clearly, the auditor does not wish to report (the recipient organization would most likely feel even more strongly) more reportable conditions and material weaknesses than necessary in order to avoid performing tests of controls.

According to SAS-60 (Consideration of Internal Control Related Matters Noted in an Audit), *reportable conditions* are "matters coming to the auditor's attention that, in his judgment, should be communicated to the audit committee because they represent significant deficiencies in the design or operation of the internal control, which could adversely affect a recipient organization's ability to record, process, summarize, and report financial data in a manner consistent with the assertions of management in the financial statements."

A *material weakness* in the internal control is "a reportable condition in which the design or operation of one or more of the internal control components does not reduce to a relatively low level the risk that errors or irregularities in amounts that would be material in relation to the financial statements being audited may occur and not be detected within a timely period by employees in the normal course of performing their assigned functions."

The auditor should document the procedures performed on internal control policies and procedures to comply with Circular A-133. The steps performed and conclusions reached and the auditor's understanding and assessment of control risk related to the internal control policies and procedures established for federal awards should be clearly evidenced in the auditor's working papers. In addition, if the auditor has not performed tests of any relevant controls (i.e., if tests of major program internal control policies and procedures are omitted because the controls are likely to be ineffective in preventing and detecting noncompliance), the auditor's rationale for omitting these tests should be clearly documented.

INTERNAL CONTROL CONSIDERATIONS IN AN AUDIT PERFORMED IN ACCORDANCE WITH GOVERNMENT AUDITING STANDARDS

As previously stated, an audit in accordance with Circular A-133 requires an auditor to perform the audit in accordance with *Government Auditing Standards* as promulgated by the Comptroller General of the United States.

As is discussed more fully in the chapter on *Government Auditing Standards*, the Yellow Book was amended in 1999 to impose an internal control standard requiring auditors to document in the working papers (1) the basis for assessing control risk at the maximum level for assertions related to material account balances, transaction classes, and disclosure components of financial statements when such assertions are significantly dependent on computerized information systems and (2) consideration that the planned audit procedures are designed to achieve audit objectives and to reduce audit risk to an acceptable level. The Yellow Book also provides additional guidance on internal controls, which the auditor should consider when performing a Circular A-133 audit. This guidance covers:

- Safeguarding of assets
- Control over compliance with laws and regulations

Safeguarding of Assets

Internal controls over safeguarding of assets (safeguarding controls) constitute a process, effected by an entity's governing body, management, and other personnel, designed to provide reasonable assurance regarding prevention or timely detection of unauthorized acquisition, use, or disposition of the entity's assets that could have a material effect on the financial statements.

> **OBSERVATION:** Auditors tend to think of safeguarding controls as controls over the theft of physical assets, such as inventory, cash, and securities. The Yellow Book expands this definition. Safeguarding controls also include, for example, a recipient organization's policies and procedures in place to prevent or detect loss from the unauthorized procurement of goods or services that result in the goods or services not being procured under the most favorable terms.

The Yellow Book specifically states the following about controls over safeguarding assets:

> Understanding the control over safeguarding of assets can help auditors assess the risk that financial statements could be materially misstated. For example, an understanding of an auditee's control over the safeguarding of assets can help auditors recognize risk factors such as:
> - Failure to adequately monitor decentralized operations;
> - Lack of control over activities, such as lack of documentation for major transactions;
> - Lack of control over computerized information systems, such as a lack of controls over access to applications that initiate or control the movement of assets;
> - Failure to develop or communicate adequate control activities for security of data or assets, such as allowing unauthorized personnel to have ready access to data or assets; and

- Failure to investigate significant unreconciled differences between reconciliations of a control account and subsidiary ledgers.

Controls over Compliance with Laws and Regulations

Auditors should design the audit to provide reasonable assurance that the financial statements are free of material misstatements resulting from violations of laws and regulations that have a direct and material effect on the determination of financial statement amounts. To meet that requirement, auditors should have an understanding of internal control relevant to financial statement assertions affected by those laws and regulations. Auditors should use that understanding to identify types of potential misstatements, consider factors that affect the risk of material misstatement, and design substantive tests. For example, the following control environment factors may influence the auditors' assessment of control risk:

- Management's awareness or lack of awareness of applicable laws and regulations,
- Auditee policy regarding such matters as acceptable operating practices and codes of conduct, and
- Assignment of responsibility and delegation of authority to deal with such matters as organizational goals and objectives, operating functions, and regulatory requirements.

> **OBSERVATION:** The Yellow Book's internal control guidance enhances GAAS by putting certain matters, particularly safeguarding controls, in a perspective auditors ordinarily do not have. The auditor should consider this guidance when planning and performing audits in accordance with *Government Auditing Standards*, but should keep in mind that it does not (other than certain documentation requirements) add any additional testwork to the procedures normally performed in financial statement audits in accordance with GAAS.

In addition to the above guidance concerning internal control, the Yellow Book includes the following examples of reportable conditions:

- Absence of appropriate segregation of duties consistent with appropriate control objectives
- Absence of appropriate reviews and approvals of transactions, accounting entries, or systems output
- Inadequate provisions for the safeguarding of assets

- Evidence of failure to safeguard assets from loss, damage, or misappropriation
- Evidence that a system fails to provide complete and accurate output consistent with the auditee's control objectives because of the misapplication of control procedures
- Evidence of intentional override of internal controls by those in authority to the detriment of the system's overall objectives
- Evidence of failure to perform tasks that are part of internal controls, such as reconciliations not prepared or not prepared in a timely manner
- Absence of a sufficient level of control consciousness within the organization
- Significant deficiencies in the design or operation of internal controls that could result in violations of laws and regulations having a direct and material effect on the financial statements
- Failure to follow up and correct previously identified deficiencies in internal controls

SUMMARY

Circular A-133 contains a number of requirements relating to the performance of tests of the internal control for administering major federal programs. In addition, the requirements of GAAS are quite specific in terms of the requirements for an auditor performing an audit of financial statements. *Government Auditing Standards,* while not imposing additional procedures on the auditor, does provide guidance on internal control as well as certain documentation requirements that the auditor must consider when planning and performing an audit in accordance with *Government Auditing Standards.*

Given the numerous internal control requirements, the auditor must be extremely careful when designing an audit strategy and planning and performing procedures relating to internal control. Auditors who fully understand the relationship between internal control procedures and the assessment of control risk, and their impact on detection risk, will be able to design the most effective and efficient audit possible despite the complex requirements.

CHAPTER 17
COMPLIANCE AND SUBRECIPIENT CONSIDERATIONS

CONTENTS

CHAPTER 17
COMPLIANCE AND SUBRECIPIENT CONSIDERATIONS

CROSS-REFERENCES

2001 MILLER NOT-FOR-PROFIT ORGANIZATION AUDITS: Chapter 4: "Internal Control Considerations"; Chapter 16, "Internal Controls over Federal Awards"

2001 MILLER SINGLE AUDITS: Chapter 9, "Compliance"

Probably the most significant element of an audit in accordance with Circular A-133 is the required testing and reporting on the recipient's compliance with laws, regulations, and terms of awards for each of the major awards programs. Following the procedures discussed in this chapter will enable the auditor to issue the required opinion on compliance with laws, regulations, and terms of award for each major program.

The auditor should determine whether the recipient has complied with laws and regulations that may have a direct and material effect on each of its major federal programs. That guidance requires that the auditor's opinion be formed using a materiality level that is determined for each major program of the recipient organization. For this reason, testing and reporting on compliance is an important part of a Circular A-133 audit.

REQUIREMENTS FOR AN AUDIT OF FINANCIAL STATEMENTS IN ACCORDANCE WITH GENERALLY ACCEPTED AUDITING STANDARDS

The requirements for the auditor to consider compliance with laws and regulations in an audit of financial statements in accordance with generally accepted auditing standards require that the auditor design the audit to provide reasonable assurance that the financial statements are free of material misstatements resulting from violations of laws and regulations that have a direct and material effect on the determination of financial statement amounts. This responsibility exists for all audits conducted in accordance with GAAS.

The auditor should obtain an understanding of the possible effects on financial statements of laws and regulations that are generally recognized by auditors to have a direct and material effect. The auditor should consider the following methods to meet these requirements:

- Assess whether management has identified the laws and regulations that could have a direct and material effect on the determination of amounts in the financial statements.

- Become familiar with those laws and regulations that could have a direct and material effect on financial statement amounts.

- Understand the characteristics of those laws and regulations that could, if they were not followed, potentially lead to a misstatement on the financial statements.

- Assess the risk that a material misstatement has occurred because of such noncompliance.

- Design and conduct an audit to provide reasonable assurance of detecting such material noncompliance.

> **OBSERVATION:** The auditor also should consider internal control activities that the not-for-profit organization has instituted to ensure compliance. This is part of the assessment of risk that a material misstatement has occurred because of such noncompliance.

When performing an audit of financial statements in accordance with GAAS, the auditor should consider audit risk at the financial statement level, which includes consideration of the financial statement assertions at the material account and class of transactions level. These considerations are also relevant to the auditor's consideration of the risk that the financial statements will be materially misstated because of violations of laws and regulations that have a direct and material effect on the financial statement amounts.

The auditor must consider the nature of the laws and regulations that may have a direct and material effect on the financial statements of the recipient organization. Many of these laws and regulations are imbedded in the compliance requirements discussed later in this chapter.

When performing an audit in accordance with Circular A-133, however, the auditor usually will satisfy many of the compliance requirements when performing test work on compliance at the major federal program level, which will limit the number of additional procedures that must be completed. The auditor should consider the requirements when planning the procedures at both the financial statement and major program levels to ensure that the most efficient manner of conducting the audit is determined.

> **OBSERVATION:** If the primary area for compliance with laws and regulations is at the major federal program level, the Circular A-133 audit requirements will meet many of the requirements for compliance considerations at the financial statement level.

REQUIREMENTS FOR AN AUDIT IN ACCORDANCE WITH GOVERNMENT AUDITING STANDARDS

The Yellow Book incorporates several generally accepted auditing standards relating to compliance. These standards include the auditor's considerations regarding fraud, illegal acts, and other acts of noncompliance, and are described below.

The auditor must design the audit to provide reasonable assurance of detecting fraud that is material to the financial statements. The Yellow Book states that auditors should:

- Design the audit to provide reasonable assurance of detecting material misstatements resulting from direct and material illegal acts. (*Direct and material illegal acts* are defined as violations of laws and regulations having a direct and material effect on the determination of financial statement amounts.)

- Be aware of the possibility that indirect illegal acts may have occurred. (*Indirect illegal acts* are defined as violations of laws and regulations having material but indirect effects on the financial statements.) If specific information comes to the auditor's attention that provides evidence concerning the existence of possible illegal acts that could have a material indirect effect on the financial statements, the auditor should apply audit procedures specifically directed to ascertaining whether an illegal act has occurred.

The Yellow Book prescribes additional requirements for instances of noncompliance that have a material indirect effect on the financial statements. Auditors must design the audit to provide reasonable assurance of detecting material misstatements resulting from noncompliance with provisions of contracts or grant agreements that have a direct and material effect on the determination of financial statement amounts. If specific information comes to the auditors' attention that provides evidence concerning the existence of possible noncompliance that could have a material indirect effect on the financial statements, auditors should apply audit procedures specifically directed to ascertaining whether that noncompliance occurred.

> **OBSERVATION:** Although the Yellow Book highlights instances of noncompliance with provisions of contracts or grant agreements that have a direct and material effect on the financial statement amounts, there is already a requirement for an audit in accordance with GAAS regarding the accounting for contingencies. Such noncompliance may well give rise to a contingency.

Auditor's Consideration of Noncompliance

The Yellow Book provides additional guidance on the meaning of *noncompliance*. According to the Yellow Book, *noncompliance* has a broader meaning than *illegal acts*. *Noncompliance* includes not only illegal acts, but also violations of provisions of contracts or grant agreements. GAAS do not discuss auditors' responsibility for detecting noncompliance other than illegal acts. But under *Government Auditing Standards*, auditors have the same responsibilities for detecting material misstatements arising from other types of non-compliance as they do for detecting those arising from illegal acts.

Direct and material noncompliance is noncompliance having a direct and material effect on the determination of financial statement amounts. Auditors should design the audit to provide reasonable assurance of detecting material misstatements resulting from direct and material noncompliance with provisions of contracts and grants.

Indirect noncompliance is noncompliance having material but indirect effects on the financial statements. A financial statement audit provides no assurance that indirect noncompliance with provisions of contracts or grant agreements will be detected. However, if specific information comes to the auditor's attention that provides evidence concerning the existence of possible noncompliance that could have a material indirect effect on the financial statements, auditors should apply audit procedures specifically directed to ascertaining whether that noncompliance has occurred.

Thus, the Yellow Book expanded the auditor's responsibility regarding the compliance requirements, material indirect noncompliance of which the auditor becomes aware, illegal acts, and the consideration given to noncompliance with grants and contracts, which is similar to the consideration given to noncompliance with laws and regulations.

COMPLIANCE AUDITING AND REPORTING REQUIREMENTS FOR AN AUDIT IN ACCORDANCE WITH CIRCULAR A-133

The requirements for compliance testing and reporting for audits performed in accordance with Circular A-133 pertain to compliance at the major federal program level.

The auditor should use the following approach or methodology for designing an audit strategy to meet the audit requirements of Circular A-133 with regard to compliance at the major federal award program level:

- Identify major federal programs administered by the not-for-profit organization.
- Determine materiality for each major federal program.
- Determine the compliance requirements applicable to each major federal program.
- Assess audit risk in terms of its components—inherent risk, control risk, detection risk, and fraud risk.
- Determine if there are any subrecipients of the major federal programs, and if so, consider them when determining required audit procedures.
- Evaluate the results of the audit procedures performed.
- Issue an opinion on the not-for-profit organization's compliance with the compliance requirements for each of its major federal programs.

SOP 98-3 identifies the following factors that an auditor should consider in planning, performing, and evaluating tests of compliance in accordance with Circular A-133:

- The assessment of inherent risk, control risk, fraud risk, and detection risk
- The assessment of materiality
- The evidence obtained from other auditing procedures
- The amount of expenditures for the program
- The diversity or homogeneity of expenditures for the program
- The length of time that the program has operated, or changes in its conditions
- The current and prior auditing experience with the program, particularly findings in previous audits and other evaluations (such as inspections, program reviews, or system reviews required by Federal Acquisition Regulations)

- The extent to which the program is carried out through subrecipients, as well as the related monitoring activities
- The extent to which the program contracts for goods or services
- The level to which the program is already subject to program reviews or other forms of independent oversight
- The expectation of noncompliance or compliance with the applicable compliance requirements
- The extent to which computer processing is used to administer the program, as well as the complexity of that processing
- Whether the program is being identified as high-risk by the Compliance Supplement

> **AUDIT COST-SAVINGS TIP:** The most efficient way for the auditor to meet the requirements of Circular A-133 for testing the recipient's compliance with compliance requirements is to perform the additional test work concurrently with the audit of the financial statements. The auditor should build the Circular A-133 related procedures into the procedures performed for an audit of financial statements.

Identify major federal programs administered by the recipient organization The chapter titled "Planning for a Circular A-133 Audit" discusses in detail the procedures for determining whether management has identified all federal programs and for determining which of the federal programs are considered major programs, including the risk assessment required to be performed by the auditor.

Determine materiality for each major federal program When testing compliance in accordance with Circular A-133, the auditor's consideration of materiality differs from that in an audit of financial statements in accordance with GAAS. In a financial statement audit, materiality is considered in relation to the financial statements being audited. In an audit of an organization's compliance with requirements for major programs, materiality is considered in relation to each major program to which the transaction or finding relates.

Circular A-133 requires the auditor to test compliance requirements. However, the auditor should apply the concept of materiality to each major program taken as a whole rather than to each individual requirement. In addition, if the tests of compliance reveal a material misstatement at the major program level, the auditor should consider its effect on the financial statements.

Although it does not relate to determining materiality at the major program level, the Yellow Book includes the following information about the materiality consideration in an audit in accordance with *Government Auditing Standards*:

> Auditors' consideration of materiality is a matter of professional judgment and is influenced by their perception of the needs of a reasonable person who will rely on the financial statements. Materiality judgments are made in light of surrounding circumstances and necessarily involve both quantitative and qualitative considerations.

Qualitative factors the auditor might consider include, but are not limited to, the cumulative effect and impact of immaterial items, the objectives of the work undertaken and the use of the reported information by the user or groups of users of the information. As part of these qualitative considerations, the Yellow Book states that in the audit of a not-for-profit organization that receives federal awards, auditors may set materiality levels lower than in audits in the private sector because of the public accountability of the auditee, the various legal and regulatory requirements, and the visibility and sensitivity of government programs, activities, and functions.

Because the auditor expresses an opinion on each major program and not on all the major programs combined, reaching a conclusion about whether the instances of noncompliance (either individually or in the aggregate) are material to a major program requires consideration of the type and nature of the noncompliance as well as its actual and projected effect on each major program. Instances of noncompliance that are material to one major program may not be material to a major program of a different size or nature. In addition, the level of materiality for a particular major program can change from one period to another.

As discussed in the chapter titled "Planning for a Circular A-133 Audit," determining materiality at the major program level is sometimes difficult for auditors because generally a program won't have its own balance sheet (or will have an atypical balance sheet) and the concept of net income does not exist for a major federal program. The auditor is basically determining materiality in relation to the federal expenditures of the program, which in the majority of cases equal the federal revenues of the program. Before considering all of the qualitative factors discussed above, the auditor probably would find that setting materiality at 5 percent of the expenditures for each major program is a good starting point that can then be fine-tuned for the recipient organization's individual circumstances.

Determine the compliance requirements applicable to each major federal program When performing an audit in accordance with the requirements of Circular A-133, the auditor tests the not-for-profit organization's compliance with the compliance requirements applicable to each major federal program. The auditor should obtain an understanding of these requirements that is sufficient to allow him or her to determine the nature, timing, and extent of procedures that the auditor will perform to provide a basis for expressing an opinion on compliance. Compliance requirements that, if not complied with, could have a material effect on a major federal awards program are based upon 14 different compliance requirements contained in the Compliance Supplement.

The Compliance Supplement is the primary tool for auditors to use to identify the compliance requirements for major federal programs. The overall features and contents of the Compliance Supplement are described in the chapter of this Guide titled "Technical Resources for A-133 Audits." Circular A-133 requires that auditors determine whether the not-for-profit organization has complied with laws, regulations, and the provisions of contracts and grant agreements that may have a direct and material effect on each of its major programs. The auditor should use the Compliance Supplement to help identify the compliance requirements whether the specific major federal program is included in the Compliance Supplement or not. The Compliance Supplement lists suggested audit procedures for each compliance requirement (as well as for each federal program that is specifically included in the Compliance Supplement). Suggested audit procedures are provided to assist the auditor in planning and performing tests of the not-for-profit organization's compliance with the requirements of the federal programs. The Compliance Supplement states that auditor judgement is necessary to determine whether the suggested audit procedures are sufficient to achieve the audit objectives as stated and whether additional or alternative procedures are needed. At the same time, determining the nature, timing, and extent of the audit procedures necessary to meet the audit objectives is the auditor's responsibility.

> **OBSERVATION:** As a practical matter, the auditor should be prepared to justify not performing any of the suggested audit procedures contained in the Compliance Supplement. This does not mean that all of the suggested procedures must be performed. However, the auditor should be able to demonstrate that he or she exercised professional judgment for the appropriate reason in omitting or substituting the procedure.

The following describes the auditor's procedures both when the specific program being audited is included in the Compliance Supplement and when the specific program is not included.

Specific programs included in the Compliance Supplement   Circular A-133 states that the principal compliance requirements applicable to most federal programs are included in the Compliance Supplement. Where the federal program is one of the specific programs included in the Compliance Supplement, an audit of the compliance requirements contained in the Compliance Supplement will meet the requirements of Circular A-133. While this appears to continue the "safe-harbor" provisions of using the Compliance Supplement in the past, there are a number of important exceptions to this rule that the auditor should be aware of in identifying compliance requirements:

1. Where compliance requirements and the changes are not reflected in the Compliance Supplement, the auditor must determine the current compliance requirements and modify his or her audit procedures accordingly.

2. The Compliance Supplement points out that the provisions of contracts and grant agreements may be included in an organization's contract or grant that would be unique to a particular not-for-profit organization's federal award program.

In addition, the Compliance Supplement can only provide a "safe harbor" as to the compliance requirements (assuming the auditor complies with steps 1 and 2); it does not provide a "safe harbor" as to the sufficiency of the suggested audit procedures. The auditor needs to consider these specific compliance requirements and, when appropriate, needs to design and perform audit procedures to test compliance. Finally, the Compliance Supplement points out that a not-for-profit organization may have agreed to additional compliance requirements with the federal grantor agency that are not otherwise required by law or regulation. These additional requirements— which may, for example, be the result of the resolution of prior-year audit findings—also need to be considered by the auditor in designing and performing tests of compliance. Finally, the Compliance Supplement specifies that the auditor has responsibilities under *Government Auditing Standards* for other requirements when specific information comes to an auditor's attention that provides evidence concerning possible noncompliance that could have a material indirect effect on a major program. The requirements as to material indirect effects are not covered by the Compliance Supplement, and the auditor needs to address them separately, when applicable.

After considering the caveats described in the preceding paragraph, an auditor who is auditing compliance for a major federal program that is included in the Compliance Supplement would first refer to the compliance matrix provided in Part 2 of the Compliance Supplement to determine which of the 14 compliance requirements (described later in this chapter) apply to that particular program. For the compliance requirements that the compliance matrix indicates as being applicable to the applicable program, the auditor would first refer to Part 3 of the Compliance Supplement, which contains information on the compliance requirements that share common characteristics among federal programs. Part 3 describes the compliance requirement, the related audit objective(s), and suggested audit procedures. The auditor should then refer to Part 4 for any special tests and provisions that pertain to the program. In addition to a more specific description of the compliance requirement for the specific program, Part 4 contains the audit objective(s) and suggested audit procedures related to the program-specific compliance requirements.

Auditors should also check to see if the program being audited is part of a cluster of programs. A cluster of programs, which is a grouping of closely related federal programs that have similar compliance requirements, is treated as a single program for the purposes of meeting the requirements of Circular A-133. Part 5 of the Compliance Supplement lists a number of clusters of programs, although a description of compliance requirements, audit objectives, and suggested audit procedures is provided for only two program clusters so far: research and development and student financial aid. However, these are particularly important to not-for-profit colleges and universities. If a program is identified as part of a cluster of programs, but the compliance requirements, audit objective(s), and suggested audit procedures are not included in Part 5, the auditor should treat the program as a part of a cluster of programs and, for determining the applicable audit procedures, should use the guidance in the following section for programs not included in the Compliance Supplement.

Programs not included in the Compliance Supplement   Circular A-133 provides that for those federal programs that are not covered in the Compliance Supplement, the auditor should use the types of compliance requirements contained in the Compliance Supplement as guidance for identifying the types of compliance requirements to test, and should determine the requirements governing the federal program by reviewing the provisions of contract and grant agreements and the laws and regulations referred to in the agreements. Part 7 of the Compliance Supplement is specifically provided to assist auditors in auditing compliance for major federal programs that are not included in the Compliance Supplement.

Part 7 describes several steps that the auditor should perform in identifying these requirements. The following questions (along with more detailed explanations) are provided to assist the auditor in following these steps:

- What are the program objectives, program procedures, and compliance requirements for a specific program?
- Which of the compliance requirements would have a direct and material effect on the program?
- Which of the compliance requirements are susceptible to testing by the auditor?
- Into which of the 14 types of compliance requirements does each compliance requirement fall?

- For special tests and provisions, what are the applicable audit objectives and audit procedures?

After addressing these questions in accordance with the specific instructions in Part 7, the auditor should be able to identify the compliance requirements, audit objectives, and audit procedures to be performed for the major programs. The same considerations described above for programs that are included in the program (changing compliance requirements, specific compliance requirements imposed on the not-for-profit organization that is being audited, etc.) should be considered when the auditor designs the audit procedures for programs not included in the Compliance Supplement.

Assess audit risk in terms of its components—inherent risk, control risk, fraud risk, and detection risk Audit risk in a compliance audit of major programs is the risk that the auditor may unknowingly fail to appropriately modify his or her opinion on compliance. Audit risk is composed of inherent risk, control risk, fraud risk, and detection risk. SOP 98-3 defines these risks in terms of a Circular A-133 as follows:

- *Inherent risk* *Inherent risk* is the risk that material noncompliance with a major program's compliance requirements could occur, assuming there is no related internal control.
- *Control risk* *Control risk* is the risk that material noncompliance that could occur in a major program will not be prevented or detected on a timely basis by the organization's internal control.
- *Fraud risk* *Fraud risk* is the risk that intended material noncompliance with a major program's compliance requirements could occur.
- *Detection risk* *Detection risk* is the risk that an auditor's procedures will lead him or her to conclude that noncompliance that could be material to a major program does not exist when, in fact, such noncompliance does exist.

Consideration of inherent risk The items listed below are identified by SOP 98-3 as related to inherent risk and should be considered when assessing inherent risk of noncompliance:

- The complexity of the compliance requirements
- The length of time the organization has been subject to the compliance requirements
- Prior experience with the organization's compliance
- The potential impact of noncompliance, both qualitatively and quantitatively

Circular A-133 provides the following examples for program characteristics with potentially higher inherent risks:

- Complex programs and the extent to which a program contracts for goods and services have the potential for higher risk.

- The phase of a federal program's life cycle at the federal agency may indicate risk (that is, newer programs may have higher inherent risks).

- The phase of a program's life cycle at the not-for-profit organization may indicate risk (the first and last years of the program may indicate high risk).

- Type B programs with larger federal awards expended would be of higher risk that Type B programs with substantially smaller federal awards expended.

In assessing inherent risk, the auditor also may consider the results of any procedures performed as part of the audit of the financial statements and the results of any tests of compliance with the general requirements.

The determination of inherent risk should be closely tied to the risk assessment performed as part of determining which programs are audited as major programs. There should be consistency in this risk assessment.

Consideration of control risk   The auditor must obtain an understanding of the internal control over major federal awards programs and assess levels of control risk. The assessment must be made regardless of whether the auditor intends to rely on internal control.

As part of his or her consideration of the internal controls over major federal programs, the auditor should:

- Plan tests of controls to the extent that when performed, the tests would be sufficient to achieve a low level of control risk to evaluate the effectiveness of the design and operation of the policies and procedures in preventing or detecting material noncompliance. This does not mean that the results of the tests must result in a low level of control risk.

- Review the recipient's system for monitoring subrecipients and for obtaining and acting on subrecipient audit reports.

- Determine whether audit procedures relating to controls are sufficient in relation to Part 6 of the Compliance Supplement.

> **OBSERVATION:** A more thorough discussion of internal controls over the administration of federal awards programs is contained in the chapter titled "Internal Control over Federal Awards." However, for purposes of the current discussion on

compliance considerations, the judgments to be made by the auditor can be summarized as follows: The auditor is required by Circular A-133 to test internal control over the administration of major federal programs. The auditor designs these tests so that a low level of control risk can be attained. If the results of the tests of control provide evidence that the controls are effective and operating properly because of a satisfactorily low error rate, the auditor can assess control risk for the assertions to which the tested controls relate at a low level. This will enable the auditor to perform less substantive testing of compliance (i.e., either different substantive procedures or lower sample sizes).

Consideration of fraud risk SAS-82 provides guidance to auditors on their responsibility to plan and perform the audit to obtain reasonable assurance about whether the financial statements are free of material misstatement due to fraud. Its requirements do not apply to an audit of a not-for-profit organization's compliance with specified requirements applicable to its major programs. However, SOP 98-3 provides that as part of assessing audit risk in a Circular A-133 audit, the auditor should specifically assess the risk of material noncompliance with a major program's compliance requirements occurring due to fraud. The auditor should then consider that assessment in designing the audit procedures to be performed.

Consideration of detection risk An audit of compliance of major federal awards programs must include the selection of an adequate number of transactions from each major program so that the auditor can obtain sufficient evidence to support the opinion on compliance. In determining the extent of audit procedures that will result in an acceptable level of detection risk, the auditor considers the assessed levels of inherent, control, and fraud risks.

> **AUDIT COST-SAVINGS TIP:** The auditor should take full advantage of the tests of controls required under Circular A-133 for minimizing control risk, which will allow the auditor to perform less substantive testing to achieve an acceptable level of detection risk.

Sampling SOP 98-3 discusses the sampling considerations an auditor should make when performing substantive tests of compliance. Circular A-133 requires the auditor to select and test a sufficient number of transactions to support an opinion on compliance related to each major program. Although the term *sampling* is not mentioned, independent auditors often perform audit sampling to achieve this objective. SAS-39 (Audit Sampling) discusses the factors to be considered in planning, designing, and evaluating audit samples. In addition, the AICPA Audit Practice Release titled "Audit Sampling" provides detailed guidance on how to implement SAS-39. Both documents discuss the use of audit sampling for tests of controls and for substantive tests.

Auditors should use professional judgment to determine sample selection methods and sample sizes for major programs. They should be sufficient to support an opinion on compliance with applicable laws and regulations relative to each major program. According to SOP 98-3, the auditor's professional judgment should be used when selecting sample sizes. The auditor should consider the specific audit objective to be achieved and should determine the audit procedures (or combination of audit procedures) to achieve that objective. The size of the sample depends on both the objective and the efficiency of the sample.

> **OBSERVATION:** See the chapter of this Guide titled "Extent of Audit Procedures and Sampling" for additional information on audit sampling.

> **OBSERVATION:** The auditor should consider all of the acceptable means of sampling to meet the professional requirements while maintaining sample sizes at a minimum acceptable level. This includes such techniques as stratifying the population of expenditures being tested and selecting more higher dollar value items than lower dollar value items. The auditor also may choose to audit all items in the population greater than a certain dollar amount and then apply sampling techniques to the items in the population below that dollar amount.

The auditor can choose to select separate samples for each major program or a sample from the total universe of major programs. In practice, the former option is somewhat more desirable, because the auditor can more readily identify the transactions selected for each major program, the sufficiency of the sample items, and the results of the test work. If the latter methodology is used, the auditor should ensure that the number of sample items for each major program is readily identified in the working papers and that there is clear indication of the items tested for each major program, the sufficiency of the sample tested, and the results of the test work.

> **OBSERVATION:** The auditor may not be able to use the approach of selecting separate samples for each major federal program if the individual transactions for each major program cannot be readily identified and sampled. In this case, the auditor will have to sample all disbursements and determine during test work whether the disbursement was actually charged to a major program. After completing the test work on the selected sample, the auditor should determine if he or she has

selected a sufficient number of transactions from each major program.

Evaluate the results of the audit procedures performed After completing the audit tests described above, the auditor must evaluate the results of those tests. When evaluating whether an entity has complied with laws and regulations that, if not complied with, could have a direct and material effect on each major federal program, the auditor should consider the effect of identified instances of noncompliance on each program. The auditor should consider the following:

- The frequency of noncompliance identified in the audit
- The adequacy of the primary recipient's system for monitoring subrecipients and the possible effect on the program of any noncompliance identified by the primary recipient or the subrecipient's auditors
- Whether any instances of noncompliance identified in the audit resulted in questioned costs, and if so, whether questioned costs are material to the program

The criteria for classifying a cost as a questioned cost vary from one federal agency to another. Congress established many of the criteria when it authorized the programs and provided the funds. Other criteria were established through agency regulations. Generally, these criteria relate to the following:

- Unallowable costs, or costs specifically not allowed under the general and special requirements or conditions of the program
- Undocumented costs, or costs charged to a program for which detailed documentation does not exist
- Unproved costs, or costs for which the program requires approval and the auditor cannot find evidence of approval, or costs not provided for in an approved budget
- Unreasonable costs, or costs incurred that may not reflect the actions of a prudent person, or the assignment of an unreasonably high value to in-kind contributions

When evaluating the effect of questioned costs on the opinion on compliance, the auditor should consider the best estimate of total costs questioned for each major program (hereinafter referred to as "likely questioned costs") not just the questioned costs specifically identified (hereinafter referred to as "known questioned costs"). When using audit sampling, as defined in SAS-39, in the tests of compliance, the auditor projects the amount of known questioned costs identified in the sample to the major program from which the sample was selected.

> **OBSERVATION:** The auditor determines whether a particular cost or group of costs is questioned. Then, to determine the effect of these questioned costs on overall compliance at the major program level, the auditor extrapolates the questioned costs, where appropriate, to determine the likely level of noncompliance. The auditor then evaluates the likely level of noncompliance in light of the materiality level for the individual major program. This is discussed further below.

Circular A-133 requires that material instances of noncompliance and questioned costs should be reported in a schedule of findings and questioned costs. (See the chapter titled "Reporting under Circular A-133" for more information on this schedule.)

The auditor should consider the following procedures for assessing whether a modification of the auditor's report is needed:

- Assess the actual error noted against the materiality level established for the individual program.

- Assess the projected error against the materiality level established for the individual program.

If the auditor determines that the actual error is material to the individual program, depending on the circumstances, the auditor's report on compliance at the major program level should be modified. If the projected error is material to the individual program, the auditor should consider whether additional audit procedures should be applied. These additional procedures should be designed to enable the auditor to more accurately assess the level of projected error, usually by auditing more sample items and developing a higher level of precision in projecting the error.

Auditors also are responsible for assessing the impact of the actual and projected error noted in the federal awards programs against the materiality level established for the basic financial statements.

Issue an opinion on the recipient organization's compliance with the specific requirements for each of its major federal programs The auditor must issue an opinion on the not-for-profit organization's compliance with the compliance requirements for each major program. The format of the auditor's opinion on compliance is more fully discussed in the chapter titled "Reporting under Circular A-133."

Compliance Auditing Considerations

Circular A-133 requires the auditor to determine whether the recipient organization has complied with laws, regulations, and the provisions of contracts and grant agreements that may have a direct and material effect on each of its major programs. The compliance testing performed should include tests of transactions and such other auditing procedures as are needed to provide the auditor with sufficient evidence to support an opinion on compliance for each major program.

Circular A-133 points to the Compliance Supplement for compliance requirements. Exhibit 17-1 gives a general description and the audit objective of each of the 14 compliance requirements contained in the Compliance Supplement. Additional details on these requirements are contained in the Compliance Supplement (which is included on the disc that accompanies this Guide).

The model audit program also contained on the disc incorporates the suggested audit procedures for each of the compliance requirements (other than this, the suggested audit procedures relate to specific programs, for which the auditor should refer to the Compliance Supplement itself).

SUBRECIPIENT CONSIDERATIONS

A *subrecipient* is a non-federal entity that expends federal awards received from a pass-through entity to carry out a federal program. Individuals and beneficiaries of such programs are not included in this definition.

> **OBSERVATION:** A subrecipient also may be a direct recipient of federal awards under other agreements.

Circular A-133 describes the following distinguishing characteristics of a subrecipient:

- Subrecipients determine eligibility for assistance.
- Subrecipients' performance is measured against the objectives of the program.
- Subrecipients are responsible for programmatic decision making.
- Subrecipients are responsible for adherence to applicable program compliance requirements.
- Subrecipients use the passed-through funds to carry out their own programs, not to provide goods or services for a program of the prime recipient.

For example, a hospital (subrecipient) may receive a federal award from a university (pass-through entity) to conduct research.

EXHIBIT 17-1
COMPLIANCE SUPPLEMENT
COMPLIANCE REQUIREMENTS
(NOT-FOR-PROFIT ORGANIZATION)

ACTIVITIES ALLOWED OR UNALLOWED

The specific requirements for activities allowed or unallowed are unique to each federal program and are found in the laws, regulations, and provisions of contract or grant agreements pertaining to the program. For programs listed in the Compliance Supplement, the specific requirements can be found in Part 4 of the Compliance Supplement. This type of compliance requirement specifies the activities that can or cannot be funded under a specific program. The audit objective for this compliance requirement is to determine whether federal awards were expended only for allowable activities.

ALLOWABLE COSTS/COST PRINCIPLES

This compliance requirement relates to the applicability of OMB Cost Principles Circulars. The compliance requirements for allowable costs and cost principles contained in the Compliance Supplement are based on the following:

- OMB Circular A-21 (Cost Principles for Educational Institutions)
- OMB Circular A-122 (Cost Principles for Non-Profit Organizations)

Not-for-profit organizations are subject to OMB Circular A-122, except those not-for-profit organizations listed in Attachment C of OMB Circular A-122. (Not-for-profit organizations listed in Attachment C are not subject to OMB Circular A-122 but are subject to the standards issued by the Cost Accounting Standards Board [48 CFR part 99] and the commercial cost principles contained in the Federal Acquisition Regulation [FAR]). All institutions of higher education are subject to the cost principles contained in OMB Circular A-21. The cost principles applicable to a not-for-profit organization apply to all federal awards an entity receives, regardless of whether the awards are received directly from the federal government or indirectly through a pass-through entity. The Circulars describe selected cost items, allowable and unallowable costs, and standard methodologies for calculating indirect costs rates (e.g., methodologies used to recover facilities and administrative costs [F&A] at institutions of higher education). The cost principles articulated in the Circulars are in most cases substantially identical, but a few differences do exist. These differences are necessary because of the nature of the federal/state/local/non-profit organization relationship, the programs administered, and the breadth of services offered by some grantees and not others.

The Compliance Supplement provides an excellent summary of when costs are generally allowed or unallowed under each of the Circulars listed above. In addition, it provides the following general criteria that affect the allowability of costs under federal awards:

- Costs must be reasonable and necessary for the performance and administration of federal awards.

- Costs must be allocable to the federal awards under the provisions of OMB's Cost Principles Circulars. A cost is allocable to a particular cost objective (e.g., a specific function, program, project, or department) if the goods or services involved are charged or assigned to such cost objective in accordance with relative benefits received.

- Costs must be given consistent treatment through application of those generally accepted accounting principles appropriate to the circumstances. A cost may not be assigned to a federal award as a direct cost if any other cost incurred for the same purpose in like circumstances was allocated to the federal award as an indirect cost.

- Costs must conform to any limitations or exclusions set forth in the Circulars, federal laws, state or local laws, sponsored agreements, or other governing regulations as to types or amounts of cost items.

- Costs must be net of all applicable credits that result from transactions that reduce or offset direct or indirect costs. Examples of such transactions include purchase discounts, rebates or allowances, recoveries or indemnities on losses, insurance refunds or rebates, and adjustments for overpayments or erroneous charges.

- Costs must be documented in accordance with OMB Circular A-110 for not-for-profit organizations.

Indirect costs are an important component of costs that are allowed to be recovered under federal awards programs. Indirect costs are those costs that benefit common activities and, therefore, cannot be readily assigned to a specific direct cost objective or project.

To recover indirect costs, not-for-profit organizations must prepare indirect cost rate proposals (IDCRPs) in accordance with the guidelines provided in OMB's Circulars. IDCRPs are submitted to the federal cognizant agency for indirect cost negotiation for approval.

Indirect costs at non-profit organizations generally include general administrative costs (e.g., the president's office, payroll, general accounting) and facility costs (e.g., rental costs, operations and maintenance, interest expense) that are not treated as direct costs.

Indirect costs at institutions of higher education include the following categories: building and equipment depreciation or use allowance, operation and maintenance expenses, interest expenses, general administrative expenses, departmental administration expenses, library expenses, and student administration expenses.

The indirect cost proposals prepared by institutions of higher education and other nonprofit organizations are based on the most current financial data supported by the organization's accounting system and audited financial statements. These indirect cost proposals can be used either to establish predetermined or fixed indirect cost rates or to establish or finalize provisional rates.

CASH MANAGEMENT

This compliance requirement focuses on the minimal of the amount of time that a not-for-profit organization has cash on hand that has been received from a federal agency for program expenses.

- Not-for-profit organizations that are funded on a reimbursement basis must expend the program costs before requesting reimbursement from the federal government.

- Not-for-profit organizations that are advanced funds must follow procedures to minimize the time elapsing between the transfer of funds from the U.S. Treasury and the disbursement of those funds. When advance payment procedures are used, recipients must establish similar procedures for subrecipients. Pass-through entities are required to establish reasonable procedures to ensure receipt of reports on subrecipients' cash balances and cash disbursements in sufficient time to enable the pass-through entities to submit complete and accurate cash transactions reports to the federal awarding agency or pass-through entity. Pass-through entities must monitor their subrecipients' cash draw-downs to assure that subrecipients conform substantially to the same standards of timing and amount as apply to the pass-through entity. Interest earned by not-for-profit entities on federal fund balances is required to be remitted to the Department of Health and Human Services.

DAVIS–BACON ACT

When required by the Davis–Bacon Act or by the federal Department of Labor, all laborers and mechanics employed by contractors or subcontractors to work on construction contracts in excess of $2,000 financed by federal assistance funds must be paid wages not less than those established for the locality of the project (prevailing wage rates) by the Department of Labor.

ELIGIBILITY

The specific requirements for eligibility are unique to each federal program and are found in the laws, regulations, and provisions of contract or grant agreements pertaining to the program. For programs listed in the Compliance Supplement, the specific eligibility requirements are in Part 4 of the Compliance Supplement. This compliance requirement specifies the criteria for determining the individuals, groups of individuals, or subrecipients that can participate in the program and the amounts for which they qualify.

> **OBSERVATION:** Many not-for-profit organizations use computerized systems to test for and determine whether they are meeting their eligibility requirements. The audit procedures contained in the Compliance Supplement focus specifically on these computerized systems. Auditors should also consider whether the Year 2000 Issue could have an impact on computerized eligibility calculations.

EQUIPMENT AND REAL PROPERTY MANAGEMENT

Title to equipment acquired by a not-for-profit organization with federal awards vests with the not-for-profit organization. *Equipment* is defined as tangible nonexpendable property charged directly to the award and having a useful life of more than one year and an acquisition cost of $5,000 or more per unit. However, consistent with a not-for-profit organization's policy, lower limits may be established.

Not-for-profit organizations are required to follow the provisions of OMB Circular A-110. Equipment records must be maintained, a physical inventory of equipment must be taken at least once every two years and reconciled to the equipment records, and an appropriate control system must be used to safeguard equipment. The equipment also must be adequately maintained. When equipment with a current per-unit fair market value in excess of $5,000 is no longer needed for a federal program, it may be retained or sold with the federal agency having a right to a proportionate (percent of federal participation in the cost of the original project) amount of the current fair market value.

MATCHING, LEVEL OF EFFORT, EARMARKING

Matching, level of effort, and *earmarking* are defined as follows:

- Matching (or cost-sharing) includes requirements to provide contributions (usually non-federal) of a specified amount or percentage to match federal awards. Matching may be in the form of cash or in-kind contributions.
- Level of effort includes requirements for (a) a specified level of service to be provided from period to period, (b) a specified level of expenditures from non-federal or federal sources for specified activities to be maintained from period to period, and (c) federal funds to supplement and not supplant non-federal funding of services.
- Earmarking includes requirements that specify the minimum and/or maximum amount or percentage of the program's funding that must be or may be used for specified activities, including funds provided to subrecipients.

The specific requirements for matching, level of effort, and earmarking are unique to each federal program and are found in the laws, regulations, and provisions of contract or grant agreements pertaining to the program. For programs listed in the Compliance Supplement, the specific requirements can be found in Part 4 of the Compliance Supplement. However, for matching, Circular A-110 provides detailed criteria for acceptable costs and contributions.

The following are the basic criteria for acceptable matching:

- Are verifiable from the organization's records.
- Are not included as contributions for any other federally assisted project or program, unless specifically allowed by federal program laws and regulations.

- Are necessary and reasonable for proper and efficient accomplish-ment of project or program objectives.
- Are allowed under the applicable cost principles.
- Are not paid by the federal government under another award, except where authorized by federal statute to be allowable for cost-sharing or matching.
- Are provided for in the approved budget when required by the federal awarding agency.
- Conform to other applicable provisions of Circular A-110 and the laws, regulations, and provisions of contract or grant agreements applicable to the program.

PERIOD OF AVAILABILITY OF FEDERAL FUNDS

This compliance requirement pertains to the situation where a federal award program may specify a time period during which the not-for-profit organization may use the federal funds. In these cases, a not-for-profit organization may charge to the award only those costs resulting from obligations incurred during the funding period and any pre-award costs authorized by the federal awarding agency. Also, if authorized by the federal program, unobligated balances may be carried over and charged for obligations of the subsequent funding period.

PROCUREMENT AND SUSPENSION AND DEBARMENT

Not-for-profit organizations must use procurement procedures that conform to applicable federal law and regulations and standards identified in OMB Circular A-110. Basically, not-for-profit organization must follow the same federal regulations applicable to procurement as are used by federal agencies themselves.

In addition to these guidelines, not-for-profit organizations must follow additional requirements relating to suspension and debarment:

Suspension and Debarment

Not-for-profit organizations are prohibited from contracting with or making subawards under covered transactions to parties that are suspended or debarred or whose principals are suspended or debarred. Covered transactions include procurement contracts for goods or services equal to or in excess of $100,000 and all nonprocurement transactions (e.g., subawards to subrecipients). Contractors receiving individual awards for $100,000 or more and all subrecipients must certify that the organization and its principals are not suspended or debarred. Not-for-profit organizations may rely upon the certification unless they know that the certification is erroneous. Not-for-profit organizations may, but are not required to, check for suspended and de-barred parties which are listed in the List of Parties Excluded from Federal Procurement or Nonprocurement Programs, issued by the federal General Services Administration (GSA).

PROGRAM INCOME

Program income is gross income received that is directly generated by the federally funded project during the grant period. If authorized by federal regulations or the grant agreement, costs incident to the generation of program income may be deducted from gross income to determine program income. Examples of program income include fees for services performed, the use or rental of real or personal property acquired with grant funds, the sale of commodities or items fabricated under a grant agreement, and payments of principal and interest on loans made with grant funds.

There are three ways for a not-for-profit organization to use program income. It may be:

- Deducted from program outlays,
- Added to the project budget, or
- Used to meet matching requirements.

However, the not-for-profit organization generally does not have a choice in how program income is used. Unless specified in the federal awarding agency regulations or the terms and conditions of the award, program income is required to be deducted from program outlays. However, for research and development activities by colleges and universities and other not-for-profit organizations, the default method is to add program income to the project budget.

REAL PROPERTY ACQUISITION AND RELOCATION ASSISTANCE

These compliance requirements relate to the equitable treatment of persons displaced by federally assisted programs from their homes, businesses, or farms. These types of relocation are rarely found in federal programs administered by not-for-profit organizations. This compliance requirement is far more likely to apply to state and local governments. Nevertheless, information on the requirements is contained in the Compliance Supplement, if needed.

REPORTING

The compliance requirements for reporting fall into three areas:

- Financial reporting
- Performance reporting
- Special reporting

The following sections briefly describe the compliance requirements for each of these three areas.

Financial Reporting

Not-for-profit organizations must report program outlays and program income on a cash basis or an accrual basis, as prescribed by the federal awarding agency. If the federal awarding agency requires accrual information and the organization's accounting records are not normally maintained on the accrual basis, the recipient is not required to convert its accounting system to an accrual basis but may develop such accrual information through analysis. The awarding agency may accept identical information from the recipient in machine-readable format, computer printouts, or electronic outputs in lieu of the prescribed formats. (The open-ended entitlement programs [Appendix 1] require quarterly reports.) The reporting requirements for subrecipients are as specified by the pass-through entity. In many cases, these will be the same as or similar to the following requirements for recipients.

The standard financial reporting forms are as follows:

1. Financial Status Report (FSR) (SF-269)—Recipients use the FSR to report the status of funds for all non-construction projects and for construction projects when the FSR is required in lieu of the SF-271.

2. Request for Advance or Reimbursement (SF-270)—Recipients use the SF-270 to request Treasury advance payments and reimbursements under non-construction programs.

3. Outlay Report and Request for Reimbursement for Construction Programs (SF-271)—Recipients use the SF-271 to request funds for construction projects unless advances or the SF-270 is used.

4. Federal Cash Transaction Report (SF-272)—Recipients use the SF-272 when payment is by advances or reimbursements.

Performance Reporting

Not-for-profit organizations must submit performance reports at least annually but not more frequently than quarterly. Performance reports generally contain, for each award, brief information on each of the following:

1. A comparison of actual accomplishments with the goals and objectives established for the period

2. Reasons why established goals were not met, if appropriate

3. Other pertinent information, including, when appropriate, analysis and explanation of cost overruns or high unit costs

> **OBSERVATION:** Performance reporting is an area that is likely to have specific compliance requirements incorporated into the award contract. Auditors should be aware of these requirements in order to consider whether they need to test for compliance with these requirements.

Special Reporting

Not-for-profit organizations may be required to submit other reporting that the federal agency may use for such purposes as allocating program funding.

SUBRECIPIENT MONITORING

As a result of the revision of Circular A-133, a not-for-profit organization has additional responsibilities as to the monitoring of subrecipients to which it passes federal program funds. The chapter of this Guide titled "Subrecipient

Considerations" provides specific information, particularly about a pass-through entity's requirement to issue management decisions as part of its monitoring activities.

A pass-through entity's responsibilities for subrecipient monitoring can be categorized as follows:

- Identifying to the subrecipient the federal award information (e.g., CFDA title and number, award name, name of federal agency) and applicable compliance requirements
- Monitoring the subrecipient's activities to provide reasonable assurance that the subrecipient administers federal awards in compliance with federal requirements
- Ensuring that required audits are performed and requiring the subrecipient to take prompt corrective action on any audit findings
- Evaluating the impact of subrecipient activities on the pass-through entity's ability to comply with applicable federal regulations.

Factors such as the size of awards, percentage of the total program's funds awarded to subrecipients, and the complexity of the compliance requirements may influence the extent of monitoring procedures.

Monitoring activities may take various forms, such as reviewing reports submitted by the subrecipient; performing site visits to the subrecipient to review financial and programmatic records and observe operations; arranging for agreed-upon procedures engagements for certain aspects of subrecipient activities, such as eligibility determinations; reviewing the subrecipient's single audit or program-specific audit results; and evaluating audit findings and the subrecipient's corrective action plan.

SPECIAL TESTS AND PROVISIONS

The specific requirements for special tests and provisions are unique to each federal program and are found in the laws, regulations, and provisions of contract or grant agreements pertaining to the program. For programs listed in the Compliance Supplement, the compliance requirements, audit objectives, and suggested audit procedures for this type of compliance requirement can be found in Part 4 of the Compliance Supplement

For programs not listed in the Compliance Supplement, the auditor should review the program's contract and grant agreements and referenced laws and regulations to identify the compliance requirements and develop the audit objectives and audit procedures for Special Tests and Provisions that could have a direct and material effect on a major program. The auditor should also ask the not-for-profit organization to help identify and understand any Special Tests and Provisions.

For the auditor to determine whether Circular A-133 requirements will apply to an entity to which federal funds are passed, a subrecipient must be distinguished from a vendor.

A *vendor* is a dealer, distributor, merchant, or other seller providing a recipient or subrecipient with goods or services that are related to the administrative support of a federal program.

Circular A-133 describes the following characteristics of a vendor:

- Vendors provide goods and services within normal business operations.
- Vendors provide similar goods or services to many different purchasers.
- Vendors operate in a competitive environment.
- Vendors are not subject to the program compliance requirements of the federal program.
- Vendors provide goods or services that are ancillary to the operation of the federal program.

The substance of the relationship is more important than the form of the relationship in the determination of whether a particular entity is a subrecipient or a vendor. There may be unusual circumstances or exceptions to the distinguishing characteristics listed above. If the determination is not clear, the recipient organization and/or its auditor should consider seeking the guidance of the cognizant agency or the federal grantor agency that provided the award.

CIRCULAR A-133 REQUIREMENTS FOR SUBRECIPIENTS

Circular A-133 provides guidance to pass-through entities relative to subrecipients. A not-for-profit organization pass-through entity should perform the following for the federal awards it makes:

- Identify federal awards made by informing each subrecipient of the CFDA title and number, award name and number, award year, if the award is research and development, and the name of the federal agency. When some of this information is not available, the best information available should be used to describe the federal award.
- Advise subrecipients of requirements imposed on them by federal laws, regulations, and the provisions of contracts or grant agreements as well as any supplemental requirements imposed by the pass-through entity.
- Monitor the activities of subrecipients as necessary to ensure that federal awards are used for authorized purposes in com-

pliance with laws, regulations, and the provisions of contracts or grant agreements and that performance goals are achieved.

- Ensure that not-for-profit subrecipients expending $300,000 or more in federal awards during the subrecipient's fiscal year have met the audit requirements of Circular A-133.

- Issue a management decision on audit findings within six months after receipt of the subrecipient's audit report and ensure that the subrecipient takes appropriate and timely corrective action.

- Consider whether subrecipient audits necessitate adjustment of the pass-through entity's own records.

- Require each subrecipient to permit the pass-through entity and auditors to have access to the records and financial statements as necessary for the pass-through entity to comply with Circular A-133.

- Keep subrecipient's report submissions (or other written notification when the subrecipient is not required to submit a reporting package) on file for three years from the date of receipt of the report.

Circular A-133 also provides guidance about the "management decision" described above. The management decision must clearly state whether or not the audit finding is sustained; the reasons for the decision; and the expected auditee action to repay disallowed costs, make financial adjustments, or take other action. If the auditee has not completed corrective action, a timetable for follow-up should be given. Before issuing the management decision, the pass-through entity may request additional information or documentation from the auditee, including a request that the documentation be audited, as a way of mitigating disallowed costs. The management decision should also describe any appeal process available to the auditee. Management's decision should reference the numbers that the auditor assigns to each audit family.

> **OBSERVATION:** The pass-through entity is acting similarly to a federal agency in issuing management decisions to subrecipients.

> **OBSERVATION:** The recipient organization's auditor should be aware of the recipient's potential liability for activities of the subrecipients. Auditors can provide a valuable service to their clients by making suggestions to improve the system the recipient organization uses to monitor subrecipients. The auditor's recommendations may limit the financial exposure of the recipient organization.

SOP 98-3 lists the following monitoring procedures that may be performed by recipient organizations:

- Review grant applications submitted by subrecipients to determine if:
  - Applications are filed and approved in a timely manner.
  - Each application contains a condition that the subrecipient comply with the federal requirements set by the federal grantor agency.
- Establish control policies and procedures to provide reasonable assurance that:
  - Funds are disbursed to subrecipients only on an as-needed basis.
  - Funds are disbursed to subrecipients only on the basis of approved, properly completed reports submitted on a timely basis.
  - Refunds due from subrecipients are billed and collected in a timely manner.
  - Subrecipients and others receiving the funds meet eligibility requirements.
- Review financial and technical reports received from subrecipients on a timely basis, and investigate all unusual items.
- Review submitted audit reports to evaluate for completeness and for compliance with applicable laws and regulations.
- Evaluate audit findings, issue appropriate management decisions, if necessary, and determine if an acceptable plan for corrective action has been prepared and implemented.
- Review previously detected deficiencies and determine if corrective action was taken.

Recipient organizations may use the above list of procedures as a guide, but the extent of monitoring procedures will vary depending on the circumstances of the particular subrecipient and must be done within the specific framework for issuing management decisions that is found in Circular A-133.

> **OBSERVATION:** When establishing a system to monitor subrecipients, the recipient organization should adopt the role of the cognizant agency and treat the subrecipient as the actual recipient organization.

Consider the following two descriptions of subrecipients:

1. The subrecipient is a large, well-known and financially sound not-for-profit organization. It has experience operating in the public eye and has a long and diverse history as both a recipient and a subrecipient of federal awards. It has a fully staffed finance department; well-designed, well-functioning internal controls; and a separate contracts management unit.

2. The subrecipient is a small, grass-roots organization. Its program manager spends a few days per week keeping the checkbook and posting accounting entries into an off-the-shelf software package, which has not yet been able to produce usable financial statements. This is the first contract the subrecipient has signed involving a federal award program.

The subrecipient monitoring system established for subrecipient 1 probably will be different from the system established for subrecipient 2. One additional consideration in this example, however, is the reliance on a subrecipient's Circular A-133 audit report as part of a recipient organization's monitoring of a subrecipient. In example 1 above, the program that the recipient organization passes through to the large organization may not be considered a major federal program, and it may receive very little audit attention as a result. On the other hand, assuming the organization in example 2 is required to have a Circular A-133 audit, the program that is passed through to it from the recipient organization is more likely to be audited as a major federal program, subject to far more extensive testing by its internal auditor than the program in example 1.

Responsibilities of the Recipient Organization's Auditor

The auditor of the recipient organization should develop an understanding of the policies and procedures used to monitor subrecipients and should determine if they have been placed in operation. The auditor should also assess the level of control risk by evaluating the effectiveness of the recipient organization's control policies and procedures for preventing or detecting subrecipient noncompliance with applicable laws and regulations.

When awards to subrecipients are part of a major program, the auditor should test the recipient organization's control policies and procedures used to monitor subrecipients. The tests of controls may include inquiry, observation, and inspection of documentation, or a reperformance by the auditor of some or all of the monitoring procedures identified above as the recipient organization's responsibilities. The nature and extent of the tests performed will vary depending on the auditor's assessment of inherent risk, understanding of the control structure policies and procedures, and professional judgment.

> **OBSERVATION:** The extent of the tests will vary depending on
> the number of subrecipients that received funds and the dollar
> amount of federal funds that flow through to subrecipients.

The recipient organization's auditor does not have to include the
instances of noncompliance reported in a subrecipient's audit in its
own audit report. However, as discussed above, the auditor should
verify that the recipient has resolved the subrecipient's audit findings directly related to the recipient organization's programs. The
auditor should consider the effects on a major program of instances
of noncompliance in subrecipient audit reports. The effects of reportable conditions, including material weaknesses, in the recipient
organization's control policies and procedures for monitoring subrecipients also should be considered. In addition, the requirements of
Circular A-133 relative to the management decision should be followed by the pass-through entity.

Recipient organizations do not always receive all subrecipient
audit reports in time to incorporate the results into their own audits.
Circular A-133 does not require that the reports for the recipient
organization and subrecipients be issued at the same time; rather, it
requires the recipient organization to have control policies and procedures to ensure that subrecipient reports are received and that
corrective action, if necessary, is taken within six months after receipt of the subrecipient's audit report.

A subrecipient's audit report may cover a previous period. In
choosing whether to use such a report to meet the above requirements, the auditor should consider the period covered by the report
and its date of issuance. As long as a subrecipient's audit report is
current, it need not cover the same period as the recipient organization's report. If the subawards are not material to the financial
statements and the major programs of the recipient organization, the
recipient organization and its auditor should be able to rely on the
subrecipient's audit cycle, even if it does not coincide with the
recipient organization's fiscal year.

For-Profit Organizations as Subrecipients

Circular A-133 does not establish audit requirements for for-profit
subrecipients. Because audit requirements are not specified, the monitoring procedures over for-profit subrecipients become more important and is the responsibility of the pass-through entity. The contract
with the for-profit subrecipient should include applicable administrative, general, and specific compliance requirements. Also, the
recipient organization should consider establishing appropriate audit requirements and including them in contracts with for-profit
subrecipients. Audit requirements that recipient organizations may
consider include the following:

- Pre-award and post-award audits to determine compliance with applicable laws and regulations
- Audit procedures and monitoring systems similar to those used when vendors are responsible for compliance

The recipient may require the for-profit subrecipient to obtain an audit that provides adequate compliance assurance for the recipient organization's programs. In this situation, the auditor's responsibilities are the same as those for a not-for-profit subrecipient except that the audit obtained is substituted for the Circular A-133 audit.

When the for-profit subrecipient has not had an audit, the recipient organization's auditor is responsible for obtaining reasonable assurance that the for-profit subrecipient materially complied with applicable laws and regulations. The auditor may obtain compliance assurances by reviewing the not-for-profit's records and monitoring procedures, performing additional procedures to determine compliance such as testing the for-profit subrecipient's records, or performing a combination of procedures. In addition, the recipient organization's auditor is responsible for determining whether the recipient organization's system for monitoring subrecipients is adequate and whether subrecipient noncompliance necessitates adjustment of the recipient organization's records.

Responsibility for Compliance of Vendors

In most cases, under Circular A-133 the recipient organization's responsibility for vendors is only to ensure that the procurement, receipt, and payment for goods and services comply with laws and regulations. Compliance requirements normally do not pass through to vendors.

However, some transactions may be structured in such a manner that the vendor also may be responsible for compliance or that the vendor's records will have to be reviewed to determine compliance. In these cases, the recipient organization is responsible for ensuring vendors' compliance. Methods to ensure this compliance include pre-award audits, monitoring during the contracts, and post-award audits. Audits may be performed or procured by the recipient organization, or the terms and conditions of the contract may require the vendor to procure the audit.

When necessary, contracts with vendors should include compliance requirements, audit and monitoring requirements, or the recipient's right to audit the vendor. Including the compliance requirements establishes a benchmark, and including audit and monitoring requirements and the right to audit gives the recipient the authority to access a vendor's records for monitoring or to obtain audit assurance.

When the vendor is responsible for compliance or when the vendor's records must be reviewed to determine compliance, the auditor is still responsible for determining vendor compliance. Circular A-133 specifies that when these types of vendor transactions relate to a major federal program, the scope of the audit should include determining whether these transactions are in compliance with laws, regulations, and the provisions of contracts or grant agreements.

When the auditor cannot obtain compliance assurances from reviewing the recipient organization's records and through monitoring procedures, the auditor will need to perform additional procedures. These procedures may include testing the vendor's records or relying on work performed by the vendor's independent auditor.

Foreign Subrecipients

Generally, Circular A-133 does not apply to non-U.S.-based organizations expending federal awards either directly as a recipient or indirectly as a subrecipient. (See the chapter titled "Planning for a Circular A-133 Audit" for more details.) According to SOP 98-3, the responsibilities that a pass-through entity and its auditor have for a non-U.S.-based entity are the same as those for a for-profit subrecipient.

SUMMARY

This chapter discusses the requirements of Circular A-133 for testing and reporting on compliance with laws and regulations. Along with the internal control considerations discussed in the preceding chapter, these compliance requirements represent significant additional procedures that the auditor must perform during an audit in accordance with Circular A-133. Any auditor conducting a Circular A-133 audit should review and understand them thoroughly.

CHAPTER 18
REPORTING UNDER CIRCULAR A-133

CONTENTS

CHAPTER 18
REPORTING UNDER CIRCULAR A-133

CROSS-REFERENCES

2001 MILLER NOT-FOR-PROFIT ORGANIZATION AUDITS: Chapter 10, "Reporting"

2001 MILLER SINGLE AUDITS: Chapter 10, "Reports"

2001 MILLER AUDIT PROCEDURES: Chapter 22, "Auditor's Reports"

There are significant additional reporting requirements under Circular A-133 that are not required in an audit of financial statements. This chapter fully explains these requirements.

Basic Reporting Requirements

This section describes the basic reporting requirements Circular A-133.

The reports and other documents required in an audit in accordance with Circular A-133 are as follows:

- Financial
  - Opinion on the basic financial statements
  - Supplementary schedule of expenditures of federal awards (with auditor's opinion in relation to the basic financial statements as a whole)
- Internal Control
  - Report on internal control at the financial statement level (Yellow Book) and on internal control related to major programs
- Compliance
  - Report on compliance with laws, regulations, and the provisions of contracts and grant agreements noncompliance with

which could have a direct and material effect at the financial statement level (Yellow Book). This report must contain an opinion as to whether the not-for-profit organization complied with laws, regulations, and the provisions of contracts or grant agreements, noncompliance with which could have a direct and material effect on each major federal program

- Schedule of findings and questioned costs, consisting of the following three components:

  — A summary of the auditor's results

  — Findings relating to the financial statements which are required to be reported in accordance with the Yellow Book

  — Findings and questioned costs for federal awards

Each of these requirements is described more fully later in this chapter.

Audit Due Dates

Circular A-133 requires that the audit be completed and the reporting package and data collection form (described below) be submitted within nine months after the end of the audit period, unless a longer period is agreed to in advance by the cognizant or oversight agency for audit. In addition, the reporting package must be submitted within 30 days after receipt of the auditor's reports even if this occurs in a period shorter than nine months after year end.

For fiscal years beginning on or before June 30, 1998, the audit must be completed and the data collection form and reporting package described below) must be submitted within the earlier of 30 days after receipt of the auditor's report(s), or 13 months after the end of the audit period.

Data Collection Form

Circular A-133 requires that the not-for-profit organization prepare a data collection form (signed by a senior official, such as the chief executive officer, chief financial officer, or director of finance) which summarizes some of the key aspects of the Circular A-133 audit. Parts II and III of the form are completed by the independent auditor, who must also sign the form.

The basic requirements for the data collection form are contained on Circular A-133, although OMB has separately prescribed a form that must be used, along with instructions for its completion. This form and its instructions are provided in Exhibit 18-1. (The form and its instructions are also available under the filenames FGD11 and FGD12, respectively, on the disc that accompanies this Guide.) In the

EXHIBIT 18-1
DATA COLLECTION FORM

OMB No. 0348-0057

FORM **SF-SAC**
(8-97)

U.S. DEPARTMENT OF COMMERCE - BUREAU OF THE CENSUS
ACTING AS COLLECTING AGENT FOR
OFFICE OF MANAGEMENT AND BUDGET

Data Collection Form for Reporting on
AUDITS OF STATES, LOCAL GOVERNMENTS, AND NON-PROFIT ORGANIZATIONS

▶ Complete this form, as required by OMB Circular A-133, "Audits of States, Local Governments, and Non-Profit Organizations."

Single Audit Clearinghouse
1201 E. 10th Street
Jeffersonville, IN 47132

GENERAL INFORMATION *(To be completed by auditee, except for Item 7)*	
1. Fiscal year ending date for this submission Month / Day / Year	**2.** Type of Circular A-133 audit ₁☐ Single audit ₂☐ Program-specific audit
3. Audit period covered ₁☐ Annual ₃☐ Other – Months ₂☐ Biennial	**FEDERAL GOVERNMENT USE ONLY** | **4.** Date received by Federal clearinghouse

5. Employer Identification Number (EIN)

a. Auditee EIN ☐☐☐☐☐☐☐☐☐   **b.** Are multiple EINs covered in this report? ₁☐ Yes ₂☐ No

6. AUDITEE INFORMATION	**7. AUDITOR INFORMATION** *(To be completed by auditor)*
a. Auditee name	**a.** Auditor name
b. Auditee address *(Number and street)* City State ZIP Code	**b.** Auditor address *(Number and street)* City State ZIP Code
c. Auditee contact Name Title	**c.** Auditor contact Name Title
d. Auditee contact telephone ( ) –	**d.** Auditor contact telephone ( ) –
e. Auditee contact FAX *(Optional)* ( ) –	**e.** Auditor contact FAX *(Optional)* ( ) –
f. Auditee contact E-mail *(Optional)*	**f.** Auditor contact E-mail *(Optional)*
g. AUDITEE CERTIFICATION STATEMENT – This is to certify that, to the best of my knowledge and belief, the auditee has: (1) Engaged an auditor to perform an audit in accordance with the provisions of OMB Circular A-133 for the period described in Part I, Items 1 and 3; (2) the auditor has completed such audit and presented a signed audit report which states that the audit was conducted in accordance with the provisions of the Circular; and, (3) the information included in **Parts I, II, and III** of this data collection form is accurate and complete. I declare that the foregoing is true and correct.	**g. AUDITOR STATEMENT –** The data elements and information included in this form are limited to those prescribed by OMB Circular A-133. The information included in Parts II and III of the form, except for Part III, Items 5 and 6, was transferred from the auditor's report(s) for the period described in Part I, Items 1 and 3, and is **not a substitute** for such reports. The auditor has not performed any auditing procedures since the date of the auditor's report(s). A copy of the reporting package required by OMB Circular A-133, which includes the complete auditor's report(s), is available in its entirety from the auditee at the address provided in Part I of this form. As required by OMB Circular A-133, the information in **Parts II and III** of this form was entered in this form by the auditor based on information included in the reporting package. The auditor has not performed any additional auditing procedures in connection with the completion of this form.

Signature of certifying official   Date
                    Month / Day / Year
 	
Name/Title of certifying official
	Signature of auditor Date
	                    Month / Day / Year

EIN: ☐☐☐☐☐☐☐☐☐

GENERAL INFORMATION – Continued

8. Indicate whether the auditee has either a Federal cognizant or oversight agency for audit. *(Mark (X) one box)*
  ₁☐ Cognizant agency   ₂☐ Oversight agency

9. Name of Federal cognizant or oversight agency for audit *(Mark (X) one box)*

01☐ African Development Foundation	83☐ Federal Emergency Management Agency	16☐ Justice	08☐ Peace Corps
02☐ Agency for International Development	34☐ Federal Mediation and Conciliation Service	17☐ Labor	59☐ Small Business Administration
10☐ Agriculture	39☐ General Services Administration	43☐ National Aeronautics and Space Administration	96☐ Social Security Administration
11☐ Commerce	93☐ Health and Human Services	89☐ National Archives and Records Administraton	19☐ State
94☐ Corporation for National and Community Service	14☐ Housing and Urban Development	05☐ National Endowment for the Arts	20☐ Transportation
12☐ Defense	03☐ Institute for Museum Services	06☐ National Endowment for the Humanities	21☐ Treasury
84☐ Education	04☐ Inter-American Foundation	47☐ National Science Foundation	82☐ United States Information Agency
81☐ Energy	15☐ Interior	07☐ Office of National Drug Control Policy	64☐ Veterans Affairs
86☐ Environmental Protection Agency			☐ Other – *Specify:*

FINANCIAL STATEMENTS *(To be completed by auditor)*

1. Type of audit report *(Mark (X) one box)*
  ₁☐ Unqualified opinion   ₂☐ Qualified opinion   ₃☐ Adverse opinion   ₄☐ Disclaimer of opinion

2. Is a "going concern" explanatory paragraph included in the audit report?   ₁☐ Yes   ₂☐ No

3. Is a reportable condition disclosed?   ₁☐ Yes   ₂☐ No – *SKIP to Item 5*

4. Is any reportable condition reported as a material weakness?   ₁☐ Yes   ₂☐ No

5. Is a material noncompliance disclosed?   ₁☐ Yes   ₂☐ No

FEDERAL PROGRAMS *(To be completed by auditor)*

1. Type of audit report on major program compliance
  ₁☐ Unqualified opinion   ₂☐ Qualified opinion   ₃☐ Adverse opinion   ₄☐ Disclaimer of opinion

2. What is the dollar threshold to distinguish Type A and Type B programs §___ .520(b)?

  $

3. Did the auditee qualify as a low-risk auditee (§___ .530)?
  ₁☐ Yes   ₂☐ No

4. Are there any audit findings required to be reported under §___ .510(a)?
  ₁☐ Yes   ₂☐ No

5. Which Federal Agencies are required to receive the reporting package? *(Mark (X) all that apply)*

01☐ African Development Foundation	83☐ Federal Emergency Management Agency	16☐ Justice	08☐ Peace Corps
02☐ Agency for International Development	34☐ Federal Mediation and Conciliation Service	17☐ Labor	59☐ Small Business Administration
10☐ Agriculture	39☐ General Services Administration	43☐ National Aeronautics and Space Administration	96☐ Social Security Administration
11☐ Commerce	93☐ Health and Human Services	89☐ National Archives and Records Administraton	19☐ State
94☐ Corporation for National and Community Service	14☐ Housing and Urban Development	05☐ National Endowment for the Arts	20☐ Transportation
12☐ Defense	03☐ Institute for Museum Services	06☐ National Endowment for the Humanities	21☐ Treasury
84☐ Education	04☐ Inter-American Foundation	47☐ National Science Foundation	82☐ United States Information Agency
81☐ Energy	15☐ Interior	07☐ Office of National Drug Control Policy	64☐ Veterans Affairs
86☐ Environmental Protection Agency			00☐ None / ☐ Other – *Specify:*

FORM SF-SAC (8-97)

Page 3

EIN:

FEDERAL PROGRAMS – Continued

6. FEDERAL AWARDS EXPENDED DURING FISCAL YEAR

CFDA number[1] (a)	Name of Federal program (b)	Amount expended (c)
		$
		$
		$
		$
		$
		$
		$
		$
		$
		$

TOTAL FEDERAL AWARDS EXPENDED → $

7. AUDIT FINDINGS AND QUESTIONED COSTS

Major program (a)	Type of compliance requirement[2] (b)	Amount of questioned costs (c)	Internal control findings[3] (d)	Audit finding reference number(s) (e)
1 ☐ Yes 2 ☐ No		$	1 ☐ A 3 ☐ C 2 ☐ B	
1 ☐ Yes 2 ☐ No		$	1 ☐ A 3 ☐ C 2 ☐ B	
1 ☐ Yes 2 ☐ No		$	1 ☐ A 3 ☐ C 2 ☐ B	
1 ☐ Yes 2 ☐ No		$	1 ☐ A 3 ☐ C 2 ☐ B	
1 ☐ Yes 2 ☐ No		$	1 ☐ A 3 ☐ C 2 ☐ B	
1 ☐ Yes 2 ☐ No		$	1 ☐ A 3 ☐ C 2 ☐ B	
1 ☐ Yes 2 ☐ No		$	1 ☐ A 3 ☐ C 2 ☐ B	
1 ☐ Yes 2 ☐ No		$	1 ☐ A 3 ☐ C 2 ☐ B	
1 ☐ Yes 2 ☐ No		$	1 ☐ A 3 ☐ C 2 ☐ B	

IF ADDITIONAL LINES ARE NEEDED, PLEASE PHOTOCOPY THIS PAGE. ATTACH ADDITIONAL PAGES TO THE FORM, AND SEE INSTRUCTIONS

[1] Or other identifying number when the Catalog of Federal Domestic Assistance (CFDA) number is not available.

[2] Type of compliance requirement *(Enter the letter(s) of all that apply to audit findings and questioned costs reported for each Federal program.)*

A. Activities allowed or unallowed	G. Matching, level of effort, earmarking	L. Reporting
B. Allowable costs/cost principles	H. Period of availability of funds	M. Subrecipient monitoring
C. Cash management	I. Procurement	N. Special tests and provisions
D. Davis - Bacon Act	J. Program income	O. None
E. Eligibility	K. Real property acquisition and	
F. Equipment and real property management	relocation assistance	

[3] Type of internal control findings *(Mark (X) all that apply)*

A. Material weaknesses   B. Reportable conditions   C. None reported

INSTRUCTIONS FOR COMPLETION OF SF-SAC, REPORTING ON AUDITS OF STATES, LOCAL GOVERNMENTS, AND NON-PROFIT ORGANIZATIONS

According to the Paperwork Reduction Act of 1995, no persons are required to respond to a collection of information unless it displays a valid OMB control number. The valid OMB control number for this information collection is OMB No. 0348-0057. The time required to complete this data collection form is estimated to average 30 hours for large auditees (i.e., auditees most likely to administer a large number of Federal awards) and 6 hours for all other auditees. These amounts reflect estimates of reporting burden on both auditees and auditors relating to the data collection form, including the time to review instructions, obtain the needed data, and complete and review the information collection.

Office of Management and Budget (OMB) Circular A-133, "Audits of States, Local Governments, and Non-Profit Organizations," requires non-Federal entities that expend $300,000 or more in a year in Federal awards to have an audit conducted in accordance with the Circular.

Circular A-133 (§__. 320(b)) requires auditees to submit a data collection form, along with other specified reports, to the Federal clearinghouse designated by OMB (currently the U.S. Bureau of the Census) at the completion of each audit.

SUBMISSION TO FEDERAL CLEARINGHOUSE

The data collection form must be completely filled out and signed by both the auditee and auditor. **Submission of anything other than a complete data collection form and reporting package as required by Circular A-133 will be returned to the auditee.**

DESCRIPTION OF THE DATA COLLECTION FORM ITEMS

PART I – GENERAL INFORMATION

The auditee shall complete this section, except for Item 7, and sign the certification statement provided in Item 6 (g).

- **Item 1 – Fiscal Year Ending Date**

  Enter the last day of the entity's fiscal period covered by the audit.

- **Item 2 – Type of Circular A-133 Audit**

  Check the appropriate box. §__.200 of Circular A-133 requires non-Federal entities that expend $300,000 or more in a year in Federal awards to have a single audit conducted in accordance with §__.500, except when they elect to have a program-specific audit conducted in accordance with §__.235.

- **Item 3 – Audit Period Covered**

  Check the appropriate box. Annual audits cover 12 months and Biennial audits cover 24 months. If the audit period covered is neither Annual nor Biennial, mark "Other" and provide the number of months covered in the space provided.

- **Item 4 – Date Received by Federal Clearinghouse**

  Federal Government use only.

- **Item 5 – Employer Identification Number (EIN)**

  (a) Auditee EIN

  Enter the auditee Employer Identification Number (EIN), which is the Taxpayer Identification Number assigned by the Internal Revenue Service (IRS). Also, using the spaces provided, enter the EIN on the top of each page.

  (b) Multiple EINs Covered in the Report

  Check the appropriate box to indicate whether the auditee (or components of an auditee covered by the audit) was assigned more than one EIN by the IRS. (Example: A State-wide audit covers many departments, each of which may have its own separate EIN.) If yes, indicate principal EIN under 5 (a).

- **Item 6 – Auditee Information**

  (g) A senior representative of the auditee (e.g., State controller, director of finance, chief executive officer, chief financial officer) shall sign a statement that the information in the form is accurate and complete as required by §__.320 of Circular A-133. Provide the name and title of the signatory and date of signature.

- **Item 7 – Auditor Information**

  The auditor shall complete this item.

  (a) Enter the name of the auditor that conducted the audit in accordance with Circular A-133. The auditor name may represent a sole practitioner, certified public accounting firm, State auditor, etc. Where multiple auditors or audit organizations are used to conduct the audit work, the auditors should use judgment in determining which auditor's name should be provided in Item 7. The auditor listed in Part I, Item 7 (a) shall be the same auditor that signs the auditor statement in Part I, Item 7 (g) of this form.

- **Item 8 – Cognizant or Oversight Agency for Audit**

  Check the appropriate box. Each auditee has either a Federal cognizant agency for audit or an oversight agency for audit, determined in accordance with §__.400(a) or (b) of Circular A-133.

- **Item 9 – Name of Federal Cognizant or Oversight Agency for Audit**

  Check the appropriate box to indicate the name of the Federal cognizant or oversight agency for audit determined in accordance with §__.400(a) or (b) of Circular A-133.

PART II - FINANCIAL STATEMENTS

The auditor shall complete this section of the form.

SF-SAC(I) (8-97)

CONTINUED ON REVERSE SIDE

INSTRUCTIONS FOR COMPLETION OF SF-SAC, REPORTING ON AUDITS OF STATES, LOCAL GOVERNMENTS, AND NON-PROFIT ORGANIZATIONS – Continued

PART III - FEDERAL PROGRAMS

The auditor shall complete this section of the form.

- **Item 1 – Type of Audit Report on Major Program Compliance**

  If the audit report for one or more major programs is other than unqualified, check boxes 2, 3, or 4, as applicable. For example, if the audit report on major program compliance for an auditee with three major programs includes an unqualified opinion for one program, a qualified opinion for the second program, and a disclaimer of opinion for the third program, then check boxes 2 and 4 but not box 1.

- **Item 2 – Dollar Threshold to Distinguish Type A and Type B Programs**

  Enter the dollar threshold used to distinguish between Type A and Type B programs as defined in §__.520(b) of Circular A-133.

- **Item 3 – Low-Risk Auditee**

  Indicate whether or not the auditee qualifies as a low-risk auditee under §__.530 of Circular A-133.

- **Item 4 – Audit Findings**

  Indicate whether or not the audit disclosed any audit findings which the auditor is required to report under §__.510(a) of Circular A-133.

- **Item 5 – Federal Agencies Required to Receive the Reporting Package**

  Check the appropriate box to indicate each Federal awarding agency required to receive a copy of the reporting package pursuant to §__.320(d) of Circular A-133. If no Federal awarding agency is required to receive a copy of the reporting package, mark "None."

- **Item 6 – Federal Awards Expended**

  The information to complete columns (a), (b), and (c) shall be obtained from the Schedule of Expenditures of Federal Awards prepared by the auditee. It is important to note that Item 6 shall include the required information for each Federal program presented in the Schedule of Expenditures of Federal Awards (and notes thereto), i.e., not only Federal programs for which audit findings and questioned costs are reported. If additional space is required, photocopy page 3 and attach the additional page(s) to the form.

  Column (a) – CFDA Number

  Enter the number assigned to a Federal program in the Catalog of Federal Domestic Assistance (CFDA) or other identifying number when the CFDA information is not available. If the CFDA information is not available, enter the identifying number provided by the Federal awarding agency or pass-through entity. Individual programs within a cluster of programs shall be listed in the same level of detail as they are listed in the Schedule of Expenditures of Federal Awards.

  Column (b) – Name of Federal Program

  Enter the name of the Federal program. If no CFDA number is provided in column (a), enter the name of the Federal program and the Federal awarding agency or pass-through entity that provided the Federal award.

Column (c) – Amount of Federal Expenditures

Enter the amount of expenditures included in the Schedule of Expenditures of Federal Awards for each Federal program. It is important to note that amounts shall be provided for the value of Federal awards expended in the form of non-cash assistance, the amount of insurance in effect during the year, and loans or loan guarantees outstanding at year end, regardless of whether such amounts were presented in the Schedule of Expenditures of Federal Awards or in a note to the Schedule.

If additional space is required, photocopy page 3, attach additional page(s) to the form, and enter the total for all pages in the "Total Federal Awards Expended" block on the last page.

- **Item 7– Audit Findings and Questioned Costs**

  The information to complete columns (a), (b), (c), (d) and (e) shall be obtained from the Schedule of Findings and Questioned Costs prepared by the auditor. Audit findings and questioned costs that relate to more than one Federal program shall be presented in the form for each Federal program for which audit findings and questioned costs are reported in the auditor's Schedule of Findings and Questioned Costs. If additional space is required, photocopy page 3 and attach the additional page(s) to the form.

  Column (a) – Major Program

  Indicate whether or not the Federal program is a major program, as defined in §__.520 of Circular A-133.

  Column (b) – Type of Compliance Requirement

  Using the list provided on the form, enter the letter that corresponds to the type(s) of compliance requirements applicable to the audit findings and questioned costs reported for each Federal program. Mark all that apply or "None."

  Column (c) – Questioned Costs

  Enter the amount of reported questioned costs by Federal program. If no questioned costs were reported, enter N/A for "Not Applicable."

  Column (d) – Internal Control Findings

  Check the appropriate box, using the list provided on the form, that corresponds to the internal control findings that apply to the Federal program. Mark all that apply or "None reported."

  Column (e) – Audit Finding Reference Numbers

  Enter the audit finding reference number(s) for audit findings included in the Schedule of Findings and Questioned Costs. If no audit finding reference numbers exist, enter N/A for "Not Applicable."

SF-SAC(I) (8-97)

near future, not-for-profit organizations and their auditors will be able to submit this form electronically to a web site, http://harvester.census.gov/sac. This capability is not presently functioning.

The independent auditor who performs the Circular A-133 audit must also sign the data collection form, which also includes a statement from the independent auditor. The statement identifies the sources of the information the auditor used to complete Parts II and III of the form as the reporting package (discussed below). In addition, the auditor makes a statement that the data collection form is meant only to accumulate certain information in a format prescribed by OMB and is not a substitute for the reporting package.

The data collection form is submitted along with the reporting package to the federal single audit clearinghouse, at the address indicated on the form.

Reporting Package Submission

Circular A-133 introduces the concept of a single audit "reporting package" for submission of single audit reports. The reporting package is defined to include the following:

- The not-for-profit organization's financial statements
- The schedule of expenditures of federal awards
- The summary schedule of prior audit findings
- Auditor's reports
- Corrective action plan

With the exception of the basic financial statements (which are discussed in Part I of this Guide) each of the other elements of the reporting package is described later in this chapter.

The reporting package (along with the data collection form) is submitted to the federal single audit clearinghouse, by the report submission deadline, at the following address:

Single Audit Clearinghouse
1201 East 10th Street
Jeffersonville, IN 47132

In addition to one copy of the reporting package for the clearinghouse's records, sufficient additional copies of the reporting package must be submitted to the clearinghouse for each federal awarding agency where the schedule of findings and questioned costs discloses audit findings relating to the federal awards of that federal awarding agency or where the summary schedule of prior audit findings relating to federal awards of that federal award agency.

> **OBSERVATION:** For example, assume that the schedule of
> findings and questioned costs has findings on the following
> major federal programs: Section 8 and the Supportive Housing
> Program (administered by the Department of Housing and
> Urban Development [HUD]) and Title I Grants to Local Educa-
> tional Agencies (administered by the Department of Education
> [ED]). The schedule of prior audit findings includes the Section
> 8 program and the Airport Improvement Program (adminis-
> tered by the Department of Transportation [DOT]). (This is a
> very diverse not-for-profit organization!) The number of copies
> of the reporting package to submit is four: one for the clearing-
> house archives, and one each for HUD, ED, and DOT.

In addition to the submission requirements described above, there
are requirements for report submission by subrecipients relating to
the pass-through entities:

- Where a program has a finding in either the schedule of findings and questioned costs or the schedule of prior audit findings and the funding was received from a pass-through entity,
  a copy of the reporting package should be sent to the pass-
  through entity.

- If there are no findings relating to the pass-through entity, the
  subrecipient may either:

  — Notify the pass-through entity in writing that an audit was
    performed in accordance with Circular A-133 (The notifica-
    tion should list the name, amount, period and CFDA num-
    bers of the awards received from the pass-through entity.
    The notification should also state that there was nothing
    relating to the pass-through award in either the schedule of
    findings and questioned costs or the schedule of prior audit
    findings.) or

  — Simply send a copy of the reporting package to the pass-
    through entity.

Dating of Auditor's Reports

In accordance with GAAS, the date of the auditor's report on the
financial statements should be the date that fieldwork, and the corresponding subsequent events review after the balance sheet date, has
been completed. The auditor should use the following guidelines
when dating the reports required by Circular A-133:

- The auditor's report on the schedule of expenditures of federal
  awards is an opinion that the schedule is fairly stated in all
  material respects in relation to the basic financial statements

taken as a whole. Therefore, the date of this report should be the same date as the date of the auditor's report on the recipient organization's basic financial statements.

- The report on internal controls and compliance with laws and regulations issued in accordance with *Government Auditing Standards* is based on the auditor's review of internal control in accordance with GAAS. The date of this report should always be the same as the date of the auditor's report on the recipient organization's basic financial statements.

- The other additional auditor's reports required by Circular A-133 are a report on internal control related to major programs and an opinion on compliance with loans, regulations, and the provisions of contracts or grant agreements that could have a direct and material effect on each major program. These reports require the performance of procedures by the auditor that are in addition to the regular audit procedures performed in the audit of the recipient organization's basic financial statements. Therefore, the date of this report does not necessarily have to be the same as the date of the financial statement related reports described above.

When audit procedures to meet the requirements of the above reports are performed after the date of the completion of fieldwork for the financial statement audit, the report should be dated as of the date of the completion of fieldwork of the additional A-133 audit procedures. The auditor should not change the date on the financial statement related reports to the date of the completion of the A-133 audit procedures, because such a change would extend the auditor's responsibility for subsequent events to the later date.

REPORTING ON FINANCIAL STATEMENTS IN ACCORDANCE WITH GENERALLY ACCEPTED AUDITING STANDARDS

Financial reporting under *Government Auditing Standards* and Circular A-133 includes the not-for-profit organization's basic financial statements and the auditor's report on the basic financial statements as required by *Government Auditing Standards*.

One controversial issue discussed during the drafting of the 1994 Yellow Book revision was whether the auditor should always state that his or her audit was performed in accordance with *Government Auditing Standards* in the opinion on the basic financial statements and whether the additional internal control and compliance information would always have to be included. The Yellow Book states in its second additional standard for financial statement audits that "audit reports should state that the audit was made in accordance with generally accepted government auditing standards." It further states that when the report on the financial statements is submitted to comply with a legal, regulatory, or contractual requirement for an audit in accordance with *Government Auditing Standards*, the report should specifically cite *Government Auditing Standards*. The report may cite GAAS as well.

The Yellow Book acknowledges that the auditee may need a financial statement audit for purposes other than to comply with requirements for an audit in accordance with *Government Auditing Standards*. In these cases, the Yellow Book does not prohibit auditors from issuing a separate report on the financial statements conforming only to GAAS. The Yellow Book indicates its preferences, however, by stating that it may be advantageous to use a report issued in accordance with *Government Auditing Standards* for these other purposes because it provides information on compliance with laws and regulations and internal controls that is not contained in a report issued in accordance with GAAS.

In summary, when issuing a report required by the Yellow Book, such as one issued to meet the requirements of either the original or the revised Circular A-133, the auditor should refer in the report to *Government Auditing Standards*. When basic financial statements are issued for purposes other than to meet the requirements of a Yellow Book audit, the auditor need not refer to *Government Auditing Standards*.

When reporting on the basic financial statements of the not-for-profit organization, the auditor should consider that Circular A-133 requires the auditor to express an opinion about whether the basic financial statements of the recipient organization as a whole are presented fairly in conformity with generally accepted accounting principles.

The cognizant audit agency has some flexibility when accepting a report on financial statements prepared on a comprehensive basis of accounting other than GAAP. This is because while Circular A-133 requires the auditor to express an opinion on whether the financial statements are presented in conformity with GAAP, it does not require the recipient organization to present the financial statements in conformity with GAAP. However, the financial statements provide the funding agencies with an understanding of an entity's accounting policies and procedures, and they may be more useful if presented in accordance with GAAP.

> **OBSERVATION:** The above discussion should *not* be interpreted as an encouragement to not-for-profit organizations and their auditors to use a basis of accounting other than GAAP. Before using a basis of accounting other than GAAP, the recipient organization should consider all of the potential users of the financial statements, such as state regulatory agencies, creditors, and donors. These users will most likely desire (if not require) financial statements in accordance with GAAP.

Presentation of the Schedule of Expenditures of Federal Awards

Circular A-133 has very specific requirements for the preparation of the schedule of expenditures of federal awards. The schedule should include expenditures of federal awards, and at a minimum Circular A-133 requires that this schedule should:

- List the individual federal programs by federal agency and major subdivision within a federal agency. For federal programs included in a cluster of programs, the individual programs included in the cluster of programs should be listed. For federal programs the organization received as a subrecipient, the name of the pass-through entity and the identifying number assigned by the pass-through entity should be included.

- Provide total federal awards expended and CFDA number (or other identifying number when the CFDA number is not available) for each individual program.

- Include notes that describe the significant accounting policies used in preparing the schedule.

- To the extent practical, pass-through entities should identify in the schedule the total amount provided to subrecipients from each federal program.

- List individual federal awards within a category of federal awards. However, when it is not practical to list each individual federal award for research and development, total expenditures should be shown by federal agency and by major subdivision within the federal agency.

- Include, in either the schedule or a note to the schedule, the value of non-cash assistance expended, insurance in effect during the year, and loans or loan guarantees outstanding at year-end.

In addition, while not required to do so, the not-for-profit organization should provide information requested, so that the schedule will be easier for federal awarding agencies and pass-through entities to use. For example, when a federal program has multiple award years, the recipient organization may list the amount of each award year separately.

> **OBSERVATION:** The Federal Clearinghouse continues to reject a high percentage of Circular A-133 data collection forms and reporting packages. A common deficiency has been improperly prepared schedules of expenditures of federal awards, including missing CFDA numbers. The above requirements should be carefully studied and followed to ensure compliance.

Exhibit 18-2 presents a sample report on the basic financial statements and the schedule of expenditures of federal awards. The auditor may also report on this schedule in the reports issued in accordance with Circular A-133 (see Exhibits 18-5 and 18-6).

REPORTING IN ACCORDANCE WITH THE YELLOW BOOK

The Yellow Book provides additional reporting standards for financial statement audits concerning:

- Reporting compliance with *Government Auditing Standards*
- Privileged and confidential information
- Report distribution
- Reporting on compliance with laws and regulations and on internal control over financial reporting

The Yellow Book requires that audit reports to comply with legal, regulatory, or contractual requirements for an audit in accordance with *Government Auditing Standards* specifically cite *Government Auditing Standards*. Since audits in accordance with Circular A-133 fall within these requirements, any Circular A-133 audit report, including the opinion on the basic financial statements, should cite *Government Auditing Standards*.

The Yellow Book includes additional standards for financial statement audits. The report on the financial statements should either (1) describe the scope of the auditor's testing of compliance with laws and regulations and present the results of those tests, as well as discuss the auditor's consideration of internal controls, or (2) refer to separate reports containing that information. When presenting the results of those tests, auditors should report fraud, illegal acts, or other material noncompliance and reportable conditions in internal control over financial reporting. In some circumstances, auditors should report fraud and illegal acts directly to parties external to the audited entity.

This chapter presents the requirements of the two reports—the report on financial statements and the report on internal control over financial reporting—and compliance. Direct reporting of fraud and illegal acts is discussed in the chapter titled "Government Auditing Standards."

Reporting on the Financial Statements

Financial reporting under the Yellow Book includes an organization's basic financial statements and the auditor's report on the basic finan-

EXHIBIT 18-2
REPORT ON BASIC FINANCIAL STATEMENTS AND
SCHEDULE OF EXPENDITURES OF FEDERAL AWARDS

Independent Auditor's Report

[*Addressee*]

We have audited the accompanying statement of financial position of [*name of recipient organization*] as of June 30, 20XX, and the related statements of activities and cash flows for the year then ended.[1] These financial statements are the responsibility of [*name of not-for-profit organization*]'s management. Our responsibility is to express an opinion on these financial statements based on our audit.

We conducted our audit in accordance with generally accepted auditing standards and the standards applicable to financial audits contained in *Government Auditing Standards* issued by the Comptroller General of the United States. Those standards require that we plan and perform the audit to obtain reasonable assurance about whether the financial statements are free of material misstatement. An audit includes examining, on a test basis, evidence supporting the amounts and disclosures in the basic financial statements. An audit also includes assessing the accounting principles used and significant estimates made by management, as well as evaluating the overall financial statement presentation. We believe that our audit provides a reasonable basis for our opinion.

In our opinion, the financial statements referred to above present fairly, in all material respects, the financial position of [*name of not-for-profit organization*] as of June 30, 20XX, and the changes in its net assets and its cash flows for the year then ended in conformity with generally accepted accounting principles.

In accordance with *Government Auditing Standards*, we have also issued our report dated [*date of report*] on our consideration of [*name of not-for-profit organization*]'s internal control over financial reporting and on our tests of its compliance with certain provisions of laws, regulations, contracts, and grants.

The accompanying schedule of expenditures of federal awards is presented for purposes of additional analysis, as required by U.S. Office of Management and Budget Circular A-133, "Audits of States, Local Governments, and Non-Profit Organizations," and is not a required part of the basic financial statements. Such information has been subjected to the procedures applied in the audit of the basic financial statements and, in our opinion, is fairly stated in all material respects in relation to the basic financial statements taken as a whole.

[*Signature*]

[*Date*]

---

[1] The titles of the financial statements should be revised to conform with the statements presented by the not-for-profit organization.

cial statements as required by GAAS. The auditor must consider three additional reporting matters when reporting on the basic financial statements as part of an audit in accordance with Circular A-133:

1. The auditor's report must state that the audit was performed in accordance with *Government Auditing Standards.*

2. The auditor's report on the basic financial statements, when issued separately from the report on internal control over financial reporting and compliance with laws and regulations, must refer to the report on internal control over financial reporting and compliance with laws and regulations.

3. If the auditor's report on the financial statements includes the report on internal control over financial reporting and compliance with laws and regulations, it should include an introduction summarizing key findings in the audit of the financial statements and the related compliance and internal control work.

Reporting on Internal Control over Financial Reporting and Compliance Policies and Procedures

Government Auditing Standards require a written report on internal control over financial reporting and compliance. Previously, separate reports were issued, one for internal control and one for compliance. However, with the revisions to Circular A-133, the AICPA has issued sample combined reports on internal control and compliance, which is now the acceptable way of reporting under "Government Auditing Standards." Exhibits 18-3 and 18-4 provide examples of the combined report in all audits.

The Yellow Book states that when reporting material fraud, illegal acts, or other noncompliance, the auditor should place his or her findings in the proper perspective. To give the reader a basis for judging the prevalence and consequences of these conditions, the instances identified should be related to the universe or the number of cases examined and should be quantified in terms of dollar value, if appropriate.

Audit findings often have been regarded as containing the elements of *criteria, condition,* and *effect,* plus *cause* when problems are found. However, the elements needed for a finding depend entirely on the objectives of the audit. Reportable conditions and noncompliance found by the auditor may not always have all of these elements fully developed, given the scope and objectives of the specific financial audit. However, auditors should identify at least the condition, criteria, and possible asserted effect. Federal, state, and local officials

---

EXHIBIT 18-3
REPORT ON COMPLIANCE AND ON INTERNAL CONTROL OVER FINANCIAL REPORTING BASED ON AN AUDIT OF FINANCIAL STATEMENTS PERFORMED IN ACCORDANCE WITH *GOVERNMENT AUDITING STANDARDS*

[No Reportable Instances of Noncompliance and No Material Weaknesses (No Reportable Conditions Identified)]

[Addressee]

We have audited the financial statements of [*name of not-for-profit organiza-tion*] as of and for the year ended June 30, 20XX, and have issued our report thereon dated [*date of report on financial statements*]. We conducted our audit in accordance with generally accepted auditing standards and the standards applicable to financial audits contained in *Government Auditing Standards*,[1] issued by the Comptroller General of the United States.

Compliance

As part of obtaining reasonable assurance about whether [*name of not-for-profit organization*]'s financial statements are free of material misstatement, we performed tests of its compliance with certain provisions of laws, regula-tions, contracts, and grants, noncompliance with which could have a direct and material effect on the determination of financial statement amounts. However, providing an opinion on compliance with those provisions was not an objective of our audit and, accordingly, we do not express such an opinion. The results of our tests disclosed no instances of noncompliance that are required to be reported under *Government Auditing Standards.*[2]

Internal Control over Financial Reporting

In planning and performing our audit, we considered [*name of not-for-profit organization*]'s internal control over financial reporting in order to determine our auditing procedures for the purpose of expressing our opinion on the financial statements and not to provide assurance on the internal control over financial reporting. Our consideration of the internal control over finan-cial reporting would not necessarily disclose all matters in the internal control over financial reporting that might be material weaknesses. A *material weakness* is a condition in which the design or operation of one or more of the internal control components does not reduce to a relatively low level the risk that misstatements in amounts that would be material in relation to the financial statements being audited may occur and not be detected within a timely period by employees in the normal course of performing their as-signed functions. We noted no matters involving the internal control over financial reporting and its operation that we consider to be material weak-nesses.[3]

This report is intended solely for the information and use of the audit committee, management, and federal awarding [*and pass-through entities*] and is not intended to be and should not be used by anyone other than those specified parties.

[Signature]

[Date]

---

[1] Any departure from the standard report on the financial statements should be described.

[2] If the auditor has issued a separate letter to management with other internal control or compliance matters that are not required to be reported under *Government Auditing Standards*, the following applicable paragraph should be included in the report at this point:

> However, we noted certain immaterial instances of noncompliance that we have reported to management of [*name of not-for-profit organization*] in a separate letter dated [*date of letter*].

[3] If the auditor has issued a separate letter to management with other internal control or compliance matters that are not required to be reported under *Government Auditing Standards*, the following applicable paragraph should be included in the report at this point:

> However, we noted other matters involving internal control over financial reporting that we have reported to management of [*name of not-for-profit organization*] in a separate letter dated [*date of separate letter*].

EXAMPLE 18-4
REPORT ON COMPLIANCE AND ON INTERNAL CONTROL OVER FINANCIAL REPORTING BASED ON AN AUDIT OF FINANCIAL STATEMENTS PERFORMED IN ACCORDANCE WITH *GOVERNMENT AUDITING STANDARDS*

[Reportable Instances of Noncompliance and Reportable Conditions Identified]

[Addressee]

We have audited the financial statements of [*name of not-for-profit organization*] as of and for the year ended June 30, 20XX, and have issued our report thereon dated [*date of report on financial statements*].[1] We conducted our audit in accordance with generally accepted auditing standards and the standards applicable to financial audits contained in *Government Auditing Standards*, issued by the Comptroller General of the United States.

Compliance

As part of obtaining reasonable assurance about whether [*name of not-for-profit organization*]'s financial statements are free of material misstatement, we performed tests of its compliance with certain provisions of laws, regulations, contracts, and grants, noncompliance with which could have a direct and material effect on the determination of financial statement amounts. However, providing an opinion on compliance with those provisions was not an objective of our audit and, accordingly, we do not express such an opinion. The results of our tests disclosed instances of noncompliance that are required to be reported under *Government Auditing Standards*, and which are described in the accompanying schedule of findings and questioned costs as items [*List related finding reference numbers*].[2]

Internal Control over Financial Reporting

In planning and performing our audit, we considered [*name of not-for-profit organization*]'s internal control over financial reporting in order to determine our auditing procedures for the purpose of expressing our opinion on the financial statements and not to provide assurance on the internal control over financial reporting. However, we noted certain matters involving the internal control over financial reporting and its operation that we consider to be reportable conditions. *Reportable conditions* involve matters coming to our attention relating to significant deficiencies in the design or operation of the internal control over financial reporting that, in our judgment, could adversely affect [*name of not-for-profit organization*]'s ability to record, process, summarize, and report financial data consistent with the assertions of management in the financial statements. Reportable conditions are described in the accompanying schedule of findings and questioned costs as items [*List related finding reference numbers*].

A *material weakness* is a condition in which the design or operation of one or more of the internal control components does not reduce to a relatively low level the risk that misstatements in amounts that would be material in relation to the financial statements being audited may occur and not be detected within a timely period by employees in the normal course of performing their assigned functions. Our consideration of the internal control over financial reporting would not necessarily disclose all matters in the internal control that might be reportable conditions and, accordingly, would not necessarily disclose all reportable conditions that are also considered to be material weaknesses. However, we believe none of the reportable conditions described above is a material weakness.[3]

This report is intended solely for the information and use of the audit committee, management, and federal awarding agencies [*and pass-through entities*] and is not intended to be and should not be used by anyone other than the specified parties.

[*Signature*]

[*Date*]

---

[1] Any departure from the standard report on the financial statements should be described.

[2] If the auditor has issued a separate letter to management with other internal control or compliance matters that are not required to be reported under *Government Auditing Standards*, the following applicable paragraph should be included in the report at this point:

> However, we noted certain immaterial instances of noncompliance that we have reported to management of [*name of not-for-profit organization*] in a separate letter dated [*date of letter*].

[3] If the auditor has issued a separate letter to management with other internal control or compliance matters that are not required to be reported under *Government Auditing Standards*, the following applicable paragraph should be included in the report at this point:

> However, we noted other matters involving internal control over financial reporting that we have reported to management of [*name of not-for-profit organization*] in a separate letter dated [*date of separate letter*].

---

need this information to determine the effect and cause of the finding and to take prompt and proper corrective action.

When presenting material fraud, illegal acts, or other noncompliance, the auditor should use the Yellow Book guidance for the contents of performance audit reports. This guidance contains report content standards for objectives, scope, and methodology; audit results; views of responsible officials; and report presentation. Auditors may provide less extensive disclosure of fraud and illegal acts that are not material in either a quantitative or a qualitative sense.

Objectives, scope, and methodology   Auditors should report the audit objectives, scope, and methodology. Audit report readers need to know the objectives of the audit, as well as of the audit scope and methodology for achieving the objectives, to understand the purpose of the audit, judge the merits of the audit work and what is reported, and understand significant limitations.

When reporting the scope of the audit, auditors should describe the depth and coverage of work conducted to accomplish the audit's objectives. Auditors should, as applicable, explain the relationship between the universe and what was audited; identify organizations, geographic locations, and the period covered; report the kinds and sources of evidence; and explain any quality or other problems with evidence. Auditors should also report significant constraints imposed on the audit approach by data limitations or scope impairments.

To report the methodology used, auditors should clearly explain the evidence gathering and analysis techniques used. This explanation should identify any significant assumptions made in conducting the audit; describe any comparative techniques applied; describe the criteria used; and when sampling significantly supports auditors' findings, describe the sample design and state why it was chosen.

Audit results   Auditors should report significant audit findings and, where applicable, auditors' conclusions. In reporting findings, auditors should include sufficient, competent, and relevant information to promote adequate understanding of the matters reported and to provide convincing but fair presentations in proper perspective. Auditors should also report any appropriate background information needed by readers to understand the findings.

Views of responsible officials   Auditors should report the views of responsible officials of the audited program concerning the auditors' findings, conclusions, and recommendations, and management's corrective action plans.

Report presentation   The report should be complete, accurate, objective, convincing, and as clear and concise as the subject permits. The Yellow Book provides a description of each of the above characteristics:

- *Complete*   To be complete, the report must contain all information needed to satisfy the audit objectives, promote an adequate and correct understanding of the matters reported, and meet the report content requirements.

- *Accurate*   Accuracy requires that the evidence presented be true and that the findings be correctly portrayed. The need for accuracy is based on the need to assure readers that what is reported is credible and reliable.

- *Objective* Objectivity requires that the presentation of the entire report be balanced in content and tone. A report's credibility is significantly enhanced when it presents evidence in an unbiased manner so that readers can be persuaded by the facts.
- *Convincing* To be convincing, the audit results must be responsive to the audit objectives, the findings must be presented persuasively, and the conclusions and recommendations must follow logically from the facts presented.
- *Clear* Clarity requires that the report be easy to read and understand. Reports should be written in language as clear and simple as the subject permits. Use of straightforward, nontechnical language is essential to simplicity of presentation. If technical terms and unfamiliar abbreviations and acronyms are used, they should be clearly defined. Acronyms should be used sparingly.
- *Concise* To be concise, the report must be no longer than is necessary to convey and support the message. Too much detail detracts from a report, may conceal the real message, and may confuse or discourage readers. Also, needless repetition should be avoided.

REPORTING IN ACCORDANCE WITH CIRCULAR A-133

Circular A-133 requires the auditor to issue the following reports:

- Reports required to be issued in an audit performed in accordance with *Government Auditing Standards*, as described in the previous sections of this chapter (Exhibits 18-3 and 18-4)
- A report on the not-for-profit organization's schedule of expenditures of federal awards (Exhibit 18-2)
- A report on compliance with requirements applicable to each major program and internal control over compliance (Exhibits 18-5 and 18-6)

Report on the Schedule of Expenditures of Federal Awards

The not-for-profit organization that is a recipient or subrecipient of a federal award is responsible for preparing a schedule of expenditures of federal awards. The contents and format of this schedule are discussed earlier in this chapter. The auditor's report on the schedule of expenditures of federal awards should be in the form of a report on supplementary information, which is reported on in accordance with the requirements of SAS-29 (Reporting on Information Accom-

---

EXHIBIT 18-5
REPORT ON COMPLIANCE WITH REQUIREMENTS
APPLICABLE TO EACH MAJOR PROGRAM AND INTERNAL
CONTROL OVER COMPLIANCE IN ACCORDANCE
WITH OMB CIRCULAR A-133

[Unqualified Opinion on Compliance and No Material
Weaknesses (No Reportable Conditions Identified)]

[*Addressee*]

Compliance

We have audited the compliance of [*name of not-for-profit organization*] with the types of compliance requirements described in the *U.S. Office of Management and Budget (OMB) Circular A-133 Compliance Supplement* that are applicable to each of its major federal programs for the year ended June 30, 20XX. [*Name of not-for-profit organization*]'s major federal programs are identified in the summary of auditor's results section of the accompanying schedule of findings and questioned costs. Compliance with the requirements of laws, regulations, contracts, and grants applicable to each of its major federal programs is the responsibility of [*name of not-for-profit organization*]'s management. Our responsibility is to express an opinion on [*name of not-for-profit organization*]'s compliance based on our audit.

We conducted our audit of compliance in accordance with generally accepted auditing standards; the standards applicable to financial audits contained in *Government Auditing Standards,* issued by the Comptroller General of the United States; and OMB Circular A-133, *Audits of States, Local Governments, and Non-Profit Organizations*. Those standards and OMB Circular A-133 require that we plan and perform the audit to obtain reasonable assurance about whether noncompliance with the types of compliance requirements referred to above that could have a direct and material effect on a major federal program occurred. An audit includes examining, on a test basis, evidence about [*name of not-for-profit organization*]'s compliance with those requirements and performing other procedures as we considered necessary in the circumstances. We believe that our audit provides a reasonable basis for our opinion. Our audit does not provide a legal determination on [*name of not-for-profit organization*]'s compliance with those requirements.

In our opinion, [*name of not-for-profit organization*] complied, in all material respects, with the requirements referred to above that are applicable to each of its major federal programs for the year ended June 30, 20XX. However, the results of our auditing procedures disclosed instances of noncompliance with those requirements that are required to be reported in accordance with OMB Circular A-133 and that are described in the accompanying schedule of findings and questioned costs as items [*List related finding reference number*].[1]

Internal Control over Compliance

The management of [*name of not-for-profit organization*] is responsible for establishing and maintaining effective internal control over compliance with requirements of laws, regulations, contracts, and grants applicable to federal programs. In planning and performing our audit, we considered [*name of not-for-profit organization*]'s internal control over compliance with requirements that could have a direct and material effect on a major federal program in order to determine our auditing procedures for the purpose of expressing our opinion on compliance and to test and report on internal control over compliance in accordance with OMB Circular A-133.

Our consideration of the internal control over compliance would not necessarily disclose all matters in the internal control that might be material weaknesses. A *material weakness* is a condition in which the design or operation of one or more of the internal control components does not reduce to a relatively low level the risk that noncompliance with applicable requirements of laws, regulations, contracts, and grants that would be material in relation to a major federal program being audited may occur and not be detected within a timely period by employees in the normal course of performing their assigned functions. We noted no matters involving the internal control over compliance and its operation that we consider to be material weaknesses.[2]

This report is intended solely for the information and use of the audit committee, management, and federal awarding agencies [*and pass-through entities*] and is not intended to be and should not be used by anyone other than these specified parties.

[*Signature*]

[*Date*]

---

[1] When there are no such instances of noncompliance identified in the schedule of findings and questioned costs, the last sentence should be omitted.

[2] There may be instances where it would be appropriate to report on the schedule of expenditures of federal awards in this report (e.g., a separate single audit package is issued). In such circumstances, a new section should be added immediately following this paragraph as follows:

Schedule of Expenditures of Federal Awards

We have audited the basic financial statements of [*name of not-for-profit organization*] as of and for the year ended June 30, 20XX, and have issued our report thereon dated [*date of report*]. Our audit was performed for the purpose of forming an opinion on the basic financial statements taken as a whole. The accompanying schedule of expenditures of federal awards is presented for purposes of additional analysis as required by OMB Circular A-133 and is not a required part of the basic financial statements. Such information has been subjected to the auditing procedures applied in the audit of the basic financial statements and, in our opinion, is fairly stated, in all material respects, in relation to the basic financial statements taken as a whole.

EXAMPLE 18-6
REPORT ON COMPLIANCE WITH REQUIREMENTS APPLICABLE TO EACH MAJOR PROGRAM AND INTERNAL CONTROL OVER COMPLIANCE IN ACCORDANCE WITH OMB CIRCULAR A-133

[Qualified Opinion on Compliance and Reportable Conditions Identified]

[Addressee]

Compliance

We have audited the compliance of [*name of not-for-profit organization*] with the types of compliance requirements described in the *U.S. Office of Management and Budget (OMB) Circular A-133 Compliance Supplement* that are applicable to each of its major federal programs for the year ended June 30, 20XX. [*Name of not-for-profit organization*]'s major federal programs are identified in the summary of auditor's results section of the accompanying schedule of findings and questioned costs. Compliance with the requirements of laws, regulations, contracts, and grants applicable to each of its major federal programs is the responsibility of [*name of not-for-profit organization*]'s management. Our responsibility is to express an opinion on [*name of not-for-profit organization*]'s compliance based on our audit.

We conducted our audit of compliance in accordance with generally accepted auditing standards; the standards applicable to financial audits contained in *Government Auditing Standards,* issued by the Comptroller General of the United States; and OMB Circular A-133, *Audits of States, Local Governments, and Non-Profit Organizations.* Those standards and OMB Circular A-133 require that we plan and perform the audit to obtain reasonable assurance about whether noncompliance with the types of compliance requirements referred to above that could have a direct and material effect on a major federal program occurred. An audit includes examining, on a test basis, evidence about [*name of not-for-profit organization*]'s compliance with those requirements and performing other procedures as we considered necessary in the circumstances. We believe that our audit provides a reasonable basis for our opinion. Our audit does not provide a legal determination on [*name of not-for-profit organization*]'s compliance with those requirements.

As described in item [*List related finding reference number*] in the accompanying schedule of findings and questioned costs, [*name of not-for-profit organization*] did not comply with requirements regarding [*identify type(s) of compliance requirement*] that are applicable to its [*identify major federal program*]. Compliance with such requirements is necessary, in our opinion, for [*name of not-for-profit organization*] to comply with requirements applicable to that program.

In our opinion, except for the noncompliance described in the preceding paragraph, [*name of not-for-profit organization*] complied, in all material respects, with the requirements referred to above that are applicable to each of its major federal programs for the year ended June 30, 20XX.[1]

Internal Control over Compliance

The management of [*name of not-for-profit organization*] is responsible for establishing and maintaining effective internal control over compliance with requirements of laws, regulations, contracts, and grants applicable to federal programs. In planning and performing our audit, we considered [*name of not-for-profit organization*]'s internal control over compliance with requirements that could have a direct and material effect on a major federal program in order to determine our auditing procedures for the purpose of expressing our opinion on compliance and to test and report on internal control over compliance in accordance with OMB Circular A-133.

We noted certain matters involving the internal control over compliance and its operation that we consider to be reportable conditions. Reportable conditions involve matters coming to our attention relating to significant deficiencies in the design or operation of the internal control over compliance that, in our judgment, could adversely affect [*name of not-for-profit organization*]'s ability to administer a major federal program in accordance with applicable requirements of laws, regulations, contracts, and grants. Reportable conditions are described in the accompanying schedule of findings and questioned costs as items [*List related finding reference numbers*].[2]

A material weakness is a condition in which the design or operation of one or more of the internal control components does not reduce to a relatively low level the risk that noncompliance with applicable requirements of laws, regulations, contracts, and grants that would be material in relation to a major federal program being audited may occur and not be detected within a timely period by employees in the normal course of performing their assigned functions. Our consideration of the internal control over compliance would not necessarily disclose all matters in the internal control that might be reportable conditions and, accordingly, would not necessarily disclose all reportable conditions that are also considered to be material weaknesses. However, we believe none of the reportable conditions described above is a material weakness.[3]

This report is intended solely for the information and use of the audit committee, management, and federal awarding agencies [*and pass-through entities*] and is not intended to be and should not be used by anyone other than these specified parties.

[*Signature*]

[*Date*]

---

[1] When other instances of noncompliance are identified in the schedule of findings and questioned costs as required by OMB Circular A-133, the following sentence should be added:

The results of our auditing procedures also disclosed other instances of noncompliance with those requirements that are required to be reported in accordance with OMB Circular A-133 and which are described in the accompanying schedule of findings and questioned costs as items [*List related finding reference numbers*].

[2] If conditions believed to be material weaknesses are disclosed, the report should identify the material weaknesses that have come to the auditor's attention. The last sentence of this paragraph should be replaced with language such as the following:

However, of the reportable conditions described above, we consider items [*List related finding reference numbers*] to be material weaknesses.

[3] There may be instances where it would be appropriate to report on the schedule of expenditures of federal awards in this report (e.g., a separate single audit package is issued). In such circumstances, a new section should be added immediately following this paragraph as follows:

Schedule of Expenditures of Federal Awards

We have audited the basic financial statements of [*name of not-for-profit organization*] as of and for the year ended June 30, 20XX, and have issued our report thereon dated [*date of auditor's report*]. Our audit was performed for the purpose of forming an opinion on the [*basic*] financial statements taken as a whole. The accompanying schedule of expenditures of federal awards is presented for purposes of additional analysis as required by OMB Circular A-133 and is not a required part of the basic financial statements. Such information has been subjected to the auditing procedures applied in the audit of the basic financial statements and, in our opinion, is fairly stated, in all material respects, in relation to the basic financial statements taken as a whole.

---

panying the Basic Financial Statements in Auditor-Submitted Documents). SAS-29 provides the following guidelines for this type of report:

- The report should state that the audit has been performed for the purpose of forming an opinion on the basic financial statements taken as a whole.

- The report should identify the accompanying information. Identification may be by descriptive title or page number of the document.

- The report should state that the accompanying information is presented for purposes of additional analysis and is not a required part of the basic financial statements.

- The report should include either (1) an opinion on whether the accompanying information is fairly stated, in all material respects, in relation to the basic financial statements taken as a whole or (2) a disclaimer of opinion, depending on whether the information has been subjected to the auditing procedures applied in the audit of the basic financial statements. The auditor may express an opinion on a portion of the accompanying information and disclaim an opinion on the remainder.

- The report on the accompanying information may be added to the report on the basic financial statements or may appear separately in the auditor-submitted document.

SAS-29 states that the auditor should consider the effect of any modification in his or her standard report when reporting on accompanying information. Any modifications to the standard report issued on the basic financial statements also should be made to the standard report on supplementary information.

When a separate single audit package is prepared without presenting financial statements, the report on the schedule of expenditures of federal awards should be included in the Circular A-133 compliance/internal control report. Sample language is provided with the accompanying samples of this report.

Circular A-133 does not require not-for-profit organizations to provide any additional supplemental information schedules other than the schedule of expenditures of federal awards. However, the federal agencies that provide the federal awards to the recipient organization may require that additional supplemental information be provided, particularly in the area of schedules related to indirect costs. The not-for-profit organization is free to include any additional supplemental schedules it deems useful or that are required by a federal awarding agency. The auditor should apply the same standards when reporting on these schedules as are applied when reporting on the schedule of expenditures of federal awards.

Report on Compliance and Internal Control over Compliance

Circular A-133 expands on *Government Auditing Standards* and requires that the auditor determine and report on whether a recipient organization has internal control to provide reasonable assurance that it is managing its federal awards in compliance with applicable laws and regulations. In addition, the auditor issues an opinion on compliance for each major federal program. (Examples of these reports are provided in Exhibits 18-5 and 18-6.)

Reporting on Program-Specific Audits

In certain circumstances that are discussed in the chapter of this Guide titled "Government Auditing Standards," a not-for-profit organization may elect to have a program-specific audit in lieu of a Circular A-133 audit. Exhibit 18-7 provides an example of an opinion on financial statements when a program-specific audit is performed. Exhibit 18-8 provides an example of a report on compliance and internal control when a program-specific audit is performed.

Reporting Findings and Questioned Costs

The guidance for reporting findings and questioned costs under the revised Circular A-133 is somewhat different than under the previous Circular A-133. Not only is the guidance more specific, but certain responsibilities for reporting the status of prior audit findings has been shifted from the auditor to the recipient organization. The general guidance provided by *Government Auditing Standards* on the requirements for reporting findings is certainly applicable to the manner in which findings are presented in the required schedules under the revised Circular A-133.

Under Circular A-133, the auditor is responsible for preparing a schedule of findings and questioned costs. The recipient organization is responsible for preparing a schedule of prior audit findings and a corrective action plan. The content of each of these documents is discussed below.

Schedule of Findings and Questioned Costs

The schedule presents the audit findings as a result of the A-133 audit. Where practical, audit findings should be organized by a federal agency or pass-through entity, and findings that relate to the same issue should be presented as a single finding. The following are the required components of the schedule of findings and questioned costs:

- *Audit findings*   The auditor is required to report the following findings and questioned costs. Each audit finding in the schedule should have include a reference number to allow for referencing the audit findings during follow-up.

    OBSERVATION: The reference number for each finding is important, since it will follow the finding in future years until it is resolved. Accordingly, a numbering scheme that indicates fiscal year (e.g., 99-xx, 2000-xx) will prove helpful in the future.

EXHIBIT 18-7
REPORT ON COMPLIANCE WITH REQUIREMENTS
APPLICABLE TO THE FEDERAL PROGRAM AND ON
INTERNAL CONTROL OVER COMPLIANCE IN
ACCORDANCE WITH PROGRAM-SPECIFIC AUDIT
OPTION UNDER OMB CIRCULAR A-133[1]

[Unqualified Opinion on Compliance and No Material Weaknesses or Reportable Conditions Identified]

[Addressee]

Compliance[2]

We have audited the compliance of [*name of not-for-profit organization*] with the types of compliance requirements described in the U.S. Office of Management and Budget (OMB) Circular A-133 Compliance Supplement that are applicable to [*identify the federal program*] for the year ended June 30, 20XX. Compliance with the requirements of laws, regulations, contracts, and grants applicable to federal program is the responsibility of [*name of not-for-profit organization*]'s management. Our responsibility is to express an opinion on [*name of not-for-profit organization*]'s compliance based on our audit.

We conducted our audit of compliance in accordance with generally accepted auditing standards; the standards applicable to financial audits contained in Government Auditing Standards; issued by the Comptroller General of the United States; and OMB Circular A-133, *Audits of States, Local Governments, and Non-Profit Organizations.* Those standards and OMB Circular A-133 require that we plan and perform the audit to obtain reasonable assurance about whether noncompliance with the types of compliance requirements referred to above that could have a direct and material effect on [*identify the federal program*] occurred. An audit includes examining, on a test basis, evidence about [*name of not-for-profit organization*]'s compliance with those requirements and performing such other procedures as we considered necessary in the circumstances. We believe that our audit provides a reasonable basis for our opinion. Our audit does not provide a legal determination of [*name of not-for-profit organization*]'s compliance with those requirements.

In our opinion, [*name of not-for-profit organization*] complied, in all material respects, with the requirements referred to above that are applicable to its [*identify the federal program*] for the year ended June 30, 20XX. However, the results of our auditing procedures disclosed instances of noncompliance with those requirements, which are required to be reported in accordance with OMB Circular A-133 and which are described in the accompanying schedule of findings and questioned costs as items [*list dated reference numbers*].

Internal Control over Compliance

The management of [*name of not-for-profit organization*] is responsible for establishing and maintaining effective internal control over compliance with the requirements of laws, regulations, contracts, and grants applicable to federal programs. In planning and performing our audit, we considered [*name of not-for-profit organization*]'s internal control over compliance with requirements that could have a direct and material effect on its [*identify the federal program*] in order to determine our auditing procedures for the purpose of expressing our opinion on compliance and to test and report on the internal control over compliance in accordance with OMB Circular A-133.

Our consideration of the internal control over compliance would not necessarily disclose all matters in the internal control that might be material weaknesses. A material weakness is a condition in which the design or operation of one or more of the internal control components does not reduce to a relatively low level the risk that noncompliance with the applicable requirements of laws, regulations, contracts, and grants that would be material in relation to a major federal program being audited may occur and not be detected within a timely period by employees in the normal course of performing their assigned functions. We noted no matters involving the internal control over compliance and its operation that we consider to be material weaknesses.

This report is intended solely for the information and use of the audit committee, management, and the federal awarding agency [*and pass-through entities*] and is not intended to be and should not be used by anyone other than these specified parties.

[*Signature*]

[*Date*]

---

[1] This is an example of a report on a program-specific audit under Circular A-133 when a federal audit guide applicable to the program being audited does not provide reporting requirements. When a federal audit guide applicable to the program is available, Circular A-133 requires that the auditor follow the reporting requirements of that federal audit guide.

[2] If issuing a qualified or adverse opinion on compliance, the auditor should modify the compliance section of this report to be consistent with the wording used in the other example Circular A-133 reports in this Guide.

EXHIBIT 18-8
UNQUALIFIED OPINION ON THE FINANCIAL STATEMENT OF A FEDERAL PROGRAM IN ACCORDANCE WITH THE PROGRAM-SPECIFIC AUDIT OPTION UNDER OMB CIRCULAR A-133

Independent Auditor's Report

We have audited the accompanying schedule of expenditures of federal awards for the [*identify the federal program*] of [*name of not-for-profit organization*] for the year ended June 30, 20XX. This financial statement is the responsibility of [*name of not-for-profit organization*]'s management. Our responsibility is to express an opinion on the financial statement of the program based on our audit.[1]

We conducted our audit in accordance with generally accepted auditing standards; the standards applicable to financial audits contained in *Government Auditing Standards*, issued by the Comptroller General of the United States; and OMB Circular A-133, *Audits of States, Local Governments, and Non-Profit Organizations.* Those standards and OMB Circular A-133 require that we plan and perform the audit to obtain reasonable assurance about whether the financial statement is free of material misstatement. An audit includes examining, on a test basis, evidence supporting the amounts and disclosures in the financial statement. An audit also includes assessing the accounting principles used and the significant estimates made by management, as well as evaluating the overall financial statement presentation. We believe that our audit provides a reasonable basis for our opinion.

In our opinion, the schedule of expenditures of federal awards referred to above presents fairly, in all material respects, the expenditures of federal awards under the [*identify the federal program*] for the year ended June 30, 20XX, in conformity with generally accepted accounting principles.[2]

[*Signature*]

[*Date*]

---

[1] In many cases, the financial statements of the program will consist only of the schedule of expenditures of federal awards (and notes to the schedule), which is the minimum financial statement presentation required by section 235 of Circular A-133. If the auditee issues financial statements that consist of more than the schedule, this paragraph should be modified to describe the financial statements.

[2] If a separate report is issued to meet the reporting requirements of *Government Auditing Standards*, an additional paragraph should be added as follows: "In accordance with *Government Auditing Standards*, we have also issued our report dated [*date of report*] on our consideration of [*name of not-for-profit organization*]'s internal control over financial reporting and on our tests of its compliance with certain provisions of laws, regulations, contracts, and grants."

—Reportable conditions in internal control over major programs. The auditor's determination of whether to report a deficiency in internal control as a reportable condition is made in relation to a type of compliance requirement for a major program or an audit objective identified in the Compliance Supplement. The auditor shall identify reportable conditions which are individually or cumulatively material weaknesses.

—Material noncompliance with the provisions of laws, regulations, contracts, or grant agreements related to a major program. The auditor's determination of whether noncompliance with the provisions of laws, regulations, contracts, or grant agreements is material is made for the purpose of reporting an audit finding is in relation to a type of compliance requirement for a major program or an audit objective identified in the Compliance Supplement.

—Known questioned costs which are greater than $10,000 for a type of compliance requirement for a major program. Known questioned costs are those specifically identified by the auditor. In evaluating the effect of questioned costs on the opinion on compliance for each major program, the auditor considers the best estimate of total costs questioned (likely questioned costs), not just the questioned costs specifically identified (known questioned costs). The auditor should also report known questioned costs when likely questioned costs are greater than $10,000 for a type of compliance requirement for a major program. In reporting questioned costs, the auditor should include information to provide proper perspective for judging the prevalence and consequences of the questioned costs.

—Known questioned costs greater than $10,000 for a federal program that is not audited as a major program. Although this should be rare (since the auditor is not performing procedures under Circular A-133 for these programs), if the auditor does become aware of these questioned costs, they should be reported.

—The circumstances concerning why the auditor's report on compliance for major programs is other than an unqualified opinion, unless such circumstances are otherwise reported as auditing findings in the schedule of findings and questioned costs.

• Known fraud affecting a federal award, unless such fraud is otherwise reported as an audit finding in the schedule of findings and questioned costs. This requirement does not require the auditor to make an additional reporting when the auditor confirms that the fraud was reported outside of the auditor's reports under the direct reporting requirements of *Government Auditing Standards.*

- Instances where the results of audit follow-up procedures have disclosed that the summary schedule of prior audit findings prepared by the recipient organization materially misrepresents the status of any prior audit finding.

> **OBSERVATION:** There are two subtle details in the above list that the auditor should consider. First, instances of noncompliance do not have to be material to a major federal program (i.e., they do not have to impact the auditor's opinion on compliance) in order to be reported in the schedule of findings and questioned costs. Second, the $10,000 questioned cost threshold does not eliminate the need to report known questioned costs below $10,000 if the likely amount of questioned costs is greater that $10,000.

Circular A-133 provides guidance for how to report the findings and questioned costs described above. Basically, audit findings should be in sufficient detail for the recipient organization to be able to prepare a corrective action plan (discussed below) and take corrective action and for federal agencies and pass-through entities to arrive at a management decision. The following specific information, where applicable, is required to be included in audit findings:

- Federal program and specific federal award identification, including the CFDA title and number, federal award number and year, name of federal agency, and name of the applicable pass-through entity. When information such as the CFDA title and number or federal award number is not available, the auditor should provide the best information available to describe the federal award.
- The criteria or specific requirement upon which the audit finding is based, including statutory, regulatory, or other citation.
- The condition found, including facts that support the deficiency identified in the audit finding.
- Identification of questioned costs and how they were computed.
- Information to provide proper perspective for judging the prevalence and consequences of the audit findings, such as whether the audit findings represent an isolated instance or a systemic problem. Where appropriate, instances identified should be related to the universe and the number of cases examined and be quantified in terms of dollar value.
- The possible asserted effect to provide information to the auditee and federal agency, or pass-through entity in the case of a

subrecipient, sufficient to permit them to determine the cause and effect in order to facilitate prompt and proper corrective action.

- Recommendations to prevent future occurrences of the deficiency identified in the audit finding.
- Views of responsible officials of the recipient organization when there is disagreement with the audit findings, to the extent practical.

Exhibit 18-9 provides a worksheet for identifying and recording single audit reportable conditions and noncompliance.

Summary Schedule of Prior Audit Findings

Circular A-133 places the responsibility for follow-up and corrective action on all audit findings with the recipient organization. The recipient organization should prepare a summary schedule of prior audit findings, which reports the status of all audit findings included in the prior audit's schedule of findings and questioned costs. The summary schedule should also include audit findings reported in the prior audit's summary schedule of prior audit findings, unless the findings were listed in the prior summary schedule as corrected, no longer valid, or not warranting further action.

> **OBSERVATION:** If the auditor concludes that the summary schedule materially misrepresents the status of a prior year's audit finding, he or she should report this as a current-year audit finding.

The following guidance is provided by Circular A-133 for preparing the summary schedule of prior audit findings:

- When audit findings were fully corrected, the summary schedule need list only the audit findings and state that corrective action was taken.
- When audit findings were not corrected or were only partially corrected, the summary schedule should describe the planned corrective action as well as any partial corrective action taken.
- When corrective action taken is significantly different from corrective action previously reported in a corrective action plan or in the federal agency's or pass-through entity's management decision, the summary schedule should provide an explanation.
- When the recipient organization believes the audit findings are no longer valid or do not warrant further action, the reasons for

EXHIBIT 18-9
SINGLE AUDIT REPORTABLE CONDITION/
NONCOMPLIANCE WORKSHEET

TYPE OF REPORTABLE CONDITION/NONCOMPLIANCE:

- Reportable Condition   _____
- Material Weakness   _____
- Material Noncompliance   _____
- Nonmaterial Noncompliance   _____

CONDITION:

CRITERIA:

CAUSE:

EFFECT:

RECOMMENDATION:

Discussed with Client Personnel:

   When: _____

   With Whom: _____

   Reaction: _____

Approved for Report: _____   Date: _____

If Not Approved, Why? _____

this position should be described in the summary schedule. A valid reason for considering an audit finding as not warranting further action is that *all* of the following have occurred:

— Two years have passed since the audit report in which the finding occurred was submitted to the federal single audit clearinghouse,

— The federal agency or pass-through entity is not currently following up with the recipient organization or the finding, and

— A management decision was not issued.

In presenting the status of prior-year findings, the recipient organization should use the reference numbers assigned by the auditor in the schedule of findings and questioned costs to facilitate cross-referencing.

Corrective Action Plan

At the completion of the audit, the recipient organization is also responsible for preparing a corrective action plan to address each audit finding included in the current year auditor's reports. The corrective action plan should provide the name of the contact person responsible for corrective action, the corrective action planned, and the anticipated completion date. If the auditee does not agree with the audit findings or believes corrective action is not required, then the corrective action plan should state this conclusion and the specific reasons for it.

SUMMARY

The reporting requirements of Circular A-133 and *Government Auditing Standards* go far beyond the opinion that the auditor issues on financial statements. The additional requirements must be fully understood to ensure the proper planning and execution of the audit and to provide a sound basis for the issuance of the required reports.

CHAPTER 19
CONCLUDING THE A-133 AUDIT

CONTENTS

CONCLUDING THE A-133 AUDIT

CROSS-REFERENCES

2001 MILLER NOT-FOR-PROFIT ORGANIZATION AUDITS: Chapter 9, "Concluding the Audit"

2001 MILLER AUDIT PROCEDURES: Chapter 21, "Concluding the Audit"

As part of the wrap-up and conclusion of an audit in accordance with Circular A-133, auditors should perform certain procedures. Although these concluding procedures track closely to those an auditor would perform in an audit performed in accordance with GAAS, additional procedures are relevant to audits performed in accordance with A-133.

As part of their effort to ensure audit quality, cognizant agencies for audit as a general rule have programs for performing quality reviews of selected A-133 audits. Although the actual number of audits examined is relatively small, auditors should complete and wrap-up their audits as if they would be ready to hand the workpapers over to the cognizant agency. This can save embarrassment and much additional work later if the auditor is selected to provide his or her working papers to the cognizant agency.

Particularly important steps in the audit conclusion process for an audit in accordance with Circular A-133 are:

- Obtain client representations.
- Resolve open items and complete the working paper review.
- Ensure that reports are appropriately filed.

The auditor should consider the guidance of the chapter of this Guide titled "Reporting" when concluding the Circular A-133 audit requirements.

Obtain Client Representations

Auditors should obtain documentation of the representations that management has made to them as part of the audit. This applies in audits performed in accordance with GAAS as well as audits performed in accordance with Circular A-133. The client representation letter should be signed by the client's executive and financial management, as of the last date of fieldwork (i.e., the date that the auditor's reports will be signed). If the reports issued in accordance with Circular A-133 are dated after the date of the reports on the financial statements and the internal control and compliance reports issued in accordance with *Government Auditing Standards*, an update to the representation letter should be obtained through the date of the A-133 reports.

For audits performed in accordance with Circular A-133, additional representations relating to the recipient organization's federal awards programs should be obtained. These additional representations are included in the sample representation letter shown in Exhibit 19-1. Auditors should modify this standard letter to include any additional items that became known during the course of the audit that, in the auditor's judgment, should be formalized by inclusion in the representation letter.

Resolve Open Items and Complete the Working Paper Review

Near the conclusion of the audit fieldwork, the auditor should begin to identify the open items that must be resolved to complete the audit fieldwork and issue the reports in accordance with Circular A-133. The chapter titled "Concluding the Audit" describes steps for the auditor to consider taking in order to ensure that all audit procedures have been properly completed and documented.

A single audit review form is shown in Exhibit 19-2 and a single audit report control form is shown in Exhibit 19-3.

Ensure That Reports Are Appropriately Filed

As discussed in the chapter titled "Reporting under Circular A-133," the distribution of reports to the cognizant agency, the grantor agencies providing the recipient organization with federal awards, and the federal audit clearinghouse is the responsibility of the recipient organization. The auditor should ask the recipient organization if this has been done and should document the distribution.

EXHIBIT 19-1
SAMPLE REPRESENTATION LETTER[1]

[*Letterhead of the Recipient Organization*]

[*Date, as of the end of fieldwork*]

[*Addressed to the audit firm*]

We are providing this letter in connection with your audit of the [*identify the financial statements*] as of and for the fiscal year ended [*date of end of fiscal year audited*] for the purpose of expressing an opinion on whether the financial statements present fairly, in all material respects, the financial position, results of operations and cash flows of [*name of recipient organization*] in conformity with generally accepted accounting principles, Further, we understand that the purpose of your testing transactions and records from the organization's federal awards programs was to obtain reasonable assurance that the organization complied, in all material respects, with the compliance requirements applicable to each of our major federal award programs. We confirm that we are responsible for the fair presentation in the financial statements of financial position, results of operations, and cash flows in conformity with generally accepted accounting principles.

Certain representations in this letter are described as being limited to matters that are material. Items are considered material, regardless of size, if they involve an omission or misstatement of accounting information that, in the light of surrounding circumstances, makes it probable that the judgment of a reasonable person relying on the information would be changed or influenced by the omission or misstatement.

We confirm, to the best of our knowledge and belief, the following representation made to you during your audit.

1. The financial statements referred to above are fairly presented in conformity with generally accepted accounting principles.

2. We have made available to you all—
   a. Financial records and related data.
   b. Minutes of meetings of the board of directors of [*name of recipient organization*] and its committees, or summaries of actions of recent meetings for which minutes have not yet been prepared.

3. There has been no—
   a. Fraud involving management or employees who have significant roles in internal control.
   b. Fraud involving others that could have a material effect on the financial statements.

c. Communications from regulatory agencies concerning noncompliance with, or deficiencies in, financial reporting practices.

4. The organization has no plans or intentions that may materially affect the carrying value or classifications of assets, liabilities, or net assets.

5. The following have been properly recorded or disclosed in the financial statements:

a. Related-party transactions and related amounts receivable or payable, including revenues, expenses, loans, transfers, leasing arrangements, and guarantees.

b. Guarantees, whether written or oral, under which the organization is contingently liable.

c. Significant estimates and material concentrations known to management that are required to be disclosed in accordance with the AICPA's Statement of Position 94-6, "Disclosure of Certain Significant Risks and Uncertainties."

6. There are no—

a. Violations or possible violations of laws or regulations whose effects should be considered for disclosure in the financial statements or as a basis for recording a loss contingency.

b. Unasserted claims or assessments that our lawyer has advised us are probable of assertion and cannot be disclosed in accordance with Financial Accounting Standards Board (FASB) Statement No. 5, "Accounting for Contingencies."

c. Other liabilities or gain or loss contingencies that are required to be accrued or disclosed by FASB Statement No. 5.

7. There are no material transactions that have not been properly recorded in the accounting records underlying the financial statements.

8. The organization has satisfactory title to all owned assets, and there are no liens or encumbrances on such assets, nor has any asset been pledged as collateral.

9. With respect to compliance with laws and regulations affecting the organization, we represent the following:

a. We are responsible for the organization's compliance with the laws and regulations applicable to it.

b. We have identified and disclosed to you all laws and regulations that have a direct and material effect on the determination of financial statement amounts and each major federal awards program.

c. We have complied with all aspects of laws, regulations, and contractual agreements that would have a material effect on the financial statements in the event of noncompliance.

10. With respect to federal awards programs—

a. We are responsible for establishing and maintaining effective internal control over compliance for federal programs that provides reasonable assurance that the organization is managing federal awards in compliance with laws, regulations, and the provisions of contracts or grant agreements that could have a material effect on its federal programs.

b. We are responsible for and have accurately prepared the summary schedule of prior audit findings to include all findings required to be included by Circular A-133.

c. We have identified in the schedule of expenditures of federal awards all assistance provided by federal agencies in the form of grants, contracts, loans, loan guarantees, property, cooperative agreements, interest subsidies, insurance, or direct appropriations, including noncash assistance.

d. We have identified the compliance requirements governing activities allowed or unallowed; allowable costs/cost principles, cash management; Davis–Bacon Act; eligibility; equipment and real property management; matching, level of effort, earmarking; period of availability of federal funds; procurement and suspension and debarment; program income; real property acquisition/relocation assistance; reporting; subrecipient monitoring; special tests and provisions.

e. We have complied, in all material respects, with the requirements in connection with federal awards.

f. Information presented in federal financial reports and claims for advances and reimbursements is supported by the books and records from which the basic financial statements have been prepared.

g. Amounts claimed for reimbursement or used for matching were determined in accordance with requirements of the Office of Management and Budget and agency requirements.

h. We have monitored subrecipients to determine that the subrecipients expend financial assistance in accordance with applicable laws and regulations, and have met the requirements of OMB Circular A-133 or other applicable federal audit requirements. When applicable, we have issued management decisions on a timely basis after receipt of subrecipients' auditors' reports that identified noncompliance with laws, regulations, or the provisions of contents or grant agreements, and have ensured that subrecipients have taken the appropriate and timely corrective action on findings.

i. We have taken appropriate corrective action on a timely basis after receipt of a subrecipient's auditor's report that identifies noncompliance with federal laws and regulations.

j. We have considered the results of the subrecipient's audits and made any necessary adjustments to the organization's own books and records.

k. We have identified and disclosed to you all amounts questioned, as well as known violations of requirements that, if not complied with, could have a material effect on a major federal award programs, and any other known noncompliance with the specific and general requirements of federal awards.

l. We are responsible for complying with the requirements in OMB Circular A-133.

m. We have disclosed whether, subsequent to the date as of which compliance is audited, any changes in internal control or other factors that might significantly affect internal control, including any corrective action taken with regard to reportable conditions (including material weaknesses), have occurred.

n. We have provided you with our interpretations of any compliance requirements that have varying interpretations.

o. The copies of federal program financial reports provided to you are true copies of the reports submitted, or electronically transmitted, to the federal agency [and/or pass-through entities].

p. We have provided you with all information on the status of the follow-up of prior audit findings by federal awarding agencies and pass-through entities, including all management decisions.

q. We have accurately completed the appropriate sections of the data collection form.

r. We have disclosed to you all contracts or other agreements with the service organizations.

s. We have disclosed to you all communications from the service organizations relating to noncompliance by the service organizations.

t. We have disclosed to you any known noncompliance subsequent to the period for which compliance is audited.

u. We have disclosed to you whether any changes in internal control over compliance or other factors that might significantly affect internal control, including any corrective action taken by management with regard to reportable conditions (including material weaknesses), have occurred subsequent to the date as of which compliance is audited.

11. To the best of our knowledge and belief, no events have occurred subsequent to the date of the statement of financial position and through the date of this letter that would require adjustments to, or disclosure in, the aforementioned financial statements.

[*Signature*]

Chief Executive Officer

[*Signature*]

Chief Financial Officer

¹ In December 1999 the AICPA issued Statement on Auditing Standards No. 89, "Audit Adjustments," which is effective for audits of financial statements for periods beginning on or after December 15, 1999, with earlier application permitted. In addition to its requirement for communicating audit adjustments to audit committees, SAS-89 adds a representation as to the effect of unrecorded audit adjustments to the financial statements to the list of matters that should be addressed in a representation letter in connection with a financial statement audit. Accordingly, the following would be added to the representation letter when SAS-89 is implemented:

> We believe that the effects of the uncorrected financial statement misstatements summarized in the accompanying schedule are immaterial, both individually and in the aggregate, to the financial statements taken as a whole.

A schedule of unrecorded audit adjustments would be added to the representation letter. However, if management believes that certain of the identified items are not misstatements, management's belief may be acknowledged by adding to the representation, for example, "We do not agree that items XX and XXX constitute misstatements because [*description of reasons*]."

Circular A-133 has some specific requirements about the preparation and filing of a reporting package. The chapter titled "Reporting under Circular A-133" describes these requirements.

SUMMARY

Working papers prepared for audits in accordance with Circular A-133 are subject to scrutiny and review by federal agencies. Particular care should be taken to ensure that the completed working papers provide adequate documentation of decisions reached and are complete in all respects.

EXHIBIT 19-2
SINGLE AUDIT REVIEW FORM

Single Audit Entity _____

Year End _____

All procedures should be completed and signed prior to the issuance of the single audit reports.

In-Charge Auditor Review

1. I have reviewed all single audit workpapers for the following attributes:
   a. All signatures (and dates) obtained
   b. Supervision indicated
   c. Indexed
   d. Cross-referenced
   e. Adequate information provided
   f. No open points remaining

2. I have reviewed the single audit programs for appropriateness and determined that all procedures have been completed and signed off by the auditor.

3. All award documents and other related documents have been obtained for the permanent file, reviewed, and cross-referenced to the appropriate workpapers.

4. All the information related to the schedule of expenditures of federal awards has been verified with the award documents and the financial records.

5. Internal control has been adequately documented and tested where necessary.

6. All reportable conditions and material weaknesses have been included in the internal control report, including those for which controls over compliance with federal laws and regulations were not effective, and thus not tested.

7. All findings and questioned costs identified in the audit workpapers have been reviewed with the recipient organization and are included in the schedule of findings and questioned costs.

8. Compliance with all applicable compliance requirements for major programs was tested.

9. All management representation letters, attorney's letters, and other confirmations have been obtained and reviewed for the audit.

10. It is my opinion that we have performed the single audit in accordance with generally accepted auditing standards, *Government Auditing Standards*, and the requirements of OMB Circular A-133. The audit procedures have been planned, conducted, and reviewed. The client's financial statements, reports, and schedules have been prepared in accordance with the criteria listed in OMB Circular A-133 and are ready to be issued as drafted.

Signed by: _____   Date: _____

Partner (or Equivalent) Review

1. I have reviewed all relevant workpapers of this single audit.

2. I have reviewed the single audit program and determined that it was appropriate in the circumstances and that all procedures have been completed and signed off.

3. I have reviewed all financial statements, single audit reports, and single audit schedules and have determined that they meet the requirements contained in OMB Circular A-133.

4. I have reviewed the financial statements, single audit reports, and single audit schedules with the recipient organization.

5. I have reviewed the management representation letter and the attorney's letter, and I believe that all matters have been considered in the audit.

6. It is my opinion that this single audit was conducted in accordance with generally accepted auditing standards, *Government Auditing Standards*, and the requirements of OMB Circular A-133, and that the reports can be issued as drafted.

Signed by: _____   Date: _____

Final Review

1. I have reviewed the other sections of this form for appropriateness and completeness.

2. I have reviewed the single audit program and related procedures and have determined that we have met the criteria established by generally accepted auditing standards, *Government Auditing Standards*, and OMB Circular A-133.

3. I have read the management representation letter and attorney's letter and believe we have handled both documents properly in our audit.

4. I have reviewed the financial statements, single audit reports, and single audit schedules and have determined that these have been prepared in accordance with generally accepted auditing standards, *Government Auditing Standards*, and OMB Circular A-133.

Signed by: _____   Date: _____

EXHIBIT 19-3
SINGLE AUDIT REPORT CONTROL FORM

Recipient Organization _____

Fiscal Year End _____

Cover of Report to Be Labeled _____

This report will include the following single audit reports:

	Yes	*No*
Auditor's Opinion	_____	_____
Financial Statements	_____	_____
Schedule of Expenditures of Federal Awards	_____	_____
Report on Schedule of Expenditures of Federal Awards	_____	_____
Internal Control and Compliance Report for GAS	_____	_____
Internal Control Report and Compliance Opinion for Single Audit	_____	_____
Data Collection Form Signature	_____	_____
Other: _____	_____	_____
_____	_____	_____
_____	_____	_____
_____	_____	_____

Audit Partner Contact _____

Audit Senior Contact _____

Date Reports to Be Issued _____

Date Reports Sent _____

Distribution of Reports (Name, Address, and Number of Copies)

1.

2.

3.

4.

5.

Final Instructions/Comments:

_____

_____

_____

_____

_____

_____

_____

_____

APPENDIXES

APPENDIX A

Form **990**		**Return of Organization Exempt From Income Tax**	OMB No. 1545-0047
		Under section 501(c) of the Internal Revenue Code (except black lung benefit trust or private foundation) or section 4947(a)(1) nonexempt charitable trust	19**99**
Department of the Treasury Internal Revenue Service		**Note:** *The organization may have to use a copy of this return to satisfy state reporting requirements.*	This Form is Open to Public Inspection

A For the 1999 calendar year, OR tax year period beginning _____ , 1999, and ending _____ ,

B Check if: ☐ Change of address ☐ Initial return ☐ Final return ☐ Amended return (required also for state reporting)	Please use IRS label or print or type. See Specific Instructions.	**C** Name of organization		**D** Employer identification number
		Number and street (or P.O. box if mail is not delivered to street address)	Room/suite	**E** Telephone number
		City or town, state or country, and ZIP+4		**F** Check ▶ ☐ if exemption application is pending

G Type of organization— ▶ ☐ Exempt under section 501(c)( ) ◀ (insert number) OR ▶ ☐ section 4947(a)(1) nonexempt charitable trust

Note: *Section 501(c)(3) exempt organizations and 4947(a)(1) nonexempt charitable trusts MUST attach a completed Schedule A (Form 990).*

H(a) Is this a group return filed for affiliates? . . . . ☐ Yes ☐ No

(b) If "Yes," enter the number of affiliates for which this return is filed: . ▶ _____

(c) Is this a separate return filed by an organization covered by a group ruling? ☐ Yes ☐ No

I If either box in H is checked "Yes," enter four-digit group exemption number (GEN) ▶ ....

J Accounting method: ☐ Cash ☐ Accrual ☐ Other (specify) ▶

K Check here ▶ ☐ if the organization's gross receipts are normally not more than $25,000. The organization need not file a return with the IRS; but if it received a Form 990 Package in the mail, it should file a return without financial data. **Some states require a complete return.**

Note: *Form 990-EZ may be used by organizations with gross receipts less than $100,000 and total assets less than $250,000 at end of year.*

Part I   Revenue, Expenses, and Changes in Net Assets or Fund Balances (See Specific Instructions on page 15.)

Revenue

1	Contributions, gifts, grants, and similar amounts received:			
a	Direct public support	1a		
b	Indirect public support	1b		
c	Government contributions (grants)	1c		
d	**Total** (add lines 1a through 1c) (attach schedule of contributors) (cash $ _____ noncash $ _____)		1d	
2	Program service revenue including government fees and contracts (from Part VII, line 93)		2	
3	Membership dues and assessments		3	
4	Interest on savings and temporary cash investments		4	
5	Dividends and interest from securities		5	
6a	Gross rents	6a		
b	Less: rental expenses	6b		
c	Net rental income or (loss) (subtract line 6b from line 6a)		6c	
7	Other investment income (describe ▶)		7	
8a	Gross amount from sales of assets other than inventory	(A) Securities 8a	(B) Other	
b	Less: cost or other basis and sales expenses.	8b		
c	Gain or (loss) (attach schedule)	8c		
d	Net gain or (loss) (combine line 8c, columns (A) and (B))		8d	
9	Special events and activities (attach schedule)			
a	Gross revenue (not including $ _____ of contributions reported on line 1a)	9a		
b	Less: direct expenses other than fundraising expenses .	9b		
c	Net income or (loss) from special events (subtract line 9b from line 9a)		9c	
10a	Gross sales of inventory, less returns and allowances . .	10a		
b	Less: cost of goods sold	10b		
c	Gross profit or (loss) from sales of inventory (attach schedule) (subtract line 10b from line 10a) .		10c	
11	Other revenue (from Part VII, line 103)		11	
12	**Total revenue** (add lines 1d, 2, 3, 4, 5, 6c, 7, 8d, 9c, 10c, and 11)		12	

Expenses

13	Program services (from line 44, column (B))	13	
14	Management and general (from line 44, column (C))	14	
15	Fundraising (from line 44, column (D))	15	
16	Payments to affiliates (attach schedule)	16	
17	**Total expenses** (add lines 16 and 44, column (A))	17	

Net Assets

18	Excess or (deficit) for the year (subtract line 17 from line 12)	18	
19	Net assets or fund balances at beginning of year (from line 73, column (A))	19	
20	Other changes in net assets or fund balances (attach explanation)	20	
21	Net assets or fund balances at end of year (combine lines 18, 19, and 20)	21	

For Paperwork Reduction Act Notice, see page 1 of the separate instructions.   Cat. No. 11282Y   Form **990** (1999)

Form 990 (1999)   Page **2**

Part II	**Statement of Functional Expenses**	All organizations must complete column (A). Columns (B), (C), and (D) are required for section 501(c)(3) and (4) organizations and section 4947(a)(1) nonexempt charitable trusts but optional for others. (See Specific Instructions on page 19.)

Do not include amounts reported on line 6b, 8b, 9b, 10b, or 16 of Part I.		**(A)** Total	**(B)** Program services	**(C)** Management and general	**(D)** Fundraising
22	Grants and allocations (attach schedule) . . (cash $_____ noncash $_____)	22			
23	Specific assistance to individuals (attach schedule)	23			
24	Benefits paid to or for members (attach schedule)	24			
25	Compensation of officers, directors, etc. . .	25			
26	Other salaries and wages	26			
27	Pension plan contributions	27			
28	Other employee benefits	28			
29	Payroll taxes	29			
30	Professional fundraising fees	30			
31	Accounting fees	31			
32	Legal fees	32			
33	Supplies	33			
34	Telephone	34			
35	Postage and shipping	35			
36	Occupancy	36			
37	Equipment rental and maintenance	37			
38	Printing and publications	38			
39	Travel	39			
40	Conferences, conventions, and meetings . .	40			
41	Interest	41			
42	Depreciation, depletion, etc. (attach schedule)	42			
43	Other expenses (itemize): a	43a			
b	....	43b			
c	....	43c			
d	....	43d			
e	....	43e			
44	**Total functional expenses** (add lines 22 through 43). *Organizations completing columns (B)-(D), carry these totals to lines 13—15* .	44			

Reporting of Joint Costs. Did you report in column (B) (Program services) any joint costs from a combined educational campaign and fundraising solicitation?   . . . . ▶ ☐ Yes ☐ No
If "Yes," enter **(i)** the aggregate amount of these joint costs $_____; **(ii)** the amount allocated to Program services $_____;
(iii) the amount allocated to Management and general $_____; and **(iv)** the amount allocated to Fundraising $_____

Part III	**Statement of Program Service Accomplishments** (See Specific Instructions on page 22.)

What is the organization's primary exempt purpose? ▶...

All organizations must describe their exempt purpose achievements in a clear and concise manner. State the number of clients served, publications issued, etc. Discuss achievements that are not measurable. (Section 501(c)(3) and (4) organizations and 4947(a)(1) nonexempt charitable trusts must also enter the amount of grants and allocations to others.)

Program Service Expenses (Required for 501(c)(3) and (4) orgs., and 4947(a)(1) trusts; but optional for others.)

a ....
....
....(Grants and allocations $_____)

b ....
....
....(Grants and allocations $_____)

c ....
....
....(Grants and allocations $_____)

d ....
....
....(Grants and allocations $_____)

e Other program services (attach schedule)   (Grants and allocations $_____)
f Total of Program Service Expenses (should equal line 44, column (B), Program services) . . . . . ▶

Form **990** (1999)

| Part IV | Balance Sheets (See Specific Instructions on page 22.) | | |

Note:	Where required, attached schedules and amounts within the description column should be for end-of-year amounts only.	(A) Beginning of year	(B) End of year
	Assets		
45	Cash—non-interest-bearing	45	
46	Savings and temporary cash investments	46	
47a	Accounts receivable **47a**		
b	Less: allowance for doubtful accounts . . **47b**	47c	
48a	Pledges receivable **48a**		
b	Less: allowance for doubtful accounts . . **48b**	48c	
49	Grants receivable	49	
50	Receivables from officers, directors, trustees, and key employees (attach schedule)	50	
51a	Other notes and loans receivable (attach schedule). **51a**		
b	Less: allowance for doubtful accounts . . **51b**	51c	
52	Inventories for sale or use	52	
53	Prepaid expenses and deferred charges	53	
54	Investments—securities (attach schedule)	54	
55a	Investments—land, buildings, and equipment: basis **55a**		
b	Less: accumulated depreciation (attach schedule). **55b**	55c	
56	Investments—other (attach schedule)	56	
57a	Land, buildings, and equipment: basis . . **57a**		
b	Less: accumulated depreciation (attach schedule). **57b**	57c	
58	Other assets (describe ▶ _____)	58	
59	**Total assets** (add lines 45 through 58) (must equal line 74)	59	
	Liabilities		
60	Accounts payable and accrued expenses	60	
61	Grants payable	61	
62	Deferred revenue	62	
63	Loans from officers, directors, trustees, and key employees (attach schedule).	63	
64a	Tax-exempt bond liabilities (attach schedule)	64a	
b	Mortgages and other notes payable (attach schedule)	64b	
65	Other liabilities (describe ▶ _____)	65	
66	**Total liabilities** (add lines 60 through 65)	66	
	Net Assets or Fund Balances		
	Organizations that follow SFAS 117, check here ▶ ☐ **and complete lines 67 through 69 and lines 73 and 74.**		
67	Unrestricted.	67	
68	Temporarily restricted	68	
69	Permanently restricted	69	
	Organizations that do not follow SFAS 117, check here ▶ ☐ **and complete lines 70 through 74.**		
70	Capital stock, trust principal, or current funds	70	
71	Paid-in or capital surplus, or land, building, and equipment fund . .	71	
72	Retained earnings, endowment, accumulated income, or other funds	72	
73	**Total net assets or fund balances** (add lines 67 through 69 OR lines 70 through 72; column (A) must equal line 19 and column (B) must equal line 21)	73	
74	**Total liabilities and net assets / fund balances** (add lines 66 and 73)	74	

Form 990 is available for public inspection and, for some people, serves as the primary or sole source of information about a particular organization. How the public perceives an organization in such cases may be determined by the information presented on its return. Therefore, please make sure the return is complete and accurate and fully describes, in Part III, the organization's programs and accomplishments.

Form 990 (1999)   Page **4**

| **Part IV-A** | **Reconciliation of Revenue per Audited Financial Statements with Revenue per Return** (See Specific Instructions, page 24.) | **Part IV-B** | **Reconciliation of Expenses per Audited Financial Statements with Expenses per Return** |

a Total revenue, gains, and other support per audited financial statements . . ▶	**a**	**a** Total expenses and losses per audited financial statements . . ▶	**a**
b Amounts included on line **a** but not on line 12, Form 990:		**b** Amounts included on line **a** but not on line 17, Form 990:	
(1) Net unrealized gains on investments . . $_____		**(1)** Donated services and use of facilities $_____	
(2) Donated services and use of facilities $_____		**(2)** Prior year adjustments reported on line 20, Form 990 . . . . $_____	
(3) Recoveries of prior year grants . . . $_____		**(3)** Losses reported on line 20, Form 990 . $_____	
(4) Other (specify): .... $_____		**(4)** Other (specify): .... $_____	
Add amounts on lines **(1)** through **(4)** ▶	**b**	Add amounts on lines **(1)** through **(4)**▶	**b**
c Line **a** minus line **b**. . . . . ▶	**c**	**c** Line **a** minus line **b** . . . . . ▶	**c**
d Amounts included on line 12, Form 990 but not on line **a**:		**d** Amounts included on line 17, Form 990 but not on line **a**:	
(1) Investment expenses not included on line 6b, Form 990 . . . $_____		**(1)** Investment expenses not included on line 6b, Form 990. . . $_____	
(2) Other (specify): .... $_____		**(2)** Other (specify): .... $_____	
Add amounts on lines **(1)** and **(2)** ▶	**d**	Add amounts on lines **(1)** and **(2)** ▶	**d**
e Total revenue per line 12, Form 990 (line **c** plus line **d**) . . . . . . ▶	**e**	**e** Total expenses per line 17, Form 990 (line **c** plus line **d**) . . . . . ▶	**e**

| **Part V** | **List of Officers, Directors, Trustees, and Key Employees** (List each one even if not compensated; see Specific Instructions on page 24.) |

(A) Name and address	**(B)** Title and average hours per week devoted to position	**(C)** Compensation (If not paid, enter -0-.)	**(D)** Contributions to employee benefit plans & deferred compensation	**(E)** Expense account and other allowances

75 Did any officer, director, trustee, or key employee receive aggregate compensation of more than $100,000 from your organization and all related organizations, of which more than $10,000 was provided by the related organizations? ▶ ☐ **Yes** ☐ **No** If "Yes," attach schedule—see Specific Instructions on page 25.

Form **990** (1999)

Form 990 (1999)

Page **5**

Part VI Other Information (See Specific Instructions on page 25.)

		Yes	No
76	Did the organization engage in any activity not previously reported to the IRS? If "Yes," attach a detailed description of each activity . **76**		
77	Were any changes made in the organizing or governing documents but not reported to the IRS? . . . **77**		
	If "Yes," attach a conformed copy of the changes.		
78a	Did the organization have unrelated business gross income of $1,000 or more during the year covered by this return?. **78a**		
b	If "Yes," has it filed a tax return on **Form 990-T** for this year? **78b**		
79	Was there a liquidation, dissolution, termination, or substantial contraction during the year? If "Yes," attach a statement **79**		
80a	Is the organization related (other than by association with a statewide or nationwide organization) through common membership, governing bodies, trustees, officers, etc., to any other exempt or nonexempt organization? . . . **80a**		
b	If "Yes," enter the name of the organization ▶		
	.... and check whether it is ☐ exempt **OR** ☐ nonexempt.		
81a	Enter the amount of political expenditures, direct or indirect, as described in the		
	instructions for line 81. . . . . `81a`		
b	Did the organization file **Form 1120-POL** for this year?. **81b**		
82a	Did the organization receive donated services or the use of materials, equipment, or facilities at no charge or at substantially less than fair rental value? **82a**		
b	If "Yes," you may indicate the value of these items here. Do not include this amount as revenue in Part I or as an expense in Part II. (See instructions for reporting in Part III.). . . . . `82b`		
83a	Did the organization comply with the public inspection requirements for returns and exemption applications? **83a**		
b	Did the organization comply with the disclosure requirements relating to quid pro quo contributions? . . **83b**		
84a	Did the organization solicit any contributions or gifts that were not tax deductible? **84a**		
b	If "Yes," did the organization include with every solicitation an express statement that such contributions or gifts were not tax deductible? **84b**		
85	*501(c)(4), (5), or (6) organizations.* **a** Were substantially all dues nondeductible by members? **85a**		
b	Did the organization make only in-house lobbying expenditures of $2,000 or less? **85b**		
	If "Yes" was answered to either 85a or 85b, **do not** complete 85c through 85h below unless the organization received a waiver for proxy tax owed for the prior year.		
c	Dues, assessments, and similar amounts from members . . . . `85c`		
d	Section 162(e) lobbying and political expenditures . . . . `85d`		
e	Aggregate nondeductible amount of section 6033(e)(1)(A) dues notices . . . `85e`		
f	Taxable amount of lobbying and political expenditures (line 85d less 85e) . . . `85f`		
g	Does the organization elect to pay the section 6033(e) tax on the amount in 85f?. **85g**		
h	If section 6033(e)(1)(A) dues notices were sent, does the organization agree to add the amount in 85f to its reasonable estimate of dues allocable to nondeductible lobbying and political expenditures for the following tax year?. . . **85h**		
86	*501(c)(7) orgs.* Enter: **a** Initiation fees and capital contributions included on line 12 . `86a`		
b	Gross receipts, included on line 12, for public use of club facilities. . . . . `86b`		
87	*501(c)(12) orgs.* Enter: **a** Gross income from members or shareholders. . . . `87a`		
b	Gross income from other sources. (Do not net amounts due or paid to other sources against amounts due or received from them.) . . . . `87b`		
88	At any time during the year, did the organization own a 50% or greater interest in a taxable corporation or partnership, or an entity disregarded as separate from the organization under Regulations sections 301.7701-2 and 301.7701-3? If "Yes," complete Part IX **88**		
89a	*501(c)(3) organizations.* Enter: Amount of tax imposed on the organization during the year under:		
	section 4911 ▶ _____ ; section 4912 ▶ _____ ; section 4955 ▶ _____		
b	*501(c)(3) and 501(c)(4) orgs.* Did the organization engage in any section 4958 excess benefit transaction during the year or did it become aware of an excess benefit transaction from a prior year? If "Yes," attach a statement explaining each transaction. **89b**		
c	Enter: Amount of tax imposed on the organization managers or disqualified persons during the year under sections 4912, 4955, and 4958. . . . . ▶ _____		
d	Enter: Amount of tax on line 89c, above, reimbursed by the organization. . . . . ▶ _____		
90a	List the states with which a copy of this return is filed ▶		
b	Number of employees employed in the pay period that includes March 12, 1999 (See inst.) . `90b`		
91	The books are in care of ▶ .... Telephone no. ▶ (____)		
	Located at ▶ .... ZIP + 4 ▶		
92	*Section 4947(a)(1) nonexempt charitable trusts filing Form 990 in lieu of **Form 1041**—Check here . . . . ▶ ☐*		
	and enter the amount of tax-exempt interest received or accrued during the tax year . . ▶ `92`		

Form **990** (1999)

Form 990 (1999)

Part VII — Analysis of Income-Producing Activities (See Specific Instructions on page 29.)

Enter gross amounts unless otherwise indicated.	Unrelated business income		Excluded by section 512, 513, or 514		(E) Related or exempt function income
	(A) Business code	(B) Amount	(C) Exclusion code	(D) Amount	
93 Program service revenue:					
a					
b					
c					
d					
e					
f Medicare/Medicaid payments					
g Fees and contracts from government agencies					
94 Membership dues and assessments . . .					
95 Interest on savings and temporary cash investments					
96 Dividends and interest from securities . . .					
97 Net rental income or (loss) from real estate:					
a debt-financed property					
b not debt-financed property					
98 Net rental income or (loss) from personal property					
99 Other investment income					
100 Gain or (loss) from sales of assets other than inventory					
101 Net income or (loss) from special events . .					
102 Gross profit or (loss) from sales of inventory .					
103 Other revenue: a					
b					
c					
d					
e					
104 Subtotal (add columns (B), (D), and (E)) . . .					

105 Total (add line 104, columns (B), (D), and (E)) . . . . ▶

Note: *Line 105 plus line 1d, Part I, should equal the amount on line 12, Part I.*

Part VIII — Relationship of Activities to the Accomplishment of Exempt Purposes (See Specific Instructions on page 30.)

Line No. ▼ | Explain how each activity for which income is reported in column (E) of Part VII contributed importantly to the accomplishment of the organization's exempt purposes (other than by providing funds for such purposes).

Part IX — Information Regarding Taxable Subsidiaries and Disregarded Entities (See Specific Instructions on page 30.)

(A) Name, address, and EIN of corporation, partnership, or disregarded entity	(B) Percentage of ownership interest	(C) Nature of activities	(D) Total income	(E) End-of-year assets
	%			
	%			
	%			
	%			

Please Sign Here | Under penalties of perjury, I declare that I have examined this return, including accompanying schedules and statements, and to the best of my knowledge and belief, it is true, correct, and complete. Declaration of preparer (other than officer) is based on all information of which preparer has any knowledge. (**Important:** See General Instruction U, on page 14.)

▶ Signature of officer | Date | ▶ Type or print name and title.

Paid Preparer's Use Only

Preparer's signature ▶		Date	Check if self-employed ▶ ☐	Preparer's SSN or PTIN
Firm's name (or yours if self-employed) and address ▶			EIN ▶	
			ZIP + 4 ▶	

Form **990** (1999)

<table>
<tr><td>**SCHEDULE A**
(Form 990)

Department of the Treasury
Internal Revenue Service</td><td colspan="2">**Organization Exempt Under Section 501(c)(3)**
(Except Private Foundation) and Section 501(e), 501(f), 501(k),
501(n), or Section 4947(a)(1) Nonexempt Charitable Trust
Supplementary Information—(See separate instructions.)
▶ **MUST be completed by the above organizations and attached to their Form 990 or 990-EZ**</td><td>OMB No. 1545-0047

1999</td></tr>
</table>

Name of the organization				Employer identification number

Part I Compensation of the Five Highest Paid Employees Other Than Officers, Directors, and Trustees
(See page 1 of the instructions. List each one. If there are none, enter "None.")

(a) Name and address of each employee paid more than $50,000	**(b)** Title and average hours per week devoted to position	**(c)** Compensation	**(d)** Contributions to employee benefit plans & deferred compensation	**(e)** Expense account and other allowances
....				
....				
....				
....				
....				

Total number of other employees paid over
$50,000 . . . . ▶

Part II Compensation of the Five Highest Paid Independent Contractors for Professional Services
(See page 1 of the instructions. List each one (whether individuals or firms). If there are none, enter "None.")

(a) Name and address of each independent contractor paid more than $50,000	**(b)** Type of service	**(c)** Compensation
....		
....		
....		
....		
....		

Total number of others receiving over $50,000 for
professional services . . . . ▶

For Paperwork Reduction Act Notice, see page 1 of the Instructions for Form 990 and Form 990-EZ. Cat. No. 11285F   **Schedule A (Form 990) 1999**

Schedule A (Form 990) 1999   Page **2**

Part III	**Statements About Activities**		Yes	No

1 During the year, has the organization attempted to influence national, state, or local legislation, including any attempt to influence public opinion on a legislative matter or referendum? **1**

If "Yes," enter the total expenses paid or incurred in connection with the lobbying activities ▶ $ _____

Organizations that made an election under section 501(h) by filing Form 5768 must complete Part VI-A. Other organizations checking "Yes," must complete Part VI-B AND attach a statement giving a detailed description of the lobbying activities.

2 During the year, has the organization, either directly or indirectly, engaged in any of the following acts with any of its trustees, directors, officers, creators, key employees, or members of their families, or with any taxable organization with which any such person is affiliated as an officer, director, trustee, majority owner, or principal beneficiary:

a Sale, exchange, or leasing of property? **2a**

b Lending of money or other extension of credit? **2b**

c Furnishing of goods, services, or facilities? **2c**

d Payment of compensation (or payment or reimbursement of expenses if more than $1,000)? **2d**

e Transfer of any part of its income or assets? **2e**

If the answer to any question is "Yes," attach a detailed statement explaining the transactions.

3 Does the organization make grants for scholarships, fellowships, student loans, etc.? **3**

4a Do you have a section 403(b) annuity plan for your employees? **4a**

b Attach a statement to explain how the organization determines that individuals or organizations receiving grants or loans from it in furtherance of its charitable programs qualify to receive payments. (See page 2 of the instructions.)

Part IV	**Reason for Non-Private Foundation Status** (See pages 2 through 4 of the instructions.)

The organization is not a private foundation because it is: (Please check only **ONE** applicable box.)

5 ☐ A church, convention of churches, or association of churches. Section 170(b)(1)(A)(i).

6 ☐ A school. Section 170(b)(1)(A)(ii). (Also complete Part V, page 4.)

7 ☐ A hospital or a cooperative hospital service organization. Section 170(b)(1)(A)(iii).

8 ☐ A Federal, state, or local government or governmental unit. Section 170(b)(1)(A)(v).

9 ☐ A medical research organization operated in conjunction with a hospital. Section 170(b)(1)(A)(iii). **Enter the hospital's name, city, and state** ▶ ....

10 ☐ An organization operated for the benefit of a college or university owned or operated by a governmental unit. Section 170(b)(1)(A)(iv). (Also complete the **Support Schedule** in Part IV-A.)

11a ☐ An organization that normally receives a substantial part of its support from a governmental unit or from the general public. Section 170(b)(1)(A)(vi). (Also complete the **Support Schedule** in Part IV-A.)

11b ☐ A community trust. Section 170(b)(1)(A)(vi). (Also complete the **Support Schedule** in Part IV-A.)

12 ☐ An organization that normally receives: **(1)** more than 33⅓% of its support from contributions, membership fees, and gross receipts from activities related to its charitable, etc., functions—subject to certain exceptions, and **(2)** no more than 33⅓% of its support from gross investment income and unrelated business taxable income (less section 511 tax) from businesses acquired by the organization after June 30, 1975. See section 509(a)(2). (Also complete the **Support Schedule** in Part IV-A.)

13 ☐ An organization that is not controlled by any disqualified persons (other than foundation managers) and supports organizations described in: **(1)** lines 5 through 12 above; or **(2)** section 501(c)(4), (5), or (6), if they meet the test of section 509(a)(2). (See section 509(a)(3).)

Provide the following information about the supported organizations. (See page 4 of the instructions.)

(a) Name(s) of supported organization(s)	**(b)** Line number from above

14 ☐ An organization organized and operated to test for public safety. Section 509(a)(4). (See page 4 of the instructions.)

                                                        Schedule A (Form 990) 1999

Schedule A (Form 990) 1999   Page **3**

Part IV-A **Support Schedule** (Complete only if you checked a box on line 10, 11, or 12.) *Use cash method of accounting.*
Note: *You may use the worksheet in the instructions for converting from the accrual to the cash method of accounting.*

Calendar year (or fiscal year beginning in) ▶	(a) 1998	(b) 1997	(c) 1996	(d) 1995	(e) Total
15 Gifts, grants, and contributions received. (Do not include unusual grants. See line 28.)					
16 Membership fees received					
17 Gross receipts from admissions, merchandise sold or services performed, or furnishing of facilities in any activity that is not a business unrelated to the organization's charitable, etc., purpose					
18 Gross income from interest, dividends, amounts received from payments on securities loans (section 512(a)(5)), rents, royalties, and unrelated business taxable income (less section 511 taxes) from businesses acquired by the organization after June 30, 1975					
19 Net income from unrelated business activities not included in line 18					
20 Tax revenues levied for the organization's benefit and either paid to it or expended on its behalf.					
21 The value of services or facilities furnished to the organization by a governmental unit without charge. Do not include the value of services or facilities generally furnished to the public without charge.					
22 Other income. Attach a schedule. Do not include gain or (loss) from sale of capital assets					
23 Total of lines 15 through 22.					
24 Line 23 minus line 17.					
25 Enter 1% of line 23					

26 Organizations described on lines 10 or 11:   **a** Enter 2% of amount in column (e), line 24. . . . ▶ | **26a** |

     b Attach a list (which is not open to public inspection) showing the name of and amount contributed by each person (other than a governmental unit or publicly supported organization) whose total gifts for 1995 through 1998 exceeded the amount shown in line 26a. Enter the sum of all these excess amounts. . . . . ▶ | **26b** |

     c Total support for section 509(a)(1) test: Enter line 24, column (e) . . . . ▶ | **26c** |
     d Add: Amounts from column (e) for lines: 18 _____   19 _____
                        22 _____   26b _____ . . . . . ▶ | **26d** |
     e Public support (line 26c minus line 26d total) . . . . ▶ | **26e** |
     f **Public support percentage (line 26e (numerator) divided by line 26c (denominator))** . . . . . ▶ | **26f** | % |

27 Organizations described on line 12:   **a** For amounts included in lines 15, 16, and 17 that were received from a "disqualified person," attach a list to show the name of, and total amounts received in each year from, each "disqualified person." Enter the sum of such amounts for each year:

     (1998) .... (1997) .... (1996) .... (1995) ....

     b For any amount included in line 17 that was received from a nondisqualified person, attach a list to show the name of, and amount received for each year, that was more than the **larger** of **(1)** the amount on line 25 for the year or **(2)** $5,000. (Include in the list organizations described in lines 5 through 11, as well as individuals.) After computing the difference between the amount received and the larger amount described in **(1)** or **(2)**, enter the sum of these differences (the excess amounts) for each year:

     (1998) .... (1997) .... (1996) .... (1995) ....

     c Add: Amounts from column (e) for lines: 15 _____   16 _____
                        17 _____   20 _____   21 _____ . . . . . ▶ | **27c** |
     d Add: Line 27a total _____   and line 27b total . _____ . . . . . . ▶ | **27d** |
     e Public support (line 27c total minus line 27d total). . . . . ▶ | **27e** |
     f Total support for section 509(a)(2) test: Enter amount on line 23, column (e) . . ▶ | **27f** |
     g **Public support percentage (line 27e (numerator) divided by line 27f (denominator)).** . . . . . ▶ | **27g** | % |
     h **Investment income percentage (line 18, column (e) (numerator) divided by line 27f (denominator)).** ▶ | **27h** | % |

28 **Unusual Grants:** For an organization described in line 10, 11, or 12 that received any unusual grants during 1995 through 1998, attach a list (which is not open to public inspection) for each year showing the name of the contributor, the date and amount of the grant, and a brief description of the nature of the grant. Do not include these grants in line 15. (See page 4 of the instructions.)

                                                                         Schedule A (Form 990) 1999

Schedule A (Form 990) 1999   Page **4**

Part V	**Private School Questionnaire** (See page 4 of the instructions.)

(To be completed ONLY by schools that checked the box on line 6 in Part IV)

	Yes	No

29   Does the organization have a racially nondiscriminatory policy toward students by statement in its charter, bylaws, other governing instrument, or in a resolution of its governing body? **29**

30   Does the organization include a statement of its racially nondiscriminatory policy toward students in all its brochures, catalogues, and other written communications with the public dealing with student admissions, programs, and scholarships? **30**

31   Has the organization publicized its racially nondiscriminatory policy through newspaper or broadcast media during the period of solicitation for students, or during the registration period if it has no solicitation program, in a way that makes the policy known to all parts of the general community it serves?. **31**
     If "Yes," please describe; if "No," please explain. (If you need more space, attach a separate statement.)

----

32   Does the organization maintain the following:
   a   Records indicating the racial composition of the student body, faculty, and administrative staff? **32a**
   b   Records documenting that scholarships and other financial assistance are awarded on a racially nondiscriminatory basis? **32b**
   c   Copies of all catalogues, brochures, announcements, and other written communications to the public dealing with student admissions, programs, and scholarships? **32c**
   d   Copies of all material used by the organization or on its behalf to solicit contributions? **32d**

     If you answered "No" to any of the above, please explain. (If you need more space, attach a separate statement.)

----

33   Does the organization discriminate by race in any way with respect to:

   a   Students' rights or privileges?. **33a**

   b   Admissions policies? **33b**

   c   Employment of faculty or administrative staff? **33c**

   d   Scholarships or other financial assistance? **33d**

   e   Educational policies? **33e**

   f   Use of facilities? **33f**

   g   Athletic programs? **33g**

   h   Other extracurricular activities? **33h**

     If you answered "Yes" to any of the above, please explain. (If you need more space, attach a separate statement.)

34a   Does the organization receive any financial aid or assistance from a governmental agency? **34a**

   b   Has the organization's right to such aid ever been revoked or suspended? **34b**
     If you answered "Yes" to either 34a or b, please explain using an attached statement.

35   Does the organization certify that it has complied with the applicable requirements of sections 4.01 through 4.05 of Rev. Proc. 75-50, 1975-2 C.B. 587, covering racial nondiscrimination? If "No," attach an explanation . . .   **35**

Schedule A (Form 990) 1999

Part VI-A   **Lobbying Expenditures by Electing Public Charities** (See page 6 of the instructions.)
(To be completed **ONLY** by an eligible organization that filed Form 5768)

Check here ► **a** ☐ if the organization belongs to an affiliated group.
Check here ► **b** ☐ if you checked **"a"** above and "limited control" provisions apply.

Limits on Lobbying Expenditures (The term "expenditures" means amounts paid or incurred.)		(a) Affiliated group totals	(b) To be completed for ALL electing organizations
36 Total lobbying expenditures to influence public opinion (grassroots lobbying)	**36**		
37 Total lobbying expenditures to influence a legislative body (direct lobbying)	**37**		
38 Total lobbying expenditures (add lines 36 and 37)	**38**		
39 Other exempt purpose expenditures	**39**		
40 Total exempt purpose expenditures (add lines 38 and 39).	**40**		
41 Lobbying nontaxable amount. Enter the amount from the following table—			

If the amount on line 40 is—   **The lobbying nontaxable amount is—**

Not over $500,000 . . . . . . .20% of the amount on line 40. . . . . . ⎫
Over $500,000 but not over $1,000,000 . .$100,000 plus 15% of the excess over $500,000 ⎪
Over $1,000,000 but not over $1,500,000 .$175,000 plus 10% of the excess over $1,000,000 ⎬ **41**
Over $1,500,000 but not over $17,000,000 .$225,000 plus 5% of the excess over $1,500,000 ⎪
Over $17,000,000 . . . .$1,000,000 . . . . ⎭

42 Grassroots nontaxable amount (enter 25% of line 41)	**42**		
43 Subtract line 42 from line 36. Enter -0- if line 42 is more than line 36	**43**		
44 Subtract line 41 from line 38. Enter -0- if line 41 is more than line 38	**44**		

Caution: *If there is an amount on either line 43 or line 44, you must file Form 4720.*

4-Year Averaging Period Under Section 501(h)

(Some organizations that made a section 501(h) election do not have to complete all of the five columns below.
See the instructions for lines 45 through 50 on page 7 of the instructions.)

Calendar year (or fiscal year beginning in) ►	Lobbying Expenditures During 4-Year Averaging Period				
	(a) 1999	(b) 1998	(c) 1997	(d) 1996	(e) Total
45 Lobbying nontaxable amount					
46 Lobbying ceiling amount (150% of line 45(e)) .					
47 Total lobbying expenditures					
48 Grassroots nontaxable amount					
49 Grassroots ceiling amount (150% of line 48(e))					
50 Grassroots lobbying expenditures					

Part VI-B   **Lobbying Activity by Nonelecting Public Charities**
(For reporting only by organizations that did not complete Part VI-A) (See page 8 of the instructions.)

During the year, did the organization attempt to influence national, state or local legislation, including any attempt to influence public opinion on a legislative matter or referendum, through the use of:	Yes	No	Amount
a Volunteers			
b Paid staff or management (Include compensation in expenses reported on lines **c** through **h.**)			
c Media advertisements			
d Mailings to members, legislators, or the public			
e Publications, or published or broadcast statements			
f Grants to other organizations for lobbying purposes			
g Direct contact with legislators, their staffs, government officials, or a legislative body			
h Rallies, demonstrations, seminars, conventions, speeches, lectures, or any other means			
i Total lobbying expenditures (add lines **c** through **h**).			

If "Yes" to any of the above, also attach a statement giving a detailed description of the lobbying activities.

Schedule A (Form 990) 1999

| Part VII | Information Regarding Transfers To and Transactions and Relationships With Noncharitable Exempt Organizations (See page 8 of the instructions.) |

51   Did the reporting organization directly or indirectly engage in any of the following with any other organization described in section 501(c) of the Code (other than section 501(c)(3) organizations) or in section 527, relating to political organizations?

			Yes	No
a Transfers from the reporting organization to a noncharitable exempt organization of:				
(i) Cash	51a(i)			
(ii) Other assets	a(ii)			
b Other transactions:				
(i) Sales or exchanges of assets with a noncharitable exempt organization	b(i)			
(ii) Purchases of assets from a noncharitable exempt organization	b(ii)			
(iii) Rental of facilities, equipment, or other assets	b(iii)			
(iv) Reimbursement arrangements	b(iv)			
(v) Loans or loan guarantees	b(v)			
(vi) Performance of services or membership or fundraising solicitations	b(vi)			
c Sharing of facilities, equipment, mailing lists, other assets, or paid employees	c			

d   If the answer to any of the above is "Yes," complete the following schedule. Column (b) should always show the fair market value of the goods, other assets, or services given by the reporting organization. If the organization received less than fair market value in any transaction or sharing arrangement, show in column (d) the value of the goods, other assets, or services received:

(a) Line no.	(b) Amount involved	(c) Name of noncharitable exempt organization	(d) Description of transfers, transactions, and sharing arrangements

52a Is the organization directly or indirectly affiliated with, or related to, one or more tax-exempt organizations described in section 501(c) of the Code (other than section 501(c)(3)) or in section 527? . . . . . . ▶ ☐ **Yes** ☐ **No**

b   If "Yes," complete the following schedule:

(a) Name of organization	(b) Type of organization	(c) Description of relationship

2001

MILLER

Not-For-Profit Organization Audits

CPE Module

Auditing Not-For-Profit Organizations

CPE REQUIREMENTS.
PLEASE READ THIS.

CPE requirements and course acceptability vary from state to state. Your state board is the final authority for the number of credit hours allowed for a particular program, as well as the classification of courses, under its specific licensing requirement. Contact your state board of accountancy for information concerning your state's requirements for the number of CPE credit hours you must earn, and the acceptable fields of study. This course is not currently registered under the Florida QA Service.

INTRODUCTION

Thank you for choosing this self-study CPE course from Harcourt Professional Publishing. Our goal is to provide you with the most clear, most concise, and most up-to-date accounting and auditing information to help further your professional development, as well as the most convenient method to help you satisfy your continuing professional education obligations.

This CPE program is intended to be used in conjunction with *2001 Not-for-Profit Organization Audits*. This course has the following characteristics:

Prerequisites: Basic knowledge of auditing

Recommended CPE credits: 10 hours

Level of Knowledge: Intermediate—Builds on a basic level of understanding in order to relate fundamental principles or skills to practical situations and extend them to a broader range of applications. This level is for participants with some exposure to the subject.

Field of Study: Auditing

The *2001 Not-for-Profit Organization Audits* Self-Study CPE Program is designed to provide 10 hours of CPE credit if the test is submitted for grading and earns a passing score.

Credit hours are recommended in accordance with the Statement on Standards for Formal Continuing Professional Education (CPE) Programs, published by the AICPA. CPE requirements vary from state to state. In accordance with the standards of the National Registry of CPE Sponsors, each credit hour awarded for this program is based on 100 minutes of average completion time.

To receive credit, complete the course according to the instructions on page 772. The module costs $64.00. Payment options are shown on the answer sheet on page 799.

Each CPE test is graded within two weeks of its receipt. A passing score is 70 percent or above. Participants who pass the test will receive a Certificate of Completion to acknowledge their achievement. The self-study CPE Program offered in conjunction with *2001 Not-for-Profit Organization Audits* will expire on December 31, 2002. Participants may submit completed tests for the program until that date.

Instructions for Taking this Course

The CPE program consists of chapter learning objectives, reading assignments, review questions and suggested solutions, and an examination. Complete each step listed below to submit your test for grading:

1. Review the chapter learning objectives.

2. Read the assigned material in *Not-for-Profit Organization Audits*.

3. Complete the review questions, and compare your answers to the suggested solutions.

4. After completing all assigned chapters, take the examination, writing each answer on the appropriate line on the answer sheet.

Methods for Sending Us Your Answers

We now have several ways for you to get your answers to the publisher.

1. **Web-based.** You can log onto our Web page for Online CPE Testing and enter your answers directly onto a self-grading answer sheet. We recommend this approach for immediate results. We'll send you a certificate upon your successful completion of the examination and our receipt of payment. (If you do not pass the exam the first time, we give you an access number so you can return to our site and retake the test without charge.) You may link to the exam on our Web site at
http://www.hpponline.com/cpetest

2. **By mail.** You can print out the answer sheet, mark your answers, and mail it to the following address:

   Not-for-Profit Organization Audits CPE Coordinator
   Harcourt Professional Publishing
   525 B Street, Suite 1900
   San Diego, CA 92101-4495

   Be sure to indicate your method of payment on the answer sheet.

3. **By fax.** You can print out the answer sheet, mark your answers, and fax it to the *Not-for-Profit Organization Audits* CPE Coordinator at (619) 699-6593. Be sure to indicate your method of payment on the answer sheet.

Note: You may make copies of the answer sheet to allow additional people to take the test and send us the answers by mail or by fax. Additional people can also take the test as delivered online at our Web site. Each additional test costs $64.00.

Self-Study Continuing Professional Education Not-for-Profit Organization Audits

PART I—FINANCIAL STATEMENT AUDITS

Introduction and Background

After completing this section, you should be able to:

- Understand the distinguishing characteristics of not-for-profit organizations.
- Identify the most common revenue sources of these organizations.
- Understand the professional accounting and auditing literature applicable to not-for-profit organizations.
- Understand the operating environment and public scrutiny in not-for-profit organizations.

Read Chapter 1, "Introduction and Background," of *2001 Not-for-Profit Organization Audits.*

Answer questions 1 and 2 on page **778**.

Preplanning Audit Activities

After completing this section, you should be able to:

- Identify the audit procedures that should be performed during the preplanning phase of an audit of a not-for-profit organization.
- Understand the considerations to make when accepting an audit engagement.
- Determine what the reporting entity should be for a not-for-profit organization's financial statements.
- Determine when the audit and reporting requirements of OMB Circular A-133 must be met for a not-for-profit organization.
- Document the pre-planning activities.

Read Chapter 2, "Preplanning Audit Activities," of *2001 Not-for-Profit Organization Audits.*

Answer questions 3–5 on page **778**.

Audit Planning

After completing this section, you should be able to:

- Properly plan the audit of a not-for-profit organization.
- Obtain an understanding of a not-for-profit organization's internal control.
- Obtain an understanding of the audit risk assessment.
- Consider the risk of material misstatement of the financial statements due to fraud.
- Understand the requirements for special audit areas, such as related party transactions, illegal acts, and use of service organizations.

Read Chapter 3, "Audit Planning," of *2001 Not-for-Profit Organization Audits*.

Answer questions 6–8 on pages **778–779**.

Internal Control Considerations

After completing this section, you should be able to:

- Understand the requirements for considering a not-for-profit organization's internal control in a financial statement audit.
- Understand the framework of SAS-55 and SAS-78 for internal control consideration.
- Describe the relationship between control risk assessment and the design of an overall audit strategy.
- Understand the effect of a not-for-profit organization's internal audit function on an audit of financial statements.

Read Chapter 4, "Internal Control Considerations," of *2001 Not-for-Profit Organization Audits*.

Answer questions 9–11 on pages **779**.

Assets, Liabilities, and Net Assets

After completing this section, you should be able to:

- Design and perform an effective audit strategy for each of the asset, liability, and net asset accounts normally encountered in an audit of the financial statements of a not-for-profit organization.

Read Chapter 5, "Statement of Financial Position," of *2001 Not-for-Profit Organization Audits*.

Answer questions 12–14 on page **779**.

Statement of Activities

After completing this section, you should be able to:

- Design and perform an effective audit strategy for each of the revenue and expense accounts normally encountered in an audit of the financial statements of a not-for-profit organization.
- Understand the accounting for contributions, including contributions receivable.
- Understand the indicators for determining the contributions and exchange portions of membership dues.
- Understand the accounting and reporting of split-interest agreements.
- Understand the nature of agency and exchange transactions, and describe the proper accounting treatment for each.

Read Chapter 6, "Statement of Activities," of *2001 Not-for-Profit Organization Audits*.

Answer questions 15–17 on page **779**.

Extent of Audit Procedures and Sampling

After completing this section, you should be able to:

- Understand the role of sampling in the audit.
- Apply audit sampling to substantive tests and tests of controls.

Read Chapter 7, "Extent of Audit Procedures and Sampling," of *2001 Not-for-Profit Organization Audits*.

Answer questions 18–20 on page **779**.

Tax Considerations

After completing this section, you should be able to:

- Understand the tax status of not-for-profit organizations for income, payroll, and sales taxes.
- Distinguish different types of organizations exempt from tax under the Internal Revenue Code.
- Determine when revenues would be considered *taxable* as unrelated business income.
- Understand the reporting of tax information to donors.

Read Chapter 8, "Tax Considerations," of *2001 Not-for-Profit Organization Audits*.

Answer questions 21 and 22 on page **779**.

Concluding the Audit

After completing this section, you should be able to:

- Draft a client representation letter.
- Perform final analytical procedures.
- Summarize and evaluate the results of audit procedures.

Read Chapter 9, "Concluding the Audit," of *2001 Not-for-Profit Organization Audits*.

Answer questions 23 and 24 on page **779**.

Reporting

After completing this section, you should be able to:

- Prepare the appropriate accountant's report based on an audit of financial statements.
- Understand the required communications to boards of directors or trustees required by generally accepted auditing standards.
- Prepare a comprehensive management letter.

Read Chapter 10, "Reporting," of *2001 Not-for-Profit Organization Audits*.

Answer questions 25 and 26 on page **779**.

PART II—SINGLE AUDITS UNDER CIRCULAR A-133

Technical Resources Necessary for the Performance of A-133 Audits (including *Government Auditing Standards*)

After completing this section, you should be able to:

- Identify the appropriate technical literature that governs the conduct of A-133 audits.

- Understand the Single Audit standards.

Read Chapters 11 and 12, "Introduction to Circular A-133 Audits" and "Technical Resources for Circular A-133 Audits," of *2001 Not-for-Profit Organization Audits*.

Answer questions 27–29 on pages **779–780**.

Audit Preplanning and Planning Activities

After completing this section, you should be able to:

- Understand the requirements of *Government Auditing Standards*.
- Determine the circumstance in which a Circular A-133 audit is required.
- Negotiate and formalize the terms of an audit engagement in accordance with Circular A-133.
- Identify the federal programs of a not-for-profit organization.

Read Chapters 13 and 14, "Government Auditing Standards" and "Preplanning for a Circular A-133 Audit," of *2001 Not-for-Profit Organization Audits*.

Answer questions 30–32 on page **780**.

Planning Considerations

After completing this section, you should be able to:

- Obtain an understanding of the recipient organization and the environment in which it operates.
- Identify major federal award programs.
- Determine materiality at the major federal award program level.
- Assess audit risk and develop an audit strategy.
- Develop a single audit strategy.

Read Chapter 15, "Planning for a Circular A-133 Audit," of *2001 Not-for-Profit Organization Audits*.

Answer question 33 on page **780**.

Internal Control Compliance and Subrecipient Considerations

After completing this section, you should be able to:

- Describe the requirements for internal control considerations contained in Circular A-133.
- Determine the effects on the overall audit strategy of the internal control considerations required under Circular A-133.
- Understand the guidance of *Government Auditing Standards* relating to internal control considerations.
- Understand the requirements of Circular A-133 for testing and reporting on compliance with laws and regulations.
- Describe the compliance requirements.
- Understand the requirements of Circular A-133 as they relate to subrecipients of federal awards programs.
- Distinguish between subrecipients and vendors.

Read Chapters 16 and 17, "Internal Controls Over Federal Awards" and "Compliance and Subrecipient Considerations," of *2001 Not-for-Profit Organization Audits*.

Answer questions 34–36 on page **780**.

Reporting and Concluding the Audit

After completing this section, you should be able to:

- Describe the reporting requirements of Circular A-133.
- Describe the reporting requirements of *Government Auditing Standards*.
- Prepare the Schedule of Expenditures of Federal Awards.
- Prepare the Schedule of Findings and Questioned Costs.
- Prepare the Summary Schedule of Prior Audit Findings.
- Prepare the Corrective Action Plan.
- Understand the process of "wrapping up an audit" in accordance with Circular A-133.

Read Chapters 18 and 19, "Reporting Under Circular A-133" and "Concluding the A-133 Audit," of *2001 Not-for-Profit Organization Audits*.

Answer questions 37 and 38 on page **780**.

REVIEW QUESTIONS

1. Name at least three of the more common revenue sources for not-for-profit organizations.

2. Which types of investments are covered by FAS-124?

3. Auditor A accepts a position as a member of the board of directors of XYZ Nonprofit Organization. Would this impair the auditor? Under what conditions can an auditor accept a position and still be independent?

4. How should a not-for-profit organization account for a majority interest in a for-profit entity?

5. Must the auditor have written or oral communication with the predecessor auditor, and if so, what types of items should be discussed?

6. What are the purposes of performing planning analytical procedures?

7. What are the two components of *audit risk*?

8. What is meant by "misstatements arising from fraudulent financial reporting" in SAS-82?

9. What five components of an entity's internal control are identified by SAS-78?

10. What are the components of the control environment identified by SAS-78?

11. What is required when assessing control risk at below the maximum level?

12. For purposes of a cash flow statement, how are *cash equivalents* defined?

13. How does FAS-124 require the amounts reported for certain investments of not-for-profit organizations to be valued, and to what types of investments does it apply?

14. How does FAS-116 define a *collection*?

15. How does FAS-116 define an *unconditional promise to give*?

16. When should a not-for-profit organization recognize a contribution with a donor-imposed condition?

17. Describe the accounting for irrevocable split-interest agreements.

18. What is *audit sampling*?

19. How does nonstatistical sampling differ from statistical sampling?

20. What are the steps in applying statistical sampling to both substantive tests and tests of controls?

21. Describe the general requirements of not-for-profit organizations in relation to federal payroll taxes in comparison to commercial enterprises.

22. What is meant by *unrelated business income* for a not-for-profit organization?

23. What are the purposes of final analytical review procedures?

24. What key information should be obtained with respect to litigation, claims, and assessments?

25. What considerations should an auditor make in determining whether he or she can be the primary auditor of financial statements when there is more than one auditor involved?

26. What is a *reportable condition*, according to SAS-60?

27. How does OMB Circular A-133 define *internal controls*?

28. When are the provisions of the Single Audit Act Amendments of 1996 generally effective?

29. What is the purpose of OMB Circular A-122?

30. Describe the requirements of *Government Auditing Standards* for a CPA's internal quality control systems.

31. What is the effect of property and other noncash federal awards in determining whether a Circular A-133 audit is required?

32. How should an auditor determine a single federal award program under A-133?

33. What types of tests of controls should auditors consider performing when testing controls to meet the requirements of the original Circular A-133?

34. Describe the basic requirements of the revised Circular A-133 for testing internal controls over federal awards.

35. List the Circular A-133 Compliance Supplement's requirements for auditing compliance of major programs.

36. When assessing whether an organization (to which federal funds are disbursed by the recipient organization) is a subrecipient of the funds or a vendor, what are the characteristics that indicate that the organization is a subrecipient?

37. When are audit reports under the revised Circular A-133 required to be completed?

38. Describe the audit reporting requirements of Circular A-133.

SUGGESTED SOLUTIONS

1. The following are some of the most common sources of revenue for not-for-profit organizations:
   a. Contributions from the general public
   b. Annual fund-raising campaigns or events
   c. Grants and contracts with foundations, other not-for-profit organizations, or governmental entities
   d. Charges for specific services rendered
   e. Investment earnings

2. The measurement standards of FAS-124 apply to equity securities that have readily determinable fair values (except where the equity method is being used or for investments in consolidated subsidiaries) and to all debt securities.

3. Yes. To maintain independence, the auditor's position must be clearly honorary and the auditor must not be able to vote or

otherwise participate in the management of the organization or the activities of the organization's board of directors or trustees. If the auditor is listed on the organization's letterhead or other externally circulated materials, the auditor's position must be clearly indicated as honorary.

4. When a not-for-profit organization has a controlling financial interest in a for-profit entity through either direct or indirect ownership of a majority of the voting interest in that for-profit entity, the not-for-profit should follow the guidance of SOP 94-3, ARB-51, and FAS-94 to determine whether the for-profit entity should be consolidated. Thus, the accounting and reporting is the same as that for commercial enterprises.

5. Yes. An auditor's inquiries of the predecessor auditor prior to accepting the engagement should include, among other things, facts that might bear on the integrity of management and on disagreements between the predecessor auditor and management, if any, about accounting principles, auditing procedures, or other similarly significant matters. The auditor should also inquire about the predecessor auditor's understanding of the reasons the client decided to change auditors.

6. Analytical procedures performed during the planning phase of the audit should focus on the following:

   a. Enhancing the auditor's understanding of the organization's business and the transactions and events that have occurred since the last audit date

   b. Identifying areas that may represent specific risks relevant to the audit

7. Audit risk consists of the following two components:

   a. The risk that the account balance or class of transactions is materially misstated, and

   b. The risk that the procedures performed by the auditor will not detect the misstatement.

8. In SAS-82, misstatements arising from fraudulent financial reporting refer to intentional misstatements or omissions from financial statements that may involve:

   — Manipulation, falsification, or alteration of accounting records or supporting documents from which financial statements are prepared.

   — Misrepresentation in, or intentional omission from, the financial statements of events, transactions, or other significant information.

   — Intentional misapplication of accounting principles relating to amounts, classification, manner of presentation, or disclosures.

9. For purposes of an audit of financial statements, SAS-78 identifies the following five elements of an entity's internal control structure:

   a. Control environment
   b. Risk assessment
   c. Control activities
   d. Information and communication
   e. Monitoring

10. According to SAS-78, the control environment sets the tone of the organization and influences the control consciousness of the organization's personnel. It includes the following factors:

    — Integrity and ethical values
    — Commitment to competence
    — Board of director's or audit committee's competence
    — Management's philosophy and operating style
    — Organizational structure
    — Assignment of authority and responsibility
    — Human resource policies and practices

11. Assessing control risk at below the maximum level involves the following:

    a. Identifying specific internal control policies and procedures relevant to specific assertions that are likely to prevent or detect material misstatements in those assertions
    b. Performing tests of controls to evaluate the effectiveness of such policies and procedures

12. Cash equivalents for purposes of preparing a cash flow statement in accordance with FAS-95 are short-term, highly liquid investments that are both:

    a. Readily convertible to known amounts of cash, and
    b. So near their maturity that they present insignificant risk of changes in value because of changes in interest rates.

13. FAS-124 requires that equity securities with readily determinable market values and all debt securities be reported at fair value in the statement of financial position.

14. FAS-116 defines a *collection* as works of art, historical treasures, or similar assets that are:

    a. Held for public exhibition, education, or research in furtherance of public services rather than financial gain;
    b. Protected, kept unencumbered, cared for, and preserved; and

    c. Subject to an organizational policy that requires the proceeds of items that are sold to be used to acquire other items for collections.

15. FAS-116 defines an *unconditional promise to give* as a promise to give that depends only on the passage of time or demand by the promisee for performance.

16. Because of the uncertainty created by a donor-imposed condition, a not-for-profit organization should substantially meet all donor-imposed conditions before recognizing the receipt of assets (including the receipt of a receivable) as a contribution.

17. Irrevocable split-interest agreements should be accounted for as part contribution and part exchange agreement. Assets under the agreement should be recorded at fair value if the organization is the trustee. Liabilities to third parties should also be recorded when the organization is the trustee.

18. *Audit sampling* is the application of an audit procedure to less than 100% of the items within an account balance or class of transactions for the purpose of evaluating some characteristic of the balance or class.

19. In nonstatistical sampling the auditor does not quantify sampling risk. Instead, conclusions are reached about populations on a more judgmental basis. When statistical sampling is used, sampling risk should be quantified.

20. Applying audit sampling to both substantive tests and tests of controls involves the following steps:

    a. Planning the sample

    b. Determining the sample size

    c. Selecting the sample

    d. Performing the tests

    e. Evaluating the sample results

21. Not-for-profit organizations are generally subject to the same payroll tax requirements as a commercial organization. However, only not-for-profit organizations classified as private foundations are subject to federal unemployment taxes.

22. *Unrelated business income* is income that a not-for-profit organization earns from an unrelated trade or business activity. An *unrelated trade or business activity* is any trade or business whose conduct is not substantially related to the performance or exercise of the not-for-profit organization's exempt purpose.

23. The purpose of analytical procedures in the final review phase is to help the auditor assess the conclusions reached during the course of the audit and to evaluate the overall financial statement presentation.

24. Auditors should obtain the following evidential matter with respect to litigation, claims, and assessments:

    a. The existence of a condition, or set of circumstances, indicating an uncertainty about the possible loss to a not-for-profit organization arising from litigation, claims, and assessments

    b. The period in which the underlying cause for legal action occurred

    c. The degree of probability of an unfavorable outcome

    d. The amount or range of potential loss

25. In determining whether an auditor may serve as the principal auditor, the following should be considered:

    a. The materiality of the portion of the financial statements he or she has audited in comparison with the portion audited by other auditors

    b. The extent of his or her knowledge of the overall financial statements

    c. The importance of the components he or she audited in relation to the not-for-profit organization as a whole

26. SAS-60 defines *reportable conditions* as:

    Matters that come to the auditor's attention that, in his or her judgement, should be communicated to the audit committee because they represent significant deficiencies in the design or operation of the internal control structure, which could adversely affect the organization's ability to record, process, summarize and report financial data consistent with the assertions of management in the financial statements.

27. OMB Circular A-133 defines *internal control* over federal programs as a process brought about by an entity's management and other personnel that is designed to provide reasonable assurance regarding the achievement of the following objectives for federal programs:

    - That transactions are properly recorded and accounted for in order to:
      — Permit the preparation of reliable financial statements and federal reports.
      — Maintain accountability over assets.
      — Demonstrate compliance with laws, regulations, and other compliance requirements.

    - That transactions are executed in compliance with:
      — Laws, regulations, and the provisions of contracts or grant agreements that could have a direct and material effect on a federal program.

— Any other laws and regulations that are identified in the Compliance Supplements.

- That funds, property, and other assets are safeguarded against loss resulting from unauthorized use or disposition.

28. The provisions of the Single Audit Act Amendments of 1996 are generally effective July 1, 1996, and apply to audits of fiscal years ending on or after June 30, 1997.

29. OMB Circular A-122 was issued to provide some standardization of the cost principles used by not-for-profit organizations to charge costs to federal financial assistance programs. It also provides guidance on the requirements for maintenance and access to records for costs associated with legislative lobbying and political activities.

30. *Government Auditing Standards* prescribe that a CPA audit organization conducting audits in accordance with *Government Auditing Standards* should maintain an internal quality control system that provides reasonable assurance to the audit organization that it has adopted and is following applicable auditing standards, and that it has established and is following adequate audit policies and procedures.

31. The value of property and other noncash federal awards should be included in the total federal awards when determining whether   an A-133 audit is required. Value generally should be determined using the same methodology and/or prices used by the federal awarding agency to value the award.

32. A single federal awards program is one that consists of all grants, contracts, and cooperative agreements with the same Catalog of Federal Domestic Assistance (CFDA) number. When no CFDA number is evident, the federal agency designation or the name of the program should be used.

33. Tests of controls that provide evidence of the design and operation of the controls and procedures performed to meet the requirements of the original Circular A-133 may include:
    a. Inquiries of appropriate personnel, including grant and contract managers.
    b. Inspection of documents and reports.
    c. Observation of the application of the specific control policies and procedures.
    d. Reperformance of the application of the policy or procedures by the auditor.

34. Circular A-133 requires the auditor to perform (a) procedures to obtain an understanding of internal control over federal

programs sufficient to plan the audit to achieve a low level of control risk for major programs and (b) testing of internal controls as planned.

35. The 14 compliance requirements contained in the OMB Compliance Supplement are:

   - Activities allowed or unallowed
   - Allowable costs/cost principles
   - Cash management
   - Davis–Bacon Act
   - Eligibility
   - Equipment and real property management
   - Matching, level of effort, earmarking
   - Period of availability of federal funds
   - Procurement and suspension debarment
   - Program income
   - Real property acquisition and relocation assistance
   - Reporting
   - Subrecipient monitoring
   - Special tests and provisions

36. The following are the distinguishing characteristics of a subrecipient:

   a. Determines eligibility for assistance.
   b. Performance is measured by the objectives of the program.
   c. Responsible for programmatic decision making.
   d. Responsible for applicable program compliance requirements.
   e. Uses the passed-through funds to carry out its own programs, not to provide goods or services for a program of the prime recipient.

37. In accordance with the revised Circular A-133 (after a transition period), the audit is required to be completed within nine months after the end of the recipient organization's fiscal year.

38. The auditor is required to complete the following audit reports:

   - Auditor's report on the financial statements
   - Report on internal controls and compliance over financial reporting based on an audit of financial statements performed in accordance with *Government Auditing Standards*

- Report on compliance with requirements applicable to each major program and internal control over compliance in accordance with OMB Circular A-133
- The schedule of findings and questioned costs prepared as a part of the single audit report

1. *Multiple choice:* Governments are prohibited from using the provisions of FASB Statements 116 and 117 as the result of which pronouncement?

    a. GASB-1

    b. FAS-116

    c. FAS-117

    d. GASB-29

2. *Multiple choice:* SOP 94-3 is applicable for all of the following types of relationships *except*:

    a. For-profit entities

    b. Incorporated joint ventures

    c. Not-for-profit entities

    d. Sole proprietorships

3. *Multiple choice:* SOP 98-2 requires all of the following disclosures *except*:

    a. Total amount allocated during the period covered by the financial statements and the portion allocated to each functional expense category

    b. Types of activities for which joint costs have been incurred

    c. A statement that such costs have been allocated

    d. A comparison of the functional costs containing joint costs for the last three fiscal years starting with the adoption of SOP 98-2

4. *Multiple choice:* The auditor determines that sufficient risk factors are present in the cash area to modify the audit procedures. Which of the following would *not* be an appropriate modification?

    a. Placing a more experienced person on the audit of cash

    b. Testing the internal controls surrounding cash receipts and disbursements

    c. Modifying the auditor's opinion with a "subject to" paragraph related to cash

    d. Performing a proof of cash

5. *Multiple choice:* For which of the following would the auditor *not* be required to follow the requirements concerning SAS-70:

   a. Bank's trust department that invests the endowment's assets

   b. Outside payroll processing company

   c. Bank's activities related to the organization's bank account

   d. Outside grants management company for the organization's federal awards

6. *Multiple choice:* Functional expenses can be shown in all of the following methods *except*:

   a. Statement of Functional Expense

   b. Inclusion in a note to the financial statements

   c. Required Supplementary Information

   d. Supplementary Information

7. *Multiple choice:* Which of the following would *not* be indicative of the risk assessment element of internal control under SAS-78:

   a. Failures in an entity's accounting software caused by Y2K concerns

   b. An entity's failure to consider the impact of FAS-124 on its investment operations

   c. An entity's failure to upgrade its software that predates FAS-116 and FAS-117

   d. An entity's failure to implement an audit committee

8. *Multiple choice:* Which of the following investments is *not* covered by FAS-124?

   a. Mutual funds

   b. All equity-type securities

   c. Foreign equity securities traded only on foreign exchanges

   d. Joint venture in an oil and gas well

9. *Multiple choice:* In Year 1, the Capital Endowment Fund suffered a market loss of $1 million in its domestic equity securities. In Year 2, the Fund's market value increased to the original market value at the beginning of Year 1. How should both Year 1 and Year 2 transactions be recorded?

   a. Year 1 reports a decrease of $1 million in the permanently restricted endowment fund, and Year 2 reports an increase of the same amount.

   b. Year 1 reports a decrease of $1 million in the temporarily restricted net assets, and Year 2 reports an increase in those net assets.

    c. Year 1 reports a decrease of $1 million in the unrestricted net assets, and Year 2 reports an increase of $1 million in the unrestricted net assets.

    d. None of the above, since there has been no permanent impairment of value.

10. *Multiple choice:* SOP 94-3 requires all of the following disclosures *except*:

    a. Summarized financial data of the other organizations being combined

    b. Instances of related party transactions

    c. Historical data of the combined entity for the previous three years

    d. Identification of the other entity and the nature of its relationship with the reporting organization that results in its inclusion

11. *Multiple choice:* The following is the new threshold for the single audits:

    a. $300,000 in federal award expenditures

    b. $400,000 in federal award expenditures

    c. $100,000 in federal revenues earned during the fiscal year

    d. The highest of the $300,000 in federal award expenditures or $500,000 in earned revenue from federal programs, whichever is greater

12. *Multiple choice:* On January 1, the Grand View Music Society starts selling advance tickets to its season music events, which are conducted from May 1 to July 1 each year. Music Society has a March 31 fiscal year end. At March 31, the Society had sold $135,000 in total advance sales. How would these sales be recorded?

    a. $135,000 as contributions in unrestricted net assets

    b. $135,000 as contributions in temporarily restricted net assets, since the events have not been held

    c. $135,000 in deferred revenue

    d. The Society will estimate, based on last year, a contribution for those patrons who do not attend the events, and the remainder will be considered sales.

13. *Multiple choice:* The International Children's Charity Organization received a $200,000 contribution from the NICE Organization, with the following restriction attached: "To be used in caring for the children around the world." Which of the following items is the proper accounting for this donation:

a. Temporarily restricted net asset

b. Unrestricted net asset

c. Permanently restricted net asset

d. Deferred contribution until the amount is spent

14. *Multiple choice:* Richie Rich gives a $50,000 donation to the United Appeal organization in his community, with the following restriction: "Restricted for the American Heart Association, or other organizations deemed appropriate by the board of directors of the United Appeal." Which of the following items is the proper accounting for this donation:

a. Agency transaction reported as an asset with an offsetting liability to the American Heart Association

b. Contribution in the Unrestricted net assets

c. Contribution in the Temporary restricted net assets

d. Deferred contribution

15. *Multiple choice:* Inherent risk would *not* involve which of the following:

a. Risk of theft or fraud

b. Amount of the average transaction

c. Quantity of transactions

d. Adequacy of the controls surrounding the transactions

16. *Multiple choice:* The auditor can assess control risk below maximum for transactions processed by service organizations for all of the following *except*:

a. Performing tests of controls at the service organization

b. Performing tests of user organization's controls over the activities of the service organization.

c. Performing an analytical review of the transactions handled by the service organization

d. Obtaining a service auditor's report on controls placed in operation and tests of operating effectiveness

17. *Multiple choice:* With regard to internal controls over areas significantly dependent on computerized information systems, *Government Auditing Standards* requires the auditor to do all of the following *except*:

a. Document the reason(s) why the internal controls were not tested

b. Document the control risk at maximum, but test the controls for possible weaknesses

    c. Document the rational for determining the nature, timing, and extent of planned audit procedures

    d. Document the types of available evidential matter produced outside a computerized information system

18. *Multiple choice:* Working paper standards contained in the *Government Auditing Standards* require all of the following *except*:

    a. Working papers must be documented with the objectives, scope, and methodology.

    b. Evidence of supervisory review must appear on the working paper.

    c. The work performed to support significant conclusions and judgments of the area being audited must be documented.

    d. The principal auditor must place conclusions on all working papers.

19. *Multiple choice:* A voluntary health and welfare organization receives a gift of common stock that does not have a readily determinable market value and thus is not covered by FAS-124. What value should the nonprofit organization record?

    a. Fair value at the end of the fiscal year

    b. Fair value at the date of gift

    c. Donor's cost basis in the stock

    d. No value should be recorded, but the gift should be disclosed.

20. *Multiple choice:* FAS-124 requires that all debt securities be reported at:

    a. Cost

    b. Amortized cost

    c. Lower of cost or market

    d. Fair value

21. *Multiple choice:* Which of the following classifications is *not* a natural expense classification?

    a. Rent

    b. Salaries

    c. Materials and supplies

    d. Fund-raising

22. *Multiple choice:* What term should be used to specify an uncertain event, the occurrence or failure of which gives the donor the right to the return of the assets transferred?

    a. An unconditional contribution

    b. A donor-imposed condition

    c. A temporary donor-imposed restriction

    d. A permanent donor-imposed restriction

23. *Multiple choice:* How should a quasi-endowment fund that has been created by the not-for-profit organization's governing body be reported?

    a. As temporarily restricted net assets

    b. As unrestricted net assets

    c. As permanently restricted net assets

    d. As a conditional net asset

24. *Multiple choice:* Which OMB Circular addresses the issue of allowable costs for a not-for-profit organization?

    a. Circular A-133

    b. Circular A-21

    c. Circular A-110

    d. Circular A-122

25. *Multiple choice:* Which of the following events may prevent a revenue item from being recorded as a contribution?

    a. The not-for-profit organization asserts that it is collecting a contribution.

    b. The resource provider asserts that it is making a donation.

    c. The method of delivery of the asset to be provided by the not-for-profit organization to third-party recipients is specified by the resource provider.

    d. The resource provider determines the amount of the payment.

26. *Multiple choice:* Which of the following events may prevent a revenue item from being recorded as membership dues?

    a. The benefits to members are negligible.

    b. There are substantive benefits to a member.

    c. The benefits are provided for a defined period.

    d. The payment is fully or partially refundable if the resource provider withdraws from membership.

27. *Multiple choice:* Which of the following is *not* a split interest agreement?

    a. Perpetual trust held by a third party

    b. Charitable lead trust

    c. Charitable remainder trust

    d. Unallocated investment trust

28. *Multiple choice:* SAS-67 lists all of the following reasons to avoid confirmations of accounts receivable *except:*
    a. Accounts receivables are not material.
    b. The use of confirmations would not be effective.
    c. The combined inherent and control risk is low.
    d. The auditor uses analytical procedures as the substantive test.

29. *Multiple choice:* Which functional expense category is *not* included in FAS-117?
    a. Program services
    b. Membership development
    c. Fund-raising
    d. Organizational costs

30. *Multiple choice:* Documentation of planning the sample would consist of all *except:*
    a. Defining the population
    b. Defining the deviation condition
    c. Determining the acceptability of the test results
    d. Defining the audit objective of the test

31. *Multiple choice:* Changes to OMB Circular A-122 include all of the following *except:*
    a. Modifying the multiple allocation base method for computing indirect costs
    b. Amending the definition of *equipment*
    c. Clarifying the treatment of several individual cost items to make them consistent with OMB Circular A-21
    d. Requiring all indirect cost plans developed after June 1, 1999, to be divided into two major components–facilities and administration

32. *Multiple choice: Government Auditing Standards* requires that the auditor perform all of the following procedures relative to fraud, illegal acts, and noncompliance *except:*
    a. Design the audit to provide reasonable assurance of detecting fraud that is material to the financial statements
    b. Be aware of the possibility that indirect illegal acts may have occurred
    c. Test controls over compliance requirements
    d. Design the audit to provide reasonable assurance of detecting material misstatements resulting from direct and material illegal acts

33. *Multiple choice:* All of the following items must be included on the Schedule of Findings and Questioned Costs *except*:
    a. Material noncompliance at a compliance requirement level
    b. Reportable conditions at a compliance requirement level
    c. All questioned costs that exceed $1,000 at a program level
    d. Known fraud affecting a federal program

34. *Multiple choice:* Regarding major programs, which of the following statements is true?
    a. Major programs are required only if the single audit is above $500,000.
    b. A single audit may have no major programs.
    c. Major programs are found in the OMB Compliance Supplement.
    d. Major programs are made up of Type A and B programs that meet certain criteria.

35. *Multiple choice:* Which of the following reports is *not* required in a single audit?
    a. Opinion on the financial statements
    b. Management letter
    c. Report on internal control and compliance over financial reporting
    d. Report on Compliance with Requirements Applicable to Each Major Program and Internal Control over Compliance for the single audit

36. *Multiple choice:* According to OMB Circular A-133, which of the following statements about the Corrective Action Plan is *not* true?
    a. The Plan must address each finding listed for the single audit.
    b. The Plan must address each finding listed for the financial audit done in accordance with *Government Auditing Standards*.
    c. The Plan must contain the name of the person in charge of corrective action.
    d. The corrective action that is planned must be taken.

37. *Multiple choice:* According to OMB Circular A-133, which of the following statements regarding the Summary Schedule of Prior Audit Findings is true?
    a. The auditor must prepare the Schedule.
    b. The Schedule must address all single audit and Yellow Book findings.

   c. The Schedule must repeat the description of the finding and must list in detail all the steps taken to correct the problem.

   d. If the corrective action taken is significantly different than that indicated in the Corrective Action Plan, then an explanation for the difference must be given.

38. *Multiple choice:* Which of the following statements regarding the auditor's reports is true?

   a. The Corrective Action Plan and the Summary Schedule of Prior Audit Findings are given an "in relation" coverage in the auditor's opinion on the financial statements.

   b. A qualified opinion on a major program should result in a qualified opinion on the financial statements.

   c. The auditor can cover the Schedule of Expenditures of Federal Awards in a separate single audit report, rather than in the financial statement opinion.

   d. The Data Collection Form must have a separate auditor's opinion issued on it in accordance with OMB Circular A-133.

39. *Multiple choice:* Which of the following statements regarding the auditor's single audit report is *not* true?

   a. The report covers both compliance and internal control on major programs.

   b. The report covers all compliance requirements contained in the OMB Compliance Supplement.

   c. The findings are indicated by reference number to the Schedule of Findings and Questioned Costs.

   d. The report address both OMB Circular A-133 and *Government Auditing Standards*.

40. *Multiple choice:* Which of the following statements regarding the Data Collection Form is true?

   a. The auditor should sign the Form on page 1 using the name of the firm rather than his or her personal name.

   b. Copies of the Data Collection Form should be sent to every federal agency that provided funding to the auditee in the current year.

   c. The information provided on page 3 of the Form must include a detailed reconciliation to the Schedule of Expenditures of Federal Awards.

   d. The Form must be filed electronically.

2001 Not-for-Profit Organization Audits

Please record your CPE answers in the space provided on the left and return this page for scoring.
Simply place the completed answer sheet in a stamped envelope and mail it to:

Not-for-Profit Organization Audits **CPE Coordinator**
Harcourt Professional Publishing
525 B Street, Suite 1900
San Diego, California, 92101-4495

METHOD OF PAYMENT

□ **Payment enclosed ($64.00).**

(Make checks payable to Harcourt, Inc.)

Please add appropriate sales tax.
Be sure to sign your order below.

Charge my:
□ MasterCard   □ Visa   □ American Express

Account number _____

Expiration date _____
Please sign below for all credit card orders.

□ **Bill me.** *Be sure to sign your order below.*

NAME _____

FIRM NAME _____

ADDRESS _____

PHONE ( ) _____

CPA LICENSE # _____

STATE REGISTERED IN: _____

ISBN: 0-15-607241-6

TO ORDER: Call Toll-Free 1-800-831-7799

Signature _____

See the reverse side of this page for the CPE evaluation.

CPE ANSWERS

1. _____   21. _____
2. _____   22. _____
3. _____   23. _____
4. _____   24. _____
5. _____   25. _____
6. _____   26. _____
7. _____   27. _____
8. _____   28. _____
9. _____   29. _____
10. _____   30. _____
11. _____   31. _____
12. _____   32. _____
13. _____   33. _____
14. _____   34. _____
15. _____   35. _____
16. _____   36. _____
17. _____   37. _____
18. _____   38. _____
19. _____   39. _____
20. _____   40. _____

Not-for-Profit Organization Audits CPE Evaluation

1. Were you informed in advance of the:
   a. Objectives of the course? Y N
   b. Experience level needed to complete the course? Y N
   c. Program content? Y N
   d. Nature and extent of preparation necessary? Y N
   e. Teaching method? Y N
   f. Number of CPE credit hours? Y N

2. Do you agree with the publisher's assessment of:
   a. Objectives of the course? Y N
   b. Experience level needed to complete the course? Y N
   c. Program content? Y N
   d. Nature and extent of advance preparation necessary? Y N
   e. Teaching method? Y N
   f. Number of CPE credit hours? Y N

3. Was the material relevant? Y N

4. Was the presentation of the material effective? Y N

5. Did the program increase your professional competence? Y N

6. Was the program content timely and effective? Y N

Please make any other comments that you feel would improve this course. We appreciate the time you take to complete this questionnaire. Be assured that all of your comments will be considered carefully.

About the CD-ROM and Quick Installation Instructions

System Requirements for the Miller Engagement System™

System Requirement	Minimum	Recommended
Microprocessor type and speed	Pentium 166 MHz	Pentium 200 MHz or faster
Operating System	Microsoft Windows 95, 98, or NT Workstation 3.51 with Service Pack	Microsoft Windows 98
Other required software	Microsoft Word and Microsoft Excel 97 (with SR-1 patch or later) or 2000; Adobe Acrobat Reader 3.0 or higher to read and print software documentation. The Reader can be downloaded free of charge from http://www.adobe.com/proindex/acrobat/headstep.html.	
System memory	32 MB	64 MB or more. Additional memory improves performance and may be required to run additional applications simultaneously.
Free hard drive space	60 MB	Additional hard drive space above the minimum may be required for storing large numbers of binders.
Other required hardware	CD-ROM drive VGA or higher-resolution video adapter (Super VGA with 256 or higher color recommended) 1.44 MB or compatible floppy drive Mouse or compatible pointing device.	
Network compatibility for workgroup and file sharing	Novell, NT Server, etc. Microsoft Mail, Microsoft Exchange, Internet SMTP/POP3, or other MAPI compliant messaging software to use network e-mail or internet e-mail.	

System Requirements without the Miller Engagement System™

- IBM PC or compatible computer with CD-ROM drive
- Microsoft® Word 7.0 for Windows™ or compatible word processor
- Microsoft® Excel 7.0 for Windows™ or compatible spreadsheet program
- 10 MB available on hard drive

The CD-ROM includes the following options:

- Miller Engagement System™
- Miller Engagement System™ User's Manual

For those users who prefer not to use the Miller Engagement System™, the CD-ROM also includes the following:

- Word 7.0 and Excel 7 (95) files in stand-alone formats

Those who use WordPerfect, WordPerfect 7.0, and above should be able to open these Word documents without difficulty. Finally, for those who would like to try the ePace! Trial Balance software, the CD-ROM also includes the following:

- Free 30-day trial version of ePace! Trial Balance software

Subject to the conditions in the license agreement and the limited warranty, which is displayed onscreen when the disc is installed and which is reproduced at the end of the book, you may duplicate the files on this disc, modify them as necessary, and create your own customized versions. Installing the disc contents and/or using the disc in any way indicates that you accept the terms of the license agreement.

ABOUT THE MILLER ENGAGEMENT SYSTEM™

The CD-ROM provided with the 2001 *Miller Not-for-Profit Organization Audits* includes the Miller Engagement System™. No other system provides you with the immediate integration of your favorite Word and Excel documents. No other system puts you in charge of workpapers instead of at their mercy. The Miller Engagement System™ is simply the best electronic workpaper management system available today.

To benefit from the Miller Engagement System™ users will need the system capabilities noted above. As a convenience to users who are not able to meet the minimum system requirements, we are providing options to install the individual documents in stand-alone formats. Please note that these formats involve stand-alone documents and that, other than some linking within the Excel Workbook, they include none of the dynamic benefits of the Miller Engagement System™.

Within the Miller Engagement System™ you can create client binders that contain and instantly update your client files, within your existing Word and Excel applications. You will be able to create master binders for specialized assignments. In addition, you can easily link and incorporate any of your existing Word or Excel documents to automatically update information throughout the workpapers. Automatic links include pertinent client data such as name, company name, and address.

THE MILLER ENGAGEMENT SYSTEM™ USER'S MANUAL

Your CD-ROM includes a copy of the User's Manual for the Miller Engagement System™, which will be installed on your computer along with the rest of the Miller system. (For convenience, the User's Manual is also available directly from the CD-ROM; it is not necessary to install the software to be able to open, read, or print the User's Manual under file name Miller User's Manual.pdf.)

Word 7.0 and Excel 7 (95) Files in Stand-Alone Formats

Microsoft® Word 7.0 files and Excel® 7 (95) formats are provided as stand-alone documents if you do not choose to use the Miller Engagement System™. (If you do not own Word 7.0 or higher, your word processing package may be able to convert the documents into a usable format. Check your owner's manual for information on the conversion of documents.) These stand-alone documents do not provide the linking capability, binder technology, or workpaper management features of the Miller Engagement System™, but the documents will still offer considerable time savings.

Quick Installation Instructions

To install all or part of the contents of the CD-ROM, first close all other applications. Place the CD-ROM in the CD-ROM drive. From the Windows Start menu, choose Settings and then Control Panel. From the Control Panel, double-click on Add/Remove Programs. Continue the installation, following the instructions provided onscreen.

The installation program will provide you with options to install individual components of the CD-ROM. These options include the following:

- The stand-alone Word and Excel files
- The Miller Engagement System™

- The Miller Engagement System™ with full ePace! Engagement trial balance capability
- A trial version of the ePace! Engagement trial balance software

Using the Stand-Alone Word, Excel, and Other Files

For using the files independently of the Miller Engagement System™, please refer to the following tips. (To use the Miller Engagement System, refer to the User's Manual, which can be read directly from the CD-ROM or installed on your system upon installation.)

Opening the Word Processing Files

Open your word processing program. If you are using Microsoft Word, choose Open from the File Menu. Select the subdirectory that contains the loaded files to list the names of the files. Highlight the name of the file you want to open and click OK or press ENTER. You can also open a document from Windows Explorer by positioning the mouse cursor over the name of the file you want to use and double-clicking your left mouse button to highlight and launch the document.

The list of the Disc Contents is also available from the installed directory of files in a file called "Contents." You can open this file and view it on your screen or print a hard copy to use for reference.

Word Processing Tips

Wherever possible, the text of the word processing documents has been formatted so that you can modify the text without altering the format of the documents.

If you are working within a table, you may find the following tips useful. To maneuver within a table, press TAB to move to the next cell, and SHIFT + TAB to move backward one cell. If you want to move to a tab stop within a cell, press CTRL + TAB. For additional tips on working within tables, consult your word processor's manual. It might be helpful to turn on the invisible table lines in Microsoft Word while modifying the document by selecting Gridlines from the Table menu.

Microsoft Word is equipped with search capabilities to help you locate specific words or phrases within a document. The Find option listed under the Edit menu performs a search in Microsoft Word 7.0.

Important: When you are finished using a file you will be asked to save it. If you have modified the file, you may want to save the modified file under a different name rather than the name of the original file. (Your word processing program will prompt you for a file name.) This will enable you to reuse the original file without your modifications. If you want to replace the original file with your modified file, save but do not change the name of the file.

Opening the Excel Spreadsheet(s)

Open Excel 7.0 or higher or a compatible spreadsheet program. Choose Open from the file menu. Select the subdirectory that contains the loaded files to list the names of the files. Highlight the name of the file you want to open and click OK or press ENTER. You can also open a spreadsheet file in Explorer by positioning the mouse cursor over the name of the file you want to use and double-clicking your left mouse button to highlight and launch the document.

Spreadsheet Tips

Initially, only one spreadsheet file will exist in the spreadsheet installation directory. This is done to preserve an original copy of the Excel or Lotus spreadsheet. After opening this file, simply select File and save to a new location and/or give the spreadsheet a different name. This will create a new file that will not be marked as read-only.

PDF Files

Some of the files on the disc are in Adobe® Acrobat® PDF (portable document format). Clicking on a PDF file will automatically launch the Adobe Acrobat Reader to enable you to view the PDF file. The Adobe Acrobat Reader can be downloaded free of charge from http://www.adobe.com/proindex/acrobat/headstep.html.

Print Troubleshooting

If you are having difficulty printing your document, the following suggestions may correct the problem:

Microsoft Word

- Select Print from the Microsoft Word File menu. Then choose the Printer function.
- Ensure that the correct printer is selected.
- From this window, choose Options.

- In the media box, make sure that the paper size is correct and that the proper paper tray is selected.
- Check your network connections if applicable.
- If you still have trouble printing successfully, it may be because your printer does not recognize the font Times New Roman. At this point, you should change the font of the document to your default font by selecting the document (CTRL + A) and then choosing Font from the Format menu and highlighting the name of the font you normally use. Changing the font of the document may require additional adjustments to the document format, such as margins, tab stops, and table cell height and width. Select Page Layout from the View menu to view the appearance of the pages before you try to print again.

Software Support

If you experience any difficulties installing or running the electronic practice aids and cannot resolve the problem using the information presented here, call our toll-free software support group hotline at (888) 551-7127, or contact us via e-mail at hpptechsupport@harcourt.com/. Hours of operation are 8:00 A.M. to 4:30 P.M., (PST), Monday through Friday.

Miller Engagement System™
Quick Reference

Note: The complete User's Manual is available from the Help menu as a PDF file.

Harcourt
Professional Publishing

 Items marked with this logo relate to Trial Balance functionality and require the installation of ePace! Engagement.

FILE ROOM WINDOW

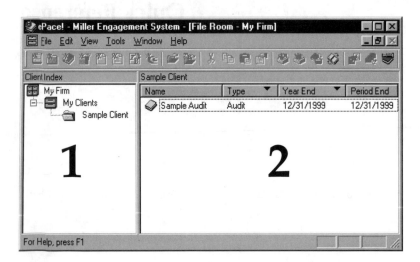

To open the File Room, double-click the Miller Engagement System™ desktop icon.

1 *Client Index Pane*—This area of the File Room displays Cabinet and Client Folder information. You may want to set up Cabinets to organize Clients by office location or by partner.

   The Client Folders hold your engagement binders. You can have Client Folders nested in other Client Folders for organizational purposes as well.

2 *Contents Pane*—This area displays the contents of the selected item in the Client Index Pane. This could be Cabinets, Client Folders, or Binders. The Contents Pane is the only area where you will see Binders. You can filter items shown in this Pane by clicking on the column drop-down for the *Type* and/ or the *Year End*.

Tip: Press **F6** to move between the panes of the File Room or Binder Window. Press **F5** to refresh the information displayed in the File Room or Binder Window.

BINDER WINDOW

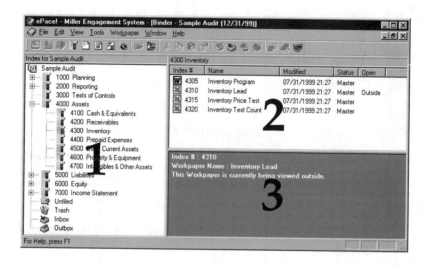

To open a Binder, double-click the Binder in the File Room. You can minimize, restore, and maximize Binders and the File Room.

1 *Binder Index Pane*—This pane displays the binder name, all Workpaper Tabs, the Unfiled, Trash, Inbox and Outbox icons. You can expand/collapse the Workpaper Tab tree by either clicking the plus/minus (+/-) sign next to the tab or you can collapse/expand all tabs by choosing Expand All/Collapse All from the View menu.

2 *Contents Pane*—From here, you can see all items contained in the selected item in the Binder Index Pane. This includes Workpaper Tabs, the Trial Balance(s), and Excel or Word workpapers, and the Unfiled, Trash, Inbox and Outbox icons. You will open and move/copy your workpapers from this window.

3 *Editing/Viewing Pane*—This pane is used for either displaying a workpaper opened inside or notifying you of a workpaper's status of being viewed outside, such being the case in the example shown above.

To open a workpaper, right-click the workpaper in the Contents Pane and either choose View Inside or View Outside. You can also double-click a workpaper to open it. This action defaults to opening a workpaper outside. See Chapter 5 in the User Guide for more.

THE MILLER ENGAGEMENT SYSTEM™ TOOLBAR

Creates a new Cabinet (File Room).

Creates a new Client Folder (File Room).

Creates a new engagement Binder (File Room).

Creates a new Workpaper Tab (Binder Window).

Creates a new Workpaper from a Template (Binder Window).

Creates a new Workpaper from an Existing File (Binder Window).

Creates a new Trial Balance database (Binder Window).

Creates a new workpaper from your Miller Templates (Binder Window).

Opens the selected item(s) (File Room & Binder Window).

Opens the Trial Balance based on your settings (outside is default). If there are more than one Trial Balance, then a list appears for you to select from (File Room & Binder Window).

Use to Cut, Copy, or Paste an item or group of items (File Room & Binder Window).

Displays the selected item's Properties (File Room & Binder Window).

Creates an Inbox/Outbox Package for file sharing (Binder Window).

Receives an Inbox/Outbox Package for file sharing (Binder Window).

Creates a Binder Package for file sharing (Binder Window).

Synchronizes or Receives a Binder Package for file sharing (Binder Window).

Exports your Trial Balance data to popular tax packages (Binder Window).

Rolls forward the selected binder to the next period.

Opens the Miller Library. Use this to view our online versions of the titles you have subscribed to (File Room & Binder Window).

THE EXCEL & WORD TOOLBARS

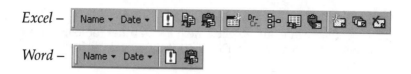

Excel –

Word –

Name ▾ Inserts Name links into the workpaper. This includes Client, Engagement, and Firm information such as the various name and address items as well as the related Workpaper Index (Excel & Word).

Date ▾ Inserts Date links into the workpaper. This includes Current, Prior, and Beginning dates. These dates will rollforward for you when you roll the entire binder forward (Excel & Word).

Refreshes all links in the workpaper. This includes Name, Date, and Trial Balance Links (Excel & Word).

Copies Trial Balance information to be linked in your workpaper. This information will update as the Trial Balance changes (Excel).

Pastes Trial Balance information into your workpaper. This information will update as the Trial Balance changes (Excel & Word).

Creates reports based on your Trial Balance. Reports include Leadsheets, Working Trial Balances, Preliminary and Final Analytics, Book-to-Tax and more (Excel).

Opens the journal entry summary. From here you can manage and book your journal entries into any Trial Balance in your Binder (Excel).

Open the Account Groupings window were you will group your accounts for financial statement and leadsheet purposes. You can import and export account grouping lists (Excel).

Open the TB Column Setup window where you can modify the columns displayed in your Trial Balance. You can set up Budget, Tax, Variance columns and more (Excel).

This imports copied cells from an Excel spreadsheet containing the trial balance data you want to import into the Trial Balance database. From here, you will simply define the columns where the information belongs and you're done (Excel).

You can add or delete comments as well as showing all comments in a workbook using these buttons (Excel).

ADDING ITEMS—FILE ROOM

New Cabinet

1. Select the Firm icon and click the **New Cabinet** toolbar button.
2. Type in the Name and Description info and click **OK** *(only Name is required)*.

New Client Folder

1. Select the item you want to add the client to *(Cabinet or other Client Folder)*.
2. Click the **New Client** button.
3. Type the Client info in the Profile tab *(only Name is required)*.
4. Click the **Contacts tab** to enter contact information.
5. Click **OK** when done.

New Binder from Blank

1. Select the Client you want to create the Binder in.
2. Click the **New Binder** button.
3. Select **Blank**, and click **OK**.
4. Enter the Binder info in the General tab *(only Name is required)*.
5. Click the **Periods tab** and enter the appropriate information *(all fields required)*.
6. Click **OK** to create the new Binder.

New Binder from a Template

1. Select the Client you want to create the Binder in.
2. Click the **New Binder** button.
3. Select **Binder Template**, and click **OK**.
4. Select the tab containing the template you want to use.
5. Select the template you want to use and click **OK**.
6. Enter the Binder info in the General tab *(only Name is required)*.
7. Click the **Periods tab** and enter the appropriate information *(all fields required)*.
8. Click **OK** to create the new Binder.

New Binder from Existing

1. Select the Client you want to create the Binder in.
2. Click the **New Binder** button.
3. Select **Existing Binder**, and click **OK**.
4. Select the Client containing the Binder you want to use from the Client drop-down list.
5. Select the engagement Binder from the list that appears.
6. Put a check in the **Clear Account Detail** box to clear the Chart of Accounts *(if you do not, the COA will remain in the new Trial Balance)*.
7. Click **OK** to create the new Binder.

ADDING ITEMS—BINDER WINDOW

New Tab

1. Select the item you want to add the tab to (*Binder icon or another Tab*).
2. Click the **New Tab** button.
3. Enter the Index and Name info and click **OK** (*only Name is required*).

New Workpaper from a Template

1. Select the tab you want to insert the workpaper in.
2. Click the **New Workpaper from Template** button.
3. Select the tab containing the template you want to use.
4. Select the template you want to use.
5. Enter the Index and Name info (*only Name is required*) and click **OK**.

New Workpaper from File

1. Select the tab you want to insert the workpaper in.
2. Click the **New Workpaper from File** button.
3. Locate the file by using the "Look in:" drop-down list. Select the file when you see it in the area below.
4. Enter the Index and Name info (*only Name is required*) and click **OK**.

New Miller Workpaper

1. Select the tab you want to insert the workpaper in.
2. Click the **New Miller Workpaper** button.
3. Select the appropriate Miller title from the "Type" drop-down list.
4. Select the tab containing the template you want to use.
5. Select the template you want to use.
6. Enter the Index and Name info (*only Name is required*) and click **OK**.

New Trial Balance

1. Select the tab you want to insert the workpaper in.
2. Click the **New Trial Balance** button.
3. Select the tab containing the template you want to use.
4. Select the template you want to use.
5. Enter the Index and Name info (*only Name is required*) and click **OK**.

SHARING WORKPAPERS—BINDER PACKAGES

Creating Binder Packages

1. From the File Room, select the Binder you want to package.
2. Click the **Create Binder Package** button.
3. Select which files you want to send as *Masters* by placing a check in the box in the Status column. Unchecked workpapers will be sent as *Carbons*.
4. Select the **Package Info tab** to type any memo text you want for this package.
5. Choose the path where you want to save the Binder Package by clicking the **Browse** button and selecting the directory to save it in from the "Save in:" drop-down list (to e-mail the file instead, click on the **Send via E-mail** checkbox). Click **Save** to save the path information.
6. Click the **Create** button to complete the process (if you chose to e-mail the file in Step 5, an e-mail message will appear with the package saved as an attachment).

Synchronizing/Receiving Binder Packages

1. From the File Room, select the Binder you want to synchronize/Receive a Binder Package to. If you do not have the Binder in your File Room, select the Cabinet you want the Binder to go into.
2. Click the **Synchronize/Receive Binder Package** button.
3. Click the **Browse** button to find the Binder Package you want to Synchronize/Receive to. Click **Open** to open the package into the Contents tab. This displays what is in the package you selected.
4. Choose either the **Synchronize Master/Carbon status after receiving** or the **Delete package after receiving** radio button to either synchronize to or to receive it.
5. Click **Next** to proceed.
   Note: If you chose to delete the package after receiving, you will be back in the File Room and the process is complete. If you chose to synchronize to the package, you will now be at the synchronize screen. This screen merges the *Master/Carbon* information between your Binder and the package.
6. Select which files you want to keep as *Masters* by placing a check in the box in the Status column. Unchecked workpapers will be sent as *Carbons*.
7. Click **Synchronize** to complete the synchronization process. The package and your Binder have both been updated with the new Master/Carbon information.

SHARING WORKPAPERS—INBOX/OUTBOX PACKAGES

Inbox   Outbox

Creating an Inbox/Outbox Package

1. From the Binder Window, select the workpaper(s) you want to send and drag them onto the **Outbox** icon in the Binder Index Pane.
2. Click the **Create Outbox Package** button.
3. Select which files you want to send as *Masters* by placing a check in the box in the Status column. Unchecked workpapers will be sent as *Carbons*.
4. Select the **Package Info tab** to type any memo text you want for this package.
5. Choose the path where you want to save the Inbox/Outbox Package by clicking the **Browse** button and selecting the directory to save it in from the "Save in:" drop-down list (to e-mail the file instead, click on the **Send via E-mail** checkbox). Click **Save** to save the path information.
6. Click the **Create** button to complete the process (if you chose to e-mail the file in Step 5, an e-mail message will appear with the package saved as an attachment).

Receiving an Inbox/Outbox Package

1. From the Binder Window, click the **Receive Inbox Package** button.
2. Click the **Browse** button to find the Inbox/Outbox Package you want to Receive. Click **Open** to open the package into the Contents tab.
3. Click **Next** to receive the package. Click **OK** on the window informing you where the files were received.
4. Click on the **Inbox** icon in the Binder Index Pane to view the files.
5. Right-click on the **Inbox** icon to either *File All Workpapers* into their respective Workpaper Tabs or *Remove All Workpapers* to delete the files from the Inbox. To file or remove individual workpapers, right-click on the file in the Content Pane and choose *File Workpaper* or *Remove*, respectively.

MASTER & CARBONS

The difference between Masters and Carbons is that a Master can be edited, while the Carbon can only be viewed (read-only). There should only be one Master of a workpaper. Both types can be opened by the user for review or to link other workpapers to them.

OTHER COMMON FEATURES

Rolling Forward Binders

1. From the File Room, select the binder you want to roll forward.
2. Click the **Roll Forward** button.
3. Enter the new Binder's name, if different, and configure the new period information if necessary.
4. Check **Save Journal Entries** to carry forward the journal entries booked in the previous Trial Balance into the new one. The journal entry amounts in the new Trial Balance will become zero.
5. Click OK to complete the roll forward process. A new binder will appear for use as the current periods engagement binder.

Moving/Copying Items

Throughout the system, there are various ways to move/copy items. You can move/copy Client Folders, Binders, Workpapers, and Workpaper Tabs. Anything contained in the item(s) being moved/copied will be transferred as well. You can even perform this function from one Binder to another.

1. Select the item or range of items you want to move/copy.
2. Use either of the following methods to move/copy the item(s):
   a. *Drag and Drop*—Click on the item(s) and hold the mouse button down. Drag the item(s) to the destination and release the mouse button. If you hold down the **Control** (Ctrl) keyboard button while you do this, the item(s) will be copied, otherwise they will be moved.
   b. *Cut, Copy, & Paste*—Click the **Cut** button to move the item(s) or the **Copy** button to copy the item(s). Click on the destination for the file(s) and click **Paste**.

Renaming Items

Throughout the system, you can easily rename items by selecting the items you want to rename, and clicking on the **Properties** button. Make your changes and click **OK** to save them.

Deleting Items

In the File Room: Select the item(s) you want to delete and press the **Delete** key on your keyboard. These items are permanently deleted.

In the Binder Window: Select the item(s) you want to delete and press the **Delete** key on your keyboard. The items are now in the *Trash*. Right-click the **Trash** icon to *Restore All* or *Empty Trash* (permanently delete). Right-click on individual workpapers in the Content Pane and choose *Restore* or *Remove*, to undelete or permanently delete an item, respectively.

INDEX

Asset transfers, classification of, 278, 279–283

Assets. *See also* Net assets; Property, plant, and equipment

  cash. *See* Cash and cash equivalents

  collections, 263–266

  contributions, 275–279

  deferred charges, 262

  exchange transactions, 279–283

  inventory, sale of, 261–262

  long-lived, 257

  prepaid expenses, 262

  transfers of, 278

Assignment of personnel, 115

Association Membership [Ethics Ruling Section 191(2)], 37

Attachments to Circular A-122, 497–500

Attestation Standards (SSAE-1), 533

Attorney letters

  audit inquiry letter, 399–400

  requirements of SAS-12, 395–398, 402

Attribute sampling, 329, 354–355

Audit

  adjustments (SAS-89), 453

  assurance, 332, 334

  compliance. *See* Compliance auditing

  economy and efficiency of, 517

  engagement, acceptance of. *See* Preplanning audit activities

  financial, 516, 534–538

  findings, elements of, 717

  findings, reporting of, 730, 734–736

  first year, 596

  frequency of, 553

  issues with Year 2000, 117–120, 124

  performance, 516–517

  prior findings, 736, 738

  prior-year, 574–577

  program, 517

  program-specific, 544–545, 546–548

  reporting. *See* Circular A-133 reporting

  single. *See* Single Audit

  standards, 124–127, 427. *See also* SAS-77

  standards and procedures, 427, 473–474

Audit and Accounting Guide. *See* AICPA Guide

Audit committee

  audit adjustments, 457

  auditor's responsibility, 453

  communication with, 451, 453, 454–456

  defined, 451

  management questions, 457, 458

  reporting requirements by auditor, 451, 453

  significant accounting policies, 456

Audit procedures

  cash and cash equivalents, 234–235

  concluding the audit. *See* Concluding the audit

  investments, 248–253

  nature, timing, and extent, 115

  preplanning. *See* Preplanning audit activities

  property, plant, and equipment, 259–261

Audit risk

  assessment, 92–98, 599–604, 679–683

  components, 93–94, 210–211

  control. *See* Control risk

  defined, 92, 599

  detection. *See* Detection risk

  inherent. *See* Inherent risk

  planning summary worksheet, 101–102

Audit Risk and Materiality in Conducting an Audit. *See* SAS-47

Audit sampling. *See also* AICPA Audit Sampling Guide; SAS-39

  approach. *See* Audit sampling approach

  conditions of, 323–324

  defined, 323

  determining necessity of, 324–328

  identifying individually significant items worksheet, 326

  in major federal programs, 681–683

  procedures when not used, 324

HARCOURT PROFESSIONAL PUBLISHING SOFTWARE LICENSE AGREEMENT FOR ELECTRONIC FILES TO ACCOMPANY *2001 NOT-FOR-PROFIT ORGANIZATION AUDITS* (THE "BOOK")

PLEASE READ THE TERMS AND CONDITIONS OF THIS LICENSE AGREEMENT CAREFULLY BEFORE INSTALLING THE FILES FROM THE CD-ROM.

THE ELECTRONIC FILES ARE COPYRIGHTED AND LICENSED (NOT SOLD). BY INSTALLING THE ELECTRONIC FILES (THE "SOFTWARE"), YOU ARE ACCEPTING AND AGREEING TO THE TERMS OF THIS LICENSE AGREEMENT. IF YOU ARE NOT WILLING TO BE BOUND BY THE TERMS OF THIS LICENSE AGREEMENT, YOU SHOULD REMOVE THE SOFTWARE FROM YOUR COMPUTER AT THIS TIME AND PROMPTLY RETURN THE PACKAGE IN RESELLABLE CONDITION AND YOU WILL RECEIVE A REFUND OF YOUR MONEY. THIS LICENSE AGREEMENT REPRESENTS THE ENTIRE AGREEMENT CONCERNING THE SOFTWARE BETWEEN YOU AND HARCOURT, INC. (REFERRED TO AS "LICENSOR"), AND IT SUPERSEDES ANY PRIOR PROPOSAL, REPRESENTATION, OR UNDERSTANDING BETWEEN THE PARTIES.

1. License Grant. Licensor hereby grants to you, and you accept, a nonexclusive license to use the Software, and any computer programs contained therein in machine-readable, object code form only, and the accompanying User Documentation, only as authorized in this License Agreement. The Software may be used only on a single computer owned, leased, or otherwise controlled by you; or in the event of the inoperability of that computer, on a backup computer selected by you. Neither concurrent use on two or more computers nor use in a local area network or other network is permitted without separate authorization and the possible payment of other license fees. You agree that you will not assign, sublease, transfer, pledge, lease, rent, or share your rights under the License Agreement. You agree that you may not reverse engineer, decompile, disassemble, or otherwise adapt, modify, or translate the Software.

Upon loading the Software into your computer, you may retain the Software CD-ROM for backup purposes. In addition, you may make one copy of the Software on a set of diskettes (or other storage medium) for the purpose of backup in the event the Software files are damaged or destroyed. You may make one copy of any additional User Documentation (such as the README.TXT file or the "About the CD-ROM" section of the Book) for backup purposes. Any such copies of the Software or the User Documentation shall include Licensor's copyright and other proprietary notices. Except as authorized under this paragraph, no copies of the Software or any portions thereof may be made by you or any person under your authority or control.

2. Licensor's Rights. You acknowledge and agree that the Software and the User Documentation are proprietary products of Licensor protected under U.S. copyright law. You further acknowledge and agree that all right, title, and interest in and to the Software, including associated intellectual property rights, are and shall remain with Licensor. This License Agreement does not convey to you an interest in or to the Software, including associated intellectual property rights, are and shall remain with Licen-

sor. This License Agreement does not convey to you an interest in or to the Software, but only a limited right of use revocable in accordance with the terms of the License Agreement.

3. License Fees. The license fees paid by you are paid in consideration of the licenses granted under this License Agreement.

4. Term. This License Agreement is effective upon your installing this software and shall continue until terminated. You may terminate this License Agreement at any time by removing all copies of the Software and returning the CD-ROM to Licensor. Licensor may terminate this License Agreement upon the breach by you of any term hereof. Upon such termination by Licensor, you agree to return to Licensor the Software and all copies and portions thereof.

5. Limited Warranty. Licensor warrants, for our benefit alone, for a period of 90 days from the date of commencement of this License Agreement (referred to as the "Warranty Period") that the Program CD-ROM in which the Software is contained is free from defects in material and workmanship. If during the Warranty Period, a defect appears in the Program CD-ROM, you may return the Program to Licensor for either replacement or, at Licensor's option, refund of amounts paid by you under this License Agreement. You agree that the foregoing constitutes your sole and exclusive remedy for breach by Licensor of any warranties made under this Agreement. EXCEPT FOR THE WARRANTIES SET FORTH ABOVE, THE PROGRAM CD-ROM, AND THE SOFTWARE CONTAINED THEREIN, ARE LICENSED "AS IS," AND LICENSOR DISCLAIMS ANY AND ALL OTHER WARRANTIES, WHETHER EXPRESS OR IMPLIED, INCLUDING, WITHOUT LIMITATION, ANY IMPLIED WARRANTIES OF MERCHANTABILITY OR FITNESS FOR A PARTICULAR PURPOSE.

6. Limitation of Liability. Licensor's cumulative liability to you or any other party for any loss or damages resulting from any claims, demands, or actions arising out of or relating to this Agreement shall not exceed the license free paid to Licensor for the use of the Software. IN NO EVENT SHALL LICENSOR BE LIABLE FOR ANY INDIRECT, INCIDENTAL, CONSEQUENTIAL, SPECIAL, OR EXEMPLARY DAMAGES (INCLUDING, BUT NOT LIMITED TO, LOSS OF DATA, BUSINESS INTERRUPTION, OR LOST PROFITS) EVEN IF LICENSOR HAS BEEN ADVISED OF THE POSSIBILITY OF SUCH DAMAGES.

7. Miscellaneous. This License Agreement shall be construed and governed in accordance with the laws of the State of California. Should any term of this License Agreement be declared void or unenforceable by any court of competent jurisdiction, such declaration shall have no effect on the remaining terms hereof. The failure of either party to enforce any rights granted hereunder or to take action against the other party in the event of any breach hereunder shall not be deemed a waiver by that party as to subsequent enforcement of rights or subsequent actions in the event of future breaches.